Banking on Kanban

Mastering Kanban to Boost Cash Flow, Minimize Inventory, and Maximize Delivery Performance

The Definitive Guide to the Math Behind the Method

Josette Russell

Published by Dynamic Kanban, Inc.

© Copyright 2016 Josette Russell

Published by Dynamic Kanban, Inc.

First edition.

ISBN: 978-0-9974941-6-7

Discounts are available for quantities of five or more books. Please visit www.kanbancalculator.com or email the author at Josette@dynamickanban.com for additional information.

Acknowledgements

I owe a deep debt of gratitude to the many people who helped me navigate and endure the long process of finishing this book.

I am especially grateful to all the **sites** that invited me to assist with their kanban and operational improvements over the last 20+ years. You contributed greatly to my expertise and I sincerely appreciate the opportunities you provided me.

Eternal thanks to my **family and friends** for encouraging me and also for letting me vent when I was frustrated. Special thanks to my parents for their lifelong support, and for tolerating my crazy notions.

I owe a huge thank you to **Timothy Galusha** for the creativity he brought to the logos and graphics I needed for this project. Tim - you are a blessing to me. (Contact the author if you'd like to connect with Timothy.)

I am incredibly indebted to **Priscilla Mullins Duckworth**, my tireless editor, for remembering all the weird rules and patiently applying her expertise to such a long and analytical topic. If there are editing errors in this book, rest assured that Priscilla got it right then I changed something and did it wrong. (Readers: If you need an editor, you can reach Priscilla at PMullins@1791.com. She is a gem!)

Thank you **Peter Bowerman** for 1) writing the book *The Well-Fed Self-Publisher*, which provided many of the insights I needed to get this book out of my computer and into readers' hands, and 2) for assisting me with the title and cover content. (www.TitleTailor.com.)

Chris Di Natale did a superb job designing a cover that communicates the book's purpose while also capturing my personality, and I love the icons she created for all the color-coded boxes. (www.DiNataleDesign.com.)

Thank you **Robbie Short** for the Kanban Master caricature. How fun is that?!? (www.RobbieShort.com.)

Rob Price at Gatekeeper Press helped me comprehend the tangled web that is the printing industry. People who are new to this process need a patient advisor, and Rob has been a great resource for me. (www.GatekeeperPress.com)

Does it irritate you when a book puts "This page intentionally left blank" on a page that has no additional content? Yes, I understand that they're informing the reader that the page is supposed to be empty, but as soon as they put that statement on the page it stopped being blank. Since that seems completely illogical to me, I'm not going to do that.

Some pages in this book are blank, such as when a chapter ends on a right-hand page. You will not find any reassurance or explanation, but there is no need to panic or conclude that the printing process randomly skipped a page.

CONTENTS

Section II.   Introduction to Kanban   65

Section III. Safety Stock Covers Supply & Demand Variation   117

INTRODUCTION

There is a direct and inseverable link between inventory and cash, and it is an inverse relationship; more inventory means less cash. In a world where cash flow is often the key to funding additional people, equipment, space, or growth projects, boosting cash is a big deal.

I often hear leaders lament about an inventory reduction goal that hangs like a time bomb over their head because 1) they don't believe in the goal, or 2) they have no idea how to achieve it.

In the first camp, some people resist inventory reduction because they operate under the misperception that high inventory is necessary for achieving on-time delivery, shortening lead times, and effectively utilizing labor. Under this erroneous concept, they choose to hold extra inventory, what could be called "just-in-case" inventory, to ensure that material availability doesn't hamper the operation. This plan often balloons into a just-in-case monster that manifests itself as large piles of raw material, work in progress,

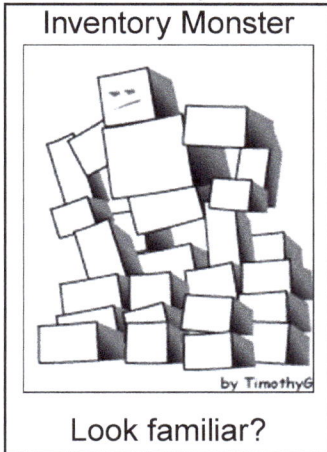

Inventory Monster

Look familiar?

and finished goods inventory in every nook and cranny of the building. One harmful side effect is that when high inventory persists over time, leaders become blind to big piles of inventory and they fail to recognize them for what they are, a huge cash drain on the business. For people with this mind-set, inventory is a security blanket and therefore any goal to reduce inventory is an operational risk that they want no part of implementing.

On the other hand, some leaders who are tackling inventory reduction can academically understand that it will require significant operational changes, but they don't know how to do it. To most people in this scenario, an inventory reduction goal is like setting a goal to swim to the moon: impossible!

Every leader should view inventory as a potential source of cash and space!

Bank On Kanban: Boost Cash By Minimizing Inventory

I bet you want to know if there's a tool to free up cash by reducing inventory, while still protecting delivery. Yes, it's called kanban. That explains why this book is about kanban, right?

Kanban is my go-to tool for inventory performance. For those who are new to Lean or the Toyota Production System (TPS), kanban is a primary Lean tool. It manages inventory replenishment signals based on the real world, where material is used.

Kanban is generally more complicated than you'd think, due to the tremendous amount of planning that is the foundation of any robust kanban system, plus the math that sits behind every kanban solution. Kanban isn't something you decide to do on a whim. There are hundreds of decisions to make when

MASTERING KANBAN TO:

Boost Cash Flow

Minimize Inventory

Maximize Delivery Performance

deploying kanban, and those decisions can make or break the system. Cash flow, inventory management, and delivery are too important to be left to chance or best guesses.

Over the years, I developed processes to design and deploy kanban with the intent of 1) protecting delivery with the right level of available material, and 2) reducing inventory to boost cash flow and free up space. At every site, I spent a lot of time teaching people how to think about kanban and also how to understand the kanban decisions that must be carefully considered. I learned that the care and feeding of kanban cards and boards is important, but the real work occurs long before that, when kanban solutions are calculated. Kanban calculations dictate *how much inventory is planned* to be in stock, and, therefore, *how much cash can be freed up* by reducing inventory.

In my experience, most kanban failures occur not in the midst of kanban cards and boards on the floor, but rather when the system is designed or *not* designed. Kanban success or failure is fundamentally based on how kanban solutions are calculated and assigned. Again, card management can derail a system, but those failures are generally easier to find and repair than a failure of kanban calculations.

Kanban comes down to math. We must get the math right in order to create a kanban system that will succeed. And if kanban depends on math, we need formulas and instructions. Yep, we're in luck because that's what this book is about.

Start with *Banking On Kanban,* Get More Help If You Need It

I've been asked the following question repeatedly over the years: "Is there a book that captures the thought processes and methodologies for designing a kanban system, specifically for calculating solutions and estimating potential inventory reduction?" Alas, when I searched for a great book, I didn't find one. There wasn't a good reference for a site that was new to kanban, or for someone who was struggling to improve or enhance an existing kanban system.

That's why I decided to write this book. It forced me to solidify my thought processes, to confirm or clarify why I do things a certain way, and to discover what causes me to deviate from standard 2-card kanban for certain items or sites.

Because I tend to work with more complicated situations, I needed something that described the process of calculating kanban solutions for even the most bizarre scenarios. I tried to be very thorough, hence the book's length. There are sections that won't apply to some sites (e.g., seasonal demand), but I'd rather provide more information than you need than to leave you lacking. With the information in this book, you can master kanban concepts and design a robust kanban system for even the most complicated situations.

One of the key elements for calculating solutions is having the right formulas, and they're all here. You're welcome. And, I'm sorry, but formulas don't make for light reading.

If you're concerned about the complexity of your situation or the overwhelming nature of your project, don't tackle it alone. There are consultants and experts all over the world who can help, so don't hesitate to hire a kanban master *early in the process* to give you rapid traction and quick success. You won't need them forever, and it will ease some of the early pain. (Yes, you can contact me at www.kanbancalculator.com. I can assist you, or help you find someone else who can.)

In addition to hiring human expertise, consider whether software could help, even if you're a kanban expert. Like the book search, I hadn't seen a great software package for calculating kanban solutions, even in the best and biggest computer systems. So, while working on this book, I also tackled that. I'd always used Microsoft Excel® for kanban calculations because I could customize it for every site, and Excel is pretty ubiquitous in the manufacturing space. With Excel, it was easy to design a tool and leave it with the site when my work there was done. The bottom fell out of that strategy when my Excel models got so large that simple tasks like inserting a column took 45 minutes, and my computer crashed regularly. I really hate that.

I needed a tool that could handle thousands of lines of data. (You'd be amazed at how many sites manage more than 10,000 part numbers when you count purchased and internal items.) The tool also had to execute the decision trees that I built into Excel. Eventually, I hired software developers and created a cloud-based tool that calculates kanban solutions, called Dynamic Kanban. If the math part of kanban scares you, DK might be a good option. (For more information, contact me or visit www.kanbancalculator.com.)

Book Layout

This book contains dozens of color-coded boxes.

Kanban Master boxes provide high-level advice or insight about kanban, processes, operations, materials, etc. Look for the Kanban Master face in the corner. (*She* looks familiar...)

Josette Russell, Kanban Master

Rule of Thumb

Green boxes with a thumb in the corner provide advice on default values or limits to use as starting points in a kanban system. When in doubt, start with a default value and adjust from there.

HINT

Think of a Hint box as a sticky note pinned to your wall. These are reminders or hints about something in the text.

Examples

Examples are in grey boxes with "e.g." in the upper right corner. These boxes contain steps, calculations, or other details to illustrate a specific topic.

Real-World Observation

I've seen many situations, both normal and strange. True-life stories are in blue boxes with binoculars in the upper right corner. Every story is anonymous.

Formulas

Formulas are in purple boxes with an equal sign in the upper right corner. Some boxes explain the math behind a formula, while others describe how to enter or use that formula in Excel. For Excel examples, sometimes formula elements are "Defined Names" instead of cell references, so the formula for lead-time demand would be "LT * DD" instead of "A2 * B2". Defined names are also used in tutorial content.

Formula Layout

Multi-level or embedded IF statements deserve special mention. In Excel, an IF statement might look like this: =IF (test_1_is_True, option_1, IF (test_2_is_True, option_2, IF (test_3_is_True, option 3, last_option)))

This formula tests 3 conditions and assigns results (options 1, 2 and 3) based on those sequential IF tests. This formula is difficult to digest as a run-on sentence, so formula boxes for multiple IF statements will be shown as separate lines for each IF test, followed at the end by the final "ELSE" in case all preceding tests were false. There will be one or more closing parentheses at the end, like this:

IF (test_1_is_True, option_1,

IF (test_2_is_True, option_2,

IF (test_3_is_True, option_3,

last_option)))

STOP boxes warn you to confirm or complete something before proceeding to the next step.

Tutorials

At the end of most chapters there is a tutorial section based on a fictitious company called Gadgets and Oddities Company, or GOCO. All of the data included in the tutorials is fictional, so don't expect every detail to be perfectly aligned. For example, GOCO ships more than $100 million per year with just 108 total part numbers. That's not very feasible, but it makes the examples easier to display.

The formulas in the Excel tutorials could be used to calculate actual kanban solutions! GOCO is fictitious, but the formulas are *very* real.

Definitions

Like many of today's business topics, inventory management and kanban have been overrun by acronyms, abbreviations, and special lingo. The following definitions ensure clarity and understanding for terms used throughout this book. Many more terms will be defined in later chapters.

ABC classification designates an item's annual spend relative to a population of purchased or manufactured parts. After sorting in descending order of annual spend, the highest spend items that sum to 80% of total annual spend are designated A items. Items that make up the next 15% of total annual spend are labeled B items, and remaining part numbers are classified as C items.

Annual demand is the sum of all demand over a twelve-month period, not necessarily a calendar year. Annual demand for a single item is usually measured in units of measure, e.g., pounds, while annual spend for a group of items or an entire site is measured in the designated currency.

Annual spend is the total annual expenditure for an item or a group of parts.

Break a bin (BaB) is a kanban timing trigger for which replenishment orders are triggered at the beginning of a bin, or when the first piece is removed.

Cost of goods sold (COGS) is the sum of standard labor, standard material, and standard overhead costs for an item.

Customer is the recipient or receiver of material, which can be an internal or external entity. The customer is a downstream process, but it isn't necessarily the last process or an external entity because there can be numerous "customer" recipients within a series of processes.

Daily demand (DD) is usage or consumption per day. For kanban, the correct denominator for calculating daily demand is workdays, instead of calendar days. So, daily demand reflects how many pieces are used during one workday. Daily demand is expressed in the same unit of measure as standard cost and on-hand balance.

Daily demand is captured several ways:

• Average daily demand is average consumption per workday, often measured for a 1-year period. Some plants call this standard daily demand. This metric is useful for sites that have limited seasonality and reasonably stable demand with no significant rate of growth or decline. This is less insightful if demand variation of any type is high.

• Current daily demand is the measured or predicted demand for today's circumstances, and it is used when resizing kanban solutions, calculating the number of cards for a multi-card solution, or calculating actual safety stock for a kanban solution.

• Low daily demand is the lowest expected daily demand for an item that exhibits seasonal or day-to-day demand variation. Low daily demand is used to calculate the kanban order quantity (KOQ) for a demand variation (DV) multi-card solution.

• High daily demand is the highest expected daily usage, which is used to calculate the maximum number of kanban cards for a demand variation multi-card solution.

Days on hand (DOH) measures inventory performance as the number of future days of demand that are covered by the current on-hand balance.

Downstream refers to processes, cells, or tasks that come later in a series or process. The recipients of a process's output are downstream. Customers are downstream.

Empty a bin (EaB) refers to triggering replenishment signals at the end of a bin, or when the last piece is removed.

Enterprise resource planning (ERP) is a computerized system to manage an organization's resources, including material, labor, equipment, etc. See Materials Requirements Planning.

Estimated inventory is a prediction of future on-hand balance based on replenishment and demand assumptions, which is important for predicting or managing inventory performance.

• Estimated minimum inventory is the expected low point or valley of an item's expected balance. This is generally tracked for individual items, not for groups of items.

• Estimated average inventory is the mid-point of the sawtooth curve for an item. This can be converted to currency and summed across multiple items to predict site-wide inventory.

• Estimated maximum inventory is the maximum on-hand balance expected for an item. This is generally tracked for individual items but it can also be insightful across all items at a site.

Finished goods (FG) is inventory that has completed all processing and is ready to ship to an external customer.

Flow is a Lean concept that progresses one unit of work (one piece, one invoice, one drawing, one purchase order) from step to step. Flow eliminates the use of batches and queues and implies the existence of pull.

An **ideal kanban solution** is the perfect kanban solution with two cards, no rounding for order quantity, and at the target lead time.

Inventory turns measures inventory performance and reports how many times per year on-hand inventory is turned over or consumed. Inventory turns compares annual usage versus on-hand balance.

Kaizen is a combination of the Japanese words "change" and "good." It is one of the most widely used Lean or continuous improvement tools and it is generally defined as "take apart and make better."

A kaizen event generally is performed by the people who do the work along with cross-functional support (think Maintenance, Purchasing, or Engineering.) A kaizen event can be a short ad hoc occurrence (e.g., a team spends 15 minutes on a specific task) or a thoroughly planned and managed event (e.g., a week-long event to redefine an entire work cell).

Kanban is a Lean tool that implements pull where flow does not exist. It is based in the real world instead of the virtual or computer world, so it is deployed and managed where material is consumed. Kanban is a visual tool that relies on observable signals or events to trigger replenishment orders for standard order quantities at standard lead times.

Kanban bin refers to either the physical container that holds kanban parts or to the kanban replenishment quantity. Interpreting this correctly generally relies on the context.

A **kanban board** holds kanban cards while they wait for replenishment orders to arrive.

A **kanban calculator** is a tool that generates kanban solutions for items with defined daily demand, lead time, and other parameters.

A **kanban card** can refer to either a physical kanban card <u>or</u> to a generic signaling method for an item on kanban, e.g., the phrase "trigger the kanban card" might be used even if a physical card does not exist, such as when an empty shelf triggers a kanban order.

Kanban order quantity (KOQ) is the standard replenishment quantity for an item on kanban. It is a calculated quantity that must meet rounding requirements for minimum order, maximum order, and standard package quantities. See replenishment quantity.

A **kanban signal** is the indicator that an order has been triggered. Most kanban signals are visual, such as an empty bin turned upside down, a kanban card hanging on a "to be scanned" peg, or an empty spot on the floor. Kanban cards are the most common signaling method.

Kanban type describes the kanban solution assigned to a kanban item: 1-card, 2-card, or multi-card.

• A 2-card solution is the default or preferred kanban solution.

• A 1-card kanban solution uses just one kanban signal or card for an item with a high minimum order quantity (MOQ).

• A multi-card solution utilizes any number of cards, from 1 to n. This solution is used in specific circumstances, including long lead times (LTs), high demand variation (DV), or maximum order quantity (MaxQ) limitations.

Lead time (LT) is the time required from order entry to receipt of parts, including transit time for external parts. Lead time should be measured in workdays instead of calendar days.

• Standard lead time is the agreed upon or expected number of days as defined in the supplier agreement. For each internal or external item, this is dictated by the supplier.

• Actual lead time is the observed or average lead time for a series of past receipts. This is a calculated number.

• Target lead time is the desired lead time for a part number (PN) or a group of parts.

Lead-time demand is the quantity of parts consumed during one lead-time period.

Lean is the generic term for the Toyota Production System (TPS), a continuous improvement philosophy based on the work of Toyota's loom and automotive businesses, Henry Ford's assembly line, Eli Whitney's and Samuel Colt's interchangeable parts, W. Edwards Deming's Plan-Do-Check-Act cycle, just-in-time replenishment, etc.

Lean is founded on the philosophies of continuous improvement with respect for people. It focuses on eliminating waste and delivering value to customers, where value is defined by the customer.

Manufactured parts are produced on site, versus purchased parts that are acquired from an external supplier.

Materials requirements planning (MRP) or **manufacturing resources planning** (also MRP) are computer systems that calculate replenishment quantities based on on-hand balance, upcoming receipts, and future demand.

Maximum order quantity (MaxQ) is the maximum number of pieces that can constitute one order. This limitation is determined by the supplier of an item, either an external company or an internal cell. It can be driven by batch processing, packaging size, or shipping requirements. MaxQ is less common than minimum order quantity (MOQ) but where it exists it must be honored.

Minimum order quantity (MOQ) is the minimum quantity that qualifies for an acceptable order. This limitation is determined by the supplier of an item, either an external company or an internal cell. It can be driven by a long set-up or change-over time that mandates a high batch quantity to balance the time allocated to set-up versus production, by batch processes that must be performed on more than one piece at a time, or by packaging requirements, such as space utilization for shipping.

On-hand balance (OHB) is the number of units on hand for a particular item. This is captured in units of measure for the particular item, e.g., pounds or feet or pieces.

On-hand currency (OHC) is the total value on hand for one or more part numbers. When reporting on-hand inventory for more than one item, OHC is required instead of on-hand balance. Use the abbreviation OH$ to indicate on-hand dollars, OH¥ for yen, OH€ for euros, etc.

On-time delivery (OTD) is the percentage of total orders, lines, or pieces that shipped by the due date. OTD measures delivery performance for a cell, process, or site. OTD is a mandatory metric for inventory performance.

Part number (PN) is the designation for a specific component, e.g., AS12345 or MT35100.

Plan for every part (PFEP) states that every part requires a robust replenishment plan that protects delivery and maximizes inventory performance, i.e., kanban, MRP, vendor management, consignment, etc.

Point of use (POU) refers to storing inventory where the work occurs. POU storage negates the use of centralized warehouses.

Pull is a Lean concept that relates to delivering products or services based on a customer signal. Pull can be used with or without flow, and pull without flow is kanban.

Purchased part (PP) refers to material that is acquired from an external supplier, including an off-site entity owned by the same parent company. See Raw material.

Raw material (RM) is supplied by an external supplier. RM becomes work in process (WIP) as soon as it is physically modified, e.g., sawed, painted, welded, etc.

Some sites differentiate between "raw material" and "purchased parts," but that is unnecessary and often adds confusion about what constitutes raw material versus a purchased part. In this book, raw material and purchased part both refer to any material from external suppliers that has not been modified into work in progress. See Purchased part and Work in progress.

Reorder point (ROP) is the on-hand balance at which a replenishment order is triggered for a 1-card solution.

Replenishment quantity is the amount ordered as one receipt. For parts on kanban, replenishment quantity is the kanban order quantity (KOQ). For both kanban and MRP parts, replenishment quantity can vary from order to order or it can be frozen or "fixed" at the same quantity for every order. Most kanban parts utilize a fixed replenishment quantity, meaning the same quantity is ordered for every kanban signal. See Kanban order quantity.

Safety stock (SS) is buffer inventory added to a replenishment plan to protect delivery from supply or demand variation.

Safety stock has both a target and actual value.

• Actual safety stock is calculated by comparing how many pieces are acquired in a lead-time period versus how many are consumed in that period.

• Target safety stock is an item's desired amount of safety stock based on expected variation in supply (supply is low) and demand (demand is high). Target safety stock is not determined by a universal formula but rather by analyzing variation in supply and demand for individual or groups of items, including supplier variation in lead time, delivered quality, or delivered quantity, plus variation in day-to-day demand. This is a theoretical number, and, therefore, is subject to change due to rounding of card count or order quantity, which mandates that actual safety stock be calculated for every item to confirm whether enough safety stock is present in the final kanban solution.

Sales, general & administrative (SG&A) is a broad category of overhead expenses that fall below standard cost. SG&A is subtracted from gross profit to get net profit.

Sawtooth curve is a pictorial representation of on-hand balance for an item, as in Figure Intro-1. A sawtooth curve peaks when a new receipt arrives, adding incoming material to the on-hand balance (OHB), and it declines as daily consumption subtracts from on-hand inventory.

Figure Intro-1. Sawtooth Curve

Seasonal demand refers to demand that varies throughout a calendar year in a predictable pattern. This can be driven by weather, events, or special occasions that occur at specific times.

Standard cost is the price per unit of measure for an item, e.g., cost per piece or cost per foot.

Standard package quantity (SPQ) is the standard container quantity for an item, i.e., the unit count per box, bag, tote, pallet, etc. Any order that meets minimum order quantity (MOQ) requirements can be increased in increments equal to the standard package. So, the kanban order quantity (KOQ) is always an even multiple of SPQ. Standard package quantity is usually driven by production batch sizes or packaging, and it can exist for internal or external parts.

Standard work in progress (WIP) is inventory that feeds each manned work station in a work cell that has two or more workers. Standard WIP gives each associate their required material for their first task.

Placing standard WIP for each worker is called keeping the line "wet." It means that at time zero, when the cell starts up, every worker within the work cell can begin his or her task without waiting for material to progress through the cell.

Standard WIP is indicated by the striped hexagon symbols near stations 3, 7, and 11 in Figure Intro-2. The raw material in front of station 1 is the standard WIP for that worker.

Figure Intro-2. Standard WIP

= Std WIP

RM

To comply with standard WIP, a work cell should not be emptied of all inventory *except* when completing a changeover. Don't drain work cells of all inventory at the end of a shift, at the close of the workday, at the end of the month, at year end, or at any other arbitrary time period.

Standard work (SW) or **standardized work** is a primary Lean tool that defines the right equipment, tools, people, inventory, and process steps to accomplish an objective. Standard work reduces variation and also serves as the foundation for employee training and future continuous improvement.

Supplier is the provider or producer of material, either an internal or external entity. A supplier can also be referred to as a sender or an upstream process.

Takt time is a Lean term that refers to the available time for one unit of production. A work cell that works 24 hours per day has 86,400 seconds of available time per day. If customer demand is 1,000 pieces per day, the takt time or allowed time per piece is [86,400 seconds / 1000 pieces = 86.4 seconds.] Takt time is a key element of the value stream map (VSM).

Target lead time is the ideal lead time for an item, and it is often based on ABC classification plus purchased versus manufactured status. Target lead time is used to define ideal kanban solutions, to calculate order quantity for a multi-card kanban solution, and to determine which items should negotiate a new lead time.

Target safety stock (TSS) is the amount of buffer inventory intended for a kanban solution to protect customer delivery from supply or demand variation.

Trigger timing refers to when replenishment signals are triggered, at the beginning, middle, or end of the consumption of a kanban bin.

• Break a bin (BaB) is one of two primary choices for trigger timing, for which a replenishment order is initiated when a kanban quantity is opened or when the first piece is taken from the "bin."

• Empty a bin (EaB) trigger timing initiates a replenishment order when a kanban quantity is depleted or when the bin is emptied.

• One-card kanban solutions utilize a mid-point trigger called the reorder point (ROP), for which signals are triggered in the middle of consuming a kanban bin.

Unit of measure (UoM) is an item's counting method for daily demand, on-hand balance, and standard cost, e.g., $1.00 per *pound* uses pounds as the unit of measure, while 100 *pieces* on hand indicates pieces as the units.

Upstream refers to processes, cells, or tasks that come earlier in a series compared to the point being discussed. A supplier is an upstream process.

Value is a Lean term that refers to the customer's definition of what is important in a product or service, e.g., high durability, short lead time, or low cost. Different customers have different definitions of value. See Value Stream Map.

Value Stream Map (VSM) is a Lean tool that illustrates how value is created and delivered to a customer. Value stream maps are created for both current and future states, and the differences between the two maps define the improvement opportunities.

Visual management (VM) is a Lean concept that utilizes observable items such as colors, shapes, lights, or other indicators to make it readily understood whether something is correct or incorrect, successful or unsuccessful, etc.

• A red tag means inventory is quarantined.

• An outline of a hammer on a peg board tells associates where the hammer belongs.

• A green up arrow ($\uparrow$) on a chart indicates high results are better than low.

Waste is a Lean term that defines the losses that occur in a process. The eight standard Lean wastes are overproduction, processing, waiting, transportation, inventory, motion, errors or defects, and underutilized human resources.

Water spider refers to a person who travels a prescribed route to find and fill open kanban signals. Specific duties vary from site to site, but most water spiders look for empty bins that need to be refilled or for kanban cards that have been triggered, such as cards hanging on a "to be scanned" peg on a kanban board.

One advantage to a water spider is that point-of-use (POU) inventory or any material in the midst of a production cell is filled by an external person so that production associates don't interrupt their work to fill bins.

Because water spiders follow a repetitive route, containers at POU can be small because they will be filled one or more times per shift. Many water spider containers hold just one to four hours of material.

Work in progress (WIP) or **work in process** is inventory that has been modified from its raw state but has not been processed into the final finished goods (FG) status. Some sites call this "intermediate inventory."

SECTION I. GENERAL DISCUSSION OF INVENTORY MANAGEMENT

Before we can comprehend kanban and design and deploy an effective kanban system, we must first understand the basic concepts of inventory management. This section covers the general functions of inventory management, the ever-insightful sawtooth curve, how to measure inventory performance, why ABC classifications are so important, and how to assign ABC.

CHAPTER 1: INVENTORY MANAGEMENT

If we're going to reduce inventory and increase cash, we must understand basic inventory concepts.

In any business that deals with physical goods, inventory must be well managed because it directly impacts customer satisfaction, cash flow, and overall operational success. Whether a business utilizes material as part of their primary role, like manufacturing or distribution, or as a support function, as in a plumbing company or hospital, every inventory management system faces the constant challenge of maintaining the correct level of on-hand material, or enough material to meet customer demand but not so much as to hinder cash flow.

The inevitable result is that balancing material availability versus cash flow is the everlasting quest for people who manage inventory. Millions of hours have been dedicated to developing systems and processes to achieve this delicate balance, yet many sites struggle to find a sustainable solution. For decades, the term "just in time" has referred to receiving or producing required material at the exact time it's needed to meet delivery or production commitments, and no sooner. For some operations this is a simple task, but for many sites JIT requires sophisticated analysis of demand forecasts (both volume and mix), customer lead-time expectations, expected supplier performance, and operational execution (e.g., production lead times, quality performance, etc.).

Supply Chain Terms

Let's briefly define inventory management.

Supply chain management (SCM) encompasses the processes to plan, negotiate, source, purchase, replenish, and transport raw mate-rial, work in progress (WIP), and finished goods (FG) from external suppliers all the way to end customers. In recent decades, SCM has become increasingly more complex and, therefore, more closely managed due to the high costs that occur across a long supply chain, specifically in a global business environment.

Sourcing occurs when on-hand inventory is required for a new or newly-negotiable item. In this subset of supply chain management, sourcing or contract experts request and review quotes, and then negotiate a supply agreement with select-ed supplier(s). A sourcing agreement can be as simple as a one-time purchase order with quantity, total price, shipping terms, and a due date. However, long-term agreements that cover a high dollar value, or that manage numerous items, are usually formal, legal contracts that specify the following: price, standard lead time, minimum order quantity (MOQ), standard package quantity (SPQ), the process for returning material, any required quality or test reports, approved supplier production locations, payment terms, defective material processes, contract termination terms, mediation processes, etc.

Inventory management is another subset of supply chain management, which commences after the sourcing decision is finalized. Inventory management processes are executed to provide the right type and amount of material to meet delivery and cash flow objectives. Unlike a sourcing decision that occurs infrequently, inventory management, or ordering and consuming material, happens over and over in an endless loop.

Every inventory management system should strive for just-in-time replenishment, providing *adequate material to achieve on-time delivery* but with *minimum on-hand inventory*, but this is difficult to do. There is a certain amount of complexity caused by the repetitive nature of inventory management tasks, i.e., managing the endless consumption and replenishment cycles for numerous items across a site. What adds even more complexity is the fact that consumption and replenishment processes are performed by numerous cross-functional players: buyers, planners, production schedulers, sourcing managers, supervisors, material handlers, operations managers, material coordinators, production associates, receiving clerks, etc. Because these processes are cross-functional and directly related to delivery and cash flow performance, the consumption and replenishment processes must be clearly defined, and associates must be well-trained and have the necessary tools to be successful.

Simple Inventory Management Model

The picture in Figure 1-1 illustrates how inventory works in its most basic form. At any point in time an item has a measurable on-hand balance —or the amount of inventory in the bucket—and that amount ranges from zero to infinity. (OK, maybe not actually to infinity, but on-hand balance can be pretty high.) As soon as the bucket contains available material, the customer can pull inventory out of the bucket (consumption, or the spigots at the bottom) and the supplier can add inventory to the bucket (replenishment, or the ladle at the top).

Figure 1-1. Inventory Bucket with Supply (Replenishment) & Demand (Consumption)

This repetitive loop of lowering the level in the bucket and refilling it must be well-managed in order to achieve inventory management success, where success means the bucket doesn't run dry and it doesn't overflow.

Some inventory managers fail to recognize that consuming and replenishing inventory is the repetitive loop that defines the entire inventory management process. Inventory consumption and replenishment processes must be designed with inventory management in mind, namely serv-

ing the customer without draining cash from the business. Manage what goes in and out of the bucket!

Receive: When a replenishment order arrives, items must be placed into available inventory as quickly as possible, which includes both *physically* and *financially* receiving the parts. These steps occur every time a full or partial replenishment order arrives from either an external or internal source.

HINT for Associates

Inspection is often part of the receiving process, but frankly it should be avoided. If suppliers are reliable and material specifications are clear, no inspection should be required. If suppliers are not reliable, fix the real problem (supplier errors) instead of covering it with an added process (inspection). In too many cases, a site neglects the supplier errors and the inspection process takes on a life of its own, adding unjustified time to the period from when an order is placed until material is ready to use.

Real-World Observation

I visited a plant that allocated a very large area to incoming material that was waiting for inspection. It was common for items to wait as long as *30 calendar days* to be inspected. Ay-yi-yi! What an atrocity! Production cells often ran short of material while the required replenishment parts sat in the inspection area. When this happened, associates left their work cell to find the needed part in the inspection wasteland, then they begged the quality team to inspect and receive what was needed. Operations frequently lacked the parts they needed, even though on-hand inventory was very high and the required parts were almost always in the building. To add insult to injury, due to the lag between physical receipt and the official "quality" receipt date, suppliers usually refused to accept the return of any failed material because it had been on site for so long. There was no way to hold suppliers financially accountable for errors. It was a disaster from every angle.

Consume: Parts are consumed when a customer or internal user takes inventory out of the bucket. Consumption can occur once a week, once per shift, or several times an hour—it depends on the process and the type of customer doing the pulling. Therefore, consumption often has a much higher occurrence rate or frequency than replenishment. Consumption might occur several times an hour, drawing down the level in the bucket gradually over time, while replenishment might happen just once a week.

Imagine that the demand spigot in Figure 1-1 on page 20 drips out small amounts almost continuously, but the supply at the top drops a full ladle once a week. Demand is more regular but in smaller quantities, while replenishment is less frequent but more lumpy.

Another consumption consideration is that it can be very predictable, e.g., the same number of pieces used every day, or it can be highly erratic. Volatility in the rate of consumption is one of the most challenging aspects of inventory management, and we'll discuss this in detail in future chapters.

HINT for Associates

For inventory accuracy, as parts are consumed they must be "relieved" or subtracted from inventory. Physical usage removes material from the bucket, but items must also be subtracted from financial and operational records so the "system" is up to date.

The difference between what is physically on hand and what the system thinks is available is a primary source of material errors and headaches, so transactions should be accurate and timely.

Replenish: After material is consumed, parts must be ordered to replenish or refill the bucket. A site must be good at getting the *right stuff* into the *right bucket* at the *right time*. Defining the details of a replenishment order is a key part of the replenishment process, so the supplier, order quantity, and due date are required for every replenishment order. Purchased parts also need a valid price on every order.

The replenishment process generates *Purchase Orders* for external material and *Manufacturing Orders* for internal material. As mentioned above, these orders should refill buckets with the right material in the right quantity and at the right time, which is much more difficult than it sounds.

HINT for Associates

A *replenishment* process is different than the process for placing and managing an *initial* order for a new part number or a new supplier. The first order for new item, or for an old item from a new supplier, usually requires special handling for placing the order, inspecting the parts, accepting the parts, and putting the parts into stock.

On the other hand, regular replenishment orders should be streamlined in how they are created and processed.

Achieving high levels of success with inventory management means defining repeatable, sustainable, and reliable processes for replenishing inventory, from order generation to putting parts in inventory. These steps should be clearly defined and easy to get right.

Real-World Observation

I assisted a plant that allowed Assembly to build customer demand in random order. Actual customer orders for 1,000 assemblies over the next four weeks were sometimes assembled entirely in one week. It was chaotic!

As you might expect, the Materials team spent most of their time expediting internal and external parts because Assembly hadn't learned the concepts of level loading and just-in-time replenishment.

Additionally, the customer refused to accept early delivery of the demand, so finished goods that were built early sat in inventory for 1, 2, or even 3 weeks until they could be shipped.

In this plant, Assembly drove high levels of chaos and on-hand inventory because they failed to recognize what their actions were doing to the rest of the operation.

Inventory Management Summary

Successful inventory management is all about balancing material availability versus cash flow. On the surface, managing inventory seems like a simple task, but it is often made up of highly complex and intertwined processes that occur repetitively for hundreds or thousands of items.

TUTORIAL: INTRODUCTION TO GOCO

Gadgets and Oddities Company (GOCO) is a US-based manufacturer of various meter and instrument assemblies for automotive, agricultural, and industrial customers. GOCO generates about $115 million a year in revenue with all sales in US dollars. Due to the competitive nature of the business, they operate on a slim profit margin, and cash flow is key to supporting and investing in the operation.

Ten years ago, GOCO's standard profit averaged 18-20% after subtracting cost of goods sold (COGS). Their net profit was 8-10% after sales, general and administrative (SG&A) overhead expenses.

In the old days, they ignored inventory dollars because cash flow from operations was sufficient to sustain company growth. Their philosophy of "stock it so we can ship it" was evident in tall stacks of raw material, high levels of work in progress (WIP), and large piles of finished goods inventory. They averaged about 80 workdays on hand, almost one third of their 250 annual workdays, tying up about $31 million of cash.

In the last few years, profit margins dropped and it became evident that they would continue to endure price pressure from their customers. The company sought ways to increase cash flow through lower costs and better asset management. After several years of reducing labor and material costs, they recently implemented an "inventory austerity program" that asked buyers and planners to minimize inventory spending and balances to free up cash. GOCO Buyers and Planners reduced on-hand balances for high-cost purchased items and certain finished goods, but improvements were limited in scope. Total inventory came down to just under 60 days, with on-hand inventory valued at about $23 million, but progress stalled there. See Figure 1-2 for more details about GOCO.

Figure 1-2. GOCO Annual Financial Results

Revenue	$	115,039,034
COGS (FG)	$	99,246,804
Operating Profit	$	15,792,230
Operating Profit Margin		13.73%
SG&A	$	11,357,902
Net Profit	$	4,434,328
Net Profit Margin		3.85%
Annual Material Spend	$	69,116,750
On-hand $	$	23,212,755
Raw Material	$	5,714,102
WIP	$	13,735,052
FG	$	3,763,601
DOH		58.47
Inventory Turns		4.28

The plant set a 12-month goal to cut inventory in half to free up cash. Mary, the newly-hired Materials Manager, had the arduous task of designing action plans to achieve this target. She had joined GOCO a couple of months ago and experienced the most recent inventory reduction activity, but she was well aware that progress had stagnated. The senior management team had no idea how to achieve the inventory reduction goal. To add even more pressure on Mary's shoulders, everyone's bonus - from managers to floor associates - depended on achieving the inventory goal.

Mary knew kanban was the right answer. At the end of each chapter, we will follow Mary and her team as they implement new kanban systems and solutions.

CHAPTER 2: CONSUMPTION, REPLENISHMENT & THE SAWTOOTH CURVE

Recall the bucket diagram from the last chapter, repeated to the left. The spigots in the lower part of the bucket represent consumption that can occur at varying rates. Inventory can slowly drip from the bucket or it can gush out like a waterfall. Spigots can run frequently or almost continually, or they can turn on and off randomly. If they run long enough the faucets can drain the bucket dry.

Replenishment is the fill ladle at the top. Theoretically, the bucket can be filled periodically or continuously, but in the real world the vast majority of inventory buckets are filled periodically instead of continuously. So conceptually, the typical bucket is filled by "periodic" ladle, not by a hose.

The bucket is a great visual image but it doesn't provide any mathematical insight about the *amplitude* or *timing* of consumption and replenishment activities.

In order to plan for and balance on-hand inventory versus cash flow, we need to predict consumption and plan replenishment. Therefore, we need an inventory management tool that accommodates the rate of consumption, defines the required replenishment pattern, and establishes the right bucket size for any item that holds inventory in stock.

• The consumption rate is how fast inventory drains out of the bucket. This is usually out of our control because it is dictated by external customers. Yes, even an inventory bucket that feeds an *internal* process instead of an *external* customer is likely driven by the behavior of an end customer.

• The replenishment pattern is the frequency of refill or how often a receipt arrives, along with the replenishment amount for every receipt. Think of this as quantity plus frequency, where both can be variable.

• The bucket size is the maximum amount of inventory that could be held in stock. Most inventory items operate with a bucket that has a relatively fixed size, e.g., we never have more than 1,000 pounds in stock, or we start making parts when we get to 1,000 and stop when the level gets to 10,000. Some buckets vary dramatically in size from day to day or season to season, so estimating maximum and minimum bucket sizes can be challenging.

The best graphical illustration of these concepts is the sawtooth curve, in Figure 2-1 on page 24. A sawtooth curve charts on-hand balance (OHB) over time as it responds to puts and takes, or pluses and minuses. Unlike the static bucket diagram above, which is one snapshot in time, a sawtooth curve is a diagram of how much inventory is in stock over a period of time.

A sawtooth curve *could* be charted for every inventory transaction, i.e., every time a unit is added or subtracted the new on-hand balance is plotted. That would be messy and difficult to interpret. Instead, one sawtooth data point is generally a defined and consistent time period, such as one day or one week, where each data point is the sum of activity for that specified period. Selecting the right time period for each data point and for the entire width of the curve can be tricky, because if the selected data points or the entire sawtooth time period are too broad the curve can mask volatility in either consumption or replenishment. Similarly, if they're too short, it can make volatility look worse than it is.

Figure 2-1. <u>Steady State Inventory Sawtooth Curve</u>

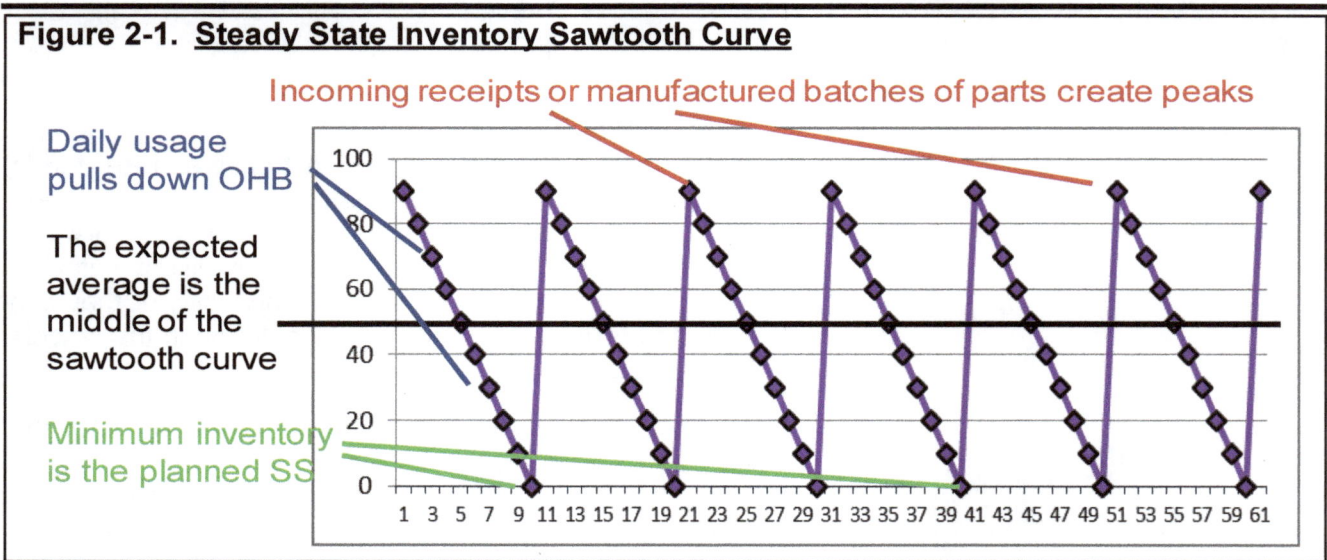

Incoming receipts or manufactured batches of parts create peaks

Daily usage pulls down OHB

The expected average is the middle of the sawtooth curve

Minimum inventory is the planned SS

We need to think about how to design a sawtooth curve, then we can figure out how to analyze it.

Factors That Determine a Sawtooth Curve

We'll start by reviewing how a sawtooth curve is constructed.

Consumption Is a Sawtooth Design Factor

The rate of consumption for any given item is a primary factor in designing a sawtooth curve because usage sets the pace of drawdown, or the slope of the downward portions of the curve.

Since the sawtooth curve covers a time period, usage *quantity* must be viewed versus *time*, where each data point represents a subset of the sawtooth period. Consumption of 10 kilograms is helpful to know, but that is only part of the formula. Do we use 10 kilograms per day, per week, or per month?

How do we know the right frequency rate for the data points in the sawtooth curve, i.e., daily or weekly or monthly?

Go back to the logic of consumption, or how customer demand pulls material out of the bucket. For most items, the timing of a demand event is random. Imagine that a bucket holds loaves of bread. The grocery store might be open 12, 16, or 24 hours per day. Whenever the store is open, a customer can walk in and select 1 or more loaves of bread. Every loaf of bread that is pulled off the shelf is a demand event, and those events are random, at the whim of the customers. Those random events can be bundled within a defined time period, such as the number of loaves demanded *per hour* or *per day* or *per week*.

That's logical, yet it takes us right back where we started, with no clear indication of the "right" time period to bundle demand events. We really need to think about this timing thing so let's flip it around. We know that demand occurs at random times and for random quantities, but does replenishment have the same randomness? We already noted that replenishment is usually periodic, or more lumpy. Does that gives better insight?

Consumption is driven by customers, which can't be perfectly controlled. But, the replenishment process is driven by the supplier, and there is usually just one supplier and, therefore, one set of replenishment rules for each item. What are the basic rules? Since the supplier sets or at least agrees to the rules, items are replenished within certain *quantity* and *lead-time* boundaries.

Suppose we need 1 custom-made birthday cake and we also need roofing nails (no, probably not from the same supplier, or for the same project). The quantity provided per delivery and the time to receive these 2 orders might be dramatically different.

Quantity: The cake will arrive as a quantity of 1, which is exactly what we ordered. A reasonable bakery won't mandate a minimum order of multiple custom cakes.

On the other hand, don't expect to purchase 1 nail at a time. They'll come in a box of 100 or 500 or even 1,000 nails, even if we need just one.

Timing: The cake requires time for the supplier to produce and deliver (or for us to pick it up) because it is a custom order. It might take a couple days to get the cake.

The time to receive nails should be short because they are standard products and should be in stock at the hardware store. So, the lead time for nails is only the transit time, whether delivered by the hardware store or picked up by us.

Replenishment Lead Time & Quantity Are Sawtooth Design Factors

Let's expand on the cake example. Suppose we run a restaurant that consumes 8 cakes per day, and the local bakery takes 3 days to replenish cakes for any order of 5 to 30 cakes. Their delivery van holds only 30 cakes, so that's the maximum allowed daily order size, and they won't deliver fewer than 5 at a time.

• Would we order 1 cake at a time? Probably not. We need 8 per day, so the minimum order of 5 isn't a big deal to us.

• Would we wait until the last minute to order cakes, placing an order only when we serve the last piece of cake? Certainly not; cake is much too important to accept the risk of running out.

• Would we order replenishment cakes every 3 days, because that's how long it takes to get more cake? That would work, but we'd have to ensure that cakes were ordered on a cycle that results in regular deliveries. One way to do this would be to place a new order when the current order arrives, so when the delivery van shows up with 3 days of cakes, which is 24 total cakes to cover 8 cakes per day, we would order 24 more to arrive 3 days later.

• Could we order cakes every day, even though it would take 3 days to receive them? Yes, that would work, too. We could place an order every day based on what we sold that day, even though it would take 3 days to get the replacement cakes. The bakery would receive daily orders for 8 cakes, and we'd receive a delivery every day for the 8 cakes that were ordered 3 days ago.

This simple example illustrates that every item has its own set of supply and demand characteristics. But how can we use timing and quantity insights to evaluate replenishment versus consumption?

First things first. When evaluating replenishment options, what do we need to know?

• Does it help to know that the bakery can't deliver more than 30 per trip or per day? Yes. Since we use just 8 per day, their upper limit doesn't impact us today. But, it would if we doubled our cake sales and needed 16 cakes per day. In that case, we'd have to order cakes every day because just 2 days of demand (16 per day x 2 days = 32 cakes) would be more than they can deliver in 1 trip. Could we run out of cake at 16 per day, if we didn't know that the bakery can deliver up to 30 cakes per trip? Yes, so knowing their maximum allowed order quantity is critical.

• Would it also be wise to know if they have a minimum order quantity of 5 cakes per delivery? Yes, that would also be required information.

• Is it possible that they require cakes to be ordered in certain multiples? Maybe they require orders in multiples of 2, so we can order 8 cakes or 10, but not 9. Yes, that would be an interesting tidbit for our planning purposes.

• Do we need to plan around their 3-day delivery time for orders of 5 to 30 cakes? Yes, that also seems pretty important.

Now we can define what is the required information.

Requirement for <u>Quantity Limit Information</u>: We definitely need to know supplier quantity limits. Minimum order quantity (MOQ), container size or "standard package" quantity (SPQ), and maximum order quantity (MaxQ) are <u>mandatory</u> pieces of information for designing a replenishment plan. Many items are delivered in "minimum order" containers, like the roofing nails discussed above, so minimum order quantity (MOQ) is a common limitation. Many items come in boxes, pails, pallets, totes, or truckloads, and every container size is a defined quantity, which defines the standard package quantity (SPQ) for an item.

Requirement for <u>Lead-Time Information</u>: Supplier lead time is a <u>mandatory</u> piece of information, measured from the time an order is placed until it's received at our site.

Remember that *lead time* dictates how much inventory we need on hand when a new order is placed. When we place a cake order, if there is nothing in production at the bakery, we must have 24 cakes on the shelf to cover 3 days of demand while we wait for the new order to arrive. If a prior order is already in the works at the bakery, that order will arrive in less than 3 days and, therefore, we need only enough cakes on hand to cover from now until the prior order arrives.

<u>Lead-Time Demand</u>: If we combine *supplier lead time, or the time it takes to receive an order,* with *daily usage,* or how many we use per day, we can calculate how many pieces must be ordered per *lead-time period* to cover total demand. This is how much is pulled out of the bucket in the time it takes the supplier to fill a new order, or the quantity that must be on hand when a new order is placed, if nothing else is on order. The quantity [daily demand * lead time] is referred to as *lead-time demand.*

It seems like lead time and lead-time demand might be sawtooth design elements. Hmmm.

Lead-time demand

Lead-time demand = daily demand * lead time

HINT for Associates

When evaluating consumption or designing replenishment plans, the right "time" to use as the analysis period is the replenishment lead time. Therefore, for every replenishment plan we must know actual lead time, measured from the time an order is placed until parts are on site.

Think about cakes. If we use 8 cakes per day, we must order 24 cakes to cover a 3-day period, which is the lead time period. We can order them once every 3 days or once per day or every 2 hours. In fact, if we planned ahead we could order them once a month to cover 30 days of demand, or 8 * 30 = 240 cakes. They might arrive as 8 deliveries of 30 each, the maximum allowed quantity of 30, which minimizes the number of delivery trips, or they might arrive every day, 8 at a time.

No matter what <u>frequency</u> of ordering we select, the <u>total number</u> of cakes ordered to cover the period between bakery deliveries must equate to a supply of at least 8 cakes per day, to cover our demand.

The conclusion is that the analysis of consumption and replenishment comes down to supplier lead time. Yes, supplier lead time is the correct time period for designing a sawtooth curve, and every sawtooth curve should cover at least 2 lead-time periods.

To create a sawtooth shape, chart on-hand balance at a frequency that is a subset of the supplier's lead time, e.g., chart daily balances for an item with a 5-day lead time or weekly balances for a 10-week lead time.

Quick Tangent About Charting Sawtooth Charts

Before we analyze sawtooth charts, let's cover a quick side topic.

When charting sawtooth curves, either the peak or the trough of the chart is slightly off versus what will be observed *mathematically* or in *reality*.

Suppose we start with a full quantity of 100 on the shelf at the *beginning* of Day 1. We use 10 pieces during the day, so the on-hand balance (OHB) at the *end* of the day is 90.

To see the difference between beginning and end of day, look at a bar graphs in Figure 2-2, which show on-hand balance for both the beginning (7:00 AM) and end (4:00 PM) for 10 days.

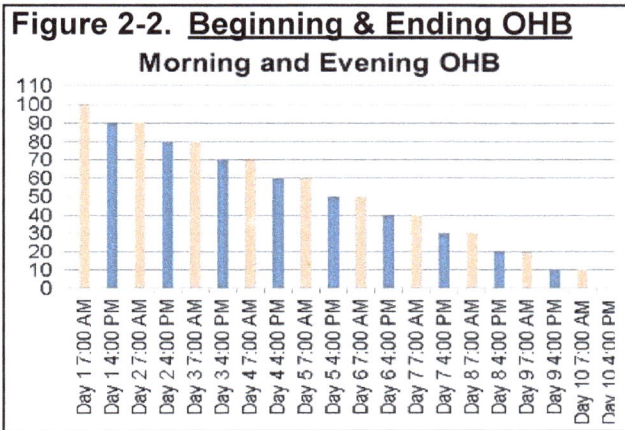

Figure 2-2. **Beginning & Ending OHB**
Morning and Evening OHB

• At 7:00 AM on Day 1, 100 pieces arrive so there are 100 on hand at the beginning of the day.

• By 4:00 PM on Day 1, or the end of the work day, 90 pieces are in stock because 10 were consumed.

• OHB at the end of Day 1 is the starting balance for Day 2, and this pattern repeats through Day 9.

• On Day 10 we start with 10 pieces on hand and use 10 during the day, ending the day with zero. With a lead time of 10 days, we expect a delivery first thing on Day 11, or 10 days after the first receipt on Day 1. So, Day 10 ends with zero on hand and 100 are expected to arrive at the beginning of Day 11.

The chart in Figure 2-2 is confusing, plotting both beginning and ending OHB in the same graph. So, when we plot on-hand balance we use either the beginning of each day or the end.

If we chart data for the *beginning* of every day, as in Figure 2-3, we have 100 pieces on Day 1, which is the balance at the start of the day, down to 10 pieces at 7:00 AM on Day 10, before the last

10 are consumed that day. This works, but it fails to report any of the consumption activity of the day being charted, so it can be misleading.

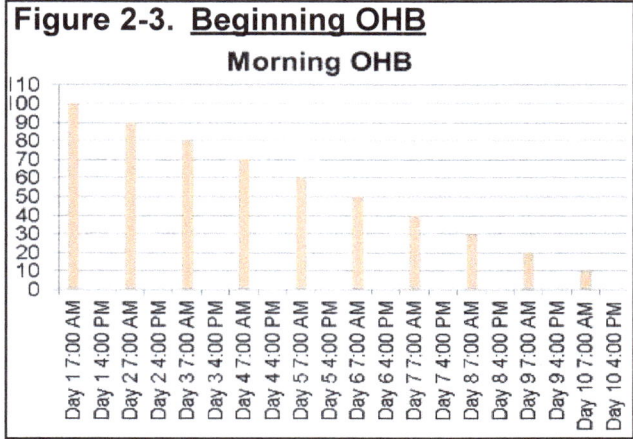

Figure 2-3. **Beginning OHB**
Morning OHB

If we chart the *end* of every day, as in Figure 2-4, Day 1 ends with 90 and Day 10 is zero by day's end, so we never see a data point of 100, the order quantity. This can be confusing since we know we order 100 pieces and therefore expect to see a peak of 100 pieces, but that is not the case for end-of-day charts. This is generally an easier error to live with (versus not seeing 0 OHB, as in beginning charts) because each data point reflects the impact of that day's replenishment and consumption activity.

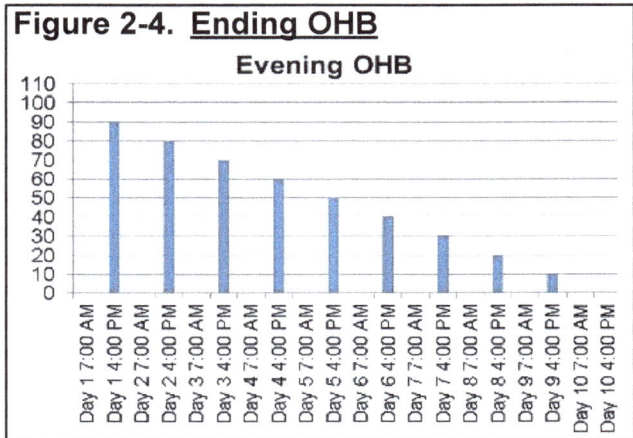

Figure 2-4. **Ending OHB**
Evening OHB

It's important to remember that whether we plot beginning or end values, one OHB will be wrong, either the maximum or minimum value. In the real world, maximum inventory occurs when a new order arrives, regardless of what time of day it arrives, and minimum inventory occurs just before an order arrives.

To create a perfect chart would require *much* more effort than it's worth because the differences between the graphs and reality are small and easily explained. Additionally, from a practical perspective, sawtooth curves should *not* be the primary tool used to predict inventory balances (we'll get to formulas soon – I can't wait!), but these curves can be insightful in some cases, even with slight errors.

The sawtooth curves in the remainder of this chapter assume <u>end-of-day</u> balances.

The Mechanics of a Sawtooth Curve

Every replenishment plan consists of both <u>timing</u> and <u>quantity</u>. When creating a sawtooth curve, we need to know supplier lead time, or the time boundary that defines the replenishment plan. But, we also need a smaller time period to bundle demand events into data points to be plotted across two or more lead-time periods. If lead time is 2 weeks, we can bundle demand events into daily sums to draw a sawtooth curve, where 10 workdays of demand, or 10 data points, equals one 10-day lead time.

Let's look at an example. Figure 2-5 is a sawtooth curve with demand summed each day. In this example, daily demand is 10 pieces. Lead time is 10 days and standard order quantity is 100. This is an example of a *theoretical* or "steady state" curve used for inventory planning because daily demand does not waver from 10 pieces, lead time is always 10 days, and a receipt is never late or early. In this simple replenishment pattern, *1* order arrives for each lead-time period, so the distance between 2 consecutive peaks equals the lead time of 10 days.

Figure 2-5. <u>Steady State Inventory Sawtooth Curve</u>

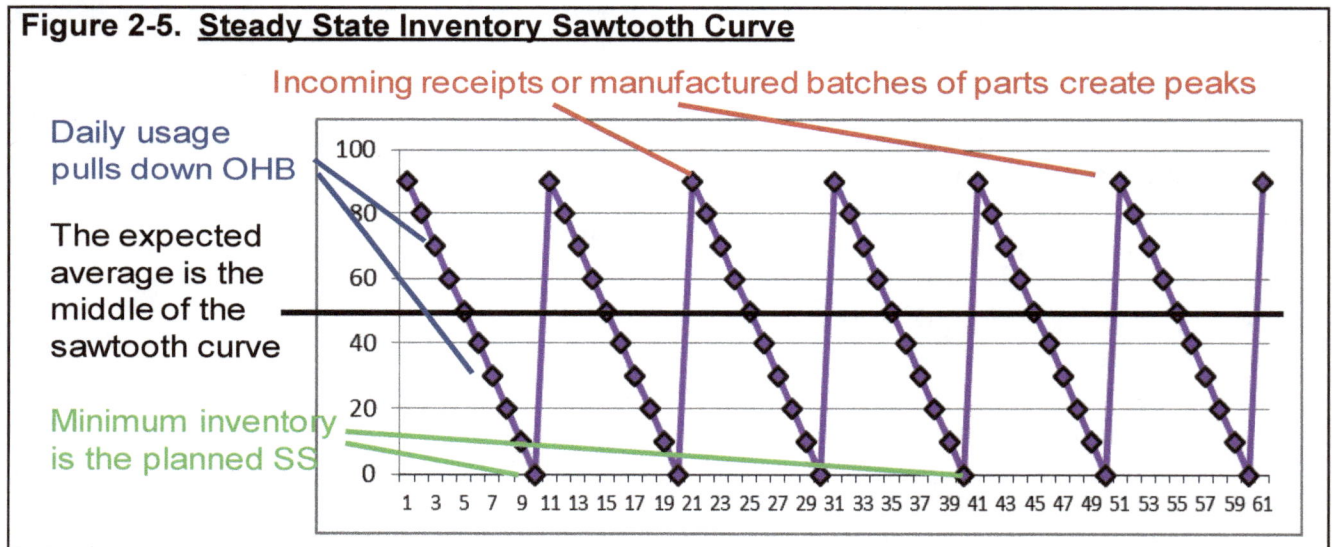

Incoming receipts or manufactured batches of parts create peaks

Daily usage pulls down OHB

The expected average is the middle of the sawtooth curve

Minimum inventory is the planned SS

Sawtooth Curve Elements

The shape of a sawtooth curve has certain expected features.

The tallest point or <u>peak</u> of a sawtooth curve is the expected maximum inventory level. The height of a peak equals any remaining OHB from the prior delivery, or material that hasn't been consumed, plus the quantity in the new receipt, minus what was used during the day. (These are end-of-day balances.)

The <u>decline</u> in on-hand balance, or the drop from point to point in the plotted line in Figure 2-5, is the total number of units consumed per *day* because it's a daily chart. The rate of daily consumption determines the slope of the decline; higher daily demand causes a steeper slope or faster decline. The rate of decline times the lead time tells us how many we need on hand when we place a new order. Think back to the cake example: we need 24 cakes on the shelf when we place an order because it will take 3 days for the new order to arrive.

The low point or <u>valley</u> of a sawtooth curve is the minimum expected inventory for that item. An item can be planned to drop to zero, as in Figure 2-5, meaning the replenishment plan matches the rate of consumption with no spare inventory. We use 10 per day with a lead time of 10 days, so we use 100 pieces per lead-time period and also receive 100 pieces. The size of the inventory bucket *exactly* matches demand, so we expect the bucket to be empty when a replenishment order arrives. Daily demand is exactly covered with nothing to spare.

To prevent the risk of allowing inventory to drop to zero, many replenishment plans include some level of cushion. In the bucket analogy, extra volume is added to the bucket beyond what is required to cover lead-time demand. This is designated as "safety stock" (SS) because it serves as a safety net to prevent inventory from dropping to zero. Any item, even those with predictable replenishment and consumption patterns, can experience risk from "non-steady-state" occurrences such as higher consumption, erratic daily demand, late deliveries, or a low replenishment quantity. When evaluating a sawtooth curve, if the *low point is greater than zero, it means safety stock has been added to the replenishment plan.*

Basic Sawtooth Curves

Let's draw a few basic curves for an item with a 10-day lead time and daily demand of 10 pieces.

One Order Per Lead Time, No Safety Stock, Stable Daily Demand, Predictable Receipts

In Figure 2-6, the blue line is the sawtooth curve, or the graph of on-hand balance. We receive 100 pieces per order, so there is no buffer in the bucket because lead time demand [daily demand * lead time] is also 100 pieces. The green bars indicate receipts of 100 pieces every 10 days.

At the end of Day 1, there are 90 pieces on hand because we received 100 (green bar) and used 10.

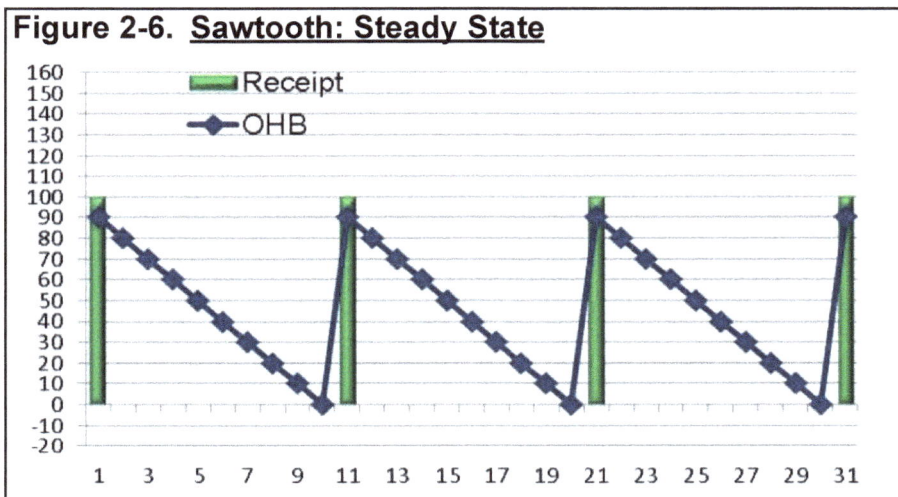

Figure 2-6. <u>Sawtooth: Steady State</u>

Over time, the steady state on-hand balance for receipts of 100 and average daily demand of 10 is very predictable and orderly because the graph assumes demand and supply are at steady state with no anomalies or outliers.

In subsequent examples we'll see that the sawtooth curve is different if we plot data that is more representative of the real world, with supplier delays, receipt quantity changes, or variation in daily demand.

One Order Per Lead Time, No Safety Stock, Stable Demand, <u>Delayed</u> Receipt

In Figure 2-7 the first receipt is delayed by just 1 day, from Day 11 to Day 12, but that gives us negative inventory for Day 11. (No, in the real world we don't really experience "negative" inventory, but OHB drops to zero and that could potentially delay production in the impacted cell because we need 10 pieces every single day.)

One hundred pieces arrive on Day 12, as indicated by the gray column that is the *delayed* receipt. The 10 pieces we missed on Day 11 *plus* 10 pieces for Day 12 are both consumed, so Day 12 receives 100 parts and consumes 20 and therefore ends at 80. (It is possible that the cell using the delayed parts might not catch up from the stock out in just *1* day, but we'll assume they are *really* fast and efficient.)

Figure 2-7. <u>Sawtooth: Delayed Receipt</u>

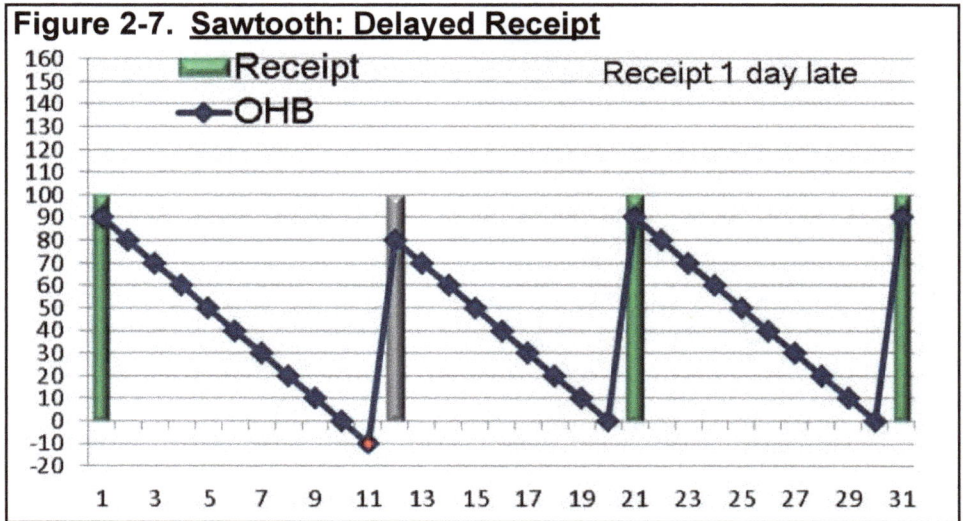

With no buffer or safety stock, this sawtooth curve is risky. Replenishment and consumption are perfectly balanced (consumption = replenishment), so a late delivery can impact production.

One Order Per Lead Time, No Safety Stock, <u>Variable</u> Daily Demand, <u>Delayed</u> Receipt

<u>Demand variation</u> is unavoidable in many environments, so in addition to supplier delays we must consider day-to-day demand changes. <u>Average</u> daily demand, the 10 per day used in the prior charts, is insightful but it doesn't capture the fluctuation that occurs from day to day.

Figure 2-8 shows a delayed receipt plus demand variation, which is an accurate snapshot for much of the real world. The OHB slope from Day 1 to Day 11 is no longer a straight line of 10 per day, because daily demand is exhibiting day-to-day variation.

There is no safety stock in this plan, and on-hand balance is "negative" for 2 days.

Figure 2-8. <u>Sawtooth: Demand Variation, Delayed Receipt</u>

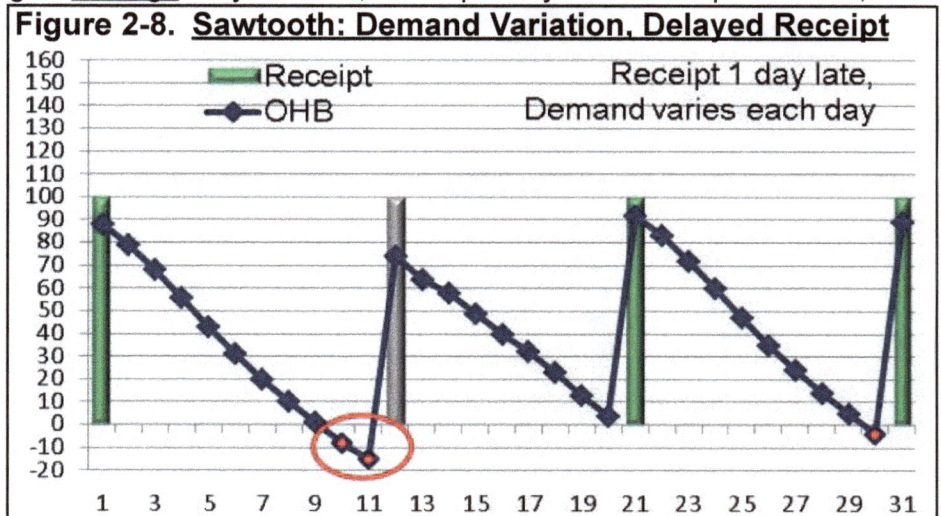

• Day 10 is negative because demand exceeded the expected 10 per day from Day 1 through Day 10, consuming more than the planned 100 pieces.

• Day 11 is "more negative" than Day 10 because the expected replenishment order did not arrive on time. So, in addition to higher demand for the first 10 days, no parts were received on Day 11.

The lack of a safety stock results in zero on-hand inventory when consumption exceeds expected demand or if supply is delayed. In this example, we experienced both risks, so the impact was big.

One Order Per Lead Time, Safety Stock = 20, Variable Daily Demand, Delayed Receipt, 120 Order Quantity, Order Every 10 Days

Suppose order quantity was increased to 120 to provide some safety stock, as in Figure 2-9. Receipts are still scheduled for every 10 days. We *expect* to see 20 pieces of safety stock (120 order quantity - lead-time demand of 100 = 20 extra pieces), but that only happens if we manage the *entire* replenishment plan.

Figure 2-9. Sawtooth: Higher Order Quantity, Demand Variation, Delayed Receipt

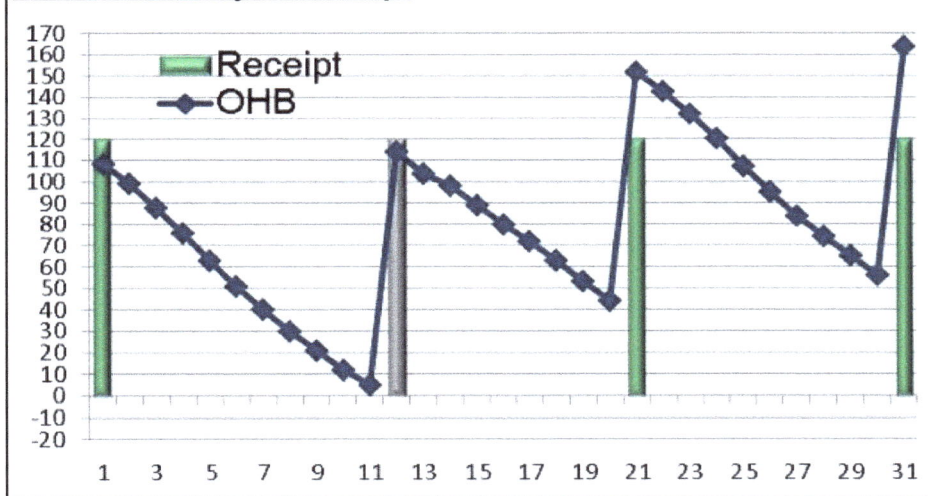

With added safety stock, Day 10 is no longer negative, even though demand was higher than expected for the first 10 days. Day 11 is also above zero, despite the delayed receipt.

Note how on-hand balance (the blue line) escalates as time progresses through several lead-time periods. This tells us that the higher order quantity *should* have changed how frequently an order was received, stretching trigger timing beyond 10 days. Orders should be processed at the correct time based on *usage*, instead of processing based on a rigid "every 10 days" schedule.

Think about cake orders again. If we ordered 32 cakes for every order instead of 24, we wouldn't need to order cakes every 3 days because each order would cover 4 days of demand (32 cakes / 8 per day = 4 days). If we had a "cake event" at the restaurant and sold 22 cakes in 2 days instead of 16 cakes, the demand variation would be covered. If the bakery was a day late delivering cakes, we'd also be covered. But, if those variations do not occur and we use 8 per day and replenishments arrive on time, we need to order cakes every 4 days and *not* every 3 days. This reinforces how important it is to understand demand and replenishment timing in a replenishment plan.

Let's look at an example where we trigger orders based on consumption instead of every 10 days.

One Order Per Lead Time, <u>Safety Stock = 20</u>, <u>Variable</u> Daily Demand, <u>Delayed</u> Receipt, <u>120 Order Quantity</u>, <u>Triggers Timed Correctly</u>

There is safety stock in this example because the <u>order</u> quantity for 1 lead-time period is greater than total <u>demand</u> for that period. When an order is triggered for 120 parts, it should take *10* days for the order to arrive, but it should take *12* days to use 120 parts. So we have 2 days or 20 pieces of safety stock.

If we're triggering orders based on consumption, we need to understand how that works. In kanban systems, orders are generally triggered *either* when a full order quantity has been completely consumed <u>or</u> when it is first opened, so an order can be triggered when piece #1 is used or when piece #120 is used. (Yes, there are mid-point trigger exceptions, and yes, the choice of first or last piece impacts the replenishment plan. More on all of that later.) Receipts are paced based on actual consumption, so if demand stays at the expected 10 per day, an order should be triggered every *12* days instead of every *10.* This prevents the inventory escalation we saw in the previous example.

In Figure 2-10, an order arrives on Day 13, 2 days later than the receipt in Figure 2-9. Why? Think about how orders are triggered. When orders are triggered based on consumption, an order is initiated 2 days later than it would be if it was based on a fixed 10-day schedule, because we have 120 pieces per replenishment (12 days of demand) instead of 100 pieces (10 days of demand.) Like the previous example, the order was delayed by one day, to day 13.

In this example, the first replenishment trigger occurred on Day 2 when the first piece was taken out of the box of 120 pieces. That order was due on Day 12 (Day 2 + 10-day lead time). This receipt was shipped 1 day late by the

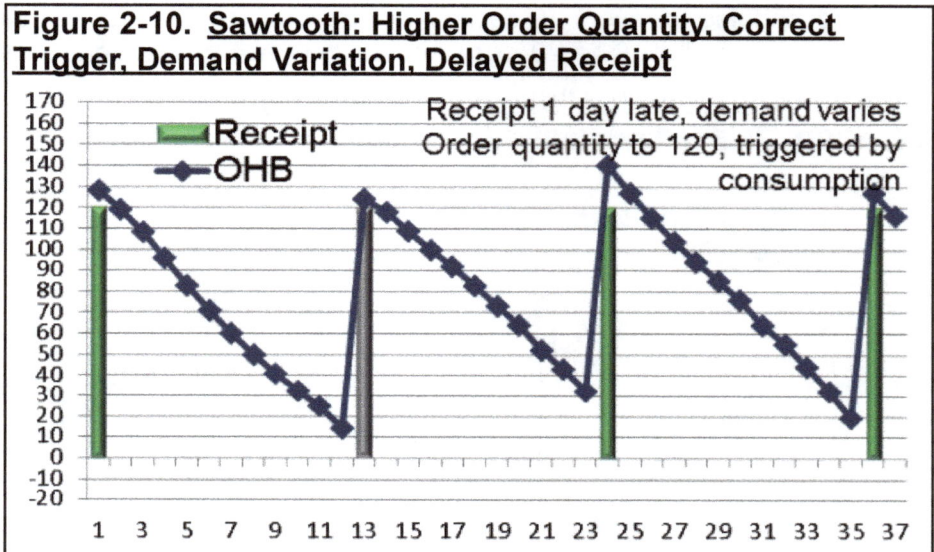

Figure 2-10. Sawtooth: Higher Order Quantity, Correct Trigger, Demand Variation, Delayed Receipt

supplier, as was the case in the prior example in Figure 2-9, but in this case it arrived on Day 13 instead of Day 11. Got all of that?

Because orders in Figure 2-10 are triggered based on consumption, and they cover more than 10 days of demand, 4 orders arrive during the charted 37 days, versus 4 orders in 31 days in Figure 2-9. Because of the safety stock, inventory does not go negative even with a late receipt plus higher demand. Similarly, OHB no longer climbs out of control over time because replenishment orders are paced by consumption.

Note that maximum and peak on-hand balances are not perfectly predictable in this diagram, as they were in some of the prior charts. This is due to demand variation plus receipt delays, and it is a common feature of real-world diagrams. In the first section of this sawtooth, demand is slightly higher than average so the balance at day 12 is below the expected safety stock of 20 pieces, but demand in the middle of the curve is lower than the 10 per day average, so on-hand balance at day 23 is higher than we would expect, or above 20 pieces of safety stock.

These simple diagrams demonstrate that we must scientifically manage replenishment plans.

• If we fail to manage the bottom of the curve we might run out of parts, which impacts delivery.

• On the other hand, if we don't manage safety stock, replenishment size, and receipt timing we might carry more inventory than we need, taking up precious cash and space.

To avoid these errors we must be able to estimate inventory balances for every replenishment plan. Here come the formulas!

Predicting Minimum, Average & Maximum Inventory for a Sawtooth Curve

When planning a replenishment solution, it's important to accurately predict the top, middle, and bottom of the sawtooth curve, or maximum, average, and minimum on-hand balances. It isn't feasible to draw a sawtooth curve for every replenishment plan. Even if we had all those graphs, we couldn't visually analyze every item to predict key inventory levels. We need formulas, and, yes, we love formulas!

Refer to the sawtooth curve in Figure 2-11. We consume 8 per day and lead time is 10 days. Every replenishment signal is for 100 parts. Maximum inventory in the chart is greater than 100 and minimum is greater than zero. So, we can conclude that safety stock has been added to this inventory plan. Now let's think through the math.

Each order for 100 pieces must cover 10 lead-time days. We use 8 parts per day, so in 10 days we

Figure 2-11. Sawtooth Curve @ Steady State

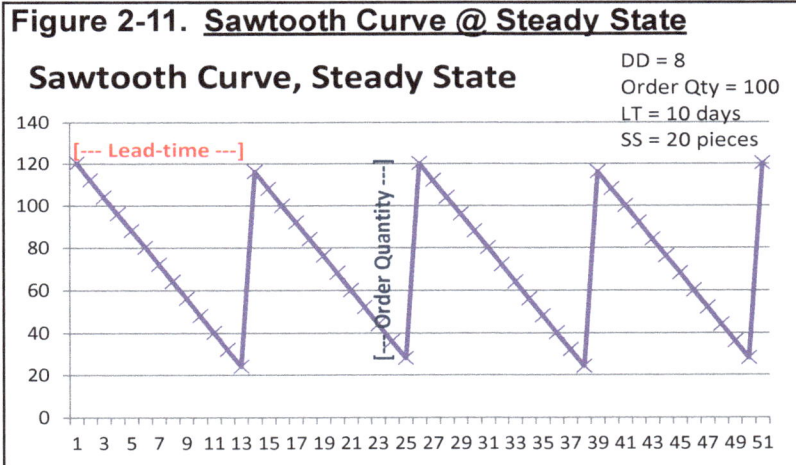

Sawtooth Curve, Steady State

DD = 8
Order Qty = 100
LT = 10 days
SS = 20 pieces

consume 80 pieces. Because we order 100 and expect to use 80 in 10 days, there are 20 pieces of safety stock in the model. If we start with 100 pieces at time zero, a full on-hand order, at steady-state demand we'd have 20 left at the end of the 10-day lead time.

If an order had been placed just before we opened this quantity of 100 parts, that "old" order is due to arrive on day 10, based on a 10-day lead time. That means our on-hand quantity at the beginning of day 11 will be 20 pieces left from the order we've been using, plus 100 pieces from the order we'll receive that day. Because there is safety stock in the system, we don't expect to get down to zero inventory unless demand is high or supply is late.

In a replenishment plan, *safety stock quantity equals the expected minimum on-hand inventory*. If safety stock is 20 pieces, the sawtooth curve has an expected minimum value of 20 units.

In Figure 2-11, the estimate of average inventory, or the value halfway up the curve, is about 70 parts on hand. That number might be surprising because it might seem logical to estimate average inventory equal to order quantity divided by 2 or [100 / 2 = 50 pieces], but that ignores the safety stock below the sawtooth curve. To accurately predict average inventory, estimate the middle of the sawtooth curve, *not* the middle of the order quantity, because order quantity sits on top of safety stock. In this case, estimate the average on-hand inventory by dividing order quantity by 2 and adding safety stock, or average inventory is [order quantity / 2 + SS = 100 / 2 + 20 = 70].

To estimate maximum inventory, add safety stock to the order quantity, or 100 pieces per order plus 20 pieces of safety stock equals an estimated maximum inventory of 120 pieces, as in Figure 2-11.

Basic Formulas to Estimate Inventory Balances

Estimated Minimum Inventory
= Actual safety stock units
= Total quantity ordered in the lead-time period
- (Lead time * Daily demand)

Estimated Average Inventory = Order quantity / 2 + Actual SS

Estimated Maximum Inventory = Order quantity + Actual SS

To estimate inventory dollars instead of units, multiply inventory units by standard cost.

Predicting inventory balances requires accurate values for actual safety stock, order quantity, daily demand, and lead time.

Things That Impact a Sawtooth Curve

Before we leave the topic of sawtooth curves, let's look at a couple factors that impact the shape or size of a sawtooth curve, and therefore ultimately effect on-hand inventory.

Sawtooth Impacts from Imposed Lead Times or Minimum Order Quantities

Because minimizing on-hand inventory is a primary inventory management goal, every replenishment plan, including kanban, seeks to avoid unnecessary inventory.

There are 2 replenishment parameters that can increase average inventory beyond what is mathematically required, which eats up cash.

High Minimum Order or Standard Package Quantity Impact on a Sawtooth

A replenishment plan should order a quantity that is equal to or slightly higher than expected consumption over a lead-time period. However, a replenishment plan that is built on an artificially high order quantity has a disastrous sawtooth curve because the entire curve is too tall.

Suppose we need to order 100 pieces every 2 weeks (10 per day) to cover the 2-week lead-time demand, but the supplier requires us to order at least 1,000 pieces per order, which covers 20 weeks of demand. The sawtooth is much taller than demand would require, and, therefore, maximum and average inventory will be very high versus what should be required for a demand of 50 pieces per week.

High order quantities can be caused by a supplier's minimum order or standard package requirements, and the impact on a sawtooth curve and the associated inventory value can be significant for on-hand inventory. This drains cash!

Lead-Time Impact on a Sawtooth

Another sawtooth curve destroyer is a long lead time. For a *typical* steady state sawtooth curve, lead time determines the *time* from peak to peak, or the length of the sawtooth pattern, because 1 receipt covers total demand for 1 lead-time period. Simultaneously, lead time determines the *height* of the peak because each receipt must be tall enough to last until the next receipt. Therefore, a long lead time drives higher on-hand inventory versus a short lead time, because the sawtooth curve has to be taller to cover a longer lead time.

Unlike a high minimum order quantity, for which there is no solution, a long lead time can be addressed by breaking the lead-time period into more than 1 replenishment order. This *changes the approach for the sawtooth curve to more than 1 peak per lead-time period*, but it is very manageable if well planned.

Let's look at a quick example of addressing a long lead time with multiple receipts per lead-time period.

Inventory Impact from More Than One Order Per Lead-Time Period

The number of receipts per lead-time period has a big impact on the height of a sawtooth curve. In the sawtooth examples starting on page 29 we assumed 1 order per lead-time period and order quantity was determined by how many were consumed in 1 lead-time period, or [lead time * daily demand + planned safety stock]. One order covered all demand for 1 lead-time period, which is the simplest replenishment plan. If we changed the model and had more than 1 receipt per lead time, we'd generate a different sawtooth curve.

In Figure 2-12 there are 3 possible scenarios.

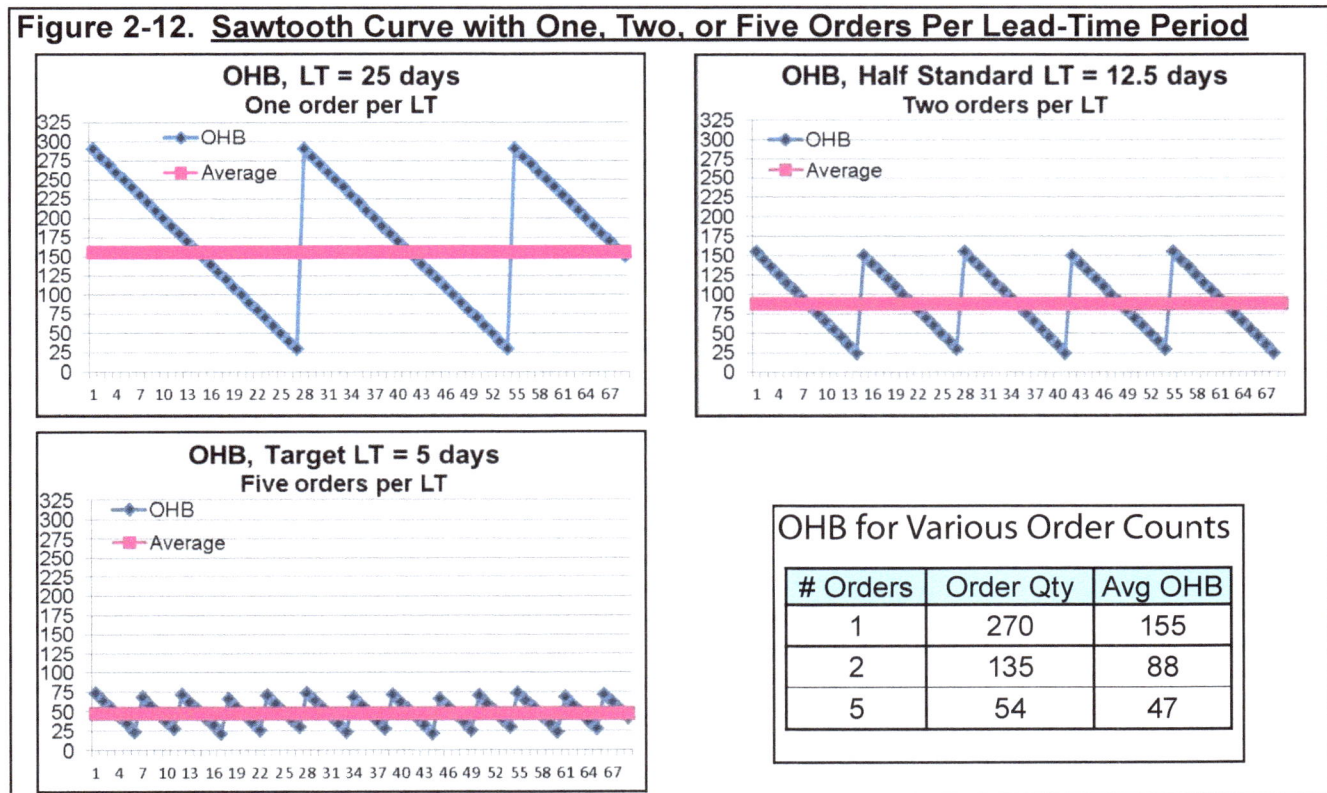

Figure 2-12. **Sawtooth Curve with One, Two, or Five Orders Per Lead-Time Period**

OHB for Various Order Counts

# Orders	Order Qty	Avg OHB
1	270	155
2	135	88
5	54	47

• The top left chart assumes a 1 order per 25-day lead-time period, daily demand of 10 pieces, and an order quantity of 270 pieces. Because lead time is 25 days and we use 10 per day, an order quantity of 270 has 20 pieces of safety stock built into the solution.

From our formulas, we calculate that average inventory is [order quantity / 2 + safety stock = 270 / 2 + 20 = 155].

• The upper right chart assumes the same 25-day lead time, but with 2 orders per lead-time period, so order quantity is 135. This solution also has 20 units of safety stock, because we receive 135 pieces per order but place 2 orders per lead-time period, so we still get 270 pieces to cover 1 lead time.

Average inventory is predicted to be [135 / 2 + 20 = 87.5].

• The bottom left graph has 5 orders in 1 lead-time period. Every order is for 54 pieces, and we still have 20 pieces of safety stock, because 5 orders of 54 sums to 270 pieces ordered for 1 lead-time period.

Average inventory is [54 / 2 + 20 = 47].

In the table at the bottom right of Figure 2-12, the values for maximum and average on-hand inventory are summarized, and they are strikingly different from 1 to 2 orders per lead-time period, and even better with 5 orders per period.

The lesson from this example? To reduce average and maximum inventory, use multiple replenishment orders per lead-time period.

But which plan is correct? If replenishment can be accomplished with any number of orders per lead-time period, how do we know which plan is correct? Why stop at 1 order every 5 days to cover a 25-day lead time? How about an order every day? Or maybe every hour? Wouldn't hourly orders be the best way to shorten the sawtooth curve and reduce on-hand inventory?

Let's think about that. Every replenishment plan has to balance delivery and inventory performance, but it isn't as simple as receiving every part number every hour or every shift or every day.

• For most purchased items, daily receipts aren't feasible or practical. Most suppliers don't want to provide hourly or daily shipments. Internally, every replenishment order is also a receiving transaction, and there are real costs for receiving (generate the order, unload the parts from the truck, transact the receipt, put parts away).

• For internal or manufactured items, there can be set-up time for every order, so it might not be practical to manufacture every part every day, though sometimes this is possible.

To settle this, we need a method for defining the proper replenishment quantity or frequency, the correct number of orders per lead-time period. Setting order *quantity* or *frequency* is at the heart of kanban design, and that decision can be more complex than it might seem, as we'll see in future chapters.

Sawtooth Curve Summary

An item's replenishment plan is the key to balancing delivery performance versus on-hand inventory because it determines the sawtooth curve. The shape and size of the sawtooth curve is dictated by demand, lead time, order quantity, and actual safety stock. Therefore, every element of a replenishment plan must be carefully planned.

Sawtooth curves can't be created for every item, but formulas can predict minimum, average, and maximum inventory for a defined replenishment plan.

CHAPTER 3: MEASURING INVENTORY MANAGEMENT

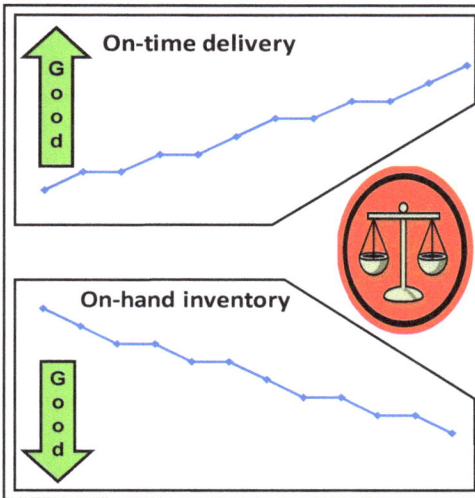

Inventory management is the set of processes that plan and control on-site material to balance customer delivery versus the cost of holding inventory. The right purchased and manufactured material must be available to complete all manufacturing processes in order to ship products on time and within a reasonable lead time. At the same time, high inventory performance means inventory balances are as low as possible to boost cash flow.

So, high *delivery* success requires enough of the right inventory to make products for internal or external customers, while *inventory performance* attempts to minimize on-hand dollars. Yikes! That's a difficult balancing act, but because customer satisfaction is an operation's top priority, it's clear that on-time delivery and short lead times are <u>more important</u> than low on-hand inventory. Serve the customer first!

Rule of Thumb

Lean is a continuous improvement philosophy based on the Toyota Production System. (If you are not familiar with Lean, read *Lean Thinking* by Womack and Jones and *The Toyota Way* by Liker.)

In the Lean world, many sites prioritize Safety, Quality, Delivery, and Cost (SQDC) as key operational metrics. These items are pursued in that order, where safety of associates and customers is the number one priority; the second priority is delivering a high quality product; meeting on-time delivery and lead-time objectives comes in third; and finally inventory, material, and labor costs are tackled. Breaking the "Cost" into Inventory (I) and Labor Productivity (P) turns SQDC into SQDIP, which is pronounced "S. Q. dip" in Lean circles.

SQDIP is an excellent way to focus on improving operational performance.

Some sites believe high delivery performance requires high inventory levels, but that is an erroneous conclusion. Many facilities consistently exhibit high delivery results and also have low on-hand balances. Perhaps it seems counterintuitive for high success on these items to be linked, but they both require *systematic* and *robust* processes to achieve success, versus processes that happen by chance, are managed by brute force, or require all-hands-on-deck emergency interventions. Simultaneous high delivery and low inventory levels are essentially two sides of the same coin, and, therefore, inventory management is measured on these two simultaneous indicators of success.

- As an operational metric, delivery has two elements.

   » <u>On-time delivery</u> (OTD) is a critical customer metric that measures the percent of time end-customer deliveries are made on time, i.e., in accordance with promised due dates.

   » Along with on-time delivery is <u>delivery lead time</u>, or how much time is allowed from customer order until the ship date. Achieving on-time delivery is more difficult with shorter lead times, but short lead times are what many customers prefer, so lead-time reduction is as important as on-time delivery. As an added bonus, shorter lead times also assist with inventory reduction.

- On-hand inventory is measured as either <u>days on hand</u> or <u>inventory turns</u>. These are often referred to as "inventory performance" metrics because they reflect how efficiently and effectively inventory is consumed and replenished. In fact, some Lean experts assert that inventory performance is the single best indicator of a site's *overall* operational performance. That makes sense!

Inventory Measurement: Delivery

From an inventory perspective, delivery performance measures whether the low points of a site's collective sawtooth curves are managed effectively, i.e., if inventory levels for every item are adequate to protect customer delivery. Delivery measurements do not capture the impact of safety stock being too *high*, which shows up as excess inventory, but delivery certainly suffers if inventory is too *low*.

On-time delivery and short lead times can only occur if the correct inventory is available when needed, but delivery also requires other things to be in place. Successful delivery mandates the right equipment in working order, trained and available labor, defined processes capable of meeting required specifications, a well-planned schedule to meet promise dates, the ability to produce high quality parts, and available material. Every one of these elements has to be "on time" to meet a due date.

A basic cause-and-effect diagram shows these forces around the central goal of high delivery performance, in Figure 3-1. If any of the "cause" items fail, delivery is at risk. Many people overlook the fact that a failure of labor, processing, equipment, quality, or scheduling can result in *material* not being available, which can *erroneously* be interpreted as a failure of the materials management system. Yes, sometimes it's easy to blame the Materials team no matter what *actually* went wrong!

Figure 3-1. Cause-and-Effect Diagram for Delivery

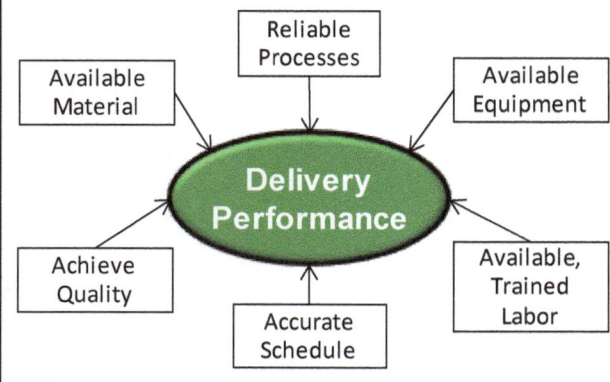

• When equipment fails, the impacted production cell might make what they <u>can</u> produce instead of what they <u>should</u> produce. If Machine A breaks but Machine B is running, the cell might make Machine B parts whether they're needed or not, but the desired Machine A parts are not being produced.

If parts aren't needed, it's not very wise to make them, but it often happens to "keep the cell busy." Yes, labor productivity and machine utilization are common excuses for stupidity. Remember that SQDIP is pursued in order. Don't produce unnecessary inventory to boost labor productivity!

• If a part fails a quality check and has to be reworked or replaced, the extra work consumes time and can also consume unexpected material. This unplanned consumption of time and material is why rework is called the "hidden factory."

• Like equipment or quality failures, if the schedule is wrong, if trained labor is not available, or if a process doesn't work, a cell might improvise their production output, which eventually disrupts the materials plan.

Any failure in the delivery cause-and-effect diagram can change *which* material or *how much* material is consumed, as well as the timing of the consumption, which disrupts material flow and puts delivery at risk.

HINT for Associates

In many sites, the weakest link in the delivery cause-and-effect diagram <u>*appears*</u> to be material shortages. Statements like "there are too many stock outs" or "we never have enough parts" might fill the "cause" portion of the delivery root cause analysis. These statements might seem factual but often there are other factors that caused stock outs or shortages, and the inventory management process is the victim of misplaced blame. When evaluating delivery, ensure that everyone accurately evaluates and understands the entire scenario.

<u>Every</u> inventory management system must have customer delivery performance in the list of key performance indicators (KPIs), and there are two necessary elements.

Delivery Metric: On-Time Delivery

In most sites, on-time delivery (OTD) measures the percent of customer deliveries that were *on time* versus the *total* number of deliveries in the identified time period. In general, on-time delivery can be measured as on-time percent of pieces, line items, orders, or currency. As you might expect, some of these approaches are better than others.

To illustrate the differences, suppose we have a customer order with ten line items, and we want to measure delivery performance for this order.

Line 1	10,000 pieces	$1,000
Lines 2 to 9	10 pieces each of 8 different part numbers, or 80 total pieces	$9,000 total
Line 10	10 pieces	$10,000
10 lines	**10,090 pieces**	**$20,000**

If we measure on-time delivery in pieces, we owe the total of [line 1 for 10,000 pieces + (lines 2 through 10) * 10 pieces each)] = 10,090 parts.

If we are measuring line items, there are 10 to be completed to be considered 100% on time.

In dollars, line 1 is worth $1,000, lines 2 through 9 sum to $9,000, and line 10 is worth $10,000, for a total of $20,000.

Suppose we ship 10,000 parts on time against line #1 and miss the other 9 lines for this order.

• If on-time delivery is based on units or pieces, OTD is 99.1% because 10,000 out of 10,090 parts were shipped on time.
• If OTD is measured by line items, we achieve 10% on time, or 1 line out of 10.
• If delivery is measured for the entire order, we are 0% on time because at least a portion of the order was late, so the entire order is counted as a delivery miss.
• If OTD is based on dollars, on-time delivery is $1,000 out of $20,000, or 5%.

What can we conclude from this quick example?

Measuring on-time delivery in pieces is not effective. It is easily manipulated, so it provides little insight about actual delivery performance. Sites that measure on-time delivery in this manner tend to chase high quantity items, to the demise of small orders, which drives bizarre operational priorities.

> If on-time delivery is currently measured in pieces, change the methodology! **STOP**

Some sites measure delivery by line items, which is better than pieces because small orders can't be ignored, but this can also be manipulated if smaller orders are prioritized over large orders.

Measuring on-time delivery by currency *seems* to focus on the right thing, i.e., cash flow, but it's an artificial indicator for delivery performance. A site might still chase subsets of orders, the high value ones, instead of working to get every order on time. Customers who place "small value" orders often suffer under this approach.

Measuring OTD as the percent of orders shipped entirely on time is usually the best approach, for two reasons. First, a customer isn't satisfied unless they receive their entire order on time. Second, all customers are important, not just the ones who spend a lot of money, order either a high quantity or small quantity of parts, or buy the easy stuff.

Every year, *Industry Week* magazine evaluates high-performing sites and selects Best Plant finalists and winners. They publish certain results in their email communications, and some results from recent years will be included in this book.

The table in Figure 3-2 on page 40 lists on-time delivery percentages for *Industry Week's* Best Plant finalists for 2014. Average OTD results are well above 90% with little variation from year to year, so one key takeaway is that most great plants consistently deliver on time.

Having said that, note the wider range for minimum results. The minimum score is just *one* plant's performance each year, the site with the worst results. The low point is 71% in 2010, and it would be interesting to see the data for that year. Perhaps the worst site saw a huge demand spike that year, which pinched their ability to deliver, or maybe that particular plant consistently exhibits lower delivery performance than the typical Best Plant finalist. I'm curious.

Figure 3-2. 2014 *Industry Week* Best Plant Data, On-Time Delivery

On-time delivery rate (% on time): *Industry Week* 2014 Best Plants Data

Year	Median	Average	Minimum	Maximum
2010	98.4	95.1	71.0	100.0
2011	98.2	96.0	82.0	100.0
2012	97.2	96.7	92.0	100.0
2013	98.0	96.6	90.0	100.0
2014	95.9	95.4	87.0	100.0
2010-2014	97.2	95.9	71.0	100.0

Setting the Due Date for Measuring On-Time Delivery

On-time delivery must be measured versus a due date, which can be set in two basic ways. Due date can be based on standard lead time, where [due date = order date + standard lead-time], or it can be based on customer request date [due date = what the customer selects]. OTD to customer request is the best method. It is certainly more difficult than standard lead-time due dates, especially if customer requests are aggressive, but it is more accurate and insightful since it considers the voice of the customer (VOC.)

Sites that switch from internal lead times to customer request often see a dramatic drop in on-time delivery performance when the switch is made. However, the new results emphasize the need to reduce internal lead times to match market preferences. Shorter lead times can be a distinct competitive advantage! Measure on-time delivery to customer request dates.

Figure 3-3 lists data from the 2013 *Industry Week* Best Plant analysis, reporting the basis for measuring on-time delivery. The results are somewhat erratic from year to year, but in general about half of the best plants measure on-time delivery versus customer request, which demonstrates that it is a common method for measuring delivery.

Figure 3-3. 2013 *Industry Week* Best Plant Data, Basis for OTD Calculation

Do you base your on-time delivery rate calculation on the date the customer requested or a date you promise the customer? (% of responses): *Industry Week* 2013 Best Plants Data

Year	Date customer requested	Date promised to customer
2009	47	53
2010	50	50
2011	44	56
2012	56	44
2013	46	54
2009-2013	49	51

Delivery Metric: Lead Time

Lead time is the time from order entry to shipment, or sometimes from order entry to customer delivery. It is measured in workdays.

If short customer lead times are the result of fast processing and *not* of holding inventory as finished goods or WIP, it is an indicator of speed. Shorter processing lead times reduce inventory (less material dwell time), and customers get shipments faster.

Lead-time reduction should be a primary focus for operational improvements!

HINTS for Leaders

First, measure lead time in workdays, not calendar days. Lead time in calendar days is nonsensical unless you run 7 days per week. If you run Monday through Friday, when an item with a 3-day lead time is ordered on Monday, it is due on Thursday [order date + 3 days]. If that same item is ordered on Wednesday, Thursday, or Friday the due date must be artificially adjusted if lead time is not in workdays. Do not use calendar days unless you and all your suppliers run 7 days per week!

Second, for external suppliers, don't calculate lead time from order entry to *shipment* from the supplier's site. Transit time might be 2 hours for a local supplier but 30 days for a trans-ocean supplier, so it must be part of the lead time for every item.

Low delivery performance, either low on-time delivery or long lead times, is a common problem and it endangers customer relationships, so improving poor delivery must be a high priority. The best way to fix delivery performance is to complete a thorough root cause analysis of the entire cause-and-effect diagram in order to find all the factors that contribute to poor delivery.

Don't focus solely on material availability when addressing low delivery performance!

On-Time Delivery & the Sawtooth Curve

In prior chapters we talked about the risk of on-hand balance dropping to zero, and how safety stock below the sawtooth curve protects delivery from running out of material. To understand the relationship between safety stock and delivery performance, let's look at different safety stock levels in sawtooth curves. In the following charts, daily demand is 10 and lead time is 10 days, so lead-time demand is 100.

Figure 3-4. OTD Risk: No SS in a Sawtooth Curve

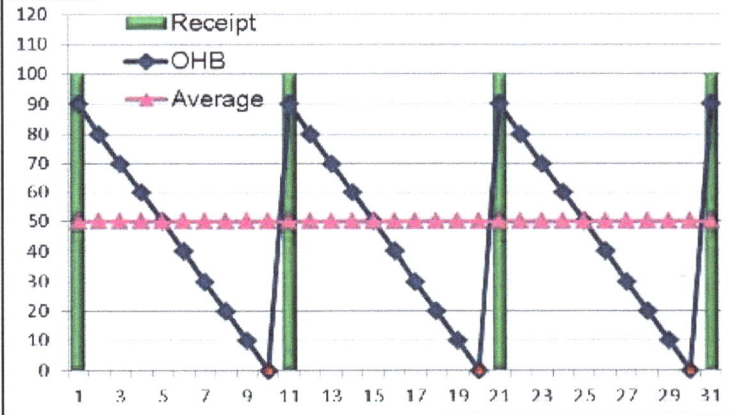

No Safety Stock

Figure 3-4 has a receipt quantity of 100 and lead-time usage of 100, so there is no safety stock because usage equals supply.

If there is any volatility in supply or demand, this is a risky replenishment plan. On-hand balance drops to zero just before every receipt, so any variation, such as higher demand or a late replenishment order, is a delivery risk.

Figure 3-5. Less OTD Risk: Moderate SS in a Sawtooth Curve

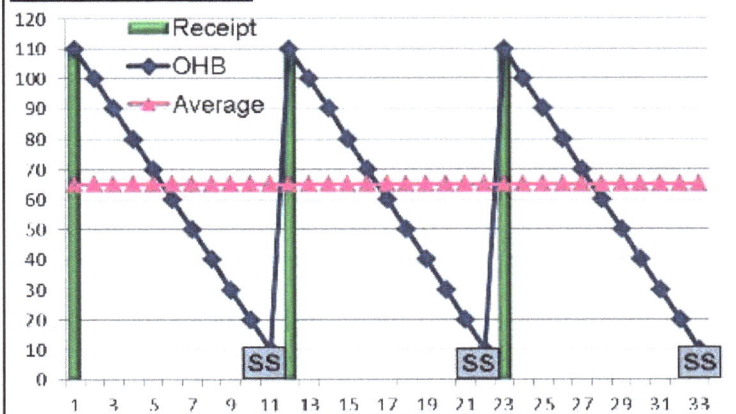

Moderate Safety Stock

Figure 3-5 is less risky than the first example. The order quantity is 110, or 10 pieces more than expected usage over the lead-time period. Safety stock sitting below the sawtooth curve means the replenishment plan doesn't intend for inventory to reach zero. The plan for this item is that inventory will drop as low as 10. In the real world, on-hand balance could go to zero if the item experiences more than 10% supply and/or demand variation.

The presence of safety stock raises minimum, average, and maximum inventories, as we would expect, but higher inventory can protect delivery if that inventory is well managed. Remember that we should achieve Delivery before we chase Cost (S-Q-D-C), so higher inventory can be the right price to pay to protect delivery.

High Safety Stock

To protect on-time delivery and also achieve high inventory performance, we can't afford to add *too* much safety stock below the sawtooth curve, as in Figure 3-6. The order quantity is 140, or 40 more pieces than will be used in one lead-time period. This puts safety stock at 40% of demand, or 40 units of safety stock versus 100 pieces of lead-time demand. If supply and demand variation are *both* high and delivery risk is significant, we <u>might</u> need this much safety stock, but verify that assumption before committing to this much extra inventory.

Figure 3-6. <u>Inventory Risk: High Safety Stock in a Sawtooth Curve</u>

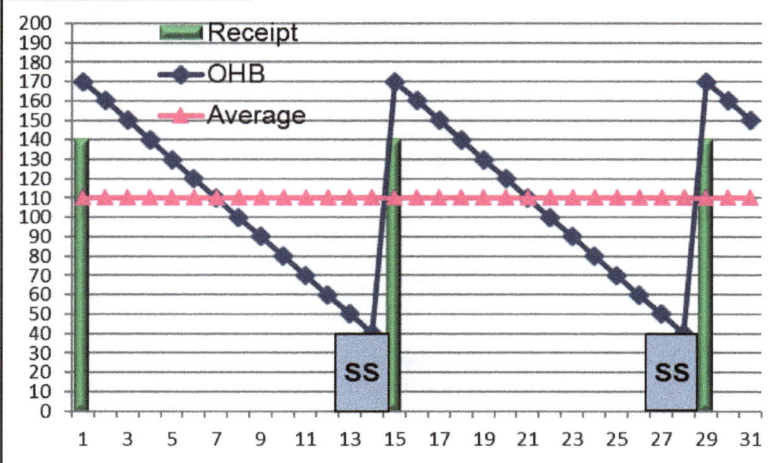

Inventory Measurement: Inventory Performance

Inventory performance reflects how well inventory assets are managed.

- Inventory is generally measured in one of two related ways.
  - » Inventory turns measures how frequently inventory "turns over" or is replaced. Turns is always an annualized number.
  - » Days on hand (DOH) measures how many days it would take to consume current on-hand inventory. It is essentially inventory dwell time.
- Inventory performance is forward looking because it compares on-hand inventory to <u>future</u> demand.
- Most sites measure site-wide inventory performance, accounting for all items. If a 1-cent item uses 100,000 per day and an item that costs $100 consumes 10 per day, it isn't reasonable to sum on-hand balances and daily units of demand for 2 such divergent parts. Therefore, when aggregating results for multiple part numbers, measure consumption and on-hand balances in currency.

Calculating turns or days on hand requires the right data for both future demand and on-hand inventory.

Inventory Performance Data: Future Demand

Inventory performance is <u>*always*</u> measured based on future demand instead of historical usage because total pieces or dollars consumed *last month* is irrelevant to how much inventory will be used *next month*. So, the demand portion of inventory performance must be predictive, i.e., a forecast.

For the demand forecast, associates who use inventory items generally think in terms of total *pieces* when evaluating demand, and that works when measuring 1 item. But, if we analyze more than 1 item, we need *currency*, namely cost of goods sold (COGS) for the defined group of items. Cost of goods sold is a standard financial measure, so it should be readily available.

The <u>correct demand forecast to use for inventory performance is 1 month of forward-looking COGS</u>, or total standard cost for the next month of sales, regardless of how much inventory is actually on hand.

First, the demand forecast for the current month or the immediate upcoming month should be rather <u>accurate because the near future should be well defined.</u>

Second, 12 turns or 20 DOH is a reasonable inventory goal. Poor inventory performance should never be an excuse to look further out to assess upcoming demand. If a site has 60 days of inventory on hand versus 250 annual workdays, they have 2.9 months on hand [60 DOH / 250 workdays * 12 months/year = 2.9 months]. But, that doesn't give permission to look at 3 months of future demand. Most sites that reach too far out for future demand do it in the hopes of grabbing a big COGS month, to make their inventory numbers look better.

Rule of Thumb

For days on hand or inventory turns, use 1 month of future demand in the calculation, regardless of current inventory performance. Sites with very low inventory turns, even as low as 2 or 3 turns per year, should still look forward just 1 month to capture the demand forecast. Sites that achieve high inventory turns (>24 turns) can also utilize 1 month of forward cost of goods sold (COGS) as an accurate demand snapshot, despite having less than 1 month of inventory on hand.

HINT for Leaders

Some sites that are under pressure to achieve high revenue elect to inflate sales forecasts above what is planned or what is even reasonable. Artificially inflating the revenue forecast also artificially increases forward cost of goods sold (COGS), which is used to calculate inventory performance. Therefore, an inflated revenue number over-estimates inventory performance.

I am amazed at the number of sites that purposefully inflate sales forecasts to avoid explaining why revenue will be low, when doing so also inflates reported inventory performance numbers and can cause Buyers and Planners to purchase and produce unnecessary material to support the false forecast.

If your site inflates sales forecasts, please stop! If this practice is out of your control and inflated sales forecasts will continue to be used, despite the insanity of it, be careful how you obtain and utilize COGS to calculate inventory performance.

Real-World Observation

Year-end inventory metrics seem to be particularly susceptible to bizarre manipulation. I worked with a company that used the last 3 months of the fiscal year's demand to calculate inventory performance for the end of that same year. For some inexplicable reason, they looked at demand from October through December to judge December's inventory turns, which broke two rules. It looked backward for the demand forecast, and it also used more than one month of demand. Instead, they should have used demand for January of the next year.

Why use year-end demand instead of the correct 1-month future demand? They claimed that January COGS was unconfirmed and therefore not reliable, but I never believe that. It was just 1 month away, and every other time in the year they could predict 1 month in the future!

The truth was they did it because the later months of the year had higher revenue than the beginning of the year. Late-year revenue growth is actually quite common, either because customers legitimately have higher demand in the fourth quarter (winter products, Christmas sales), or because the site forces revenue out the door to close the year on a high note. Using those higher Q4 demand numbers to calculate year-end inventory performance artificially increases turns, whether the high year-end revenue was legitimate or not. This is illogical!

As mentioned before, the excuse for this practice is often that future demand isn't a firm forecast, but as a site closes the current year and reports inventory performance they certainly have a forecast for month one of the new year, so they could use forward COGS, as recommended.

Be wary of this reporting stunt!

Inventory Performance Data: On-Hand Balance

In addition to future demand, the other required data for calculating either turns or days on hand is current on-hand inventory or the <u>all-in</u>, total, nothing excluded inventory balance. Yes, count everything, including raw material (RM), work in progress (WIP), finished goods (FG), excess, obsolete, and vendor-managed inventory. If anything is excluded for any reason, the reported inventory performance looks better than it truly is. Count everything when capturing on-hand balances!

As with demand, when measuring a single item, capture on-hand balance and demand in units of measure <u>or</u> in currency. However, when assessing more than 1 item, on-hand balance must be in currency.

Inventory Performance Metric: Inventory Turns

<u>Inventory turns</u> measures how many times inventory *turns over* or is replaced during one year. The advantage to turns versus days on hand (DOH) is that it can be combined with accounts receivable and accounts payable into a cash flow "turns" metric to indicate how well cash is managed overall.

The disadvantage to turns is that it is difficult to explain. Many people, even some who have worked in Materials for years, struggle to explain the turns calculation, e.g., why it goes up (good) or down (bad) and how to move it in the right direction (up).

Turns is an annualized number. To get an annual result, adjust the turns formula based on the period of time for the future cost of goods sold number. And what *should* COGS be? One month. Yes, one month of forward COGS is the right demand forecast to use when calculating inventory performance.

Inventory Turns

Annual Turns = (1-month COGS * 12) / Total On-hand currency

With monthly COGS, multiply by 12 to get an annual number. If COGS is quarterly, multiply by 4, but please don't use quarterly COGS for the reasons discussed earlier in this chapter. Use 1 month!

Real-World Observation

While helping a site, I learned that they held inventory on the books as raw material until all processing was complete. At Shipping they transacted everything directly to finished goods (FG). There was no work in progress (WIP) in the plant!

In most plants, material progresses from raw material to WIP to finished goods. Progress is reported or "back-flushed" throughout the production process to capture material and labor costs as they occur. Because standard cost includes standard material, labor, and overhead, the value of material escalates as labor and overhead are added to the cost of the raw material.

This plant manipulated on-hand inventory dollars by back-flushing only when items achieved finished status. It might have been acceptable if the time from raw material to finished goods was 1-2 days, but it ranged from several days to two weeks, so on-hand inventory was *severely* understated.

Inventory performance metrics are supposed to compare *actual* on-hand dollars versus forecasted cost of goods sold, but if COGS includes total standard cost while on-hand dollars only includes raw material plus a few finished goods waiting to be shipped, on-hand dollars is significantly lower than the COGS value it is compared to. This is cheating! Make sure financial and operational reporting is linked to reality.

HINT for Leaders

Visual management: When posting any results, include a green arrow that indicates which way is "good" so associates can instantly recognize a positive trend.

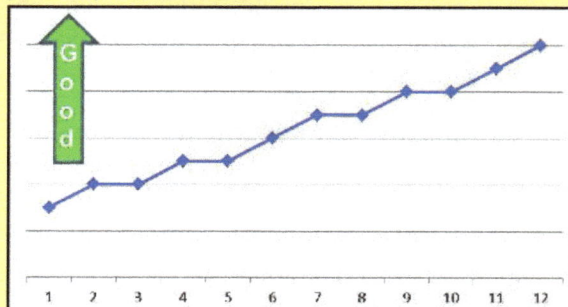

Inventory Performance Metric: Days on Hand (DOH)

Days on hand (DOH) measures how many days of usage are in stock or how many days it would take to consume what is on hand. Unlike turns, DOH is easy to explain. Ask any work call associate, "How many of these do you use per day?" They can usually answer with high confidence and accuracy. Then ask, "How many do you have?" They estimate how many are on hand by looking at the storage location for that item. Voila! Divide on-hand balance by daily usage to get DOH.

Like turns, when measuring more than one part number, measure DOH in currency.

> **Days on Hand**
>
> $$\text{DOH for one item} = \frac{\text{OHB (units of measure or currency)}}{\text{Daily Demand (units or currency per day)}}$$
>
> $$\text{DOH for multiple items} = \frac{\text{Total OHB in Currency}}{\text{Summed Daily Demand in Currency}}$$
>
> Summed daily demand in currency is daily COGS for the population of items being evaluated

> **HINT for Leaders**
>
> Most employees think in workdays not calendar days, so measure days on hand in workdays, e.g., 20 days is 1 month, 5 days is 1 week.

Convert Days to Turns or Turns to Days

Days on hand and turns can easily be converted back and forth, so don't hesitate to utilize both reporting metrics if they are beneficial to various recipients of performance reports. For example, Operations can report DOH by cell, value stream, or across an entire site, and Finance can report inventory turns.

When converting from turns to days on hand or vice versa, ensure that daily cost of goods sold

(COGS) was based on the same divisor, i.e., calendar days or workdays. If daily COGS is based on 20 workdays per month as the denominator [i.e., Daily COGS = Monthly COGS / 20 days per month], DOH must be measured the same way.

It's best to use workdays instead of calendar days. Plants that work 365 days a year are obvious, but most plants work 250 to 260 days per year after subtracting weekends and holidays, so adjust each month accordingly.

> **Convert DOH to Turns or Turns to DOH**
>
> $$\text{Turns} = \frac{\text{Monthly Workdays } or \text{ Calendar Days}}{\text{DOH}}$$
>
> $$\text{DOH} = \frac{\text{Monthly Workdays } or \text{ Calendar Days}}{\text{Turns}}$$

> **HINT for Leaders**
>
> Associates must comprehend every metric that they own or refer to. For inventory performance, days on hand is usually better on the factory floor instead of turns. If inventory turns is required for financial reports, use it *only* where it is fully understood.

> **Inventory Performance with Annualized COGS Versus 1-month COGS**
>
> Annual cost of goods sold is $12 million over 250 workdays. September closed with $1.4M in inventory. If we calculate DOH using annual COGS ($12 million):
> DOH = On-hand $ / Annualized daily COGS in $
> = $1.4M OH$ / ($1,200,000/250 workdays)
> = $1.4M / ($48K / workday) = 29.2 DOH
> Turns = Annual Workdays/DOH = 250 / 29.2 = 8.6 Turns
>
> Next month's COGS is estimated at $1.5M due to high seasonal demand. If we calculate DOH using 1-month forward COGS instead of the full-year monthly average:
> DOH = $1.4M OH$ / ($1,500,000/20 workdays)
> = $1.4M / ($75K / workday) = 18.7 DOH
> Turns = 250/18.7 = 13.4, which is much better!
>
> Use the right data!

Inventory Performance Benchmarks

Inventory performance varies significantly based on industry and other conditions, but 20 to 25 workdays on hand or about 10-12 turns is a reasonable target for most sites in most industries.

The following limitations can hamper inventory performance.

1. Short customer lead times, measured from customer order date to ship date, might require more work in progress (WIP) or finished goods (FG) inventory to service quick deliveries, thereby reducing inventory performance.

2. Significant daily demand variation can require more safety stock, which raises inventory levels and reduces performance.

3. High minimum order quantities for purchased or manufactured parts drives taller sawtooth curves, reducing inventory performance.

4. High mix and low volume means a large count of active items, but most items have very low volume. This slows down how fast each individual item is consumed, thereby reducing turns.

Some business situations force companies to excel at inventory management.

1. Some industries manage inventory very carefully due to obsolescence or expiration issues (think cakes from the prior chapter, fresh fruit, fashion, monthly magazines). Due to the required inventory diligence for these kinds of products, their manufacturers tend to have higher inventory performance.

2. Industries with narrow profit margins keep inventories low as a way to maximize cash flow. The automotive industry is a great example of high turns driven in part by low margins.

The tables in Figure 3-7 and in Figure 3-8 list days on hand and inventory reduction data from *Industry Week*'s Best Plant finalists.

Figure 3-7. *Industry Week* Best Plant Data, 2015 RM & 2011 FG DOH

Change in raw-materials inventory, last three years* (%):
Industry Week Best Plant Data 2015

Year	Median	Average	Minimum	Maximum
2011	-8.5	-21.4	-70.0	21.0
2012	-12.1	-11.6	-70.0	49.0
2013	-25.0	-12.3	-35.0	57.0
2014	-27.3	-27.8	-58.1	0.0
2015	-15.9	-17.4	-57.0	28.0
2011-2015	-15.0	-17.9	-70.0	57.0

Average days of finished-goods inventory:
Industry Week 2011 Best Plants Data

Year	Median	Average	Minimum	Maximum
2007	6.6	16.2	0.0	76.8
2008	9.7	13.6	0.0	41.3
2009	4.1	16.1	0.0	91.0
2010	5.0	14.3	0.0	63.0
2011	4.0	13.1	0.0	55.0
2007-2011	5.6	14.9	0.0	91.0

Figure 3-8. *Industry Week* Best Plant Data, 2015 3-year % RM and FG Reductions

Change in raw-materials inventory, last three years (%):
Industry Week Best Plant Data 2015

Year	Median	Average	Minimum	Maximum
2011	-8.5	-21.4	-70.0	21.0
2012	-12.1	-11.6	-70.0	49.0
2013	-25.0	-12.3	-35.0	57.0
2014	-27.3	-27.8	-58.1	0.0
2015	-15.9	-17.4	-57.0	28.0
2011-2015	-15.0	-17.9	-70.0	57.0

Change in finished-goods inventory, last three years (%):
Industry Week Best Plant Data 2015

Year	Median	Average	Minimum	Maximum
2011	0.0	48.3	-45.0	860.0
2012	-7.0	-1.3	-52.0	80.0
2013	-9.5	-5.5	-57.0	120.0
2014	-2.0	-13.2	-67.0	32.0
2015	0.0	-5.9	-72.0	58.0
2011-2015	-1.0	5.0	-72.0	860.0

Other Inventory Metrics

In addition to on-time delivery, lead time, and inventory turns or days on hand, several other metrics can provide useful insights about inventory success or failure.

HINT for Leaders

Caution: please don't track too many metrics! Sites that attempt to track more than about 8 or 10 metrics per team usually discover that metric tracking takes so much time that they can't complete root cause analysis and solve underlying issues. Limit each team, even the senior management team to no more than a dozen metrics.

No supplier should exhibit high failures over an extended time. Like poor delivery, if a supplier fails to solve quality problems within a reasonable time, replace them.

Note: Supplier OTD and quality performance come up again when we talk about supplier safety stock.

Supplier On-Time Delivery

Average on-time delivery for individual suppliers and also for the entire supply base are excellent starting points for inventory performance. If suppliers generally ship late, we must carry more safety stock to cover late receipts and avoid missing delivery dates to our customers.

With very few exceptions, low supplier delivery performance should not be tolerated. Instead, work with suppliers to improve their processes or find new suppliers that are more reliable.

Figure 3-9 lists *Industry Week* Best Plant data for supplier on-time delivery for 2013.

Figure 3-9. 2013 *Industry Week* Best Plant Data, 2013 Supplier On-time Delivery

Supplier orders delivered on time, by the request date (%): *Industry Week* 2013 Best Plants Data

Year	Median	Average	Minimum	Maximum
2009	95.8	94.8	84.0	99.0
2010	96.2	95.1	85.0	99.0
2011	96.0	95.1	80.0	99.7
2012	94.0	89.6	50.0	99.3
2013	91.0	90.0	75.0	99.5
2009-2013	95.0	93.2	50.0	99.7

Supplier Quality

Poor supplier quality is also a delivery risk, so it should be measured where it exists, e.g., parts per million (ppm), percent of received parts that fail to meet accepted quality criteria, etc.

Supplier Count

Measuring how many suppliers are maintained for a site is a common metric, and there are a couple valid reasons to minimize supplier count.

1. There is a cost for maintaining suppliers and their associated data in an inventory system, including contract negotiation processes and data maintenance. The more suppliers there are, the higher the cost of that maintenance.

2. There are potential freight savings if a supplier ships enough material to fill trucks. Conversely, spreading purchases across multiple suppliers can eliminate potential truckload freight savings.

3. Inventory reduction can occur if a supplier ships enough volume to justify numerous shipments per week, which reduces the supplier's lead time because orders leaving their facility don't wait more than a day or so for the next shipment to depart. On the contrary, suppliers that wait 2 weeks or more to fill a truck or container automatically add lead time to every item (or they increase freight expenses), and longer lead times mean taller sawtooth curves.

4. Sites *might* have leverage with a supplier that ships high dollars or numerous items, but only if those items could easily be moved to an alternate supplier. It isn't always true, but sometimes supplier consolidation presents price, lead time, or minimum order quantity negotiating opportunities.

While these advantages can be valid, there are risks with the many-eggs-in-one-basket approach. If a supplier ships a high percentage of a site's total material, that supplier has enormous power over the operation. If they demonstrate dependable performance, it is certainly an advantage. But, if the supplier is weak, arrogant, or uncooperative, they will be a site-wide burden.

As with many metrics, some people go off the deep end on supplier count, such as deciding to reduce supplier count by buying from mediators or consolidators, which are entities that purchase a wide range of products from hundreds of companies and ship them in combination, e.g., screws, gaskets, and wiring harnesses from 3 different suppliers arrive as 1 shipment from the consolidator. Consolidators charge a mark-up or handling fee, so even if they have tremendous buying power and acquire individual items for less than we could, their total cost might still be higher due to the added fees. In theory, this practice can remove dozens of suppliers from the list but there is a financial toll to be paid. Be careful with these types of services.

Be wise when setting goals for supplier count, and never reduce the supply base at the expense of quality or operational flexibility.

Annual Purchase Transactions

Even if the process of issuing a purchase order or manufacturing order is highly automated, every purchasing transaction has an associated cost that might include maintaining ordering systems or paying associates who process orders.

Managing transaction costs is a valid concern in an inventory management system, but this is another balancing act. A higher number of transactions does add cost and complexity, but too few transactions can lead to unreasonably high purchase quantities. If one purchase order covers several months of demand in order to avoid multiple transactions, the trade-off for the lower transaction cost is a very tall sawtooth curve and high on-hand inventory. Use common sense!

Sites that wish to increase efficiency and effectiveness by reducing transactions often measure annual transactions for purchased or manufactured items, or per buyer or planner, to estimate workload and track reduction activity. Transaction count by subcategory, such as purchased versus manufactured items, can be a good indicator for the expected effort to issue purchase orders, receive external parts, set-up internal items, etc.

Annual or monthly transaction count can be insightful, but some sites try to equalize transaction count or managed dollars across all buyers or planners to make things "fair." These initiatives rest on the assumption that *every* order and *every* dollar requires the same effort, and that is rarely true. An order for an item that requires price negotiation for every purchase is much more difficult and time-consuming than on order for a commodity product like hardware. Again, use common sense. Don't attempt to equalize effort based on an incomplete indicator like transaction count, but rather recognize when transactions occur too frequently or too rarely. More on this later.

Stock Outs

Tracking stock outs, the what-where-why of production cells running out of a required item, is a tactical measure that tracks one of the most egregious failures in an inventory management system. Any stock out, even of the simplest or cheapest component, can have an immediate and far-reaching impact on production processes and customer delivery.

This is tedious to track in a large plant, but until robust replenishment systems successfully eliminate stock outs, it might be necessary to force root cause analysis of all stock outs when they occur. This should *not* be a long-term metric because stock outs are errors that should be eliminated by improving the replenishment processes.

Percent Low Cost Region Sourcing

This is a bit of an artificial metric, but it is quite common so it's worth a quick discussion. This refers to measuring how much of a site's annual purchasing spend comes from low-cost regions (LCRs). The theory is that a site can reduce the cost of material, and therefore reduce total cost and boost cash flow, by sourcing material from low-cost countries. It sounds like a great concept, but many sites fail to measure "total landed cost" as their purchased spend. In many cases, as the percent of low-cost region (LCR) sourcing increases, the material *acquisition* cost (e.g., cost per piece) comes down as planned. However, other hidden or unmeasured costs increase as much or even more than purchase price savings. To be accurate, total cost must include freight, handling, customs, inspections, the cost of holding extra inventory, and any other LCR costs. If total cost is not accurately captured, this metric can be very misleading.

In some sites, low-cost sourcing has a devastating impact on inventory turns.

• Shipping containers are always filled to capacity in order to get the most material per freight charge, and therefore items that cross the ocean are purchased in higher quantities, raising total inventory.

• If numerous items from multiple suppliers are consolidated to fill a shipping container from a low-cost region, lead time is often extended due to that consolidation activity because items wait on the shipping pier while other parts trickle in. This delay raises on-hand inventory because either order quantity or underlying safety stock must be increased to cover the longer lead time.

Real-World Observation

Many facilities have fallen prey to the low-cost sourcing trap and often the "overseas" sourcing program is deeply entrenched before the damage to inventory turns is fully identified and quantified. By the time the root cause for higher DOH is linked to low-cost sourcing, the site has numerous contracts and agreements to retract or modify, and if those contracts cover multiple years the damage is long term.

I visited a site that purchased numerous items from an overseas supplier under a contract with harsh and strict annual minimum purchase requirements. Imagine the site's dismay when they received several shipping <u>containers</u> of material in late January because numerous items failed to meet the prior year's minimum annual requirement. They thought they had a great deal until the total *annual* cost arrived on their doorstep.

Be cautious with LCR sourcing. If it is utilized, be judicious about tracking total cost and inventory.

Expedited Freight Expenditure

Freight is an unavoidable expense for any site that utilizes material. Expedited freight is a different matter, because it is a *premium* fee for accelerated delivery of either incoming or outgoing material. Expedited freight for incoming material is particularly troubling if it is a normal course of business. And, yes, in some sites it is just another daily expense because they regularly expedite parts to cover inventory gaps. How crazy is that? Fix the inventory management system!

If expedited incoming freight is a regular expense, track it and determine the root cause for the repetitive expense, e.g., safety stock is too low so stock outs occur, or suppliers ship late so parts must be expedited. This stuff is frightening and unnecessary.

If expedited outgoing freight is common, understand whether it is an unavoidable cost of doing business in your industry (i.e., everything ships "overnight" in your industry) or if the expediting is internally generated because on-time delivery or lead times are poorly managed.

For most sites, measuring expedited freight should only exist until the underlying error is eliminated or significantly reduced.

Excess & Obsolete Inventory

As mentioned earlier in this chapter, when evaluating inventory performance, we must include all inventory dollars, even excess and obsolete (E&O) inventory. E&O is a financial sum of 1) on-hand inventory that exceeds the reasonable level to hold for future demand, called "excess" inventory, plus 2) inventory that has been designated as no longer valid or as "obsolete" material, including items that are discontinued. Sites often have a financial reserve to cover the eventual write-off of the E&O value, but this is a drain on profit. A reserve should never be viewed as a good answer to this problem.

Excess inventory is any amount above what is considered reasonable for the business. For many plants, 24 to 36 months of demand is the maximum allowed "active" inventory. However, in an environment characterized by rapid innovation, the limit for excess inventory might be as short as 2 to 6 months. (Think women's fashion, where 8 to 12 weeks might be the right definition for active inventory, due to rapid seasonal and fashion trend changes.)

To calculate excess inventory, compare the on-hand balance for every item to the financial definition of excess inventory, e.g., 24 months is considered valid inventory but any quantity greater than 24 months is categorized as excess.

Obsolete inventory includes items that have been designated as no longer active, along with active items with zero future demand. All inventory for an obsolete item is considered part of E&O.

Though it is common to have excess or obsolete inventory, it means an error has occurred, which can be caused by numerous things.

• Inventory produced or purchased under the expectation of high shipments (perhaps a new product launch) might be too high once real demand numbers become available. A portion of this inventory will be classified as excess inventory.

• High minimum order quantities can force an extremely high inventory position, which can exceed the financial definition of active inventory.

• To save on purchase price, some sites agree to enormous purchase contracts with strict expiration dates and minimum quantities. When the order deadline arrives, the supplier exercises the clause that forces the remaining open quantity to be purchased all at once. (Recall the prior Real-World Observation, related to low-cost sourcing, and also see the next Real-World box.)

• One item replaced by another adds to obsolete inventory if we don't bleed off the old item before putting the new part number in service.

• Changes in market or customer preferences can quickly drop an item's demand status from active to inactive. If demand drops to zero, the item is obsolete.

E&O Hints

E&O shouldn't be accepted as inevitable. Most root causes can be prevented or minimized by more effective Sales, Inventory, and Operations planning (SIOP).

1. Don't let a low unit price entice a contract for more pieces than are needed. The reduced standard cost masks other costs that must be paid when we are forced to make a mandatory but unnecessary contractual purchase. In the real world, E&O is eventually written off.

In addition to the E&O risk, the entire time the artificially low standard cost is in the system, the cost that was lowered by over-committing to inventory, we will price finished goods at a level that doesn't begin to cover the total cost of the item in question.

Real-World Observation

A site needed 50,000 computer chips over the upcoming 2-year period for a new product. The supplier quoted $100,000 for 50,000 chips or $105,000 for 100,000 chips, due to the high cost of tooling. Engineering committed to 100,000 because it reduced chip cost by almost half, $1.05 instead of $2.00, which helped meet the cost target.

The selling price of the product assumed the lower chip cost of $1.05. Over 2 years of selling the product, the company claimed a profit of $250,000. However, that figure did not include writing off the excess chips, so profit was overstated. The false profit figure was used to calculate margins, bonus payouts, etc.

At the end of 2 years, 50,000 of the original 100,000 chips remained on the supplier purchase contract. The site was forced to buy them, though they would never be used.

When the Operations team completed root cause analysis to explain the 50,000 excess chips and E&O hit, it took several weeks to discover the cause. Buried in Engineering's records, they saw that the demand estimate of 50K units was ignored.

This is a real example of how a bad decision can have a long-term negative financial impact on an entire operation.

Don't be stupid!

2. When considering purchasing contracts, don't over-commit to quantities because Sales says they'll sell a million of something. Sales people always say that, so use common sense.

3. When calculating turns or days on hand, <u>include E&O even if there is a financial reserve to cover it</u>. This ensures that improvement plans attack the largest piles of inventory, and E&O might be the top of that list. Remember that a reserve account sets aside *profit* to cover E&O!

4. In addition to looking at the current level of E&O, study the trend over the last 12 to 24 months to see if it is growing in absolute currency *or* as a percent of total on-hand inventory. If it is, look for systemic failures that add E&O to total inventory.

Summary of Measuring Inventory Management

There are numerous metrics to indicate inventory success, but every site <u>must</u> measure delivery and inventory performance. Delivery metrics should include both on-time delivery and customer lead time, and inventory performance is generally inventory turns or days on hand.

Select other inventory metrics that will genuinely improve problem solving, aid root cause analysis, or point to projects to improve inventory or operational performance.

Don't track too many metrics! Focus on strategic or critical metrics that link to your operational priorities.

TUTORIAL: GOCO INVENTORY PERFORMANCE

When Mary joined GOCO, she studied financial and inventory results from the prior 12 months, November through October. See Figure 3-10 on page 52.

The chief financial officer told Mary that GOCO measured inventory turns based on annual workdays. The plant used the formula [annual cost of goods sold / annual workdays] to determine daily cost of goods sold (COGS), and that was used to calculate monthly turns, which was the GOCO barometer for cash flow success.

GOCO Annual COGS = $99,246,804, Annual Workdays = 250

Daily COGS = $99,246,804 / 250 = $396,987, or approximately $397K

Inventory turns were calculated every month by dividing on-hand inventory dollars by the <u>annualized</u> daily COGS of $396,987. Mary knew there was seasonal demand variation, with increased sales during spring and summer. So, she wondered if it was reasonable to use <u>annualized</u> daily COGS to calculate inventory turns and DOH because daily cost of goods sold varied based on season.

To test her suspicion, she compared two different calculations for the most recent 12 months of data, from November through October. As an alternative way to calculate turns, Mary decided to compare one month of forward-looking COGS data, or the forecasted upcoming daily COGS, versus actual on-hand inventory dollars.

The highest monthly COGS was $9,500,000 and the lowest was $6,750,000, so the range was wide. This supported Mary's suspicion that the company was overstating inventory turns during winter months.

The table in Figure 3-10 and the chart in Figure 3-11 demonstrated that DOH and turns varied dramatically based on time of year, or the state of seasonal demand. The "annualized" DOH results (the black line in Figure 3-11) looked acceptable as the slow period began in September, with days on hand descending toward 60 days. But, if she looked at actual COGS values (the blue line in the chart), DOH was much higher as daily COGS came down compared to on-hand dollars.

Figure 3-11. GOCO Inventory Chart

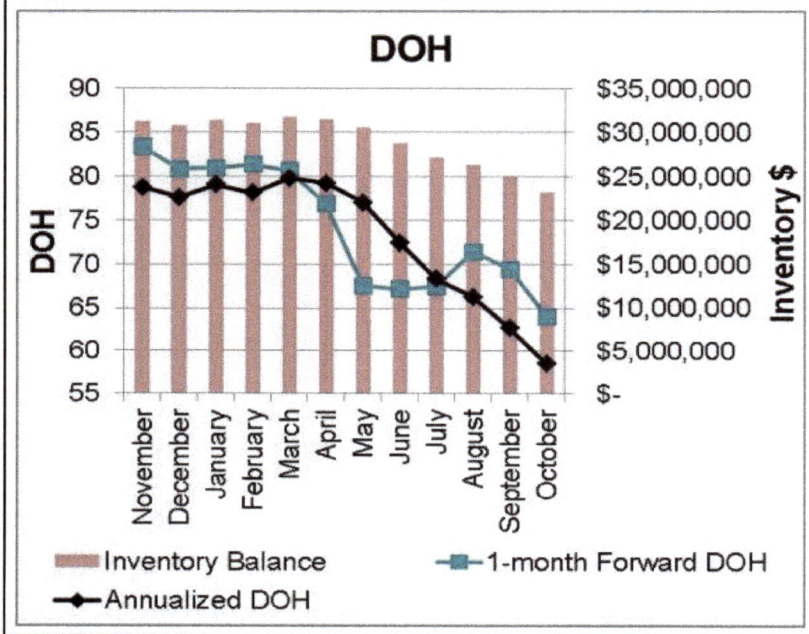

Mary and the rest of the team agreed that ignoring seasonality in daily COGS resulted in inaccurate DOH and inventory turns for many months of the year. During peak season, days on hand was too high and inventory performance was better than indicated by the annualized numbers. During the slow season, just the opposite occurred and they had more inventory on hand than was needed.

Going forward they decided that inventory results would be calculated with a 1-month forward COGS estimate.

Figure 3-10. GOCO Inventory Turns & DOH

	November	December	January	February	March	April	May	June	July	August	September	October
Inventory Balance	$ 31,260,323	$ 30,808,924	$ 31,368,933	$ 31,010,532	$ 31,689,302	$ 31,436,990	$ 30,557,589	$ 28,767,934	$ 27,118,903	$ 26,295,632	$ 24,889,234	$23,212,755
Est Next Month COGS	$ 6,750,000	$ 8,000,000	$ 7,750,000	$ 8,000,000	$ 8,250,000	$ 9,000,000	$ 9,500,000	$ 9,000,000	$ 9,250,000	$ 7,000,000	$ 8,250,000	$ 7,250,000
Annualized Turns	3.2	3.2	3.2	3.2	3.1	3.2	3.2	3.4	3.7	3.8	4.0	4.3
Annualized DOH	78.7	77.6	79.0	78.1	79.8	79.2	77.0	72.5	68.3	66.2	62.7	58.5
1-month Forward Turns	3.0	3.1	3.1	3.1	3.1	3.3	3.7	3.7	3.7	3.5	3.6	3.9
1-month Forward DOH	83.4	80.9	81.0	81.4	80.7	76.8	67.5	67.1	67.4	71.4	69.4	64.0

ABC
easy as 123...

CHAPTER 4: INVENTORY ABC CLASSIFICATION

ABC classification is a universal inventory management tool that plays a central role in kanban planning. ABC classifications designate parts as high, medium, or low annual expenditure. High-spend items receive more time and attention and are carefully guarded to minimize inventory dollars. Low spend items are the opposite, taking much less time and effort but also allowing for higher purchase quantities (and therefore fewer annual transactions) due to the lower expenditure.

ABC classification is used for setting safety stock and lead-time targets and also for allocating appropriate effort to managing a population of items. The goal is to accurately classify every item.

• Target safety stock is primarily driven by supply and demand variation, but those targets must also make the best use of safety stock dollars.

• Target lead time sets the desired replenishment cadence for an item. A high-value item should arrive in smaller quantities, or more frequently, versus an item with a lower expenditure. A cheap item might order a quantity to cover 3 to 8 weeks of demand, but that would be a high inventory commitment for an expensive item.

• Last but certainly not least, items with high annual expenditure deserve the most human effort and oversight because an error that results in too much inventory can be very costly.

Material spend is the defining factor for ABC classification. When thinking about material spend, *standard* cost comes to mind, but that's only half of the equation. A $200 motor used once a year has a lower annual impact ($200 * 1 = $200) than a 2¢ screw used a million times ($.02 * 1,000,000 = $20,000).

When defining ABC classifications, annual spend is generally the right data for deciding which parts are expensive and which are cheap because it smooths seasonal demand or erratic usage more effectively than monthly or quarterly demand. So, use annual data unless demand for a shorter time period is more representative of what the business will look like going forward. For example, if a new product was launched 8 months ago, don't use average usage over 12 months, but rather use a shorter period to get an accurate estimate of spend.

ABC Classification Definitions

A items are those with the highest annual spends, accounting for 80% of total annual spend, or 80% of total payments to external suppliers for purchased parts. The total of all A items usually accounts for 5-20% of total item count, e.g., 20% of *part numbers* cover 80% of annual *spend*.

1. A items are usually high usage items, but some A parts have very high cost and low usage. A $400,000 laser can be an A item even if demand is just a few per year.

• A *typical* A item is critical to the operation due to its high usage. If a shortage occurs for an A item, it probably impacts numerous shipments.

2. For buyers, planners, or other associates who manage replenishment orders, A items should receive the majority of time and attention due to the amount of money spent annually.

• High annual spend implies a risk of high inventory dollars if the wrong replenishment plan is deployed and inventory is pushed too high.

3. A items benefit greatly from low replenishment quantities and shorter sawtooth curves due to the high associated cost.

• A's are often replenished every 3 to 5 days, which means lower replenishment quantities and more frequent receipts than B's or C's.

• A's are negotiated the most fiercely to control annual spend and on-hand balance. Special attention is given to managing standard cost, minimum order quantity (MOQ), standard package quantity (SPQ), and lead time. Minimum order and standard package quantities can have significant impacts on replenishment orders because they determine how an order quantity is rounded up from the calculated replenishment quantity.

4. In most sites, A items account for about 60-70% of on-hand value, depending on target safety stock and lead-time decisions.

B Items make up the next 15% of total spend and are generally 15-30% of the number of items. They have a moderate impact on annual spend and inventory value.

1. B parts are usually consumed on a regular basis, i.e., they aren't sporadic but have "middle of the road" annual usage, standard cost, or both. Like A items, there can be outliers with higher cost and more sporadic usage.

2. These parts should be actively tracked and managed, but not as obsessively as A items.

3. B's are replenished in modest quantities, usually 2 to 4 weeks of demand, to control the height of the sawtooth curve without pushing the number of transactions too high.

4. B items usually account for approximately 15-25% of on-hand dollars.

C items are the bottom 5% of total annual spend. This usually includes 50-70% of the total number of items.

1. C parts are often low-priced parts such as screws, washers, brackets, or literature. But, they can also be more expensive parts with low annual usage, like a costly motor used once or twice per year.

2. These parts should receive little attention because if a buyer or planner spends much time on C items, they are probably ignoring an A or B item.

• Sites with tens of thousands of C items must manage them automatically as much as possible. Even 1 minute per month on each of 10,000 C items is 167 hours of effort or 1 full-time job. Try to avoid huge time commitments for low-spend items.

• C items should carry enough safety stock to make stock outs <u>very</u> rare and therefore prevent the human intervention required to correct a

shortage. Expediting a C item takes precious time away from planning and managing A and B items.

3. C's should be purchased in large enough quantities to prevent excessive transaction activity and the associated costs from tasks such as issuing a purchase order, receiving and inspecting incoming material, delivering parts to point of use, setting up a manufacturing run, etc. It's silly for an order's transaction cost to exceed the value of the order itself, but it does happen. To minimize this, C parts should be purchased in larger quantities than A or B parts, e.g., 3 to 8 weeks of demand.

4. C parts should account for about 5-20% of on-hand dollars.

Rule of Thumb 👍			
ABC General Targets			
	% of Total Annual Spend	% of Total On-Hand $	Typical Target Lead Time (Workdays)
A	80%	60-70%	3-10 days
B	15%	15-25%	5-15 days
C	5%	5-20%	15-30 days

Determine ABC Classification

ABC classifications are determined by sorting parts in descending order of annual spend, with purchased parts separated from manufactured parts.

1. First, separate purchased items from manufactured parts to create two different lists.

Do not analyze all items in one consolidated list! If purchased and manufactured parts are combined for ABC analysis, manufactured parts tend to push high-spend purchased parts out of A and sometimes out of B classifications. Finished goods (FG) and work in progress (WIP) have higher costs than purchased parts, resulting in higher annual spends, so don't mix purchased with manufactured! **STOP**

HINT for Leaders

Be accurate when designating items as purchased or manufactured. Purchased parts include all external parts, or anything that is delivered to your site. Don't classify a part from a sister plant as "internal" because that plant is owned by your parent company.

When listing purchase parts for ABC analysis, include MRO and other non-production purchased items (gloves, light bulbs, safety glasses, batteries, etc.). Any non-production or support item with high annual spend will be appropriately assigned an A or B classification, so it gets the attention it deserves, and items that don't have high annual spends will be—and should be—classified as C items.

2. Gather standard cost and annual usage data for all purchased parts and create a spreadsheet that lists every item's part number, standard cost, and annual demand in units. Make sure the unit of measure for annual demand aligns with standard cost, i.e., don't buy a part with standard cost in pounds then consume it in inches.

3. Multiply annual demand times standard cost to get annual spend for each item.

4. Sum annual spend for all purchased parts to get total annual purchased spend for all items.

5. Sort the list of part numbers in descending order of annual spend, with high spend at the top.

6. Add a column that cumulates annual spend down the rows, providing a running total item by item of annual spend from high spend to low. Ensure the cumulative total formula is working correctly by testing a couple rows, e.g., the cumulative annual spend for the 4th item on the list equals the sum of the annual spends for items 1 through 4. Do a quick check on a couple rows to verify the numbers. The cumulative number for the last item on the list should equal the sum of all annual spends from Step 4.

7. Calculate the required total annual spend for all A items by multiplying 80% times total annual spend for all purchased parts, from Step 4.

Target Purchased A Total Annual Spend

Target purchased A total annual spend = 80%* total annual purchased spend

8. In the cumulative annual spend column, find the first row that exceeds the target total annual spend for A items, from Step 7. We'll finalize where to draw the final cutoff in the next steps, but this is our first guess for the cutoff for A items. Make note of the annual spend for the selected item where the cutoff occurs. This is the rough estimate of the minimum spend that would qualify an item as an A.

9. To make the threshold easier to remember and use, the cutoff for annual spend should be rounded <u>down</u> to the next integer. If the exact cutoff for an A item was $12,345.12, an annual spend of $12,345.20 would be an A item, but $12,345.10 would be a B item. That doesn't make sense, particularly when an Excel spreadsheet could hide two decimal places and make it look like an annual spend of $12,345 was assigned two *different* ABC classifications, both A and B. To prevent this, round the cutoff down to $12,345.

Sometimes rounding to an even "rounder" number is better than simply rounding down to the next integer. A cutoff of $12,300 might be better than $12,345 when utilizing or remembering cutoff levels. Look at items 1 or 2 rows above and below the exact cutoff line and set a reasonably rounded number for the annual spend threshold.

In Figure 4-1, the target cumulative annual spend for all A items is $10,476,823, as listed in the last row of the table. At part number 113 the cumulative annual spend is $10,482,789, or about $6,000 above the target number, and annual spend is $10,000 for this item. The cumulative number is pretty close, considering the target exceeds $10.4 million.

Figure 4-1. <u>A Item Threshold Rounding Example 1</u>

Part	Annual Spend	Cumulative Annual Spend
111	$ 11,476	$ 10,462,639
112	$ 10,150	$ 10,472,789
113	$ 10,000	$ 10,482,789
114	$ 9,243	$ 10,492,032
115	$ 9,091	$ 10,501,123
Target Cumulative $		$ 10,476,823

Part number 112, one row up, has an annual spend of $10,150, so it's slightly higher than the annual spend for part 113 at $10,000. The cumulative total for 112 is about $4,000 below the target of $10,476,823, so it's also pretty close. Excluding part 113 from the A parts is a valid consideration.

Before we decide what to do, let's look at part 114. Annual spend is $9,243, which is well below part 113's annual spend of $10,000. There's a nice "numerical" break between part 113 at $10,000 and 114 at $9,243, so it makes sense to put the cutoff between those rows. An A item cutoff of greater than or equal to $10,000 works, or we could lower it to $9,500, or any number between $9,243 and $10,000.

Let's consider another scenario. Suppose the item just below the initial cutoff has an annual spend of just a few dollars less than the initial threshold. Does it make sense to have such a narrow difference between an A item and a B? Probably not.

Look at the data in Figure 4-2. Like the previous example, target cumulative annual spend is achieved at part number 113 with an annual spend of $10,000. The two part numbers just below 113 have annual spends of $9,956 for 114 and $9,924 for 115. Those are so close to the $10,000 annual spend for part 113 that it seems inappropriate to put a cutoff between them.

Figure 4-2. Threshold Rounding Example 2

Part	Annual Spend	Cumulative Annual Spend
112	$ 11,236	$ 10,472,789
113	$ 10,000	$ 10,482,789
114	$ 9,956	$ 10,492,745
115	$ 9,924	$ 10,502,669
116	$ 9,712	$ 10,512,381
Target Cumulative $		$ 10,472,823

Part number 116 has an annual spend of $9,712, which does provide a gap from part 115, so it might make sense to include part numbers 114 and 115 with A items and set the A item cut off between $9,712 and $9,924. A cutoff of $9,900 for

A items, close to item 115's annual spend, would be reasonable.

If there were a dozen parts within a few dollars of the annual spend for part 113, instead of just 2 parts as in Figure 4-2, we wouldn't want to go way down the list to find a "clean break" or a gap between A and B annual spends because it would dramatically alter total annual spend for A items. With target cumulative annual spend at $10,472,823, if we add a couple A items at about $10,000 each, it really isn't a big deal. But, if we add 12 parts at $10,000 each, we would far exceed the target for A items, adding too much money and too many items to the A list. In that case, go up 1 row, above item 113, and set the cutoff at $10,100.

The other choice in this example would be to exclude part 113 from the list of A parts and put the cutoff slightly higher than that annual spend, such as $10,100.

10. Insert another column and enter "A" for all items identified by the cutoff defined in Step 9. Use an Excel formula if the list of items is long. To save steps, insert the formula after figuring out the cutoff for B items and manufactured items so one formula assigns A, B, and C classifications for purchased and manufactured items. See Step 12 for formula examples.

11. After completing A items, calculate the target cumulative total annual spend for B items by multiplying 95% times total annual purchased spend, from step 4. B items are 15% of the annual spend after A items, so they are part numbers from the item just below the last A down to where cumulative annual spend hits the target number for B items, or 95%.

If we added a couple items to the list of A items when we rounded the cutoff for A annual spend, it isn't necessary to adjust the target annual spend for B items. Use 95% as the multiplier for target cumulative annual spend for B items *even if* A items were above or below 80% of total spend.

Target Purchased B Total Annual Spend

Target purchased B total annual spend = 95%* total annual purchased part spend

Repeat Steps 8 through 10 to identify B items, then everything else is a C item. In the ABC classification column, insert a formula to assign the correct class.

HINT for Associates

If ABC assignments rely on Excel formulas, ensure they work correctly. If the cutoff is $10,400 and any number greater than or equal to that value should be an A, this formula won't work because it excludes any item that is equal to $10,400: IF (Annual Spend > 10400, "A")

To include an annual spend of $10,400 as an A item, use $10,399 in the greater than function or change the formula to greater than or equal to 10400:

IF (Annual Spend >= 10400, "A")

ABC Assignment Formula

IF (AND (Purch or Mfd = "P", Annual Spend > Purch A Min Spend), "A",

IF (AND (Purch or Mfd = "P", Annual Spend > Purch B Min Spend), "B",

IF (Purch or Mfd = "P", "C",

IF (Annual Spend > Mfd A Min Spend, "A",

IF (Annual Spend > Mfd B Min Spend, "B",

ELSE = "C")

The beginning of this formula assigns ABC based on two criteria, an item's purchased status and annual spend. After purchased items are assigned, remaining items are manufactured and therefore annual spend is the only criteria.

12. Repeat the process for manufactured items, but keep in mind a couple of philosophical notes.

Total annual spend for manufactured items often looks *inordinately* high due to the double and triple counting that occurs with these items. If a subassembly is used in a top assembly and that assembly is used in a finished good, the subassembly, top assembly, and finished good part numbers are all in the list of manufactured items so the cost of the subassembly is counted 3 times.

The mathematical impact on total annual spend depends on the amount of vertical integration at a site, or how many items are counted more than once. For this reason, the *sum* of annual manufactured spend can far exceed total annual cost of goods sold. And, the cumulative spend targets for assigning A and B classifications to manufactured items can be *really* big numbers.

Manufactured items can also have strange item counts versus the expected mix of A, B, and C, and they can have weird ratios for the percent of total on-hand dollars for A, B, and C.

Purchased parts are generally more orderly than manufactured parts, so don't be concerned if the data for manufactured items looks odd. The ABC assignment process is still valid and applicable for manufactured items.

Rule of Thumb

ABC classifications are assigned separately for purchased and manufactured items by sorting items in descending order of annual spend. The cutoff for an A item is the annual spend for the item at which cumulative annual spend hits 80% of total annual spend, and B items cumulate to 95% of total annual spend, or the next 15% of annual spend after A items.

ABC Classification Hints

Update ABC at Least Annually

Reassign ABC when it makes sense. For most sites the analysis should not be a monthly or quarterly event but should be done annually or when a large number of standard costs are updated, such as in a cost roll or when major business changes occur. Examples of changes that warrant ABC analysis include adding or deleting numerous parts, adding or deleting a product family, any significant change to spending patterns such as adding a new customer, expanding to a new region, increasing revenue by 10%, etc.

Use Thresholds for ABC Classifications

To assign or update ABC classifications, compare each item's annual spend to the cutoffs for A and B items and assign ABC accordingly. It is not necessary to redo ABC analysis if an ABC classification is needed for a few items, but if the population of parts changes noticeably, i.e., 10% change in annual spend or count of items, rerun the ABC analysis and set new thresholds for A and B items.

HINT for Associates

It is important to define annual spend thresholds or cutoff values for purchased and manufactured A and B items, instead of repeatedly running ABC analysis to determine or update an ABC assignment. To assign ABC, compare a part's annual spend to the defined thresholds.

Don't Mess with ABC Definitions

Don't modify the ABC codes to make it more "flexible" or to mold it to "special" circumstances. If it is necessary to flag items as inactive, end of life, new product introduction, or anything else, use another field. ABC classification is utilized for target lead time and often for target safety stock, and it's ridiculous to have to convert every weird D, E, F, or G item into what it should be. Don't monkey with ABC categories!

Real-World Observation

One site classified items as A, B, C, D, or E. They used standard definitions for A, B, and C, but then it got weird. D items had no current demand, but they thought they might bounce back so they didn't want to deactivate them. Alas, they also didn't want to lump them with C items. What?!? These should have been C items, because C includes items with zero demand.

E parts were new products, so they didn't have any demand history. Again, these should have been C items, and as demand climbed they would have become B or A items.

Don't Assign ABC in Subgroups

Do not assign ABC by subgroups within purchased and manufactured part lists. Subdividing parts by product family, value stream, manager, supplier, internal warehouse, or anything else just creates artificial spending thresholds for A and B items, which destroys the validity of ABC assignments. Sub-dividing parts also makes assigning ABC more cumbersome because it requires annual spend plus purchased versus manufactured plus some other attribute. ABC thresholds should be universally applied based only on annual spend versus purchased or manufactured status.

ABC by Product Family Example

A site decided to assign ABC based on product family so each family would have its own set of A, B, and C parts. Product family YSC had low revenue and a limited number of items while product family CMS was a large, high-spend family with a very high item count.

In the ABC analysis, YSC parts with a relatively low spend were artificially elevated to A and B status, while CMS parts that should have been A's or B's slipped into B and C classifications since every family had to have A, B, and C items.

Similarly, several A items in the YSC product family had low annual spends that didn't warrant A classifications and the associated low replenishment quantities, frequent transactions, and high attention from a buyer.

The site repeated the ABC analysis to get it right, then created new replenishment plans. They lost four weeks of project time due to this silliness.

Current or Recommended ABC

When calculating kanban solutions, we must decide whether to use current or recommended ABC classification, since ABC impacts target lead time and often target safety stock. Note that this decision is only required if the kanban calculator is sophisticated enough to calculate ABC.

The advantage to using current ABC is that ABC stays consistent over time. Parts that are on the edge of A versus B or B versus C don't bounce back and forth based on daily demand at the time of re-sizing. Think about that. Annual spend determines ABC, and daily demand times standard cost equals annual spend, so when daily demand changes it can impact ABC. If daily demand varies from time to time, an item that hovers on the edge of A-B or B-C will change classification if we use recommended ABC, because as demand bumps up or down the annual spend changes. That results in chaos for target safety stock and lead times if those are based on ABC. This is significant for sites with seasonal demand.

The disadvantage to using current ABC is that items that are improperly classified remain in error, which causes inaccurate safety stock and lead-time targets. If errors exist in current ABC assignments, use recommended ABC if available or rerun the entire ABC analysis.

For most sites it's best to use current ABC classifications, but always ensure that ABC classifications are verified at least once per year or when standard costs are updated.

ABC Summary

ABC classification makes it instantly clear whether a part is high value or low, which tells us if it deserves minimum or maximum time and attention, long or short target lead times, high or low replenishment quantities, and possibly higher or lower safety stock. These are important decisions when designing kanban solutions. Ensure all parts are evaluated correctly, with accurate purchased versus manufactured designations, standard costs, and annual demand data.

> **HINT for Associates**
>
> When improving inventory performance, focus on parts with high annual spend because they move the needle for both inventory turns and on-hand dollars. We need to know where the money lives, and that's generally in A and B items.
>
> One caution: ensure that C items don't become a financial anchor for inventory performance, which can happen if they are ignored. By definition, C items account for just 5% of annual spend but they are likely to have higher order quantities when measured as days of demand, i.e., 20 days of coverage for a C item versus 5 for an A. Because of this, C items will be greater than 5% of total *on-hand dollars* even though they are 5% of *spend*. But, don't let them get out of control just because they are "cheap."

How can this be an A item? It's a bolt.

We use 7,500 a day, 250 days a year, at four cents each. Do the math. That's $75,000 a year! You spend more on that bolt than you spend on me.

That's amazing.

For me, it's a little depressing.

by TimothyG

TUTORIAL: GOCO ABC CLASSIFICATION

Mary knew that about half of the items in the MRP system had no ABC classification. The buyers told her the data hadn't been updated in more than 5 years, so even items that had a classification could not be assumed to be correct. GOCO had 44 purchased parts and 64 manufactured parts, including 50 work in progress and 14 finished goods.

Purchased Parts

Mary separated purchased parts from manufactured parts and sorted them in decreasing order of annual spend. Figure 4-4 on page 61 shows the list of purchased parts.

The data summed to an annual spend of $69,116,750, in Figure 4-3.

• A items should include all items through the cumulative annual spend of $55,293,400, or 80% of total annual purchased spend.

Figure 4-3. ABC Purchased Target Spending Levels

PP Total Spend	$	69,116,750
A Item Target Total Annual Spend (80%)	$	55,293,400
B Item Target Total Annual Spend (95%)	$	65,660,913

• B parts should include items below the last A and up to the cumulative annual spend of $65,660,913, or 95% of total annual purchased spend.

• C items would be the rest of the list.

The next step was to determine the annual spend threshold for an individual A or B item, or the level of spend that qualified a purchased part to be an A or a B. Mary inserted a column that summed cumulative annual spend for the list of parts. See the last column in Figure 4-4 on page 61. (Due to space limits, the list of parts is cut off at the bottom. Not all purchased parts are listed in the table.)

Mary reviewed the cumulative annual spend column until she found where it hit the A item target of $55,293,400. That occurred at part number 100.50 Trim with a cumulative spend of $56,894,471. See the red line in Figure 4-4 on page 61. Mary checked the part one row up from 100.50 Trim, Rand4, and cumulative spend at that row was $55,164,868, which was also really close to the target.

The item below 100.50 Trim had a much lower annual spend, from more than $1.7M for 100.50 Trim to less than $1.2M for 67389, so the cutoff had to be at 100.50 Trim or Rand4.

Mary looked at annual spend for the 100.50 Trim and Rand4 to see how they compared. Item 100.50 Trim had an annual spend of $1,729,602 while Rand4 right above had an annual spend of $2,122,020, which was a big gap. Since Rand4's cumulative annual spend was so close to the 80% target for A items, it made sense to put the cutoff for A items at Rand4 and set the annual spend threshold for an A item at $2,000,000, taking 100.50 Trim off the A item list.

For B items, the cumulative annual spend target was achieved at part number 50.50 Face with a cumulative spend of $65,893,560, which just exceeded the target of $65,660,913. See the blue line in Figure 4-4 on page 61. The annual spend for 50.50 Face was $368,307 and the item just above, part number 22624, was $406,726 with cumulative spend of $65,525,253. Because this was a big gap and the cumulative annual spend numbers for each item were close to the target of $65,660,913, Mary set the cutoff for B items at $400,000, which made 50.50 Face a C item.

Figure 4-4. Purchased Parts Sorted by Annual Spend, with Cumulative Spend

Part Number	Description	Group	RM/WIP/FG	Std Cost	Demand	Annual Spend	Annual $	
Steel 12	Sheet Steel, 12 Gauge	All	RM	$ 3.17	4,383,838	$ 13,887,999	$ 13,887,999	
Steel 20	Sheet Steel, 20 Gauge	All	RM	$ 1.40	9,017,661	$ 12,660,796	$ 26,548,795	
PressSens	Pressure Sensor	All	RM	$ 3.12	2,985,201	$ 9,307,857	$ 35,856,652	
PressHarn	Pressure Harness	All	RM	$ 1.79	2,985,201	$ 5,340,525	$ 41,197,176	
Steel 16	Sheet Steel, 16 Gauge	All	RM	$ 1.87	2,080,280	$ 3,894,284	$ 45,091,460	
75.50 Trim	750 x 500mm Trim	All	RM	$ 3.67	813,115	$ 2,984,132	$ 48,075,592	
DispHarn	Display Harness	All	RM	$ 1.85	1,461,062	$ 2,703,695	$ 50,779,288	
DD 75.50	Digital Display, 750 x 500r	All	RM	$ 2.79	811,603	$ 2,263,561	$ 53,042,848	
Rand4	Random Purch Part 4	Auto	RM	$ 1.68	1,263,107	$ 2,122,020	$ 55,164,868	A or B?
100.50 Trim	1000 x 500mm Trim	Ind	RM	$ 5.86	295,154	$ 1,729,602	$ 56,894,471	A or B?
67389	Angle Iron 1/8" x 1" - 6'	All	RM	$ 1.84	639,007	$ 1,174,122	$ 58,068,593	A or B?
50.50 Trim	500 x 500mm Trim	Auto	RM	$ 3.05	350,452	$ 1,067,126	$ 59,135,719	
50R12	1/2" Rubber Hose, 12"	All	RM	$ 1.29	815,926	$ 1,051,729	$ 60,187,448	
75.50 Face	750 x 500mm Face Plate	All	RM	$ 1.17	805,984	$ 944,049	$ 61,131,497	
DD 50.50	Digital Display, 500 x 500r	Auto	RM	$ 2.59	352,351	$ 911,532	$ 62,043,029	
DD 100.50	Digital Display, 1000 x 500	Ind	RM	$ 3.01	296,317	$ 890,877	$ 62,933,906	
Rand3	Random Purch Part 3	Auto	RM	$ 0.71	859,419	$ 610,187	$ 63,544,093	
75.50 Gasket	750 x 500mm Gasket	All	RM	$ 0.74	805,212	$ 597,870	$ 64,141,963	
22824	#8 1 1/2" Phillips head	All	RM	$ 0.15	3,562,452	$ 534,368	$ 64,676,331	
100.50 Face	1000 x 500mm Face Plate	Ind	RM	$ 1.49	296,776	$ 442,196	$ 65,118,527	
22624	#6 1 1/2" Phillips Head	All	RM	$ 0.13	3,253,805	$ 406,726	$ 65,525,253	B or C?
50.50 Face	500 x 500mm Face Plate	All	RM	$ 1.00	369,933	$ 368,307	$ 65,893,560	B or C?
Rand2	Random Purch Part 2	Ag	RM	$ 0.61	578,677	$ 352,993	$ 66,246,553	B or C?
75R12	3/4" Rubber Hose, 12"	All	RM	$ 1.48	237,368	$ 351,067	$ 66,597,620	
10R12	1" Rubber Hose, 12"	All	RM	$ 1.53	227,814	$ 349,467	$ 66,947,087	
33824	U-Bolt, 2"	All	RM	$ 0.61	514,152	$ 313,890	$ 67,260,977	
100.50 Gasket	1000 x 500mm Gasket	Ind	RM	$ 1.01	299,080	$ 300,874	$ 67,561,851	
CB08	8" Corner brace	Auto	RM	$ 5.04	47,780	$ 241,026	$ 67,802,877	
FlowSens	Flow Sensor	All	RM	$ 4.25	49,304	$ 209,542	$ 68,012,419	
TempHarn	Temp Harness	All	RM	$ 1.67	120,825	$ 201,899	$ 68,214,318	
338	#8 Nuts	All	RM	$ 0.04	4,548,914	$ 181,957	$ 68,396,275	
50.50 Gasket	500 x 500mm Gasket	Auto	RM	$ 0.45	352,318	$ 158,543	$ 68,554,818	
TempSens	Temp Sensor	All	RM	$ 1.14	120,788	$ 137,759	$ 68,692,576	
22824H	#8 1 1/2" Hex head	All	RM	$ 0.19	591,427	$ 112,371	$ 68,804,947	
Rand1	Random Purch Part 1	Ind	RM	$ 0.31	290,970	$ 90,201	$ 68,895,148	
FlowHarn	Flow Harness	All	RM	$ 1.74	49,304	$ 85,986	$ 68,981,134	
336	#6 Nuts	All	RM	$ 0.02	3,426,437	$ 68,529	$ 69,049,663	
22824A	#8 1 1/2" Allen head	All	RM	$ 0.15	415,168	$ 60,199	$ 69,109,862	
Misc14	Misc Purch Part 14	Auto	RM	$ 0.04	54,174	$ 2,275	$ 69,112,138	
Misc13	Misc Purch Part 13	Ind	RM	$ 0.03	49,465	$ 1,583	$ 69,113,721	
Misc12	Misc Purch Part 12	Auto	RM	$ 0.02	52,143	$ 1,147	$ 69,114,868	

Manufactured Parts

Mary repeated the same steps for manufactured parts, using the list in Figure 4-7 on page 63. She knew they might have strange results due to the "double counting" that occurred with annual spends, but the analysis was necessary to fix ABC records. She combined WIP and FG into one list and sorted them in descending order of annual spend, as she had done with purchased parts.

Figure 4-5 lists the data for manufactured items. For A items, the target cumulative annual spend was achieved at IHous2 with cumulative annual spend of $256,966,597, which was above the target of $252,127,494, which was very close to the target. See the red line in Figure 4-7 on page 63. The part

Figure 4-5. ABC Manufactured Target Spending Levels

Mfd Total Spend	$	315,159,368
A Item Target Total Annual Spend	$	252,127,494
B Item Target Total Annual Spend	$	299,401,399

number one row above, IBrace3, had cumulative spend of $252,054,663. The two annual spends were really close, $4,958,212 and $4,911,934, so it made sense to count anything above $4,900,000 as an A item, leaving the cutoff in the original location.

Target cumulative annual spend for B items was $299,401,399, which was achieved at part number MBkt1 with cumulative spend of $300,064,724. See the blue line in Figure 4-7 on page 63. That exceeded the target by a bit, but the next part number up the list set cumulative spend at $298,140,780, which was not as close to the target. The annual spend values were close for the 2 parts, and the next part number down the list, IBrace2 demonstrated good separation from MBkt1 for annual spend. Based on annual and cumulative spends, Mary chose the original cumulative number and set the cutoff for manufactured B items at $1,900,000.

GOCO ABC Summary

When the analysis was done, Mary created an ABC reference table (Figure 4-6) and had the buyers correct all ABC classifications in the system.

Figure 4-6. A and B Item Cutoffs

	Purchased Parts	Manufactured Parts
A Item Cutoff	$ 2,000,000	$ 4,900,000
B Item Cutoff	$ 400,000	$ 1,900,000

Figure 4-7. Manufactured Parts Sorted by Annual Spend, Partial List

Part Number	Description	Cust Group	RM/WIP/FG	Std Cost	Annual Demand	Annual Spend	Cumulative Annual $	
Gaggle	Gaggleflute	Auto	FG	$ 36.66	690,609	$ 25,317,726	$ 25,317,726	
ISub1	Instrument Subassy 1	Ag	WIP	$ 30.84	692,390	$ 21,351,646	$ 46,669,372	
ISub3	Instrument Subassy 3	Ag	WIP	$ 30.44	635,666	$ 19,349,673	$ 66,019,045	
IHous1	Instrument Housing 1	Ag	WIP	$ 24.42	694,306	$ 16,954,119	$ 82,973,164	
Angle	Angleflater	Ag	FG	$ 26.15	611,027	$ 15,978,356	$ 98,951,520	
IHous3	Instrument Housing 3	Ag	WIP	$ 22.98	629,984	$ 14,477,032	$ 113,428,553	
MSub3	Meter Subassy 3	Ag	WIP	$ 26.32	508,726	$ 13,389,668	$ 126,818,221	
What	Whatchamacallit	Auto	FG	$ 71.97	185,412	$ 13,344,102	$ 140,162,323	
Dimmer	Crescendimmer	Ind	FG	$ 38.31	313,788	$ 12,021,218	$ 152,183,541	
IBkt1	Instrument bracket 1	Ag	WIP	$ 8.53	1,358,280	$ 11,586,128	$ 163,769,669	
MSub2	Meter Subassy 2	Ind	WIP	$ 29.87	382,899	$ 11,437,193	$ 175,206,862	
IBkt3	Instrument bracket 3	Ag	WIP	$ 8.22	1,267,851	$ 10,421,735	$ 185,628,598	
DiddyDoo	Diddydoo	Ag	FG	$ 23.07	386,818	$ 8,923,891	$ 194,552,489	
DSub1	Doodle Subassy 1	Ag	WIP	$ 21.52	358,538	$ 7,715,738	$ 202,268,227	
MSub1	Meter Subassy 1	Auto	WIP	$ 28.73	246,097	$ 7,069,875	$ 209,338,101	
MHous3	Meter Housing 3	Ag	WIP	$ 13.76	503,633	$ 6,929,990	$ 216,268,091	
ISub2	Instrument Subassy 2	Auto	WIP	$ 34.02	202,595	$ 6,892,282	$ 223,160,373	
Subfasc	Subfascinator	Auto	FG	$ 104.92	62,619	$ 6,569,985	$ 229,730,359	
DoodHop	Doodlehopper	Auto	FG	$ 80.28	73,903	$ 5,932,933	$ 235,663,291	
MHous2	Meter Housing 2	Ind	WIP	$ 14.92	388,649	$ 5,798,643	$ 241,461,935	
IBrace1	Instrument Brace 1	Ag	WIP	$ 4.07	1,384,470	$ 5,634,516	$ 247,096,451	A or B?
IBrace3	Instrument Brace 3	Ag	WIP	$ 3.97	1,248,920	$ 4,958,212	$ 252,054,663	A or B?
IHous2	Instrument Housing 2	Auto	WIP	$ 24.99	196,556	$ 4,911,934	$ 256,966,597	A or B?
Bangle	Banglenok	Auto	FG	$ 5.80	626,804	$ 3,635,463	$ 260,602,061	
MHous1	Meter Housing 1	Auto	WIP	$ 14.36	251,036	$ 3,605,881	$ 264,207,942	
OSub2	Other Subassy 2	Auto	WIP	$ 18.76	183,190	$ 3,436,644	$ 267,644,586	
OSub1	Other Subassy 1	Auto	WIP	$ 19.52	169,577	$ 3,310,143	$ 270,954,729	
IBkt2	Instrument bracket 2	Auto	WIP	$ 8.53	383,444	$ 3,270,777	$ 274,225,506	
MBkt3	Meter bracket 3	Ag	WIP	$ 3.22	997,054	$ 3,210,514	$ 277,436,020	
Krinkle	Krinklehorn	Ag	FG	$ 75.52	40,324	$ 3,045,268	$ 280,481,289	
MBkt2	Meter bracket 2	Ind	WIP	$ 3.93	767,406	$ 3,015,906	$ 283,497,194	
DHous1	Doodle Housing 1	Ag	WIP	$ 8.26	357,769	$ 2,955,172	$ 286,452,366	
DSub2	Doodle Subassy 2	Ind	WIP	$ 21.63	121,159	$ 2,620,669	$ 289,073,036	
DBkt1	Doodle Bracket 1	Ag	WIP	$ 3.42	713,170	$ 2,439,041	$ 291,512,077	
Pingle	Pingleloom	Ind	FG	$ 28.80	83,437	$ 2,402,902	$ 293,914,979	
MBrace3	Meter Brace 3	Ag	WIP	$ 2.21	1,001,074	$ 2,212,374	$ 296,127,353	B or C?
MBrace2	Meter Brace 2	Ind	WIP	$ 2.52	798,979	$ 2,013,427	$ 298,140,780	B or C?
MBkt1	Meter bracket 1	Auto	WIP	$ 3.79	507,905	$ 1,923,944	$ 300,064,724	B or C?
IBrace2	Instrument Brace 2	Auto	WIP	$ 4.52	392,594	$ 1,774,525	$ 301,839,249	
Thing	Thingamabob	Auto	FG	$ 41.57	36,904	$ 1,534,099	$ 303,373,348	
OHous2	Other Housing 2	Auto	WIP	$ 7.98	181,739	$ 1,450,277	$ 304,823,625	
DBrace1	Doodle Brace 1	Ag	WIP	$ 1.71	714,699	$ 1,222,135	$ 306,045,761	
OHous1	Other Housing 1	Auto	WIP	$ 7.26	165,440	$ 1,201,094	$ 307,246,855	
MBrace1	Meter Brace 1	Auto	WIP	$ 2.39	497,468	$ 1,190,938	$ 308,437,793	
DHous2	Doodle Housing 2	Ind	WIP	$ 8.19	120,543	$ 987,247	$ 309,425,040	
ONkt1	Other bracket 1	Auto	WIP	$ 2.72	345,037	$ 938,501	$ 310,363,541	
OBkt2	Other bracket 2	Auto	WIP	$ 2.51	361,760	$ 908,018	$ 311,271,559	
DBkt2	Doodle Bracket 2	Ind	WIP	$ 3.76	231,961	$ 872,173	$ 312,143,732	
OBrace1	Other Brace 1	Auto	WIP	$ 1.71	351,219	$ 600,584	$ 312,744,317	
OBrace2	Other Brace 2	Auto	WIP	$ 1.65	344,406	$ 568,270	$ 313,312,586	
Diddy	Doowadiddy	Ag	FG	$ 73.25	6,862	$ 502,642	$ 313,815,228	
DBrace2	Doodle Brace 2	Ind	WIP	$ 1.62	253,099	$ 410,020	$ 314,225,248	

Section II.
Introduction
to Kanban

This section introduces the basic concepts of kanban, to give the reader a general understanding of the entire process from gathering data through sustaining a kanban system.

We'll start by comparing kanban to MRP, since that is such a common replenishment tool. From there we'll look at how kanban works in the real world.

There are a couple elements of kanban that are often overlooked, and we'll begin covering those in this section. First we'll cover the different types of kanban solutions and the associated trigger timing options, then we'll look at the concept of an ideal kanban solution, followed by the related topics of target lead time and order quantities.

This section will just introduce these concepts, and we'll cover additional details when we get to Section V, where we'll go through the steps to calculate kanban solutions. It might seem redundant to cover these topics twice, but it's easier to comprehend the entire kanban topic if we cover the big picture first then dive into the mechanics of actually calculating kanban solutions at a later time.

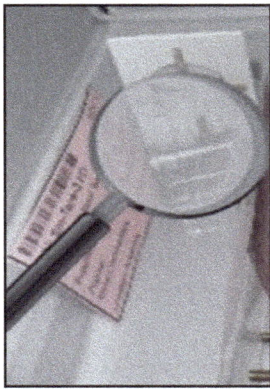

Kanban vs. MRP

CHAPTER 5: KANBAN VS. MRP REPLENISHMENT SYSTEMS

A successful replenishment plan for an item requires an order quantity and safety stock plan that does not torpedo inventory turns yet still protects on-time delivery and lead times. To design such a solution, we need a replenishment planning and management tool. There are two primary methods to consider: MRP and kanban.

What Is MRP?

For many decades, manufacturers have used material requirements planning (MRP) or manufacturing resource planning (also MRP) to drive the acquisition and production of purchased and manufactured materials. MRP is the generic term for a computerized system that calculates an item's required replenishment quantity by comparing on-hand balance plus upcoming receipts versus expected future demand through the defined time period.

It's really easier than it sounds. Essentially, if future demand for a time horizon exceeds what will be available from the addition of current on-hand balance plus what will arrive in that time, MRP recommends a replenishment order, either a purchase order for external parts or a manufacturing order for internal parts.

Basic MRP Order Quantity Formula

MRP order quantity = On-hand balance + upcoming receipts – future demand

A negative result means a replenishment order is required

MRP replenishment recommendations are *theoretically* sound and, therefore, *should* define accurate replenishment orders. But, there are inherent limitations to MRP because recommended actions are based on data stored in the system, specifically on-hand balance (OHB), upcoming receipts, and future demand. These data points must be *accurate and timely* in order for MRP recommendations to be correct, and that's where MRP often breaks down. There are some plants that can obtain and manage the data that feeds MRP, but many plants struggle. See Figure 5-1.

Figure 5-1. MRP Replenishment View
MRP's view is focused on system data: on-hand balance, upcoming receipts, and future demand. When demand in the selected analysis period is greater than on-hand balance plus upcoming receipts, a replenishment order is triggered. If system data is incorrect or incomplete, MRP recommendations are wrong.

A Few MRP Characteristics

• MRP looks at a specified time horizon, often called the planning horizon, to pull the correct data for each item. This applies to demand and supply data.

• The due date for an MRP order is usually determined by a complicated algorithm, but essentially it can be based on a need date determined by MRP or it can be driven by the standard lead time for that item.

» If standard lead time is used to generate the replenishment due date, that due date can be further out than the required timing for additional pieces, e.g., we need pieces in 2 weeks, but standard lead time is 3 weeks, so the MRP order is entered for a date that is too far out.

» If the due date is based on a date created by MRP, the date can be sooner than the lead time required by the supplier, e.g., MRP says we need parts in 2 weeks, but the supplier's lead time is 3 weeks, so the MRP order is entered for a date the supplier can't meet.

• MRP analysis runs at a defined frequency. Many MRP systems run every night, but some systems run once a week. As expected, MRP recommendations are out of date if they are not fed by real-time data.

• Some MRP systems have the option to "auto-release" orders without human approval, while others generate what is commonly called an "exception report" that lists actions to be taken.

» Auto-release means the system executes whatever it discovers, which streamlines the process but adds definite risk if MRP recommendations contain errors.

» MRP exception reports must be reviewed by humans if a site does not use auto-release. This review cycle can consume significant time to review and respond to MRP suggestions. In some sites an MRP exception report is thousands of lines, so it can be overwhelming.

MRP Data

MRP depends on several values that are pulled from its data repository.

MRP Data: On-Hand Balance

On-hand balance is the reported in-stock quantity for a given item, in the unit of measure for that part number, e.g., feet, pieces, or grams. Accurate on-hand balances depend on accurate and timely reporting of <u>every</u> replenishment and consumption transaction.

The need for accurate <u>and</u> timely reporting disrupts many sites in their quest to obtain balances that match what is actually on site, because at any given time the on-hand balance is subject to a number of puts and takes that can be out of step with reality. Any <u>physical</u> transaction that increases or decreases on-hand inventory should be associated with a matching real-time <u>system</u> transaction.

• Have all scrap and rework units been reported?

• Are Sales and Engineering samples immediately subtracted from the system's on-hand balances?

• Are manufacturing transactions completed in a timely manner to "backflush" consumed material?

• Is received or produced material reported in the system so it is available for consumption?

MRP OHB Examples

Cell 45 works for 2 or 3 days then reports all production quantities at once. Since they "batch" their production reporting, on-hand balance is usually incorrect because what shows as available has in fact been partially consumed.

Cell 99 experiences high scrap on one part number. They report production and relieve inventory at the end of every shift, but they let scrap accumulate throughout the week then report it on Friday afternoon. Obviously, on-hand balance is incorrect whenever scrap goes unreported. Additionally, if the actual scrap rate is higher than the MRP planning assumption, e.g., MRP assumes 1% scrap but actual scrap is 2%, MRP won't plan enough parts to cover the higher loss rate.

How many does MRP say we have?

Negative 40.

Hmm. This looks like more than that.

by TimothyG

MRP Data: Upcoming Receipts

Purchase orders initiate receipts from suppliers, and manufacturing orders trigger production from internal cells. If these orders are maintained and updated in MRP from the time of order entry through order completion, MRP conclusions about upcoming receipts should be accurate. However, errors often exist for either the timing (<u>actual</u> receipt date versus <u>original</u> due date) or quantity (<u>actual</u> receipt quantity versus <u>order</u> quantity) of upcoming receipts.

MRP Supplier Quantity Examples

A major supplier is notorious for shipping the wrong quantity. Sometimes they over-ship by 5%, but more often they under-ship by as much as 15%. If we can't predict actual receipt quantities for an open purchase order, MRP assumptions and recommendations are wrong.

Another supplier has intermittent quality rejects, so an incoming lot of 100 can be reduced to 85 or 90 after sorting out bad parts. Since this is unpredictable, MRP recommendations are incorrect.

MRP Data: Future Demand

MRP relies on a forward-looking view of demand, so future demand must be populated by a combination of firm customer orders and/or a demand forecast. This must include all usage sources: customer shipments, Sales samples, scrap, Engineering test items, etc. If there are gaps between what MRP estimates as total need (future *forecast*) versus what will actually ship (future *demand*), MRP recommendations are incorrect for that demand period.

Inaccuracy is exacerbated if demand data is entered in MRP for a time period that is shorter than the production planning horizon. If customer orders exist for the next 4 weeks, but the production planning horizon requires 8 weeks of demand insight, there is an unavoidable gap.

Likewise, if customer demand is subject to random adjustments for either timing or quantity, there is a gap between the data available for planning versus what will actually occur. If customers provide a 12-month forecast but change the product mix or quantity on a weekly basis, the system data is inaccurate. It might be close enough to estimate overall output to plan capacity, but planning individual items is difficult with last-minute changes.

Future demand accuracy also relies on accurate bills of material (BOMs). Customer orders or demand forecasts are usually entered at the finished goods (FG) level, and they cascade down to lower components via the bills of material in the system. When BOMs are wrong, so is MRP.

MRP Future Demand Example 1

The MRP forecast indicates shipments of 50 finished goods in the next 4 weeks. The BOM says 4 screws are required, or 200 screws to make 50 assemblies. But, it actually takes 6 screws per assembly, so the MRP recommendation to order 200 screws is inaccurate *even if the customer orders exactly 50* assemblies, as predicted in the forecast.

MRP Future Demand Example 2

Our biggest customer loads demand on Monday of each week for the following 4 weeks, including new and updated orders. So, at any given time we have 3 to 4 weeks of visibility depending on which day of the week we check the system. Several expensive purchased parts have lead times of 6 to 8 weeks, so we don't have customer visibility at the time we must place orders. To accommodate this, we estimate how many are needed for weeks 5 to 8.

We're tasked with reducing inventory, so we tend to order on the low side and expedite parts when a new forecast reveals increased demand for the long lead-time items. As expected, this happens every week for one or more items, so we spend lots of time and energy updating orders and expediting parts. It's no surprise that suppliers often charge expedite fees when we rush an order. So, this practice costs real money in addition to the human effort that is expended.

MRP Data: Supplier Minimum Order & Standard Package Quantity Requirements

Once MRP analysis is complete, the system recommends purchasing or manufacturing orders for everything that is managed by MRP. These orders should accommodate supplier requirements for minimum order quantity (MOQ) and standard

package quantity (SPQ). But, that works only if MRP is programmed to round for MOQ and SPQ <u>and</u> if those limitations are accurate in the system. For most facilities, maintaining MOQ and SPQ data is another source of errors.

Let's face it - in most facilities, MRP is full of errors.

* BOMs are inaccurate, and scrap is reported too late or not at all.

* Minimum order quantities and standard package quantities are missing or out of date, so MRP recommendations are not correctly rounded to meet supplier limitations.

* Replenishment orders are not updated with new due dates or quantities when internal or external suppliers modify open orders, so incoming material orders are wrong in the system.

* Lead times are out of date, so orders are planned for the wrong due dates.

Don't get lulled into a false sense of security that MRP is correct and timely because it's in a Great Big Computer. In actuality, few sites have highly accurate data; OHB, upcoming receipts, and future demand are difficult to get 100% right.

Suppose we have these conditions:

» On-hand balance is 98% correct.

» Incoming purchased and manufactured orders are right ~95% of the time, both quantity and due date.

» Forecasted demand is 85% accurate.

This is pretty high data integrity, yet MRP calculations would be just 79% correct [98% * 95% * 85% = 79%]. This means MRP is wrong on 1 out of every 5 order recommendations. That's amazing, yet these results would be considered quite good for many MRP sites around the world.

What Is Kanban?

In the Lean world, kanban is a subset of the concept of pull. Think of it as a combination of "visual" plus "signal" or "card." As the name implies, kanban relies on the physical or observable world, sending a replenishment signal when a certain set of conditions exist, such as emptying or opening a bin of material.

HINT for Associates

As mentioned before, Lean is a continuous improvement philosophy based on the Toyota Production System. If you are not familiar with Lean, read *Lean Thinking* by Womack and Jones and *The Toyota Way* by Liker.

Figure 5-2. Kanban Replenishment View

Kanban's view is focused on actual, physical inventory, or how many parts are in the kanban bin. As consumption occurs, replenishment orders are triggered.

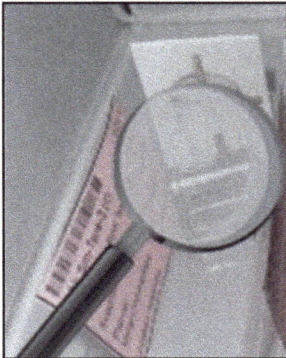

Unlike MRP, kanban's vision is on the physical world, not system data, as in Figure 5-2, so it is synchronized with actual inventory. When an associate consumes inventory to the level of the trigger point, a kanban signal is generated for a replenishment order. No system functionality or data is required, so if the system is wrong, kanban still works correctly. This is one of the most significant benefits to utilizing kanban instead of MRP!

To generate valid replenishment orders, kanban has two primary functions:

1. Calculate kanban solutions to plan inventory levels that balance delivery goals versus inventory performance. Like MRP, kanban solutions must accommodate supplier lead-time and batch-size limitations as well as supply and demand variation.

2. Trigger replenishment orders in response to material consumption, using physical or visible signals such as cards or spots on the floor.

A typical kanban execution process is rather simple, as in Figure 5-3 on page 72. Start in the upper left corner and go clockwise.

What is missing in the execution diagram is kanban sizing, the foundation of a kanban system and a necessary planning step to determine the right replenishment plan for every item.

Kanban systems require calculated solutions for every item: the number of assigned signals or cards for each item, the rounded kanban order quantity per signal, and the standard lead time to receive an order. The math behind defining kanban solutions is significant and if done incorrectly the entire system will fail. Fortunately, calculating kanban solutions is what this book is about. How amazing!

Some MRP advocates insist that an MRP fixed order point (FOP) process, for which an order is placed as soon as on-hand balance reaches a certain trigger point, is the same as kanban because orders are triggered based on consumption and are issued for a standard quantity and lead time, just like kanban.

Aaahhh, that's not entirely accurate. Fixed order point can be effective, but it depends on data integrity, just like any MRP recommendation. Ensuring that MRP is in sync with the real world is the biggest challenge for most systems. So, MRP or fixed order point - or any system-based replenishment system - is generally not as accurate as kanban when it comes to generating replenishment orders.

Figure 5-3. Typical Kanban Execution Process

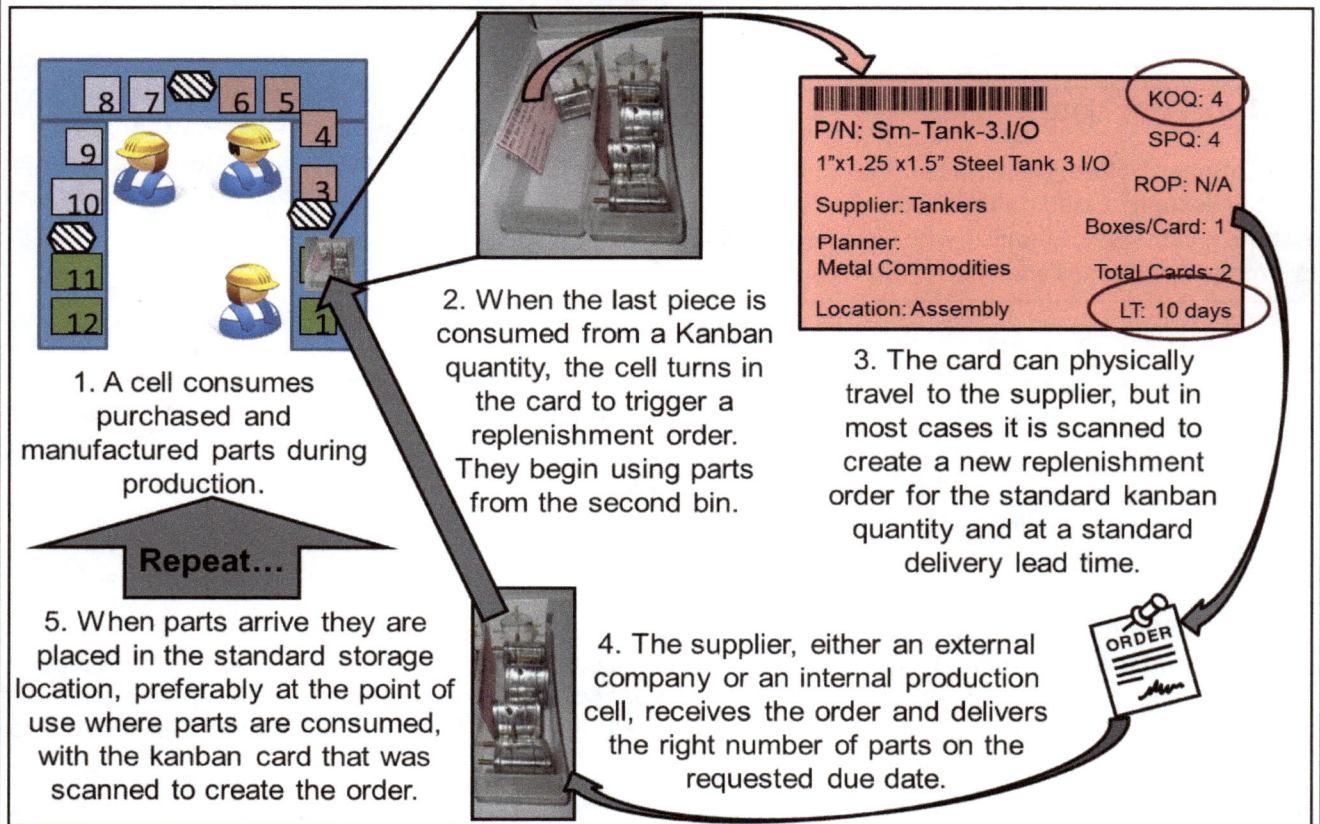

1. A cell consumes purchased and manufactured parts during production.

Repeat...

2. When the last piece is consumed from a Kanban quantity, the cell turns in the card to trigger a replenishment order. They begin using parts from the second bin.

P/N: Sm-Tank-3.I/O
1"x1.25 x1.5" Steel Tank 3 I/O
Supplier: Tankers
Planner: Metal Commodities
Location: Assembly

KOQ: 4
SPQ: 4
ROP: N/A
Boxes/Card: 1
Total Cards: 2
LT: 10 days

3. The card can physically travel to the supplier, but in most cases it is scanned to create a new replenishment order for the standard kanban quantity and at a standard delivery lead time.

ORDER

5. When parts arrive they are placed in the standard storage location, preferably at the point of use where parts are consumed, with the kanban card that was scanned to create the order.

4. The supplier, either an external company or an internal production cell, receives the order and delivers the right number of parts on the requested due date.

Associates consume parts from Inventory (Step 1). When an item hits the trigger point, the card is pulled (Step 2) and processed (Step 3) to create a replenishment order. The card is placed on a kanban board to wait for replenishment parts to arrive. (The board is not shown here...we'll cover that later.) The internal or external supplier fills the order for the correct quantity and at the standard lead time (Step 4). When parts arrive they are delivered to the cell, usually at point of use, and the card that originated the order is placed with the parts (Step 5). This process is repeated over and over for every kanban item.

Kanban Versus MRP Characteristics

• MRP is virtual, while kanban is physical and visual. MRP is only visible to buyers, planners, supervisors, and other "system" users with the right access. Kanban is visible to everyone.

• MRP lives in the system, with invisible and indescribable algorithms and decisions. Kanban lives where the work gets done, usually at point of use, and is managed by the people who are closest to that work.

• MRP relies on a demand forecast or firm customer orders to trigger replenishment orders, while kanban relies on consumption. If parts are not consumed,

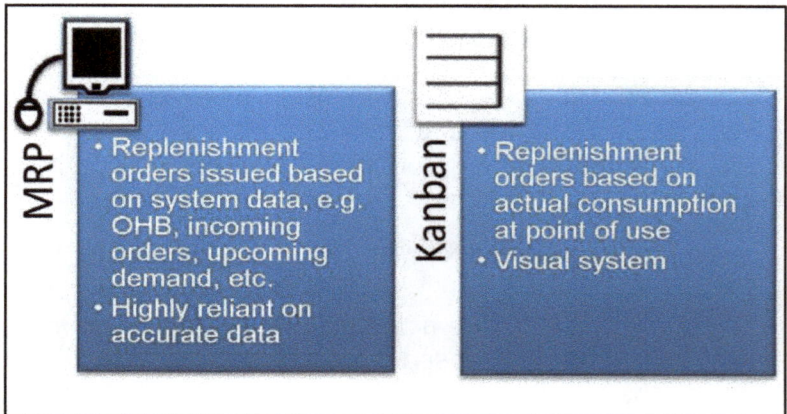

MRP
• Replenishment orders issued based on system data, e.g. OHB, incoming orders, upcoming demand, etc.
• Highly reliant on accurate data

Kanban
• Replenishment orders based on actual consumption at point of use
• Visual system

kanban does not trigger an order, so parts don't pile up due to inaccurate usage forecasts.

• MRP uses system data to calculate inventory needs. Kanban uses actual on-hand inventory and consumption.

• Because kanban is visual and exists where the work occurs, kanban empowers associates because they see what is actually happening. They participate in the replenishment process. Associates know if an order arrives late because they can compare the receipt date to the due date on the kanban card. If an order arrives for the wrong quantity, they know immediately because the kanban order quantity is part of the kanban plan. They can track which items stock out by simply noting which cards are placed on the "Stock Out" peg on the kanban board. They live at the heart of a kanban system every single day!

• MRP has been around for decades, but so has kanban.

• MRP triggers new orders for external or internal parts, and so does kanban.

• Kanban solutions provide data to estimate on-hand inventory per item, which can be used to create prioritized action plans to improve on-time delivery while reducing inventory. Trust me - MRP doesn't do that very well.

Managers who are considering kanban to supplement or replace MRP often ask how many sites have succeeded with kanban. The answer? Thousands and thousands, all over the world, in every industry. In fact, many sites disable or ignore MRP once kanban is in place because MRP is no longer needed. (That's a frightening thought for MRP zealots.) Avoiding MRP definitely saves the time of reviewing exception reports but it can also save money. MRP maintenance costs can be significant, but even if the MRP "system" is maintained after kanban deployment for financial reports or storing item master data, costs are reduced when hard copies of MRP reports are no longer printed and reviewed.

Figure 5-4. *Industry Week* Best Plant Data
Kanban with Suppliers

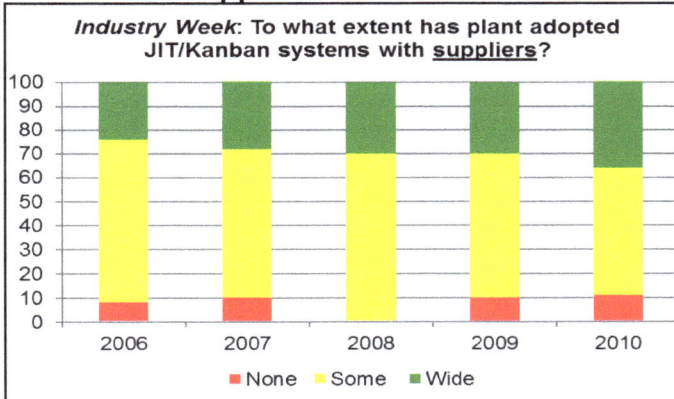

Industry Week: To what extent has plant adopted JIT/Kanban systems with suppliers?

Kanban for Internal Items

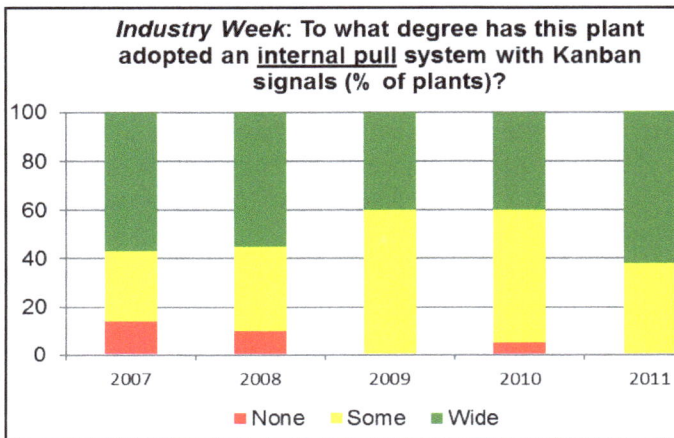

Industry Week: To what degree has this plant adopted an internal pull system with Kanban signals (% of plants)?

Kanban Is Used By the "Best Plants"

For 2010 and 2011, *Industry Week's* Best Plant surveys included questions about the use of kanban with suppliers or for internal processes. See Figure 5-4.

Of the finalists for 2006 to 2010, 25% to 35% had widespread kanban with external suppliers, 55% to 70% had some kanban, and just 10% did not use kanban.

In the 2011 survey, at least 40% of Best Plant finalists utilized kanban internally to implement pull replenishment systems. For 4 of the 5 survey years, no more than 10% of sites reported zero internal kanban systems.

Kanban is everywhere and the message is clear: kanban works. If MRP was consistently achieving high inventory turns and high on-time delivery, kanban would be a narrowly applied tool. Instead, kanban is one of the most widely utilized tools in the Lean toolbox.

If you have not tried and succeeded with kanban, you are already behind the times. Don't delay the potential improvements that can be gained from a well designed kanban system.

Stop dawdling! Deploy kanban!

HINT for Associates

Every item needs a replenishment plan, an approach that is often called Plan for Every Part or "P-Fep" for short. As you might expect, every item must be planned to protect delivery while maximizing inventory performance.

Kanban provides a plan for every part. Items that are not on kanban can be planned by MRP, vendor-managed inventory (VMI), consignment, or some combination of the above. We'll discuss why an item might not be on kanban in future chapters.

Summary of MRP Versus Kanban

On the surface, MRP sounds like a logical replenishment system based on pull logic, but in reality it is riddled with risk.

Kanban is a better alternative because it is linked to real consumption and physical on-hand balances, which accommodates demand or supply errors or anomalies. Kanban is a proven system that has been successful for decades in thousands of sites across innumerable industries. It works!

TUTORIAL: GOCO MRP

GOCO utilized an antiquated "green screen" MRP system coupled with frequent human intervention and expediting. They ran MRP every day at midnight. Buyers and planners reviewed MRP recommendations every morning and entered or released purchase and manufacturing orders in the system.

The Materials team expedited internal and external parts on a daily basis, so it was obvious that MRP recommendations did not provide adequate solutions. Due to the daily expediting activity, on some days the Buyers struggled to review new MRP recommendations from the prior MRP run because they spent so much time expediting parts that had stocked out during second or third shift.

Due to the history of daily expediting, Buyers and Planners had an informal practice of holding extra safety stock, which they called "just in case" (JIC) inventory. Only a few external suppliers agreed to hold extra inventory ready to ship. So, 95% of JIC safety stock was on site at GOCO, adding to inventory space and dollar requirements. Yet even with the JIC safety stock, they still had stock outs almost every day.

Mary reviewed MRP item masters for a couple dozen items and found numerous errors for lead time, minimum order quantity (MOQ), standard package quantity (SPQ), ABC classification, etc. It was evident that low data integrity was part of the problem with MRP recommendations.

The Materials team increased cycle counts for 2 weeks to see how actual on-hand balances compared to system balances, and the results were striking. More than 80% of counted items had fewer pieces on the floor than were in the system, which certainly contributed to MRP errors. They knew cycle counts were a form of waste because it was an inspection function that did not add value. (In Lean, inspection is considered over-processing waste). Cycle counts were definitely not the correct long-term solution, but it verified their suspicion that inventory was not being properly relieved on the floor, that bills of materials (BOMs) might have errors, and that on-hand balances in the system were highly suspect.

The Materials team recognized that stock outs were a major concern that had to be solved by kanban, but they also hoped to reduce inventory.

Kanban Loop

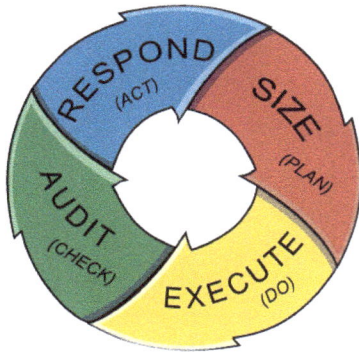

CHAPTER 6: HOW KANBAN WORKS

Before calculating kanban solutions, it is necessary to have a basic understanding of how kanban works and what it does. From the prior chapter, kanban has two primary functions:

1. "Calculate kanban solutions to plan inventory levels that balance delivery goals versus inventory performance. Like MRP, kanban solutions must accommodate supplier lead-time and batch-size limitations as well as supply and demand variation."

2. "Trigger replenishment orders in response to material consumption, using physical or visible signals such as cards or spots on the floor."

This sounds pretty basic, which is why some people incorrectly describe kanban as a "simple pull system." That drives me crazy. Kanban's basic functions are *described* with relative ease, but most people severely underestimate what it takes to <u>design</u> (create a plan), <u>deploy</u> (put every element in place), <u>execute</u> (perform daily and periodic processes), and continuously <u>improve</u> (tweak, adjust, modify) an effective kanban system. Kanban is a tremendous tool, but it requires significant planning, robust plans and processes, and tenacious discipline. The benefits are worth the effort, but kanban practitioners should understand and accept the required effort from the very beginning.

When people describe a kanban system they almost always mention kanban cards, point-of-use storage, and kanban boards, which are the most visible portions of kanban replenishment. What is often missed is that those elements depend on an inordinate amount of unseen planning and process design to achieve consistent success, as measured by delivery and inventory performance.

Dozens of questions must be answered to create, deploy, execute, and sustain a kanban system. These questions are particularly critical if kanban is new for a site or if an existing kanban system is being completely redesigned.

- Which part numbers belong on kanban?
- Which items should be deployed first?
- What kind of kanban solution fits each item?
- How do we determine the correct kanban order quantity for each item? How about the right number of signals?
- How long will it take to receive parts after an order is placed?
- Does each part number have an existing storage location at point of use (POU)? If not, do we need to define those before we deploy kanban?
- When externally-supplied items are delivered to point of use, are they stored in the box they came in or in a different container?
- How do we store and display kanban cards with their respective parts?
- Where do kanban cards go after an order is triggered, while they're waiting for parts to arrive?
- Can we use visual signals other than cards? Would those options provide tangible benefits?
- How much inventory could potentially be on the shelf at any given time for each part number, or how much storage space will each item need?
- How do we track actual lead time for internal and external suppliers?
- Do our suppliers ship the right quantities?
- Can we measure or verify supplier on-time delivery and quality performance?
- Do we have accurate lead time, minimum order quantity (MOQ), and standard package quantity (SPQ) limits for external and internal part numbers?
- How do ensure we won't run out of an item?
- What demand data should we use in the kanban calculator, historical usage or a demand forecast?

- Can we measure or estimate demand variation?
- Do we experience seasonal demand variation, day-to-day variation, or both?
- If an item is used in multiple cells, where will parts be stored and how will orders be triggered?
- What kind of kanban cards will we use? What will be printed on the cards?
- What is the best kanban board design? How many do we need and where should they be located?
- How often should we resize kanban solutions, and how do we deploy new cards and solutions?

High-Level Kanban Processes

In the previous chapter, we briefly reviewed a basic kanban process, as in Figure 6-1.

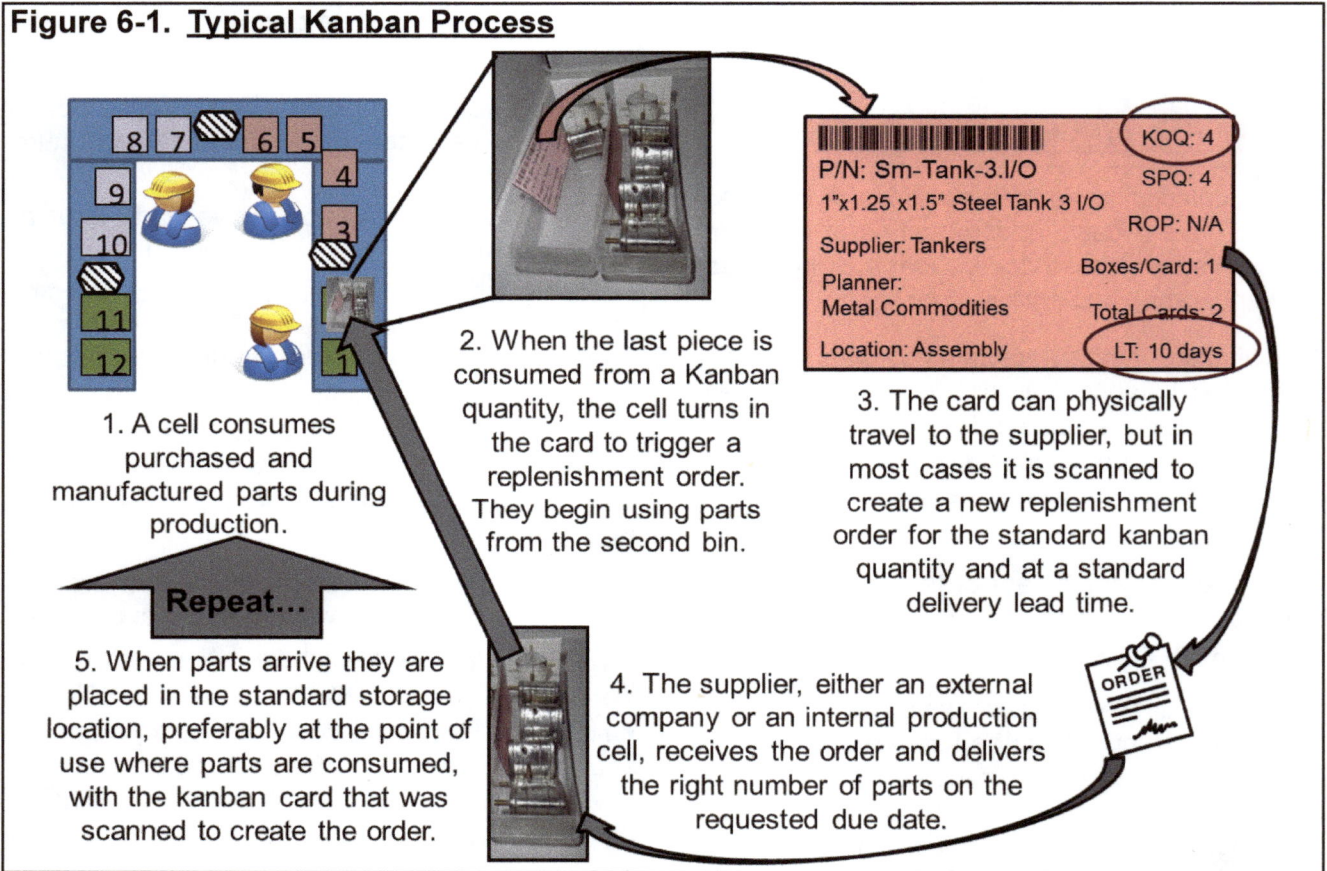

Figure 6-1. Typical Kanban Process

1. A cell consumes purchased and manufactured parts during production.

2. When the last piece is consumed from a Kanban quantity, the cell turns in the card to trigger a replenishment order. They begin using parts from the second bin.

3. The card can physically travel to the supplier, but in most cases it is scanned to create a new replenishment order for the standard kanban quantity and at a standard delivery lead time.

4. The supplier, either an external company or an internal production cell, receives the order and delivers the right number of parts on the requested due date.

5. When parts arrive they are placed in the standard storage location, preferably at the point of use where parts are consumed, with the kanban card that was scanned to create the order.

Repeat...

P/N: Sm-Tank-3.I/O
1"x1.25 x1.5" Steel Tank 3 I/O
Supplier: Tankers
Planner:
Metal Commodities
Location: Assembly
KOQ: 4
SPQ: 4
ROP: N/A
Boxes/Card: 1
Total Cards: 2
LT: 10 days

The above diagram assumes robust processes exist: valid kanban solutions were calculated and deployed, standard work exists for all processes, and errors are corrected when they occur. For the entire process to work effectively, we must successfully perform all aspects of a kanban system. Figure 6-2 on page 77 illustrates these steps in the form of the Plan-Do-Check-Act cycle.

- SIZE or PLAN kanban solutions by setting system parameters and limits, gathering relevant data, calculating kanban solutions, and deploying kanban cards.
- EXECUTE or DO inventory replenishment and material storage processes (the steps in Figure 6-1) by executing defined processes to consume parts, generate kanban signals for replenishment orders, receive parts into inventory, and place parts in assigned storage locations.

Figure 6-2. Kanban Process PDCA Loop

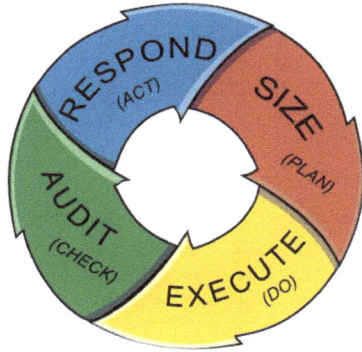

• AUDIT or CHECK results and process status by auditing parts, cards, and kanban boards, and also by tracking data integrity, performance metrics, and other status indicators.

• RESPOND to or ACT on findings or insights from kanban and other inventory processes and audits to tweak the system, modify standard work, correct errors, train associates, and update kanban data.

Most of the rest of this book is about calculating kanban solutions, which is part of the Size or Plan portion of the kanban cycle. But, to effectively execute the sizing process, we must understand all kanban processes. So, the rest of this chapter reviews the four high level kanban elements: Size, Execute, Audit, and Respond.

Sizing = PLAN

A kanban plan 1) sets the parameters that will scope and define the system, 2) gathers necessary data, 3) calculates kanban solutions for all kanban items, and 4) deploys accurate and timely kanban solutions, as in Figure 6-3.

Every kanban solution is a combination of the number of signals plus the order quantity per signal, e.g., 8 cards of 100 pounds each or 2 floor spots for 1 barrel each, and lead time is also required for every solution. A kanban solution must be defined before cards can be deployed or triggered, so sizing must be the first step in the kanban Plan-Do-Check-Act loop. Kanban doesn't exist until sizing occurs.

Figure 6-3. The Sizing Loop

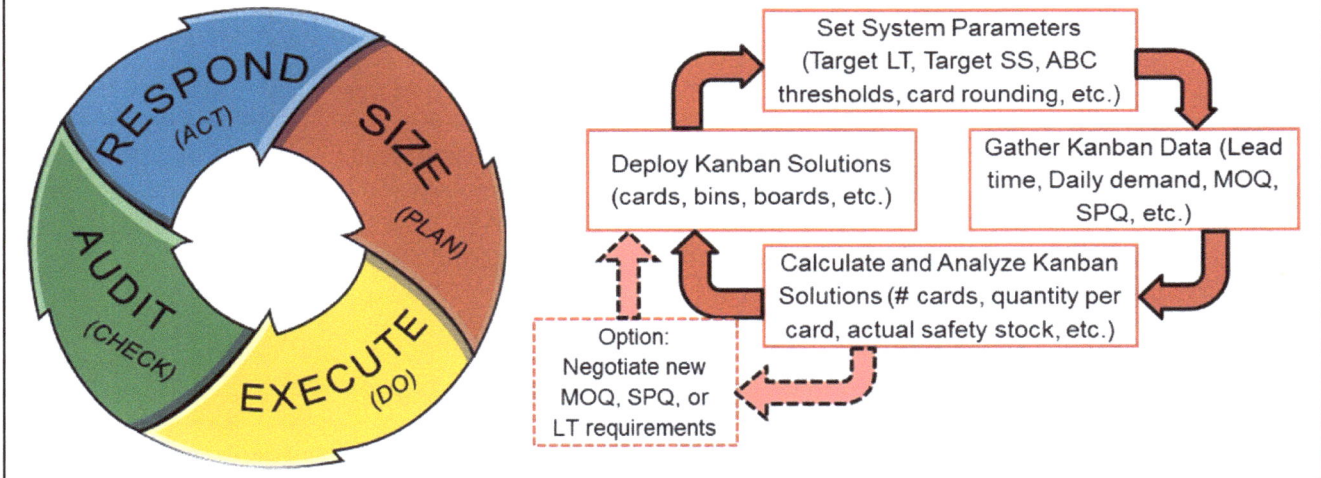

Sizing is performed by a kanban calculator, usually an Excel tool or software program that evaluates demand, lead time, and demand and supply variation to determine the number of signals and the associated order quantity for every item. For most sites it isn't practical to put *every* item on kanban, so the sizing process should also differentiate which parts go on kanban and which do not.

We'll cover details for the Sizing portion of kanban in great detail in later chapters, but this section provides a basic overview. Refer to Figure 6-4

Figure 6-4. <u>Sizing Loop: Kanban Calculator Steps</u>

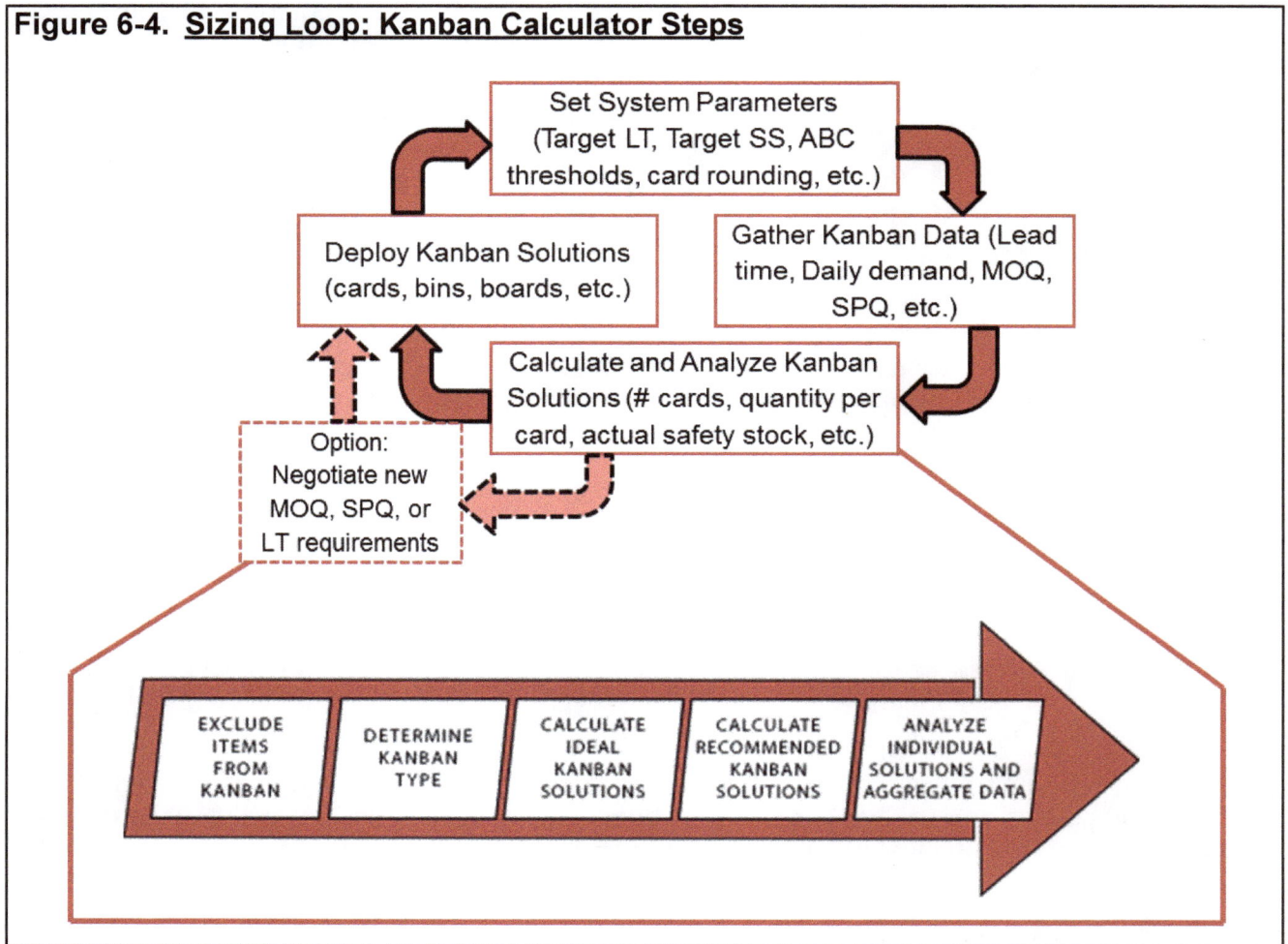

Sizing Step 1: Set System Parameters

A kanban system uses a decision tree with defined criteria to determine which part numbers go on kanban and what type of kanban solution is assigned to every kanban item. To do that, a calculator needs baseline or default values. Typical criteria include thresholds for ABC classifications, target lead times, and target safety stock values. These values must exist prior to calculating solutions.

Sizing Step 2: Gather Kanban Data

Every kanban solution is based on targets and limits from Step 1, plus a data set that covers every item. Obtaining accurate data is often the most challenging and time-consuming step in a new kanban system, particularly for external items, so start this early.

Some system parameters, such as ABC cutoffs, can only be determined after data is available, so there is a bit of back-and-forth between the steps for system parameters and data gathering.

Real-World Observation

I advised a site that faced significant kanban issues: poor supplier performance, numerous stock outs, low on-time delivery, and high on-hand inventory dollars. I finally uncovered the root cause when they admitted that they didn't have accurate lead-time data for purchased parts, so they guessed that *every* external item had a 2-week lead time. Yep, they made it up. How stupid is that?!? I told them to halt kanban until they had accurate data, then start over and recalculate and deploy valid kanban solutions.

Sizing Step 3: Calculate Kanban Solutions

Calculating kanban solutions is a major subset of the sizing loop, as in the red arrow at the bottom of Figure 6-4 on page 78.

A robust kanban calculator performs five steps, and these can only occur after targets, limits, and the entire data set is loaded into the calculator.

1. <u>Divide</u> items into those that go on kanban and those that will utilize an alternative replenishment method, such as MRP or vendor management.

2. Assign the right kanban <u>type</u> to every kanban item.

3. Calculate an <u>ideal</u> kanban solution for every item, to be used as a benchmark for planning inventory improvement or negotiation activity.

4. Calculate the appropriate <u>recommended</u> or resized kanban solution for every kanban item.

5. <u>Analyze</u> kanban solutions and estimate expected on-hand inventory by part number, as well as the inventory reduction potential by item and overall. This provides insights for inventory reduction action plans and timing.

Unfortunately, sizing is an afterthought for many kanban systems. Some sites focus on designing and deploying cards, hanging kanban boards, notifying suppliers of the "new and mandatory kanban process," and predicting glorious results. But, everything depends on correctly sizing kanban solutions up front. Valid solutions can't be deployed until kanban calculations are correct!

A kanban solution requires two elements: order quantity and the number of signals or cards, e.g., 2 cards at 100 pieces or 5 buckets of 3 gallons each. Upcoming chapters will discuss kanban calculations in great detail, but there are two formulas that demonstrate basic logic behind order quantity and number of cards. The first calculates replenishment quantity and the second calculates the number of cards required for a kanban item with a defined order quantity. These formulas DO NOT work in every case, but they are the foundation for kanban calculation logic, so they must be understood.

Basic Kanban Formulas

$$\text{Empty a bin (EaB) kanban order quantity, 2 cards} = \frac{(\text{Actual LT} * \text{Daily demand} + \text{Target SS units})}{(2\text{ cards} - 1)}$$

$$\text{EaB \# cards for defined order quantity} = \frac{(\text{Actual LT} * \text{Daily Demand} + \text{Target SS units})}{\text{KOQ}} + 1$$

$$\text{Break a bin (BaB) kanban order quantity, 2 cards} = \frac{(\text{Actual LT} * \text{Daily demand} + \text{Target SS units})}{(2\text{ cards})}$$

$$\text{BaB \# cards for defined order quantity} = \frac{(\text{Actual LT} * \text{Daily demand} + \text{Target SS units})}{\text{KOQ}}$$

Empty a bin (EaB) and break a bin (BaB) will be covered later, including the requirement to adjust EaB card count, i.e., minus 1 card when calculating order quantity and plus 1 card when calculating card count.

Sizing Step 3A: Resizing

Sizing occurs before the first kanban solutions are deployed, but the sizing step is *repeated* frequently to keep kanban solutions up to date. <u>Resizing</u> confirms whether current solutions accommodate the latest daily demands, lead times, package requirements, and system-wide parameters, such as target lead times or safety stock levels. New or updated data sets, targets, and limits must be in the kanban calculator before resizing occurs. If current deployed solutions do not work for the latest conditions, new or resized solutions must be generated and deployed.

There are a few differences between sizing and resizing, so technically we could say that sizing is just the first time through the calculation loop, while the repetitive process is resizing. Resizing assumes that there are active kanban solutions in place. So, the calculator must know what is currently deployed by item so it can confirm which solutions must be changed, or resized, and which part numbers can keep current kanban solutions.

Rule of Thumb 👍

Resizing analysis should be performed on every kanban item at least once per quarter, but sites with high demand variation might resize monthly or even weekly.

Resizing recommends kanban updates to support on-time delivery (i.e., protect delivery by deploying "bigger" kanban solutions) and inventory performance (i.e., reduce inventory by fixing items that need "smaller" kanban solutions). Resizing can also reveal opportunities to negotiate better minimum order quantities (MOQ) and lead times from internal or external suppliers. Note that the negotiation step happens only if ideal kanban solutions are provided as part of the resizing effort.

The terms "sizing" and "resizing" are used interchangeably because resizing is the same *basic* logic as sizing, but we'll see in a future chapter that there are differences that must be accommodated in a resizing calculator. Sizing the *first time* deploys only new solutions, but resizing implies a high probability of *changing* deployed solutions, which could involve reprinting cards, deploying new or additional cards, and pulling cards out of active circulation. Resizing can add or take away cards.

HINT for Associates 📌

In some sites, resizing is a major EVENT in which every active item is analyzed and hundreds of new "resized" cards are deployed in a short time period. This makes resizing very time-consuming and everyone dreads it.

Instead, resizing should be a fluid part of inventory management. For that to occur, the resizing process must be easy to perform. A robust kanban calculator that runs frequently (e.g., weekly) finds out-of-balance kanban solutions soon, so only a few parts are updated at any given time. This is better than the pain of a Massive Resizing Event.

HINT for Associates 📌

Be aware of the differences in calculator logic for sizing versus resizing. A resizing process or tool must have access to current kanban solutions so the tool, such as an Excel kanban calculator, or user can determine which solutions must be changed (resized) and which stay the same. The resizing process also has to know which solutions utilize a fixed or frozen kanban order quantity versus a fixed number of signals. We'll discuss these nuances later.

Sizing Step 4: Deploy Kanban Cards

Kanban solutions should be deployed immediately so associates can trigger orders and manage on-hand inventory using the best and most recent solutions. The sizing or resizing process is not complete until new solutions are deployed!

HINT for Associates 📌

A kanban calculator must provide all necessary data to generate kanban cards, so when sizing and deploying kanban for the first time, design kanban cards in advance so it is clear what has to be printed on the card. Everything that is printed must be available from the calculator or another reliable data source.

Execute = DO

Kanban execution includes all the processes that manage kanban orders, cards, and boards.

Order Loop

Order management is a repetitive loop, in Figure 6-5, which includes triggering a replenishment order, waiting for the order to be filled, restocking parts when they arrive, and consuming parts. It is repeated ad infinitum for every kanban part, as in the pictorial diagram in Figure 6-1 on page 76.

Figure 6-5. Order Loop

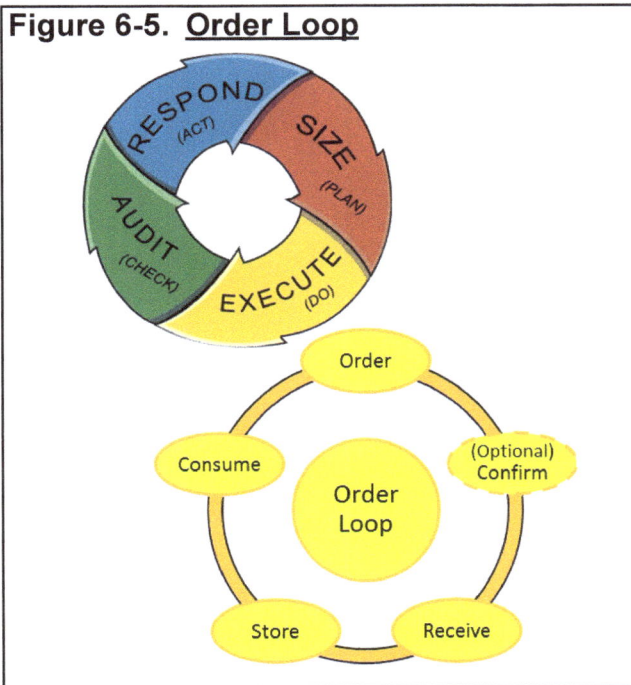

Order: An order is triggered by a physical event such as using the first or last piece in a kanban bin, at which point a replenishment order is issued for the specific kanban order quantity and at the standard lead time for that item. If the first piece in a kanban quantity is the trigger event, it is called break a bin (BaB), while a last-piece trigger is called empty a bin (EaB).

Kanban orders should be immediately issued when a trigger point is reached. Human intervention or approval should not occur because it causes two kinds of waste: over-processing (review the order) and waiting (the order waits to be reviewed), both of which add lead time.

(Optional) Supplier Confirmation: This is an optional step in which a supplier is required to confirm or acknowledge a new order. It is common and acceptable to use the "no news is good news" philosophy. So, if a supplier accepts the order as submitted and intends to meet both the due date and quantity, then no response is necessary.

Unreliable suppliers should not be members of a site's supply base, and unreliable order transmission methods should not be utilized. Given these 2 conditions, mandatory confirmations should be rare because this is another form of the Lean over-processing waste.

To safely eliminate the need for supplier confirmations, use an error-proof order transmission method such as supplier portals, traceable emails, or electronic data interchange (EDI). Eliminate confirmations for all suppliers who have demonstrated the ability to meet requested order specifications, both quantity and due date. In any circumstance, even if confirmations are not required, suppliers are expected to communicate any change to either due date or quantity at the time the order is initiated <u>or</u> at any later point in the replenishment process. No surprises!

Receive: When parts arrive, close the open replenishment order, match incoming parts to the waiting kanban card, and send everything to the correct storage location, preferably at point of use (to keep inventory close to where it is consumed).

Store: Since kanban is a visual system, parts should be stored at point of use or within "eye shot" of the consuming cell or the process that uses the parts. Each item should have a standard storage location so it's easy to find the right home and put them away.

It is tempting to use rotating or random storage locations so that any open spot can be used for any item, which seems like efficient space utilization. The downside is that every item gets a new storage location each time it's put away, which hampers visual management.

Some sites utilize centralized "internal warehouses" to store material, instead of putting items at point of use, but this breaks a couple Lean rules. First, it removes one of the visual elements of kanban, the preference to have inventory in sight of those who use it. Second, it adds transportation to the process, which is one of the eight Lean wastes.

Figure 6-6 gives examples of designating storage locations.

Figure 6-6. Storage Logic & Markings

For effective point-of-use locations, define standard work for how locations are identified and labeled.

In this diagram, the posts on the left of the shelf units are labeled with a letter, the shelves are designated 1 to 3 from bottom to top, and spots on the shelves are numbered 1 on the left and 2 on the right. (See the black letters and numbers on the shelves.) Yellow labels on the front of each shelf location or on the floor indicate which part number belongs in each spot.

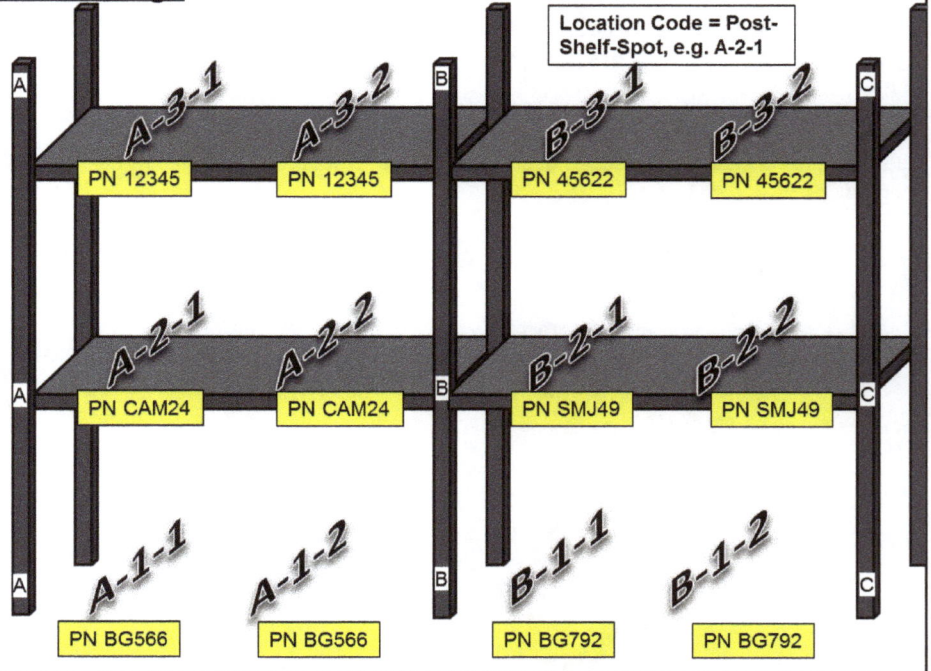

Location Code = Post-Shelf-Spot, e.g. A-2-1

A-3-1 PN 12345   A-3-2 PN 12345   B-3-1 PN 45622   B-3-2 PN 45622

A-2-1 PN CAM24   A-2-2 PN CAM24   B-2-1 PN SMJ49   B-2-2 PN SMJ49

A-1-1 PN BG566   A-1-2 PN BG566   B-1-1 PN BG792   B-1-2 PN BG792

HINT for Leaders

As part of any kanban project, it is wise to eliminate centralized warehouses unless specific conditions require them, such as space allowances or environmental requirements (e.g., store large 200-gallon totes in a central place, or maintain 40% to 50% humidity in a special room).

At some sites, centralized storage is seen as the only way to control inventory. They believe their locked, fenced, restricted-access warehouse is the single biggest secret to inventory success and therefore it can't be eliminated. They think the people who work in the "Cage" are trustworthy and trained and that's why inventory is controlled, and the people in production cells are unaware and undisciplined, so releasing precious material to the masses would result in complete and immediate failure. Wow. Did they hire great workers for the warehouse and idiots for the rest of the site? If so, kanban and inventory management is the _least_ of their worries!

In every "central control" site I've been in, the command-and-control perception is horribly out of line with reality. Associates who perform value-added production work are just as capable (usually more so) and as dedicated (ditto) as the non-value-add resources hovering in central storage. Inventory is best managed where it is used, not in a segregated location.

Consume: Kanban systems trigger replenishment orders based on consumption, so kanban relies on a physical or observable signal, e.g., empty spot on a shelf, empty bin, newly-opened container, re-order line on the wall, etc. See Figure 6-7.

Figure 6-7. <u>Visual Replenishment Signals</u>

→ Empty spots for additional barrels signal the replenishment need without using cards. A pump or even a simple barrel magnet that says "OPEN" can indicate which barrel is being consumed.

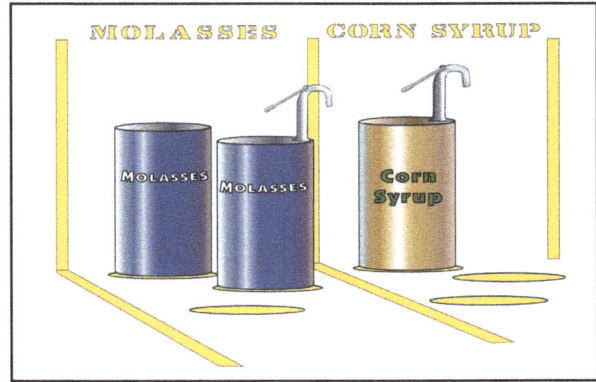

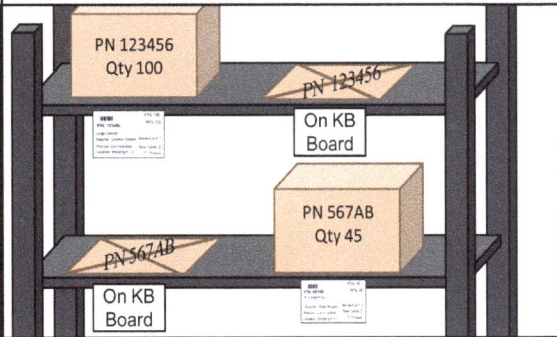

← Kanban cards are stored in clear sleeves on the front of the shelf that holds kanban items. The inside background of the sleeve says "On KB Board," which is visible when the card is pulled out of the sleeve to be put on the board.

→

Each stack of boxes is one part number. When the green line on the wall is visible, i.e., just one box in stock, a replenishment order is triggered for another box. Kanban cards are kept on the pole to the left of each pair of items. The two top cards are for the item on the left side and the bottom cards are for the item on the right side.

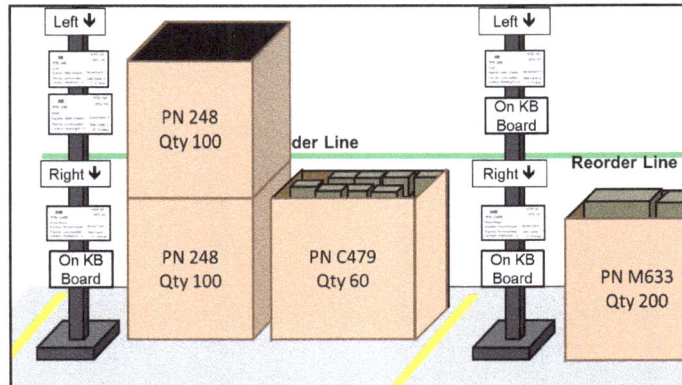

← An empty bin turned upside down signals the replenishment. A water spider or kanban coordinator sees this visual signal and knows to refill the bin. Like empty spots, this can eliminate the need for kanban cards.

Can kanban succeed without cards? Alternative visual signals, such as those in Figure 6-7 work well in the right situations, but I've never seen an entire kanban system run successfully without any cards.

Please don't set "zero cards" as a kanban goal.

Card Loop

Kanban cards require a robust support infrastructure. Like sizing and order management, cards live in a loop (Figure 6-8), which is a subset of kanban execution. In general, at any given time a kanban card is in one of three states.

1. Many cards are linked to on-hand inventory and stored with the associated parts. Cards need a home when they are with parts, e.g., in the bin with the parts, on the front of the shelf, or on a post next to the storage rack. Refer back to Figure 6-7 on page 83 for some examples.

2. Sometimes cards wait for a short time to be processed to create a replenishment order. This status should never last more than a couple of hours, so it's just a blip in the life of a card, but this step must be planned so it doesn't result in unnecessary delays.

If card scanning is done in real-time at point of use, it isn't necessary to designate a place for cards to wait to be processed because they are scanned as soon as they are taken from a parts bin at point of use. After cards are scanned, they are placed on the kanban board.

If real-time scanning does not occur, designate a place for cards to pause while waiting to be scanned, such as a "To Be Scanned" peg on the kanban board.

Figure 6-8. Card Loop

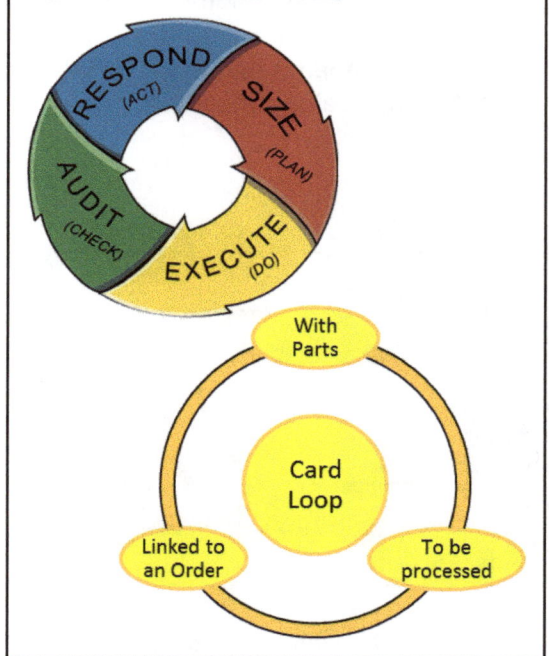

Rule of Thumb

Find a way to scan cards in real-time at point of use (POU) to avoid even the short delays caused by periodic scanning (e.g., scan at 10:00 AM, 2:00 PM, 6:00 PM, 10:00 PM). Scanning at point of use also reduces the risk of lost cards from moving them away from where they reside. Carrying cards out of a cell to an office or other area runs the risk of a card being dropped or left at the other location. Make the card travel path as simple and as short as possible.

For real-time or periodic scanning, cards should never wait more than 4 hours (half of an 8-hour shift) to be processed, and scanning must occur on every active shift.

---

3. A high number of cards are linked to replenishment orders and stored "on hold" until those orders arrive. In most sites, cards hang on a "calendar board" with each card on the date that the respective order is scheduled to arrive, as in the next example.

A typical kanban board has a peg for each date in a month, i.e., the numbers 1 to 31. In January, the fourth and fifth might be Saturday and Sunday so they aren't workdays, but in February of that year the fourth and fifth will fall on Tuesday and Wednesday. A board with 1 to 31 accommodates any monthly or workday configuration.

When an order is processed, an item's standard lead time determines the order's due date. [Order date + lead time = due date]. Hang the card on the peg that stands for the assigned due date. If the order is due in more than 31 days from today put the card on the "Next Month" peg. If some items have very long lead times, add a "Two Months Out" peg for orders that are more than 60 calendar days in the future.

Kanban Board Example

We're consuming parts and triggering kanban orders on Monday, May 5th. Part number 105 has a lead time of 5 workdays, so its order is due 1 week later, on May 12th. Because today is May 5th, the "12" peg on the kanban board does stand for May 12th. We hang the card on that peg to wait for parts to arrive.

Part number 135 has a lead time of 35 workdays, which would normally make it due on June 16th. But, we need to add one day for the holiday (red "H" on the board), putting it on June 17th. Because today is May 5th, the "17" peg on the board stands for May 17th. So, the card for June 17th goes on the "Next Month" peg and we'll move it to the "17" peg on May 18th, when the "17" peg will indicate June 17th instead of May 17th.

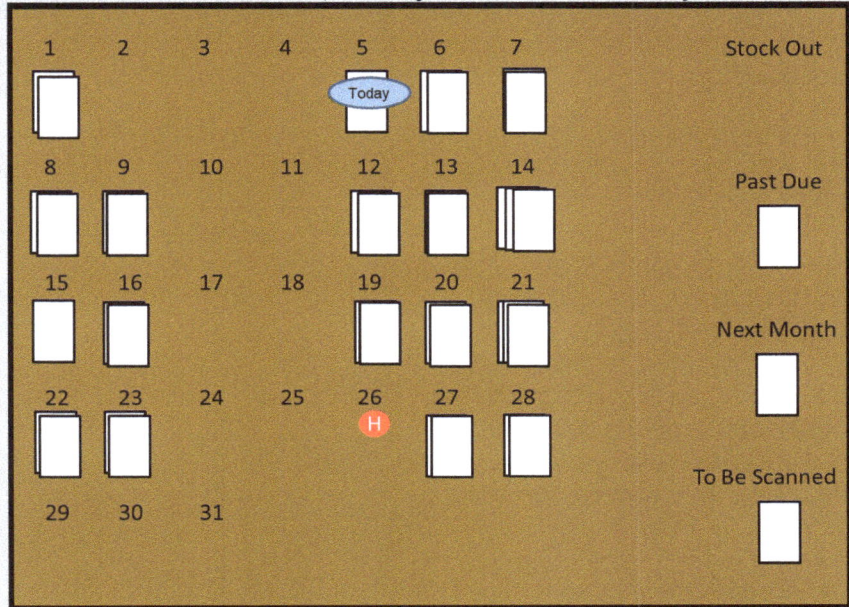

The above board layout and process works very well. Once associates are familiar with the board it will be second nature to put cards on the right peg and errors will be rare. The key to effectively managing a kanban board is to understand what each peg means. Standard work should document how to use the board and everyone should be fully trained.

HINT for Associates

If signals other than cards are utilized, every signaling method needs a management process similar to what was described for cards to control how signals are communicated and tracked.

HINT for Associates

We don't necessarily need a kanban card for every container, e.g., every box, bin, bag, or tote. If a pallet holds 16 boxes, don't automatically put 16 cards on the pallet and make one box equal to the replenishment quantity. Even if parts are sent to point of use in single boxes instead of the pallet, emptying or opening the pallet can serve as the trigger indicator, with just one card per pallet.

I don't perceive kanban as simple, particularly when a site designs a new system from scratch. Don't fall into the trap of thinking kanban is a straight-forward project that can be designed and deployed in a few weeks. Kanban requires and deserves adequate time for thinking, planning, designing, executing, and modifying the various elements. Don't rush the process or shortchange the allotted time.

If kanban is new for your site, ensure that you have the necessary internal or external expertise to design a system that will work.

Audit = CHECK

Kanban systems should be audited periodically to find and correct data or process errors. Figure 6-9 lists sample categories for kanban audits, though this is not an exhaustive list. Any audit category could contain numerous checklists, audit points, or verification processes, so design the audit process to fit the business.

• Auditing cards and kanban boards is an essential part of the audit process, so it is wise to write standard work for how a kanban board is utilized *and* audited and how cards are verified to be in the correct spot.

• It is useful to visually audit point-of-use storage to ensure that kanban bins have cards where they are expected. This is easier for empty a bin (EaB) kanban, where every bin has a card. Also ensure that none of the cards at POU *should have been turned in* for scanning but are still with their parts, which is a higher risk for break a bin (BaB) kanban systems.

Figure 6-9. Audit Categories

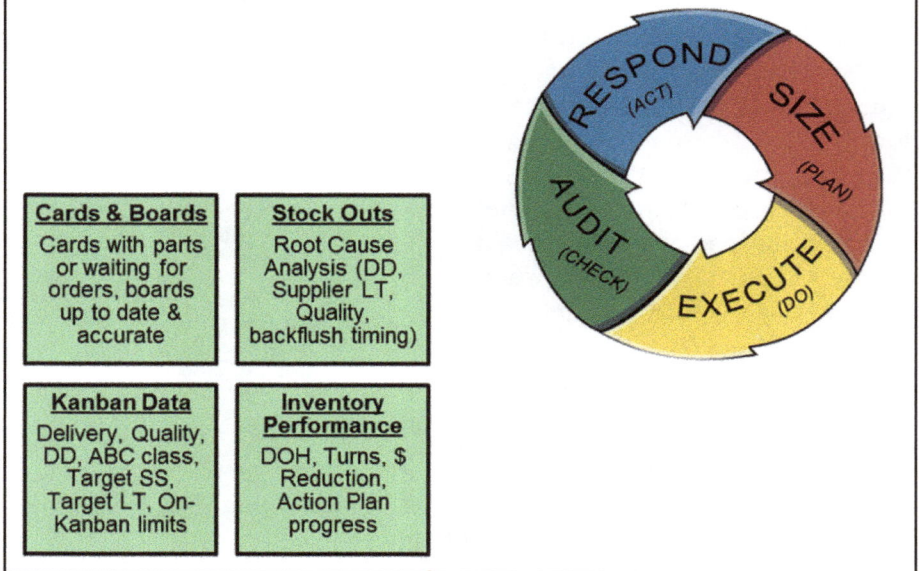

Cards & Boards	Stock Outs
Cards with parts or waiting for orders, boards up to date & accurate	Root Cause Analysis (DD, Supplier LT, Quality, backflush timing)

Kanban Data	Inventory Performance
Delivery, Quality, DD, ABC class, Target SS, Target LT, On-Kanban limits	DOH, Turns, $ Reduction, Action Plan progress

RESPOND (ACT) — SIZE (PLAN) — EXECUTE (DO) — AUDIT (CHECK)

• If stock outs are an issue they should be audited every day. A stock out is a high-risk scenario for on-time delivery so it must be viewed as a failure and the correct response is to determine root cause. Is the actual replenishment lead time longer than expected? Is daily demand higher than what was planned? Was there an unexpected demand spike from external customers or perhaps from internal rework or scrap?

Auditing stock outs does *not* imply or mandate that "daily stock out count" must be a performance metric for kanban or inventory management, but continue to audit for outages until stock outs decline to a rare occurrence.

• Kanban data should be tracked to verify that the assumptions used in the latest resizing process are still valid. Data errors might result in less safety stock than planned, which is a stock out risk, or more on-hand inventory than planned, which is a cash drain. Manage data ferociously!

• Inventory performance is how we verify results versus what was in the plan. If we expected kanban deployment to reduce on-hand inventory dollars by $200,000 in 6 months, track actual on-hand dollars to ensure we achieve the goal. Along with operational or financial results, verify that action plans are being executed successfully, whether it's negotiating better lead times, bleeding off excess inventory, or driving down minimum order quantities (MOQ) for external and internal parts.

Respond = ACT

Kanban process and audit results plus daily observations require immediate responses to correct or update processes and data sets, as in Figure 6-10.

Figure 6-10. Respond Plan

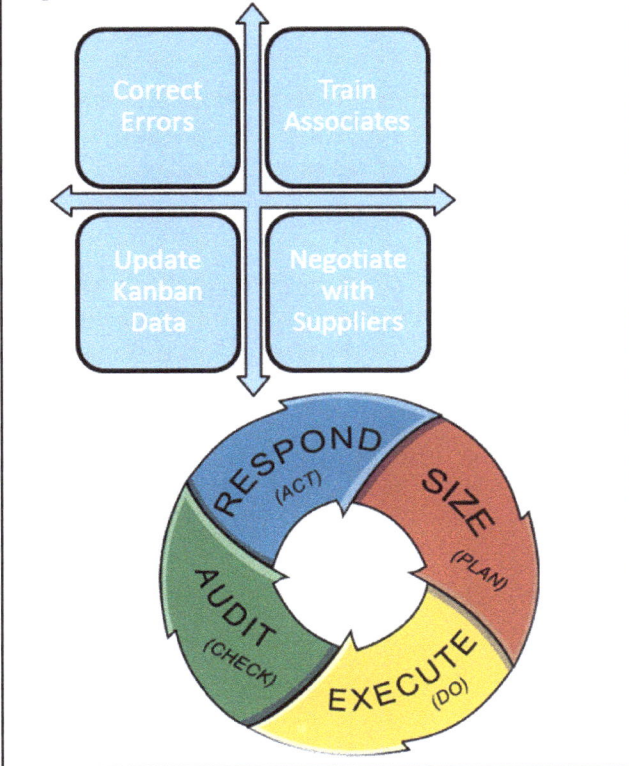

When errors occur, recognize the difference between lack of training (aptitude) and lack of effort or adherence (attitude). The former is a valid and reasonable occurrence, particularly for new employees. The latter is unacceptable and should be grounds for termination if the offense is repeated. Yes, kanban is that important.

Data: One of the most important tasks in a kanban system is maintaining thorough and accurate data. Updating or maintaining data is often overlooked or delayed until a formal event occurs to tackle kanban updates, but skipping or delaying data upkeep means the system operates on "garbage-in-garbage-out" and it <u>will</u> fail. We can't achieve positive results if the data is a mess, so don't wait for a special event to fix it.

Perhaps we assigned a 15-day lead time to an internal part but it exhibits an 18-day actual lead time. We can ask the supplying cell if 18 days is truly necessary, but don't keep an inaccurate lead time in the kanban calculator just because we *wish* it was true.

Negotiate: Supplier negotiation is another common outcome from reviewing kanban processes. If inventory is higher than the goal because a supplier is not achieving what they committed to, communicate the concern and verify if their performance gap is short-term or if the target should be adjusted in the data set.

If it is discovered that minimum order quantities or lead times are driving high inventory balances, set a plan to negotiate with associated suppliers to improve those limitations.

Correct: When errors occur (e.g., cards on the wrong date peg, cards that should have been scanned but weren't turned in, missing cards, cards in the wrong bin, inaccurate lead time, wrong minimum order quantity, stock outs), correct them immediately so the system returns to good health. This might be as simple as moving a card to the right peg, or it might require resizing kanban solutions or updating standard work to modify how a task should be performed.

Train: Some of the items discovered in an audit require training or a refresher course for associates who perform kanban processes. But, as kanban systems mature there should be fewer and fewer errors due to lack of understanding.

HINT for Leaders

If leaders don't audit <u>and</u> respond to kanban systems and processes, associates lose confidence in both the kanban system and the leaders. Don't let it flounder!

Real-World Observation

Sites sometimes say, "We don't have the discipline to manage kanban." They think it's a handy excuse to delay kanban, but it really means leadership has failed to instill a culture of discipline or an adherence to standard work. A lack of discipline is a failure of leadership, not of the associates.

In many cases, standard work does not exist or people aren't properly trained to perform to the standard. But, in the most egregious cases standard work exists and everyone is trained but nobody is held accountable to perform the defined standard work. How sad is that?!?

If associates know what to do and how to do it, which is the definition of standard work, most people will adhere to the instructions. When we encounter someone who insists on breaking rules or ignoring instructions even after being "coached," we owe it to the rest of the team to terminate their employment. Our good employees, those who follow the rules and contribute in a valuable way, shouldn't have to work with someone who refuses to follow the process.

Summary of How Kanban Works

Kanban is a great system, but it depends on several intertwined processes. It can be thought of as a version of the Plan-Do-Check-Act cycle, where sizing is the Plan, execution is Do, auditing is the Check, and responding is the Act portion of the loop.

Managing kanban sizing, orders, cards, and storage is critical for achieving on-time delivery and managing on-hand inventory balances.

Kanban is not a "Materials Project," so when deploying or updating a kanban system it should be a site-wide priority, not a departmental task. The Materials team usually leads the project, but Operations, Finance, Engineering, and other teams should participate in gathering data, deploying cards, analyzing results, sustaining the system, and accomplishing improvements.

TUTORIAL: GOCO KANBAN STATUS

GOCO had never tried kanban so they had no expertise or systems in place. Mary knew she had to design and deploy the necessary processes to Size, Execute, Audit, and Respond to kanban systems, data, and audits. Sizing had to be done first, and it had to be correct in order for the rest of the processes to work. But, the sizing process required much more than just gathering and confirming data.

Based on her prior experience deploying kanban, Mary knew leaders and associates had to understand how kanban worked so she began holding short training sessions with various departments to teach people about kanban concepts, such as the various kinds of kanban types and triggers.

BEGINNING, MID, & END TRIGGERS
1, 2, & MULTI-CARD KANBAN SIGNALS

CHAPTER 7: KANBAN TYPES & TRIGGER TIMING

There are three options for trigger timing, or when a replenishment order is issued, and this must be decided before completing kanban calculation steps.

There are also three types of kanban signal sets, or the number of cards per part number, and this is determined by characteristics such as minimum order quantity, actual lead time, and demand variation.

Trigger Timing

A kanban system initiates replenishment orders based on actual consumption. Because of that direct link to demand, the concept of trigger "timing," or when a replenishment order is signaled, deserves serious consideration.

There are three trigger timing options: the beginning of a kanban bin, the end of a bin, or some point in the middle. Before we get into details, let's clarify what is meant by the word "bin" when discussing trigger timing. In this context, a bin is the kanban order quantity (KOQ). If the order quantity is 100 pieces, but it arrives in 4 boxes of 25 each, the *bin* is the total of 100 pieces, not each box of 25. Referring to triggering at the "end" or "beginning" of a bin does *not* refer to the physical bin or box but rather to the entire order quantity.

Break a Bin = Beginning Trigger

Break a bin (BaB) triggers an order as soon as the <u>first</u> piece is removed from the kanban bin, so it is designated as a "beginning" trigger point.

BaB Process & Formulas

In BaB, a kanban signal is triggered at the beginning of the bin, so a replenishment order is generated when the bin is first opened or at [100% full - one piece]. When that "active" bin is emptied, the next bin is opened, and that triggers another order.

Because a BaB card is triggered when the first piece is used, if that one card requested the entire kanban quantity, there would be no need for a second card. Two cards are always preferred for a robust kanban solution, so it is better to submit <u>two</u> orders during the lead-time period and have each order cover half of lead-time demand. This means that each card in a 2-card BaB kanban solution orders half of the lead-time demand quantity, which is a distinguishing feature for BaB.

A card is triggered as soon as a bin is opened, so most of a BaB card's life is spent hanging on the kanban board waiting for material to arrive. In fact, BaB items *expect* to have *both* cards on the board and linked to upcoming orders as a regular occurrence. Conversely, BaB should not see both cards with parts on the shelf unless demand stops and cards are not being triggered.

A kanban solution has to order enough material to cover lead-time demand plus safety stock. For a BaB kanban solution, the order quantity per card is the required total quantity divided by the number of cards, and this formula works for any number of cards from 1 to n.

If we rearrange the formula to solve for the number of cards, for those occasions when the order quantity is fixed or frozen and the number of cards must be calculated, the required quantity is divided by order quantity to determine card count. Card count is always rounded to an integer, and we'll discuss rounding options later.

BaB Formulas

$$BaB \ KOQ = \frac{(Actual \ LT * Daily \ demand + Target \ safey \ stock)}{(\# \ cards)}$$

$$BaB \ \# \ Cards = \frac{(Actual \ LT * Daily \ demand + Target \ SS \ units)}{KOQ}$$

$$BaB \ Actual \ SS = (\# \ cards * KOQ) - (Actual \ LT * Current \ Daily \ Demand)$$

Safety stock, the buffer built into a kanban solution to ensure that inventory stays above zero, is the difference between what is ordered during a lead-time period versus what is consumed.

BaB Pros & Cons

+ Because a BaB 2-card order is for half of [lead-time demand + safety stock], a BaB sawtooth curve is shorter than an empty a bin (EaB) solution for the same item. This can be a significant benefit for BaB versus EaB for 2 card solutions. It does not come into play for multi-card solutions.

- The penalty for a lower order quantity is that BaB items process more orders than EaB items, as seen in the illustrations later in this chapter. Note the number of pink arrows in the BaB diagram starting on page 92, versus EaB starting on page 93.

- The biggest downside to BaB is that it is difficult to audit because only a <u>full</u> kanban bin has a card. If a BaB kanban order quantity is 100 parts, a full bin of 100 pieces should have a card, but a bin with 99 pieces has no card because the card was turned in when the first piece was consumed. Visually it is difficult to tell which bins *should* have a card and which bins should *not* have a card, e.g., there is no card but the bin *looks* full. It is also challenging to identify cards that should have been turned in but were not, e.g., a card is present but *maybe* 1 piece has been taken. Unless parts are organized in very orderly patterns, such as physical and <u>visual</u> layers with a spot for each part (think egg carton), it's difficult to see the difference between [100%] and [100% - 1]. So, a BaB audit might require counting parts, weighing parts, or implementing visual cues for a full bin, e.g., a line or other mark on the bin.

Empty a Bin = End Trigger

Empty a bin (EaB) is an end-point trigger because the card or signal is triggered at the end of a kanban quantity, or when the bin is emptied.

EaB Process & Formulas

In EaB, the card waits with on-hand inventory until the last piece in the bin is consumed. Therefore, while 1 card idles in the active bin as parts are consumed, another card must trigger a replenishment order to provide parts when that current bin runs dry. That other card must have signaled an empty bin or "last piece" consumption at the end of the <u>prior</u> bin, before the current bin was opened. The prior order must provide replenishment parts by the time we empty the current active bin.

Order quantity for EaB equals lead-time demand plus safety stock, while BaB ordered half of that quantity.

Most of the time, for EaB cards in a 2-card solution, 1 card is with parts and the other is on the kanban board waiting for an incoming order. If there is safety stock to prevent inventory from dropping to zero, when the active bin gets down to that safety stock quantity, the prior order arrives and for a short time there are 2 cards on the shelf linked to on-hand inventory. (See the EaB diagram on page 93.) Unlike BaB, EaB does not have both cards on the kanban board unless there is a stock out.

Due to this end-of-bin process, each of the cards in a 2-card EaB solution represents a quantity of parts equal to total lead-time demand plus target safety stock, or [Lead time * Daily demand + Target safety stock].

EaB Formulas

$$EaB \ KOQ = \left[\frac{(Actual\ LT * Daily\ demand + Target\ safety\ stock)}{(\#\ cards - 1)} \right]$$

$$EaB \ \#\ Cards = \frac{(Actual\ LT * Daily\ Demand + Target\ SS\ units)}{KOQ} + 1$$

$$EaB \ Actual\ SS = (\#\ cards - 1) * KOQ - (Actual\ LT * Current\ Daily\ Demand)$$

Don't forget the +1 or -1 card adjustment for EaB!

For special multi-card situations, which we'll cover later in this chapter, it won't work to assign lead-time demand plus total safety stock as the order quantity. It's also clear that we can't divide the required quantity by card count, because for 2 cards that would order only half as many parts as are needed.

For EaB there is a "card count" factor in the order quantity formula: divide the required quantity by the number of cards minus 1, as in the formula box above. Similarly, when calculating the number of cards required for a specific order quantity, add 1 card to the result to get the required number of EaB cards.

Safety stock follows the same principle as for BaB, but to calculate the amount of material ordered during 1 lead-time period, multiply order quantity by the number of signals minus 1. As usual, card count is rounded to an integer, and order quantity must comply with minimum order and package limits.

EaB Pros & Cons

+   EaB is the easiest trigger method to audit because the kanban card stays with parts until the last piece in the bin is used, which means any quantity - from 1 up to a full order quantity - has an associated card. Every EaB kanban item on the shelf should have a card, and any pile of parts without a card is a kanban error.

-   EaB has a higher order quantity than BaB for 2-card solutions, so the disadvantage to this approach is more on-hand inventory versus for BaB solutions.

Trigger Method Examples

Review the BaB and EaB diagrams in Figure 7-1 on page 92 and Figure 7-2 on page 93 to see how the trigger methods differ. In each diagram, daily demand is one piece, lead time is 10 days, and safety stock is 2 pieces or 2 days of demand. For the BaB example, order quantity is 6, because 2 cards cover the lead-time demand quantity. For EaB, the order quantity goes to 12, so the sawtooth for EaB would be twice as tall as for BaB.

The brown kanban boards show the 31 date pegs. The 1st day of the month is a Monday, the 6th and 7th are a weekend, and on through the month.

Notice the timing for order triggers and arrivals, and differences between how cards travel from point of use to the board and back to point of use. Note also that BaB often has both cards on the board, while EaB has both cards with inventory.

Figure 7-1. **Break-a-Bin Diagram**

Gray discs are consumed by an assembly cell and replenished by an external supplier.
Daily demand = 1, Lead time = 10 days, Safety stock = 2 pieces

In the 10-day lead-time period, BaB triggers 2 cards

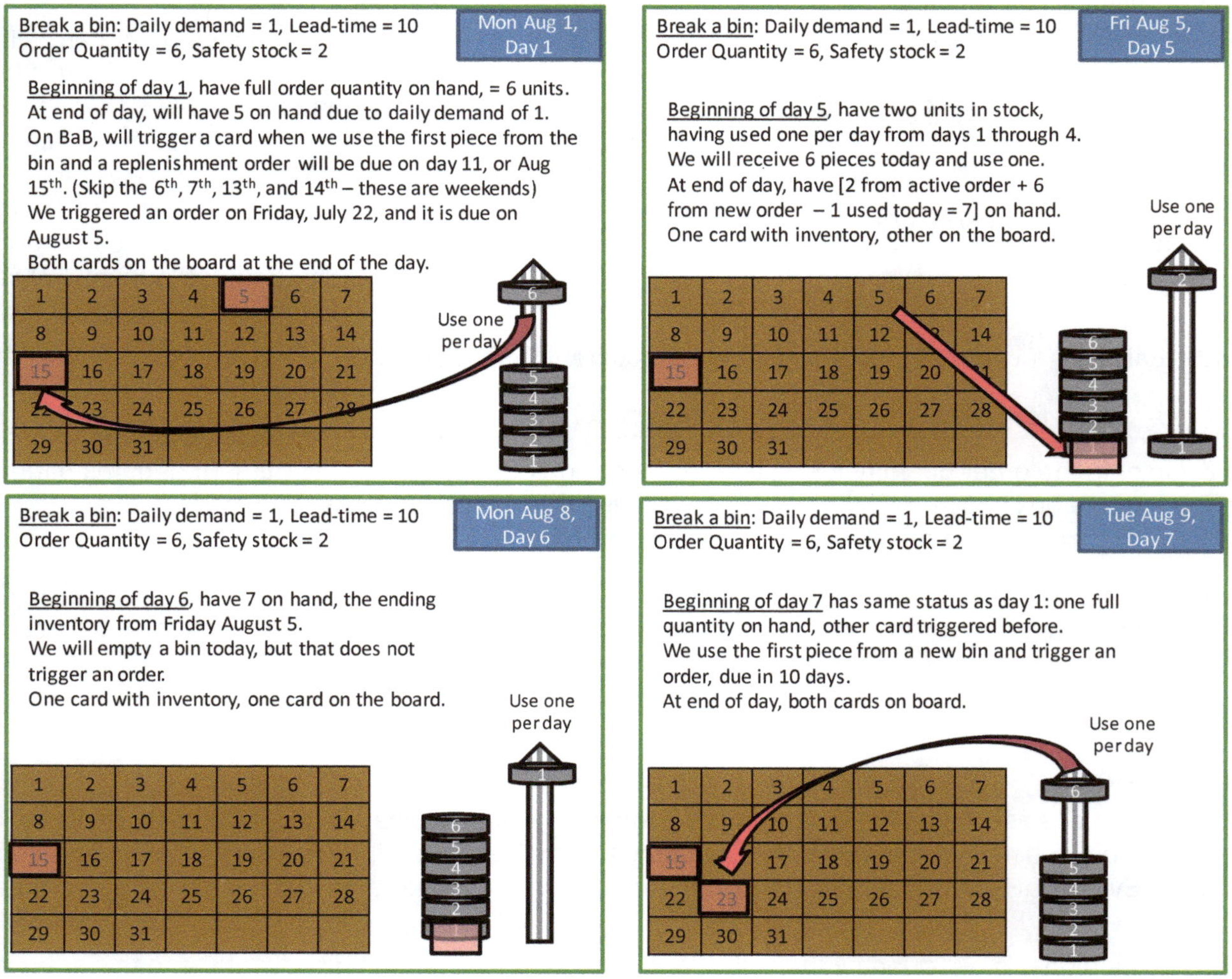

Break a bin: Daily demand = 1, Lead-time = 10
Order Quantity = 6, Safety stock = 2

Mon Aug 1, Day 1

Beginning of day 1, have full order quantity on hand, = 6 units.
At end of day, will have 5 on hand due to daily demand of 1.
On BaB, will trigger a card when we use the first piece from the bin and a replenishment order will be due on day 11, or Aug 15th. (Skip the 6th, 7th, 13th, and 14th – these are weekends)
We triggered an order on Friday, July 22, and it is due on August 5.
Both cards on the board at the end of the day.

Use one per day

Break a bin: Daily demand = 1, Lead-time = 10
Order Quantity = 6, Safety stock = 2

Fri Aug 5, Day 5

Beginning of day 5, have two units in stock, having used one per day from days 1 through 4.
We will receive 6 pieces today and use one.
At end of day, have [2 from active order + 6 from new order – 1 used today = 7] on hand.
One card with inventory, other on the board.

Use one per day

Break a bin: Daily demand = 1, Lead-time = 10
Order Quantity = 6, Safety stock = 2

Mon Aug 8, Day 6

Beginning of day 6, have 7 on hand, the ending inventory from Friday August 5.
We will empty a bin today, but that does not trigger an order.
One card with inventory, one card on the board.

Use one per day

Break a bin: Daily demand = 1, Lead-time = 10
Order Quantity = 6, Safety stock = 2

Tue Aug 9, Day 7

Beginning of day 7 has same status as day 1: one full quantity on hand, other card triggered before.
We use the first piece from a new bin and trigger an order, due in 10 days.
At end of day, both cards on board.

Use one per day

HINT for Associates

When designing a kanban system, choose the same trigger timing (EaB or BaB) for every item with two or more cards. Mixing trigger methods within a work cell or from cell to cell is very confusing and cards will inevitably be turned in late (associates accustomed to EaB, but working with BaB) or early (accustomed to BaB, but in an EaB cell). Late triggers increase stock out risks and early triggers drive excess inventory. Neither outcome is good.

Remember that 2-card BaB solutions often have both cards hanging on the kanban board but rarely have both cards waiting with parts. Conversely, EaB kanban solutions rarely have both cards hanging on the kanban board but often have both cards waiting with parts.

Figure 7-2. Empty-a-Bin Diagram

Gray discs are consumed by an assembly cell and replenished by an external supplier.
Daily demand = 1, Lead time = 10 days, Safety stock = 2 pieces

In the 10-day lead-time period, EaB triggers 1 card.

Panel 1 — Mon Aug 1, Day 1

Empty a bin: Daily demand = 1, Lead-time = 10
Order Quantity = 12, Safety stock = 2

Beginning of day 1, have full order quantity on hand, = 12 units. At end of day, will have 11 on hand due to daily demand of 1.
On empty a bin, if starting new bin (12) today, must have emptied one Friday (prior workday) so a replenishment order is due on day 10, or Aug 12. One card with inventory, one on board.

Use one per day

1	2	3	4	5	6	7
8	9	10	11	12	13	14
15	16	17	18	19	20	21
22	23	24	25	26	27	28
29	30	31				

Panel 2 — Fri Aug 12, Day 10

Empty a bin: Daily demand = 1, Lead-time = 10
Order Quantity = 12, Safety stock = 2

Beginning of day 10, have three units in stock, having used one per day from days 1 through 9. Will receive order of 12 pieces today and use one piece today.
At end of day, have [3 from active bin + 12 from new order − 1 used today = 14] on hand. Both cards with inventory at end of day.

Use one per day

1	2	3	4	5	6	7
8	9	10	11	12	13	14
15	16	17	18	19	20	21
22	23	24	25	26	27	28
29	30	31				

Panel 3 — Tue Aug 16, Day 12

Empty a bin: Daily demand = 1, Lead-time = 10
Order Quantity = 12, Safety stock = 2

Beginning of day 12, have one unit in stock, the last piece from the active bin. Will use 1 piece and process the kanban card for an order due on the 30th. (Skip 20th, 21st, 27th, and 28th because are weekends.)
At end of day, have full bin of 12 in stock. One card with inventory, one card on board.

Use one per day

1	2	3	4	5	6	7
8	9	10	11	12	13	14
15	16	17	18	19	20	21
22	23	24	25	26	27	28
29	30	31				

Panel 4 — Wed Aug 17, Day 13

Empty a bin: Daily demand = 1, Lead-time = 10
Order Quantity = 12, Safety stock = 2

Beginning of day 13 has same status as day 1: one full quantity on hand, other card triggered prior day.
We will start a new bin today, but that does not trigger an order for empty a bin. One card with inventory, one on board.

Use one per day

1	2	3	4	5	6	7
8	9	10	11	12	13	14
15	16	17	18	19	20	21
22	23	24	25	26	27	28
29	30	31				

Mid-Point Triggers

The remaining trigger method is a special case used only for a 1-card solution, which is covered later in this chapter. Not only is this a special trigger timing, but it's also a specific type of kanban.

Which trigger method is best? In most cases, EaB is better because it's easier to audit. For new kanban sites, or if there are concerns about process discipline, use empty a bin (EaB).

Break a bin (BaB) works if items are easy to assess visually and therefore associates can always tell if a bin is "open" and the card should be gone. Break a bin can result in lower inventory, so if the audit hurdle can be overcome then BaB is attractive.

Kanban Types: 2 Cards, 1 Card, or Multiple Cards

2-Card Kanban Type

Two kanban cards is the ideal solution and therefore the default kanban type. In short, 2 cards is ideal because 1 card is available to be with parts on the shelf while the second waits for an order to be received.

When determining kanban signal sets, a kanban calculator must check for special circumstances that warrant a 1-card or multi-card solution, and if nothing is special the item defaults to the preferred 2-card solution.

1-Card Kanban Type

A 1-card kanban solution is deployed when minimum order quantity (MOQ) covers more days of demand than the sum [lead-time days + target safety stock days]. In other words, if the minimum order quantity is high, each replenishment order from a default 2-card solution would order more parts than are required to cover lead-time demand plus safety stock, so just 1 card is required.

There is some flexibility in the rule for how many days are covered by a minimum order quantity, called the MOQ allowance. If a minimum order covers slightly more than what should be acquired by each card in a 2-card solution, the item can still utilize 2 cards, but it will have slightly higher safety stock than what was desired.

The MOQ allowance is usually 10 to 20 percent above the desired quantity of [lead-time in days of demand + target safety stock as days of demand]. This allowance introduces extra safety stock, but that is often better than putting an item on 1 card due to the high maintenance of 1-card kanban solutions.

To determine if we need a 1-card solution, we compare minimum order quantity to [lead-time demand + target safety stock], with safety stock in days of demand. Convert MOQ into days of de-

mand and compare that to [LT days + target SS days * the MOQ allowance factor].

> **1-Card Kanban Scenario**
>
> MOQ Days Demand
> = MOQ / daily demand
>
> IF (MOQ Days Demand > [(Actual lead time + Target Safety stock days) * MOQ Allowance], THEN utilize 1 card)

> **Rule of Thumb**
>
> Items receive 1-card solutions if MOQ days of demand exceeds [Actual LT days + Target SS days], times a reasonable allowance factor.
>
> Default MOQ days demand allowance is 10%, or IF MOQ > 110% * [Actual LT + Target SS] THEN use one card.

Mid-Point Trigger = 1-Card Kanban Type

One-card kanban solutions are quite common in kanban systems but they are *fiercely* detested due to the manual effort required to manage them. Single cards have mid-point triggers because a replenishment order is triggered when a specific number of parts remain in the bin. The point at which the replenishment order is triggered is called the reorder point (ROP) and it is not how many parts are consumed *before* an order is placed, but rather how many parts *remain* when the order is triggered.

> **ROP Formula**
>
> ROP = Daily demand * Lead time + Target safety stock

Notice that the ROP formula is the same one used to calculate kanban order quantity for a 2-card empty-a-bin solution.

Since ROP varies based on daily demand, lead time, and target safety stock, there is a unique result for every item. The kanban order quantity remains static (equal to minimum order quantity), unless MOQ, daily demand, lead time, or safety stock changes enough to move the desired order quantity above the MOQ. The calculated ROP should be verified periodically as part of resizing.

Kanban order quantity must be rounded for standard package quantity, but ROP does not have to be rounded, though that can be advantageous for the associate who has to trigger the order. For example, items in bags of 25 can have an ROP of 42 or 50, but 50 is much easier to determine since it is 2 full bags, while 42 would require counting parts. See the 1-card diagram in Figure 7-3 on page 96.

HINTS for Associates

If rounding reorder point (ROP) for package quantities, always round up not down, so the order timing is slightly early instead of a little late.

When daily demand, actual lead time, or target safety stock changes, recalculate ROP.

For items with high demand variation, it is feasible to deploy additional safety stock to avoid frequent ROP updates on the floor that can be driven by changes in daily demand. For example, if the current reorder point is 400 pieces but ROP goes as high as 500 pieces when daily demand climbs to its highest level, it can be acceptable to set the reorder point to a constant 500 pieces to avoid periodic ROP resizing. The drawback is the higher safety stock that results from an early trigger, at times when the ROP should really be 400 instead of 500.

1-Card Kanban Process

1. Parts arrive in an order quantity equal to the minimum order quantity, since a high MOQ is what drives a 1-card solution. If the minimum order quantity is 100, the kanban order quantity is 100.

2. Calculate ROP based on current daily demand, actual lead time, and safety stock, or [DD * LT days + target SS]. For this discussion, suppose ROP is calculated to be 40 out of the order quantity of 100.

3. For 1-card solutions, associates can't use the beginning or end of the kanban bin as an indication of when to trigger an order. Instead, parts arrive as one kanban order quantity, e.g., a box of 100, but they are separated into one pile equal to the ROP quantity and another equal to the remainder. If the order quantity is 100 and the reorder point is 40, the remainder is 60.

4. Count the number of parts equal to the ROP, or how many parts are in the bin when we trigger an order, and put that quantity in a separate container. This is often a bag or box within the main container, and as mentioned above this can be rounded up to match a certain package size. Obviously, if the remainder quantity is smaller than the ROP, count out the remainder instead of counting the higher ROP.

Remember that ROP is how many parts are *left* when an order is placed. For this example, we count 40 parts out of 100 and put those 40 parts in a bag labeled "ROP" and leave 60 loose parts with the 40 bagged parts in the bin. When the loose parts are gone, we open the bag of 40 parts and trigger the order.

Some ROP items can be managed by marking the bin with a visual indicator for the ROP, versus using an actual count. Imagine that a box of 100 parts is dumped into a plastic tote and the tote has a line around the inside showing the height of parts in the tote when it reaches a quantity that approximates the ROP of 40 pieces. This works in many scenarios, but the challenge with this method is if we ever have to resize the ROP. If the ROP count is placed in a separate bag, a new ROP means a different quantity can be counted into the bag and the bag or "segregation" method still works. If the container itself is marked to indicate the ROP, the visual marker must be modified to indicate a new ROP, if ROP conditions ever change.

5. The ROP can be treated as EaB or BaB because there is very little practical difference. If EaB, put the kanban card with the loose parts (the quantity that is used first) and trigger the order when the last piece is used. For BaB, put the card with the ROP parts and process the card when the first piece is used out of the ROP quantity. There is virtually no difference in these methods so use whatever matches other kanban solutions in that cell.

6. After the card is processed, the ROP quantity is consumed while waiting for the replenishment order to arrive.

Figure 7-3. 1-Card Diagram

Gray discs are consumed by an assembly cell and replenished by an external supplier.
Daily demand = 1, Lead time = 10, Safety stock = 2 pieces, Minimum order quantity = 50

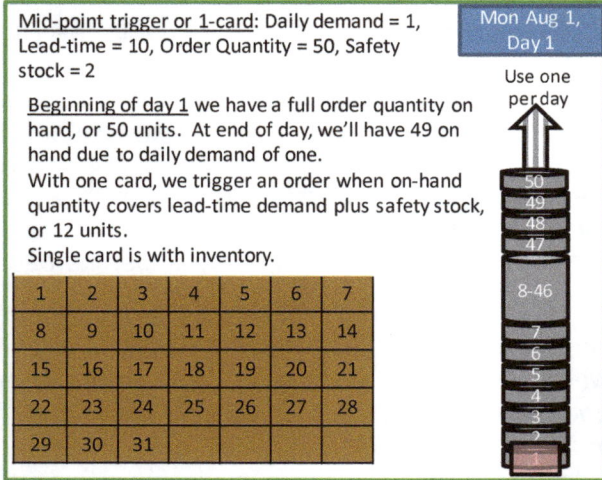

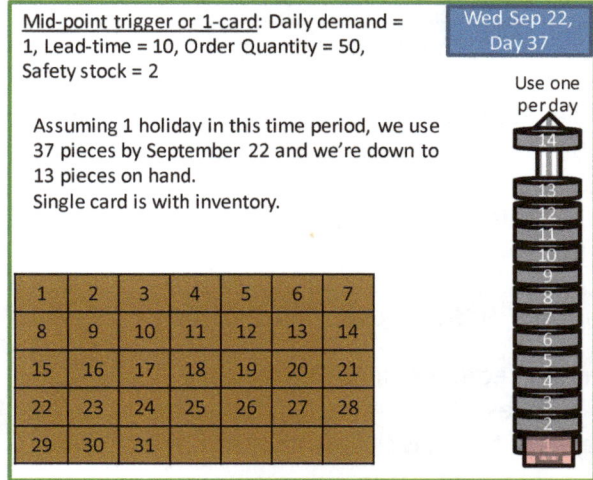

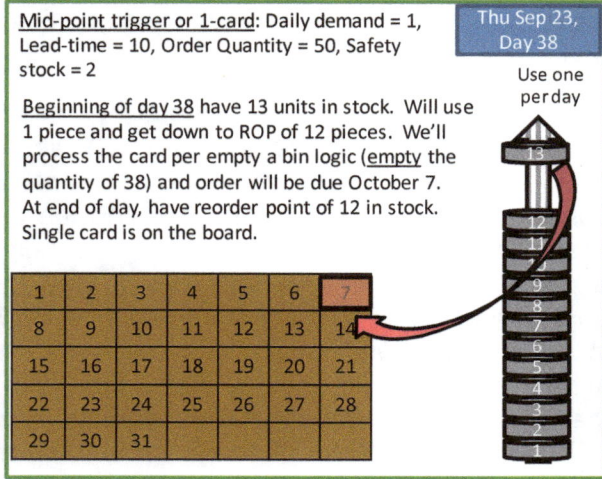

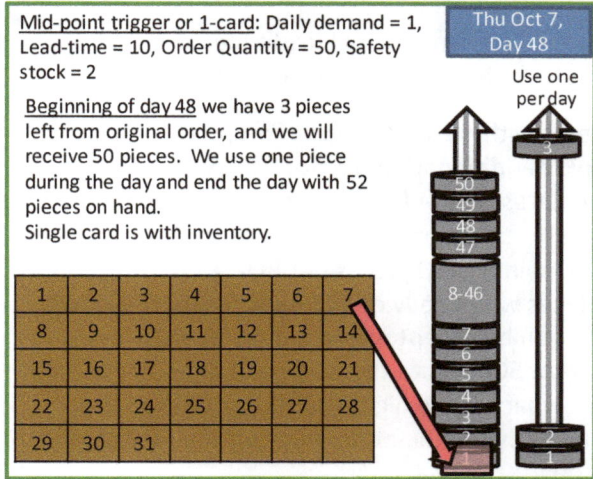

<u>Mid-point trigger or 1-card</u>: Daily demand = 1, Lead-time = 10, Order Quantity = 50, Safety stock = 2

Mon Aug 1, Day 1

Use one per day

<u>Beginning of day 1</u> we have a full order quantity on hand, or 50 units. At end of day, we'll have 49 on hand due to daily demand of one.

With one card, we trigger an order when on-hand quantity covers lead-time demand plus safety stock, or 12 units.

Single card is with inventory.

1	2	3	4	5	6	7
8	9	10	11	12	13	14
15	16	17	18	19	20	21
22	23	24	25	26	27	28
29	30	31				

<u>Mid-point trigger or 1-card</u>: Daily demand = 1, Lead-time = 10, Order Quantity = 50, Safety stock = 2

Wed Sep 22, Day 37

Use one per day

Assuming 1 holiday in this time period, we use 37 pieces by September 22 and we're down to 13 pieces on hand.

Single card is with inventory.

1	2	3	4	5	6	7
8	9	10	11	12	13	14
15	16	17	18	19	20	21
22	23	24	25	26	27	28
29	30	31				

<u>Mid-point trigger or 1-card</u>: Daily demand = 1, Lead-time = 10, Order Quantity = 50, Safety stock = 2

Thu Sep 23, Day 38

Use one per day

<u>Beginning of day 38</u> have 13 units in stock. Will use 1 piece and get down to ROP of 12 pieces. We'll process the card per empty a bin logic (<u>empty</u> the quantity of 38) and order will be due October 7. At end of day, have reorder point of 12 in stock. Single card is on the board.

1	2	3	4	5	6	7
8	9	10	11	12	13	14
15	16	17	18	19	20	21
22	23	24	25	26	27	28
29	30	31				

<u>Mid-point trigger or 1-card</u>: Daily demand = 1, Lead-time = 10, Order Quantity = 50, Safety stock = 2

Thu Oct 7, Day 48

Use one per day

<u>Beginning of day 48</u> we have 3 pieces left from original order, and we will receive 50 pieces. We use one piece during the day and end the day with 52 pieces on hand.

Single card is with inventory.

1	2	3	4	5	6	7
8	9	10	11	12	13	14
15	16	17	18	19	20	21
22	23	24	25	26	27	28
29	30	31				

HINT for Associates

1-card solutions are by far the most difficult kanban type to manage. They serve a specific and necessary purpose so utilize them where needed, but ensure that every ROP is clearly and accurately defined at point of use and that cards are processed properly. The ROP must be obvious so associates know when to process the card.

The need for 1-card solutions can be minimized by negotiating reasonable internal and external minimum order quantities, so don't ignore minimum order quantities!

1-card Trigger Example

Daily demand = 10, MOQ = 1,000, MOQ Days Demand = 1,000 / 10 = 100 days

Lead time = 20 days, Target safety stock = 50 pieces (5 days)

If this item is on a 2-card system, replenishment orders will arrive long before they are required. Whether we "break" or "empty" a bin to place a replenishment order, the cell will require 100 days to use 1,000 parts in the bin (1,000 per bin / 10 per day) but the order will arrive in 20 days. That's 80 days of un-planned safety stock!

A better solution is to turn in the card at the right ROP.

ROP = [Lead time * Daily demand + Target safety stock] = [20 day LT * 10 per day + 50] = 250

When 1,000 pieces arrive, segment 250 parts as the ROP. After 750 parts are consumed and 250 ROP parts remain, turn in the card. Replenishment parts will arrive in 20 days when we have about 50 parts left, which is the safety stock quantity.

When the replenishment order arrives, separate 250 of the new parts (follow first-in-first-out) as the ROP quantity, add the 750 new parts to the 50 "old" parts in the bin, then consume those 800 parts before submitting the next order. If FIFO by order is critical, i.e., order #1 must be fully consumed before order #2 is started, keep the 50 old pieces segregated from the new order and consume those first.

Multi-Card Kanban Signals

Recall from the Sawtooth Curve chapter that lead-time demand can be covered by one or more replenishment orders, but two cards is preferred. There are three general circumstances that justify a multi-card solution.

When to Use a Multi-Card Solution

1. **Demand Variation Multi-Cards** are deployed to address changes in average daily demand that would require periodic resizing, such as with seasonal demand. (Seasonal demand is covered in detail in the section about safety stock.) When resizing occurs to accommodate demand changes, the *number of cards* must be adjusted. It is best to adjust the number of active cards instead of changing the order quantity, because order quantity impacts planned storage space, container size, and packaging.

With a multi-card solution, cards are activated (added to the deployed solution) when daily demand increases and deactivated (taken off the floor) when demand decreases. In order to follow basic kanban rules, the goal is to utilize *two* cards during the lowest demand period and resize up from there. Target lead time drives the order quantity, to prevent the sawtooth curve from being too tall. Therefore, kanban order quantity for a demand variation multi-card solution is based on *target* lead time, the *lowest* expected daily demand, and *target* safety stock associated with *low* demand.

Figure 7-4 on page 98 is a seasonal daily demand pattern, with the lowest daily demand occurring at the far right of the graph. Imagine that this is the demand curve for swimming supplies, where spring and summer are busy and fall and winter are slow.

Figure 7-4. **Set the Order Quantity for a Seasonal Demand Item Based on the Lowest Daily Demand**

The correct kanban order quantity is the quantity that results in 2 cards at the lowest demand of the year, with target lead time as the daily demand multiplier to set the order quantity. When the kanban solution is resized for higher daily demands, kanban cards are activated as necessary.

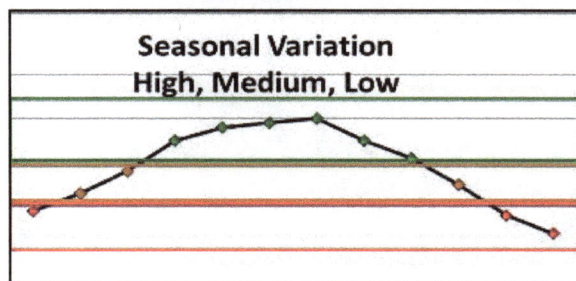

Seasonal Variation
High, Medium, Low

Lowest daily demand multiplied by target lead time calculates kanban order quantity, plus target safety stock, and the deployed kanban solution increases from 2 cards to n cards as daily demand climbs. Though we use target lead time and lowest daily demand to set order quantity, the resizing process calculates the required number of cards based on actual lead time, current daily demand, and target safety stock, as in the formula box below. Kanban order quantity still has to honor minimum order, standard package quantity (SPQ), and maximum order (MaxQ) limits. The 1-card adjustment for empty a bin still applies, but order quantity is the same for EaB or BaB.

Demand Variation Multi-Card Kanban Formulas

Rounded Demand Variation Multi-card KOQ, assume 2 cards, target LT, lowest demand =

$$\text{MIN} \, [\, \text{MaxQ}, \, \text{MAX} \, \{\text{MOQ}, \, \text{MROUND}[(\text{Target LT} * \text{Low DD}) * (1 + \text{Low Target SS \%})], \text{SPQ}\} \,]$$

Use the calculated order quantity to determine how many cards are required for current daily demand. This is the solution that is deployed to production.

Multi-card kanban order quantity formulas FIRST round calculated KOQ based on standard package quantity, THEN the larger of rounded order quantity or minimum order quantity is selected.

$$\# \text{ EaB cards for defined KOQ} = \frac{[(\text{Actual LT} * \text{Current DD}) * (1 + \text{Target SS \%})]}{\text{DV Multi–card KOQ}} + 1$$

$$\# \text{ BaB cards for DV KOQ} = \frac{[(\text{Actual LT} * \text{Current DD}) * (1 + \text{Target SS \%})]}{\text{DV Multi–card KOQ}}$$

Safety stock is covered later in great detail and we'll discuss why multi-card safety stock is a percent of total lead-time demand. We'll also cover the card rounding threshold.

---

2. Long lead-time multi-card solutions are used when actual lead time would result in high on-hand inventory due to an inflated order quantity. In Figure 7-5 on page 99, taken from the sawtooth curve chapter, the lead time is 25 days and the 2 diagrams span approximately 2.5 lead-time periods. The left diagram assumes 1 order covers 1 lead-time period, while the right diagram assumes 5 orders cover each lead-time period using a multi-card solution. Note the shorter sawtooth and therefore lower inventory level for the multi-card solution on the right.

Figure 7-5. Sawtooth Curve with One Order or Five Orders Per Lead-Time Period

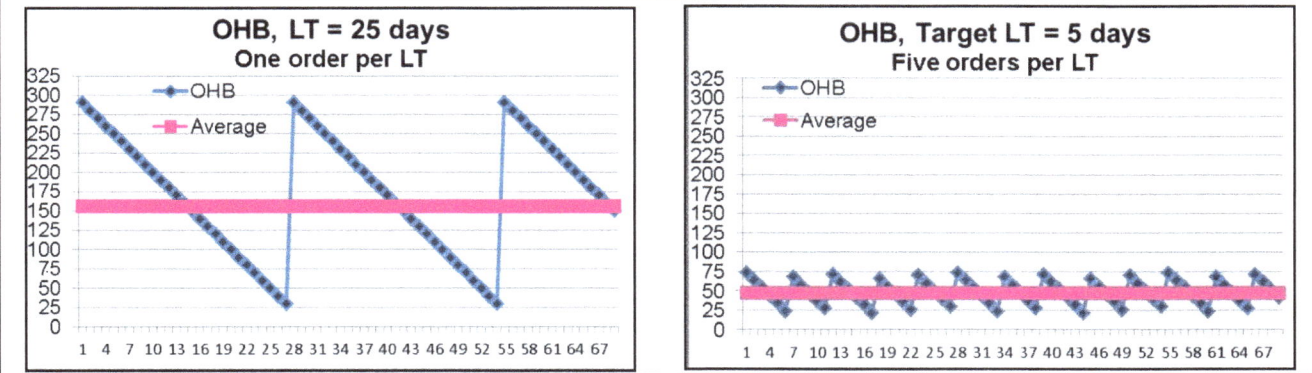

Long lead times are the most common reason for deploying a multi-card solution. To determine if actual lead time is long enough to justify a multi-card solution, compare actual lead time to the item's target lead time to get a lead-time ratio. If that result is greater than the allowed ratio, the item is assigned a multi-card solution. In general, actual lead time has to be two times the target lead time before a multi-card solution is justified.

Rule of Thumb

Items receive a multi-card solution for a long lead time when actual lead time is at least twice the target lead time for that item. IF [Actual LT days / Target LT days > 2] THEN use a multi-card solution.

Default Long LT Multi-card limit = 2, or actual LT at least 200% of target LT.

Long Lead-Time Multi-Card Ratio

$$\text{LT/TLT Ratio} = \text{Actual LT} / \text{Target LT}$$

IF [Actual LT / Target LT] > Long LT Multi-card Limit, THEN utilize LT Multi-card solution

For long lead-time multi-cards that do not have demand variation to deal with, use average daily demand or a reasonable "permanent" daily demand along with target lead time. Like all multi-cards, kanban is resized by adjusting card count for current daily demand, actual lead time, and target safety stock.

Long Lead-Time Multi-Card Kanban Formulas

Long LT Multi-card KOQ, assume 2 cards at target lead time =

$$\text{MIN} [\text{MaxQ}, \text{MAX} \{\text{MOQ}, \text{MROUND} [(\text{Target LT} * \text{Average DD}) * (1 + \text{Target SS \%})], \text{SPQ}\}]$$

$$\text{\# EaB cards for defined KOQ} = \frac{[(\text{Actual LT} * \text{Current DD}) + (1 + \text{Target SS \%}]}{\text{LT Multi–card KOQ}} + 1$$

$$\text{\# BaB cards for defined KOQ} = \frac{[(\text{Actual LT} * \text{Current DD}) + (1 + \text{Target SS \%})]}{\text{LT Multi–card KOQ}}$$

As with demand variation multi-card solutions, round order quantity for standard package, minimum order and maximum order quantity requirements. Round card count to an integer, using the card-rounding threshold.

HINT for Associates

If variation analysis (described later) reveals that every item at a site has seasonal demand variation, kanban types come down to 3 choices: Not Kanban, 1-card, or DV Multi-card. First sort those that qualify for kanban, then test for the need for just 1 card. Once "not kanban" and 1-card items have been identified, everything else gets a demand variation multi-card solution.

If conditions for both lead time <u>and</u> demand variation multi-cards exist for an item, i.e., a long lead time *plus* seasonality, treat it as a demand variation item and use target lead time and the lowest expected daily demand to set the kanban order quantity. Demand variation multi-cards require a bit more analysis than lead time or MaxQ multi-cards, so it's best to sort for demand variation first.

3. <u>**MaxQ Multi-Card**</u>: A maximum allowed order quantity, or MaxQ, means an item has a ceiling for how many units of measure can be in one order. If the MaxQ is smaller than the calculated kanban order quantity for a standard 2-card solution, use more than 2 cards to order an adequate quantity over the lead-time period. For example, if we need to order 1,000 parts to cover the lead-time period but the maximum per order is 200, deploy more than 2 cards.

MaxQ Multi-Card Test

$$\text{IF } (MaxQ < [\text{Actual lead time} * \text{Current daily demand} + \text{Target SS units}]),$$
$$\text{THEN utilize MaxQ multi-card solution}$$

Assign MaxQ as the order quantity, then calculate the number of required cards.

MaxQ Multi-Card Kanban Formulas

$$\text{MaxQ kanban order quantity} = MaxQ$$

$$\text{Empty a bin \# MaxQ cards} = \frac{[(\text{Actual LT} * \text{Current DD}) * (1 + \text{Target SS \%})]}{MaxQ} + 1$$

$$\text{Break a bin \# MaxQ cards} = \frac{[(\text{Actual LT} * \text{Current DD}) * (1 + \text{Target SS \%})]}{MaxQ}$$

MaxQ Process Example

Part number MQ-888 is processed through a heat treat oven and the baskets can only hold 500 parts. MaxQ = 500, Trigger = Break a bin, Daily demand = 140, Actual lead time = 10 days, Target safety stock = 2 days

Target KOQ = [Daily demand * Lead time + Target safety stock] = [140 * 10 + 280] = 1,680 parts

Because the trigger method is BaB, we order 840 parts per card, which exceeds MaxQ, so use a MaxQ multi-card solution and calculate how many cards are required. Kanban order quantity = MaxQ = 500

cards = 1680/500 = 3.36, round up to 4 cards.

MaxQ Package Example

Parts are stacked on a pallet that holds 64 per pallet, or 4 rows of 16 each. The calculated kanban quantity is 178 per kanban card but that means 1 kanban card covers 3 pallets at 64 each, or 192 per kanban card.

The site stores these pallets in tall racks and it is not visually feasible for one card to represent several pallets. Instead, the site elects to assign one card per pallet, which is essentially a MaxQ scenario.

MaxQ = 64, Trigger = Break a bin, Daily demand = 16.2, Target SS = 1 day, Lead time = 10 days

cards = [(Lead time + Target SS days) * Daily demand] / MaxQ = [(10 + 1) * 16.2] / 64 = 178.2/ 64 = 2.78 cards, round up to 3 cards

---

HINT for Associates

A MaxQ multi-card solution works very well when a process or shipping limitation prevents high order quantities, but another logical fit for a MaxQ multi-card is when a site elects to put a kanban card with every container and the calculated order quantity is more than one container. If a site puts a card on every pallet of 2,000 pounds of material and the order quantity is 10,000, use 2,000 as the MaxQ and therefore the order quantity, and calculate the required number of cards per item.

HINT for Associates

Batch-size reduction is a key theme for Lean practitioner, since it works toward one-piece flow. For an item that is undergoing batch reduction, deploy a MaxQ solution and change the MaxQ limit as the batch size is reduced. This will make it easy to resize the kanban solution as the order quantity comes down.

Some kanban designers recommend "multi-bin solutions," which means the number of cards is fixed (usually 2) and the kanban order quantity changes, hence the name multi-bin for a variable order quantity. (Yes, it's very confusing.)

A fixed number of cards is sometimes recommended if a site deploys generic physical cards or cards with limited information, e.g., no kanban order quantity is printed on the card. This is supposedly advantageous for resizing kanban solutions without changing the deployed cards. In theory it makes sense, but generic kanban cards are difficult to manage and audit. When an associate attempts to match a kanban card to a quantity of parts to put parts away or complete an audit, the card doesn't tell them how many parts are associated with the card so they need an additional reference source to complete the task, which adds extra work and increases the chance for errors.

Some sites with virtual cards (no physical cards) use varying order quantities to manage order quantities more exactly. When an order is generated the supplier receives an electronic order for a specific quantity based on current daily demand, actual lead time, and target safety stock. The next order might be for a different quantity if any of those values change. This only works if both the supplier and customer can handle varying quantities, i.e., container size, shelf space, packaging, etc.

In my experience, there is rarely a need to deploy multi-bin solutions with a fixed number of cards and a floating order quantity. They add confusion and provide very limited upside, so don't go down this hazardous road.

Types & Triggers Summary

Kanban designers should select either break a bin or empty a bin as the standard trigger timing for a site. Empty a bin is easier to audit and therefore is the best option for sites that are new to kanban. Break a bin can result in lower inventory, which can be a distinct advantage, but process discipline must be very high due to the difficulty of auditing BaB items.

Before a kanban solution can be calculated for a kanban item, we must first define what type of kanban solution is required. The ideal solution has two cards, but one card is used when minimum order quantity is high. Multi-card solutions are deployed when demand variation requires frequent resizing (i.e., add or subtract cards), when actual lead time is at least 2 times the target lead time, or when a maximum order quantity dictates more than 2 cards.

TUTORIAL: GOCO KANBAN TYPES

Mary and the team elected to use EaB for all kanban solutions due to the ease of auditing. The team hoped 1-card solutions would be few and far between, but they wouldn't know if they needed any 1-card solutions until kanban types were determined for all items.

The team suspected they might need demand variation multi-card solutions due to the seasonality in some channels of their business.

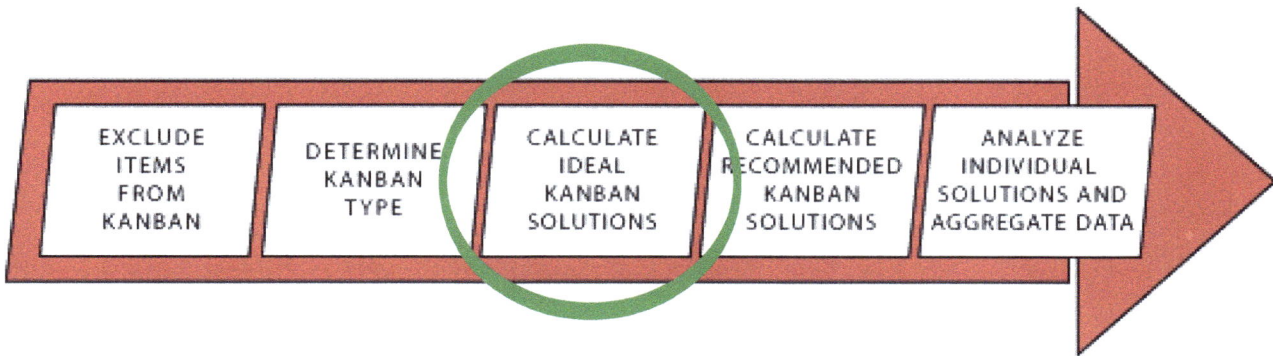

CHAPTER 8: IDEAL KANBAN SOLUTIONS

Recall from the chapter about how kanban works that there are five steps that a sophisticated kanban calculator completes to provide kanban solutions.

1. Divide items into those that go on kanban and those that will utilize an alternative replenishment method, such as MRP or vendor management.

2. Assign the right kanban type to every kanban item.

3. Calculate an ideal kanban solution for every item, to be used as a benchmark for planning inventory improvement or negotiation activity.

4. Calculate the appropriate recommended or resized kanban solution for every kanban item.

5. Analyze kanban solutions and estimate expected on-hand inventory by part number, as well as the inventory reduction potential by item and overall. This provides insights for inventory reduction action plans and timing.

Defining and calculating the correct kanban type and recommended kanban solution for a kanban item requires some insight about that item's _ideal_ kanban solution.

The Logic for an Ideal Kanban Solution

For every item's supply and demand characteristics, there is an ideal kanban solution that orders the perfect quantity of parts for every replenishment order, with no rounding for minimum order quantity (MOQ) or standard package quantity (SPQ), and no multi-card solution for a long lead times or a maximum order quantity. Yes, in an ideal kanban system, there could be multi-card solutions for demand variation. But, long lead time and/or order quantity limitations are considered out-of-bounds and therefore are not present in an ideal world.

Let's walk through the logic.

1. Inventory management is expected to achieve short lead times and high on-time delivery, with minimal on-hand inventory. Less inventory, more cash. Kanban should be _designed_ to pursue these goals.

2. Lead-time demand, or the number of pieces utilized from the time a replenishment order is placed until it is received, must be covered by a replenishment plan. In addition to lead time demand, safety stock might be required for some items to cover variation in supply or demand.

3. <u>An ideal kanban solution is 2 cards</u>, 1 card linked to on-hand inventory and another waiting for an incoming receipt.

4. Kanban formulas rely on daily demand, lead time, and target safety stock.

a. Daily demand is driven by the customer and generally can't be changed or adjusted. For kanban, there is no "ideal" condition for daily demand.

b. Every item has an actual lead time and a target lead time. The target lead time is the ideal state and the goal is to achieve target lead times for internal and external items.

c. Target safety stock is driven by supply and demand variation. Supply variation should be eliminated (more on that later), but demand variation is generally uncontrollable. Therefore, target safety stock for the purposes of protecting delivery against demand variation is difficult to adjust.

Kanban Formulas: 2 Cards, Calculate Order Quantity ⊜

EaB kanban order quantity, 2 cards =

$$\frac{(\text{Actual LT} * \text{Daily demand} + \text{Target SS units})}{(2 \text{ cards} - 1)}$$

BaB kanban order quantity, 2 cards =

$$\frac{(\text{Actual LT} * \text{Daily demand} + \text{Target SS units})}{(2 \text{ cards} - 1)}$$

From this quick analysis, it's evident that <u>target lead time is the parameter that drives an ideal kanban solution!</u>

5. Inventory performance is measured as inventory turns or days on hand, each of which is reported in currency for a population of parts. It seems like there should be something about managing money when maximizing kanban solutions for inventory performance.

Aha! We know that ABC classification designates an item's annual spend as high, medium, or low versus the population of parts to which that item belongs. And, it seems logical that A parts, the highest expenditure items, would arrive more frequently than C parts in order to minimize the height of the sawtooth curve for expensive items.

This ABC insight implies that if two items have identical daily demand in <u>units</u> but have very different standard <u>costs</u>, the more expensive item should arrive in smaller batches and more frequently than the cheaper item, even though total lead-time demand is the same number when measured in units.

<u>When setting target lead time, an ideal kanban solution utilizes ABC classification to ensure inventory value is reduced by receiving high-spend items more frequently than low-spend items.</u>

6. For each item, <u>target lead time assists with the decision of whether an item needs a lead-time multi-card solution</u> instead of the preferred 2-card solution.

7. For both ideal and "actual" kanban solutions, we can calculate expected minimum, average, and maximum inventory levels. We then <u>compare ideal to recommended or actual results to clarify which items have the biggest negative impact from *not* achieving perfection</u>.

Estimated Inventory Levels ⊜

Estimated minimum inventory = Actual safety stock

EaB Actual SS, more than 1 card = (# cards - 1) * KOQ - (Actual LT * Current Daily Demand)

BaB Actual SS, more than 1 card =(# cards * KOQ) - (Actual LT * Current Daily Demand)

Actual SS for 1 card = Reorder point - (Actual LT * Current Daily Demand)

Estimated average inventory = KOQ/2 + Actual Safety stock

Estimated maximum inventory = KOQ + Actual Safety stock

To determine what is causing a recommended kanban solution to divert from ideal, look at lead time, MOQ, SPQ, and MaxQ to see if those limitations impose something other than the ideal solution.

For example, one "C" item might have a package quantity of 25, which rounds the ideal order quantity for 2 cards from 112 up to 125. That probably doesn't have much impact. But, another item might have an actual lead time of 8 weeks versus a target of 1 week, and the minimum order quantity might prevent a multi-card solution from being utilized to address the long lead time. This can have a huge impact, particularly if it is an "A" item with high annual spend.

Define the Ideal Kanban Solution

It took a long path to get to what sounds like a simple answer: <u>focus on target lead-time</u>. In order for an ideal kanban solution to reflect the correct order *frequency* and receipt *quantity*, the parameter that must be defined to design an ideal kanban solution is <u>target</u> lead time. Daily demand and target safety stock can't be adjusted without adding risk, but long lead time can be accommodated by increasing the order count per lead-time period. This depends on target lead time.

That long discussion clarified the math and the logic. Now we're ready to design ideal kanban solutions. Yep, this is easy.

Fact 1: An ideal kanban solution is 2 cards.

Fact 2: Target lead time is the value that defines an overall ideal kanban solution, by calculating the right order quantity for 2 cards at the target lead time.

Fact 3: ABC classification breaks items into stacks of most expensive to least expensive, captured by annual spend, and A items should have a shorter target lead time than B's, which are shorter than C's.

Therefore, the first step when determining ideal kanban solutions is to define target lead times by ABC classification, with a slight adjustment for purchased versus manufactured status. We'll cover this in detail in the next chapter.

Using those target lead times, calculate <u>ideal</u> 2-card kanban solutions based on the correct frequency for every item using standard kanban order quantity formulas, but substitute <u>target</u> lead time in place of <u>actual</u> lead time.

Ideal Kanban Order Quantity for 2 Cards

$$\text{EaB, 2 card KOQ} = \frac{(\text{Target LT} * \text{Daily demand}) + \text{Target SS}}{(2 \text{ cards} - 1)}$$

$$\text{BaB, 2 card KOQ} = \frac{(\text{Target LT} * \text{Daily demand}) + \text{Target SS}}{(2 \text{ cards})}$$

If target lead time can't be achieved in today's world, the *ideal* solution is still used as a model for how to design the *recommended* kanban solution. In other words, if a long lead time can't be shortened, use target lead time to define the correct order quantity then calculate the correct number of kanban cards for that order quantity.

Rule of Thumb

An ideal solution is <u>2</u> cards with an order quantity that matches the ideal receipt frequency for that item. Target lead time dictates the ideal frequency of receipt and, therefore, the ideal quantity for a replenishment order. So, target lead time draws the ideal sawtooth curve including both lead time and order quantity.

Insights from an Ideal Kanban Solution

The advantage to defining a perfect solution for every kanban item is that it sets the benchmark for what <u>should</u> be deployed to protect delivery and minimize on-hand inventory. This doesn't imply that ideal solutions *will* be achieved, but a kanban calculator should provide these benchmarks for planning kanban deployment or improvements.

To be clear on our terms, a current kanban solution is what is deployed today for a kanban item, or the active kanban solution. The ideal solution is the goal for a perfect kanban world, and the recommended or calculated kanban solution is based on an item's current conditions for daily demand, lead time, and package quantity limitations.

Every current and recommended kanban solution can be compared to an item's ideal solution to assess the magnitude of inventory reduction that would be possible if the ideal kanban solution was achieved.

Inventory Reduction Based on Ideal Kanban Solutions

Potential inventory reduction for Current OH$ versus Ideal kanban OH$ = Estimated OH$ for Current Kanban Solution - Estimated OH$ for Ideal Kanban solution

Potential inventory reduction for Recommended OH$ versus Ideal kanban OH$ = Estimated OH$ for Recommended Kanban Solution - Estimated OH$ for Ideal solution

A positive result from these formulas indicates an inventory reduction. If we prefer to see reductions as negative numbers, reverse the formula and subtract current or recommended OH$ from Ideal OH$.

A large gap between an item's recommended kanban solution versus the ideal solution indicates that the ideal solution is significantly different than what the calculator can recommend today for that item, given current limitations. The calculator accommodates current lead time and package limitations, so a large gap from recommended to ideal means the calculator had to compromise when it determined the resize solution. Items with large currency gaps should go to the top of the negotiation list to address lead times or package quantity limitations.

If we sum the estimated on-hand currency for ideal solutions across an entire population of items, we have the *best-case estimate* for how much inventory should be on hand.

Rule of Thumb

The sum of ideal expected on-hand currencies defines the best inventory performance that could be achieved. By definition, this is the ideal level of inventory.

If your inventory goal is a lower number than the sum of the ideal inventory levels, the goal is completely unrealistic!

HINT for Associates

Calculate estimated on-hand inventory dollars for all current or "resized" kanban solutions and compare to ideal solutions to estimate how much inventory reduction could be achieved for every item if minimum order, standard package, and lead time penalties were eliminated.

When defining inventory reduction plans, or where to negotiate better MOQs or lead times, start with items with the greatest opportunities to reduce on-hand dollars.

Summary of Ideal Solutions

Target lead time is one of the most powerful elements in a kanban system because it defines ideal conditions. An ideal solutions sets the benchmark for one item, and the aggregate of all ideal solutions is the best possible performance for an entire population of parts.

This topic will be expanded in the next chapter, along with target MOQs and SPQs.

Target Lead Time (TLT)
Target Minimum Order Quantity (MOQ)
Target Standard Package Quantity (SPQ)

CHAPTER 9: TARGET LEAD TIME & ORDER QUANTITIES

When we calculate kanban solutions, we need an ideal and a recommended solution for every kanban item, and each solution requires the kanban order quantity and the associated number of signals or cards. Ideal kanban solutions require a target lead time for every kanban item, and target lead time (TLT) drives associated targets for MOQs and SPQs.

Target Lead Time (TLT)

Target lead time serves four primary purposes in kanban planning.

1. Target lead time determines the ideal kanban solution by defining the correct order quantity for a perfect 2-card solution.

2. An item's target lead time is the benchmark comparison when identifying items that need shorter or longer lead times, which is a negotiation task for improving inventory performance.

3. The gap between an items's actual and target lead time determines if a multi-card solution is required to reduce on-hand inventory for a long lead-time item.

4. Target lead times for a population are the benchmarks for categorizing short, medium, and long lead times for purchased and manufactured parts, which is beneficial when filtering or grouping items for analysis.

Target lead times are usually based on ABC classification plus purchased or manufactured status.

• A items have the shortest target lead times and C's have the longest, which is logical because A items have the highest spend so we want shorter lead times to drive lower inventory dollars.

• Internal parts have slightly shorter target lead times than external parts since there is minimal transit time for items from within the same site.

HINT for Associates

Target lead time defines the perfect order quantity for any item. If every part number was managed at its ideal order quantity, as determined by target lead time, each order would be neither too small nor too large. As items deviate up or down from their ideal order quantity, the impact gets bigger and bigger, either as higher inventory (when order quantity exceeds the target) or as higher transactions (if order quantity is less than the ideal.)

Target Lead-Time Hints

Target lead times must be reasonable, neither too short nor too long, and they must be accurately assigned to every item.

Target Lead-Time Hint: Carrying Cost Versus Transaction Cost

What makes a target lead time too short or too long? Target lead times balance the opposing goals of low on-hand dollars, which is a function of short lead times, versus low transaction costs, which is driven by longer lead times. Low inventory dollars usually wins this battle because those costs are more visible, but both elements should be considered.

Inventory is a financial investment, so carrying cost is one expenditure for holding inventory, along with other expenses like space and transit costs. Higher inventory means higher carrying cost, so inventory reduction activity seeks low order quantities to minimize the height of sawtooth curves, which implies buying in small quantities to reduce carrying cost.

Transaction cost includes all expenses associated with ordering and receiving internal or external parts. Every manufacturing or purchase order takes time to create (define the order, enter it in the system, send it to the supplier) and also to close (produce or receive parts, put them away, transact the receipt in the system). The cost to process an order is generally independent of the order quantity, i.e., an order for 100 pieces takes essentially the same time and effort as an order for 20,000 pieces. Smaller order quantities increase the *count* of orders required to cover annual demand. So, while the cost is constant for a *single* transaction, the *number* of transactions per year is why total transaction cost increases with lower order quantities. Transaction cost is inversely correlated to order quantity, so high quantities give low transaction costs and vice versa. This is another reason why C items are purchased in larger quantities because it is silly for the transaction cost for a C item to exceed the value of the parts being ordered. Minimizing transaction cost means buying in large quantities.

Target lead time determines the balance between holding cost versus transaction cost, so be prudent when setting target lead times. Target lead times provided on the next page are a good pace to start.

Target Lead-Time Hint: BaB Versus EaB

For the same target lead time, the kanban order quantity (KOQ) for a 2-card break-a-bin kanban solution is half of the quantity for empty a bin. This means BaB items have higher transaction costs than EaB, which can have an impact if transaction cost or receiving and processing activities are a primary consideration.

Ideal Kanban Order Quantity (KOQ)

$$EaB, 2\ card\ KOQ = \frac{(Target\ LT * Daily\ demand) + Target\ SS}{(2\ cards - 1)}$$

$$BaB, 2\ card\ KOQ = \frac{(Target\ LT * Daily\ demand) + Target\ SS}{(2\ cards)}$$

Target Lead-Time Hint: Accommodate Special Circumstances Where It Makes Sense

Items with special circumstances, such as vendor managed (VMI) or consigned inventory, can often accommodate shorter target lead times than traditional purchased parts, so base each target lead time on the specific scenario. If vendor-managed parts are checked at least twice a week by the supplier, VMI target lead time should be no more than three days.

Target Lead-Time Hint: Confirm ABC

Since target lead time often depends on ABC, ensure that all ABC classifications are complete and correct before assigning target lead times.

Ratio of Actual to Target Lead Time

If actual lead time for an item is much longer or shorter than the target, the item should be on the negotiation list. To assess how far each actual lead time is from its target, calculate the ratio of actual lead time versus target lead time.

Actual Lead Time/Target Lead-Time Ratio
LT/TLT Ratio = Actual LT / Target LT

Some actual lead times that miss the target do not have a significant impact on inventory performance. An actual lead time of 22 days compared to a 20-day target might not move the needle for on-hand inventory. And, an actual lead time of 4 days versus a target of 5 might not add to transaction costs. Therefore, prioritize which lead times to attack by setting minimum and maximum lead-time ratios that justify lead-time negotiation or improvement activity.

Rule of Thumb

IF [Actual LT / Target LT] > 2, THEN pursue a shorter LT

IF [Actual LT / Target LT] < 0.5, THEN pursue a longer LT

Default Target Lead Times

Target lead times must be reasonable, which raises another question of balance. Like the need to balance higher inventory to protect delivery performance versus lower inventory to reduce on-hand inventory, there is also a necessity to balance low transaction costs versus low inventory. In the debate about delivery versus on-hand inventory, delivery wins that battle until delivery performance can be successfully achieved while at the same time reducing inventory. Never let delivery suffer!

For transaction costs versus carrying costs, the debate isn't as clear. Many sites fail to fully understand this conundrum and underestimate both transaction costs and carrying cost, giving neither element adequate consideration.

In general, carrying costs climb faster than transaction costs because carrying more inventory adds handling, space, and transit costs. Higher transaction occurrences certainly require more labor to handle internal and external orders and

those costs can add up. But, for most sites the additional labor is a small amount and therefore the impact is not extreme. For that reason, err on the side of shorter target lead times, but don't reduce target lead times to the point of lunacy. If a site spends an inordinate amount of time generating orders, receiving material, and putting parts away, the cost of all of that activity will increase labor costs due specifically to a higher number of transactions!

As stated before, target lead times are usually based on ABC classification plus purchased versus manufactured status. Target lead times for internal parts are shorter than for purchased parts due to the lack of transit time. A 2-day extension for external items is generally adequate. These default target lead times balance carrying costs versus transaction costs.

Rule of Thumb

Default target lead times in workdays:

	Purchased	Manufactured
A	5	3
B	10	8
C	20	18

HINT for Leaders

Don't set unreasonable target lead times as an excuse to beat up suppliers.

Asking for an ultra-short lead time with a secret hope that the supplier will grant a price concession *instead of* achieving the short lead time is not negotiating in good faith. Be fair!

The opposite is also true. Don't set ridiculously long target lead times simply because the site elected to pursue "global sourcing partners" that are half a world away. Global sources might look great when evaluating cost per piece, but extended lead times are a noteworthy penalty. Set target lead times based on inventory management goals, not cost per piece. Instead of accommodating the lead time for remote suppliers, target lead times should make it obvious that long lead times to cross an ocean are out of touch with broader inventory management goals.

Target Lead Time (TLT) & Estimated Days on Hand (DOH)

A site set a goal of 12 inventory turns or 21 days on hand in a work year with 250 workdays. They wondered if their defined target lead times would achieve the goal with target safety stock set to 20% of target lead time.

They estimated the resulting days on hand (DOH) for each type of part using the formula for average inventory [Average Inventory = KOQ/2 + SS], with order quantity and safety stock both captured in <u>days</u> so the formula estimated inventory <u>days on hand</u>.

A items are 80% of spend, B's are 15%, and C's 5%, so they weighted the estimated DOH by ABC classification then summed those values to get a blended DOH value.

The blended DOH will be well under 5.0, even if purchased parts are a large percentage of on-hand dollars. Five days on hand equates to about 50 inventory turns over 250 annual workdays. So, they should hit the 12 turn goal even if more than half of on-hand dollars fail to achieve their ideal kanban solutions. They decided to verify the expected result after recommended kanban solutions were confirmed.

This demonstrates that reasonable lead times and target safety stock levels result in high inventory performance <u>if kanban execution is successful</u>, which necessitates actively and wisely managing kanban order quantities through reasonable minimum order quantities (MOQs), standard package quantities (SPQs), and lead times (LTs).

Currrent TLT	P	M
A	5	3
B	10	8
C	20	18

Target SS Days	P	M
A	1.0	0.6
B	2.0	1.6
C	4.0	3.6

Estimated DOH	P	M
A	3.5	2.1
B	7.0	5.6
C	14.0	12.6

Weighted DOH	P	M
A (Est DOH * 80%)	2.8	1.7
B (Est DOH * 15%)	1.1	0.8
C (Est DOH * 5%)	0.7	0.6
Blended DOH	4.6	3.2

Real-World Observation

I visited a site with a 1-day target lead time for purchased A items. It might have worked if they bought full truckloads <u>every</u> day from <u>every</u> supplier, or if key suppliers were 20 minutes away, but that wasn't the case. The site achieved a 1-day lead time on less than 10% of purchased A items.

Unreasonable goals are bad for morale because associates become convinced that they can't succeed, and they're detrimental to individual and team performance reviews because the boss says, "You missed your goal by a mile." Consider both transaction and carrying costs for target lead times, but be reasonable.

Short, Medium, & Long Lead-Time Thresholds

When categorizing items for kanban analysis, it is sometimes beneficial to group them by lead-time category, e.g., short, medium, or long. Defining "short" versus "long" is based on target lead times.

Rule of Thumb

Default LT Category values:

If Actual LT < 1.5 * [A Purchased target LT], THEN LT Category = Short
If Actual LT > 1.5 * [B Purchased Target LT], THEN LT Category = Long
For all others, LT Category = Medium

In most sites, both purchased and manufactured items can be <u>categorized</u> versus Short and Long limits for purchased items. But because target lead times are usually different for purchased and manufactured items, a site might elect to use the different targets when assigning lead-time categories.

Multi-Card Example: [Actual LT / Target LT] = 8

Item A405 has a target lead time of 5 days and actual lead time of 40 days. Daily demand is 10 and target safety stock (SS) is 1 day or 10 pieces. [Actual LT / Target LT] = 8.0 or 40 days divided by 5.

<u>Ideal</u> EaB 2-card KOQ = [Target LT * DD + Target SS] / (2 cards - 1) = [5 days * 10/day + 10] / (2 - 1) = 60

<u>EaB calculated 2-card KOQ</u> = [Actual LT * DD + Target safety stock] = [40* 10/day + 10] / (2 - 1) = 410

Estimated average inventory @ 410 KOQ = KOQ/2 + SS = KOQ / 2 + [KOQ * (# cards - 1) - (LT * DD)]
= 410/2 + [410 * (2-1) - (40 * 10)] = 205 + [410 - 400] = 205 + 10 = 215

If we use a long lead-time multi-card at the ideal KOQ of 60: # cards = [(Actual LT * DD + Target safety stock) / Ideal KOQ] + 1 = [40 * 10 + 10] / 60 + 1 = 410 / 60 + 1 = 6.83 + 1 = 7.83, round to 8 cards

Estimated average inventory for 8 cards @ 60 = KOQ / 2 + SS = 60 / 2 + [60 * (8-1)) - (40 * 10)]
= 30 + [420 - 400] = 50

What if it was BaB?
<u>Calculated</u> 2-card KOQ = [Actual LT * DD + Target SS] = [40 * 10/day + 10] / 2 = 205

Estimated average inventory @ 205 KOQ = KOQ/2 + [KOQ * # cards - (LT * DD)]
= 205/2 + [205 * 2 - (40 * 10)] = 102.5 + 10 = 112.5

If we use a lead-time multi-card at the ideal KOQ of 60: # cards = [(Actual lead time * Daily demand + Target safety stock) / Ideal KOQ] = [40 * 10 + 10] / 60 = 410 / 60 = 6.83 round up to 7

Estimated average inventory for 7 cards @ 60 = KOQ / 2 + SS = 60 / 2 + [60 * 7 - (40 * 10)]
= 30 + [420 - 400] = 50

For multi-card, BaB has 1 less card and the same average inventory as EaB.

	Empty a Bin	Break a Bin
2-Card KOQ	410	205
2-Card Estimated Average Inventory	**215**	**112.5**
Multi-Card KOQ	60	60
# Multi-Cards	8	7
Multi-Card Estimated Average Inventory	**50**	**50**

Multi-Card Example: [Actual LT / Target LT] = 1.6

e.g.

Item A508 has a target lead time of 5 days and an actual lead time of 8 days. Daily demand is 10 per day and target safety stock is one day.

The ratio [Actual lead time / Target lead time] is 1.6, or 8 days divided by 5 days.

The ideal 2-card EaB order quantity = [5 days * 10/day + 10 SS] = 60.

EaB 2-card calculated kanban order quantity = [8 * 10/day + 10] / (2 - 1) = 90

Estimated average inventory @ KOQ of 90 = KOQ / 2 + [(# cards - 1) * KOQ - (Actual LT * DD)]
= 90 / 2 + [90 * (2-1) - (8 * 10)] = 45 + [90 - 80] = 45 + 10 = 55

For a long lead-time multi-card, KOQ is the same as EaB Ideal KOQ of 60:
cards = [(Actual lead time * Daily demand + Target safety stock) / Long LT KOQ] + 1
= [8 * 10 + 10] / 60 + 1 = 90 / 60 + 1 = 1.5 + 1 = 2.5, round to 3 cards

Estimated average inventory = 60 / 2 + [(3-1) * 60 - (8 * 10)] = 30 + [120 - 80] = 30 + 40 = 70

If BaB, 2-card calculated KOQ = [8 * 10/day + 10] / 2 = 45, or half of the EaB quantity

Estimated average inventory = KOQ / 2 + [# cards * KOQ - (Actual LT * DD)] = 45/2 + [2 * 45 - (8 * 10)]
= 22.5 + [90 - 80] = 22.5 + 10 = 32.5

For a lead-time multi-card at the Long LT KOQ of 60: # cards = [(Actual lead time * Daily demand + Target safety stock) / Ideal KOQ]: # cards = [8 * 10 + 10] / 60 = 90 / 60 = 1.5 cards, round to 2 cards

Estimated average inventory = KOQ / 2 + SS = 60 / 2 + [60 * 2 - (8 * 10)] = 30 + [120 - 80] = 70

	Empty a Bin	Break a Bin
2-Card KOQ	90	45
2-Card Est Average Inventory	**55**	**32.5**
Multi-Card KOQ	60	60
# Multi-Cards	3	2
Multi-Card Est Average Inventory	**70**	**70**

Because the lead-time ratio is less than 2.0 in this example, the multi-card solution is a detriment to on-hand inventory for both EaB and BaB. Therefore 2 cards is the best solution, even though it results in some unplanned safety stock.

Target Minimum Order Quantity (TMOQ)

The perfect minimum order quantity (MOQ) is a unit of "1" because that allows the *final* replenishment quantity to equal the *calculated* KOQ, with no rounding. An MOQ of 1 for every part number is unrealistic, but low minimum order and standard package quantities prevent the calculated order quantity from rounding up too much, which minimizes the height of the sawtooth curve and keeps average inventory low.

Calculate target minimum order as a function of target lead time. Because target MOQ varies by part number, there is no target MOQ "threshold" or cutoff in the targets and limits tab. Instead, the calculator retrieves the appropriate target lead time for every item and calculates target MOQ accordingly.

Target MOQ

Target MOQ = Target lead time * Daily demand + Target safety stock

Actual MOQ vs. Target MOQ Ratio

Divide each item's current MOQ by target MOQ (TMOQ) to measure the gap, then identify items that need a lower MOQ. It is not necessary to identify parts that need a higher MOQ.

Actual MOQ/TMOQ Ratio and Negotiation Decision

Actual MOQ/TMOQ Ratio = Actual MOQ/ TMOQ

IF (Actual MOQ / Target MOQ > 2.0), THEN mark the part for MOQ negotiation.

Rule of Thumb

An actual MOQ must be at least 2 times the target MOQ to justify negotiating a new MOQ with an internal or external supplier.

Target Standard Package Quantity (TSPQ)

A calculated kanban order quantity (KOQ) is rounded up or down by the standard package quantity (SPQ), keeping in mind that first the order quantity match or exceed MOQ. Negotiate a package quantity that provides rounding flexibility. Think of package quantity as a percent of MOQ and set a goal for package quantity to be 10% to 30% of the target MOQ.

Rule of Thumb

Default Target SPQ = 20% * Target MOQ

Target Lead Time, MOQ, SPQ, & On-Hand Balance

Purchased A item, EaB
Daily demand = 125
Actual lead time = 30 workdays (6 weeks)
Current minimum order quantity = 4,000 = KOQ
Current standard package quantity = 1,000
Target lead time = 5 days
Target safety stock = 1 day (125 pieces)

Target MOQ = Target LT * DD + Target SS
= 5 days * 125 + 125 = 625 + 125 = 750

Target SPQ = 20% * TMOQ = 20% * 750 = 150

2-card current EaB solution = (30 days * 125) + 125 = 3,875, round for MOQ: 2 cards @ 4,000

Actual SS = (# cards - 1) * KOQ - (Actual LT * DD) = (2 - 1) * 4,000 - (30 * 125) = 4000 - 3750 = 250, or 2 days of SS

Estimated average inventory, current solution = KOQ / 2 + SS = 4,000 / 2 + 250 = 2,250

2-card ideal EaB solution = (5 days * 125) + (1 day * 125) = 750, no rounding: 2 cards @ 750

Actual ideal SS = (2 - 1) * 750 - (5 * 125) = 750 - 625 = 125 or 1 day of SS

Estimated ideal average inventory, ideal solution = 750 / 2 + 125 = 375 + 125 = 500

Get MOQ down to [5 days target LT * 125 + 125 = 750], and SPQ down to [20% * 625 = 125].

HINTS for Associates

Minimum order quantity (MOQ) is always greater than or equal to standard package quantity (SPQ).

Kanban order quantity (KOQ) must be greater than or equal to MOQ and also evenly divisible by SPQ.

Kanban order quantity must be less than or equal to the maximum order quantity (MaxQ).

Extended Example from Sawtooth Curve Chapter (continued on next page)

A purchased A item on EaB has an actual lead time of 25 days and target lead time of 5 days. We use 10 per day and want 2 days of safety stock, or 20 pieces. If we buy on a standard 2-card system, we buy 270 parts at a time.

KOQ = [25 days * 10 per day + 2 days SS * 10 per day] = 250 + 20 = 270.

Figure 9-1. Sawtooth Curve, KOQ 270

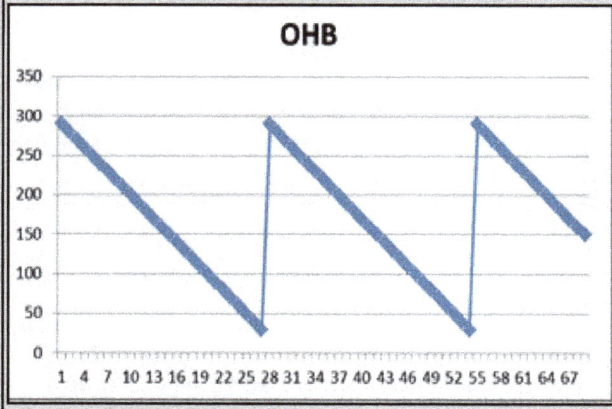

OHB

Expected Minimum Inventory = SS = 20

Expected Average on-hand = KOQ / 2 + SS = 155

Expected Maximum Inventory = KOQ + SS = 290

The sawtooth curve for this solution is in Figure 9-1. The width of the sawtooth equals [Actual lead time + 2 days of safety stock = 27 days]. The height of the sawtooth is driven by the long lead time since KOQ = [LT * DD + Target SS].

Figure 9-2. Sawtooth Curve, KOQ 135

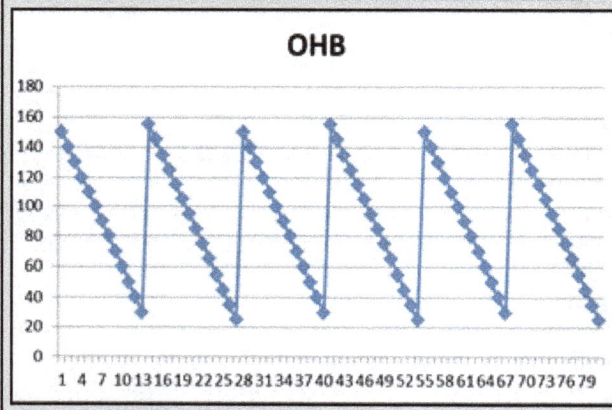

OHB

Suppose we cut the order quantity in half. We still wait 25 days to receive replenishment orders but would order twice as often.

KOQ = 135

cards = [Actual LT * DD + Target SS] / KOQ + 1 = [25 * 10 + 20] / 135 + 1 = 3

Actual SS = (3 cards - 1) * 135 - (25 * 10) = 20

Expected Min Inventory = SS = 20

Expected Avg Inventory = KOQ / 2 + SS = 135 / 2 + 20 = 87.5

Expected Max Inventory = KOQ + SS = 135 + 20 = 155

The sawtooth is in Figure 9-2. These are much better results just from dividing the 2-card order quantity in half, but this was just a guess. Instead of guessing, we should use target lead time to set the order quantity, at the top of the next page.

Standard lead time is 25 but target lead time is 5 days. We'll set target safety stock as a percentage of target lead-time demand, a topic we'll cover in more detail in a later chapter.

KOQ = [(Target LT * DD) + (1 + Target SS %)] = [(5 day target LT * 10 / day) * (1 + 20/250) = 50 * 1.08 = 54 with no MOQ or SPQ limits

A KOQ of 54 makes sense. Target lead time is 5 days and we use 10 per day, so our order quantity should be in the 50-60 range, including safety stock.

Extended Example from Sawtooth Curve Chapter (continued from previous page)

cards = [(actual LT * DD) * (1 + Target SS %)] = [(25 days * 10/day) * (1.08)] / 54] + 1
= 270/ 54 + 1 = 5 + 1 = 6 cards

Actual SS = (# cards - 1) * KOQ - (LT * DD) = (6 - 1) * 54 - (10 * 25) = 270 - 250 = 20

We achieve the right target safety stock since we didn't round the number of cards to an integer, nor did we round kanban order quantity for MOQ or SPQ. Look at the sawtooth curve for 6 cards at 54 per card in Figure 9-3.

Figure 9-3. Sawtooth Curve, KOQ 54

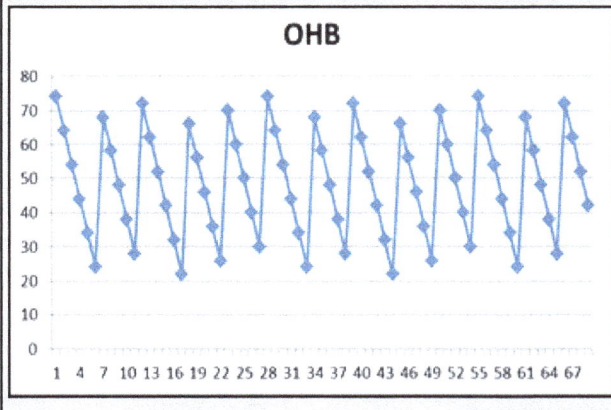

OHB

We trigger an order every 5 or 6 days.

Expected Max inventory = 54 + 20 = 74

Expected average inventory = 54 / 2 + 20 = 47

Expected minimum is still 20 units of safety stock

Remember that we did not round the order quantity in this example, which is rare. There was no unintended safety stock from rounding the order quantity or card count.

HINT for Associates

A recommended or resize KOQ is based on <u>actual</u> lead time and <u>current</u> daily demand, rounded for minimum order and standard package quantity limits.

An ideal order quantity is based on <u>target</u> lead time with no quantity limits.

Though actual lead time is important, a low KOQ is the best lever for improving a recommended kanban solution because a long actual lead time can be addressed by a multi-card kanban solution, but high order quantity limits can't be overcome.

Focus on achieving reasonable minimum order and standard package quantities!

Target Safety Stock

In addition to target lead time and quantities, every ideal kanban solution requires a target safety stock value. The complex and multi-faceted concept is covered in the next section.

Target Lead Time & Quantity Summary

Target lead time is the foundation for kanban solutions and target values must be set with consideration for minimizing inventory while also managing transaction costs. From target lead time, we calculate target minimum order and standard package quantities. Target lead time is generally based on ABC classification plus purchased or manufactured status.

TUTORIAL: GOCO TARGET LEAD TIME

Mary and the Materials team agreed on target lead times for internal parts, purchased parts, vendor managed inventory, and finished goods, in Figure 9-4.

Figure 9-4. Target Lead times in Days

Target LT	P	M
A	5	3
B	10	8
C	20	18
VMI	2	
FG	3	

VMI items were refilled by suppliers at least twice a week so they chose 2 days as the target lead time. Technically it should have been 2.5 days for 2 refills per week, but they knew the items would have some safety stock, so they were comfortable with 2 days.

All work in progress (WIP) and most finished goods could be produced in 3 days if raw material was available, so 3 days was a reasonable goal for A manufactured items and all finished goods.

With target lead times, they established cutoffs for short and medium lead times, in Figure 9-5.

Figure 9-5. LT Categories

LT Categories (Site preference)				
Short LT Category	7.5	If Std LT is less than this number, is Short LT	
Medium LT Category	15	If Std LT is > Short Category but < this number, is Medium LT	

SECTION III. SAFETY STOCK COVERS SUPPLY & DEMAND VARIATION

Target safety stock, or the amount of buffer inventory required to protect on-time delivery from supply and demand variation, is one of the most complex and challenging topics when designing a kanban system or evaluating inventory management models.

Most sites have a sense about the need for safety stock, whether required for supply or demand variation, but it is safer to measure it than to guess.

Yes, the math behind variation analysis and safety stock can be frightening, but if variation is part of your reality it is vital that you understand this complex topic.

Sizing Loop: The Kanban Calculator

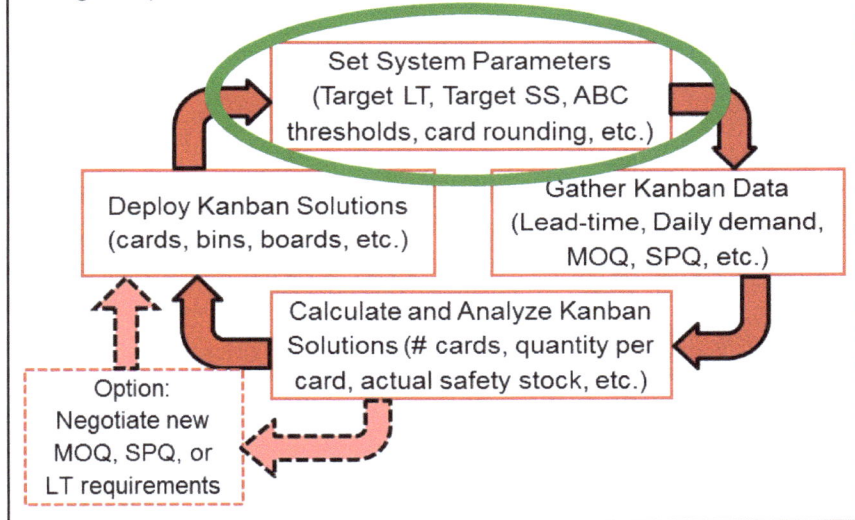

Set System Parameters
(Target LT, Target SS, ABC thresholds, card rounding, etc.)

Gather Kanban Data
(Lead-time, Daily demand, MOQ, SPQ, etc.)

Calculate and Analyze Kanban Solutions (# cards, quantity per card, actual safety stock, etc.)

Deploy Kanban Solutions
(cards, bins, boards, etc.)

Option: Negotiate new MOQ, SPQ, or LT requirements

CHAPTER 10: TARGET SAFETY STOCK CONCEPTS

Safety stock (SS) is added to an inventory plan to prevent stock outs caused by 1) demand that is *higher* or *earlier* than expected or 2) supply that is *lower* or *later* than expected.

Recall from the sawtooth chapter that every item has an expected maximum, minimum, and average on-hand quantity based on the item's demand and replenishment plan. An item's maximum inventory is the top of the sawtooth curve or the volume of the full bucket. (See Figure 10-1 for a basic sawtooth curve at steady state.) Minimum inventory is planned safety stock or the lowest level we expect inventory to reach, and average inventory is halfway between expected maximum inventory and the safety stock value.

Figure 10-1. Steady State Sawtooth Curve

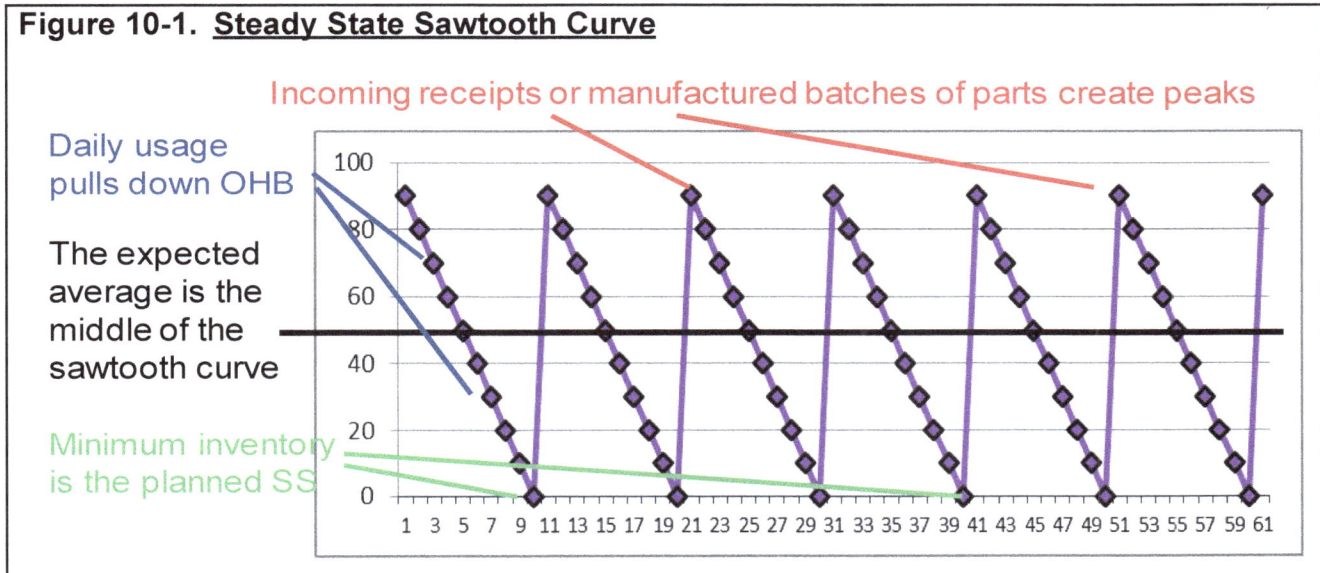

Incoming receipts or manufactured batches of parts create peaks

Daily usage pulls down OHB

The expected average is the middle of the sawtooth curve

Minimum inventory is the planned SS

In order for safety stock to protect delivery it must cover variation in both <u>supply</u> (push variation) and <u>demand</u> (pull variation).

<u>Target safety stock</u> equals the amount of planned replenishment material that exceeds lead-time demand. In the formula box below, target safety stock is added to the quantity [lead time * daily demand] to increase the number of pieces that are replenished during a lead-time period. Target safety stock is included in formulas for kanban order quantity and for the number of required cards.

Basic Kanban Formulas

$$\text{Kanban order quantity 2 cards EaB} = \frac{(\text{Actual LT} * \text{Daily demand} + Target \text{ SS units})}{(2 \text{ cards} - 1)}$$

$$\text{Kanban order quantity 2 cards BaB} = \frac{(\text{Actual LT} * \text{Daily demand} + Target \text{ SS units})}{(2 \text{ cards})}$$

$$\text{\# cards empty a bin} = \frac{(\text{Actual LT} * \text{Daily Demand} + Target \text{ SS units})}{\text{KOQ}} + 1$$

$$\text{\# cards break a bin} = \frac{(\text{Actual LT} * \text{Daily demand} + Target \text{ SS units})}{\text{KOQ}}$$

What Is Variation?

To understand safety stock we must first understand variation. The term "six sigma" has gained popularity in the last few decades and "sigma" is the statistical term for variation or standard deviation. Standard deviation is exactly what it says: the typical variation for a data population, or how far the typical data point varies from the overall mean or average. The formula for sigma or standard deviation is complicated, as listed in the next formula box, but Excel calculates it easily.

Standard Deviation

Math: Standard Deviation = Sigma = s =

$$\sqrt{\sum_{i=1}^{n} \frac{(x_i - \bar{x})^2}{(n-1)}}$$

Instructions: Sum the square of each data point minus the mean, divide that total by the number of observations minus one, and calculate the square root of that result. Got it?

Excel is much easier: STDEV (Values 1 to n)

Standard deviation is always a positive number because it measures the *absolute* value of the gap between data points and the mean, since the difference of a data point minus the mean is squared.

When evaluating a kanban item for required safety stock, the first step is assessing inherent variation for both supply and demand, and standard deviation is the best way to accomplish that.

Variation of supply or demand inserts risk in inventory management plans, making safety stock a necessary additive to protect delivery, but safety stock increases average inventory. It is better to reduce variation instead of covering it with safety stock, but that isn't always possible. When variation can't be avoided, add safety stock.

Supply Variation

Supply or "push" variation is driven by supplier performance. If suppliers miss delivery dates, ship short quantities, or experience quality rejects, safety stock must be present to cover those gaps.

Supply variation generally means there are errors in the supply chain, so adding safety stock to accommodate those errors is a countermeasure that covers one kind of waste (errors) with another (inventory). For this reason, *supply-side safety stock should be a short-term or temporary countermeasure until supply issues are resolved.*

Demand Variation

Demand or "pull" variation is driven by how material is consumed by the customer, either an external or internal consumer. High seasonality, unpredictable mix changes, and high day-to-day volatility can all contribute to the need for safety stock. These risks can be broken into three general categories of demand variation, as in Figure 10-2 on page 121. Day-to-day demand volatility is illustrated in the top chart. The middle chart shows random shifts in average daily demand, and seasonal demand is in the bottom illustration.

Daily Demand Volatility

Demand that bounces up and down from day to day or week to week with no apparent pattern or predictability is classified as daily demand variation. An item with daily volatility can exhibit the same <u>average</u> daily demand over time, but predicting any <u>specific</u> day is challenging due to the randomness, e.g., average demand is 100 but the day-to-day range is zero to 1,000 parts per day.

Daily demand volatility is covered by safety stock.

Figure 10-2. **Demand Variation Patterns**

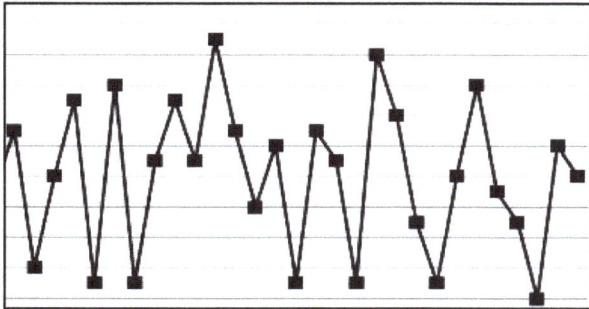

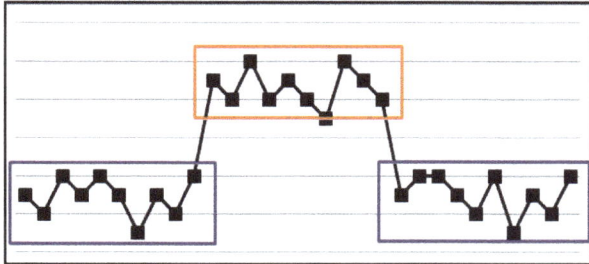

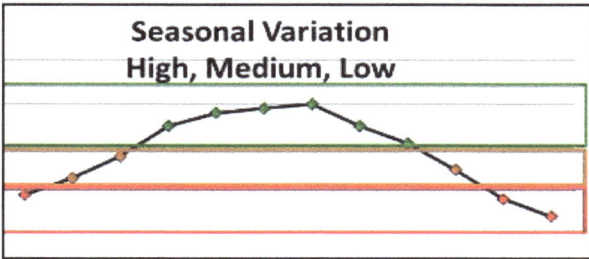

**Seasonal Variation
High, Medium, Low**

If demand shifts are *unpredictable*, e.g., not driven by a defined event, the risk of a *potential* demand change must be covered by higher safety stock. In this case, a shift in daily demand acts like demand volatility because the range for daily demand is as wide as the highest to the lowest average daily demand, so safety stock can be used to cover that wide range.

Seasonal Variation

In seasonal variation, <u>average daily demand</u> experiences somewhat predictable changes due to weather (snow plows), seasons (boating season), events (recurring sporting events, the start of the school year), and holidays (Valentine's Day or New Year's Day).

In general, seasonal variation is covered by resizing kanban solutions, using multi-card solutions to allow for easy resizing via card count changes. Adding enough safety stock year-round to cover seasonal demand shifts is <u>not</u> a good plan!

Average Daily Demand Shifts

Shifts in average daily demand can occur at any time with no predictable link to time of year, season, holidays, events, etc. Marketing promotions or price incentives often generate demand shifts but these changes do not necessarily connect to a seasonal factor. Changes in the overall economy can also move average demand up or down.

The biggest difference between daily demand volatility and daily demand shifts is that day to day volatility hovers around the same average daily demand, while a shift in demand actually moves average daily demand up or down.

If daily demand shifts can be *predicted* they should be covered by resizing kanban solutions in advance of the change. Items that experience *frequent* but *predictable* shifts should be on multi-card kanban solutions to allow for regular resizing via adding or subtracting active kanban cards.

HINT for Associates

In general, use historical data for demand variation analysis instead of forecast data. Forecasts are always unconfirmed (a guess) so they automatically introduce uncertainty. Additionally, they might not reflect all demand sources, such as Engineering or Sales samples or process scrap.

One caution to keep in mind is that in order for kanban solutions and demand variation analysis to be accurate, historical demand data must be representative of current and near-term business conditions, so don't reach too far into history.

If historical demand is truly unrelated to the expected future demand, you must use forecasted demand for calculating kanban solutions, but demand variation analysis might still be based on historical demand. Be smart about this.

Target Safety Stock Versus Actual Safety Stock

Target safety stock is the required buffer for an item that exhibits supply and/or demand volatility. It can be assigned to individual items or to groups of parts, and it can be calculated or estimated.

Target safety stock must be distinguished from *actual* safety stock. Kanban formulas include a factor for target safety stock, but order quantities and card counts are almost always rounded so a deployed kanban solution often differs from the originally calculated and "un-rounded" solution. This can result in higher or lower actual safety stock versus the target for safety stock.

Actual safety stock is calculated by comparing the total number of pieces acquired during a lead-time period versus the expected demand in that period, and the formula changes based on the kind of kanban solution.

> Actual Safety Stock
>
> 2 or more cards, EaB Actual SS = (# cards - 1) * KOQ - (Actual LT * Current DD)
>
> 2 or more cards, BaB Actual SS = (# cards * KOQ) - (Actual LT * Current DD)
>
> 1 card Actual SS = Reorder Point - (Actual LT * Current Daily Demand)

When deploying kanban solutions, it is absolutely necessary to confirm actual safety stock is greater than zero, to prevent stock-out risk. We'll cover this in the section about analyzing kanban solutions.

Ways to Express Target Safety Stock

Recall the kanban order quantity formulas for empty a bin and break a bin solutions, listed at the beginning of this chapter. The safety stock variable in these formulas is <u>target</u> safety stock, or how much buffer inventory is needed in the kanban plan to protect customer delivery from supply and demand variation. The same is true for formulas that calculate the number of kanban cards.

In these formulas, safety stock must be in *units of measure*, i.e., pieces or kilograms, but target safety stock isn't always expressed in units of measure for a kanban item. Therefore, it's important to understand how safety stock can be expressed before calculating kanban solutions.

Target Safety Stock in Units of Measure

In the formulas on page 119, safety stock is in the same units of measure as daily demand, e.g., safety stock equals 100 pounds and daily demand is also in pounds. Though this is how target safety stock is expressed in many kanban formulas, it is not the most common way to express target safety stock because it isn't very insightful. One hundred pieces of target safety stock for an item that consumes 1,000 per day is very different than 100 pieces of safety stock for an item that uses 10 per day, so expressing safety stock in units is not very informative to a kanban practitioner.

However, there are specific scenarios that fit well with a unit of measure safety stock target. Suppose we periodically sell a box of 50 aftermarket parts of an item that is primarily used in original equipment manufacturing (OEM) shipments. We win more aftermarket orders if we can meet a 3-day lead time from customer order to shipment. We might elect to add 50 <u>pieces</u> of safety stock to the kanban solution to increase the chance that parts will be in stock when aftermarket requests arrive. This adds a specific *quantity* to the kanban solution to provide aftermarket coverage.

The risk with adding random units of measure as safety stock is that the calculated average daily demand would likely have included historical OEM <u>and</u> aftermarket orders, unless different part numbers are used for each type of usage, so adding a full 50 pieces of safety stock specifically for aftermarket orders is more safety stock than is actually needed, but it should provide the desired on-hand inventory to cover both types of orders.

Target Safety Stock in Days of Demand

Expressing safety stock as a number of days of demand, e.g., target safety stock equals two days of demand, is the most common method for defining and communicating target safety stock. When expressed in days, the safety stock variable in kanban formulas must be replaced by [Target safety stock days * Daily demand] to convert to units of measure, e.g., convert from days of demand to kilograms of demand by multiplying target safety stock days by daily demand in kilograms.

Target safety stock in days of demand makes it easy to communicate, calculate, and compare safety stock targets across numerous items.

Safety Stock in Pieces Versus Days of Demand

Items TUV and XYZ have standard deviations equal to 50 pieces each for their 2-week lead times, but TUV consumes 100 parts in two weeks (10 per day) while XYZ consumes 1,000 (100 per day). We can't imply that target safety stock for the two parts is equivalent because they both need 50 <u>pieces</u> of safety stock, but we can compare <u>days</u> of safety stock.

Part number TUV needs 50 pieces at an average demand of 10 per day, or 5.0 days of safety stock, while XYZ needs 50 pieces at 100 per day, or 0.5 days of safety stock. Obviously, item TUV is much more volatile.

Target Safety Stock As a Percent of Lead Time

Target safety stock as a percent of lead time demand, e.g., 20% of a 10-day lead time is two days of safety stock, is useful in certain circumstances such as multi-card solutions, which we'll discuss later. In fact, for multi-card solutions this approach is the correct mathematical solution.

For items that do not need a multi-card solution, defining safety stock based on lead time can be driven by either demand or delivery risk. At first it seems like an oxymoron to use *supplier* lead time or lead-time demand to estimate target safety stock that's supposed to cover *demand* risk, but the logic is that in many cases a longer lead time makes it more difficult to <u>predict</u> what daily demand will be when the parts actually arrive. For example, it's easier to predict daily demand for the next two weeks than for ten weeks from now, so long lead-time items might need more safety stock to cover a potential increase in *average daily demand*, in additional to or instead of safety stock to cover a potential increase in *demand variation*. Yes, it's a little confusing.

In addition to implying more demand risk, sometimes lead time is a proxy for supply complexity, i.e., an item with a 40-day lead time is fundamentally more complex to produce than an item with a 5-day lead time, so *supply* risk increases with lead time. Higher risk implies more safety stock, so it's convenient that safety stock as a percent of lead time automatically increases safety stock coverage as lead time extends.

When safety stock is measured as a percent of lead time, it doesn't necessarily imply that lead time is the *source* of the variation

---

Lead Time and Demand Variation

We have numerous C items with low demand that is erratic. The supplier does not hold raw material to produce these items so they have long lead times because the supplier must procure material (25 days) then process it to completion (another 15 days). The long lead time is due to the erratic demand and the lack of raw material, so it would be erroneous to conclude that high variation is a function of the long lead time. Actually it's the opposite; the long lead time is a function of the erratic demand.

ABC Classification & Target Safety Stock

ABC classification is often a deciding factor for assigning target safety stock.

Suppose we define a simple safety stock rule to add 20% to the lead-time demand, or [safety stock = 20% * lead time * daily demand]. If an item consumes 100 parts in one lead-time period, we order 120 during that time to provide the extra 20%.

This approach is easy to explain and execute, but does it make sense to have the same safety stock philosophy for a $200 circuit board and a 2¢ steel washer?

Twenty percent of an item that costs $100 per month is much less money below the sawtooth curve than 20% of an item that costs $100,000 per month. So, to minimize on-hand dollars while protecting delivery, safety stock must be added judiciously.

A items generally have less planned safety stock than B items, which have less than C items. The exception to this rule is if A items demonstrate more variation than B or C items, but that is rather rare.

Demand Variation Target Safety Stock Usually Set for Groups of Items

The easiest way to assign target safety stock to items in a kanban calculator is to create a reference table that defines *target safety stock based on parameters* that exist for every part number that needs a target safety stock value. When grouping items to assign safety stock, many sites use ABC classification, purchased versus manufactured status, customer channel, or other basic parameters.

Figure 10-3 contains three sample reference tables for use by a kanban calculator. The first table assigns target safety stock by the market being served: pharmaceutical, food, or water treatment. The second table assigns days of safety stock by ABC classification and purchased or manufactured status, e.g., purchased A items or manufactured C items. The third table is safety stock by ABC classification versus short, medium, or long lead-time categories.

Figure 10-3. Target SS Examples

Market	SS Days
Pharmaceutical	7
Food	2
Water Treat	1

SS Days	Purch	Manf
A	2	1
B	3	2
C	4	3

SS Days	Short LT	Med LT	Long LT
A	1	3	4
B	2	5	6
C	4	8	9

When using any of these tables, a kanban calculator could use a VLOOKUP or INDEX function to find the right target safety stock value for any item in the population of part numbers. In any case, every possible safety stock scenario must be covered by the reference table.

The alternative to a table is to assign safety stock for every individual part number, which is incredibly cumbersome and generally unnecessary because most populations have patterns of variation. We'll discuss this later.

Target safety stock can be assigned in groups for both supply and demand variation, but it is more common for demand variation.

Demand Target Safety Stock: Group Items Based on Demand Variation

Sorting items according to demand variation patterns or behavior is quite common, but using sub-groups for target safety stock only works if parts within each sub-group exhibit similar variation characteristics.

There are many potential grouping options for target safety stock, and demand variation must be measured in days of demand.

Options for Finding Similar Demand Variation

Every population of items is unique so there is no universal answer for defining groups of parts that exhibit similar demand variation patterns, but certain parameters deserve consideration due to a tendency to correlate with demand variation.

- ABC classification
- Purchased vs. manufactured
- Industry or market, e.g., Textile, Automotive, or Aerospace
- Channel
  - » OEM versus Service
  - » Retail versus Distribution
  - » Business versus Consumer
- Product family or value stream
  - » Steel, Aluminum, or Brass
  - » Motors, Sensors, or Displays
- Geography, e.g., North America, Europe, Pacific Rim, Latin America, Africa, etc.

The list of examples could go on and on but suffice to say that potential groups should be defined based on common sense for the business. (Common sense is always a great analytical tool.) If we know intuitively that Textile demand is more volatile than Automotive, don't assign equivalent target safety stock to those two divergent groups of items.

Let's review a few categories in more detail.

1. ABC Classification is probably the most broadly applied categorization for demand variation because it is common for lower usage parts to have higher variation when measured as days of demand, so C parts often exhibit higher variation than A items, and B items fall somewhere in between.

2. Purchased Versus Manufactured: Internal and external parts generally exhibit different variation patterns, but this is often related to the pooled demand effect mentioned above.

a. Purchased parts exhibit lower variation if they are used across multiple demand streams. This is particularly valid for generic things like screws, cardboard packing material, or coil steel. These might be used on numerous customer channels or product families, which can have a damping effect on the variation from any single end-product, value stream, customer, or channel.

b. It is possible for purchased parts as a group to have more variation than manufactured parts, but it isn't common. Higher volatility for certain purchased parts can occur if items are purchased for a volatile end-market, but it generally isn't a universal characteristic for all purchased parts. If an automotive aftermarket business supplies purchased parts for the Ford Model T, those items would be very erratic compared to manufactured parts for a late-model Toyota, but the volatility would be a feature of the market served not the purchased versus manufactured status. Be careful not to assign causation to the wrong indicator.

HINT for Associates

Some sites elect to assign lower safety stock for manufactured parts because there is more control over when internal parts are delivered and how they can be expedited. This assumes that an internal cell can respond more effectively to expedite requests, but the other underlying assumption with this philosophy is that expediting is an answer to demand variation. Yikes! Expediting is not the appropriate planned response for demand or supply variation.

Manufactured parts might have less supply variation, which can reduce the overall need for safety stock, but they usually have higher demand variation. Don't mix two safety stock decisions inappropriately. Instead, clarify if lower overall variation for manufactured items is due to lower supply variation, not lower demand variation. If manufactured parts experience fewer stock outs than purchased parts, it might be true that internal cells are better at supplying parts, not that manufactured parts are less volatile.

3. Universal Versus Niche Items: Universal or generic items experience "pooled" demand, or demand from numerous customer streams, while "niche" components have narrower demand streams.

Diversified end-markets or customers that experience independent demand don't generally exhibit the same demand ups and downs, either in timing or amplitude, so a diversified and pooled demand stream shouldn't experience <u>simultaneous</u> peaks and valleys from different market segments. If an item is used for aerospace and automotive applications, we don't expect those two markets to move up and down in lock step. A steel bracket used in five different market segments should exhibit lower variation than a bracket used in just one market.

This does not mean that independent demand streams can't or won't have similar demand <u>cycles</u>. Macro-economic factors can impact even the most unrelated markets, but from a variation perspective a pooled demand stream should exhibit less day-to-day variation than a demand stream for a narrow market.

Niche components are used in narrow applications (think antique sewing machines) and they exhibit the same demand variation as their parent demand product or value stream, so if that parent product is highly volatile the niche components will be as well.

Though the universal versus niche concept is generally valid, it can be difficult to categorize individual items as universal or niche, which can make it challenging to utilize this grouping option since every item would have to be classified as Universal, Automotive, Aerospace, Textile, etc., in order to utilize a reference table based on market served. If this kind of segmentation is utilized, entering a "Market" or "Industry" code in a specific field in the item master is a viable option.

4. <u>Product Family</u> or value stream can also be an insightful way to subdivide parts, and this is essentially a subset of the universal versus niche segmentation. With the right market intelligence, we might group parts by industry (e.g., automotive versus aerospace), channel (distribution versus wholesale versus retail), end user (consumers or businesses), etc. There are many options for this segmentation so each business must define segmentations that might fit.

When segregating parts based on product family or value stream, there are usually items that cross multiple segments and exhibit lower variation from the pooled demand effect. For those components, it is wise to create a "general" classification to designate parts that are used in multiple seg-

ments and therefore require less safety stock, as in the universal versus niche discussion above.

Like universal versus niche, if product family or value stream is the right segmentation, consider using an item master field to assign the correct category to every item, e.g., the "Family" field indicates Automotive, Aerospace, or General.

5. <u>Service vs. OEM</u>: If an item is sold to original equipment manufacturers (OEM) and also ships as a standalone component for service or aftermarket orders, it is likely to have different variation patterns for service shipments versus OEM. (When you hear "OEM", think Chevrolet, Honda, Kubota, John Deere, Ingersoll Rand, Parker Hannifin, Siemens, Eaton, Dell, Apple, etc. These manufacturers purchase components for use in their manufactured equipment.) Manufacturers with a strong aftermarket business will experience significant parts demand on top of their OEM demand. Imagine the service parts business for a company like John Deere, as compared to Apple.

Like product family or value stream, there is no universal rule for service versus OEM but it's wise to test this characteristic as a possible demand variation grouping if service shipments are a significant portion of demand.

6. <u>Geography</u>: Geographic markets can exhibit different demand variation for a couple reasons. One market might be early in the adoption stage for a product, while another market is more fully penetrated, and a new market generally has higher volatility. One market might have strong brand loyalty, which dampens volatility, while another market is more affected by competitive advertising or price cuts, which can add volatility.

Geography can be difficult to utilize for item groupings, particularly if some part numbers are used in more than one geographical region, but a field in the item master can be used to designate the right geographic segmentation. Like product family groupings, it is beneficial to include a "universal" category for items that cross numerous geographies.

7. <u>Short, Medium, & Long Lead Time</u>: As discussed before, in most cases lead time is <u>not</u> a factor that drives demand variation since lead time is a supply feature and demand variation is a demand characteristic, but there is often an *apparent* correlation between demand variation and

lead time. Usually the correlation between lead time and demand variation is a false indicator, meaning it isn't actually the lead time that drives the variation, but rather the type of parts that have long lead times and also have high variation.

Evaluate Grouping Options for Range & Overlap

After defining grouping options, it is necessary to select the right parameters for segmentation. To do this, we need to assess each grouping option to see if demand variation is consistent across the segmenting option, analyzing for both the range of demand variation (e.g., A items range from two to four days of demand variation) as well as the overlap from sub-group to sub-group (e.g., A items have two to four days of demand variation and B items have two to five days of variation).

A wide range of demand variation within a sub-group indicates that items within that group don't behave similarly. If A items have demand variation that ranges from two days up to ten days, it isn't reasonable to assume that A items behave similarly when it comes to demand variation. Wide ranges are not a good fit when the purpose is to find items with similar demand variation.

The other consideration is how much overlap there is from one sub-group to the next. If every sub-group has similar variation, i.e., the range of minimum to maximum days of demand variation is consistent from sub-group to sub-group, the groupings are meaningless. Some level of overlap is usually present, perhaps two or three sub-groups overlap and others diverge, but minimal overlap is preferred.

The best grouping option is the combination of parameters that exhibit the narrowest ranges and least overlap. We'll spend more time on this in the demand variation chapters.

Assign Logical Target Safety Stock Groups

Once demand variation groups are finalized, it has to be straightforward to assign parts to the appropriate group. Think about how to create a reference table for the kanban calculator.

1. Groups should be mutually exclusive whenever possible, so an item doesn't belong to multiple groups. The kanban calculator must be able to easily assign the right group to every part number.

2. Don't define groups that are so cumbersome that they are impossible to manage. More than a dozen sub-groups becomes unwieldy unless part number data is extremely easy to manage in an automated way. If we can assign a part number to a group by combining one feature with another, e.g., ABC classification plus product family, it's easy to manage, but if group assignments require extensive analysis it is likely that mistakes will occur and the data won't be kept up to date. In general, don't try to assign groups that require more than two or three parameters. ABC classification plus purchased versus manufactured (P/M) would be easy to manage. ABC plus P/M plus value stream plus geography would be a mess.

Group Assignment Example

A site concludes that purchased or manufactured coupled with OEM and Service sales are the best product groupings. Every item has a code in the item master where O = OEM, S = Service, and O+S = OEM + Service. Purchased or manufactured status is also known, so any part number is assigned to one of six demand variation groups:

P / O	P / S	P / (O+S)	M / O	M / S	M / (O+S)
Purchased	Purchased	Purchased	Manufactured	Manufactured	Manufactured
OEM	Service	OEM & Service	OEM	Service	OEM & Service

Supply Target Safety Stock: Group Items Based on Supply Variation

When evaluating supply-side variation, don't assume that all items from a supplier have the same supply risk. Sometimes items from a supplier share a common risk factor based on that supplier, e.g., parts from Acme Axles or internal assemblies built by the motor cell are always late, but this is not as common as supply risk for individual items. Therefore, it is not as common to group items based on *supplier* when assigning target safety stock. Most cases require target safety stock values by part number for supply-side risk.

Supply Risk by Supplier

Items from Steve's Spades demonstrate universal supply risk because the supplier tends to miss due dates on everything they ship. For this supplier, group items based on supplier name to assign supply-side safety stock, but do this only until Steve's delivery issues are solved. If they don't fix the issues, find a more reliable supplier!

Items from Shane's Shovels are generally on-time and generate little supply risk, except for one part number with a risky manufacturing process. In this case, items from Shane's Shovels don't require universal supply-side safety stock, but one item warrants special treatment.

Zero Target Safety Stock?

Technically it is possible for kanban solutions to exist without safety stock. If daily or random demand variation is low and supply risk does not exist, kanban solutions can be deployed without safety stock but this requires very stable demand, highly accurate forecasts, or very long customer lead times. When in doubt, include a small amount of safety stock as a precaution against delivery risks and reduce safety stock over time if it proves to be too high.

Target Safety Stock Concept Summary

Safety stock exists to protect customer deliveries against variation in either supply or demand. We must quantify push (supply) and pull (demand) risks accurately so we can assign target safety stock to each impacted item.

Demand safety stock is usually assigned in days of demand to groups of items. Each business must determine the right segmentation to group items with similar demand variation.

TUTORIAL: GOCO SAFETY STOCK UNITS & GROUPS

The Materials team agreed that expressing target and actual safety stock in "days of demand" was the right choice for GOCO part numbers. They also thought there were a couple grouping options that would exhibit similar demand variation patterns, specifically the different markets served (industrial versus automotive versus agriculture.) They suspected that there might be more variation in manufactured parts than in purchased parts.

There saw very little supply-side risk, since most of their suppliers shipped on time with high quality.

To be safe, they set aside plenty of time to complete supply and demand variation analysis to confirm their assumptions.

CHAPTER 11: TARGET SAFETY STOCK FOR SUPPLY VARIATION

Supply or "push" variation can exist for external or internal suppliers due to any one of three potential supply errors.

1. Late shipments: receipts that miss due dates.

2. Short shipments: received quantity is less than what was ordered.

3. Poor quality: rejecting or reworking some or all of a receipt.

A reliable supplier should require no safety stock because lead times, shipping quantities, and product quality should be accurate. Shipments that *meet all criteria* are the standard expectation for supplier performance, and therefore adding target safety stock for suppliers should only be used as a short-term fix.

Low or high quantities should not be a repetitive occurrence and therefore should not add safety stock.

• If suppliers ship short in order to meet the promised due date, it is a due date issue, not a quantity problem. If imposed due dates are sooner than what the supplier requires, adjust the allowed lead time so the supplier can ship the correct quantity on time.

• If shipments are short because order quantities don't adhere to minimum order, maximum order, or standard package quantities, fix the rounding process for order quantities.

For lead time and quality gaps, analyze the data to assess the impact, then size target safety stock accordingly.

Supplier Lead-Time Safety Stock

Before going through a lot of analysis, remember that the ultimate goal is to eliminate lead-time safety stock, and there are a couple ways this can be accomplished.

1. Ask the supplier what lead time they can consistently meet, then use that number. This lead time should be no longer than the longest observed time in recent history. This is the most collaborative approach and the supplier's commitment should eliminate the need for any lead-time safety stock.

2. Assign a lead time equal to the maximum observed lead time in recent history, and eliminate the need for safety stock. This approach impacts kanban calculations, raising the order quantity and the height of sawtooth curve due to picking the longest lead time, so it is generally not preferred. This also runs the risk of early deliveries, so with this method you must instruct the supplier to ship on the due date and not before. Early shipments cause problems for storage space, because early shipments mean a higher level of inventory than what is planned.

HINT for Associates

As discussed in prior chapters, target and actual lead times are extremely important for kanban solutions, so ask suppliers to meet target lead times. If target lead times are not feasible, ask suppliers to commit to an achievable lead time for every item.

Supplier lead time can be analyzed based on performance in the recent past, and this data should be readily available. Capture the number of days for a typical delivery from order entry to receipt. Look at each supplier's overall performance across all items that they supply, and also look at individual items.

HINT for Associates

Supplier lead time days should be measured in the same method used for daily demand.

If daily demand is in workdays, e.g., monthly demand divided by 20 workdays per month equals average daily demand, then lead time is also in workdays.

For lead time analysis and calculating kanban solutions, lead time must be from order entry to receipt. For external suppliers, lead time includes transit time.

To evaluate lead time and calculate kanban solutions, we need accurate data for every item. If a supplier always delivers in about 18 days, don't calculate a kanban solution based on a 15-day lead time simply because we *wish* actual lead time was 15 days or because the supplier says they will *soon* achieve 15 days. It's reasonable for 15 days to be the target lead time for negotiation purposes but use the actual lead time of 18 days in the kanban calculator.

HINT for Associates

When calculating kanban solutions, don't use a lead time that is shorter than actual lead time then inflate safety stock to cover the erroneous lead time.

Never lie to the kanban calculator!

Supply lead-time safety stock covers supply <u>variation</u>, which is based on actual or "observed" lead times. Therefore, measure the standard deviation of a series of actual lead times using Excel's STDEV function.

Supplier Lead-Time Variation

Supplier lead-time variation
$$= STDEV (LT_1, LT_2, LT_3...LT_n)$$

LT_1 to LT_n are actual lead times over the analysis period for the item being analyzed

---

One way to benchmark the amount of variation is to compare standard deviation to average lead time to decide how big the risk is. If standard deviation is low compared to total lead time, up to about 10% of average lead time, there likely isn't enough variation to justify safety stock. Remember that lead-time deviation is a result of early *and* late deliveries and only late deliveries are a stock out risk.

Lead-Time Risk Based on Lead-Time Standard Deviation

Lead-time Standard Deviation Ratio
= LT standard deviation / Average LT

HINT for Associates

If lead-time standard deviation is greater than 10% of average lead time, contact the supplier and ask them to commit to a lead time they can achieve then hold them to that lead time. If they continue to exhibit high variation, inform them of the consequences of their unsatisfactory performance and if they fail to correct the error, replace them with a more reliable source.

If supplier lead-time performance is erratic after attempts to encourage them to hit due dates, there are a couple options for setting target safety stock.

1. Set target safety stock equal to the calculated standard deviation of delivery times. If average lead time is 12 days and standard deviation is two days, use 12 days as actual lead time and add two days of safety stock. Standard deviation was calculated based on all variation, both late and early shipments, so two days might be more buffer than is needed. Try it for a while and reduce it when possible.

2. Measure standard deviation for just the shipments that arrived late and use that number for safety stock. This is a safe approach but the underlying assumption is that late deliveries are a permanent problem, and that should not be the case for reliable suppliers. Use reliable suppliers!

HINT for Associates

Supplier conversations should be collaborative. Don't bully your suppliers!

HINT for Associates

When calculating average lead time or lead-time variation by supplier, don't blame suppliers for imposed expediting activity and erratic due dates. If we regularly place orders with due dates based on a supplier's standard lead times then beg for early shipment, we are contributing to their variation. Standard lead time might be 15 days but if we ask them to rush 50% of their orders, they show high lead-time variation and probably demonstrate an average LT that is less than the standard 15 days.

When setting standard lead time, ask the supplier to verify how much time they need, <u>outside</u> of any expedite activity. Maybe they promised a 15 day lead time in the past because they knew we expedite frequently, so committing to 15 days when they could actually do 12 made them look like heros! Use the correct lead time and stop expediting.

If expediting is a constant reality, find the root cause and solve that problem.

• Driven by demand variation? Add demand safety stock.

• Driven by incorrect on-hand balances in MRP? Kanban solves that with replenishment based on actual on-hand balances and point-of-use replenishment triggers.

• Orders not being placed on time? Ensure that orders are processed quickly. If on MRP, respond to MRP exception reports immediately. If on kanban, process triggers at least two times per shift.

Supplier Quality Safety Stock

Quality errors exist even in the best supply chains, but they should be rare. It's also true that not every quality issue justifies adding safety stock.

Rule of Thumb

In most cases, rejecting less than 1-2% of received orders requires no safety stock.

If safety stock is necessary for quality variation, i.e., rejects or rework for certain items, follow these basic steps.

1. Quantify the percentage of a particular item's deliveries that exhibit a quality problem. This isn't the percent of *parts* that are rejected, but the percent of *orders* that have rejects within the shipment. This scopes the reject occurrence rate for an item. We want this to be less than 2%.

2. Determine the required action when an incoming receipt contains rejects.

a. If only a portion of an order is rejected and parts are sorted in order to use the good ones, production continues while bad parts are replaced by the supplier, so there is no immediate stock out risk if the reject rate is low. If the supplier provides replacement parts quickly, safety stock shouldn't be necessary.

b. If a rejected order is automatically sent back to the supplier without sorting good from bad parts, immediate replacement parts are required for every rejected delivery. For this case, quantify how many days it takes for the supplier to replace a rejected shipment.

3. For quality issues that result in stock-out risk, as in paragraph 2.b above, add "quality" safety stock.

a. Shift the safety stock requirement to the supplier by requiring risky suppliers to stock additional finished goods at their site for immediate shipment in the event of a quality reject.

b. If the option in 3.a isn't possible, add minimal safety stock equal to a multiple of the answer to #1 (the percent of orders with a quality issue) times the answer to #2.b (number of days for replacement parts to arrive). Suppose 10% of an item's receipts have quality issues and it takes an average of five days to recover. Supplier quality safety stock is [10% * 5 days = 0.5] days of safety stock.

c. For some sites, the minimal safety stock in paragraph 3.b is too risky. Instead, the required safety stock is the entire expected delay, e.g., 5 days in this example. In other words, even though only 10% of orders have rejects, add safety stock for the total time it takes to receive replacement parts. This drives very high inventory levels so it should not be a long term solution. Fix or replace the supplier!

Suppliers usually need more time to correct quality issues than to address lead time, so safety stock for quality is more common than lead-time safety stock, but it should still be short term.

HINT for Associates

Don't add supplier lead-time or quality safety stock without first contacting the supplier to clarify expectations. Kanban activity sometimes highlights issues that were overlooked in the past and suppliers deserve fair notice that commitments must be met. Have an open conversation before adding safety stock or extending lead times. Supplier safety stock should be rare and short term. Don't carry extra inventory to cover supplier mistakes.

Supplier Target Safety Stock Summary

Supplier safety stock should be rare and only deployed as a short-term fix.

• <u>Safety stock to cover inaccurate quantities should not occur</u> because suppliers should fix this immediately, even if it means granting a longer lead time for the standard order quantity.

• <u>Safety stock for lead time issues should be short term</u>, only until the delivery issues are addressed by the supplier.

• <u>Safety stock for quality issues is sometimes necessary but it shouldn't be permanent</u>. Don't allow the supplier to push the burden of poor quality onto the kanban system. Instead, make them carry additional inventory at their site to protect inventory and delivery performance.

See Figure 11-1 for a supply-side safety stock decision tree.

Figure 11-1. <u>Supply Safety Stock Decision Tree</u>

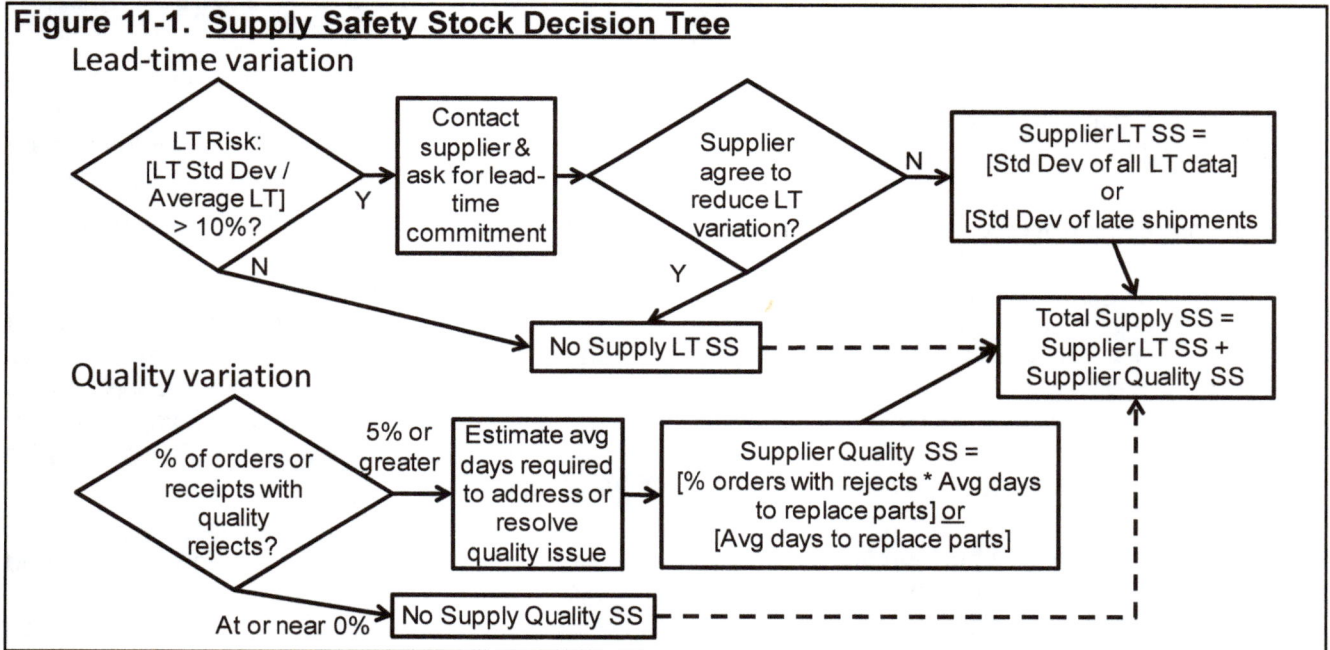

TUTORIAL: GOCO SUPPLIER SAFETY STOCK

GOCO suppliers demonstrated very reliable quality and delivery. There were some *internal* quality concerns but Operations was tackling those, so Mary didn't believe they needed supplier safety stock for the initial kanban roll-out.

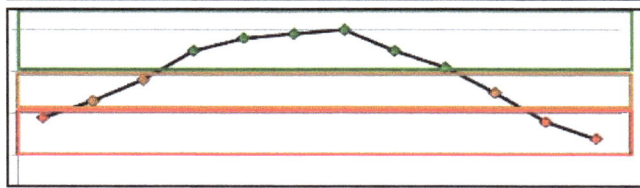

CHAPTER 12: SEASONAL DEMAND VARIATION

Before we can evaluate day-to-day demand variation we need to determine if seasonal demand variation is present, because seasonality changes the process for analyzing demand variation.

Seasonal demand variation means there are times of the year when business is slow and other times when it is more active. (Think lawn mowers and snow shovels.)

For this discussion, seasonal variation does not refer to businesses or products that only operate for part of the year. Christmas trees have infinite variation because the demand for November and December is infinitely greater than January through October, when the business is closed.

What Is Seasonality?

Seasonal variation means the demand in one portion of the year is much higher—or lower, depending on how we look at it—than the rest of the year. Seasonal variation is present if a chart of monthly, weekly, or daily demand for one or more years exhibits a pattern of high and low periods that consistently align with certain times of the year, e.g., Christmas or snow skiing season is always high or summer is always low.

Figure 12-1 has two illustrations of average daily demand by month for January through December. The business on top is weak in the winter, medium in spring and fall, and strong in the summer. Note that medium demand occurs in two time periods, February and March plus October for a total of three months, but those medium months are not sequential. We could dismiss those medium months and conclude that the top chart has just high and low periods. But, sometimes identifying an "average" time of year or medium demand lev-

el is advantageous for estimating what "normal" looks like.

Demand in the bottom chart exists in the extremes, either high or low, with an abrupt spike from March to April, a strong summer season, then a steep drop from September to October. This business is strong in the summer and weak from October through March and there is no obvious average or medium period.

Figure 12-1. Seasonal Variation

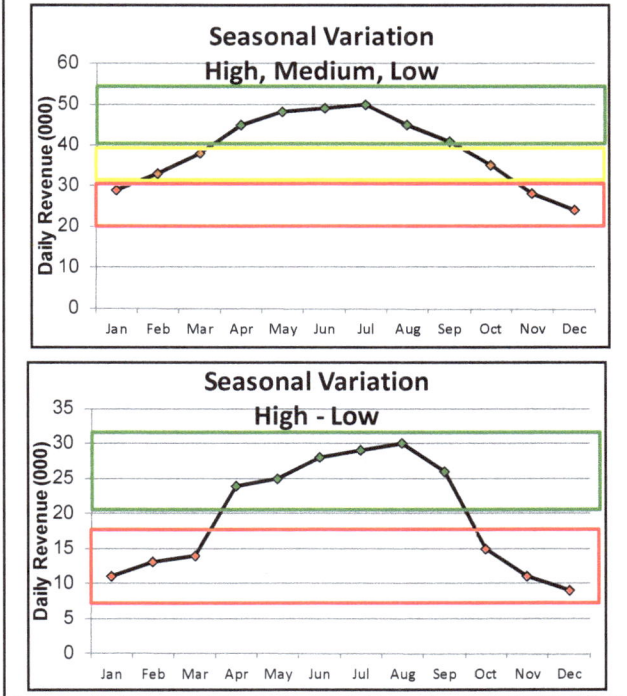

As you might expect, there is a process for analyzing seasonality.

How to Check for Seasonality

1. Gather one year of revenue data for all finished good items that are potentially impacted by seasonal demand changes.

a. To study seasonality we need at least 12 months of demand data. Don't look at the latest *calendar* year. Instead use the most recent 12 months of demand.

Most sites know intuitively if seasonal demand exists, but use 24 or 36 months of data if it is necessary to confirm the seasonal pattern over more than one year.

Demand history is easier if it's reported in monthly buckets. Weekly buckets work, but they are more difficult to analyze due to the higher number of data points per item and per season.

b. When aggregating across numerous items, seasonality is analyzed in revenue instead of units of measure. If a two-cent gasket goes from shipping 1,000 per day in the summer to 1,500 per day all winter, don't let that high daily demand in units mask seasonal changes in other more expensive items that ship in *lower* quantities. The gasket will still be treated and planned as a seasonal item, but look for patterns at the higher spend level, where the money lives.

c. Finished goods is where seasonality is studied because they are the only items with direct links to customer demand, while raw material and work in progress are at least one step removed from customer pull signals.

• If some finished good items are flat (think underwear) while others are seasonal (think snow suits), segregate the FG items and evaluate just the seasonal items so nonseasonal items don't dampen seasonal peaks and valleys. It can be difficult to sort items to just the seasonal ones, but it is a beneficial step if it's feasible.

• If the presence of seasonality can't be predefined or if it is impossible to sort items to just those that exhibit seasonality, study all finished goods. This kind of "aggregate" analysis works, but the process must result in a viable method to categorize individual items as seasonal or nonseasonal based on mathematical results.

d. Avoid using forecast data for seasonality analysis because it is never as accurate as actual usage. If future demand is expected to differ dramatically from past demand, the forecast is even more suspect because it is not based on anything concrete unless actual customer orders are available. If future demand is undergoing a major shift in mix, timing, or daily demand, add general safety stock across the board until there is enough demand history to analyze for demand variation. But, use historical data to determine the magnitude of seasonality.

2. Sum monthly revenue for all finished goods over the entire analysis period.

3. Obtain the number of <u>standard</u> workdays for every month in the analysis. This is a bit tricky. If the business runs 5 days per week during low and medium seasons but 6 days per week during

peak. If we analyze daily revenue using 5 days per week for part of the year and 6 days per week for another part of the year, the daily revenue will look too low during peak season because we divided by 6 days per week. Therefore, it's best to use a consistent number of workdays for the entire analysis, even if the work schedule changes during peak season.

4. For each item, divide every month's summed revenue by that month's workdays to get average daily revenue by month. It is important to divide by workdays instead of calendar days to accurately assess months with abnormally high or low workdays. If March has 23 workdays and December has 15, we can't treat those months as equivalent demand periods just because they each have 31 calendar days.

Also capture minimum and maximum daily revenue for each month. This reveals if certain months are more volatile within the month.

To get a demand comparator, divide annual revenue by total annual workdays to get average daily revenue for 1 year.

5. Chart the sum of daily revenue by month from step 4 for all items.

6. Review the graph visually as a first check, then complete the mathematical analysis to divide the year into chunks of high, low, and possibly medium periods.

Calculate average, minimum, and maximum daily revenue by month for the entire analysis period, as in the table in Figure 12-2.

	Min Daily Revenue	Average Daily Revenue	Maximum Daily Revenue	Label	% of Annual Average
Jan	8	11	13	Low	56.7%
Feb	9	13	15	Low	67.0%
Mar	11	14	16	Low	72.2%
Apr	17	24	28	High	123.7%
May	21	25	28	High	128.9%
Jun	24	28	31	High	144.3%
Jul	26	29	33	High	149.5%
Aug	27	30	33	High	154.6%
Sep	22	26	29	High	134.0%
Oct	9	15	21	Low	77.3%
Nov	8	11	13	Low	56.7%
Dec	5	9	11	Low	46.4%
Annual		19.4			

Figure 12-2. <u>Seasonal Variation</u>

To set initial high, medium, and low labels for each month, compare each month's average daily revenue to the annual average. In general, a swing of 30% from one category to the next, e.g., from Low to High, constitutes a noteworthy "shift." Recall from Figure 12-1 on page 133 that periods do not have to be sequential months.

Calculate daily revenue per <u>period</u> by summing revenue for low, medium, and high months and dividing by the corresponding number of workdays.

Seasonal Daily Demand (DD)

$$\text{High DD} = \frac{\text{SUM (High period revenue)}}{\text{Total high period workdays}}$$

$$\text{Low DD} = \frac{\text{SUM (Low period revenue)}}{\text{Total low period workdays}}$$

$$\text{Medium DD (if needed)} = \frac{\text{SUM (Medium period revenue)}}{\text{Total medium period workdays}}$$

HINT for Associates

Review a graph or data table and look for steep inclines or declines in daily revenue, as from March to April or September to October in the bottom chart in Figure 12-1 on page 133. This indicates a shift from high to low or vice versa without going through a medium demand period, which means demand shifts are sudden and significant and therefore the site <u>must be prepared in advance</u>. These abrupt changes the highest resizing and customer delivery risks.

Sometimes it is insightful to calculate daily revenue for high and low periods as a percent change from the average to use when estimating low and high daily demands across a large population of parts. If the aggregate business moves up about 40% from medium season to high and down 30% from medium to low, we can use these multipliers to set high daily demand and low daily demand for every seasonal item.

Divide average daily revenue for the entire high season by average daily revenue during the average season to get the ratio of high season versus average, e.g., $120 per day in peak season divided by $100 during average demand means high season is 1.2 times or 120% of the average.

Seasonal Daily Demands by Percent Change

High daily revenue as % of average = Average daily revenue during high season / Average daily revenue during average season

High DD for any seasonal item = Average DD * High daily revenue as % of average

Low daily revenue as % of average = Average daily revenue during low season / Average daily revenue during average season

Low DD for any seasonal item = Average DD * Low daily revenue as % of average

7. Compare high and low daily demands to assess the magnitude of seasonal shifts. If high daily demand is at least 130% of medium or low daily demand, seasonal demand variation is significant and demand variation should be analyzed in seasonal periods instead of across the entire year.

Seasonality Assessment

For 3 seasonal periods (High, Medium, Low): IF (High Revenue / Medium Revenue > 1.3 OR Medium Revenue / Low > 1.3), THEN seasonality is significant

or

For 2 seasonal periods: IF (High Rev / Low Rev > 1.3), THEN seasonality is significant

Seasonality Assessment Example

We ship 65% of annual units from October through March, so the year is divided into two 6-month buckets: peak season is from October through March and low season is from April to September.

High daily revenue is $1,289 and low is $654

High daily revenue/Low daily revenue = 1,289/654 = 197%

With a result well above the 130% threshold, seasonal demand is very significant.

Rule of Thumb

To confirm if seasonal demand variation is significant enough to warrant special analysis, at the very least it is necessary to calculate low and high daily revenue. If high daily revenue is greater than or equal to 130% of medium or low daily revenue, seasonal variation justifies analyzing demand variation in seasonal time periods.

HINT for Associates

In some seasonal businesses, demand *variation* is different during peak season than it is during low or medium periods. It's important to understand the variation within each period so that target safety stock matches the variation pattern.

8. Seasonality is analyzed for finished goods but every item that exhibits seasonality must be assigned a multi-card solution to handle the required resizing from season to season. The kanban calculator has to be able to identify any part number that is seasonal, so it requires some kind of flag or indicator to assign *yes* or *no* for seasonality. Add a column to the calculator, and enter "Yes" or "1" to indicate the presence of seasonal demand and "No" or "0" for items that have no seasonality. These flags can be assigned based on individual part number data or in groups. For example, individual items might have an item master field in the calculator data that indicates the presence of seasonality. Or entire groups of parts might be designated as "seasonal" based on the item's product family, like snow shovels.

HINT for Associates

In Excel, use "1" instead of "Y" to indicate the presence of a certain condition, such as seasonality. This allows that data column to be summed to indicate the count of items that meet the condition.

9. A demand variation multi-card solution requires an estimate of the lowest daily demand in order to establish the correct kanban order quantity for 2 cards in low season. So, for every seasonal item, define the lowest expected daily demand throughout a calendar year.

Daily Demand for Seasonal Items

By definition, seasonal items experience predictable shifts in daily demand over a calendar year. Every seasonal item has expected daily demands for each of the seasonal periods, i.e., an item with high and low demand periods must have estimated high and low daily demands.

Expected low and high daily demands are necessary to design a multi-card kanban solution. But, when resizing multi-card kanban solutions, the current daily demand is always used to calculate the required number of cards.

• Current daily demand = daily usage in current conditions, used for resizing and calculating actual safety stock

• Low daily demand = daily usage during the low season, which is used to set the kanban order quantity

• Average daily demand = average usage over an entire year or during the medium or average period, generally used as a reference for demand analysis

• High daily demand = daily usage during the peak season, used to calculate the maximum number of kanban cards for a given item

Seasonal Demand Summary

To check for seasonal variation, finished goods demand must be summed in monthly buckets to determine if the highest demand period of the year differs from the lowest period by 30% or more, as measured by daily revenue. If so, seasonality is significant and must be accommodated by multi-card solutions for ease of resizing from period to period.

Seasonal demand also requires that demand variation, not just daily demand, be evaluated for each seasonal period. This topic is up next.

TUTORIAL: GOCO SEASONALITY

Mary obtained the most recent 12 months of demand data, from November through October, in Figure 12-3. Top rows are *monthly* revenue by customer group, bottom rows are average *daily* revenue by customer group.

Figure 12-3. 12 Months of Demand

	November	December	January	February	March	April
Auto	$ 5,094,082	$ 4,395,487	$ 5,295,068	$ 5,113,280	$ 5,236,060	$ 5,214,464
Ag	$ 1,936,361	$ 2,081,893	$ 2,695,638	$ 3,059,192	$ 3,273,590	$ 3,655,393
Ind	$ 1,074,989	$ 1,045,790	$ 893,431	$ 1,232,584	$ 1,595,047	$ 1,480,502
Total	$ 8,105,432	$ 7,523,170	$ 8,884,136	$ 9,405,057	$ 10,104,697	$ 10,350,359
Auto DD	$ 254,704	$ 244,194	$ 252,146	$ 255,664	$ 249,336	$ 248,308
Ag DD	$ 96,818	$ 115,661	$ 128,364	$ 152,960	$ 155,885	$ 174,066
Ind DD	$ 53,749	$ 58,099	$ 42,544	$ 61,629	$ 75,955	$ 70,500
Total	$ 405,272	$ 417,954	$ 423,054	$ 470,253	$ 481,176	$ 492,874

	May	June	July	August	September	October
Auto	$ 5,664,740	$ 5,032,842	$ 5,457,645	$ 5,765,956	$ 4,950,154	$ 5,776,736
Ag	$ 3,463,506	$ 3,459,112	$ 3,222,255	$ 3,017,694	$ 2,350,989	$ 2,279,622
Ind	$ 1,821,516	$ 1,941,278	$ 1,924,703	$ 2,333,460	$ 1,232,206	$ 971,768
Total	$ 10,949,763	$ 10,433,233	$ 10,604,603	$ 11,117,109	$ 8,533,350	$ 9,028,126
Auto DD	$ 257,488	$ 239,659	$ 259,888	$ 250,694	$ 260,534	$ 251,162
Ag DD	$ 157,432	$ 164,720	$ 153,441	$ 131,204	$ 123,736	$ 99,114
Ind DD	$ 82,796	$ 92,442	$ 91,653	$ 101,455	$ 64,853	$ 42,251
Total	$ 497,716	$ 496,821	$ 504,981	$ 483,353	$ 449,124	$ 392,527

Their biggest demand variation concern was seasonal demand in the agricultural and industrial customer groups. Mary had to analyze annual production to determine the magnitude of seasonal variation in those channels, as well as whether automotive also exhibited seasonality. She charted monthly revenue and daily revenue in Figure 12-4 to see the pattern.

Figure 12-4. 12 Months of Demand, Monthly and Daily Revenue

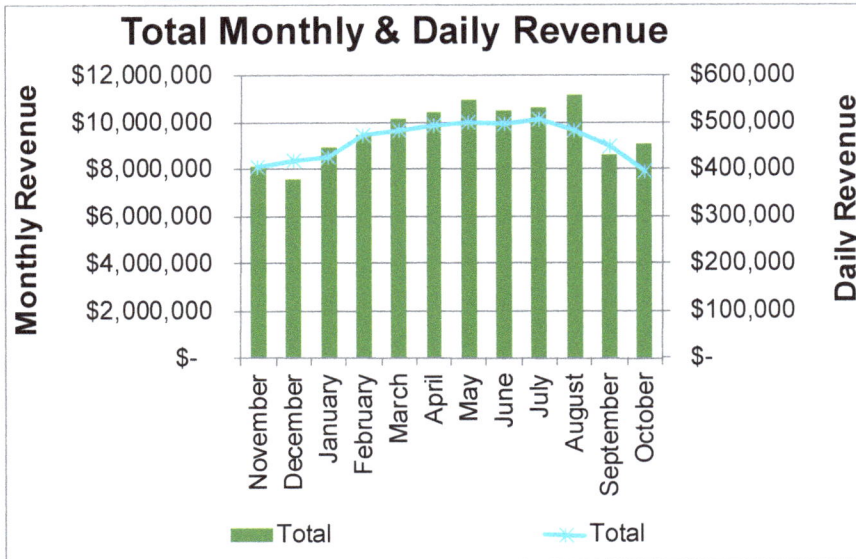

Total Monthly & Daily Revenue

As expected, spring and summer were higher than the rest of the year, so further analysis was necessary. Average daily revenue was greater than $450,000 from February through August, but below that level the rest of the year, with some low months at or below $400,000.

Mary had to confirm if the agriculture and industrial customer groups caused the high months for total revenue. So, she charted average daily revenue by customer group in the stacked bar chart in Figure 12-5. The orange automotive bars were flatter than the other 2, indicating less volatility.

Figure 12-5. Average Daily Revenue by Customer Group

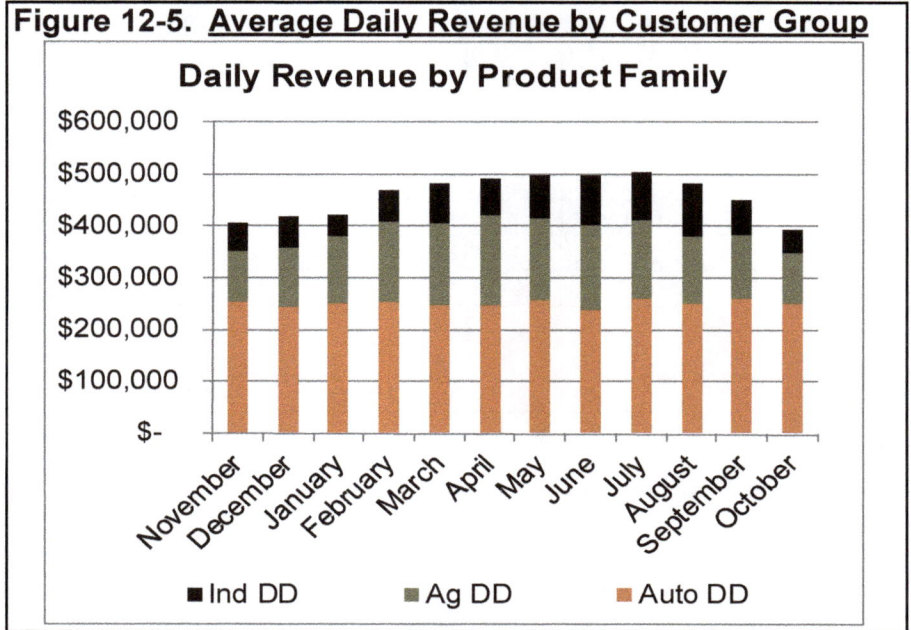

She charted daily revenue for agriculture and industrial without automotive in Figure 12-6, which made it clear that they exhibited seasonal demand. Mary and the Materials team decided to break the year into two seasons: high season from February to August and low season from September through January, but only for agriculture and industrial products.

The team decided that every part number would have a flag in each item master to indicate product family, i.e., Ag, Ind, Auto, or All.

Figure 12-6. Average Daily Revenue for Agriculture and Industrial

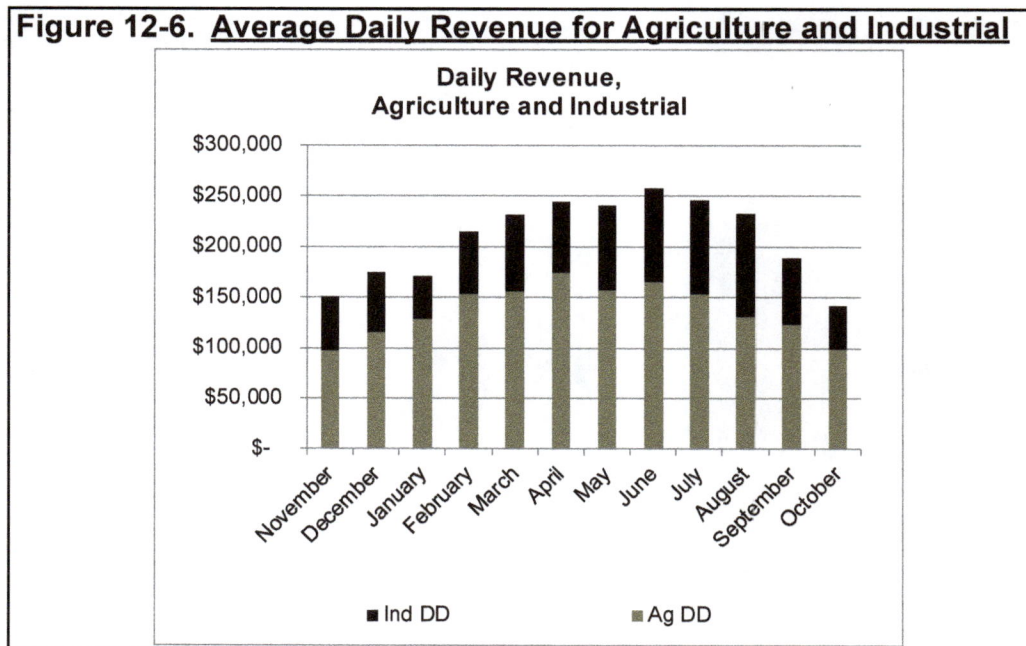

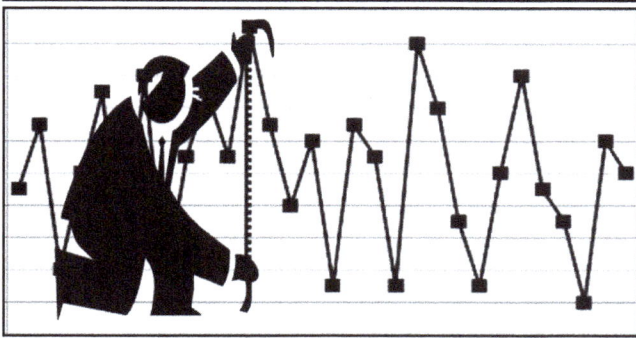

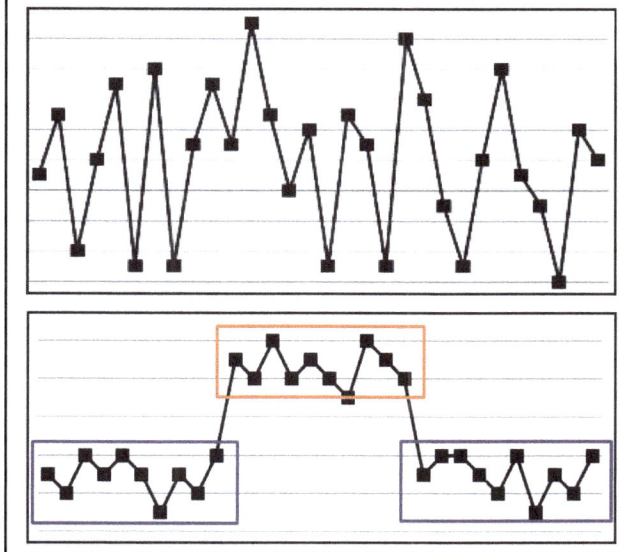

Figure 13-1. Demand Variation Patterns

CHAPTER 13: QUANTIFY DEMAND VARIATION

Of all the topics and concepts in kanban, quantifying demand variation might generate the most debate for both kanban practitioners, who want to know how much variation constitutes a "significant" amount, as well as analysts, who seek the perfect statistical method to assess demand variation and assign safety stock.

It is possible to *estimate* demand variation instead of *calculating* actual values. A team can estimate demand variation for segments of the business or groups of parts based on market or demand insight. There is no "math" if this method is used, but there is also no assurance that estimates are correct. So, the risk can be high for either inventory levels (over-estimate the amount of safety stock required) or for delivery (under-estimate required safety stock).

A better approach is to run the numbers and quantify actual demand variation. As discussed in the chapter about safety stock concepts, demand variation can occur as daily demand volatility, which is random ups and downs like the top chart in Figure 13-1. Or it can occur as daily demand shifts, which are changes in average daily demand, including cyclical demand variation caused by macro forces, such as changes in consumer spending. See the second chart in Figure 13-1.

Daily demand variation and demand shifts are separate from seasonal variation, and either type of daily variation can exist in conjunction with seasonal demand, adding even more complexity.

Understand Demand Patterns

A demand pattern often looks like the top chart in Figure 13-1, a seemingly random graph of high and low points. To create a demand graph, individual demand signals are summed in equal time periods so each data point represents a defined time period, e.g., each point is one *day* or one *week* of demand. Like sawtooth curves, a production cell might receive demand signals all day from internal customers, but all of those signals are summed into one number for each day of demand.

Let's look at 4 demand patterns, each 4 weeks in length with average daily demand of 10 pieces, as in Figure 13-2 on page 140. The yellow area represents average daily demand of 10, the blue line is actual demand from day to day, and the red line is the weekly average in discrete weeks of Monday through Friday. These 4 patterns are very different visually even though they share the same daily and monthly averages of 10 and 200 pieces respectively.

1. Data set #1 has minimal variation from day to day or week to week. It is very stable.

2. Data set #2 has high variation from day to day, with requests for as many as 23 and as few as zero. This demand pattern has week to week and day to day variation.

3. Data set #3 has no demand from Monday to Thursday then 50 units are requested every Friday. This is predictable from week to week. Standard deviation of <u>daily</u> demand would show high variation due to the wide range of zero or 50. But, in the graph it's obvious there is a weekly pattern of 4 days off followed by 1 day at 50. This demand has high predictability and low variability <u>if</u> it is viewed in weeks.

4. Data set #4 has demand for 200 pieces on the first day of the 4-week period then zero demand for the next 19 days. This is high variation from day 1 to day 2 and for week 1 to week 2, but weeks 2, 3, and 4 are identical at zero. This data set has high variation if we look at the first day compared to the rest of that week, or at week 1 compared to other weeks, but there is no variation if we look at the entire 4-week period. It is predictable but erratic: 200 pieces demanded on just 1 day out of 20.

We can draw a couple of conclusions from these charts.

• Demand variation patterns can be rather obvious if charted over time, but even if this works it isn't practical to create a demand graph for every item with demand variation.

• Demand patterns must be viewed in the correct time horizon. Data set #3 looks highly variable if we look at individual days, but it is perfectly smooth if we look at weeks.

Figure 13-2. <u>Demand Pattern Examples</u>

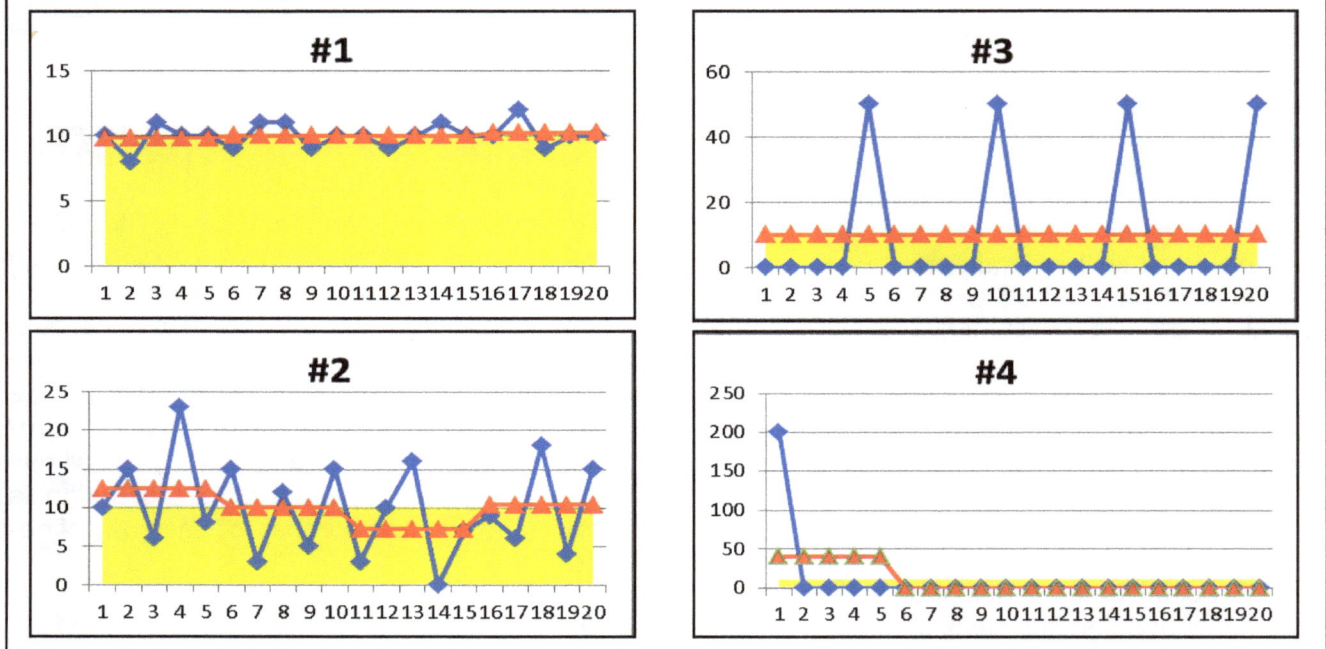

HINT for Associates

Most demand variation is rooted in external forces, e.g., effects from the customers or markets served. But, there are cases when what looks like demand variation is really internal chaos. Poor internal planning or scheduling can introduce more variation than what is driven in the demand stream.

Be aware of internal nonsense, and fix it!

If demand is truly and unavoidably erratic, one of the goals of a Lean process is to smooth or "level load" that *demand* into more stable *production* quantities. A demand pattern might vary wildly from day to day, but the supplying cell is more successful if they produce a similar quantity from hour to hour and day to day. Kanban can assist with this.

Estimate Demand Variation

Estimating instead of calculating demand variation should be done only when variation is known to be low and therefore target safety stock values are minimal, or when accurate demand data simply does not exist and standard deviation calculations are impossible. Estimating demand variation is a "last resort" option that should be avoided when possible.

Frankly, the "lack of demand data" excuse should be rare because a lack of data is a catastrophic and systematic failure that should be corrected, not accommodated. Some sites misinterpret "lack of demand data" to mean that if every demand quantity is not 100% correct and confirmed then the data can't be used, but that is an extreme view. Use common sense to define "unavailable" data. If we lack demand data for 50 out of 1,000 parts, calculate demand variation and apply what is learned from 950 items to the remaining 50. It might be wise to watch those 50 parts for a while and tweak them at a later date if necessary, but even that might be overkill.

Similarly, if you believe there are data errors due to bill of material, scrap reporting errors, or other anomalies, perform the data analysis as described below and be aware that data gaps could potentially understate or overstate the need for safety stock. If in doubt, target safety stock values can be increased slightly if data errors are a concern.

Truly "inaccurate" data means available data is so highly suspect that any results garnered from the analysis would be rejected as impossible to validate or utilize.

• If we believe demand data is 80% accurate or better, run the analysis.

• If data is 50% to 80% accurate, run the analysis on the entire population then select a subset of items to validate via further analysis, even if that analysis has to be manually performed, e.g., build a manual data set for a small number of parts or collect usage observations for a specific time period.

• If demand data is less than 50% accurate and variation calculations are impossible, rely on human intelligence to form an educated guess about

variation for different sub-groups of parts. Yes, some teams can literally guess the correct safety stock targets for groups and get pretty close, but data collection and analysis is a better approach.

Steps to Assign Estimated Safety Stock Values in Groups

1. Define demand variation groups based on intelligence about variation patterns. This is the most critical step in estimating target safety stock, so interview key associates (production workers, supervisors, buyers, planners, material handlers, receiving clerks, etc.) to discover which items tend to be more volatile, or which items cause the most stock outs or expediting exercises. Selecting potential grouping options was covered in the chapter about Target Safety Stock Concepts. (See page 124).

2. For each group, select a manageable yet representative sample of items, usually no more than 50 to 100 items per subgroup.

3. For each sample item, review available data such as stock outs, expedite history, aggregate demand data, purchasing records, etc.

4. Based on business intelligence and sample item reviews, establish target safety stock values in days of demand for every item type or subgroup.

5. Create a target safety stock table for the kanban calculator to use as a reference.

HINT for Associates

When using anecdotal or limited data, be careful not to designate *supply* issues as *demand* variation. If steel is expedited on a regular basis, it might not be caused by demand volatility. Find a way to confirm if steel actually has high variation or if there is another root cause behind the expediting activity, e.g., the supplier ships late, we don't order enough each week, or we ignore the supplier's delivery rule that they only ship once per week.

If end-of-quarter or year-end demand looks more volatile, consider whether it was internally induced by shipping orders early to "make higher revenue numbers" and finish on a high note. Ay-yi-yi, when will that madness stop?

Calculate Demand Variation

Demand variation analysis assesses the predictability, or lack thereof, of a demand stream. The purpose of this analysis is to scope demand variation to use as a basis for establishing target safety stock levels.

There are two metrics that describe the fundamental nature of a demand stream: average demand and demand standard deviation.

1. <u>Average demand</u> is the average or mean for a demand series, e.g., average daily demand for the last 20 workdays or average weekly demand over the prior year. Demand should be reported for workdays instead of calendar days, so workdays with zero demand will lower the overall average, while unscheduled days, e.g., weekends and holidays, do not count as zero but are left blank and therefore not evaluated by the average demand formula.

Average Demand

$$\text{Math: Mean} = \mu = \frac{\sum_{i=1}^{n}(\text{Demand}_i)}{n}$$

Excel: AVERAGE (Demand values 1 to n)

<u>Daily</u> demand is necessary for every kanban solution. Daily demand exists in numerous forms, including current or actual daily demand, the average daily demand over a defined period (such as annual daily demand), and also lowest and highest daily demands if it varies seasonally.

2. As mentioned in the chapter about safety stock concepts, demand volatility is measured by <u>standard deviation</u>, or how far the typical data point deviates from the mean. The higher the standard deviation, the more instability the item or population exhibits.

Standard Deviation

$$\text{Standard Deviation or Sigma } (\Sigma) \text{ or } s = \sqrt{\sum_{i=1}^{n}\frac{(x_i - \bar{x})^2}{(n-1)}}$$

Excel = STDEV (Values 1 to n)

Remember that standard deviation or "sigma" is not the positive or negative gap from the mean but is the *absolute value* of that gap. So, any change *up* or *down* from the mean contributes to standard deviation.

Demand Analysis Example of Average Demand and Standard Deviation **e.g.**

Consider daily demand that alternates between 25 and 75 (25, 75, 25, 75, 25, 75...), as in the diagram below.

The average is 50 and standard deviation is 25.4 over 30 observation days. We might expect standard deviation to be exactly 25.0, but it varies slightly due to the [n-1] factor in the standard deviation formula. If we added more days of demand data, standard deviation would gravitate toward 25.0.

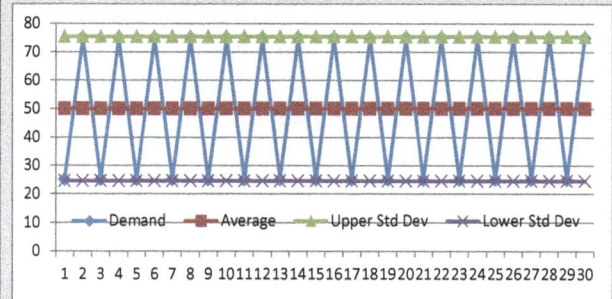

A standard deviation of 25.4 means the typical data point deviates from the mean of 50 by an average 25.4 units, either up or down. See the blue and purple lines in the chart. This makes sense for demand that vacillates from 25 to 75.

Analyze Demand Variation in Lead-Time Buckets

To analyze demand variation for kanban applications, demand data must be divided into the correct buckets or periods of time. As we saw in the demand charts earlier in this chapter, some data exhibits wide variation day to day but virtually no variation week to week. So, for those items, *daily* demand variation is high but *weekly* variation is low. Which is the correct viewpoint? Ah, this is where it gets complicated.

We touched on this topic when we covered sawtooth curves. For kanban, every item is automatically "time fenced" by its lead time, and the correct time period for demand variation analysis is an item's lead time, or the time it takes from an order to receipt of parts. This is perhaps the least understood concept about analyzing demand variation.

Why use lead time as the defined time period for demand variation? Kanban formulas utilize daily demand, so why not measure standard deviation of daily demand? Why not choose one week or one month as the analysis period for everything? The answer to these questions is both logical and mathematical.

Logically there is no need to add safety stock if demand variation within a typical lead-time period is minimal. If we allow one week to produce an item and demand variation in a typical week is low but day-to-day variation is high, it isn't important that daily variation is *high*, but rather that weekly variation is *low* because we are allowed one week to supply parts. Evaluating demand variation in lead-time buckets avoids unnecessary safety stock that can be introduced by an artificially short evaluation period. Refer to chart #3 in Figure 13-2 on page 140 for an illustration of why individual days can look more volatile than weeks, when weeks are perfectly predictable.

Mathematically, kanban solutions are designed to purchase a quantity equal to [lead time * daily demand + target safety stock] during the lead-time period. This might be produced as one order or signal, or it can be multiple orders. Safety stock in a kanban solution is the buffer quantity necessary to cover variation that could occur *within one lead-time period*. Therefore, to avoid over-estimating or under-estimating demand variation, every item must be analyzed in the right time horizon, which is lead time.

Weekly Bucket Example

Assembly A15 is only produced on Friday for shipment the following Monday, 50 per week. The item has a 5-day lead time. The demand pattern in the table to the right is repeated throughout the year.

Day	1	2	3	4	5	6	7	8	9	10
Demand	0	0	0	0	50	0	0	0	0	50

If we calculate average and standard deviation of <u>daily</u> demand we get an average of 10 per day and standard deviation of 21, because 4 out of 5 days have zero demand and day 5 has a demand of 50.

This standard deviation is extremely misleading because demand is entirely predictable. On an average day we use 10, or 50 pieces per week divided by 5 days per week. The standard deviation for any <u>week</u> is zero since <u>every</u> week has the same demand of 50. If we calculate standard deviation in weekly buckets, average lead-time demand is 50 per week, or 10 per day, and standard deviation is zero! There is no variation!

If we mistakenly use <u>daily</u> standard deviation to set safety stock, we incorporate high safety stock when in fact we don't need any!

HINT for Associates

Demand variation analysis is performed in lead-time buckets, defined per item. Don't short-cut the analysis process by selecting random or universal demand buckets. This is one of the most critical steps in demand variation analysis.

Basic Logic for Lead-Time Buckets in Excel

Evaluating demand variation in lead-time buckets certainly adds more work to the analysis versus a universal approach like daily or weekly demand variation, but it is the only way to get valid results. Therefore, to properly analyze demand variation we need a series of lead-time buckets of demand, not just one lead-time snapshot of demand. Ideally we'd like at least 6 or 8 demand *buckets* per item.

1. Demand data is usually downloaded from an Materials Requirements Planning (MRP) or Enterprise Requirements Planning (ERP) system and will likely contain daily or weekly values. Mathematically, either days or weeks will work, but daily demand dumps hundreds of columns for just a few months of data so it's easier to use weeks because most items have lead times that are longer than 2 or 3 days. If daily demand is all that is available, convert daily data into weeks by summing data in calendar weeks.

2. In the Excel spreadsheet, put demand data in weekly columns, as in Figure 13-3. This can easily be 26 (about 6 months) to 78 (about 18 months) columns of demand data, depending on how far back demand data reaches.

Figure 13-3. <u>Demand History in Weekly Buckets</u>

PN	LT	DD	Wk 1	Wk 2	Wk 3	Wk 4	Wk 5	Wk 6	Wk 7	Wk 8	Wk 9	Wk 10
1	5	3.0	11	13	18	17	14	18	12	15	17	16
2	5	23.6	128	105	122	93	130	126	131	121	115	107
3	10	3.0	11	13	18	17	14	18	12	15	17	16
4	10	23.6	128	105	122	93	130	126	131	121	115	107
5	15	3.0	11	13	18	17	14	18	12	15	17	16
6	15	23.6	128	105	122	93	130	126	131	121	115	107
7	20	3.0	11	13	18	17	14	18	12	15	17	16
8	20	23.6	128	105	122	93	130	126	131	121	115	107
9	25	3.0	11	13	18	17	14	18	12	15	17	16
10	25	23.6	128	105	122	93	130	126	131	121	115	107

3. Because demand data is in weeks, it's best if every lead time is also in weeks in order to make Excel formulas easier to write. There are a couple of ways to convert workdays into lead-time weeks, as shown in this formula box.

Convert Lead Time to Weeks

ROUND Function: Lead-time Weeks = MAX (1, ROUND (LT Days/5, 0))

This formula divides lead-time days by 5 (LT Days / 5) then rounds up or down based on standard rounding (ROUND function) to get lead-time weeks as an integer. The "0" at the end of the ROUND function means the result is an integer. Lead times and daily demand must be in workdays, so this formula assumes lead times are in workdays and 5 days equals one week. For any value that rounds down to zero, the formula assigns a minimum value of 1 week using the MAX function.

IF Function: Lead-time Weeks = IF (LT Days < 7, 1, IF (LT Days < 12, 2, IF (LT Days < 19, 3.....)
If mathematical rounding is not desired, an IF formula uses prescribed limits for how many lead-time days convert to 1 week, 2 weeks, etc. This is cumbersome if lead times extend to 8 or more weeks.

HINT for Associates

Short lead times can be quirky when converted to weeks of lead time. For lead times of less than 3 days, weekly demand buckets might not accurately calculate standard deviation. So, those items *might* need daily demand data, but this should be the exception and not the rule. Test the weekly approach first, and if the data is suspect, use a daily approach for items with lead times of less than 3 days.

4. We need 6 to 8 buckets of data to perform demand variation analysis, so long lead-time items require many demand weeks to create an effective series of lead-time buckets. One calendar quarter, or 13 weeks of data, would be 13 buckets for an item with a lead time of 1 week. But, it is just 1 bucket if the lead time is 13 weeks.

A site with numerous long lead-time items should gather more than 13 weeks of data, but that might not be possible if historical data has to be divided into 2 or 3 seasonal periods. If more data is not possible, one fix is to establish a cutoff value for the longest lead-time bucket that will be created, e.g., 6 weeks is the maximum lead-time bucket regardless of actual lead time. Actual lead times might range from 1 week to 14 weeks, with just a few items over 10 weeks. But, if 6 weeks is the longest allowed lead-time bucket then every item with a lead time of 6 weeks or greater will be broken into 6-week buckets, not 10-week or 14-week buckets. This approach violates the rule of analyzing demand variation in lead-time buckets, but for some sets of data this is the only option that will work mathematically.

To use this option, any lead time that is greater than the defined cutoff must be set to the new lower value, which can be done in the same formula that converts lead-time days to weeks.

Lead-Time Weeks with Max Value to Accommodate Long Lead Times

Add a MIN function to ROUND and IF functions when converting workdays into weeks.

Lead-time Weeks = MIN (6, MAX (1, ROUND (LT Days/5, 0)))

Lead-time Weeks = MIN (6, IF (LT Days < 7, 1, IF(LT Days < 12, 2, IF (LT Days < 19, 3.....)))

Rule of Thumb

Limit the number of demand weeks in lead-time buckets only when there isn't enough available data. For most populations, long lead times can be limited to 6-8 weeks of demand without severely impacting variation analysis, but do not go below 4 weeks as the allowed maximum.

5. Now that we've assigned the right number of lead-time weeks to every item, we're ready to create buckets of demand for variation analysis. Every lead-time demand "bucket" for an item will contain as many weeks of demand data as the assigned number of weeks in the item's lead time. An item with a 1-week lead time will have 1 week of demand in every lead-time bucket, while an item with a 6-week lead time will have 6 weeks of demand in every lead-time bucket.

Insert Excel formulas to sum weekly demand into correct lead-time buckets by using lead-time weeks to size the lead-time buckets. This is tricky, but Excel makes it relatively easy. The first lead-time bucket uses data in the first week of demand data, and any item with a lead time of greater than 1 week is left blank for the first bucket. The second bucket uses weeks 1 and 2 of the demand data, pulling just 1 week (which is week 2 at this point) for items with a 1-week lead time and adding weeks 1 and 2 for items with a 2-week lead time. The third bucket uses weeks 1 to 3 of the demand data. This continues until we hit the maximum lead-time bucket length.

Excel formulas are listed in the next formula box, with 4 weeks as the maximum allowed lead-time bucket, just to make the list of formulas a little shorter.

Excel Formulas for LT Buckets

Bucket 1 (the first LT bucket column): IF (LT Weeks = 1, Week 1 Demand, "")

Bucket 2: IF (LT Weeks = 1, Week 2 Demand, IF (LT Weeks = 2, SUM (Week 1 to Week 2 Demands), ""))

Bucket 3: IF (LT Weeks = 1, Week 3 Demand, IF (LT Weeks = 2, SUM (Week 2 to Week 3 Demands), IF (LT Weeks = 3, SUM (Week 1 to Week 3 Demands),"")))

Bucket 4: IF (LT Weeks = 1, Week 4 Demand, IF (LT Weeks = 2, SUM (Week 3 to Week 4 Demands), IF (LT Weeks = 3, SUM (Week 2 to Week 4 Demands), SUM (Week 1 to Week 4 Demands))))

Buckets 5 to 15 follow the same logic as Bucket 4 because all long lead-time items have 4-week buckets.

These formulas leave cells blank (the "" entry at the end of the first three formulas) for buckets with no data, so Excel will ignore those cells when calculating standard deviation. Buckets 1 to 3 are blank for every 4-week lead-time item.

6. Weekly demand data ends up in properly summed lead-time buckets, as in Figure 13-4. For the first bucket, an item with a standard lead time of up to 5 days (1 week) pulls one data point of weekly demand, and items with longer lead times have no data and are blank. In the second rolling bucket, the column is populated for parts with up to 10-day lead times (2 weeks) and the third column adds items with up to 15-day (3 weeks) lead times.

Figure 13-4. Demand Rolling Buckets, Sorted in Ascending Order of Lead-Time Days

PN	LT	LT Weeks	DD	Bucket 1	Bucket 2	Bucket 3	Bucket 4	Bucket 5	Bucket 6	Bucket 7	Bucket 8	Bucket 9	Bucket 10
1	5	1	3	11	13	18	17	14	18	12	15	17	16
2	5	1	24	128	105	122	93	130	126	131	121	115	107
3	10	2	3		24	31	35	31	32	30	27	32	33
4	10	2	24		233	227	215	223	256	257	252	236	222
5	15	3	3			42	48	49	49	44	45	44	48
6	15	3	24			355	320	345	349	387	378	367	343
7	20	4	3				59	62	67	61	59	62	60
8	20	4	24				448	450	471	480	508	493	474
9	25	5	3					73	80	79	76	76	78
10	25	5	24					578	576	602	601	623	600

7. Once lead-time buckets are defined, calculate standard deviation for every item's series of buckets using the STDEV formula in Excel. See the next-to-last column in Figure 13-5 on page 147.

The data is in lead-time periods, so the standard deviation is the expected deviation for the lead-time bucket. If the bucket size was artificially limited with a ceiling of allowed number of weeks, standard deviation is for that period, but it will be applied as the standard deviation for the actual lead time. Got that?

8. Divide lead-time standard deviation by average daily demand for the entire analysis period to convert deviation into days of safety stock. See the last column in Figure 13-5. This is one of the reasons that seasonal demand periods must be evaluated separately, because average daily demand is different for a low period versus high.

Figure 13-5. Rolling Demand Standard Deviation

PN	LT Weeks	DD	Bucket 5	Bucket 6	Bucket 7	Bucket 8	Bucket 9	Bucket 10	Std Dev	Days Demand
1	1	3.0	14	18	12	15	17	16	2.5	0.8
2	1	23.6	130	126	131	121	115	107	12.6	0.5
3	2	3.0	31	32	30	27	32	33	3.3	1.1
4	2	23.6	223	256	257	252	236	222	15.8	0.7
5	3	3.0	49	49	44	45	44	48	2.7	0.9
6	3	23.6	345	349	387	378	367	343	21.4	0.9
7	4	3.0	62	67	61	59	62	60	2.8	0.9
8	4	23.6	450	471	480	508	493	474	21.6	0.9
9	5	3.0	73	80	79	76	76	78	2.5	0.8
10	5	23.6	578	576	602	601	623	600	17.5	0.7

Rolling Versus Discrete Lead-Time Buckets

Now that we understand the need for lead-time demand buckets and the basic logic to use them, we can consider two ways to create buckets, either rolling or discrete. Consider the demand pattern in Figure 13-6. This item has a lead time of 5 weeks and average daily demand equal to 10.

Figure 13-6. Demand Pattern & Data

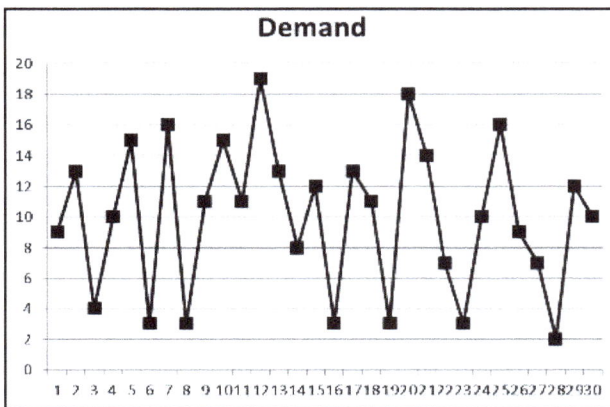

Week	Demand	Week	Demand
1	9	16	3
2	13	17	13
3	4	18	11
4	10	19	3
5	15	20	18
6	3	21	14
7	16	22	7
8	3	23	3
9	11	24	10
10	15	25	16
11	11	26	9
12	19	27	7
13	13	28	2
14	8	29	12
15	12	30	10

Rolling Lead-Time Buckets

In Figure 13-7, column 1 is the week number and column 2 is total demand for that week. This item has a 5-week lead-time, so 5 weeks of demand are summed to create 1 lead-time bucket.

Rolling lead-time buckets are *sequential* data sets with the number of summed observations equal to the number of weeks in the lead time. Buckets are created using a rolling data selection. So, if a part number has a 5-week lead time, there will be 5 observations in each bucket and each bucket in the series starts with the next consecutive observations, e.g., bucket #1 starts with observation #1 and bucket #2 starts with observation #2. In Figure 13-7, column 3 contains 5-week rolling buckets created by summing weeks 1 to 5, 2 to 6, 3 to 7, and so on.

The rolling bucket approach is the easiest to set up in a spreadsheet.

1. Start at the first demand data point and count down to the cell that captures the required number of lead-time weeks per bucket, which is 5 rows in this case.

2. From that cell, go one cell to the right and enter a formula to total the data points up to and including the row that was selected. Use a SUM formula, e.g., SUM (B7:B11).

3. Copy that formula to the bottom of the column to sum every 5 rows of data in series, creating rolling 5-week buckets next to the column of demand data. This puts a lead-time bucket in every row except the first rows that lacked sufficient data to create the proper sum. In this example, the first 4 rows are blank because there wasn't adequate weekly data to sum a lead-time bucket until we reached 5 weeks of demand data.

This approach provides the maximum possible number of lead-time buckets because most observations are used more than once. So, *seven* data points provide *three* 5-week lead-time buckets: bucket 1 is weeks 1 through 5, bucket 2 is weeks 2 through 6, and bucket 3 is weeks 3 to 7.

The number of final lead-time buckets for any item is dictated by the number of available data points and the number required to create 1 bucket.

Figure 13-7. Rolling & Discrete Data

Week	Column 2 Weekly Demand	Column 3 5-Week Rolling Buckets	Column 4 5-Week Discrete Buckets
1	9.0		
2	13.0		
3	4.0		
4	10.0		
5	15.0	51.0	51.0
6	3.0	45.0	
7	16.0	48.0	
8	3.0	47.0	
9	11.0	48.0	
10	15.0	48.0	48.0
11	11.0	56.0	
12	19.0	59.0	
13	13.0	69.0	
14	8.0	66.0	
15	12.0	63.0	63.0
16	3.0	55.0	
17	13.0	49.0	
18	11.0	47.0	
19	3.0	42.0	
20	18.0	48.0	48.0
21	14.0	59.0	
22	7.0	53.0	
23	3.0	45.0	
24	10.0	52.0	
25	16.0	50.0	50.0
26	9.0	45.0	
27	7.0	45.0	
28	2.0	44.0	
29	12.0	46.0	
30	10.0	40.0	40.0
Average	10.0	50.8	50.0
Weekly Demand	10.0	10.2	10.0
Std Dev	4.9	7.4	7.5
Min	2.0	40.0	40.0
Max	19.0	69.0	63.0
Std Dev/ Mean	49%	15%	15%

For an item with a lead time of 1 week, the number of lead-time buckets equals the number of data points, or 1 data point per bucket. This is the maximum number of lead-time buckets that is possible for the data set.

An item with a long lead time will have fewer lead-time buckets due to the requirement for more demand weeks per lead-time bucket. The lowest or minimum number of created buckets is determined by the *longest* lead time to be evaluated. If the longest lead time is 8 weeks, rolling lead-time buckets are weeks 1 to 8, 2 through 9, 3 to 10, etc. Therefore, 10 data points provide 3 lead-time buckets for an item with an 8-week lead time.

As usual, we can create a formula to determine the lowest number of lead-time buckets that can be created from a series of demand observations.

Lowest Rolling LT Bucket Count

Lowest # rolling LT buckets, or # of lead-time buckets for longest LT = # demand observations - (observations required for the longest LT - 1)

For 30 weeks of demand data and a 5-week lead time, [30 - (5-1)] = 26 LT buckets

---

Rolling Weekly Buckets Example

With 50 weeks of data...

If lead time = 1 week, obtain 50 lead-time buckets since 1 demand week = 1 lead-time bucket

If LT = 2 weeks: 49 buckets because bucket 1 is created by summing [week 1 + week 2]

If LT = 3 weeks: 48 buckets

If LT = 48 weeks: 3 buckets (1-48, 2-49, 3-50)

If LT = 49 weeks: 2 buckets (1-49, 2-50)

If LT = 50 weeks: 1 bucket

This illustrates why it is sometimes advantageous to limit lead times to a reasonable number, e.g., 6 to 8.

For the lead-time buckets in column 3 of the data table, calculate average demand and standard deviation for that column, as in the bottom of Figure 13-7. Remember that average demand for column 3 is for 5-week periods while column 2 is average demand for 1 week.

Rolling buckets under-weight certain observations and over-weight others. In this data set, demand weeks 1 and 30 are used only once in a lead-time bucket, i.e., the first and last buckets containing demand weeks 1-5 and 26-30, while demand weeks 5 through 26 are each used 5 times. In most cases this is insignificant but it can skew the data. If observations 1 through 4 or 27 to 30 differ from the rest of the data set, the rolling buckets might not be as accurate because those observations aren't included in as many buckets as the other data points. To avoid these concerns, obtain as much data as possible but ensure that it represents reality.

Discrete Lead-Time Buckets

Discrete lead-time buckets are separate and distinct entities, e.g., weeks 1 to 5, 6 to 10, 11 to 15, etc. Each data point is used only <u>once,</u> so this method provides fewer lead-time buckets than the rolling lead-time approach. For our data set, we have 30 observations and a 5-week lead time, so the data will provide [30 / 5 = 6] lead-time buckets.

Follow these steps to create discrete buckets.

1. Count down to the first cell that sums the right number of weekly observations and insert a sum formula to the right, as was done for rolling buckets. See column 4 in Figure 13-7.

2. For discrete buckets, we can't copy this formula to the bottom of the column because it would repeat what we did for rolling buckets. Instead, copy the <u>block</u> of cells from the top of the column to the first formula. In this case copy 4 empty cells plus 1 cell with the sum formula.

3. In the next 25 rows, every fifth cell will have a formula and all other cells are blank. By copying the block of 5 rows, we maintain 4 blank cells followed by 1 formula. Do *not* enter zero in empty cells because Excel interprets that as data to evaluate in the standard deviation formula. Empty cells must truly be empty.

If the number of demand observations is not evenly divisible by the number of weeks in a lead time, the last lead-time bucket will not have enough demand weeks to create a bucket. If 26 weeks of demand are in the data set, any item with lead time of 3, 4, 5, or 6 weeks in the lead time will not evenly divide into the number of observations. If using later data is preferable versus using early data, skip the early weeks of data and start the lead-time buckets at the correct week of demand. For example, if we have 27 weeks of demand data and a 5-week lead time, we can skip weeks 26 and 27 by cutting off the end of the data, or skip weeks 1 and 2 by cutting off the beginning of the data. Yes, you could also skip weeks 1 and 27 and use weeks 2 through 26, or skip weeks in the middle if the data in a couple middle weeks was "weird."

Discrete LT Bucket Count

\# Discrete Lead-time Buckets
= ROUNDDOWN (# observations / observations per LT, 0)

This rounds the result down to the next integer if the number of observations is not evenly divisible by lead-time weeks.

---

4. Like rolling buckets, calculate average and standard deviation for the list of data points, as in the bottom of Column 4 in Figure 13-7 on page 148.

Rolling Versus Discrete Lead-Time Bucket Results

In most cases, rolling and discrete buckets provide similar results. Look at average weekly demand in our table of results.

• In column 2 of Figure 13-7 on page 148, average weekly demand is 10.0.

• When we use rolling 5-week buckets in column 3, 5-week demand is 50.8 and weekly demand is 10.2 (50.8 / 5 = 10.2).

• With discrete buckets in column 4, 5-week demand is 50.0, and weekly demand is 10.0 (50.0 / 5 = 10.0). We expect discrete results to exactly match the weekly calculation in column 2 because each observation was used just 1 time in discrete buckets. This would not be the case if the number discrete of demand observations was not evenly divisible by lead-time bucket weeks.

The results indicate that the data points used less than 5 times in the rolling buckets were smaller numbers than the overall average, so by using those numbers less frequently the average daily demand was pulled slightly up, but it isn't a big change.

Standard deviation for the lead-time buckets in columns 3 and 4 versus weekly data in column 2 is a noticeable difference, as in Figure 13-7 on page 148.

• In the weekly data, standard deviation is 4.9 pieces per week.

• For rolling buckets, standard deviation is 7.4 pieces per 5 weeks.

• Standard deviation for discrete buckets is 7.5 pieces per 5 weeks.

The standard deviation numbers are what would be used as target safety stock for the lead-time bucket period. So, it is the right number to use in kanban formulas, e.g., [(Daily demand * lead time in workdays) + Target safety stock in pieces].

Convert target safety stock into days of demand if that is the preferred method for specifying target safety stock.

HINT for Associates

Don't assume that *weekly* demand variation, or the standard deviation of a series of weekly demands, can be multiplied by an item's lead time in weeks to get "lead-time standard deviation" for that item.

Imagine the error that would occur in the above example if we assumed weekly demand variation was an accurate way to assess lead-time variation by multiplying the weekly standard deviation of 4.9 pieces times a 5-week lead time! That would add (4.9 * 5) = 24.5 pieces of safety stock to the kanban solution instead of the correct 7.5 pieces.

Demand Variation for Seasonal Demand

Items that exhibit seasonal demand variation must be analyzed in seasonal periods. Break the weekly demand data into seasonal periods, e.g., high and low or high, medium, and low, as discussed in the chapter about seasonal demand. Evaluate each period <u>independently</u> for demand variation.

Seasonality Deviation Example

We calculate standard deviation for item SDV3600 at 28.6 units over the 25-day lead time during the low season. Daily demand is 10 pieces, so lead-time demand is [25 days * 10 / day = 250]. During low season, standard deviation is [28.6 / 10 per day = 2.9 days].

During peak season, daily demand climbs to 14 units, or 350 units per lead-time period, and standard deviation is 33.2 pieces or 2.4 days of demand.

Demand variation ranges from 2.4 to 2.9 days whether in peak or low season, so a safety stock target of 3 days would be appropriate all year regardless of season.

Summary of Quantifying Demand Variation

Demand variation is evaluated in lead-time buckets!

• Don't forget to separate demand data into the correct periods if seasonal demand variation exists, and repeat the variation analysis for each seasonal period.

• For every item, break demand data into lead-time buckets, either discrete or rolling. It is beneficial to have at least 6 to 8 buckets for every item.

  » For most sites, rolling buckets work well to create lead-time buckets, and they are much easier to create in Excel, particularly for long data sets.

• If numerous items have long lead times versus the available demand data, set a maximum lead-time bucket size to shrink those buckets to more manageable levels.

• Calculate standard deviation for every item based on the series of lead-time demand buckets.

In the next chapter we'll cover how to create target safety stock values based on demand variation.

TUTORIAL: GOCO DEMAND VARIATION

Mary had monthly data from the seasonality analysis, but she needed weekly data to create lead-time buckets. So, she downloaded 50 weeks of data from the MRP system and put it in Excel.

The data set was 1 year, November to October, but Mary's seasonal periods were February to August and September to January. To make the data fit her defined seasons, she put February through August in the first 29 columns in her Excel sheet, removing November through January from the front of the data. She moved September and October data from the end of the original data to the front with the prior year's November through January in the next columns. Whew! She ended up with February through August followed by September through January. She colored the high season with green fill at the top of the columns and added pink fill to the low months to give her visual clues for the seasons.

She used VLOOKUP to pull data into the tab, like New LT (the lead time confirmed by suppliers), New ABC, P/M (purchased or manufactured), Std Cost, etc. See Figure 13-8 on page 153 for an abridged version of Mary's Excel sheet, with weekly demand data and a few calculated demand statistics.

Mary wrote formulas to create rolling lead-time buckets with a cutoff of 4 weeks as the longest allowed lead-time bucket.

She needed 4 different formulas to create the lead-time buckets: 1 for lead times of 1 week in the first bucket, a second for 1-week and 2-week lead times starting with the second lead-time bucket, a third for week 3 and up to 3 weeks of summed weekly data, and a fourth for 4 weeks beyond.

LT Bucket Formulas:

=IF (LT_Weeks=1, L3, "")

This formula was used only in the first lead-time bucket column. It pulled week 1 of the demand data (L3) for every part that had LT_Weeks = 1 and left all other rows blank.

=IF (LT_Weeks=1, M3, IF(LT_Weeks=2, SUM(L3:M3), ""))

This formula was used only to populate lead-time bucket 2. It pulled week 2 of the demand data for every part that had LT_Weeks = 1, summed weeks 1 and 2 for all parts with LT_Weeks = 2, and left other rows blank.

=IF (LT_Weeks=1, N3, IF(LT_Weeks=2, SUM(M3:N3), IF (LT_Weeks=3, SUM(L3:N3), "")))

This formula populated LT Bucket 3. It pulled week 3 of the demand data for every item that had LT_Weeks = 1, summed weeks 2 and 3 for all parts with LT_Weeks = 2, summed Weeks 1 to 3 for all parts with LT_Weeks = 3, and left all other rows blank.

=IF (LT_Weeks=1, O3, IF(LT_Weeks=2, SUM(N3:O3), IF(LT_Weeks=3, SUM(M3:O3), SUM(L3:O3))))

This formula was used for LT Buckets 4 through 50 because the maximum number of demand weeks for any lead-time bucket was 4 weeks. It pulled week 4 (column O) of the demand data for every part with LT_Weeks = 1, summed weeks 3 and 4 for all parts with LT_Weeks = 2, summed Weeks 2 to 4 for all parts with LT_Weeks = 3, and summed weeks 1 through 4 for all remaining rows.

Once the buckets were ready, Mary calculated low and high season standard deviations for the data sets. She then calculated statistics for high season lead-time buckets in subsequent columns, with standard deviation in days of demand and high season filled with green. She added statistics for the low season, with standard deviation in days of demand and pink in the column headers. See Figure 13-8 on page 153 and Figure 13-9 on page 154 for snapshots of Mary's Excel file.

Mary would use this data to begin grouping parts based on similar demand variation.

Figure 13-8. __GOCO LT Bucket Data__

Green column headers indicate high season weeks, while pink means low demand season.

To the right of colored columns are statistics about the demand data, such as annual demand or average daily demand.

Part Numb	Week 26	Week 27	Week 28	Week 29	Week 30	Week 31	Week 32	Week 33	Annual Demand	Average DD	Annual Spend	New AB	High Weekly Avg	High Season DD	Low Weekly Average	Low Season DD	New L
50.50 Face	7,404	7,422	7,342	7,219	7,464	7,441	7,419	7,348	369,933	1,479.7	$ 368,307	C	7402.3	1480.5	7393.7	1478.7	20
75.50 Face	15,169	16,978	16,788	16,495	15,720	16,429	16,162	16,735	805,984	3,223.9	$ 944,049	B	16150.0	3230.0	16077.8	3215.6	10
100.50 Face	5,905	5,937	5,972	5,969	5,948	6,045	5,945	5,803	296,776	1,187.1	$ 442,196	B	5927.4	1185.5	5946.7	1189.3	10
50.50 Gasket	7,199	7,021	7,045	7,028	7,018	7,001	7,085	7,022	352,318	1,409.3	$ 158,543	B	7096.3	1419.3	6977.4	1395.5	20
75.50 Gasket	15,463	15,268	15,075	14,776	15,006	14,708	14,416	14,000	805,212	3,220.8	$ 597,870	B	17726.7	3545.3	13863.8	2772.8	10
100.50 Gasket	5,759	6,094	6,029	6,029	6,006	5,907	5,810	5,871	299,080	1,196.3	$ 300,874	C	5994.7	1198.9	5963.5	1192.7	15
50.50 Trim	7,026	6,941	7,057	6,927	6,527	7,097	7,070	7,090	350,452	1,401.8	$ 1,067,126	B	7056.0	1411.2	6944.2	1388.8	20
75.50 Trim	15,027	15,837	15,649	16,359	16,582	16,293	16,009	16,605	813,115	3,252.5	$ 2,984,132	A	16005.1	3201.0	16617.4	3323.5	12
100.50 Trim	5,944	6,075	5,907	5,802	5,884	5,778	5,776	5,929	295,154	1,180.6	$ 1,729,602	B	5918.8	1183.8	5881.4	1176.3	12
TempSens	2,326	2,398	2,472	2,431	2,462	2,421	2,382	2,424	120,788	483.2	$ 137,759	C	2416.3	483.3	2415.0	483.0	20
PressSens	59,106	59,409	60,721	60,654	59,475	59,413	60,373	60,891	2,985,201	11,940.8	$ 9,307,857	A	59678.4	11935.7	59739.3	11947.9	10
FlowSens	986	974	964	1,047	1,060	1,043	1,026	1,002	49,304	197.2	$ 209,542	C	993.9	198.8	975.3	195.1	20
TempHarn	2,426	2,498	2,472	2,431	2,462	2,424	2,382	2,424	120,825	483.3	$ 201,899	C	2412.8	482.6	2421.6	484.3	20
PressHarn	59,106	59,409	59,721	59,654	59,475	60,413	61,373	59,891	2,985,201	11,940.8	$ 5,340,525	A	59712.9	11942.6	59691.7	11938.3	10

Figure 13-9. GOCO Bucket Standard Deviations

Mary calculated standard deviation of lead-time buckets for both high and low demand periods, in the columns to the right of color-coded lead-time buckets.

Part Numb	LT Wee	Bucket 1	Bucket 2	Bucket 3	Bucket 4	Bucket 30	Bucket 31	Bucket 32	Bucket 33	High Average LT Bucket	High Season LT Std Dev	High Season Std Dev Days	Low Average LT Demand	Low LT Std Dev	Low Std Dev Da
50.50 Face	4				29517	29447	29466	29543	29672	29631.42	161.7	0.11	29545.52	115.2	0.08
75.50 Face	2		32564	32782	31674	32215	32149	32591	32897	32308.43	656.0	0.20	32169.9	547.7	0.17
100.50 Face	2		11696	11723	11775	11917	11993	11990	11748	11855.82	94.8	0.08	11891.19	116.2	0.10
50.50 Gasket	4				28492	28112	28092	28132	28126	28395.35	177.0	0.12	27921.43	146.5	0.11
75.50 Gasket	2		33034	33767	34899	29782	29714	29124	28416	35586.43	2570.7	0.73	27693.57	2061.8	0.74
100.50 Gasket	3			17498	17618	18064	17942	17723	17588	17990.3	185.3	0.15	17890.71	313.0	0.26
50.50 Trim	4				28354	27452	27608	27621	27784	28228.69	169.1	0.12	27783.24	214.3	0.15
75.50 Trim	3			49160	49930	48590	49234	48884	48907	47994.7	1166.8	0.36	49817.81	613.0	0.18
100.50 Trim	3			18027	17787	17593	17464	17438	17483	17748.74	156.5	0.13	17642.86	137.4	0.12
TempSens	4				9504	9763	9786	9696	9689	9668.731	107.8	0.22	9664.81	62.7	0.13
PressSens	2		118667	119121	119835	120129	118888	119786	121264	119327.6	1147.7	0.10	119548	1304.4	0.11
FlowSens	4				4011	4045	4114	4176	4131	3969.385	83.1	0.42	3907.714	165.5	0.85

CHAPTER 14: TARGET SAFETY STOCK FOR DEMAND VARIATION

The purpose of analyzing demand variation is to assign appropriate target safety stock to each kanban item to prevent demand variation from emptying the inventory bucket. Once variation numbers are calculated, the open question is whether target safety stock should be assigned to groups of parts with similar demand variation patterns or to every part number individually.

Option 1. Calculate actual demand variation based on demand data for every item, then aggregate those safety stock results in groups of parts. In this method, target safety stock *must* be in days of demand so that it can be applied to a variety of items. Segmentation options are based on groups that exhibit similar variation patterns in the mathematical results. If all items in a site have essentially the same demand variation, no subgroups are necessary.

In this method, target safety stock is assigned to an item based on which group it belongs to, not on the calculated standard deviation for that particular item. Yes, it seems like a waste to calculate all the *individual* data then not use them *individually*, but grouping items is an excellent approach and it is much easier to manage in the kanban calculator than individual safety stock targets.

Option 2. Calculate actual demand variation based on usage data for every item, then utilize each individual result to assign target safety stock for that specific item. This method calculates individual standard deviations using the process in the prior chapter, but no groups are created from the results.

This is not a common approach for assigning target safety stock, first because there are very few scenarios that require the complexity of unique target safety stock values for each individual item. Second, maintaining a valid list of individual safety stock values is tedious. Finally, assigning individual safety stock targets can be difficult if there are thousands of items because the kanban calculator has to have an all-inclusive target safety stock list by part number, which would be a very large Excel file.

Option 1: Calculate Demand Variation Target Safety Stock Values & Assign in Groups

Calculate individual standard deviations, then aggregate those results in logical groups.

Steps to Assign Calculated Safety Stock Values in Groups

Once demand variation is quantified as standard deviations of lead-time buckets, test different groups of parts to find similar variation patterns. The goal of this process is two-fold.

• Find the correct grouping method for assigning target safety stock. The only way to confirm that the best grouping has been identified is to calculate several different options and find the combination with the best mathematical fit for the defined subgroups.

• Using the safety stock values for the defined groups, create a target safety stock reference table to be used by the kanban calculator to select the correct target safety stock for every kanban item.

Follow these steps.

1. Complete demand variation analysis for all items and convert those results into days of demand, as described in the previous chapter.

2. Define basic grouping options that might fit with the business, e.g., ABC, purchased versus manufactured, product family, lead-time category, market served, and so on. Each grouping option must have clearly defined and mutually exclusive choices, i.e., the ABC grouping contains A, B, and C types, and each type excludes the existence of another assignment, so an item can't be both an A and a B classification.

3. Consider how grouping options from step 2 might be combined to form more complex subgroups, e.g., ABC <u>with</u> PM, ABC <u>with</u> product family, market served <u>plus</u> lead-time category, etc. Select those that *should* demonstrate divergent variation patterns based on business intelligence, e.g., the Sales observation that one channel is more volatile than another.

4. Items that exhibit similar variation amplitude will be grouped, so standard deviation results for individual items in their groups must be averaged to generate the numbers to populate the safety stock reference table. To do that, calculate the average of all the standard deviations in days of demand for each <u>type</u> or <u>subgroup</u>. We'll also want minimum and maximum standard deviation for each grouping so we can look at range and overlap.

For example, if ABC is one of the grouping options, calculate average, minimum, and maximum standard deviation days of demand for all A parts, all B parts, and all C parts, representing the three *types* of parts within the ABC grouping. If ABC plus purchased or manufactured (PM) is another grouping option, calculate average, minimum, and maximum standard deviation in days of demand for every combination, i.e., A purchased parts, B purchased parts, C purchased parts, A manufactured parts, B manufactured parts, and C manufactured parts.

Average Standard Deviation for a Subgroup of Items

Excel Average standard deviation = AVERAGE (Std Dev 1, Std Dev 2,...Std Dev n)

This calculates the average of the standard deviation of values 1 through n, where values 1 to n represent all the items within a certain subgroup, e.g. all A items. MIN and MAX functions complete the trio of information we need for each grouping.

Excel Minimum value = MIN (Std Dev 1, Std Dev 2,...Std Dev n)

Excel Maximum value = MAX (Std Dev 1, Std Dev 2,...Std Dev n)

For options with just two dimensions, e.g., ABC versus PM, a pivot table works well to calculate average standard deviation by type. Select one dimension as the row label and the other as the column. Then choose average, minimum, or maximum standard deviation days as the value in the pivot table.

In Figure 14-1, the graphic on the right shows the field settings to create the "average" standard deviation pivot table and the table to the left is the result. Repeat this twice more for Min and Max instead of Average.

Figure 14-1. <u>**Standard Deviation Pivot Table**</u>

Pivot table fields -->

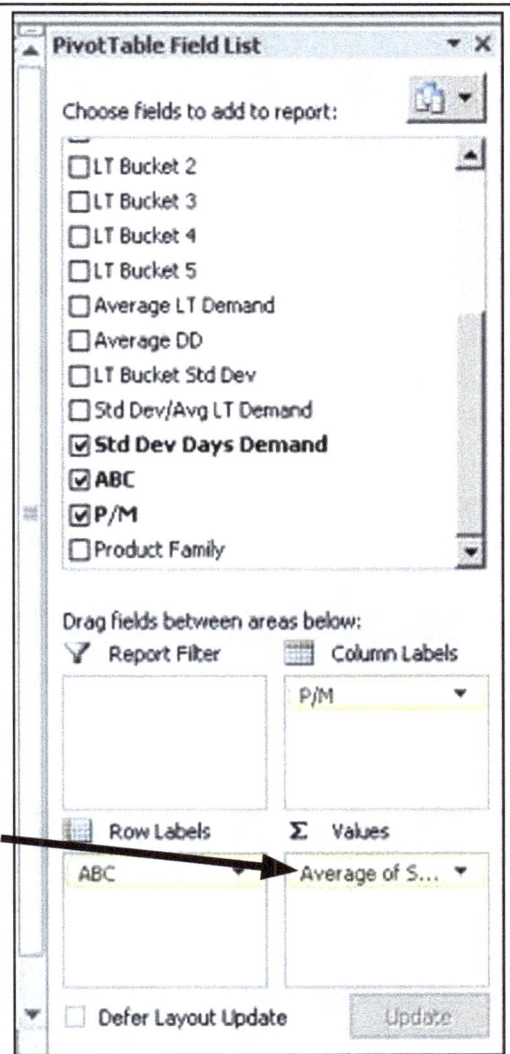

Resulting pivot table.

Average of Std Dev Days Demand	Column Labels	
Row Labels	M	P
A	0.6	0.6
B	0.8	0.8
C	1.4	0.9

This table reports the <u>average</u> value for every combination of ABC plus P/M.

Click on the option in the "Values" box and choose "Value Field Settings" for a menu of options for how this data is reported. We need the *average* of all of the standard deviations, as well as *minimum* and *maximum*. So, create <u>three</u> pivot tables for every grouping option to capture these three statistics.

For groupings that require more than two dimensions, e.g., ABC <u>plus</u> P/M <u>plus</u> lead-time category, a pivot table won't work. Instead, it is necessary to add columns to the spreadsheet, one for every subgroup, and in each new column grab an item's standard deviation <u>if</u> the item matches the subgroup for that column. This adds many columns to the spreadsheet! The number of subgroups equals the product of the number of types in each grouping parameter. If we have ABC plus purchased or manufactured, we have 3 ABC choices times 2 P/M choices, or 6 subgroups for ABC plus P/M.

At the bottom of each column, average all of the standard deviation numbers that were pulled into that column to get the aggregated standard deviation for that subgroup. Yes, this sounds like a lot of work, and it can be. It seems more complicated than the math actually is, but it is tedious and it increases the size of the kanban spreadsheet very rapidly. See the following example of how to calculate standard deviations for complex groups. For a more extended example, see the chapter starting on page 171.

5. For every subgroup, e.g., purchased A items or manufactured C items, find the smallest and largest standard deviation values within that subgroup to define the <u>range</u> for every subgroup.

If standard deviation data is in a pivot table, create three pivot tables and in one table choose the value field setting "Min," in another select "Average," and in the third select "Max." Refer to the pivot table example in Figure 14-1 on page 157.

If the data is in columns due to more than two grouping dimensions, insert Excel MIN, AVERAGE, and MAX functions at the bottom of every column to find the smallest, average, and largest standard deviations for each subgroup.

Repeat these steps for several grouping options.

Standard Deviations for Complex Groups

We are analyzing <u>average standard deviation</u> for the combination of ABC classification (A, B or C), purchased versus manufactured (P or M), and product family (Textile or Auto). There are **12** possible combinations, or [3 * 2 * 2] for [3 ABC * 2 PM * 2 Product Family].

In the Excel tab, column N collects standard deviation days for items that are <u>A</u> classification, <u>purchased</u>, and the <u>textile</u> product family. Column O is <u>B</u> classification, <u>purchased</u>, and <u>textile</u>, Column P is <u>C</u>, <u>purchased</u>, and <u>textile</u>. This continues until every possible combination has a column, which adds 12 columns of data to the Excel tab, one for every type definition.

	N	O	P	Q	R	S	T	U	V	W	X	Y
	A	B	C	A	B	C	A	B	C	A	B	C
	Purch	Purch	Purch	Manf	Manf	Manf	Purch	Purch	Purch	Manf	Manf	Manf
	Tex	Tex	Tex	Tex	Tex	Tex	Auto	Auto	Auto	Auto	Auto	Auto
PN 1	If the part number in a certain row is A + Purch + Tex, the standard deviation value is pulled into column N.						For every part number or row of the data set, standard deviation is only populated into ONE of the 12 columns because every part number has a specific combination of ABC plus P/M plus product family.					

Column N Formula: IF (AND (ABC = "A", PM = "P", Prod Fam = "Tex"), = Std Dev Days Demand, "")

For every row in the kanban calculator, if the defined conditions for the AND statement are all true (A <u>and</u> P <u>and</u> Tex) the formula grabs that item's Standard Deviation Days Demand, or the days of safety stock required for this item. Every item that meets the conditions for the particular column has a standard deviation value in this column, and parts that don't match are blank.

At the bottom of every subgroup standard deviation column, calculate average standard deviation days for that column, then use those 12 values to build a reference table like the one to the left. Also find the min and max for each column.

	Textile	Auto
AP	Enter the average of all standard deviation days contained in Column N	Column T
BP	Column O	Column U
CP	Column P	Column V
AM	Column Q	Column W
BM	Column R	Column X
CM	Column S	Column Y

Pivot tables are much easier than adding columns, but with more than two dimensions the column approach is really the only method.

---

6. Create a table with minimum, average, and maximum values from step 5 for every grouping option, as in Figure 14-2.

Figure 14-2. <u>Target SS Tables: Min, Average & Max</u>

ABC versus P/M with just <u>average</u> standard deviation days of demand requires 6 values [3 ABC choices * 2 P/M choices = 6]. A table with just average standard deviation works for a safety stock reference table, but it doesn't provide minimum and maximum deviation values, which are needed when selecting the best grouping option.

Reporting minimum, average, and maximum deviations triples the number of data points to 18, but this provides better insight about how standard deviation varies from type to type.

	M	P
A	0.6	0.6
B	0.8	0.8
C	1.4	0.9

	Min	Avg	Max
A/M	0.3	0.6	0.7
B/M	0.2	0.8	1.5
C/M	0.2	1.4	1.9
A/P	0.2	0.6	1.1
B/P	0.3	0.8	1.0
C/P	0.1	0.9	1.6

Several grouping options should be tested to ensure the best fit is selected. We might test ABC classification by itself, ABC plus purchased or manufactured, and ABC plus product family. For each of these, capture minimum, average, and maximum standard deviations, then create a consolidated table as shown in Figure 14-3. This allows us to see the grouping options in one organized table.

Yes, it's difficult to digest this many data points, even in a table, so we can create a graph of these values. Since we need three data points for each type (minimum, average, maximum), use Excel's stock charting option and select markers and fill colors that make minimum, average, and maximum easy to discern, as in Figure 14-4 on page 160.

Figure 14-3. <u>Target SS Standard Deviation Data in Table</u>

We have 3 different grouping options under consideration:

1. ABC classification

2. ABC and purchased or manufactured

3. ABC and product family

This table shows minimum, average, and maximum values for each of the three grouping options. From this data we need to select the grouping option that has the most safety stock similarity among the items in any given subgroup, but that also has divergence from subtype to subtype.

	Min	Avg	Max
A	0.2	0.6	1.1
B	0.2	0.8	1.5
C	0.1	1.1	1.9
A/M	0.3	0.6	0.7
B/M	0.2	0.8	1.5
C/M	0.2	1.4	1.9
A/P	0.2	0.6	1.1
B/P	0.3	0.8	1.0
C/P	0.1	0.9	1.6
A Food	0.5	0.7	1.1
B Food	0.6	1.1	1.5
C Food	1.6	1.8	1.9
A Pharm	0.3	0.5	0.8
B Pharm	0.3	0.7	1.0
C Pharm	0.8	0.8	0.9
A Water	0.2	0.2	0.2
B Water	0.2	0.2	0.2
C Water	0.1	0.2	0.2

Figure 14-4. Stock Chart of Min-Avg-Max Standard Deviations

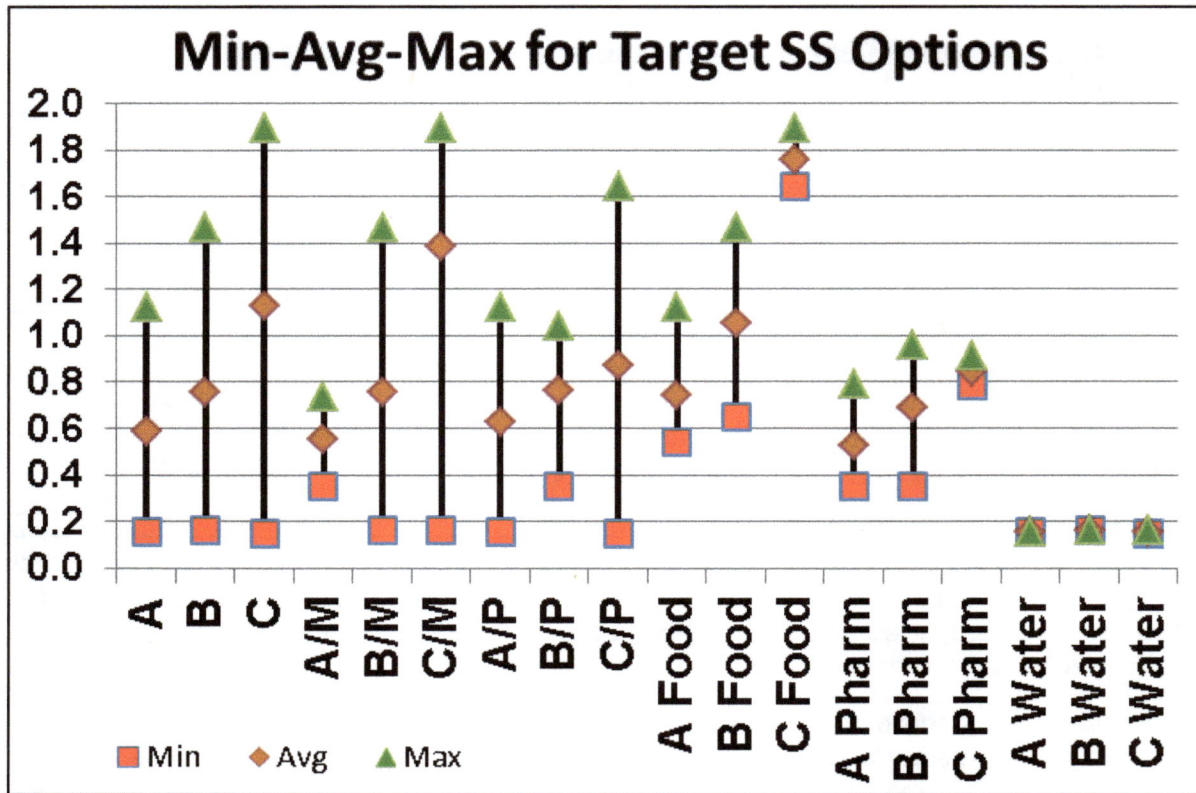

7. Using either a data table, like Figure 14-3 on page 159, or a chart like the one in Figure 14-4, select the best way to group parts, or the grouping option with the narrowest ranges within each type and the most divergence from type to type. Start by reviewing the data above and on the prior page, and make note of characteristics we can see from the data.

• The data for ABC classification, the first 3 plots in the graph above, shows a wide range from minimum to maximum and a lot of overlap. Every subgroup (A, B, and C) has a minimum standard deviation of 0.1 or 0.2, so there isn't much difference from A to B to C at the minimum standard deviation. Average and maximum values show some difference from class to class, but there is extensive overlap since the C classification covers the entire spread for A and B items, and the B range covers the entire A range. This tells us that items do not behave similarly based on ABC classification alone, so this grouping method is not a good fit.

• ABC versus purchased or manufactured is slightly better. The ranges are narrower for manufactured A items and purchased B items, but the overlap from type to type is still significant, and the other ranges from minimum to maximum are wide.

• ABC plus product family is the best option based on the stock chart above.

» The Water product family has standard deviation values of less than 0.2 days of demand across A, B, and C classifications. Water items need little or no target safety stock and there is no benefit to subdividing Water items by ABC or purchased or manufactured status.

» Pharmaceutical volatility has reasonable ranges from min to max, but there is some overlap for A and B items. It is interesting to note that C items are consistent at about 0.8 days of safety stock.

» The Food sector has the highest target safety stock needs, with A items needing slightly less than B's, and C's needing the most, at about 1.8 days. B items have the widest range but C items are surprisingly narrow. There is overlap from A to B but that overlap occurs in every grouping option that was studied.

Notice the narrower standard deviation ranges for C items when divided by product family, versus C items in total. This tells us that not <u>all</u> C items exhibit high volatility, just those in Food and somewhat in Pharmaceuticals.

When completing this exercise, always remember that <u>every</u> item with the same parameters (i.e., <u>all</u> Water items or <u>all</u> C Food items) will be given exactly the <u>same</u> target safety stock. In this case, every C item from the Food product family will have 1.8 days of target safety stock for a kanban solution. With proper grouping, every kanban item should succeed in protecting delivery from demand volatility with target safety stock equal to the <u>average</u> days of deviation from its assigned group. It might be tempting to use the maximum standard deviation for a subgroup as the target safety stick value, but that would be very aggressive and would assign too much safety stock to the vast majority of items. This is why it's important to find reasonable groups!

HINT for Associates

As an error check, calculate how many types exist within a defined grouping option to ensure that the correct number of results are created. The total number of group types for all possible combinations equals [N1 * N2 * N3...* Nn], where N1 to Nn are the count of "choices" within each defined parameter. ABC classification has three types (N = 3) due to the three choices of A, B, or C. If we evaluate ABC versus purchased or manufactured, we have three options for ABC and two for PM, so there are six possible combinations, or [3 * 2 = 6].

Compare the count of average standard deviations in a table or chart to the number of types we expect to have to ensure none were missed. If we expect six types but only have five average standard deviation values, we missed a combination. This is a great error-proofing tool when there are multiple grouping options in combination, e.g., ABC plus purchased versus manufactured plus lead-time category plus market served, and therefore a large number of combinations.

8. Once the right grouping option is selected, create a safety stock reference table like the one to the right. For this data set, target safety stock is based on ABC versus product family.

	Water	Pharmaceutical	Food
A	0.2	0.5	0.7
B	0.2	0.7	1.1
C	0.2	0.8	1.8

HINT for Associates

For item populations that are highly volatile, there might not be a grouping option that minimizes the range from small to large and simultaneously limits overlap from type to type. When faced with that dilemma, ensure that multiple options have been tested, and if none of the grouping options look any better, choose the best fit from the selection of reasonable options. If nothing comes at all close to being a good fit, it might be necessary to assign target safety stock by part number, as described in the next section.

9. Demand analysis must be kept up to date, which requires periodic repetition of the demand variation analysis. For most sites, calculated target safety stock values should be valid for up to a year. It would be <u>very</u> rare for demand variation analysis to be necessary every time kanban solutions are resized or when new items are added to kanban.

If demand changes due to a change in product mix or overall demand, it might be necessary to repeat the demand variation analysis to confirm that variation patterns have not changed and the selected grouping option is still valid.

How to Handle Seasonality & Other Demand Shifts

When demand exhibits seasonality, each season's demand data must be analyzed separately. Once seasons are defined, as discussed in the Seasonal Demand chapter, evaluate each season's demand data to set <u>target safety stock by season</u> using the steps described above.

Option 2: Calculate Demand Variation Target Safety Stock for Individual Part Numbers

It is sometimes necessary to calculate standard deviation days of demand and assign target safety stock for every individual item, but this method is difficult to sustain and should only be used if grouping is impossible.

Steps to Assign Calculated Safety Stock Values to Individual Part Numbers

1. Calculate standard deviation for every item, as described in the previous chapter.

2. Create an Excel look-up list with a target safety stock value for every part number. Target SS is equal to the average standard deviation in days of demand, or in units of measure for that specific item.

3. In the kanban calculator, use Excel's VLOOKUP or another index function to pull the correct safety stock value from the reference table for every kanban item.

Pulling individual data from a reference list might seem simple, but maintaining that list of safety stock values is extremely tedious. Sites with a large number of part numbers will soon discover that managing large spreadsheets is challenging. Thousands of rows of data is the first challenge, and keeping it up to date is a nightmare.

Sometimes Measure Standard Deviation As Percent of Lead-Time Demand

It can be insightful to compare standard deviation measured in units versus total lead-time demand to see how significant the variation is.

• If standard deviation is 100 and total lead-time demand [Actual lead time * daily demand] is also 100, the ratio of standard deviation to demand is 1:1, so standard deviation is 100% of total lead-time demand. That's really high, but it happens in the real world.

• If standard deviation is 100 and lead-time demand is 100,000 it's a much different story. The ratio of standard deviation to total lead-time demand is 1:1000, so there is much less variability and standard deviation is just 0.1% of demand.

This can also be done as standard deviation in days of demand versus actual lead time in days.

Highly volatile items should be on multi-card solutions, to enable frequent and easy resizing. Remember that a multi-card solution does not address high demand variation, which must be covered by safety stock. A multi-card solution just makes it easier to move the kanban solution slightly up or down if average daily demand shifts as part of the volatility.

If multi-card solutions are used for highly volatile items, any part number that needs a multi-card solution can be categorized based on standard deviation as a percent of lead-time demand.

Consider the following data for a population of items.

	[Standard deviation in units / Lead-time demand in units]
Minimum ratio across all items	.005
Average ratio	0.4
Maximum ratio	1.3

The range of ratios is a high of 1.3 down to .005, with an average of 0.4. For this population of parts, the most volatile item has a standard deviation that is 1.3 times the total lead-time demand, so if lead-time demand was 100, the standard deviation for a single lead-time period would be 130 pieces.

Based on the ratios of standard deviation versus lead-time demand across a population of items, we can define high and low benchmarks for variation categories. This is not an exact science, but high volatility items generally exhibit twice as much volatility as the average item in the population. For this example, the average ratio is 0.4, so two times that number is 0.8.

	[Standard deviation / Lead-time demand] ratio
High demand variation category	0.8 or greater
Low demand variation category	0.2 or less

Rule of Thumb

Benchmarks vary from site to site, but if an entire population of items exhibits [Standard deviation units / Lead-time demand] ratios of less than about 0.2 to 0.3, the volatility is manageable without special handling. Don't force multi-card solutions unless variation is greater than 0.3 times total lead-time demand.

To identify <u>highly volatile</u> items, consider a cutoff of [standard deviation / lead-time demand] greater than 2 times the average standard deviation ratio for the population of items.

Assign Demand Variation Target Safety Stock for Multi-Card Solutions

When assigning target safety stock, 1-card and 2-card solutions are easy to manage but caution is required for multi-card solutions. A multi-card kanban solution establishes the standard order quantity, then calculates the correct number of cards based on the item's current daily demand, actual lead time, and target safety stock. Some people fall into the trap of basing a multi-card order quantity on [Target Lead time * Daily Demand + Target SS], which puts all required safety stock into the order quantity and ignores the switch to target lead time. To fix this, multi-card solutions utilize a target safety stock <u>multiplier</u> to prevent the kanban order quantity from being artificially increased by too much safety stock.

To prevent the error of putting all safety stock into the order quantity, express target safety stock as a percent of total lead-time demand, as described before, and assign target safety stock as a multiple of lead-time demand.

> ### Target Safety Stock Percent
>
> Target SS % = (Target safety stock days * Daily demand / (Actual LT * Daily demand)
>
> or
>
> Target safety stock days/ Actual Lead-time days

The first formula in the box is easier to understand, but it is more complicated than it needs to be and is mathematically redundant. It isn't necessary to include "Daily demand" in both the numerator and denominator, but that redundancy clarifies that target safety stock *units* are compared to total lead-time demand in *units*. The simplified formula at the bottom of the formula box [Target SS Days / Actual LT Days] works as long as target safety stock is expressed in days of demand to compare to lead-time days.

The kanban order quantity for a multi-card solution is based on target safety stock as a percent of daily demand times lead time.

> ### Kanban Order Quantity for Multi-Card Solution
>
> Multi-card kanban order quantity = (Target lead-time * Daily demand) * (1 + Target SS %)

> ### Target Safety Stock Percent Example
>
> A multi-card part has a lead-time of 25 days, daily demand of 10, and target safety stock of 2 days. Target lead-time is 5 days and the item is EaB.
>
> Total demand over the lead-time period is 250, but the quantity to be ordered during one lead-time period including safety stock is [(25 days lead-time + 2 days safety stock) * 10 per day = 270].
>
> Suppose we intend to manage this item with a multi-card solution to address actual lead-time of 25 versus target lead-time of 5 days. Target safety stock is 20 parts out of lead-time demand of 250 pieces, so if we add 20 pieces of safety stock to every card in a multi-card solution, or to the target lead-time quantity using the formula [Target lead-time * Daily demand + Target safety stock units], we end up with a kanban order quantity = [5 days * 10 per day) + 20 pieces = 70 pieces. Let's see if that is correct.
>
> With a target lead-time of 5 days, this item should have 6 cards: 5 cards for the 25-day lead-time divided by the 5-day target plus 1 for EaB. If we use 6 cards and the inflated KOQ of 70, actual safety stock is really high.
>
> Actual safety stock = (# cards - 1) * KOQ - (Actual lead-time * Daily demand) = (6-1) * 70 - (25 * 10) = 350 - 250 = 100 pieces of safety stock versus the target of 20
>
> We need to correct the KOQ. Instead of adding the entire safety stock quantity to the order quantity, multiply target lead-time demand by target safety stock as a percent of lead-time.
>
> Target SS % = 2 days target safety stock / 25 days actual lead-time = 8%
>
> KOQ = (5 days target lead-time * 10 per day) * (1.08 SS factor) = 54
>
> Actual safety stock = (6 cards - 1) * 54 - (25 days * 10 per day) = 270 - 250 = 20, which is the target.

Total Target Safety Stock = Supply Safety Stock + Demand Safety Stock

The final target safety stock value for every item must include safety stock for both supply and demand variation. If any items need both supply (push) and demand (pull) safety stock, use three columns in the spreadsheet to express safety stock. The first column is how much safety stock is required to cover variation in supply, the next column indicates demand safety stock, and the third column sums supply plus demand safety stock to get total target safety stock. Ensure the units of safety stock are consistent, e.g., always units of measure or days of demand.

Demand Target Safety Stock Summary

Calculating standard deviations across a population of part numbers is a chore, but that's just half the battle. Deciding how to assign safety stock based on standard deviation results is just as critical as getting the math right.

Assigning safety stock to individual part numbers is generally not necessary. Instead, group items wisely and create a reference table to assign safety stock based on an item's characteristics.

Don't forget to add required supplier safety stock to get total target safety stock per item.

The steps required to analyze demand variation and assign safety stock can be summarized in a decision tree, in Figure 14-5.

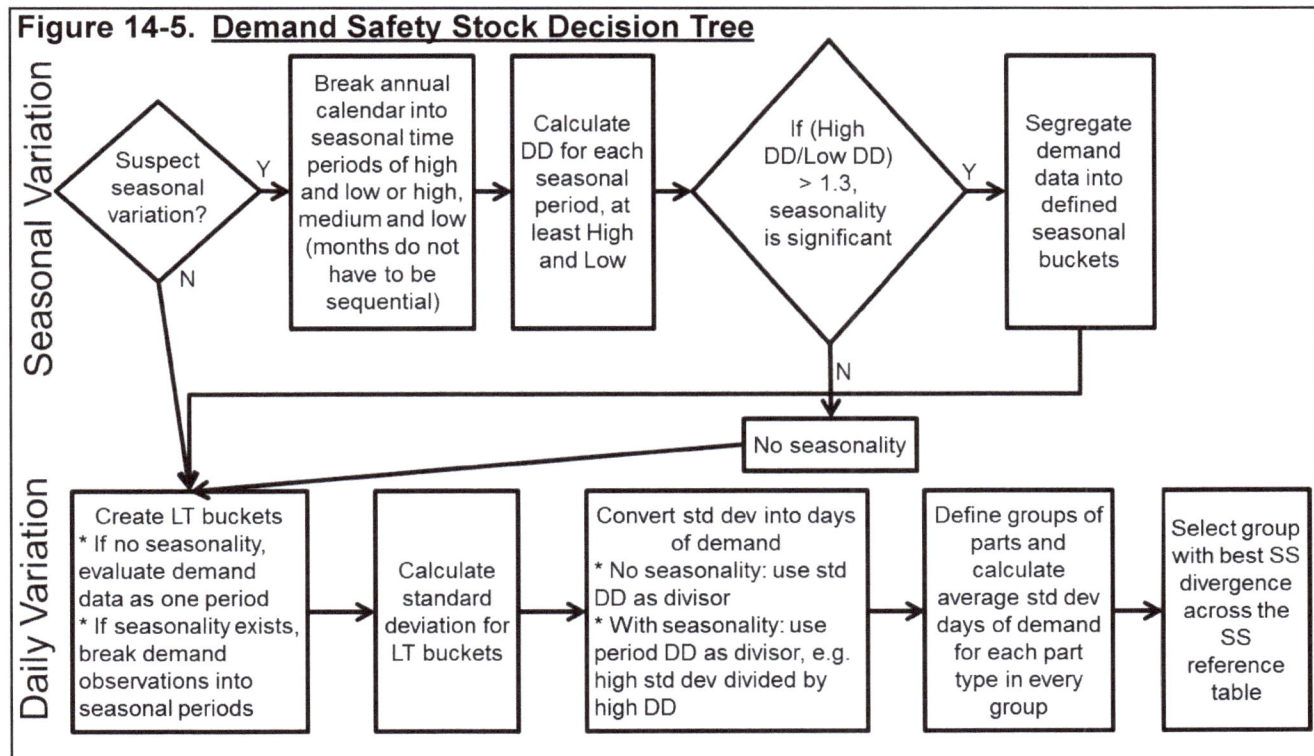

Figure 14-5. **Demand Safety Stock Decision Tree**

TUTORIAL: GOCO DEMAND SAFETY STOCK

Mary wasn't sure how to group items to assign target safety stock for demand variation, so she created a series of pivot tables to group parts by combinations of ABC, Purchased or Manufactured, and lead-time category (Short, Medium, or Long). The pivot tables captured minimum, average, and maximum standard deviation in days of demand. Average values are displayed in Figure 14-6.

Figure 14-6. Pivot Tables for Average Days of Standard Deviation

High

Average of High Season Std Colu ▼

Row Labels ▼	S	M	L	Grand Total
A	0.57	0.27	0.33	0.52
B	0.22	0.73	0.21	0.58
C	0.51	1.25	0.90	0.87
Grand Total	0.53	0.74	0.80	0.69

Average of High Season St Colu ▼

Row Labels ▼	M	P	Grand Total
A	0.63	0.24	0.52
B	0.86	0.24	0.58
C	1.14	0.57	0.87
Grand Total	0.89	0.41	0.69

Average of High Season Std umn L ▼

Row Labels ▼	Ag	Auto	Ind	All	Grand Total
A	0.73	0.41	0.69	0.22	0.52
B	1.44	0.33	0.52	0.31	0.58
C	2.07	0.44	0.87	0.48	0.87
Grand Total	1.34	0.40	0.72	0.37	0.69

Average of High Season St umn L ▼

Row Labels ▼	Ag	Auto	Ind	All	Grand Total
S	0.73	0.41	0.63	0.35	0.53
M	1.45	0.45	0.72	0.35	0.74
L	2.22	0.38	0.76	0.42	0.80
Grand Total	1.34	0.40	0.72	0.37	0.69

Low

Average of Low Std Dev Day Colu ▼

Row Labels ▼	S	M	L	Grand Total
A	0.60	0.26	0.52	0.55
B	0.36	0.94	0.24	0.75
C	0.34	1.25	1.34	1.19
Grand Total	0.53	0.89	1.18	0.89

Average of Low Std Dev Da Colu ▼

Row Labels ▼	M	P	Grand Total
A	0.65	0.30	0.55
B	1.16	0.23	0.75
C	1.63	0.70	1.19
Grand Total	1.17	0.49	0.89

Average of Low Std Dev Day umn L ▼

Row Labels ▼	Ag	Auto	Ind	All	Grand Total
A	0.77	0.36	0.94	0.26	0.55
B	1.43	0.40	1.08	0.31	0.75
C	1.85	0.50	2.71	0.39	1.19
Grand Total	1.27	0.44	1.87	0.34	0.89

Average of Low Std Dev Da umn L ▼

Row Labels ▼	Ag	Auto	Ind	All	Grand Total
S	0.77	0.32	0.94	0.27	0.53
M	1.37	0.52	1.41	0.32	0.89
L	2.01	0.45	2.53	0.44	1.18
Grand Total	1.27	0.44	1.87	0.34	0.89

The tables at the top of the sheet, with the green band in the top row, were for the high months of the year, February through August. The bottom tables, below the pink band, were the same pivot table designs for the low season. She drew basic conclusions from the pivot tables of average standard deviations.

1. For the High season:

• From the Grand Total <u>column</u> in the top left table, A items at 0.52 days had slightly less variation than B's at 0.58, and C's were the highest at 0.87, as shown in the far right column of the top left table.

• From the Grand Total <u>row</u> in the top left table, short lead-time items at 0.53 days were better than medium at 0.74, and long lead-time items demonstrated the highest variation of 0.80 days.

• In the Grand Total row on the top right table, purchased items were more stable than manufactured, at 0.41 versus 0.89 days.

• In the Grand Total row in the second table on the left, All averaged 0.37, Auto was 0.40, Industrial was 0.72, and Ag was a very 1.34. Mary noticed that Auto and "All" parts had flat variation, with Auto ranging from at 0.33 to 0.44 days and All from 0.22 to 0.48 days.

• It looked like Short, Medium and Long LT versus Customer Group was the pivot table with the best divergence in target safety stock days.

2. For the Low season:

• Low season variation was slightly higher than the High season, but the patterns were similar.

» A items at 0.55 days had slightly less variation than B's at 0.75, and C's were the highest at 1.19, which matched the pattern for the High seasons but with higher variation for B and C items.

» Purchased items were more stable than manufactured, 0.49 days versus 1.17, both of which were higher than during High season.

» Short lead-time items at 0.53 days were better than medium at 0.89, and long lead-time items demonstrated the highest variation of 1.18 days.

» Auto and "All" parts had flat variation, with Auto from 0.36 to 0.5 days and All from 0.26 to 0.39 days.

» Ag and Industrial parts had the highest variation by far, above 2.0 days in several areas.

Mary created data tables from the results in the pivot tables so she could create charts of minimum, average and maximum standard deviation values using the Excel stock chart. See Figure 14-7.

Figure 14-7. <u>Data Table Created from Pivot Tables</u>

With such a broad range of possible grouping options, Mary's data list was very long, and selecting the best grouping option was impossible without charting each possible option.

	Min	Average	Max
A	0.06	0.52	0.90
B	0.08	0.58	1.75
C	0.05	0.87	3.24
P	0.05	0.41	1.74
M	0.17	0.89	3.24
Short	0.05	0.53	0.90
Med	0.08	0.74	1.75
Long	0.10	0.80	3.24
Ag	0.63	1.34	3.24
Auto	0.10	0.40	0.87
Ind	0.08	0.72	1.48
All	0.05	0.37	1.07
A Purch	0.06	0.24	0.52
B Purch	0.08	0.24	0.73
C Purch	0.05	0.57	1.74
A Manf	0.21	0.63	0.90
B Manf	0.20	0.86	1.75
C Manf	0.17	1.14	3.24
A Short	0.06	0.57	0.90
A Med	0.10	0.22	0.43
A Long	0.05	0.51	0.79
B Short	0.10	0.27	0.52
B Med	0.08	0.73	1.75
B Long	0.76	1.25	1.64
C Short	0.26	0.33	0.40
C Med	0.10	0.21	0.36
C Long	0.11	0.90	3.24

	Min	Average	Max
A Ag	0.63	0.73	0.90
B Ag	1.19	1.44	1.75
C Ag	1.32	2.07	3.24
A Auto	0.21	0.41	0.54
B Auto	0.10	0.33	0.58
C Auto	0.12	0.44	0.87
A Ind	0.62	0.69	0.82
B Ind	0.08	0.52	1.16
C Ind	0.15	0.87	1.48
A All	0.06	0.22	0.52
B All	0.10	0.31	0.73
C All	0.05	0.48	1.07
Ag Short	0.63	0.73	0.90
Ag Med	1.19	1.45	1.75
Ag Long	1.73	2.22	3.24
Auto Short	0.21	0.41	0.54
Auto Med	0.20	0.45	0.76
Auto Long	0.10	0.38	0.87
Ind Short	0.43	0.63	0.82
Ind Med	0.08	0.72	1.29
Ind Long	0.15	0.76	1.48
All Short	0.05	0.35	0.79
All Med	0.10	0.35	0.73
All Long	0.11	0.42	1.07

Mary first charted the most basic grouping options with just one parameter, e.g., ABC <u>or</u> P/M <u>or</u> Customer Group <u>or</u> lead-time category, for a total of 12 plots. See Figure 14-8.

Figure 14-8. <u>Basic Standard Deviation Group Options</u>

Every grouping option had a lot of overlap from subgroup to subgroup, and the range from minimum to maximum was wide for C items, Manufactured items, long lead-time items, and Industrial items in the low season. These high season plots showed no potential to serve as the final grouping option.

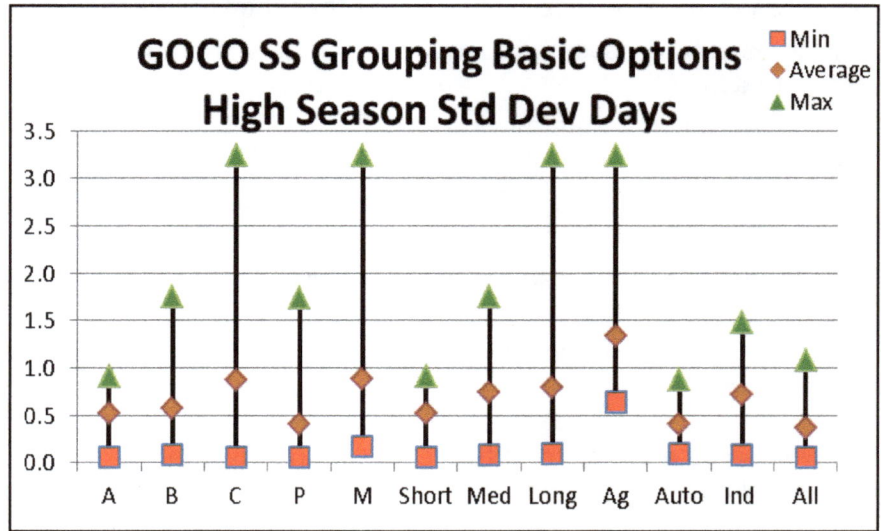

GOCO SS Grouping Basic Options High Season Std Dev Days

Legend: ■ Min   ◆ Average   ▲ Max

(X axis categories: A, B, C, P, M, Short, Med, Long, Ag, Auto, Ind, All)

Mary noticed that the scale for the Y axis on the Low season chart was one day higher than the high season, confirming the observation from the original data tables that demand variation was higher during the low season. She also recognized that these basic sorting options also had a lot of overlap and min/max ranges were tall.

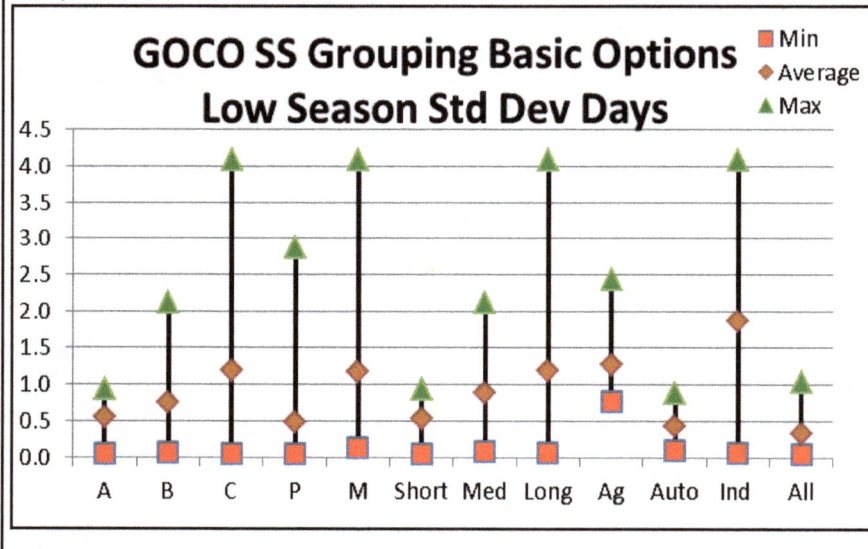

GOCO SS Grouping Basic Options Low Season Std Dev Days

Legend: ■ Min   ◆ Average   ▲ Max

(X axis categories: A, B, C, P, M, Short, Med, Long, Ag, Auto, Ind, All)

In both high and low season, Customer Group showed the most promise. Auto and All items had much lower variation, and Ag was the highest.

None of the simple grouping options looked like a good fit due to their wide ranges and high overlap, so Mary created charts for more complex options. See Figure 14-9 on page 169 for the various combinations. Mary marked the chart with comments, using red for unfavorable or "bad" conditions and green for good conditions, in true Lean visual management style.

Figure 14-9. Complex Standard Deviation Group Options, High & Low Seasons

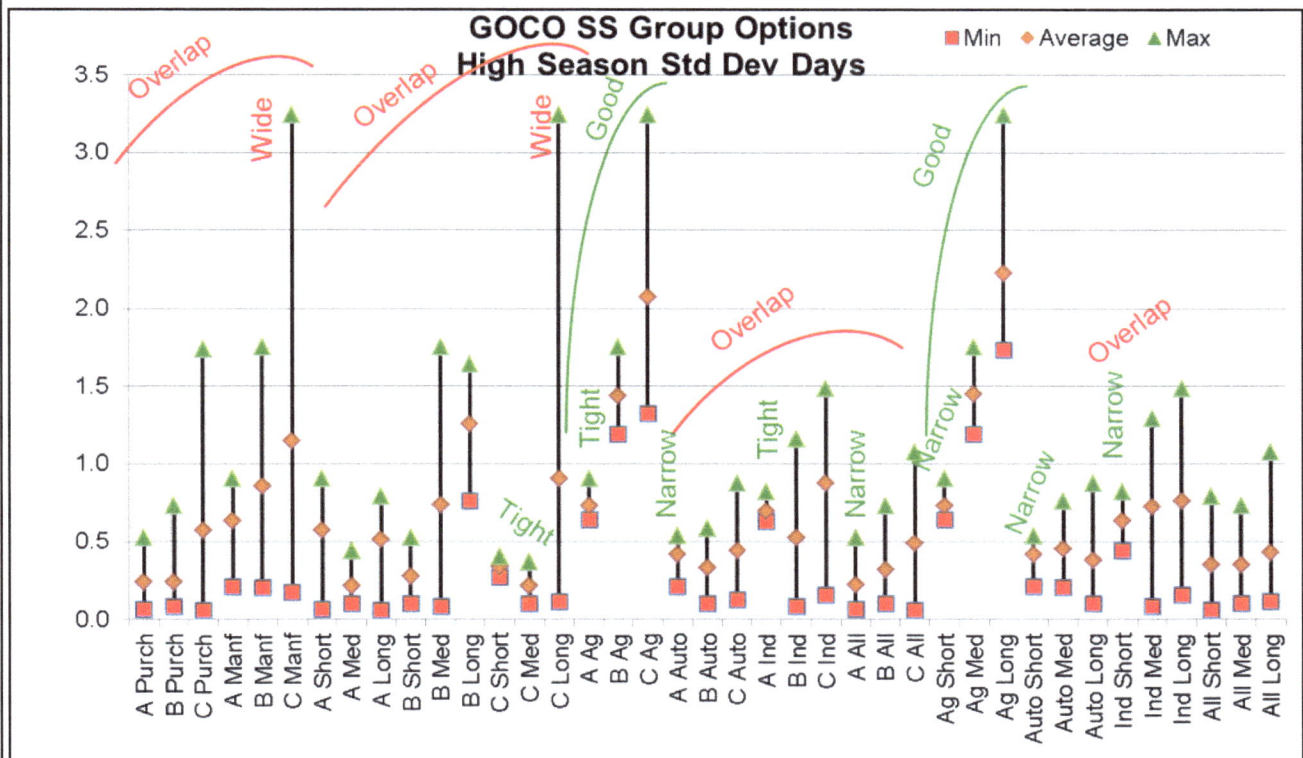

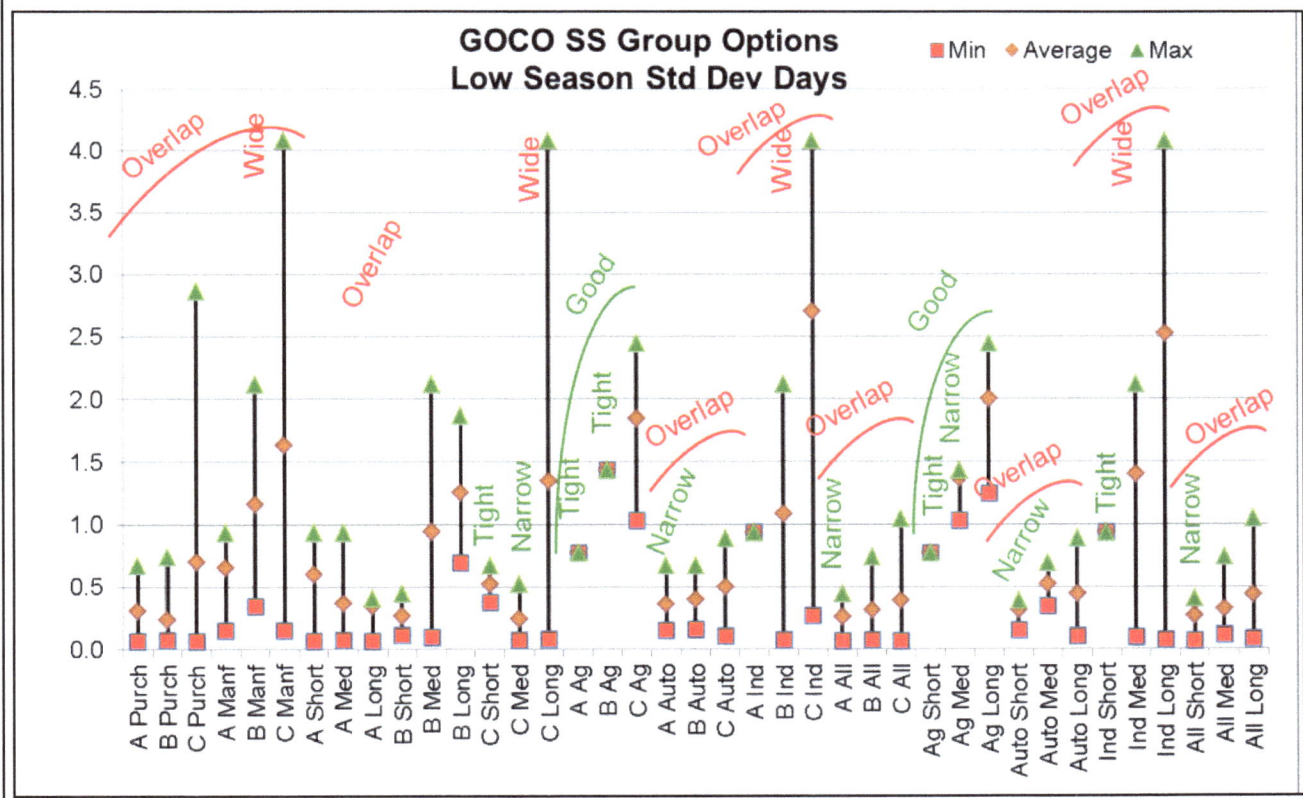

• "Overlap" meant the subgroups or types within a grouping option demonstrated overlap from type to type, indicating a lack of divergence for safety stock days. Mary noted that overlap occurred in every grouping option.

• A "Good" comment meant overlap for a segment of a grouping was minimal.

• "Wide" pointed out a range from minimum to maximum that was particularly tall. She had noticed before in the basic chart that C items, manufactured, long lead-time items, and Industrial parts all had wide ranges, so she wasn't surprised that so many chart lines were tall.

• "Narrow" and "Tight" indicated ranges that were pretty good, with little spread from minimum to maximum.

3. For both seasons, ABC versus Customer Group <u>or</u> Lead-time Category versus Customer Group looked the most promising.

• Due to the different variation patterns across the Customer Groups, it was clear it had to be one of the safety stock assignment parameters. This confirmed what Mary observed when she plotted just the different Customer Groups.

• For simplicity, Mary concluded that she could set one target safety stock number for Auto and All, regardless of season. Auto items needed 0.4 days regardless of season and All parts needed 0.5 days.

• For the remaining parts, Mary has to choose Customer Group versus either A, B, and C or versus Short, Medium, and Long lead-times. Both choices displayed similar divergence, so Mary chose ABC because it was simpler to apply because ABC classification was always available as an item attribute and short, medium, or long lead-time would have to be calculated.

Mary entered target safety stock data on the Targets & Limits tab shown in Figure 14-10.

Figure 14-10. <u>GOCO Target SS Values</u>

High Months	Ag	Auto	Ind	All
A	0.70	0.40	0.70	0.20
B	1.40	0.30	0.50	0.30
C	2.10	0.40	0.90	0.50
VMI	1.00			

Low Months	Ag	Auto	Ind	All
A	0.80	0.40	0.90	0.50
B	1.40	0.40	1.10	0.50
C	1.80	0.50	2.70	0.50
VMI	1.00			

• She rounded standard deviation values to one decimal place.

• She overwrote Auto and All safety stock values to 0.5 for Auto and 0.4 for All and highlighted them in yellow as a reminder that the values had been modified.

• She set all VMI parts to one day of target safety stock. VMI parts were reviewed at least twice a week when the supplier checked inventory. So, target safety stock wouldn't actually drive the level of stock on the floor. But, providing a safety stock value for the calculator would allow it to accurately calculate a KOQ that would be a reference for how to size the physical bin for every VMI part so that the supplier couldn't overfill the shelves.

CHAPTER 15: DEMAND VARIATION EXAMPLE

Demand variation analysis warrants a long example so let's analyze a simple data set with the following features.

- 24 part numbers (PN)
- Three industry categories: Food, Pharmacy, and Water Treatment
- Lead times range from 1 to 3 weeks
- ABC classification plus purchased or manufactured status indicated in the data set
- Five weeks of demand history. No, we wouldn't really run analysis on just 5 weeks of data, but that's what fits on a page for this example. Humor me.
- Rolling lead-time buckets, so 5 possible lead-time buckets for items with 1-week lead time, but just 3 buckets for 3-week lead-time part numbers
- No seasonality

The data set is in Figure 15-1 on page 172.

Column labels (A, B, C, etc.) are in the first row and row numbers are listed in the left-most column so that we can locate the cells that are mentioned in formulas.

Figure 15-1 also contains lead-time buckets and statistics calculated about those buckets, starting in column I.

The formulas that created lead-time buckets and calculated bucket statistics are listed in Figure 15-2 on page 173 and in Figure 15-3 on page 174.

Figure 15-1. Demand Data, LT Buckets, LT Bucket Statistics

	B	C	D	E	F	G	H	I	J	K	L	M	N	O	P	Q	R
A1	Part	LT Weeks	Demand Week 1	Demand Week 2	Demand Week 3	Demand Week 4	Demand Week 5	LT Bucket 1	LT Bucket 2	LT Bucket 3	LT Bucket 4	LT Bucket 5	Avg LT Demand	Avg DD	LT Bucket Std Dev	Std Dev/Avg LT Dem	Std Dev Days Demand
3	1	1	10	15	12	18	13	10	15	12	18	13	13.6	2.7	3.0	0.22	1.12
4	2	2	26	36	30	42	44		62	66	72	86	71.5	7.2	10.5	0.15	1.47
5	3	3	36	52	42	66	48			130	160	156	148.7	9.9	16.3	0.11	1.64
6	4	1	20	27	24	30	25	20	27	24	30	25	25.2	5.0	3.7	0.15	0.73
7	5	2	31	42	39	51	41		73	81	90	92	84.0	8.4	8.8	0.10	1.04
8	6	2	38	42	42	54	66		80	84	96	120	95.0	9.5	18.0	0.19	1.89
9	7	1	31	36	33	39	34	31	36	33	39	34	34.6	6.9	3.0	0.09	0.44
10	8	2	44	52	48	62	50		96	100	110	112	104.5	10.5	7.7	0.07	0.74
11	9	3	57	72	63	81	66			192	216	210	206.0	13.7	12.5	0.06	0.91
12	10	1	40	45	42	48	43	40	45	42	48	43	43.6	8.7	3.0	0.07	0.35
13	11	2	50	62	55	70	69		112	117	125	139	123.3	12.3	11.8	0.10	0.96
14	12	3	69	71	70	73	67			210	214	210	211.3	14.1	2.3	0.01	0.16
15	13	1	50	54	51	53	52	50	54	51	53	52	52.0	10.4	1.6	0.03	0.15
16	14	2	66	70	67	70	71		136	137	137	141	137.8	13.8	2.2	0.02	0.16
17	15	3	87	90	88	92	86			265	270	266	267.0	17.8	2.6	0.01	0.15
18	16	1	52	63	70	66	61	52	63	70	66	61	62.4	12.5	6.7	0.11	0.54
19	17	2	71	81	75	87	77		152	156	162	164	158.5	15.9	5.5	0.03	0.35
20	18	2	106	108	97	68	80		214	205	165	148	183.0	18.3	31.6	0.17	1.73
21	19	1	60	88	69	75	70	60	88	69	75	70	72.4	14.5	10.3	0.14	0.71
22	20	2	80	80	84	96	86		160	164	180	182	171.5	17.2	11.1	0.06	0.65
23	21	1	105	78	111	85	84	105	78	111	85	84	92.6	18.5	14.5	0.16	0.78
24	22	2	86	92	90	108	92		178	182	198	200	189.5	19.0	11.1	0.06	0.59
25	23	1	111	122	98	88	90	111	122	98	88	90	101.8	20.4	14.5	0.14	0.71
26	24	2	93	92	96	122	144		185	188	218	266	214.3	21.4	37.6	0.18	1.75

Figure 15-2. Formulas for LT Buckets

Column I: LT Bucket 1 = IF ($C3 = 1, D3, "")

If the LT for this part is 1 week, select Demand Week 1 in cell D3

If LT is not 1, leave the cell blank

Column J: LT Bucket 2 = IF ($C3 = 1, E3, IF ($C3 = 2, SUM (D3:E3), ""))

If the LT for this part is 1 week, select Demand Week 2 in cell E3

If the LT for this part is 2 weeks, sum Demand Week 1 to Demand Week 2

If the LT is not 1 or 2, leave the cell blank

Column K: LT Bucket 3 = IF ($C3 = 1, F3, IF ($C3 = 2, SUM (E3:F3), IF ($C3 = 3, SUM (D3:F3))))

If the LT for this part is 1 week, select Demand Week 3 in cell F3

If the LT for this part is 2 weeks, sum Demand Week 2 to Demand Week 3

Else sum Demand Week 1 to Demand Week 3

Column L: LT Bucket 4 = IF ($C3 = 1, G3, IF ($C3 = 2, SUM (F3:G3), IF ($C3 = 3, SUM (E3:G3))))

If the LT for this part is 1 week, select Demand Week 4 in cell G3

If the LT for this part is 2 weeks, sum Demand Week 3 to Demand Week 4

Else sum Demand Week 2 to Demand Week 4

Column M: LT Bucket 5 = IF ($C3 = 1, H3, IF ($C3 = 2, SUM (G3:H3), IF ($C3 = 3, SUM (F3:H3))))

If the LT for this part is 1 week, select Demand Week 5 in cell H3

If the LT for this part is 2 weeks, sum Demand Week 4 to Demand Week 5

Else sum Demand Week 3 to Demand Week 5

The last three portions of the formulas for columns K, L, and M instruct Excel to sum 3 weeks of data no matter how long the lead time is. So, a part with a lead time of 6 weeks would sum 3 weeks of demand data in each bucket, not 6 weeks. This data set only has lead times up to 3 weeks, so this formula doesn't cut off any lead-time data. In the real world, 3 weeks is too short to use as a maximum allowed lead time. I recommend at least 6 weeks, if lead-time has to be restricted to a cutoff.

Lead-time weeks is in column C, with blue shading in the heading. Note that lead-time bucket formulas use the "locked" reference format for the lead-time column (refers to cell $C3, not a defined name reference), where "$" locks the reference to column C but no "$" in front of the row number allows the row reference to float. This formula can be copied from one column to the next and still refer correctly to lead-time weeks in column C for each subsequent formula.

Figure 15-3. **Formulas for LT Bucket Statistics**

Column N = Average LT Demand = AVERAGE (I3:M3)

This simply calculates the average of the 5 demand weeks.

Column O = Average DD = N3 / (MIN ($C3,3) * 5)

This pulls Average LT demand (column N) and divides it by the number of workdays in the LT period. Because we limited LT buckets to 3 weeks of demand, we can't divide Average LT demand (column N) by the LT workdays. The formula assumes that there could have been lead times in the data that were longer than 3 weeks. In this example, there weren't any long lead times but there could have been in the real world. To accommodate the 3-week limitation, divide by the smaller of either [LT weeks in column C or 3 weeks] times 5 days per week. An alternate formula for this cell is to average the demand week data and divide that by 5, e.g., = AVERAGE (D3:H3) / 5

Column P = LT bucket std dev = STDEV (I3:M3)

Column Q = Std Dev / Avg LT Dem = P3 / N3

Column R = Std Dev Days Demand = P3 / O3

Figure 15-5 on page 175 shows the group option labels in columns S, T and U: ABC, purchased versus manufactured, and Industry group (Food, Pharmacy, and Water.)

We can obtain average standard deviation days for one or two grouping parameters, i.e., ABC plus P/M, but if we want to combine all three parameters we need to add columns to Excel for each subgroup.

Starting in column V in Figure 15-5 on page 175, there is a column for each of the 18 combinations of ABC plus PM plus industry, e.g., A/P Food, C/M Pharm, C/P Water, etc.

The formulas that populated columns V through AM are in Figure 15-6 on page 176, along with the resulting target safety stock table for the 18 combinations.

Using pivot tables (not shown) and the target safety stock table at the bottom of Figure 15-6 on page 176, we can assemble possible target SS tables for the various grouping options, as listed in Figure 15-4.

To complete the analysis we would add minimum and maximum values, to look at ranges and overlap.

Note: If we had more than 24 part numbers and 5 weeks, ABC/PM with Industry might prove to be the best fit. But, with such limited data we can't calculate all the values necessary for 18 sub-groups. This demonstrates why it's necessary to have a broad data set!

Figure 15-4. **Target Safety Stock Tables**

A	0.6
B	0.8
C	1.1

	M	P
A	0.6	0.6
B	0.8	0.8
C	1.4	0.9

	Food	Pharm	Water
A	0.7	0.5	0.2
B	1.1	0.7	0.2
C	1.8	0.8	0.2

	Food	Pharm	Water
A/P	1.1	0.6	0.2
B/P	1.0	0.7	#DIV/0!
C/P	1.6	0.8	0.1
A/M	0.6	0.3	#DIV/0!
B/M	1.1	0.7	0.2
C/M	1.8	#DIV/0!	0.2

Figure 15-5. Demand Data, LT Buckets, LT Bucket Statistics

A1	B	C	R	S	T	U	V	W	X	Y	Z	AA	AB	AC	AD	AE	AF	AG	AH	AI	AJ	AK	AL	AM
2	Part	LT Weeks	Std Dev Days Demand	ABC	P/M	Product Family	A/P Food	B/P Food	C/P Food	A/M Food	B/M Food	C/M Food	A/P Pharm	B/P Pharm	C/P Pharm	A/M Pharm	B/M Pharm	C/M Pharm	A/P Water	B/P Water	C/P Water	A/M Water	B/M Water	C/M Water
3	1	1	1.12	A	P	Food	1.1																	
4	2	2	1.47	B	M	Food					1.5													
5	3	3	1.64	C	P	Food			1.6															
6	4	1	0.73	A	M	Food				0.7														
7	5	2	1.04	B	P	Food		1.0																
8	6	2	1.89	C	M	Food						1.9												
9	7	1	0.44	A	P	Pharm							0.4											
10	8	2	0.74	B	M	Pharm											0.7							
11	9	3	0.91	C	P	Pharm									0.9									
12	10	1	0.35	A	M	Pharm										0.3								
13	11	2	0.96	B	P	Pharm								1.0										
14	12	3	0.16	C	M	Water													0.2					
15	13	1	0.15	A	P	Water															0.1			
16	14	2	0.16	B	M	Water																	0.2	
17	15	3	0.15	C	P	Water																		0.2
18	16	1	0.54	A	M	Food				0.5														
19	17	2	0.35	B	P	Pharm								0.3										
20	18	2	1.73	C	M	Food						1.7												
21	19	1	0.71	A	P	Pharm							0.7											
22	20	2	0.65	B	M	Food					0.6													
23	21	1	0.78	C	P	Pharm									0.8									
24	22	2	0.59	A	M	Food				0.6														
25	23	1	0.71	B	P	Pharm								0.7										
26	24	2	1.75	C	M	Food						1.8												
	Average						1.1	1.0	1.6	0.6	1.1	1.8	0.6	0.7	0.8	0.3	0.7	#DIV/0!	0.2	#DIV/0!	0.1	#DIV/0!	0.2	0.2
	Count						1	1	1	3	2	3	2	3	2	1	1	0	1	0	1	0	1	1

Figure 15-6. Formulas for Standard Deviations by ABC, P/M, Industry Groupings

Each formula in row 3 checks for the right conditions using an IF formula with AND. If the part number matches all the parameter conditions, the AND formula is TRUE and Std Dev Days Demand is pulled from column R. If the item does not match all conditions, the cell is left blank.

Column V = A/P Food = IF (AND ($S3 ="A", $T3 ="P", $U3 = "Food"), $R3, "")

Column W = B/P Food = IF (AND ($S3 ="B", $T3 ="P", $U3 = "Food"), $R3, "")

Column X = C/P Food = IF (AND ($S3 ="C", $T3 ="P", $U3 = "Food"), $R3, "")

Column Y = A/M Food = IF (AND ($S3 ="A", $T3 ="M", $U3 = "Food"), $R3, "")

Column Z = B/M Food = IF (AND ($S3 ="B", $T3 ="M", $U3 = "Food"), $R3, "")

Column AA = C/M Food = IF (AND ($S3 ="C", $T3 ="M", $U3 = "Food"), $R3, "")

Column AB = A/P Pharm = IF (AND ($S3 ="A", $T3 ="P", $U3 = "Pharm"), $R3, "")

Column AC = B/P Pharm = IF (AND ($S3 ="B", $T3 ="P", $U3 = "Pharm"), $R3, "")

Column AD = C/P Pharm = IF (AND ($S3 ="C", $T3 ="P", $U3 = "Pharm"), $R3, "")

Column AE = A/M Pharm = IF (AND ($S3 ="A", $T3 ="M", $U3 = "Pharm"), $R3, "")

Column AF = B/M Pharm = IF (AND ($S3 ="B", $T3 ="M", $U3 = "Pharm"), $R3, "")

Column AG = C/M Pharm = IF (AND ($S3 ="C", $T3 ="M", $U3 = "Pharm"), $R3, "")

Column AH = A/P Water = IF (AND ($S3 ="A", $T3 ="P", $U3 = "Water"), $R3, "")

Column AI = B/P Water = IF (AND ($S3 ="B", $T3 ="P", $U3 = "Water"), $R3, "")

Column AJ = C/P Water = IF (AND ($S3 ="C", $T3 ="P", $U3 = "Water"), $R3, "")

Column AK = A/M Water = IF (AND ($S3 ="A", $T3 ="M", $U3 = "Water"), $R3, "")

Column AL = B/M Water = IF (AND ($S3 ="B", $T3 ="M", $U3 =" Water"), $R3, "")

Column AM = C/M Water = IF (AND ($S3 ="C", $T3 ="M", $U3 = "Water"), $R3, "")

At the bottom of each column is calculated average standard deviation days of demand for that subgroup, and also the count of items in the column. When working with such a small data set, it's important to know if subgroups are so small that "average" values are based on too few data points to accurately reflect a population of part numbers. In this data set of 24 part numbers and 18 defined groups, some columns have no results, and the best is just 3 items for a subgroup. Therefore, average standard deviations are essentially meaningless for all subgroups due to the lack of data, but the purpose of the example was to demonstrate the method for generating the standard deviation data for 3 simultaneous parameters (ABC, P/M, and Industry.)

If this was real data, we'd use average standard deviation for each column to build the target safety stock reference table, to the right.

	Food	Pharm	Water
A/P	1.1	0.6	0.2
B/P	1.0	0.7	#DIV/0!
C/P	1.6	0.8	0.1
A/M	0.6	0.3	#DIV/0!
B/M	1.1	0.7	0.2
C/M	1.8	#DIV/0!	0.2

SECTION IV.
SCOPE & DESIGN A
KANBAN SYSTEM

Scope a Kanban System

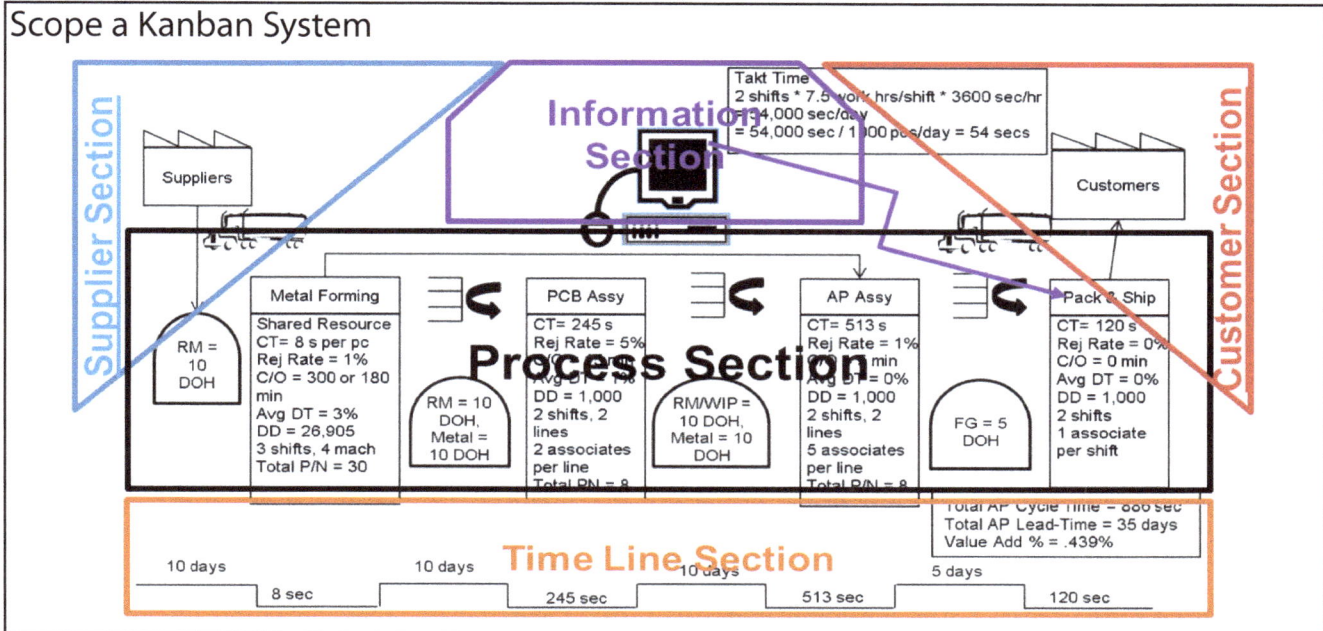

One part of calculating kanban solutions is determining where kanban fits and where it doesn't. A knowledgeable kanban designer or a robust kanban calculator must be capable of determining where kanban does not fit.

Sometimes kanban is excluded for all the right reasons, such as where flow exists and hence inventory is not needed.

Other times kanban is excluded for specific items that are burdened by difficult characteristics, like an extremely high minimum order quantity or an unstable supply situation.

Successful kanban deployment must look beyond the immediate tactical issues of deploying cards and boards and also tackle the strategic opportunities to enhance kanban by expanding and contracting it appropriately.

This section introduces tools and thought processes to review the broader implications of kanban, specifically where kanban should and should not be utilized.

CHAPTER 16: INVENTORY PLANNING & MANAGEMENT & THE VALUE STREAM MAP

This chapter and the next will cover one of the most powerful tools in the Lean toolbox, the value stream map (VSM). A VSM diagrams a series of processes or tasks that accomplish an objective, such as assembling a car, purchasing raw materials, designing software, or prioritizing Emergency Room patients. Value stream mapping is incredibly helpful - even indispensable - when designing a kanban system.

The VSM is a *strategic* Lean tool because it reveals opportunities to improve how we deliver value to customers. But, it is also very informative for designing inventory action plans because a VSM indicates where on-hand inventory is high, where inventory must be planned because flow does not exist, where flow should occur to avoid inventory, where push can be replaced by pull, and where delivery is at risk due to materials or process issues. Every inventory plan should include value stream analysis!

HINT for Associates

Learning to See by Mike Rother and John Shook is an excellent book about Value Stream Maps. For hospital VSMs, read *Making Hospitals Work* by Marc Baker and Ian Taylor.

Brief Value Stream Map Review

A VSM has five primary sections, as shown in Figure 16-1.

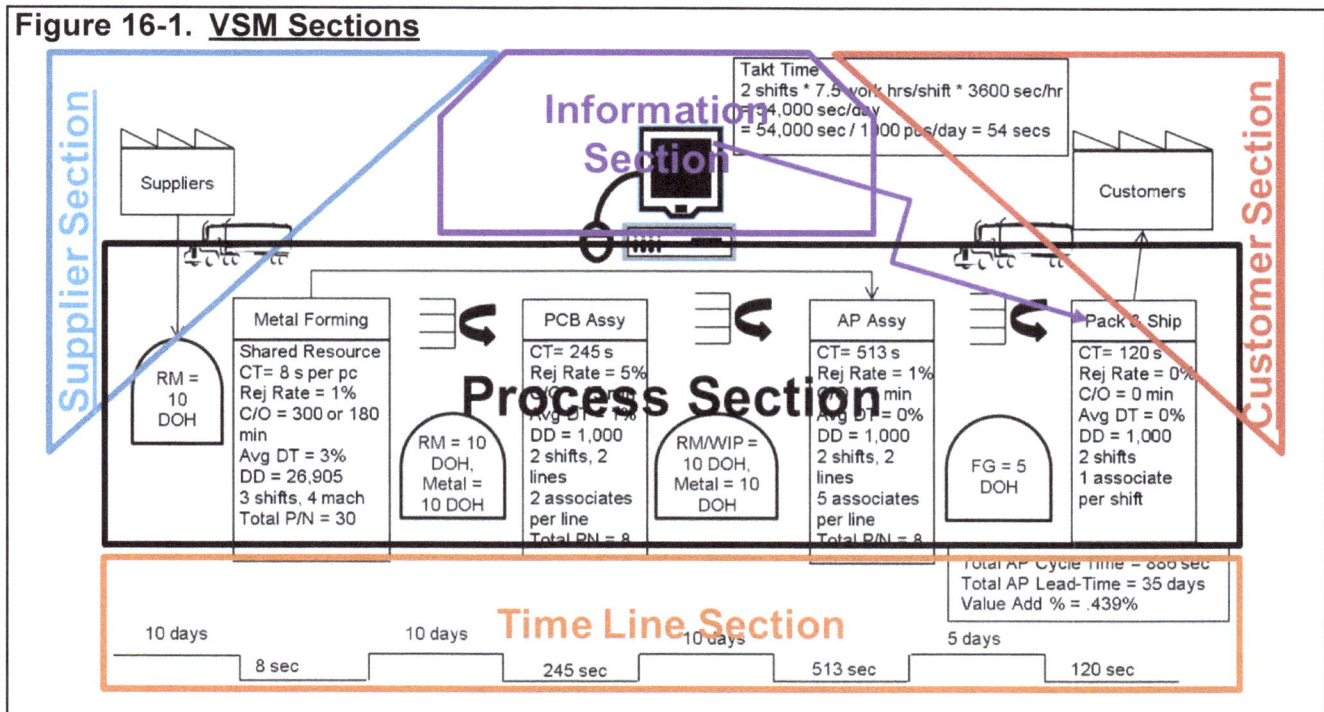

Figure 16-1. **VSM Sections**

• The Customer Section (top right) lists takt time (the allowed work time per unit of demand), delivery methods, expected demand, and other customer-centric items. Volume is usually expressed as annual demand but there might be notes about seasonality, expected changes in future demand, or other delivery, demand, and customer information.

• The Process Section (horizontally across the middle of the page) diagrams the series of processes in the value stream. Two sequential VSM process boxes imply that <u>flow does not exist between those processes</u>, so <u>inventory should be found between every pair of boxes</u>. This is a key component of VSM creation and interpretation! Flow exists within each box but breaks down between boxes. No kidding. Get this right on every VSM!

The Process Section provides details such as machine count, number of work shifts, assigned head count, cycle time, drop rate, reject or scrap rates, average down-time, days of inventory waiting for a process, etc. This is where we find most of the information required for inventory and kanban planning.

• The Supplier Section (upper left) lists how much inventory is on site from external suppliers, as well as how it is delivered, plus other relevant supply details.

• The Information Section (top center) shows how information is delivered to each process and how it is shared with suppliers and customers. This includes how processes receive production schedules, whether visual checks are part of information management, and what type of information is shared with customers or suppliers.

• The Time Line Section (bottom) is a square-tooth wave that puts inventory days on hand (DOH) on high lines and process times on low lines. Days on hand from every process is summed across the entire VSM to get total lead time at the bottom right. The sum of all cycle times is divided by total lead time to get percent of value-add time in the value stream. This is somewhat misleading because there is no requirement to verify that *every* second of cycle time adds value. So, the calculated percent of value-add is generally higher than actual value-add at the work cell level. Even so, the percent of value-add time is almost always a really low number, usually less than 5% and often less than 1%.

A current-state VSM illustrates today's status and a future state map defines what should exist in 12-18 months. An improvement plan or lean deployment plan defines how to go from current to future state.

HINT for Leaders

If the current or future-state map is incomplete, or drawn at such a high level that process and data boxes are meaningless, start by creating new maps that accurately reports process details for the value stream.

Beware of so-called "enterprise-wide" VSMs that list high-level or generic process boxes, as in this example of the process section of a future-state VSM. This map is <u>useless</u> when evaluating kanban. Use a real VSM!

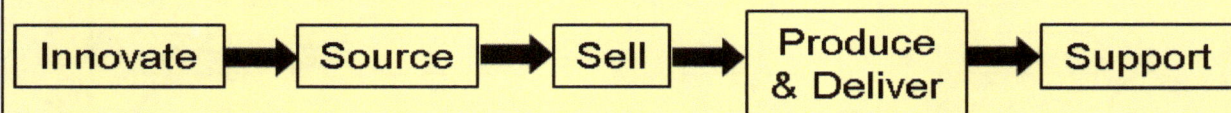

| Innovate | ➡ | Source | ➡ | Sell | ➡ | Produce & Deliver | ➡ | Support |

VSM Inventory Insights

A VSM explains the relationship between sequential cells, such as how work is scheduled, who is in charge of planning material flow, etc. Due to the interdependence of two sequential cells as supplier and customer, one process sets the production plan for the other via either push (supplier is in charge of material replenishment) or pull (the customer is in control).

VSM Insight: Flow

Flow, or one-piece flow, means an item does not stop when going through a series of tasks. Flow negates the use of queues (flow = non-stop, no waiting) and eliminates batches (flow = 1 at a time). Flow exists within every VSM process box.

One side effect of this VSM design requirement is that a site with very little flow has a current-state value stream map that is extremely long because essentially every step is an individual process box. That's always enlightening to see on paper!

Flow implies pull because material progresses to the next step only when a downstream process signals for the next work unit. It isn't practical to achieve flow without *pull* because *pushed* material is sent at the will of the supplier, which isn't flow. If the supplier works ahead of the receiving process in a push environment, it eliminates flow because inventory piles up. Flow breaks down when material sits and waits, so flow plus push is not valid in the real world.

However, *pull exists with or without flow* and is actually quite beneficial in the absence of flow.

• Pull with flow means the downstream process signals the upstream supplier to send the next unit, one at a time. There is no need to plan inventory between processes because pieces don't wait. By definition, flow means parts arrive one at a time. So, where flow exists, inventory is not "planned" because it doesn't exist between processes other than the single piece that is requested by the customer's pull signal.

Pull with flow is often managed by some kind of visual signal. In Figure 16-2, the empty green spot on the left side of the table indicates that Station 3 is ready for the next piece.

Figure 16-2. Open Pull Spot, One-Piece Flow

The associate at Station 2 (not visible in the diagram, but to the left of Station 3) sees the green spot and provides a part for Station 3, filling the visual pull signal with a single piece.

• Pull without flow also means material is produced to a downstream signal. But, it is sent in batches of 2 or more instead of 1 at a time, so it sits in inventory in front of the receiving process. Yes, that's kanban.

HINT for Associates

At the most basic level, pull plus flow is one piece at a time, while pull without flow requires material to be delivered in batches.

Pull without flow means "think kanban."

VSM Insight: Pull vs. Push

Pull means material requests go from the customer back to the supplying process. This puts the downstream or customer process in charge of the upstream supplier. "Just in case" inventory is avoided because items are produced *only* when the receiving cell signals a need.

Pull is a great replenishment system because it manages both what is produced and how many are produced, based on specific customer signals.

The opposite of pull is push, where the upstream or supplying process is in control and material is delivered at the will of the supplier, not the receiver. In most cases, push is managed by a schedule, such as MRP or a production plan.

Remember that two sequential VSM process boxes indicate a lack of flow, which implies some kind of planned inventory, either push or pull. In a VSM, pull versus push is indicated in the process section between process boxes, as in Figure 16-3. Pull is a solid arrow between two process boxes, while push is a striped arrow.

Figure 16-3. Pull vs. Push

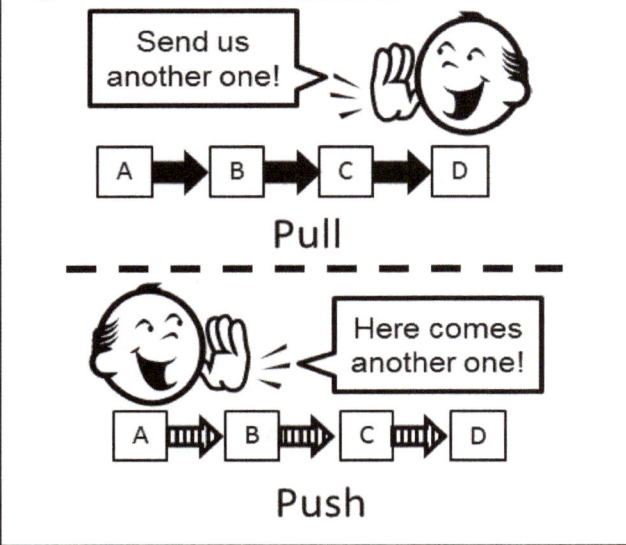

Send us another one!

A → B → C → D

Pull

Here comes another one!

A ⫸ B ⫸ C ⫸ D

Push

For a Lean site, pull between two VSM boxes is almost always a kanban system, which has a distinct symbol instead of the solid pull arrow, as in Figure 16-4. Between the two process boxes, the icon on the left is a shelf that represents a kanban "store" or shelf. The solid curved arrow means parts are pulled from kanban storage by the customer. So, "shelf plus curved arrow" means pull (the solid arrow) from planned kanban inventory (the shelf).

Figure 16-4. Kanban Pull Symbol in VSM

| AP Assy | ≣ ⌇ | Pack & Ship |

Real-World Observation

I've been to dozens of sites that produce parts based on schedules that mandate which items to produce, in what quantity, and to which due date. Schedules are based on push logic, so they are disrupted when a customer cell needs something different than what was planned, and therefore expediting is a common practice.

Suppose Subassembly decides to produce part number TUVWX instead of the formerly scheduled LMNOP. If all of Subassembly's suppliers followed the "Great Master Schedule," they supplied parts for LMNOP, not TUVWX, so TUVWX parts must be expedited to feed Subassembly. For this reason, cells running to production schedules often have HOT lists or other expediting tools that override the planned schedule.

A robust pull system is a great way to eliminate push schedules, along with those annoying HOT lists.

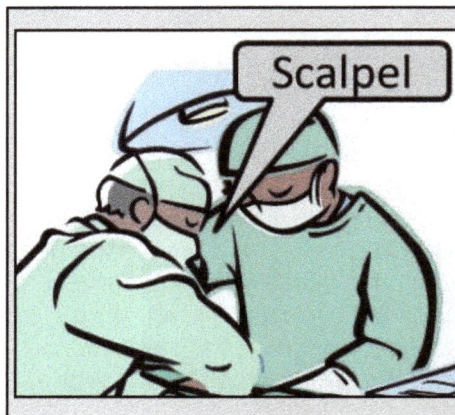

Scalpel

Pull signals are usually visual, but they can be verbal or electronic.

HINT for Associates

Don't get hung up on the words used for "supplier" or "customer" in a process.

This book uses the words *supplier, feeder, sender,* or *upstream process* to refer to a cell or process that supplies a downstream or subsequent process. Likewise, the words *customer, downstream, recipient* or *receiver* refer to a cell or process that obtains input from a supplier.

Don't interpret *customer* or *supplier* to always refer to an outside entity.

Why Flow Gets Interrupted

One-piece flow eliminates batches, queues, waiting, and also on-hand inventory. In a Lean environment, flow is the ultimate goal but there are numerous reasons why flow isn't always possible.

1. Batches = No Flow

Heading into or out of a batch process means inventory will exist.

• Purchased or external parts: Even if a supplier is right next door, external parts can't arrive in synchronized one-piece flow. Instead, they arrive in batches. Therefore, some parts wait in inventory, and there is no flow.

• Batch processes: Some manufacturing processes require a certain batch size. (For example, when baking cookies, you don't bake them one at a time, unless they're really, really big.) A batch is automatically a lack of flow.

• Shared resources: Shared machines or cells feed multiple downstream cells, like an injection molding machine supplying multiple assembly cells. It is nearly impossible for one cell to feed multiple cells without resorting to batches, particularly if set-up or changeover times are significant. Shared resources mean flow does not exist, and kanban is a great fit.

2. Holding Inventory in Stock = No Flow

There are several reasons why inventory might be held in stock as a standard practice, which means there is no flow.

• Mismatched work schedules: If shifts or workdays are not in sync between two sequential processes, flow breaks down at least temporarily. If a 1-shift operation feeds a 2-shift operation, the mismatched work schedules necessitate inventory between the cells, even if it sits just long enough for the cell with the shorter work schedule to catch up, e.g., inventory waits for one shift.

• Lead-time gaps: If a supplying process has a longer lead time than the allowed time from customer order to required delivery, material must be held in inventory in advance of customer requests because there isn't enough time to produce parts after a customer order is received. In other words, if customers expect delivery in 2 days but the process takes 5 days, inventory must be produced in advance of orders.

• Build to stock (BTS) or Make to Stock (MTS) is the practice of producing goods in advance of customer orders. It is often implemented to meet lead-time requirements, as described above, but it can also occur due to demand variation or supply constraints. Building to stock is an automatic commitment to on-hand inventory.

• Demand variation or capacity shortages: If customers order varying quantities that can't be covered by last-minute production adjustments, or if customer demand can spike above available

production capacity, inventory is held in stock to protect customer on-time delivery.

• Supplier concerns: Concerns about a supplier's ability to consistently provide material make it necessary to hold inventory to assure that the receiving process always has material. When this occurs, think Lean and fix the supplier so that an inventory countermeasure is not needed to cover supplier performance shortcomings. Until then, hold inventory as a buffer, in SQDC fashion.

HINT for Associates

If an item stops for a short time it might still be treated like "flow" with no need for planned inventory. This requires proper controls to ensure that 1) over-production does not occur, 2) the right order sequence is followed (e.g., first-in-first-out, or FIFO) by all processes, and 3) if expected short hold times become too long, associates respond to and correct the breakdown of flow.

When Flow Is Interrupted, Create an Inventory Plan

A lack of flow means material stops or pauses, which means it sits in inventory. This necessitates an inventory plan, or a plan for every part (PFEP), to determine what will be held in inventory, how many will be held, for how long, and under what replenishment method. The inventory plan doesn't have to be kanban, but that is often the best tool for planning, managing, and improving inventory performance.

Lock this kanban truth in your brain!

Think of kanban as a countermeasure for the lack of flow. When flow is not possible, material sits in inventory, and kanban is the most effective way to manage and plan that inventory.

Flow is always preferred but the absence of flow should prompt the question, "How can we make kanban work effectively?"

VSM Insight: Days on Hand (DOH)

Due to the rules for drawing a VSM, namely that flow does not exist between process boxes, we expect that every sequential pair of process boxes has inventory between them. The amount of inventory is reported as days on hand (DOH) in an inventory triangle or "tombstone" in front of each VSM process box.

If there is no inventory between process boxes, figure out why. This indicates that something is out of balance. It might mean that the supplying cell is struggling to keep pace with the receiving cell. In that case, determine if the capacity of the supplying cell is sufficient to meet demand from the receiving cell. If the supplying cell has adequate capacity, determine if one or more receiving cells are over-producing or working ahead, pulling more inventory than necessary, which can take on-hand balance to zero.

Rule of Thumb

Unless the level of work is very low, it is rare to find zero inventory between two VSM process boxes, since 2 sequential boxes imply a lack of flow that should mandate on-hand inventory. If zero inventory occurs, figure out why it happened because it is not a normal state.

Analyze DOH in a VSM

To analyze inventory, count what is physically in front of each process then convert those quantities into the number of days on hand. Easy, right? Ahh...no. Not as easy as it sounds.

Raw material in front of a stamping machine should be easy. Count bundles of steel and divide by the number of bundles used per day to get DOH. Simple and straightforward.

Inventory waiting for a mixed model cell, one that makes a variety of items, isn't as easy, nor is counting inventory for a cell that consumes numerous components. Raw material and work in progress (WIP) are likely to be in front of a mixed model cell, and it's possible to have several hundred or even thousands of parts. No, it isn't reasonable to count everything. Instead, count a representative

sample of raw material and WIP, preferably those with the highest dollar value, and convert those counts to DOH for that inventory pile. The goal for a value stream map is to count big contributors to *days on hand*, but high dollar components should also be a priority.

HINT for Associates

Some VSM teams skip the step of counting inventory in front of each process, thinking it takes too much time, is too tedious, or is unnecessary for a high level tool like a VSM. Not true!

Inventory or time-line data is necessary for completing the time line at the bottom, summing total lead time, or designing inventory action plans.

Don't skip this step!

HINTS for Associates

The time line at the bottom of the VSM captures DOH and cycle time for every process box. Total VSM lead time equals the sum of individual inventory locations, in days on hand. This is not the same as the inventory performance metric that is also called days on hand.

Total VSM lead time is the number of sequential days it would take for new material inserted at the beginning of the value stream to make it to the end, without jumping ahead of any inventory that is currently in the stream.

Days on hand as an inventory performance metric is *average* days of inventory based on a site's on-hand dollars versus daily usage.

Therefore, inventory DOH is usually a smaller number than total VSM lead time because VSM lead time is not weighted by dollars. Forty days on hand for "inexpensive" inventory counts as 40 days of VSM lead time, but total dollars for that pile might not impact average DOH when measured in dollars for a financial DOH metric.

VSM Insight: Delivery Risk

Delivery risk comes from anything that can cause inventory stock outs or extend cycle times and lead times. The most common risks are scrap, rejects, machine downtime, long changeover or set-up times, and capacity constraints. Each of these items should be reported in the data boxes for every VSM process in order to identify and quantify delivery risk.

A capacity constraint is sometimes less obvious than other delivery risk factors because it can be difficult to measure. Capacity constraints are often erroneously excluded from VSM data boxes, but understanding them is necessary for designing valid inventory plans. The theory of constraints, or finding the bottleneck for any sequence of processes or tasks, is a great way to identify capacity risks. We'll touch on bottlenecks or pacemakers in the next chapter.

HINT for Associates

Don't overlook delivery risks or "red flags" when designing a kanban system! Every hurdle - rework, rejects, scrap, capacity constraints, long changeovers, machine downtime, quality risks - must be covered by the inventory replenishment plan until improvements are made to address the root cause for the risk.

Improvement Plans from a VSM

Use VSM insights to plan the right improvement activities. Think very broadly when planning improvements. It is expected that a current-state VSM should have numerous kaizen bursts for events such as standard work (SW), pull or kanban deployment, flow, error-proof, set-up reduction (SUR), and total productive maintenance (TPM), as in Figure 16-5. Bursts can be drawn on either the current or future-state map but they are usually easier to understand on the current-state map because that's where issues exist today.

Figure 16-5. Example of Current-State VSM with Kaizen Bursts

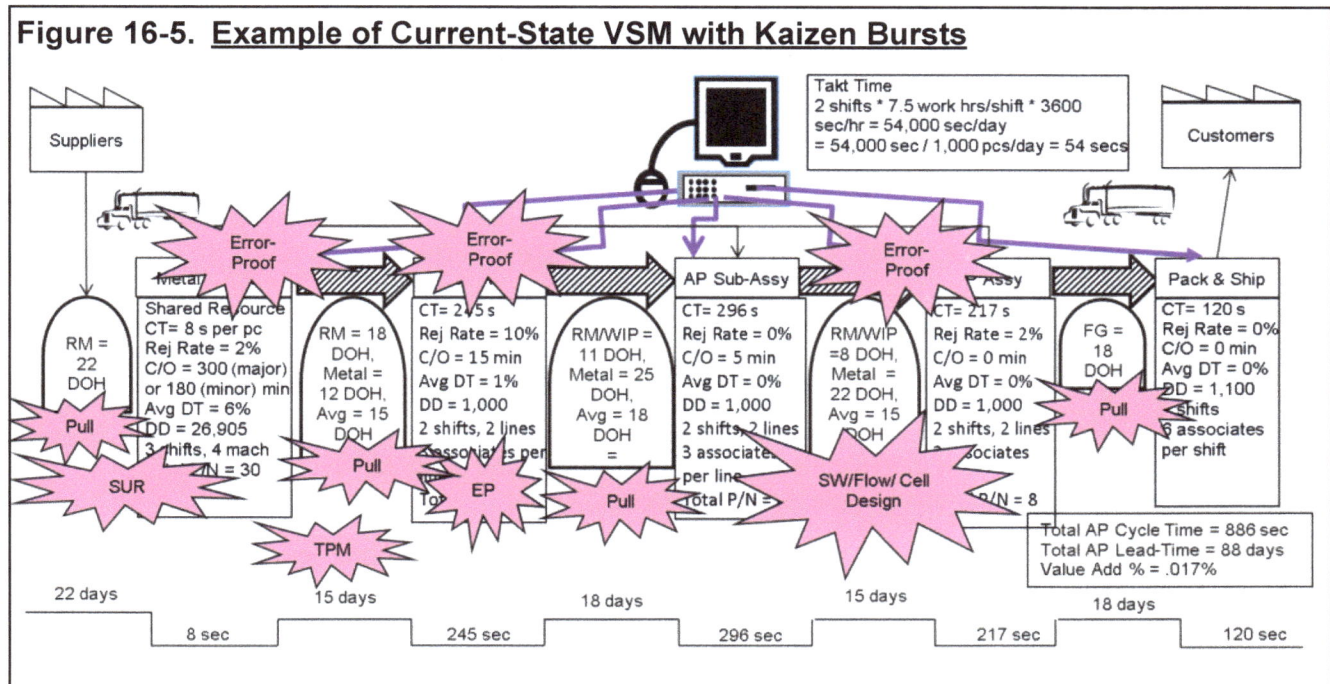

When planning inventory improvements versus general operational improvements, action plans should address all inventory opportunities.

• Every inventory triangle between sequential boxes indicates that flow does not exist, so implementing flow should be one of the first priorities to eliminate inventory and reduce total lead time.

• High days on hand at any point in the VSM requires an inventory reduction plan via flow, lower order quantities, better timing of replenishment orders, or lower safety stock in the replenishment plan. Kanban helps all of these goals.

• Scrap and rework reduce material availability, which can negatively impact on-time delivery. An error-proofing kaizen can improve process quality, but *never* pursue error reduction without first verifying that standard work is defined and followed. Error -proofing a process without standard work is like wearing muddy shoes to mop a floor: valiant effort, but a waste of time. Deploy robust standard work, error-proof the standardized process, update standard work for the error-proofing activity, and deploy supply-side safety stock *only* if reject rates remain high enough to negatively impact delivery.

• Shared resources are challenging because they supply multiple customers (internal or external) and items must be produced in batches. Kanban is the logical solution to manage order quantities and timing. Always consider batch-size reduction for shared resources.

• Long changeover or set-up times force items to be produced in batches. The first goal is to reduce long changeover times via set-up reduction. If long set-up times are unavoidable, then items must be produced in the right batch sizes. Again, look for ways to reduce batch sizes.

Rule of Thumb

The target for changeover time is less than one takt time, where takt time is defined as the allowed time to produce one unit. If available work time per day is 7.75 hours (or 27,900 seconds) and customer demand is 465 pieces per day, we are allowed [27,900 / 465 = 60 seconds per unit].

If takt time is 60 seconds, a cell or machine should change from one set-up or production run to another in about 1 minute.

• Unplanned downtime is also risky for delivery, so safety stock should be planned until downtime causes are resolved.

By their very nature, inventory improvement activities will significantly aid overall operational performance, so make these efforts part of a cross-functional, site-wide strategy.

HINT for Leaders

Random kaizen events are common (how sad) but generally not very useful in the big picture. One site told me they held a 5S event (Sort, Straighten or Set in Order, Shine or Scrub, Standardize, Sustain) because they hadn't done one in a while. How stupid!

Every improvement activity should link directly to a performance improvement plan or strategy, not to fake goals like holding the "right" number of events or involving a certain percentage of people.

VSM Example for Inventory Action Plans

A site produces Aviation & Plane (AP) assemblies. The current-state VSM is in Figure 16-6.

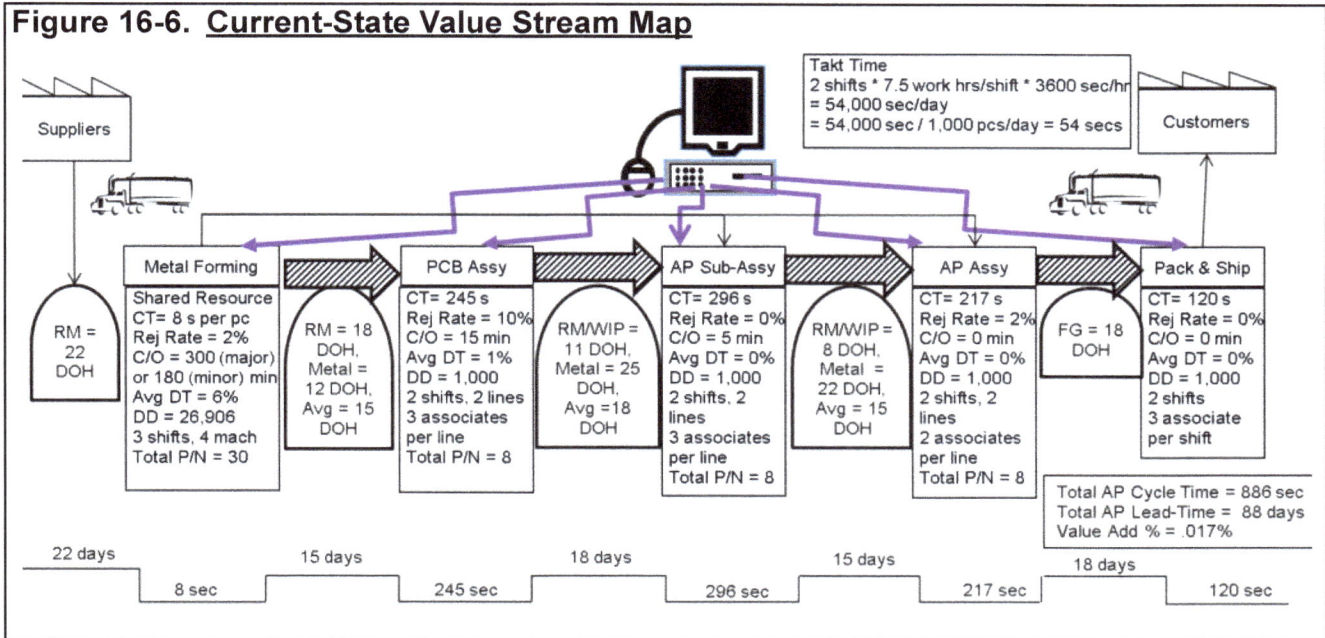

Figure 16-6. Current-State Value Stream Map

Initial VSM Conclusions

1. Printed-circuit-board (PCB) Assembly, AP Subassembly, and AP Assembly each work 2 shifts with 2 lines per cell.

   a. PCB Assembly has a 10% reject rate.

2. Metal Forming

   a. Works 3 shifts, versus 2 shifts for all other cells.

   b. Has a cycle time of 8 seconds.

   c. Has high changeover times: 5 hours for a major change and 3 hours for a minor.

   d. Loses 2% of production to rejects that must be reworked.

   e. Suffers 6% machine downtime.

   f. Produces just 30 part numbers, but with a combined average daily demand of 26,905 parts.

3. Days on hand is high in several areas, particularly coming out of Metal Forming.

   a. Raw material inventory is 22 days in front of Metal Forming.

   b. Inventory at PCB Assembly is 18 days for purchased parts and 12 days of metal parts.

   c. Inventory waiting for AP Subassembly averages 18 days, with 25 days of metal parts.

   d. Inventory in front of AP Assembly is 15 days, and metal parts are again the cause of the high inventory, at 22 days.

   e. There are 18 days of finished goods inventory in Pack/Ship.

Note: some sites report the highest DOH for each inventory location, but average DOH is a reasonable approach. If most items in front of a process box have 10 to 15 DOH, but 1 component has 40 DOH, it can be misleading to report 40 days as the on-hand inventory at that point. Technically, if the value stream was tasked with reducing all inventory to some new target, it would take more time to use up 1 component with 40 DOH. But, reporting DOH based on the worst case in front of every process box is misleading because it gives the impression that inventory reduction is a much bigger opportunity than it truly is.

Flow Reduces On-Hand Inventory

The first priority is always to deploy flow wherever possible.

The Assembly manager says AP Subassembly and AP Assembly utilize similar equipment and skills, so it makes sense to combine those cells to achieve flow. With multiple production lines in each area we should have the flexibility to link subassembly and assembly lines and eliminate inventory in between, which is 15 DOH. Even if the combined cell achieves no improvements in cycle time, changeover time, or reject rates, the reduction of 15 days of inventory between the cells is a huge victory.

To accomplish this, execute a kaizen event that tackles flow, standard work, and cell design to combine subassembly and assembly activities.

Kanban Reduces Overproduction

An obvious opportunity for inventory and lead-time reduction is the high inventory for metal parts. Metal inventory is much higher than what should be necessary for an internal supplier. The fact that metal inventory is high everywhere indicates that they overproduce as a standard practice. If Metal Forming ran reasonable quantities as a general rule, we'd expect to see at least 1 or 2 inventory points with low DOH, maybe 5 days or less. Because every pile is at least 12 DOH, it looks like they always overproduce. This tells us

we have a systematic process issue, probably related to how Metal Forming replenishment orders are scheduled or sized.

To reduce metal inventory, link Metal Forming output to actual consumption in each of the receiving cells so they don't overproduce. Yes, use kanban.

Kanban Works for Batch Parts

Kanban makes sense for raw material from external suppliers. Current state shows 22 DOH for raw material, so there is opportunity to reduce inventory by applying kanban.

Find & Fix Delivery Risks

Any process with reject or scrap above 0.5% should undergo a standard work review, with emphasis on error-proofing.

Downtime should be reduced via preventive maintenance (PM) or total productive maintenance (TPM) events.

A reasonable goal for the future state is to cut every scrap, reject, and downtime rate in half within 6 months. When that's done, repeat the same approach and try to cut everything in half again.

As long as supply or delivery risks exist, cover them with safety stock, as discussed in the prior section. Remember that the ultimate goal is to eliminate all supply risks so safety stock countermeasures are not required.

Future State VSM

In the future-state VSM in Figure 16-7 on page 189, AP Subassembly and AP Assembly are combined, kanban is implemented to reduce inventory in front of every process, reject and downtime rates are reduced, and pull is implemented from customer orders to AP Assembly, so multiple production schedules are no longer required. Total lead time drops from 88 days to 35 days.

Figure 16-7. Future-State VSM with Pull, Combined Subassembly & Assembly

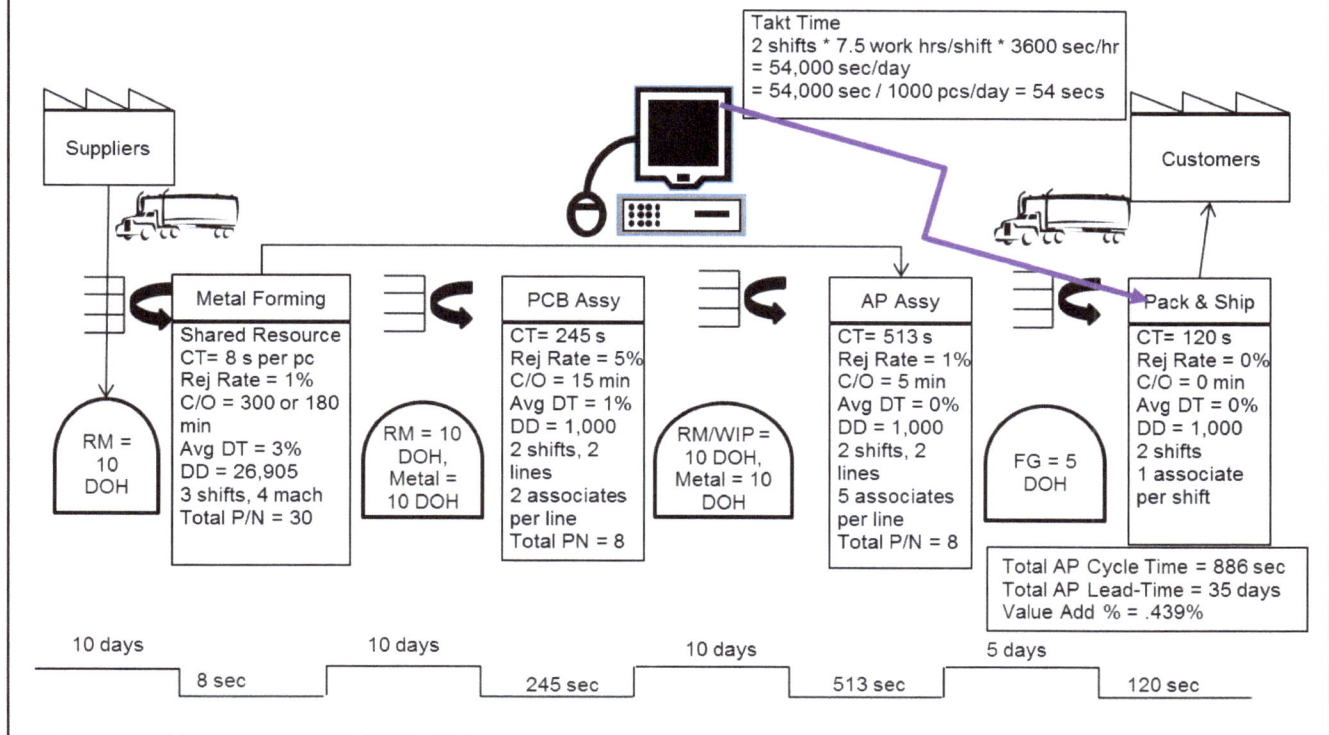

Takt Time
2 shifts * 7.5 work hrs/shift * 3600 sec/hr
= 54,000 sec/day
= 54,000 sec / 1000 pcs/day = 54 secs

Suppliers

Customers

Metal Forming
Shared Resource
CT= 8 s per pc
Rej Rate = 1%
C/O = 300 or 180 min
Avg DT = 3%
DD = 26,905
3 shifts, 4 mach
Total P/N = 30

RM = 10 DOH

RM = 10 DOH, Metal = 10 DOH

PCB Assy
CT= 245 s
Rej Rate = 5%
C/O = 15 min
Avg DT = 1%
DD = 1,000
2 shifts, 2 lines
2 associates per line
Total PN = 8

RM/WIP = 10 DOH, Metal = 10 DOH

AP Assy
CT= 513 s
Rej Rate = 1%
C/O = 5 min
Avg DT = 0%
DD = 1,000
2 shifts, 2 lines
5 associates per line
Total P/N = 8

FG = 5 DOH

Pack & Ship
CT= 120 s
Rej Rate = 0%
C/O = 0 min
Avg DT = 0%
DD = 1,000
2 shifts
1 associate per shift

Total AP Cycle Time = 886 sec
Total AP Lead-Time = 35 days
Value Add % = .439%

10 days   10 days   10 days   5 days

8 sec   245 sec   513 sec   120 sec

VSM Summary

A VSM points out numerous opportunities to improve operational performance. It also indicates where kanban should be considered to improve inventory performance.

1. Use kanban where flow can't be implemented and inventory sits in stock, but always pursue flow first. More on this topic in the next chapter.

2. Deploy kanban for processes that must produce parts in batches.

3. Eliminate supply and delivery risks as quickly as possible, but until they are addressed cover them with safety stock.

TUTORIAL: GOCO VALUE STREAM MAPS

Mary led a VSM exercise with a team that included associates from Materials, Operations, Finance, and Engineering. The team spent the first day working on the current-state map (see Figure 16-8 on page 191), then they reviewed the map for conclusions.

1. Subassembly cells in each product family pushed material to Assembly cells, but it seemed unnecessary to keep Subassembly separate from Assembly. Mary marked the current-state map with a kaizen burst to achieve flow from Subassembly to Assembly for each product family.

2. There were large piles of inventory throughout the VSM, but the Doodle product was very high. The Planner for those products was risk averse, and he overstocked everything to prevent shortages. He had 171 DOH from Housing through Assembly plus 5 days of finished goods. Yikes!

3. The current promised lead time for customer orders was 5 days, but customers had universally requested 3 days, so lead-time reduction had to be part of the overall materials strategy. Operations was confident that 3 days was adequate to provide finished goods, so this would assist with inventory efforts by reducing the need for finished goods.

4. The 3% reject rate in Doodle Assembly had to be reduced to avoid the risk of shortages in Shipping.

5. GOCO was proud of their on-time delivery rate, which consistently topped 98%, but they were carrying inventory at every point to support that result. Mary marked 4 areas to insert kanban and reduce inventory:

• In front of Metal Form, coming from Suppliers

• In front of Housing cells, coming from Metal Form and Suppliers

• In front of the new Assembly cells, coming out of Housing, Sensor Assembly, and Suppliers

• Mary intended to eliminate finished goods inventory over time, but she planned to start by dropping down to just 3 DOH for each part number that had demand of at least 10 per day. She identified Automotive finished goods as the one possible exception to this plan, because GOCO received accurate and timely forecast data from those customers, and, therefore, building to stock was not necessary.

On the second day the team created the future-state map in Figure 16-9 on page 192. The blue text boxes on the map describe kanban deployments.

1. Purchased parts in Receiving

2. Purchased and metal parts in front of the housing cells

3. Purchased, metal, and housing parts in front of Assembly

4. Finished goods in Pack.

Mary had no way to estimate future days on hand in front of each cell until kanban solutions were done, so she put question marks in every DOH box.

When the future state was done, Mary and the rest of the VSM team decided to start with Metal Form as the first kanban cell. It fed every value stream, handled a large number of part numbers, and was heavily impacted by summer peak demand. Success there could also reduce high on-hand dollars sitting in front of Housing and Sensor cells. Purchased parts (PP) were the second priority.

The Operations team held kaizen events to combine Subassembly and Assembly for all product families, and they successfully created new cells that achieved flow and reduced inventory.

Figure 16-8. GOCO Current-State Value Stream Map

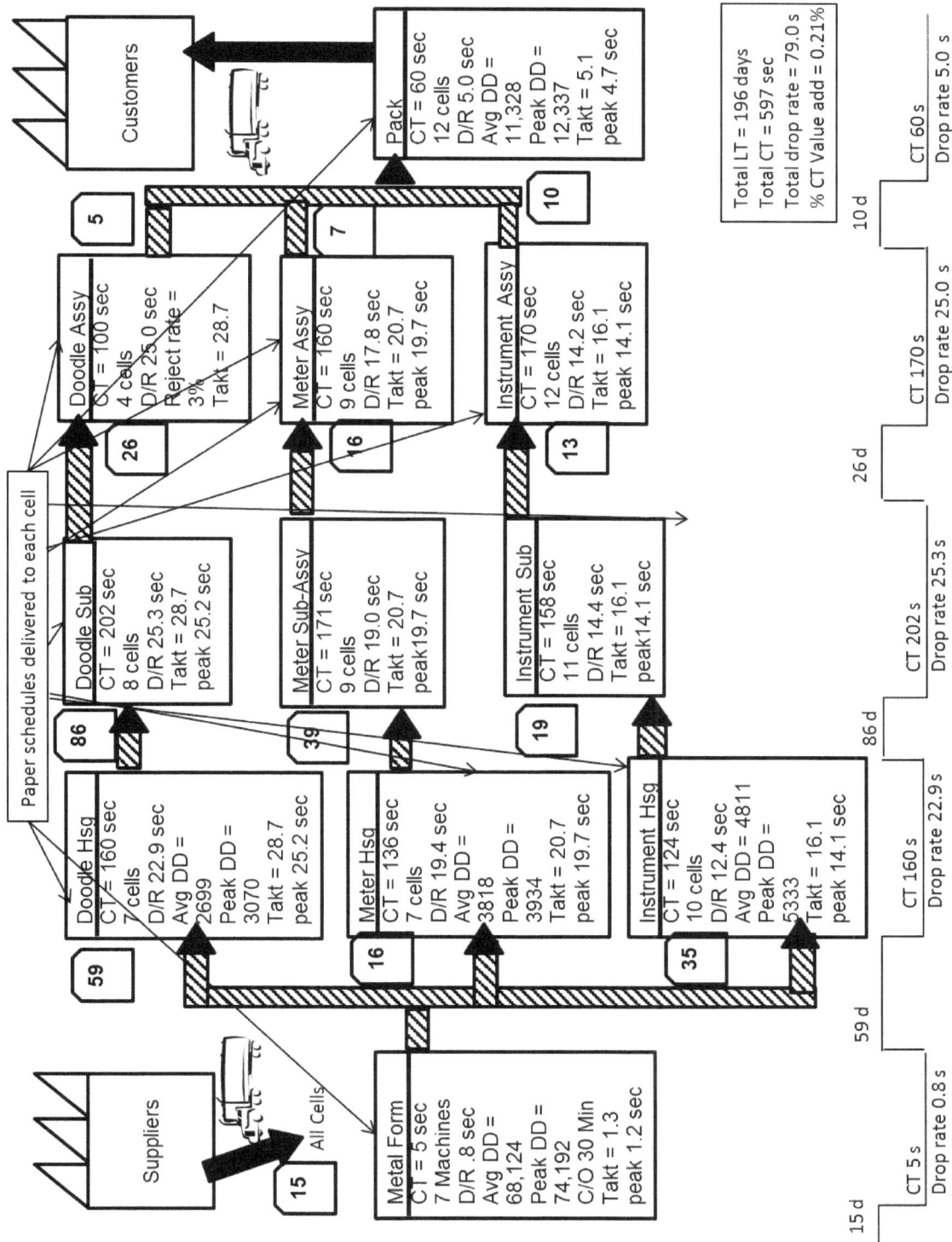

Figure 16-9. <u>GOCO Future-State Value Stream Map</u>

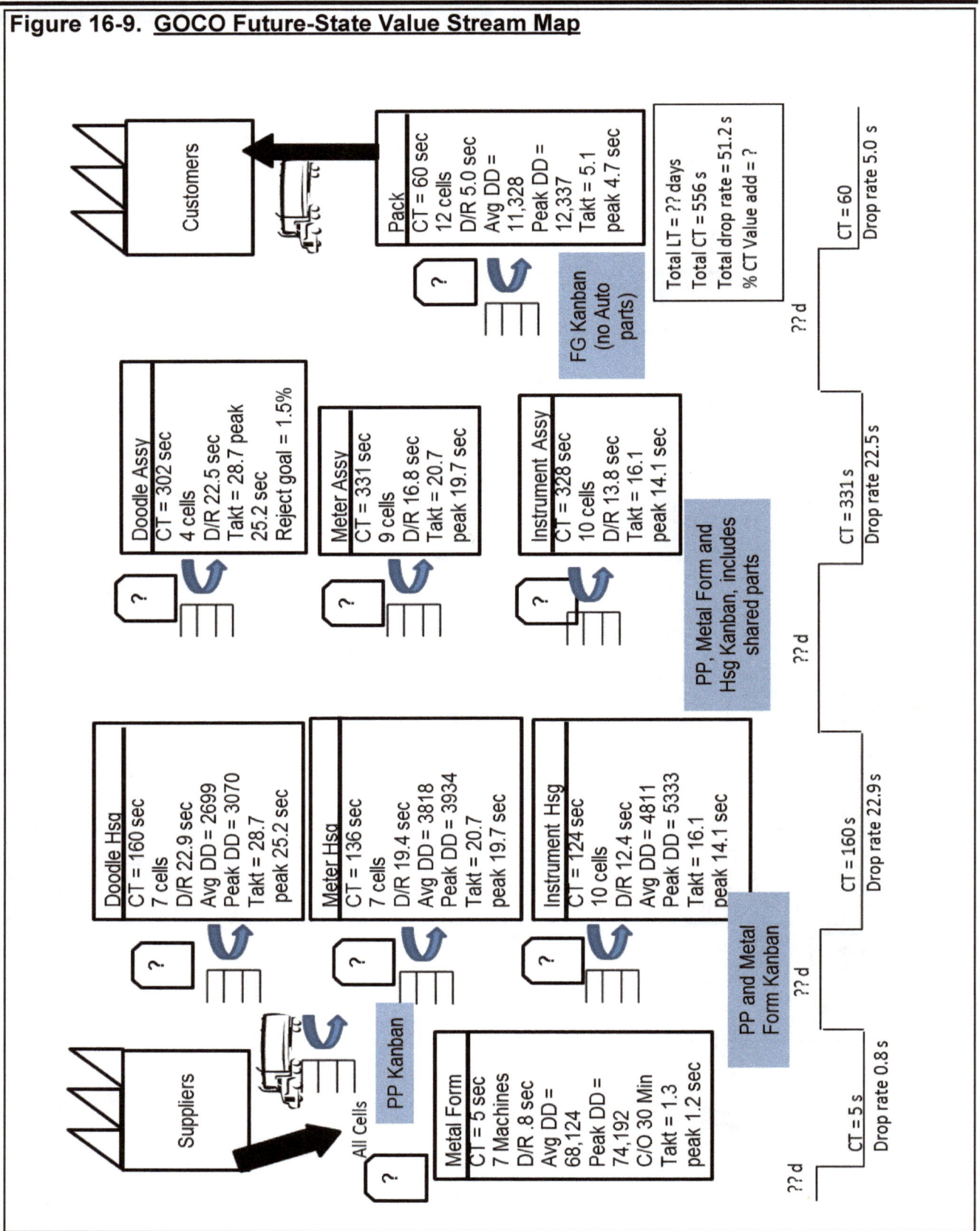

Customers

Pack
CT = 60 sec
12 cells
D/R 5.0 sec
Avg DD = 11,328
Peak DD = 12,337
Takt = 5.1
peak 4.7 sec

FG Kanban (no Auto parts)

Total LT = ?? days
Total CT = 556 s
Total drop rate = 51.2 s
% CT Value add = ?

Doodle Assy
CT = 302 sec
4 cells
D/R 22.5 sec
Takt = 28.7 peak 25.2 sec
Reject goal = 1.5%

Meter Assy
CT = 331 sec
9 cells
D/R 16.8 sec
Takt = 20.7
peak 19.7 sec

Instrument Assy
CT = 328 sec
10 cells
D/R 13.8 sec
Takt = 16.1
peak 14.1 sec

PP, Metal Form and Hsg Kanban, includes shared parts

Doodle Hsg
CT = 160 sec
7 cells
D/R 22.9 sec
Avg DD = 2699
Peak DD = 3070
Takt = 28.7
peak 25.2 sec

Meter Hsg
CT = 136 sec
7 cells
D/R 19.4 sec
Avg DD = 3818
Peak DD = 3934
Takt = 20.7
peak 19.7 sec

Instrument Hsg
CT = 124 sec
10 cells
D/R 12.4 sec
Avg DD = 4811
Peak DD = 5333
Takt = 16.1
peak 14.1 sec

PP and Metal Form Kanban

Suppliers

PP Kanban

All Cells

Metal Form
CT = 5 sec
7 Machines
D/R .8 sec
Avg DD = 68,124
Peak DD = 74,192
C/O 30 Min
Takt = 1.3
peak 1.2 sec

CT = 60
Drop rate 5.0 s

?? d

CT = 331 s
Drop rate 22.5 s

?? d

CT = 160 s
Drop rate 22.9 s

?? d

CT = 5 s
Drop rate 0.8 s

?? d

Where does kanban belong?

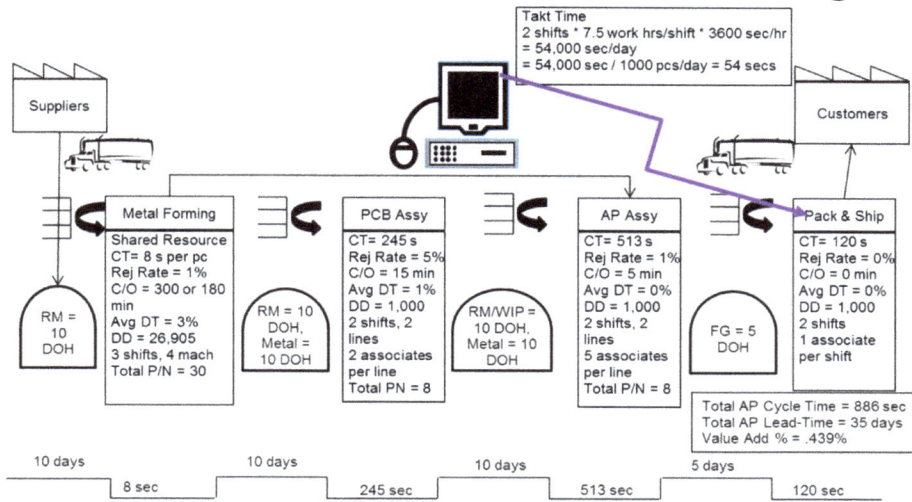

Takt Time
2 shifts * 7.5 work hrs/shift * 3600 sec/hr
= 54,000 sec/day
= 54,000 sec / 1000 pcs/day = 54 secs

Suppliers

Customers

Metal Forming
Shared Resource
CT= 8 s per pc
Rej Rate = 1%
C/O = 300 or 180 min
Avg DT = 3%
DD = 26,905
3 shifts, 4 mach
Total P/N = 30

RM = 10 DOH

RM = 10 DOH, Metal = 10 DOH

PCB Assy
CT= 245 s
Rej Rate = 5%
C/O = 15 min
Avg DT = 1%
DD = 1,000
2 shifts, 2 lines
2 associates per line
Total PN = 8

RM/WIP = 10 DOH, Metal = 10 DOH

AP Assy
CT= 513 s
Rej Rate = 1%
C/O = 5 min
Avg DT = 0%
DD = 1,000
2 shifts, 2 lines
5 associates per line
Total P/N = 8

FG = 5 DOH

Pack & Ship
CT= 120 s
Rej Rate = 0%
C/O = 0 min
Avg DT = 0%
DD = 1,000
2 shifts
1 associate per shift

Total AP Cycle Time = 886 sec
Total AP Lead-Time = 35 days
Value Add % = .439%

10 days   10 days   10 days   5 days

8 sec   245 sec   513 sec   120 sec

Chapter 17: Analyze the VSM to Decide Where to Put Kanban Stores

Kanban practitioners gain excellent insight from current and future-state value stream maps (VSMs) because the maps reveal places where changeovers are too long, scrap is too high, flow could be achieved, or inventory could be reduced. As stated in the prior chapter, we *expect to find inventory between every sequential pair of process boxes in a VSM*. So, the future-state VSM illustrates process sequences (the order of the boxes) and where we plan to hold inventory (between the boxes). We can't stress this too much in kanban analysis: flow exists within VSM process boxes, but it does not exist between boxes.

Most future-state VSMs assume that every pair of sequential processes requires a kanban store between them. The logic is that kanban is the Lean pull solution for a lack of flow and flow doesn't exist between process boxes. Therefore, kanban should be deployed between every pair of process boxes. This is an appropriate *first assumption*, but it isn't necessarily the right *final answer*. In fact, there are specific cases where pull or kanban is not the best answer.

Although a pull system is generally better than push, sometimes pull and push can be combined to our advantage. *Pull* used with *FIFO plus push* can be a better inventory plan than inserting kanban stores between every pair of sequential process boxes.

Process Sequence Insights

There are valuable insights to be gained by reviewing the sequence of processes in a current-state value stream map.

Process Insight: Flow Exists Within Every VSM Process Box

Yes, it's true that flow exists within a VSM process box, and kanban should not be required where flow is achieved. Therefore, kanban should <u>not</u> exist within a value stream process box except in very specific circumstances, such as a piece of equipment within a cell that has frequent breakdowns and therefore needs a certain level of planned inventory. In that case, the kanban store is a temporary countermeasure to protect the cell from machine breakdowns.

HINT for Associates

Don't confuse "inventory" with "standard WIP." Within a process that achieves flow, standard work in progress or standard WIP is the inventory required to run the cell. Every associate needs the right material at their work station, and this material is called "standard WIP" or "keeping the line wet." See the definition and picture on page 14.

A dry line means that when the cell starts up, such as after a changeover, material has to progress from the first work station through each of the subsequent stations, and those later stations are idle until new material arrives. A wet line allows each work station to be productive from the first minute while a dry line forces all but the first worker to wait for material to arrive at their station. Standard WIP is part of the regular set-up for every cell or process, even those that achieve flow. Flow does not eliminate standard WIP.

Process Insight: Find the Bottleneck in Every Sequence

A bottleneck process sets the work pace for an entire sequence, which is why bottlenecks are also called pacemakers. The task or process with the longest cycle time or slowest drop rate dictates the overall pace of an entire sequence.

The pacemaker concept is the central theme of the Theory of Constraints. (Read *The Goal* by Eliyahu Goldratt.) Just as the weakest link determines the strength of a chain, the pacemaker is the limiting factor in the production sequence. A pacemaker sets the pace for all associated tasks, particularly if demand is at or above the pacemaker's capacity. If a process is operating at the pacemaker's capacity, the pacemaker throttles the entire sequence up or down and the kanban system must be determined by the pacemaker's daily capacity, instead of by customer daily demand. As long as other processes abide by the pacemaker's limits, the entire sequence avoids over-production and the associated waste of piles of inventory waiting for the bottleneck.

From a process analysis perspective we need to recognize the basic fact that every sequence of processes has a bottleneck that is the output constraint for that series. There is always a bottleneck resource, whether it is being strained or not.

A kanban system must accommodate the process bottleneck in order to avoid replenishment plans that stretch the bottleneck beyond its capacity. To be safe, a kanban plan should put the pacemaker in charge of setting the production pace for a sequence, but that doesn't necessarily mean that the kanban store is directly linked to the bottleneck, i.e., kanban does not necessarily have to exist immediately before or after the pacemaker cell.

A bottleneck constraint that is operating at capacity does mandate that kanban order quantities and card counts are designed around the pacemaker process. If a specific cell is the pacemaker and we deploy hundreds of cards that sum to an expected weekly output that exceeds the capacity of that cell, we're in trouble.

HINT for Associates

To accommodate a bottleneck cell, one or more kanban stores can be anywhere in the process sequence, but the overall kanban system must be designed and planned around the bottleneck.

Process Insight: Total Lead Time Versus Customer Lead Time

If the allowed lead time from a customer order to the promised ship date is long enough to accommodate a sequence of manufacturing processes, skip kanban within that sequence and build to order. This is a primary consideration for deciding whether finished goods should be on kanban.

It is rather straightforward to determine where inventory should be held to cover lead-time gaps: start at "Ship" and go backward or upstream until the sum of the process lead times exceeds the allowed customer lead time. Somewhere between that point and the final process (at or near shipping) there must be planned inventory.

In Figure 17-1, each process has a defined cycle time and there is an allowed customer lead time of 3 days. The block arrows below the process boxes sum the total required time from shipping back to a specific upstream step. The top arrow shows that cell C plus Ship takes 1.5 days, which is less than the customer lead time of 3 days, so finished goods inventory is not necessary in front of Ship.

Figure 17-1. Lead Time in a Sequence

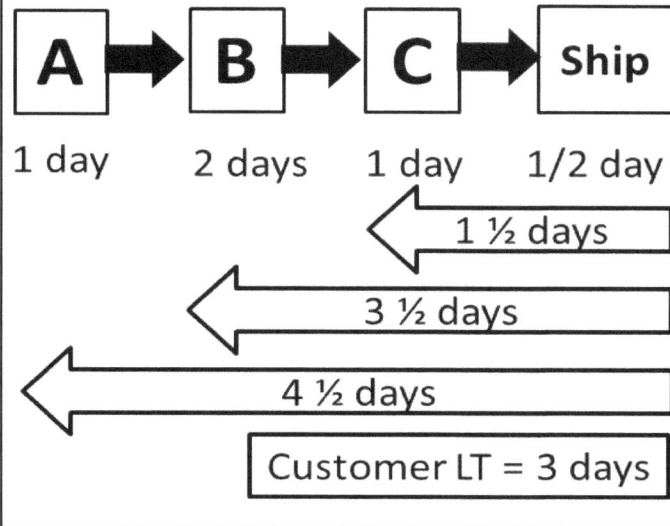

If we go as far back as cell B, the second block arrow, the summed process time of 3.5 days exceeds the allowed 3 days, so we need inventory somewhere in that span.

If we reduced the lead time for cells B and C by half a day, we could hold inventory before cell B and still meet customer shipments. Reducing the combined lead time would be a great improvement priority to move the kanban store further upstream, in front of cell B, where inventory is cheaper to hold. Until that happens, hold work in progress (WIP) inventory after cell B to protect customer delivery.

Customer Versus Internal Lead Times

Consider the sequence from Stamping through Pack & Ship. The customer allowed lead time is 3 days.

We can complete Subassembly, Assembly, and Pack & Ship within the 3-day customer lead time, but we can't complete the entire sequence from Stamping through Ship. If we put Plated parts on kanban we divide total processing time into 2 sequences, 6 days from Stamping through Plating plus 2.5 days from Subassembly through Ship. When we receive a customer order, we pull plated parts out of kanban to feed Subassembly then push those parts through Assembly and Pack & Ship. As soon as a kanban quantity of plated parts is consumed by Subassembly, a replenishment signal is sent back to Stamping to refill the kanban store.

This illustrates that although flow does not exist from Subassembly to Assembly, it is not necessary to put a kanban store between those cells. As customer orders arrive, Subassembly produces the required items and pushes them to Assembly, where they are finished and sent to Pack within the 3 days allowed by the customer.

Kanban stores can place inventory where it is needed to close the gap between process lead time and customer lead time. But, kanban is not an acceptable substitute for lead-time reduction. Kanban is planned inventory, and inventory is one of the eight Lean waste categories. Pursue flow and lead-time reduction wherever possible and eliminate the need for inventory and kanban. Lead-time and cycle-time reductions are always good improvement priorities, particularly for processes that are the bottleneck or the cause of an inventory store.

Eight Lean Wastes: Overproduction, Defects, Waiting, Transportation, Inventory, Motion, Processing, and Underutilization

Internal vs. Customer Lead-Time Examples

• If total lead time is 5 days from raw material (RM) to finished goods (FG), and customer lead time is 10 days, hold RM in stock and process to finished status for every customer order.

• If customer lead time is 5 days, and total processing lead time is 10 days, but parts can be processed "half way" and held as work in progress (WIP), hold RM and the right "half-way" WIP in stock and process WIP into FG in response to customer orders.

• If customer lead time is 3 days, and process lead time is 5 days from RM to WIP and 10 days from WIP to FG, carry FG inventory to meet customer demand. We might also need WIP somewhere in the sequence to facilitate the replenishment of FG as inventory is shipped to customers, but that would depend on process details.

Rule of Thumb

Finished goods (FG) inventory is more expensive than raw material (RM) or WIP, so it should be avoided when possible. But, there are at least two conditions that justify holding FG inventory.

1. If customer lead time is shorter than the process lead time, FG must be in stock when the customer places an order. In this case, look for ways to reduce internal lead times. If that can't be accomplished, consider holding WIP that can be quickly converted to FG status, often called "late point definition" or "late point conversion," to avoid holding FG in inventory.

2. If customer demand exhibits high demand variation, FG inventory provides a buffer against that variation.

Process Insight: Part Numbers Used in More Than One Location

It is common for some items to be used in more than one cell within a site, and there are two basic options for managing shared parts.

Decentralized: A shared item has a kanban store at each cell where it is used, as in Figure 17-2 on page 197. Each cell manages replenishment at point of use, which can be an advantage. Cells that use the item send kanban orders to the supplier.

The biggest risk with this method is holding more inventory than is necessary, which is driven by a couple factors.

Figure 17-2. Decentralized Common Part

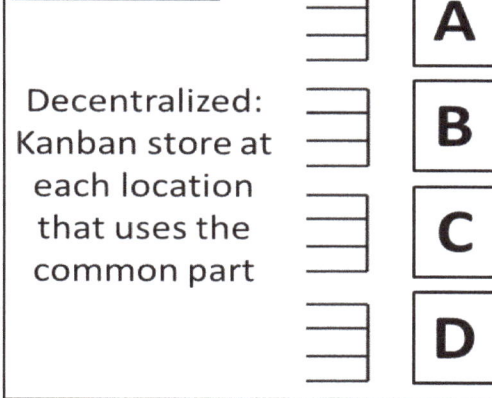

Decentralized: Kanban store at each location that uses the common part

First, if minimum order quantity (MOQ) or standard package quantity (SPQ) limitations cause kanban order quantities to be rounded up for one or more of the cells, the kanban stores at those cells will have excess inventory (unplanned safety stock from higher order quantity) caused by that rounding.

Second, each cell holds safety stock for their specific demand and supply variations. Since unpooled demand generally exhibits higher variation than pooled or combined demand, the sum of safety stock for individual cells is likely to be higher than it would be if inventory was centralized.

Centralized: The shared item is in inventory at every cell that uses it but there is a kanban store at just one location, generally the biggest user, and other cells pull what they need from that consolidated store. In Figure 17-3, the main cell stores the parts and other cells refill from there. Total inventory will

Figure 17-3. Centralized Common Part

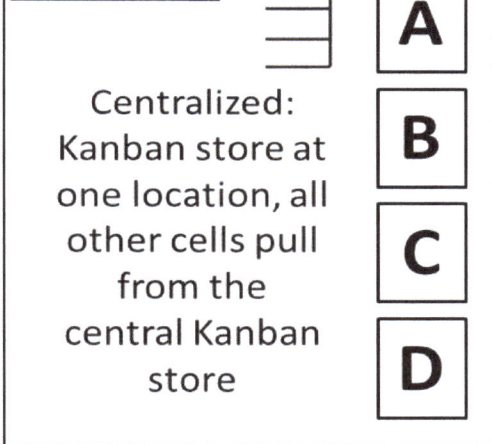

Centralized: Kanban store at one location, all other cells pull from the central Kanban store

likely be lower than in the decentralized method. The main cell is the only store that issues kanban orders to the supplier.

A standard process is needed for outlying cells to obtain "refill" parts from the main kanban store. This can be accomplished by having associates from outlying cells go to the store to get parts, which means associates must leave their work cell to get parts. Another option is to have a water spider refill the outlying cells.

In addition to determining who refills the outlying cells, a refill quantity must be calculated. The centralized method works well if outlying cells use "transfer" cards to request standard refill quantities to prevent those cells from requesting too much inventory from the store. (See the section about transfer cards in the chapter about deploying kanban cards, on page 296.) A transfer card requests a standard refill quantity from the kanban store, but it does not generate a replenishment order for pieces to be produced or procured. Transfer card quantities are usually based on a standard refill cycle, e.g., refill every shift or every 2 days. Multiply the planned replenishment cycle by the right demand number, e.g., refill every [two days * daily demand], to calculate the standard refill quantity.

Another alternative is to use an item's standard package quantity (SPQ) as the refill quantity, but this works only for items that come in reasonably sized containers. If a box holds a quantity that covers 1 to 5 days of demand for an outlying cell, requesting 1 box per refill is reasonable. But, this doesn't work if 1 box is more than a week of demand because it forces outlying cells to pull material in very lumpy quantities that then must be stored at point of use.

HINT for Associates

Choose the right kanban approach for shared items. Centralized stores generally minimize on-hand inventory, but if usage is high at every cell then decentralized kanban stores might be best.

Process Sequence Structures & Where Kanban Belongs

We also review process sequences to determine where kanban fits.

Process Structure: Straight Line, or Linked Processes in a Sequence

The simplest process structure is a straight line, where cells are linearly linked. In Figure 17-4, parts can follow only one path through the sequence of cells: A to B to C to D. Linked processes *should be* easy to schedule because accurately planning one cell essentially plans every other cell in the sequence via either push or pull. But, it's amazing how many sites mess this up by independently scheduling every process in the most disconnected and oblivious (yes, oblivious, not obvious) ways. The safest approach is to plan the pacemaker cell, since it is the limiting factor, then use a combination of push and pull for the rest of the sequence.

Figure 17-4. Linked or Sequential Processes

I know what you're thinking. "Does that mean <u>push</u> is OK?" I'm fully aware that some people have an aversion to push because some Lean experts say it is the antithesis of Lean. However, in some scenarios push is a reasonable solution, particularly when designed to work with a pull mechanism as a control.

Let's consider a couple of structures.

Linked Sequence with One Kanban Store at the End

In many cases a sequence of linked processes is successful with just <u>one</u> kanban store. It's generally wise to put the kanban store right in front of the pacemaker so that their pull pattern sets the pace of the entire sequence. But, that isn't mandatory. It might make sense to place the kanban store at the end of the sequence, just before or after the final process as in Figure 17-5.

As parts are consumed by cell D, kanban replenishment signals go all the way back to cell A. Material is <u>pulled</u> by cell D all the way back to cell A, then <u>pushed</u> from A through cells B and C. This works with any pacemaker location (front of the sequence, middle, or end of the sequence) as long as the pacemaker is accommodated in the kanban plan.

Figure 17-5. Linked Processes with Kanban Store at End

Linked Sequence with One Kanban Store in the Middle

There are situations where a kanban store doesn't work well at the end of the process sequence. Think about a Final Assembly cell that requires 5 different part numbers for each assembly. Each part exists in 10 different colors, so the combination of 5 physical components and 10 different colors drives a total of 50 part numbers as inputs to Assembly, but Assembly consumes just 1 color at a time.

In Figure 17-6 on page 199, a kanban store in front of Paint holds unpainted parts that are painted when Assembly requests parts to fill customer orders. Assembly sends signals to Paint for a specific color based on customer orders, so no kanban store is required between Assembly and Paint. Assembly signals Paint for specific quantities and colors based on demand, so it's a make-to-order pull system without a kanban store. Paint consumes parts from the kanban store, and when the store needs to be refilled they send pull signals back to cell A, which pushes parts to B and then to the store.

This works only if the lead time for Paint plus Assembly is less than the lead time from customer order entry to shipment. If the process lead time for Paint plus Assembly is longer than the allowed customer lead time, hold painted parts in front of Assembly or finished goods after assembly, whichever is appropriate.

Figure 17-6. Linked Processes with Midway Kanban Store

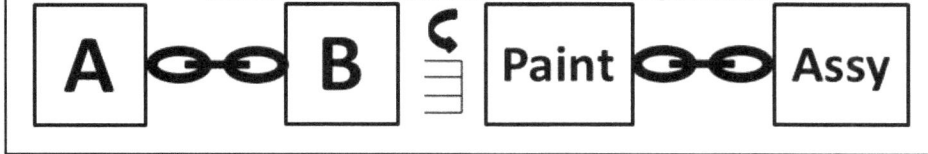

Linked Sequence with More Than One Kanban Store

There are cases where more than one kanban store is necessary, even in a linked sequence.

• Shorter sawtooth curves: Some sites prefer short lead times from kanban signal to order fulfillment in order to limit the height of the sawtooth curve by producing material in smaller batches. If short lead times are desired and total lead time from start to finish is longer than customer-allowed lead time, install more than one kanban store to break up the long sequence.

Suppose we have fifteen processes in a linked sequence with a total lead time of 13 days and a cycle time of 3 days for cell 15. Customer lead time is 3 days, so we can only complete cell 15's work within the allowed customer lead time. We have a goal to fill kanban signals for internal parts in 7 days or less, so we need at least 1 kanban store midway through the sequence in order to split the summed cycle time from cell 1 through cell 14 (10 processing days) into 2 segments.

In Figure 17-7, there is a kanban store in front of cell 8 and another in front of cell 15. The store at cell 8 is filled in a time equal to the sum of the lead times for cells 1 through 7, and the store in front of cell 15 requires the sum of the process times from cells 8 to 14. Cells 8 and 15 send replenishment signals back to the earliest process in that segment and material is pushed from those cells forward.

Figure 17-7. Linked Processes with Two Kanban Stores, Lengthy Sequence

• Process risk: If one of the tasks or processes within a sequence has a high risk of failure, e.g., machine downtime or a high scrap rate, it is wise to hold inventory right after the risky process to protect the overall sequence from shutting down due to that one high-risk process. Another alternative is holding extra inventory at the end of the entire sequence. Late-point parts would have a higher cost because more processing has occurred by the end of the sequence, so it's better to hold the safety stock as early in the sequence as possible, i.e., right where the risk exists.

In Figure 17-8 on page 200, process 2 has high risk, so we hold inventory at the output of cell 2 to protect the subsequent processes from a delivery failure out of cell 2. This "extra" kanban store after cell 2 should be temporary, until the supply risk is eliminated.

Figure 17-8. Linked Processes with Two Kanban Stores, Risk in the Sequence

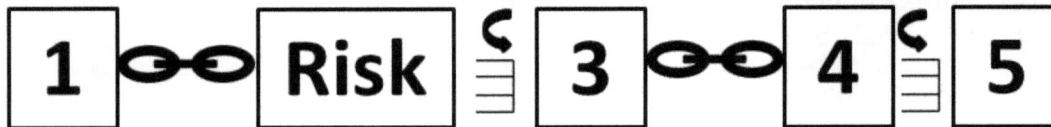

- Batch sizes: If sequential processes have incompatible batch limits, such as divergent minimum and maximum batch quantities, use 2 or more kanban stores to resize batch quantities from process to process. In Figure 17-9, the *maximum* quantity cell 2 can process is 1,000 pieces, but the *minimum* quantity that can go through cell 4 is 1,500 pieces. Put a kanban store after cell 2 or after cell 3 and limit kanban order quantities to 1,000 parts or less. Put a second store after cell 4 or cell 5 with order quantities of 1,500 pieces or more so that order quantities pulled from cell 4 have the right minimum order quantity.

The store after cell 2 will process replenishment signals more frequently than the store after cell 4 due to the lower order quantities, but the sequence should stay in balance. This approach does increase inventory due to duplicate kanban stores, so think Lean and find ways to reduce the required MOQ for cell 4.

Figure 17-9. Linked Processes with Two Kanban Stores, Divergent Batch Sizes

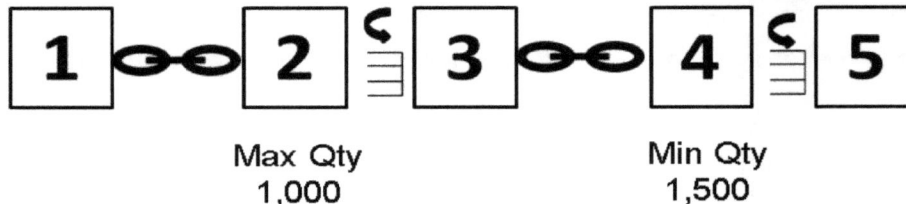

Max Qty
1,000

Min Qty
1,500

Process Structure: Multiple Suppliers at the Front of a Value Stream

If a process in the middle of a sequence is fed by more than one supplier, such as Heat Treat receiving parts from two independent streams, there are potential scheduling challenges in the cell with multiple inputs.

In Figure 17-10, cell C is fed by A and B and cells C and D are sequentially linked. To schedule these cells, put a kanban store in front of cell C and send replenishment signals back to cells A and B, where parts will be produced according to standard kanban rules for order quantity and due date.

Figure 17-10. Multiple Suppliers at Front

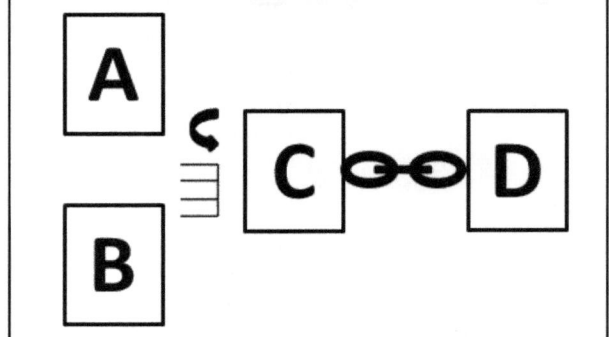

Process Structure: Shared Resource at the Front of a Value Stream

Sometimes the opposite situation exists, where an upstream cell produces parts for two separate production sequences. In Figure 17-11 on page 201, cell A supplies parts to cells B and D, so we need a robust way to plan production out of cell A to feed two streams.

Cell A has higher daily output than the receiving cells because it feeds both the B-C and D-E streams.

Figure 17-11. Shared Resource at Front

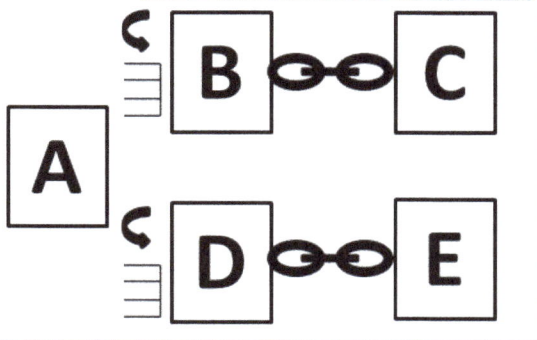

It might also experience different demand variation than the linked sequences. (Demand variation analysis for parts coming out of cell A would confirm if that was the case.)

The challenge is how to schedule cell A to feed two streams. Kanban stores in front of cells B and D would provide point-of-use kanban storage for each receiving cell, and they would send kanban replenishment signals back to cell A.

Rule of Thumb

When push and pull are used together, kanban signals are sent as far back as the cell that initiates the work for the replenishment order, which is back to the next kanban store or planned inventory location.

If cell D has the kanban store and there are no kanban stores at cells B or C, the signal goes all the way back to cell A. See Figure 17-5 on page 198.

If cell 15 pulls stock out of kanban store and there is also a kanban store in front of cell 8, as in Figure 17-7 on page 199, the signal from cell 15 goes all the way back to cell 8.

Process Structure: Shared Resource at the End of a Value Stream

In some operations the shared resource resides at the end of the process sequence. For this discussion, assume a shared resource at the end of a process is something other than pack or ship, maybe an assembly cell or paint process that completes every item to finished goods status.

Figure 17-12. Shared Resource at End

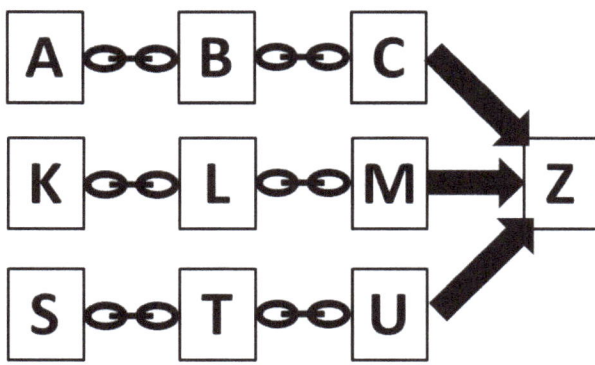

In Figure 17-12, the Z cell is the end of the value stream for the three separate sequential processes: ABC, KLM, and STU. Even if cell Z is not the pacemaker for the overall operation, it can still stop the entire show if it is poorly managed and either falls behind or produces the wrong parts.

Suppose everything comes through the Paint shop, cell Z in the diagram, as the last step before Shipping. Every value stream depends on timely output from Paint to meet delivery due dates. So, the Paint cell must process items in the right order, but Paint also has to manage set-ups as they convert from one color to the next. For that reason, they batch their production sequence by color to avoid added downtime to change colors unnecessarily. Of course they should reduce changeover time so it is short enough to avoid scheduling issues. But, maybe they haven't achieved that yet and in today's world every changeover results in lost paint when they flush the lines, so both scrap cost and minimizing wastewater are valid concerns.

If the separate value streams that feed Paint *always* produce to the right cadence, the streams can push material to Paint, which will process orders based on customer due date with an eye to first-in-first-out (FIFO).

If the three different value streams do <u>not</u> produce to correct due dates and lead times, Paint can't solve that incoming scheduling problem on its own. Supplying cells must solve their scheduling and delivery problems, but until they do, there should be inventory in front of Paint.

In Figure 17-13, the left diagram shows that Paint utilizes push plus FIFO with no kanban stores from the three value streams. The three value streams push work to Paint based on customer due dates, and Paint works on whatever comes their way. Paint has to diligently manage several things.

First, they must know the due date for each order that gets pushed to them, so they process work orders in the right priority.

Second, they should utilize FIFO in conjunction with order due dates so the value streams that get their work to Paint on time are rewarded by being at the front of the processing line if there are multiple orders with the same due date.

Finally, Paint must manage their queue time, or how long each order waits before being processed.

Figure 17-13. <u>Paint Cell at End: Push Plus FIFO *or* Three Kanban Stores</u>

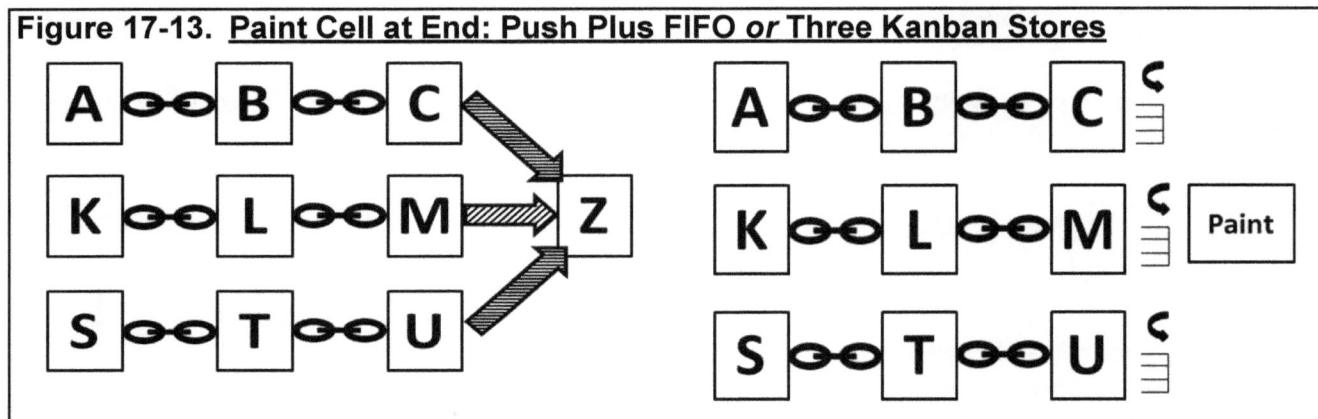

The diagram on the right side of Figure 17-13 illustrates how a kanban store at the end of each of the three value streams could feed Paint, putting Paint in charge of managing customer due dates. Paint pulls what they need from kanban stores to fill customer orders, and replenishment signals are sent by Paint all the way back to cells A, K, and S. Those upstream cells push material through subsequent processes. Note that the store in front of Paint could be considered one kanban store instead of three.

Suppose the promised lead time from customer order to shipment is less time than it takes to complete the entire process sequence. Therefore, inventory must be held as FG or WIP. If customer lead time is very short, we might hold finished goods in inventory and pull from Ship back to cells A, K, and S to replenish FG as they are consumed. This would put a finished goods kanban store after Paint, which might prevent the need for a kanban store before Paint.

Regardless of what kind of cell or process is at the end of multiple value streams—Paint, Assembly, Test, Pack, Polish—the analysis is the same. Compare customer lead times versus process lead times to determine where inventory must be held. Determine if pull is preferred, with one or more kanban stores, or if push with FIFO will work to balance what comes out of distinct value streams.

Always ensure that the bottleneck won't be overloaded.

Kanban Planning Nuances

Manage the Implications of Pull + Push

Combining pull with push does not require that impacted cells be on the same work schedule or that the kanban store be in a specific location within the process sequence, but the kanban system must be balanced. If Stamping works one shift and Heat Treat works two, pull plus push still works, but the workload must be balanced to prevent either cell from working ahead or falling behind. As discussed above, within any sequence of processes that utilize push with pull, identify the bottleneck and ensure that it is not overloaded by kanban signals.

If combining push with pull results in erratic output, stock outs, schedule interruptions, poor planning, or other non-Lean results, go back to basic pull systems. Don't allow a desire to reduce the number of kanban stores to abolish common sense and Lean thinking.

Keep an Eye on Purchased Parts, WIP, & Finished Goods

Once the value stream has been studied and we know where to hold inventory, establish inventory performance goals for purchased parts, work in progress (WIP), and finished goods (FG), measured in days on hand or inventory turns. To do this, estimate expected on-hand inventory dollars for every item and sum those dollars by inventory category (e.g., ABC classification and/or purchased parts, WIP, and FG) to assess inventory performance. If any category of items gets out of control, use root cause analysis to find out what is causing excess inventory.

If kanban stores do not include finished goods, yet FG inventory is always higher than it should be, find out why. If purchased inventory runs 20% higher than the prediction, find the root cause. If C items are sky high, figure out why. Be relentless about managing on-hand balances!

> ## Rule of Thumb
>
> **Make it a priority to hold inventory as far upstream as possible to minimize cost: RM is better than WIP, and WIP is better than FG.**

Summary of Analyzing the Value Stream Map for Kanban

Analyzing process sequences in a VSM allows us to refine where kanban is needed instead of blindly putting kanban stores between every pair of process boxes.

• An accurate future-state map is essential for analyzing process sequences to determine where kanban is required. The structure of a VSM provides insight about where kanban could be utilized.

• Lead-time analysis versus allowed customer lead time is essential for defining where kanban stores are required to meet delivery requirements. Short process lead times provide opportunities to eliminate kanban stores in favor of build to order.

• Process sequences that can use a combination of pull and push can avoid putting kanban stores at every process intersection, limiting them to where they make sense.

Figure 17-14 illustrates where kanban should be considered in a value stream map.

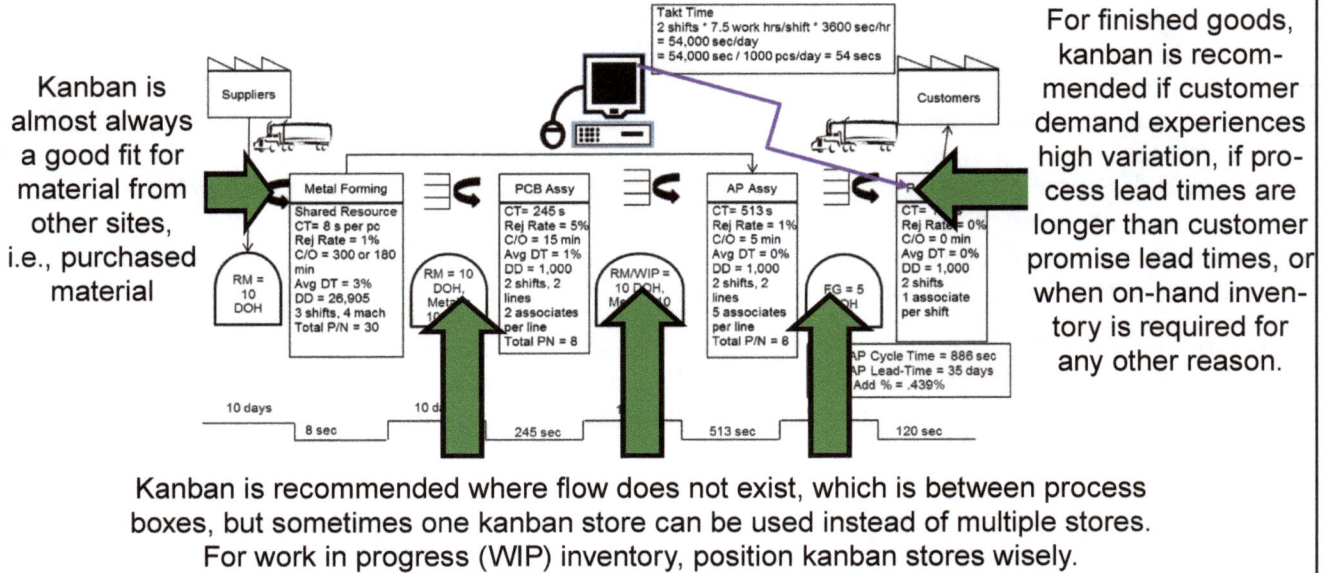

Figure 17-14. VSM Sections & Kanban Fit

Kanban is almost always a good fit for material from other sites, i.e., purchased material

For finished goods, kanban is recommended if customer demand experiences high variation, if process lead times are longer than customer promise lead times, or when on-hand inventory is required for any other reason.

Kanban is recommended where flow does not exist, which is between process boxes, but sometimes one kanban store can be used instead of multiple stores. For work in progress (WIP) inventory, position kanban stores wisely.

Tutorial: GOCO VSM Analysis for Kanban

Mary and the team reviewed the future state VSM and concluded the original plan made sense. They decided to deploy kanban stores at all of the locations on the future state map.

Kanban = Y or Kanban = N?

CHAPTER 18: KANBAN SCOPE—EXCLUDE THE RIGHT ITEMS & INCLUDE THE REST

After determining where kanban stores fit, we must decide which items belong in those stores. We can't assume that every part number should be considered for kanban, which makes excluding items from kanban the first step in defining kanban solutions.

Excluding items from kanban requires three steps:

1. Exclude *groups* of parts from kanban based on how they move through the value stream or where stores are placed.

2. Exclude *groups* of parts based on certain attributes, such as new product introduction.

3. Decide which *specific* parts should be excluded from kanban, even when an item qualifies for kanban consideration based on its place in the value stream and other characteristics.

Kanban calculators often use data out of a Materials Requirements Planning (MRP) or Enterprise Resource Planning (ERP) system. There are part numbers in the "system" that should not be on kanban, and the calculator has to know how to divide items into those that qualify for kanban and those that do not. This means the topic of eliminating items from kanban opens a related discussion about part numbers in general. After we cover that, we'll get into eliminating groups of items then individual items.

Part Numbering Considerations for Kanban Exclusion

Discussing the logic of how part numbers (PNs) change as material travels through a value stream might seem like an unnecessary tangent in a discussion about how to exclude items from kanban. But, a kanban calculator relies on PN designations and associated data to determine how to treat every item, so understanding where and how part numbers are created is essential.

A part number designates a specific physical form of material. Part numbers are necessary for ordering and receiving purchased parts, backflushing (a common term for inventory transactions in a materials or financial system), accepting and filling customer orders, material planning, financial analysis, labeling items, etc.

Part Numbers Can Be Created at Various Points in the Value Stream

Processes that utilize physical goods <u>consume</u> incoming part numbers as inputs and <u>create</u> new PNs as their outputs. The PN change indicates a change in status, e.g., a painted item has a different PN than the very same item in an unpainted form.

PN Created at the End of a Process or Cell

Changing PNs at the end of a process or at the output of a cell is easy to see and understand: incoming PNs go through the process, and different items exit the process as newly created PNs.

From value stream analysis it is evident that PNs created at the end of or "between" value stream process boxes should be *considered* for kanban because flow does not exist from one process box to the next. The new PN that exits one process box and enters the next box sits in inventory between those processes. But, as we learned in the last chapter it might not be appropriate to put every inventory item on kanban. Therefore, individual parts and groups of parts must be assessed for kanban applicability.

PN Created in the Middle of a Process or Cell, During Flow

Some part numbers are created in the middle of a process, and these items are not as obvious for kanban consideration as are those created at the end of a process. By definition, a PN created in the middle of a process box is in the midst of flow because it's within a value stream process box. Therefore, we can't assume that *every* PN created within a process is a good fit for kanban.

As you might guess, there are times when an item that experiences flow might be on kanban. Suppose a housing is created in the middle of a subassembly cell, and the housing progresses through that process to become a subassembly. In addition to being used in the subassembly, the housing is also sold as an aftermarket component, and that's why it needs a standalone PN. When we get a list of all the part numbers in the system, the housing that achieves flow but is sold to the aftermarket will show up on the list. Should it be on kanban? That's a great question. If aftermarket sales or another feature require inventory to be held in stock, put it on kanban even though within its manufacturing process it achieves flow.

If it isn't necessary to hold a "flow" item in inventory or to ship it as a standalone part number, it would be appropriate to eliminate that PN from the system. Yes, I'm saying that the part number itself should be eliminated - taken out of the system - if it isn't required for a valid reason!

HINT for Leaders

Eliminate unnecessary part numbers so they don't clog up kanban calculators and other analysis tools. Keeping unnecessary part numbers drives over-processing waste.

Smart Part Numbers

When setting action plans or analyzing data by part number, it helps if we can sort items easily. Smart part numbers are a great option.

Smart Part Numbers Describe the Item

Suppose we buy 20 different kinds of screws. It would make sense to have numbers that clarify some of the key features.

1. That the item is a screw.

2. The material it is made of, if different materials are used.

3. The size of the screw.

4. The pitch of the threads.

5. The type of head on the screw, e.g., straight, hex, Phillips, etc.

We might end up with something like "SCR-SST-125.20-PH" to indicate a screw made of stainless steel that is 1.25 inches long and has a thread pitch of 20 with a Phillips head. When sorting part numbers, we can extrapolate any of these features as a sorting characteristic. If we have an inventory action plan to consolidate all 1.25" screws to 1 item, we can easily find the list of contenders.

Smart Part Numbers Indicate Process Point

It can be beneficial to indicate a process point within a PN. Suppose items can go through up to five processes in a series, processes A through E. If an item is held in inventory at each step along the way, it would be beneficial to track it step by step via the PN, making it possible to easily find items coming out of or going into a certain process step based on the content of the PN.

To create this type of smart PN, assign a leading or trailing extension for every process step and tack it onto the base PN as it travels through the process. Part number 12345-CF is item 12345 just out of Cold Form and 12345-HT is from Heat Treat.

Smart Part Numbers & Flow

Part numbers should be assigned only to items that are expected to be held in inventory or shipped to a customer. If a part achieves flow or is pushed via first-in-first-out (FIFO) from Cold Form to Heat Treat to Plating, there is no need to have an interim PN at Heat Treat because the part doesn't stop there. Using interim PNs adds unnecessary transactions to report the item as cold formed, heat treated, and plated. There is no value because parts process through the sequence without delay.

The transaction impact from multiple PNs might seem trivial, but when determining which items to consider for kanban, unnecessary PNs clog up the analysis if there is no way to cleanly divide them into "Yes" or "No" for kanban consideration.

Suppose we have PNs for both Cold Form and Grind, but we never hold parts in inventory that have not been through the grinding step because parts go straight from Cold Form through the grinder in the same cell.

If we have PNs for both Cold Form and Grind, imagine what the kanban analysis looks like for these parts. First, we have two times the required number of items. Second, we need to sort the parts into those that should be considered for kanban (parts that have been through the grinder) and those that should not (parts that just came out of Cold Form.) Smart PNs make it easy to sort them; anything that ends in "CF" is not on kanban and anything that ends in "GR" is eligible for kanban.

Methods for Excluding Part Numbers from Kanban Within the Calculator

Telling the kanban calculator which parts to exclude is one of the biggest challenges when designing a kanban calculator. Excluding PNs from

kanban means identifying items that should be skipped, and then accepting all other items as kanban eligible. It is preferable that this be done in an automated way instead of manually reviewing the entire item list and designating line by line which items will not be on kanban.

There are several methods to provide the calculator with the information needed to make those decisions.

Kanban Exclusion Method: Smart Part Numbers

A smart PN is easily interpreted by a human or a spreadsheet based on the content or order of characters in the PN, which allows the calculator to find relevant data using basic functions such as FIND, LEFT, and RIGHT.

> **Exclude PN from Kanban Using Smart PN to Indicate Process Status**
>
> IF (Left (PN, 2) = "HT", 0, 1)
>
> This formula excludes a PN from kanban (assigns a "0" value) if the number starts with the characters "HT," so parts created at heat treat are not on kanban.

Some sites insert a specific character in any PN that is excluded from kanban, e.g., 187-R425X is not eligible for kanban, as indicated by the X at the end of the PN. This works, but it can be tedious to maintain.

> **Exclude PN from Kanban Using Smart PN to Indicate Exclusion**
>
> IF (Right (PN, 1) = "X", 0, 1)
>
> This excludes from kanban any PN that ends with "X."

> **HINT for Leaders**
>
> It is a daunting task to renumber every item that needs a smart PN, but the benefits can be enormous. At the very least, use smart numbering schemes when a new PN is created.

Part Number Kanban Exclusion Example

A process has a series of steps that transform parts from raw material to final assembly. In the current-state value stream map, parts are held in inventory between every pair of processes, Cut to Rough Sand to Finish Sand to Stain to Clear Coat. The PNs were created years ago and there is no rhyme or reason to any of them. In the future-state VSM, parts don't stop from Cut to Clear Coat, they flow from process to process so that only raw material (wood) and coated parts are held in inventory. To sort parts for kanban consideration, we need to separate coated parts from all other part numbers.

1. Eliminate PNs: We could eliminate all PNs between raw material and Clear Coat, and actually take them out of the system. If we do this, we no longer capture data at those intermediate steps. This is probably the best approach, but Finance, Operations, and Materials might be concerned about losing data associated with those parts, particularly if designations are used to track scrap, labor, etc.

2. Item Master Flag: We could create a field in each part's item master that indicates Yes or No for whether the part should be considered for kanban. This allows us to sort parts easily, but it requires significant effort up front and on-going maintenance thereafter. Item master fields often sound like a great idea, but they are incredibly difficult to maintain. Consider this as a last resort.

3. New PNs: We could create new smart PNs for every existing item in order to continue capturing data at every step, yet also easily sort parts for kanban consideration. In kanban analysis, we would include a formula that assigns "Not Kanban" to items that end in RS for Rough Sand, FS for Finish Sand, or ST for Stain, etc.

In truth, there is generally no need to keep intermediate PNs so Option 1 is the best. People might insist that tracking operational data requires it, but maintaining unnecessary PNs to track data is waste (over-processing) that should be stopped. Consider what is best for the long-term and find a way to get rid of intermediate PNs. Eliminating PNs is the cleanest and most Lean approach.

If we believe current PNs will be active for years, consider all three options and determine the best approach.

If we believe current PNs will go away in the next couple years, we can probably eliminate option #3 for current part numbers, and design a new part numbering system that makes it easy to create and sort new PNs in the future. In the meantime, stop creating PNs for steps between raw material and Clear Coat.

Kanban Exclusion Method: Reference List

A site can create a list of excluded parts to be inserted as a separate tab in the Excel kanban calculator. If a PN in the calculator appears in the exclusion list, the part is excluded from kanban consideration. This method is helpful if excluded parts have no smart numbering or if the list of parts to exclude is truly random in nature and not easily defined by process status, item attribute, etc.

In Excel, the MATCH function in combination with ISNUMBER and IF is one of the best ways to utilize an exclusion list.

Exclude Items on an Exclusion List

The excluded PNs for a kanban calculator are 12, 34, 56, 78, and 90. These are listed in column A of a reference sheet called "Exclusions." In the kanban calculator, add a column to check every PN versus the exclusion list.

Formula: IF (ISNUMBER (MATCH (PN, 'Exclusions'!A2:A6, 0)), 0, 1)

This is simpler than it looks. Trust me, it's easy.

1. The MATCH function compares the selected PN to the exclusion list (cells A2 to A6 on the exclusion tab) and checks for an exact match, specified by the 0 at the end of the MATCH function. The MATCH formula returns the number that correlates to where the item was found in the list, or the error "#N/A" if no match is found. The MATCH function for PN 12 we would get "1" as the result because it is in the first cell of the list.

2. The ISNUMBER function returns TRUE if a number is found and FALSE if a result is not a number. We use this to prevent the Excel error "#N/A" (the result of no match) from ruining the IF formula.

3. The IF function checks to see if ISNUMBER generated a "true" result, meaning a number was found by the MATCH function. If ISNUMBER is true, the PN was excluded so "0" is assigned to the item to exclude it from kanban.

• Instead of using a single Yes/No field in the item master, use multiple fields to reflect specific attributes that exclude kanban consideration, such as the presence of flow, new product introduction (NPI), vendor managed inventory (VMI), consignment, or end of life (EOL). The advantage of multiple fields is that some items have more than one noteworthy attribute and associates who use the calculator might want to see them all. This requires numerous field definitions and *robust* maintenance of item masters. But, every item is well defined and therefore easily sorted or filtered because all defined fields can be used by the calculator to decide kanban validity.

Exclude PN from Kanban Using Item Master Attributes

IF (OR (Column B = "Y," Column C = "Y," Column D = "Y"), 0, 1)

This excludes an item from kanban if the entry in columns B, C, or D is "Y."

Designated columns contain attribute fields such as NPI (new product introduction) or VMI (vendor managed inventory) and the formula interprets "Y" in any column as kanban exclusion.

Exclude Groups of Items from Kanban

Exclude Group of Items: Where Flow Exists

If items achieve flow and therefore do not require planned inventory, flag them as excluded from kanban. This can be difficult to do if there are a large number of parts to exclude. But, to accomplish this automatically, find a way to identify flow based on the process that creates the PNs.

Kanban Exclusion Method: Item Master Fields

An item master is a set of data fields that describes the associated item. In most ERP or MRP systems, the item master includes fields such as PN, description, supplier, standard cost, buyer or planner, etc.

There are two ways to use item master fields to eliminate items from kanban.

• Use a single Yes/No or 1/0 field in the item master to indicate if kanban is valid for that item. This field is pulled into a column in the kanban calculator as part of the data upload.

How to Exclude Items That Flow

Smart PNs are a great way to identify which process creates a specific PN, and an insightful numbering scheme is often the easiest way to segregate kanban based on the process that creates the PNs.

If smart PNs won't work, one or more item master fields is another option to indicate PNs that exhibit flow. However, this means updating every item master for parts that achieve flow, so it's very tedious if the exclusion list is long.

A reference list is also possible, but this has the same challenges as the item master in that it can be a daunting task to correctly list all PNs that achieve flow.

HINT for Leaders

When possible, consider deleting PNs that achieve flow. If an item achieves flow, it shouldn't sit in inventory, so why is a PN required?

I can't say this too much. Kanban is wonderful, but achieving one-piece flow is always preferred. When flow can't be achieved, inventory must be planned, and kanban is a great inventory planning tool. Use it wisely, but only where it is necessary. Achieve flow wherever possible.

Exclude Group of Items: No Kanban at Some Process Intersections

A process sequence consists of Stamping, Heat Treat, Plating, and Subassembly, as in Figure 18-1. Flow does not occur from Stamping through Subassembly because parts are produced in batches. But, it might not be necessary to put kanban stores between all processes, as we discussed in prior chapters.

Instead of multiple kanban stores, or a store at every intersection, suppose we put one kanban store in front of Subassembly. Material will wait between the other processes for as long as it takes to move through the sequence, which should be hours and not days. Stamping, Heat Treat, and Plating will utilize first-in-first-out (FIFO) along

Figure 18-1. Future state VSM, Kanban at Subassembly

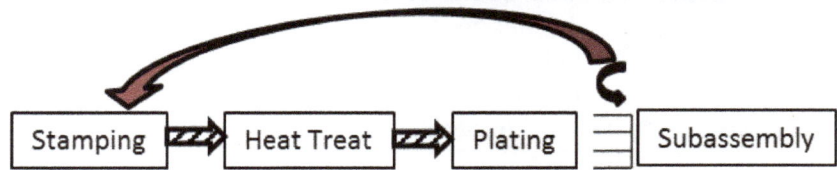

Stamping → Heat Treat → Plating ≡ Subassembly

Kanban store in front of Subassembly. Kanban replenishment signal goes from Subassembly to Stamping, then parts are pushed through Heat Treat and Plating.

with replenishment due dates to determine the correct production sequence for incoming orders.

Because every item is produced in standard kanban order quantities and pushed from Stamping to Heat Treat to Plating, inventory exists at a minimal level between processes. But, the only kanban store is between Plating and Subassembly. The replenishment signal from Subassembly to Stamping is a traditional kanban pull signal, and the replenishment quantity is driven by the total lead time from Stamping through Plating.

As discussed in the last chapter, this is actually quite simple in practice. Parts move from Stamping to Heat Treat to Plating and then to the kanban store, with minimal time at each stop until the kanban store after Plating. The impact on the kanban calculator is that a PN for a plated part will qualify for kanban, but a Heat Treat or Stamped PN will be excluded.

There are some nuances that must be recognized and accommodated in this plan:

1. Think about the prior discussion about when PNs change or are created. Subassembly might consume one PN but request a different PN for the replenishment signal. If Subassembly consumes PL3456 as the plated part, it might leave Stamping as **ST**3456 and come out of Heat Treat as **HT**3456. This is a case where it is beneficial to have smart PNs, so any item that starts with "PL" is from Plating, "ST" is a stamped part, and "HT" is heat treated. Smart PNs allow Subassembly to easily interpret which part to *order* based on the PN they *consume*, and Stamping can quickly determine which stamped part becomes the correct plated part for Subassembly.

2. Push plus pull does not require that sequential cells be on the same work schedule, or the same number of shifts per day or days per week, but the kanban system must be balanced. If Stamping works one shift and Heat Treat works two, pull plus push will work, but the workload must be balanced to prevent cells from working ahead or falling behind.

3. Within any sequence of processes that are linked, one process is the bottleneck. Identify that process and ensure that it is not overloaded by kanban signals.

How to Exclude Items at Process Intersections

We can use the "supplier" column in a kanban calculator to determine where PNs are created then exclude items based on that column. (Supplier is a required data point for all items, so this data should be available.) If Stamping and Heat Treat parts are excluded from kanban, exclude every PN that lists those cells as the supplier.

Of course, smart PNs are another way to exclude parts from kanban when process status is included in the numbering scheme, as described above.

Exclude Group of Items: Not Kanban Due to Short Process Lead Time vs. Available Customer Lead Time

If the lead time from customer order to promised ship date is long enough to accommodate the sequence of manufacturing processes, skip kanban within that sequence and build to order. This often eliminates finished goods from kanban consideration.

In order to flag items with a short enough lead time to avoid holding inventory, determine which processes fall within the build-to-order sequence, or those with enough time to go from their position in the value stream to the Shipping process. Compare "time to completion" for each process versus the lead time for customer orders and designate every item created by an excluded process as excluded from kanban.

How to Exclude Items with a Short Lead Time

To exclude an item based on lead time requires a way to identify the process that produces the item, as described above. Smart PNs work best, but exclusion lists and item master fields also work.

Exclude Group of Items: Not Kanban Due to Supply Characteristics

Some supply characteristics exclude items from kanban.

• Parts being moved to a new supplier or those being re-negotiated with the current supplier do not have a valid supply contract. That makes it difficult to define a confirmed kanban order quantity because lead time, minimum order quantity, or standard package quantity might be unconfirmed.

• Parts that are managed and replenished by the supplier don't need to be on kanban, such as vendor managed inventory (VMI) and some forms of consignment inventory. We might choose to use kanban with VMI items to calculate for the supplier the standard quantity for a full bin, but a kanban card won't be processed to generate orders.

HINT for Leaders

Investigate opportunities for parts to be replenished as "vendor managed inventory" (VMI), in which the supplier manages on-hand balances by making regular visits to the site to assess and replenish inventory. In many cases, this is as good or better than kanban because it avoids kanban cards, replenishment signals and transactions, etc. This only works for suppliers that offer this service in a controlled and predictable manner, which requires frequent replenishment visits (generally at least weekly) and reasonable refill quantities.

Real-World Observation

The most common VMI error I've seen is allowing *suppliers* to size the containers for every VMI item. Given a choice, suppliers use large bins so they can deliver more parts. One site had 2-3 weeks of inventory in every bin, yet parts were replenished twice a week. That's crazy! I know what you're thinking: "But the supplier only refills as much as we use." You might think it works that way, but some VMI suppliers overfill every bin when they need to boost their revenue for a certain month. Oversized bins consume space and dollars. Use relentless batch-size reduction logic for VMI, as for everything else.

• Parts that are sourced from numerous suppliers or those that undergo contract negotiation for every order can't automatically issue replenishment orders when a kanban card is scanned.

   » If Flux Capacitors are renegotiated for every purchase order, a kanban card is still useful for triggering orders based on consumption. But, human review is required for every signal in order to define the correct supplier.

   » Similarly, parts with multiple sources can be managed by kanban, but submit the kanban card for review, as described in the next HINT box. If bolts come from any one of three different distributors based on spot price and availability, the order signal can easily be managed by a kanban card even though it requires human intervention to finalize the order.

• In rare cases, a supplier's business is at risk due to financial strain, loss of assets (e.g., a fire), potential ownership changes, or other conditions that could impede the supplier's future ability to fill orders. Remove affected parts from kanban until issues are resolved, or at least require manual review when a replenishment order is triggered. Again, kanban cards are beneficial, but human review is necessary.

HINT for Associates

For items that are not on kanban or for kanban items that require human intervention to manage replenishment orders, consider using a variation of a standard kanban process with modified cards. Print "Give to Buyer/Planner" on the card instead of a barcode.

These "unscannable" cards work well for parts that are renegotiated for each order, acquired from different sources from order to order, and even for parts that are not on kanban. Associates turn in a card to signal that replenishment action is required, so all items are managed by kanban logic and the same point-of-use process. Having a card for every part also makes kanban audits much simpler to perform because every item has a card at point of use.

How to Exclude Items from Certain Suppliers

To exclude parts from specific suppliers, use an Excel formula that excludes an item if "supplier" equals a certain name, or use a PN or supplier exclusion list as described earlier in this chapter.

Exclude Parts Based on Supplier Characteristics

e.g.

This is our exclusion list of supplier names: Adam's Apples, Benjamin's Benches, Caleb's Clocks, Daniel's Decking, and Ephraim's Edgers.

If items are excluded for several suppliers, we can use the OR function in a column in the calculator: IF (OR (Supplier = "Adam's Apples", Supplier = "Benjamin's Benches", Supplier = "Caleb's Clocks", Supplier = "Daniel's Decking", Supplier = "Ephraim's Edgers"), KB_Flag = 0, 1)

With this approach, if the list of excluded suppliers changes we must change the formula.

Consider a Match function instead with a list of excluded suppliers: IF (ISNUMBER (MATCH (Supplier, 'Supplier Exclusions'!A2:A26, 0)), 0, 1)

If the list of excluded suppliers changes, simply update the exclusion tab. To facilitate easy future changes, refer to plenty of rows in the exclusion tab, e.g. cells A2 through A99 instead of just A2 to A6, so more cells are considered in case more supplier names are added to the list.

Exclude Group of Items: Not Kanban Due to Attributes

Some life-cycle conditions should be excluded from kanban.

• End of life (EOL) items are being discontinued, replaced, or obsoleted and therefore should not be automatically replenished.

• New product introduction (NPI) includes components at the beginning of their life cycle, so they have no demand history and possibly also lack an accurate demand forecast. Keep in mind that if a "new" part simply replaces an old PN, there is demand history under the old PN so that data can be used to create kanban solutions for the new PN.

• Parts that exhibit zero or very low demand during certain times of the year should be removed from kanban as demand winds down, e.g., snow shovels or swim suits. Kanban places orders au-

tomatically, so as the "minimal demand" time period approaches, it is necessary to prevent automatic orders from being placed. In these cases, a replenishment order generated late in the demand season might be appropriate, but it should likely be for a smaller quantity than the standard order quantity. This is another good place for a "Give to Buyer/Planner" kanban card, as described above.

How to Exclude Parts Based on Attributes

Item master fields are generally the best way to eliminate parts based on life-cycle status or other attributes that are unrelated to process or flow. A single item master field that can reflect new product introduction (NPI), end of life (EOL), vendor managed inventory (VMI), or any other exclusion factor is insightful for the user. But, multiple fields are best if the list of relevant attributes is more than two or three.

Using a smart PN that reflects various life cycle conditions is not a good approach for excluding a part. This is because every status change that occurs over time will require PN updates, and it is tedious to modify PNs every time a condition changes. We wouldn't want PN12345 to go from NPI12345 when it's a new product to 12345 when it's a standard part to EOL12345 when it reaches end of life. Think of the bill of material impacts that would result from this approach! It might work to insert an exclusion character in the part number, such as 12345X, but that raises similar concerns due to the PN changes that would have to occur.

Exclude **Specific** Items from Kanban

After groups of parts are designated as eligible for kanban, individual items can be excluded for two basic reasons.

Exclude Specific Items: Not Kanban Due to Low Daily Demand

Items with low demand deserve special consideration. Because kanban is an automatic ordering method, kanban is best for items that have sufficient demand to warrant automatic ordering when a trigger point is reached.

Every site must determine a reasonable minimum daily demand for putting items on kanban. A minimum daily demand of 1 unit per day is a common "on kanban" threshold, which equates to about 250 parts per year if a site works 5 days per week and 50 weeks per year. A daily demand value as low as 0.1 (25 per year or about 2 per month) is valid for some sites, while other sites set a daily demand of at least 4 (1,000 pieces per year). The low daily demand limit must be reasonable for each individual business.

> ## Rule of Thumb 👍
>
> **Every site must define the appropriate threshold to qualify an item's daily demand for kanban.**
>
> **Default: Daily demand < 1.0 = not on kanban**

Because the "On Kanban Daily Demand Limit" depends on the business, setting this limit requires some analysis coupled with common sense. In general, it is reasonable to link this to the related goal that a certain percentage of the annual expenditure for purchased parts should be on kanban. The annual spend goal might target at least 90% of annual spend to be managed by kanban. If analysis of initial kanban assignments indicate that the annual external spend on kanban is less than 90%, adjust the daily demand cutoff to a lower number to put more items on kanban. Suppose a daily demand cutoff of 1 per day results in 80% of external annual spend on kanban, we might reduce the daily demand cutoff to 0.5 per day and see if that approaches 90% of annual purchased spend on kanban. Yes, it's a bit of trial and error.

How to Exclude Items with Low Daily Demand

To exclude parts from kanban for low daily demand (DD), use an Excel formula to compare each item's daily demand to the minimum DD threshold.

> **Daily Demand Kanban Exclusion** =
>
> IF (Daily demand < DD On Kanban Limit), THEN exclude from kanban

> ## Rule of Thumb 👍
>
> **Daily demand (DD) varies widely from site to site, so there is no right or perfect answer for the DD kanban limit.**
>
> **If an initial DD limit excludes a large portion of items and results in a low percent of spend on kanban, adjust the limit until the percent on kanban increases to near 90%. As mentioned before, decreasing the DD limit is usually not a big deal, within reason.**

Specific Parts: Not Kanban Due to High Minimum Order Quantity

Minimum order quantity (MOQ) is defined as the minimum production or purchase quantity for an item. When excluding individual items from kanban, a "high" MOQ is not determined by the actual order quantity itself but rather by how many days of demand the quantity covers. An order for 10,000 parts is fine if DD is 1,000, but it would be a disaster if we use only 1 per day.

A high minimum order as measured in days of demand causes us to order more than we normally would, i.e., the calculated kanban order quantity is rounded up to accommodate the MOQ.

A high MOQ raises the risk of excess or obsolete inventory. For example, if a minimum order would take 12 months to consume, it might not be a good fit for kanban because every order commits to a long-term inventory quantity.

Eliminating high MOQs is less critical for C items than for A and B items. Be very careful with those high-spend items.

High MOQs is another case when a kanban card with "Give to Buyer/Planner" instead of a barcode might be a great solution. This keeps high MOQ items on modified kanban but inserts the necessary human review to avoid the potential for unnecessary orders. Manual review should be minimized due to the wastes of over-processing and waiting, but it works well in some scenarios.

How to Exclude Items with a High MOQ

To exclude parts from kanban based on MOQ, set a limit for the maximum <u>demand coverage</u> allowed by the MOQ, or the highest number of days of demand that can be covered by one order quantity.

Convert MOQ into days of demand. Then compare MOQ Days Demand to the On Kanban MOQ Days Demand Limit.

MOQ Days Demand

MOQ Days Demand = MOQ / Daily Demand

IF (MOQ Days Demand > On Kanban MOQ Days Limit), THEN exclude from kanban

---

If the MOQ Days Demand limit eliminates a large number of items from kanban, which reduces kanban coverage measured as percent of annual spend on kanban, the response isn't as easy as it was for daily demand. Increasing the MOQ Days Demand limit is more disconcerting than lowering the daily demand threshold because if we raise the allowed number of days of demand for an item to qualify for kanban, we're accommodating high MOQs and therefore raising inventory levels.

Rule of Thumb

Define the maximum number of days of demand that can be covered by one MOQ in order for an item to qualify for kanban.

Default: MOQ Days Demand > 6 months (125 workdays for 250 annual workdays) = not kanban

HINT for Leaders

An MOQ allowance of more than 6 months of demand indicates a drastic failure to manage MOQs. Tolerating high MOQs results in more on-hand inventory, so negotiate lower MOQs from external suppliers and work diligently to reduce batch quantities from internal cells.

Use One Column in Calculator to Aggregate Exclusion Results

If more than one column in the kanban calculator can exclude an item from kanban consideration, such as multiple item master fields <u>and</u> DD <u>and</u> MOQ limits, it is helpful to add a summary Yes/No or 1/0 column labeled "Consider for kanban." If any of the attribute columns exclude a part number from kanban, the kanban consideration flag is set to "0" or "N" and that item is skipped when kanban calculations are performed.

There are a few advantages to doing this.

1. The person who uses the calculator can quickly see which items were excluded.

2. This simplifies the formula to assign kanban type because the calculator checks just one column to determine if an item receives a kanban solution.

3. If the kanban exclusion designation is "0" instead of "No" and kanban consideration is "1" instead of "Yes," the kanban consideration column can be summed to total the number of parts that are eligible for kanban, and a "COUNT" function can be used on that column to find the number of items with a "0" value.

Exclude Parts from Acme, All Finished Goods, and Items with DD & MOQ Misses **e.g.**

A site excluded all finished goods (FG) inventory, items from the supplier "Acme," DD less than 1, and MOQ Days Demand > 125 from kanban consideration, using this formula:

IF (OR (Material Category = "FG", Supplier = "Acme", DD <1, MOQ Days Demand >125), 0, 1)

This assigns "0" (not kanban) to any item that meets one or more of the listed criteria, and 1 to all other parts.

Manage Parts That Are Not on Kanban

No matter what the reason for excluding items from kanban, ensure that the alternative replenishment process (MRP, VMI, etc.) for every non-kanban item is robust and will protect both on-time delivery and inventory performance. Remember, we need a plan for every part.

Real-World Observation

I worked with a site that put kanban cards with _every_ item on the floor, whether managed by kanban or not. It was brilliant! They used empty-a-bin (EaB) timing so inventory auditors and associates on the floor expected to find a kanban card with _every item_ on the floor. Anything that was not actually managed by kanban, such as vendor managed inventory (VMI), had a kanban card that said "Give to Buyer/Planner for Replenishment" and those cards were processed by the appropriate planner for each PN.

This method implemented a site-wide and consistent replenishment process on the floor: when you use the last piece in a kanban bin, turn in the kanban card. Standard kanban cards were scanned to automatically place orders and "Give to Buyer/Planner" cards were reviewed by the appropriate experts. It was easy to train new associates in the production cells and also in support areas like Material Handling or Purchasing. It was an excellent process!

Kanban Exclusion Summary

Some items do not belong on kanban so a kanban system and the associated calculator must be designed to exclude parts that don't fit.

• A kanban calculator works best if designed with automatic methods to exclude groups of parts or individual parts from kanban consideration. Smart PNs, item master fields, and exclusion lists can be used to exclude groups of parts from kanban.

• Process flow, or where a PN is created within the value stream, and item attributes can exclude groups of parts from kanban.

• Individual parts can be eliminated from kanban based on a low DD or a high MOQ measured as days of demand.

The goal for a kanban system should be to put at least 90% of the annual expenditure for purchased parts on kanban. In most sites the same DD and MOQ limits are used to eliminate both purchased and manufactured parts from kanban.

Use the goal of "90% of annual purchased spend on kanban" to scope whether DD limits are properly sorting which parts should go on kanban, or if too many parts are being eliminated.

TUTORIAL: KANBAN EXCLUSIONS AT GOCO

Because Operations combined Subassembly and Assembly cells, Mary and the Materials team eliminated Subassembly part numbers from MRP because they would no longer report production or hold inventory for those items. They also modified item master and bill of material information for Assembly PNs to accommodate the change.

The first kanban priority was Metal Forming due to their high on-hand balances. Purchased parts were also a priority but Mary knew it would take time to get all the required lead times and order quantity data from external suppliers, so that was the second priority.

Mary confirmed that GOCO received accurate forecast information from automotive customers so she also excluded Automotive finished goods from kanban consideration. This is her formula:

Kanban Consideration
=IF (AND (Cust_Group= "Auto", RM_WIP_FG = "FG"), "0", "1")

The team hoped to eventually eliminate all finished goods inventory, but they decided that Agriculture and Industrial needed that extra customer coverage for the initial roll-out.

They set a DD limit of 10 pieces per day as the on-kanban limit and set MOQ days of coverage at less than 125 workdays.

SECTION V. CALCULATE KANBAN SOLUTIONS

Now that we've covered how kanban works, kanban types, trigger timing, ideal kanban, target lead time and quantities, supply and demand variation, safety stock, and how to scope a kanban system, we're ready to actually calculate kanban solutions.

The next few chapters are intended to be an extended practical example of how to perform the steps required to calculate kanban solutions, including analyzing kanban solutions to plan inventory reductions, a key element of kanban planning.

"Plan" Kanban = Calculate Kanban Solutions

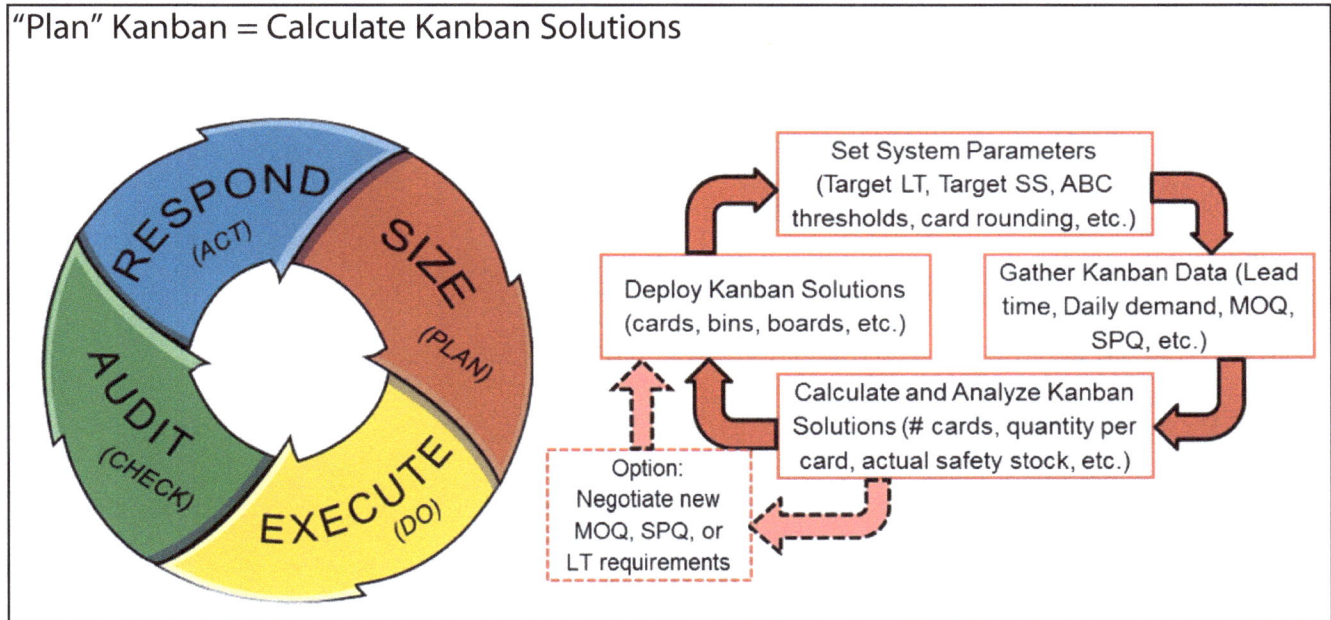

RESPOND (ACT)

SIZE (PLAN)

AUDIT (CHECK)

EXECUTE (DO)

Set System Parameters (Target LT, Target SS, ABC thresholds, card rounding, etc.)

Gather Kanban Data (Lead time, Daily demand, MOQ, SPQ, etc.)

Calculate and Analyze Kanban Solutions (# cards, quantity per card, actual safety stock, etc.)

Deploy Kanban Solutions (cards, bins, boards, etc.)

Option: Negotiate new MOQ, SPQ, or LT requirements

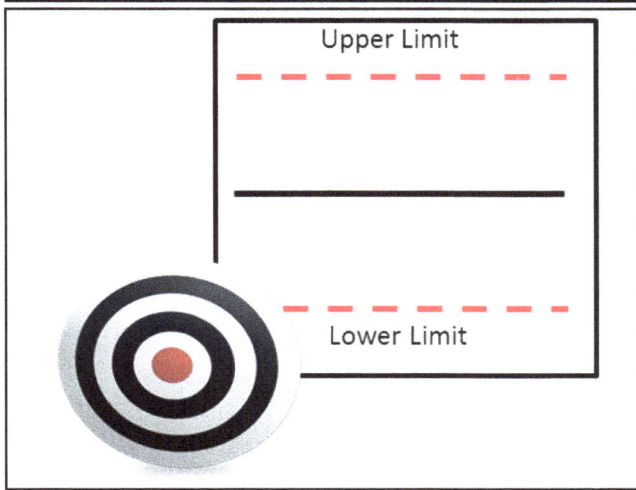

Upper Limit

Lower Limit

CHAPTER 19: KANBAN CALCULATOR TARGETS & LIMITS

Create Excel Tabs

If an automated or software-based calculator is not available, an Excel workbook is a very viable tool for calculating kanban solutions. The Excel file will contain several tabs of data and results, so it's important to design the file effectively. The following tabs should be included.

1. Targets and Limits Tab: Include all required limits or comparison values: target lead times, target safety stock values for groups of parts or individual part numbers, actual versus target lead-time ratio for a multi-card solution, rounding threshold for card count, ABC classification cut-offs for purchased and manufactured items, etc.

HINT for Leaders

For simplicity, Targets and Limits should be listed in one or more separate tabs in the kanban calculator file for easy reference by both kanban users and the calculator itself.

Targets and Limits are usually an assortment of look-up tables from which the Calculator tab obtains data. Populating the Targets and Limits tab depends on several other exercises, such as ABC classification or demand variation analysis. So, it will evolve over time but it must be completely populated before kanban solutions can be calculated. We'll list the required references later in this chapter.

2. ABC Tabs: If new ABC classifications will be used instead of current ABC assignments, create one tab to perform ABC analysis on purchased parts and a separate tab for manufactured parts. Then enter resulting A and B spending thresholds on the Targets and Limits tab. If current ABC classifications will be used, there is no need to add ABC tabs.

3. Kanban Calculator Tab: Calculate kanban solutions in the Calculator tab. If there is a separate tab or file that contains a data download, such as an MRP flat file, it is easy to use VLOOKUP formulas to pull data from that Source tab into the Calculator tab. It is also possible to use the Data Download tab as the starting point for the Calculator tab. Deciding which route to take generally comes down to how many extraneous or unnecessary columns are in the data download. If it is loaded with unneeded columns, start on a new tab.

After kanban solutions are calculated, additional kanban analysis columns will be added for data such as estimated inventory reduction or weekly bleed-off dollars per item, as described in the chapters about analyzing kanban solutions.

4. Summary Tab: This tab isn't necessary to run kanban calculations or deploy solutions, but a Summary tab helps manage and communicate actual or predicted results and action plans.

Create a summary of kanban results for financial reports, goal setting, and action plan tracking and include aggregate data such as total current on-hand dollars, estimated on-hand dollars after resizing, number of items that need a negotiated shorter lead time, etc.

It is *possible* to put summary data at the bottom of the columns in the Calculator tab or in a separate area of that spreadsheet, but if that tab has thousands of data rows and dozens of columns, it is difficult to navigate and track the summary data.

The Summary tab is populated as part of kanban analysis.

5. Sorted and Filtered Action Plan Tabs: Once kanban solutions are defined and analyzed, create action plans to address stock outs, add items to kanban, take items off kanban, resize existing kanban solutions, or negotiate lead times and package sizes with suppliers.

One option is to create action lists as new columns within the main Calculator tab, but that becomes unwieldy due to the large number of columns required. It can also get messy to resort the master data for every new view of action plans, e.g., sorting by supplier or by Buyer/Planner.

Instead, create multiple Planning tabs to avoid sorting or filtering the main tab. Copy key columns from the main tab or copy the entire sheet as many times as are necessary to cover the various action lists. Sort and filter the created Action Plan tabs to facilitate kanban analysis, action plan design and execution, and deployment prioritization and tracking.

There are several common sorting options that might need one or more tabs for action plan management.

- Resize to fix negative safety stock
- Resize to recommended kanban
- Put on kanban
- Take off kanban
- Update ABC
- All items in descending order of inventory reduction from kanban resizing, measured in currency
- Items by Buyer/Planner (might need one tab per person)
- Items by Supplier (might need a tab for every supplier, with negotiation activity)
- Items by in descending order of inventory impact from negotiating a new MOQ or lead time
- Items by inventory category, i.e., raw material, WIP, FG, ABC classification, or purchased or manufactured status

If each list is a separate tab, action plans can be managed and tracked by various owners. If that occurs, it might make sense to create new action plan files instead of keeping them as separate tabs in the same Excel file.

Required Targets & Limits

Recall the five steps a Kanban calculator completes.

1. Determine which items are excluded from kanban, in groups or individually.

2. Decide the correct kanban type for every kanban item.

3. Calculate an ideal kanban solution for every kanban item.

4. Calculate the correct kanban solution, sometimes called the "recommended" or "resizing" kanban solution.

5. Analyze kanban solutions for action planning.

Several of these steps require comparison values or references for decision making. This section lists the targets and limits that are utilized by a kanban calculator to make these choices. Most of these topics were discussed in previous chapters.

Targets & Limits for the Data Set

ABC Classification

Valid ABC classifications are an absolute requirement for kanban solutions, so these should be determined or verified before calculation steps occur. ABC classification can be set by obtaining existing ABC assignments, completing ABC analysis for the entire population, or comparing each item's annual spend to established ABC thresholds for purchased and manufactured items.

> **Rule of Thumb**
>
> ABC classifications are assigned separately for purchased and manufactured items by sorting items in descending order of annual spend. The cutoff for an A item is the annual spend for the item at which cumulative annual spend hits 80% of total annual spend, and B items cumulate to 95% of total annual spend, or the next 15% of annual spend after A items.

Targets & Limits for Step 1: Exclude Items from Kanban

Individual Item Kanban Exclusions

Individual items are eliminated from kanban based on daily demand or MOQ days of demand. In the Targets and Limits tab, include the limitations for these parameters.

> ## Rule of Thumb 👍
>
> From Chapter 17 about excluding items from kanban starting on page 205:
>
> **Default DD < 1.0 = not on kanban**
>
> **Default MOQ Days Demand > 125 not kanban**

Other Excluded Items

If items are eliminated based on an exclusion list or item attributes, gather the required data in a tab or file that can be accessed by the kanban calculator.

Targets & Limits for Step 2: Determine Kanban Type

There are three basic types of kanban solutions: 2-card (the default), 1-card, and multi-card. A kanban calculator selects the right solution for every item based on comparing each item's characteristics to various thresholds. These must be included in the Targets and Limits tab.

Target Safety Stock

To determine kanban type and an eventual kanban solution, the calculator needs target safety stock for every item that is assigned a kanban solution.

If safety stock is assigned by attributes such as ABC versus lead-time category, create a SS reference table in the Targets and Limits tab, as in the examples in Figure 19-1.

It is impossible to establish a generic rule of thumb for target safety stock. Instead, it's best for each site to analyze supply and demand patterns to determine how much safety stock is required.

Figure 19-1. Target SS Table Examples

Market	SS Days
Pharmaceutical	7
Food	2
Water Treat	1

SS Days	Purch	Manf
A	2	1
B	3	2
C	4	3

SS Days	Short LT	Med LT	Long LT
A	1	3	4
B	2	5	6
C	4	8	9

Use an INDEX or IF statement to select the correct target safety stock from a reference table.

> **Look Up Target Safety Stock from a Table** =
>
> IF (AND (ABC="A", Purch_Mfd = "P"), B2,
>
> IF (AND (ABC = "B", Purch_Mfd = "P"), B3,
>
> IF (AND (ABC = "C", Purch_Mfd = "P"), B4,
>
> IF (ABC = "A", C2,
>
> IF (ABC = "B", C3, C4)))))
>
> This selects target safety stock by referring to a specific cell based on an item's ABC and purchased or manufactured attributes.
>
> Target SS = INDEX ('Final Targets & Limits'!$B$2:$C$4, ABC_Row, Purch_Mfd_Column)
>
> An alternate approach is to look at a cell array (cells B2 to C4 in this case) and select the row that matches the ABC row designation (e.g., A = 1, B = 2, C = 3) and the column that matches P/M status. For a purchased A item, it would pull the value from cell B2, and a manufactured C item would pull data from cell C4.

If safety stock is assigned by individual PN, insert a Target Safety Stock tab with values for every item and refer to that list from the kanban calculator.

> **Look Up Target SS from a PN List** =
>
> Target SS = VLOOKUP (PN, 'Target SS PN List'!$A$1:$B$9999, 2, FALSE)
>
> This looks up a PN on the tab called Target SS PN List, in cells A1 through B9999. When it finds the right PN, it pulls the value from column 2 of the identified row.

1-card Limit: MOQ Days Demand Allowance

An item is put on a 1-card kanban solution if the required MOQ covers more days than the sum of [actual lead-time days + target days of safety stock * MOQ allowance factor]. Add the MOQ Days Demand allowance value to the Targets and Limits tab.

> **Rule of Thumb** 👍
>
> Default 1-card MOQ days demand allowance
>
> = 110% * [Actual LT + Target SS]

Target Lead Time

Target lead time is required to determine kanban type.

> **Rule of Thumb** 👍
>
> **Default target lead times in workdays:**
>
> | | Purchased | Manufactured |
> |---|-----------|--------------|
> | A | 5 | 3 |
> | B | 10 | 8 |
> | C | 20 | 18 |

Lead-Time Multi-Card Limit: Target Lead-Time Ratio

To determine if a lead-time multi-card solution is required, the calculator needs target lead times to compare to every A or B item's actual lead time.

> **Rule of Thumb** 👍
>
> IF [Actual LT / Target LT] > 2 for an A or B item, THEN consider a multi-card solution.

Lead-Time Categories

If lead-time category (e.g., short, medium, or long) is used for a grouping identifier for demand variation analysis, establish cutoffs to determine assigned categories. These categories can also be used for kanban analysis, which would put it under Step 5, analyzing kanban.

> **Rule of Thumb** 👍
>
> Default LT category values:
>
> If Actual LT < 1.5 * [A Purchased Target LT], THEN LT Category = Short
>
> If Actual LT > 1.5 * [B Purchased Target LT], THEN LT Category = Long
>
> For all others, LT Category = Medium
>
> Remember that purchased and manufactured items can usually be <u>categorized</u> versus Short and Long limits for purchased items, even though target lead times are different for purchased versus manufactured.

Standard Deviation Ratio to Lead-Time Demand

To determine if demand variation is significant, a site can set a threshold for the ratio of standard deviation versus lead-time demand, where any item that exceeds the threshold is assigned a demand variation multi-card solution.

Rule of Thumb

Benchmarks vary from site to site, but if an entire population of items exhibits [Standard deviation units / Lead-time demand] ratios of less than about 0.2 to 0.3, the volatility is manageable without special handling. Don't force multi-card solutions unless variation is greater than 0.3 times total lead-time demand.

To identify highly volatile items, consider a cut-off of [standard deviation / lead-time demand] greater than 2 times the average standard deviation ratio for the population of items.

Seasonality Ratio

Seasonality is evaluated as high versus low demand, or possibly as high, medium, and low seasons. In order for seasonality to be significant enough to warrant demand variation multi-card solutions, it should exceed a defined threshold.

Rule of Thumb

To confirm if seasonal demand variation is significant enough to warrant special analysis, at the very least it is necessary to calculate low and high daily revenue. If high daily revenue is greater than or equal to 130% of medium or low daily revenue, seasonal variation justifies analyzing demand variation in seasonal time periods.

Targets & Limits for Step 3: Calculate Ideal Kanban Solutions

Ideal kanban solutions require target safety stock, target lead times, and the target lead-time ratio, all of which were listed above.

Targets & Limits for Step 4: Calculate Kanban Solutions

Once we know kanban type and have ideal solutions, the next step is finalizing the right kanban order quantity for every 1-card and 2-card kanban solution and the exact number of signals for every multi-card solution.

Card Rounding Threshold

It is extremely rare for a calculated card count to result in an exact integer so the calculated number of cards must be rounded to the right integer, either higher or lower than the calculated result.

Standard mathematical rounding increases a number to the next integer when the decimal value or "remainder" is greater than or equal to 0.5, e.g., 2.49 rounds down to 2 and 2.50 rounds up to 3. Mathematical rounding of the calculated number of kanban cards results in stock outs if card count is rounded down by a large adjustment. If we calculate a required 2.49 cards and mathematical rounding is employed, the solution ends up with just 2 cards, which is too low.

In addition to the stock out risk, if card count is rounded down to the next integer, actual safety stock is less than what was planned. Conversely, if card count is rounded up, actual safety stock is higher than target safety stock.

To manage this, define a rounding threshold that makes the calculator round up to the next whole card when the remainder is greater than the rounding threshold. This replaces basic mathematical rounding of card count, using a slightly more complicated formula.

In Excel, the MOD function returns the remainder when one number is divided by a second number. Use calculated card count as the first number and "1" as the second value to obtain the decimal portion of the calculated card count.

MOD Function

MOD (value 1, value 2) = remainder when value 1 is divided by value 2

MOD (9, 2) = 1 and MOD (9, 3) = 0

MOD (card count, 1) = decimal value of calculated card count, e.g., MOD (1.23, 1) = .23

Round up card count to the next integer if the remainder exceeds the rounding threshold.

Round Calculated Card Count

IF [MOD (card count, 1) > rounding threshold, ROUNDUP (card count, 0), ELSE ROUNDDOWN (card count, 0)]

Rule of Thumb

For the rounding threshold, use a value ranging from 0.1 to 0.3 as a starting point.

The alternative to a rounding threshold is to require all calculated card counts to round up, so a calculated value of 2.01 rounds up to 3.0. This is simpler than setting a rounding threshold, but it can result in too much unintended safety stock.

Targets & Limits for Step 5: Analyze Kanban Solutions

There are no required targets or limits for kanban analysis, but a couple comparators are optional.

Minimum Inventory Reduction Threshold

Some sites choose to set minimum inventory reduction values to filter the negotiation list down to those items that justify the effort of negotiating with suppliers for better lead times or lower minimum order and standard package quantities.

Rule of Thumb

Optional: IF [Estimated Inventory Reduction in Currency < Reduction Limit], THEN negotiation or resizing priority is Low.

MOQ Negotiation Ratio

In order to justify the effort of negotiating a lower MOQ, set a ratio that is the minimum requirement for actual MOQ versus target MOQ.

Rule of Thumb

An actual MOQ must be at least 2 times the target MOQ to justify negotiating a new MOQ with an internal or external supplier.

Lead-Time Negotiation Ratios

Like MOQ, actual lead time must miss the target lead time by a certain ratio in order to justify lead-time negotiation. For most sites, the ratio to pursue a short lead time is same that is used to justify a lead-time multi-card solution.

Rule of Thumb

IF [Actual LT / Target LT] > 2, THEN pursue a shorter LT

IF [Actual LT / Target LT] < 0.5, THEN pursue a longer LT

Target SPQ as Percent of Target MOQ

Target SPQ is used when deciding what to negotiate with suppliers.

Rule of Thumb

Default Target SPQ = 20% * Target MOQ

Targets & Limits Summary

Many of the decisions that a kanban calculator makes depend on the thresholds in the Targets and Limits tab. Ensure that these values are accurate and in line with your business.

Put all targets and limits in a tab in the kanban calculator workbook for easy reference by the calculator and the user.

Figure 19-2 on page 225 is an example of a tab for Targets and Limits.

Figure 19-2. Example Targets & Limits Tab, with Default Values

	Purchased annual spend minimum	Manufactured annual spend minimum
A	$9,900	$15,500
B	$3,450	$4,440

On Kanban Limits		
Min Daily demand		1.0
Max MOQ Days Demand		125

Target lead time	P	M
A	5	3
B	10	8
C	20	18
LT vs. TLT, or Long LT Multi-card cutoff		2.0
Example: IF [LT / TLT] > 2.0, use Multi-card		
MOQ Days vs. [LT + SS Days], or 1-card cutoff		110%
Example: IF [MOQ Days Demand / (LT + SS Days)] > 110%, use one card		

LT Categories		
Short LT (<1.5 * Purch A TLT)		< 7.5 days
Long LT (>1.5 * Purch B TLT)		> 15 days

LT Negotiation Cutoffs, LT/TLT		
Negotiate Longer LT		< 0.5
Negotiate Shorter LT		> 2.0

Card Rounding Threshold		0.25

Tutorial: GOCO Targets & Limits

Mary and the Materials team had already agreed on their required targets and limits, so they created reference tables on a tab in the kanban calculator, in Figure 19-3.

Figure 19-3. Target Lead Times in Days

	Purchased Parts	Manufactured Parts
A Item Cutoff	$ 2,000,000	$ 4,900,000
B Item Cutoff	$ 400,000	$ 1,900,000

Target LT	P	M
A	5	3
B	10	8
C	20	18
VMI	2	
FG	3	

LT Categories (Site preference)		
Short LT Category	7.5	If Std LT is less than this number, is Short LT
Medium LT Category	15	If Std LT is > Short Category but < this number, is Medium LT

On Kanban Daily Demand Min	10	IF DD < this number, not on KB
On Kanban MOQ Days Demand Max	125	IF MOQ Days Demand > this number, not on KB
1-card MOQ Days Demand Allowance	110%	IF MOQ Days Demand/(Actual LT + Target SS Days) > this number, use 1-card
Rounding Threshold	0.2	Round up # cards if remainder > this number
LT Multi-card Multiple	2.5	IF [Actual LT/Target LT] > this number, use LT Multi-card
Negotiate Shorter LT	2.0	If Actual LT > Target LT times this limit, negotiate shorter LT
Negotiate Longer LT	0.5	If Actual LT is less than Target LT times this limit, negotiate longer LT

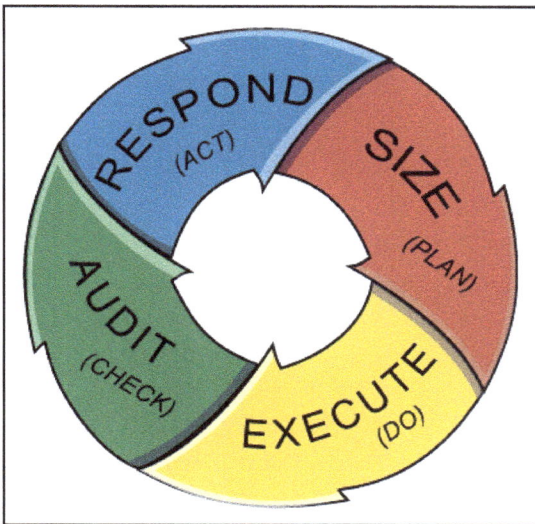

CHAPTER 20: PRIMARY & SECONDARY DATA

In the "How Kanban Works" chapter we compared a kanban system to the Plan-Do-Check-Act cycle, with kanban sizing as the planning portion. (See diagram to the left.) Every kanban process—managing kanban orders and cards, auditing processes and results, and responding to audit and process results—depends on accurate kanban solutions. Every kanban solution is calculated based on available data for that item. Therefore, accurate data is a mandatory element of calculating correct kanban solutions.

In Figure 20-1, the sizing process starts with setting target and limits then proceeds to gathering necessary data to calculate kanban solutions. Yes, technically we need annual usage and standard cost data to calculate ABC classifications, so data gathering has to occur to set those cutoffs, but most of the data set for kanban calculations is not required to set targets and limits.

The columns of primary and secondary data are the initial content for the Calculator tab in the Excel spreadsheet. The data set includes numerous part-specific values ranging from ABC classification to daily demand to supplier name. In addition to columns of item data, the data set also needs aggregate or summary values that are used in kanban calculation steps, such as total annual purchased spend or total on-hand dollars.

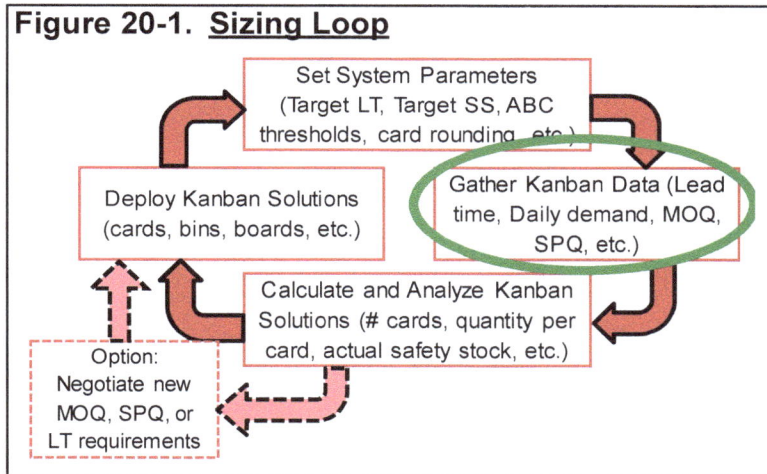

Figure 20-1. Sizing Loop

• Primary data are those independent parameters that are not derived from any other data source, such as supplier name or standard cost. This is often raw data pulled from MRP or another data repository. Much of the required primary data is available internally but some comes from, or at least should be confirmed by, external suppliers.

• Secondary data are calculated from primary data. Some of this will be available from a source like MRP, but much of it will be calculated by the kanban calculator.

Gathering data can be very time consuming and many kanban efforts fail *not* because of a lack of effort but because the team failed to obtain and scrub the necessary data. This is generally the most significant pre-work for a kanban project, and it often reveals data gaps or errors, which is another reason to begin gathering data early. Allow external suppliers enough time to collect and review requested data, and ensure they understand that what they provide is considered firm commitments for lead time, minimum order quantity (MOQ), standard package quantity (SPQ), and other boundaries.

This chapter lists primary and secondary data for individual items. (We'll cover aggregate data when we get to the analysis portion.) Required fields are indicated with ** in the header. Some fields are required for kanban calculations, some are required for printing kanban cards, and others are for sorting or filtering kanban action plans and task lists.

Internal Primary Data

Internal data is available from inside sources such as MRP downloads, existing kanban data, or operational records.

To facilitate data maintenance, use planner codes instead of names so that when individual names or assignments change, the codes are still correct.

Part Number (PN) **

Part number is the universal identifier for kanban analysis and reporting. Because kanban spreadsheets often swap data using reference formulas like VLOOKUP, ensure that PNs are exactly the same in all data sets. If errors occur when trying to utilize VLOOKUP or another similar function that relies on matching PNs from one source to another, check for trailing spaces or other anomalies from data downloads.

Description **

This text field describes the item and it is required for kanban cards but not for calculations. Description can sometimes be beneficial for sorting or filtering inventory action plans.

Supplier **

Supplier is required for kanban cards and is also advantageous for sorting or filtering items and action plans by supplier. This can be supplier name, identification number, or both.

Buyer, Planner, or Kanban Owner **

This field is printed on most kanban cards and is necessary for sorting and filtering kanban results, so it is required. Enter data that makes sense for the site, e.g., if "buyers" source parts and negotiate supplier contracts while "planners" manage inventory transactions and replenishment orders, list the planner as the kanban contact.

Purchased or Manufactured (P/M) **

This field designates internal and external parts. Any part that comes from outside the facility, including items from sister plants, are considered purchased parts (PP) because transit time and a receiving process is required for the part.

Inventory Category: RM or PP, WIP, & FG

A kanban calculator must be able to distinguish between external and internal items, as in P/M mentioned above, but many sites subdivide internal items into work in progress (WIP) and finished goods (FG). For example, a site might decide not to put finished goods on kanban so "FG" would be a key attribute for excluding items from kanban.

ABC Classification **

ABC classification is required for kanban calculations, so if current ABC is not available or is incorrect, ABC analysis must be completed as a precursor to kanban calculations. Technically, if ABC is readily available it is a primary data field, but if it must be calculated, it is secondary data.

Unit of Measure (UoM)

Unit of measure is how an item is counted, e.g., pieces, feet, or kilograms. This must be consistent for standard cost, on-hand balance, and demand, so if unit of measure for standard cost is metric tons, usage and on-hand inventory must also be metric tons. If left blank, assume "each."

On-Hand Balance (OHB) **

Current on-hand balance in units of measure is required for inventory analysis, but not for calculating kanban solutions.

Standard Cost **

Standard cost drives ABC classification, on-hand dollar estimates, and inventory reduction estimates and priorities, so ensure values are correct. Standard cost and demand should be measured in the same unit of measure.

Zero is not a valid standard cost!

Where Used

This is the cell that consumes an item and it is usually printed on the kanban card, particularly if the consuming cell is also where the item is stored. If it is the storage location, it is a required field. If it is simply a sorting or filtering aid for analyzing results, it is not a required field.

Storage Location **

Storage location is where an item is stored, which is required on the kanban card.

Product Family or Value Stream

To track progress and manage workloads, some sites segregate action plans or priorities by product family, mini-factory, customer, channel, or value stream. Any of these fields can be added as attributes.

Annual Demand **

Annual demand is total demand for twelve consecutive months, reported in unit of measure for the item. This is required if ABC analysis occurs.

Daily Demand (DD) **

Technically, DD should be considered secondary data because it is calculated. But, some MRP or ERP systems provide this data automatically, so we'll include it with primary data. If it comes from a system report, verify how it is calculated to ensure it is correct per kanban restrictions, e.g., daily demand must be measured for workdays.

Average Daily Demand

Average daily demand is average demand per workday over an extended time, generally a year. This is the number to use when calculating annual usage or annual expenditure.

Current or Actual Daily Demand **

Current daily demand is average consumption for one workday at today's demand levels. It can be measured historically or with forecast data. Current DD is used when sizing kanban solutions for current conditions and also to calculate actual safety stock.

Every part needs current DD, but it can be obtained in two basic ways.

1. Download current DD.

If the ERP or MRP system maintains a value for current DD, it can be downloaded as primary data, but only if historical data is correct. To be accurate, the system must select the right time horizon for which to calculate average DD, and it must be calculated in workdays. Demand must consider all workdays, even when usage was zero, so ensure that MRP includes days with zero demand when calculating DD, but it should exclude holidays and non-workdays.

2. Calculate current daily demand.

If DD is not available as a primary data field, calculate it by dividing total usage over a certain time period by the number of workdays in that period. Select a period that accurately reflects upcoming or expected demand, with enough weeks of data to provide a valid baseline. In general, three to twelve months is a good time period. Use shorter periods if seasonality exists or if demand is trending up or down.

Lowest or Highest Daily Demand

Two special DD values are used for items that experience demand variation.

Lowest daily demand is the minimum DD expected during a calendar year. This is used to calculate the kanban order quantity for a multi-card kanban solution.

Highest DD is used to estimate the maximum number of cards required for a multi-card solution.

> ### HINT for Associates
>
> Daily demand that is based on calendar days, i.e., annual demand divided by 365, confuses people who use the parts. When they see that the "official" DD for a part is 71.4 but they *know* they use 500 per week or 100 per day, they immediately question the accuracy of the data and of the kanban system. Calculate all daily demands based on workdays.

Trigger Timing **

If EaB and BaB trigger timing are both used at a site, set EaB=1 and BaB=0 in the data to make calculating kanban solutions easier to do, since EaB has to add or subtract 1 card in various kanban formulas.

This must be defined before kanban solutions are calculated.

Include this on kanban cards if both EaB and BaB are used in the same facility. If just one method is used, it is not required for cards.

Item Designations or Attributes

Codes can be used to delineate special circumstances or attributes. These are good sorting or filtering aids and they also assist with deciding which parts should be considered for kanban.

Several of these were mentioned in the chapter about excluding parts from kanban.

- **MRP:** Always managed by MRP, eliminated from kanban consideration
- **EXP :** Expense items
- **VMI :** Vendor managed inventory is restocked by the supplier. VMI parts don't need kanban solutions but unscannable kanban cards are advantageous for identifying, managing, and auditing parts on the floor.
- **CON:** Consignment inventory is stored on site, but is not owned by the site until a specific event (e.g., opening a container) transfers ownership. These items can be managed by the supplier via VMI or by traditional kanban solutions.
- **EOL:** End of life, or a part nearing the end of active demand, means demand history is not indicative of future demand.
- **LTB:** Parts that have experienced a last-time buy do not qualify for kanban until a new source is identified, which might be "never" if the part is obsolete.
- **NPI:** A new product introduction (NPI) item is in the early stages of active demand and has no demand history. Kanban is usually delayed until adequate demand history is gathered or until usage reaches a certain level.

Consider for Kanban

If a value stream map (VSM), flow analysis, or anything else indicates that certain groups of parts are not considered for kanban, this field is one way to exclude them from receiving kanban solutions.

Technically this is not a required field because a kanban solution can be required and calculated for every item, but there are risks with that approach. Kanban calculators estimate future on-hand balance for every kanban solution. If there are items in the list that will not be on kanban, estimated balances based on kanban solutions are erroneous for items that won't deploy the recommended kanban solutions. This makes the aggregate of estimated on-hand dollars inaccurate. If just a few parts are excluded from kanban, the impact is minimal, but if a broad range of parts are excluded, the error could be large when estimating future on-hand balances.

Current Kanban Solution **

If a part is currently on kanban, the associated data is required for the kanban calculator.

On Kanban Now **

Designate 1 = Yes and 0 = No so that multiplying the "on kanban" indicator times parameters such as on-hand currency or annual spend can easily exclude non-kanban items.

On Kanban Now

On Kanban Now =
IF (Current # cards > 0, 1, 0)

This assigns "1" if an item has cards currently assigned. Other versions of this formula would be valid, such as checking for current KOQ or for an item master field that designates if an item is on kanban.

By setting "On Kanban Now" to 1, we can easily populate a column for Annual Spend on Kanban = On Kanban Now * Annual Spend

Current Kanban Order Quantity (Current KOQ) **

This is the quantity ordered for each card or signal.

Current # Kanban Cards **

This is the number of active cards or signals for an item.

Current 1-Card Reorder Point (ROP) **

If a kanban item has a 1-card solution, the reorder point is the number of pieces on hand when a replenishment order is triggered. This applies only to 1-card solutions, but it is a required field for those items.

Trigger Timing **

Add this field again if it is different than what was listed above for recommended kanban solutions.

Fixed Kanban Order Quantity (Fixed KOQ) **

If an item has a fixed or frozen order quantity, such as items on multi-card solutions, indicate that so the calculator knows the order quantity can't be adjusted.

Other Data Fields

Add anything that helps calculate, sort, or prioritize data and actions. This could include industry, channel, geography, commodity code, etc.

Supplier Primary Data

Numerous parameters are set by internal or external suppliers based on process limits, package design, geographic distance, contracts, etc.

Minimum Order Quantity (MOQ) **

This is the minimum required production or purchase quantity to qualify as an order.

Standard Package Quantity (SPQ) **

This is standard box or container quantity.

Maximum Order Quantity (MaxQ) **

MaxQ is the maximum number of parts in a single order. This is not nearly as common as minimum order or standard package limits, but it does occur, and when it does it is a mandatory field.

Lead Time (LT) **

Lead time is the time required from order entry to receipt of parts, including transit time.

Comments or Special Instructions

Some suppliers have rules such as shipping just one day per week, requiring truckload quantities, etc. Capture these requirements so that they are readily available to the kanban user.

Secondary Data

Once primary data is available, calculate secondary data in preparation for determining kanban solutions.

Annual Spend **

Multiply annual demand in units of measure times standard cost to get annual spend, which is required for ABC calculations.

> **Annual Spend**
>
> Annual spend = Annual demand * Std cost

Days on Hand (DOH)

Days on hand is calculated by dividing on-hand balance by DD. If DOH is measured across multiple PNs, use currency as the unit of measure.

> **Days on Hand**
>
> DOH for one part =
> OHB / Daily demand (units per day)
>
> DOH for multiple parts =
> Total on-hand $ / Total daily demand in $

On-Hand Currency (OHC) **

Multiply current on-hand balance times standard cost to get current on-hand currency, such as on-hand dollars. This is required to estimate potential inventory reduction per item.

> **OH$**
>
> OH$ = On-hand balance * Standard cost

Recommended ABC

Recommended ABC is determined by completing ABC analysis or comparing annual spend to established ABC thresholds. This is an alternative to current ABC.

Weekly Bleed-Off Units & Currency **

With current DD and standard cost, calculate inventory consumption in both units of measure and currency, then convert daily consumption into weekly usage for each item. This determines how fast inventory will decrease or bleed off, which is necessary when predicting future on-hand inventory levels.

Inventory reduction is a primary function of kanban, so kanban analysis must consider the timing of any planned reduction.

> **Weekly Bleed-Off in Units of Measure**
>
> Weekly bleed-off =
> Current daily demand * 5
>
> Multiply by standard cost to get currency

Demand Variation or Seasonality

If just certain items experience demand variation or seasonal demand, add a field to flag those items to indicate the need for multi-card solutions.

Lead-Time Weeks

If demand variation analysis is required, include actual lead time in weeks in addition to workdays. Round lead-time weeks to integers so that demand variation analysis can occur in lead-time buckets. This also allows items to be grouped based on lead-time weeks.

LT Weeks

ROUND Function: Lead-time Weeks = MAX (1, ROUND (LT Days/5, 0))

This formula assigns lead-time weeks in whole numbers, using 5 days per week as the divisor.

IF Function: Lead-time Weeks = IF (LT Days < 7, 1, IF (LT Days < 12, 2, IF (LT Days < 19, 3.....)

This assigns lead-time weeks using defined cut-offs for each integer.

MOQ Days Demand **

Minimum order quantity (MOQ) divided by current DD assesses how many days of coverage are provided by the MOQ.

MOQ Days Demand

MOQ days demand = MOQ/Daily demand

"On Kanban" Safety Stock Data

For parts currently on kanban, calculate safety stock statistics.

Actual Safety Stock Units **

Actual safety stock measures how many parts are acquired in a lead-time period versus how many are consumed. The formula depends on whether the trigger point is EaB or BaB, and 1-card solutions need special treatment.

Actual Safety Stock Units

1-card: Actual Safety Stock Units = Reorder point - (Lead time * Current DD)

2 or more cards BaB: Actual SS Units = (# Kanban Cards * Kanban order quantity) - (Lead time * Current DD)

2 or more cards EaB: Actual SS Units = (# Kanban Cards -1) * KOQ - (LT * Current DD)

Actual Safety Stock Days

Convert safety stock units to days of coverage by dividing safety stock units by current DD.

Current Safety Stock Days

Actual SS Days = Actual SS units/ Current DD

Stock-Out Risk **

If current safety stock is less than zero, the kanban solution acquires fewer parts in each lead-time period than are expected to be consumed, so there is a definite stock-out risk. This is a required field because it flags parts that need immediate attention to repair stock-out risks.

Stock-Out Risk

IF (Current Safety Stock units < 0, THEN Stock-out risk = Yes or 1)

Data Management & Excel Hints

Excel can be quirky, so here are a few hints for pulling and referencing data from MRP or spreadsheets.

Data Type

In Excel, some PNs look like a number (e.g., 12345) and others look like text (A98-765), so Excel treats them differently. If look-up functions are used to extract data from different spreadsheets, create a modified PN to avoid mismatched data formats. A quick solution is to add a leading text character to every PN to force everything to text format.

Part Numbers for Excel Look-up

CONCATENATE ("V", part number)

Creates a text PN to use in look-up functions, where V stands for VLOOKUP part number. Any text character can be used at the front of the actual PN.

Rounding

Excel formulas result in more decimal places than are necessary. So, get in the habit of rounding results to a reasonable number of decimals based on the type of data.

> ROUND in Excel
>
> ROUND (Value, decimals)
>
> ROUND (10.46238, 2) = 10.46
>
> ROUND (10.46238, 1) = 10.5

To round a number by another value, such as rounding kanban order quantity (KOQ) for the standard package quantity (SPQ), use MROUND. This function assumes mathematical rounding.

> MROUND in Excel
>
> MROUND (Value, Rounding #)
>
> Examples
>
> MROUND (127, 25) = 125
>
> MROUND (144, 25) = 150
>
> MROUND (1103, 100) = 1100
>
> MROUND (1149, 100) = 1100
>
> MROUND (1151, 100) = 1200
>
> MROUND (99, 5000) = 0
>
> MROUND (KOQ, SPQ) rounds KOQ for SPQ

If values must be rounded up or down regardless of the decimal value, such as to round up the number of cards, use ROUNDUP and ROUNDDOWN functions.

> ROUNDUP or ROUNDDOWN in Excel
>
> ROUNDUP (Value, decimals)
>
> ROUNDUP (10.46238, 0) = 11
>
> ROUNDDOWN (10.46238, 0) = 10

Blank Is Not the Same As Zero

Some MRP or other data downloads leave data fields blank to indicate zero. But, that confuses Excel because a blank or empty cell is skipped by formulas like AVERAGE or STDEV.

To make formulas work correctly, enter zero in cells that are actually zero, such as workdays with zero usage, items with zero on-hand balance, etc. Do not interpret a blank cell to be the same as zero in Excel.

Similarly, do not enter zero in fields that should be blank. This can wreak havoc with Excel data!

Eliminate Extra Spaces

Some MRP systems add trailing spaces at the end of data strings in order to fill the field, which interferes with Excel lookup functions. Trim extra spaces from data fields.

> Eliminate Spaces
>
> TRIM (part number)
>
> Removes leading or trailing spaces, but not those between words.

Index Functions

Kanban calculators often involve creating and referring to a number of data tables, and in those instances the INDEX function is beneficial.

When pulling information based on common attributes, such as ABC classification or purchased vs. manufactured, use standard row and column assignments when designing tables. For example, always put ABC down the left side of tables so that ABC is a *row* indicator, and A is always row one. Put purchased versus manufactured across column headings so they are always *column* indicators, and purchased is always column one.

For even more error-proofing in formula design, the MATCH function is an excellent way to select the correct row or column within an INDEX function, as in the example on the next page.

INDEX Function Example

Target lead time is found in a table in the upper left corner of an Excel tab, covering cells A1 through C4. We have several options when pulling data from this table.

Functional: Simple but cumbersome

IF (AND (ABC = "A", P/M = "P"), $B$2, IF (AND (ABC = "B", P/M = "P"), $B$3, IF (AND (ABC = "C", P/M = "P"), $B$4, IF (ABC = "A", $C$2, IF (ABC = "B", $C$3, $C$4)))))

Better: Create look-up fields

	Column A	Column B	Column C
Row 1		P	M
Row 2	A	5	3
Row 3	B	10	8
Row 4	C	20	18

Add columns to the data set for the ABC row and P/M column. The index formula will refer to these cells to get the right row and column references.

ABC Row: IF (ABC = "A", 1, IF (ABC = "B", 2, 3))

P/M Column: IF (P/M = "P", 1, 2)

INDEX ($B$2:$C$4, ABC Row, P/M Column)

This points to the table in cells B2 to C4 and pulls the value that is in the ABC row and the PM column.

Advanced: Use MATCH function

The Match function returns the number for where a look-up value is located in a list, e.g., MATCH ("A", A2:A4, 0) returns the answer "1" because "A" is the first cell from A2 to A4. Embed "MATCH" in the INDEX function to designate the right row and column for each item.

INDEX ($B$2:$C$4, MATCH (ABC, $A$2:$A$4), MATCH (P/M, $B$2:$B$3))

For this to work, "ABC" and "P/M" reference cells must match exactly to corresponding rows and columns, e.g., "P" in one cell won't match "Purch" in the other cell.

Data Summary

Gathering and confirming kanban data must not be underestimated because this is where many kanban systems fail. Spend enough time and effort on this! Kanban success is highly susceptible to the "garbage in, garbage out" phenomenon, so review and validate your data.

Figure 20-2 on page 236 lists Primary and Secondary data for a kanban calculator.

Figure 20-2. **List of Required Primary & Secondary Data**

Parameter	Required for Kanban calculations?	Required for Kanban Analysis	Recommended for Kanban cards?	Beneficial for sorting and filtering?
Part Number	Y	Y	Y	Y
Description	N	N	Y	Y
Supplier	N	Y	Y	Y
Buyer/Planner or Kanban Owner	N	Y	Y	Y
Purchased or Manufactured	Y	Y	N	Y
ABC Classification	Y	Y	N	Y
On-Hand Balance (OHB)	N	Y	N	N
Standard Cost	Y	Y	N	N
Storage Location	N	N	Y	Y
Annual Demand	Y	Y	N	N
Daily Demand (DD)	Y	Y	N	N
Trigger Timing	Y	Y	N	N
Current Kanban Solution (# cards, KOQ)	N	Y	Y	Y
Minimum Order Quantity (MOQ)	Y	Y	Y	N
Standard Package Quantity (SPQ)	Y	Y	Y	N
Maximum Order Quantity (MaxQ)	Y	Y	Y	N
Lead Time (LT)	Y	Y	Y	N
Annual Spend	Y	Y	N	Y
On-Hand Currency (OHC)	N	Y	N	Y
Weekly Bleed-Off Units & Currency	N	Y	N	Y
MOQ Days Demand	Y	Y	N	Y
Actual Safety Stock Units	N	Y	N	Y
Stock-Out Risk	N	Y	N	Y

Tutorial: GOCO Primary Data

Mary drafted a letter to send to all external suppliers. Each supplier would also receive an Excel data template that the supplier would fill out to confirm part number data, in Figure 20-3 on page 238.

GOCO Supplier Letter

Dear [Supplier contact name],

GOCO is undertaking a new inventory replenishment system called kanban. You are probably familiar with this and might already use it for internal material or with other customers.

Our kanban process will have two obvious impacts on how we order parts from you.

1. We will always order a standard kanban quantity, which will accommodate your minimum order and standard package quantity limits.

2. We will always order at the standard lead time for each part, so the due date for every order will be order date plus standard lead time, in workdays.

Kanban will not only allow us to manage on-hand inventory more effectively, it will also eliminate much of the erratic order and expediting activity you might have experienced from us in the past.

Over the next few months we will deploy kanban across all cells, but first we need to gather accurate data. The attached template lists the items you supply to us with the current data from our system. Please fill out this template and email it back to us with your verified data. (Please do not send it back in paper or pdf format.)

The columns with Blue headings contain our requested figures, such as target lead time or target minimum order quantity (MOQ). In some cases, we might request a longer lead time than what you currently provide, and we ask that you convert to our requested lead time instead of keeping the current shorter time, so that we don't receive orders earlier than we want them.

If you have any special instructions, such as consolidated shipping or returnable packaging, please provide those in the template.

Please do not enter "text" in the data fields, e.g., the words "days" or "pieces" after a numeric answer. Only use numeric values so that they can be pulled directly into our Excel data file.

Definitions

Lead time (LT) is the number of workdays from when we place an order until we receive parts at our door. We realize transit time can be difficult to predict, but please estimate a reasonable lead time from your facility to ours when you quote lead time for any item.

Minimum order quantity (MOQ) is the minimum quantity that qualifies as an order. MOQ must be greater than or equal to SPQ, and it must be an integer-multiple of the SPQ.

Standard package quantity (SPQ) is the package quantity (box, skid, tub, etc.) that will increment the order quantity above MOQ. For example, the MOQ and SPQ for eggs might be one dozen, so an order for 24 is acceptable but 18 is not.

Maximum order quantity (MaxQ) is the maximum order quantity for an item. This doesn't apply to many items, but please include it for any of your items with a maximum order limitation.

We provided requested values for lead time, minimum order quantity, and standard package quantity, so please accommodate these values when possible.

We'd like to have your data as soon as practical, and we ask that you take no more than three weeks from the date of this letter.

Please contact me or your GOCO Buyer if you have any questions.

Mary attached the Excel template in Figure 20-3 to each email, with just the data for that specific supplier on the sheet in order to protect confidentiality. For purchased parts she sent the letter via email so the supplier would receive the template electronically. Internal cells also received an Excel file, but Mary met individually with department managers to review the template.

Target lead times were already established, as were target safety stocks, but when creating the template Mary realized she needed target MOQ and SPQ values for every item, which relied on daily demand, target lead time, and target safety stock.

- She estimated target MOQ at [target lead time * current daily demand + Target SS]. If that value was higher than the current MOQ, she requested a value equal to current MOQ so that it would not increase.
- She set target SPQ at 20% of target MOQ.

Mary did not intend to pursue cost decreases in exchange for higher MOQs because she knew that would extend the time required to come to an agreement, and she wanted to hold to the rapid time line for deploying kanban.

As internal and external suppliers returned the data, Mary pulled it into the master Excel spreadsheet using "VLOOKUP" formulas.

Figure 20-3. Supplier Template Example (Supplier = GTP)

P/N	Description	Supplier P/N	Std Cost	UOM	Requested MOQ	Current MOQ	Supplier Agreed MOQ	Requested SPQ	Current SPQ	Supplier Agreed SPQ	Requested LT	Current LT	Supplier Agreed LT	MaxQ	Comments or Special Instructions
50.50 Face	500 x 500mm Face Plate		$ 1.00	Ft	29,595	40,000		5,000	5,000		20	15			
75.50 Face	750 x 500mm Face Plate		$ 1.17	Ft	32,239	40,000		5,000	5,000		10	10			
100.50 Face	1000 x 500mm Face Plate		$ 1.49	Ft	11,871	40,000		1,187	5,000		10	10			
50.50 Gasket	500 x 500mm Gasket		$ 0.45	Ea	20,000	20,000		1,000	1,000		20	15			
75.50 Gasket	750 x 500mm Gasket		$ 0.74	Ea	30,000	30,000		1,000	1,000		10	10			
100.50 Gasket	1000 x 500mm Gasket		$ 1.01	Ea	20,000	20,000		1,000	1,000		20	15			
50.50 Trim	500 x 500mm Trim		$ 3.05	Ea	14,018	15,000		1,000	1,000		10	20			
75.50 Trim	750 x 500mm Trim		$ 3.67	Ea	16,262	20,000		1,000	1,000		5	20			
100.50 Trim	1000 x 500mm Trim		$ 5.86	Ea	10,000	10,000		1,000	1,000		10	20			

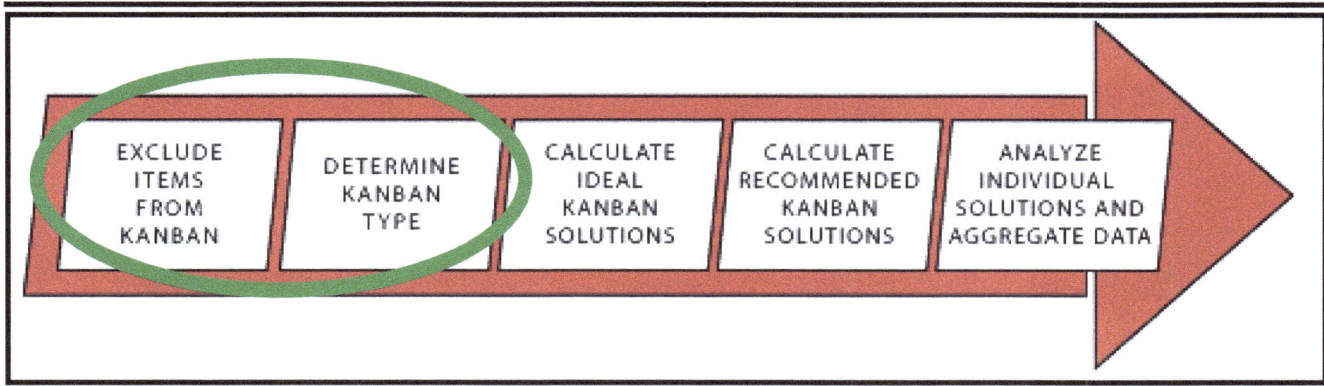

CHAPTER 21: STEP 1 EXCLUDE ITEMS & STEP 2 DETERMINE KANBAN TYPE

With targets and limits and a complete data set, the Calculator tab is ready to generate kanban solutions.

Step 1: Exclude Items from Kanban

The first step for a kanban calculator is excluding groups of parts and individual items from kanban, and there are several ways to do that.

1. Write formulas to refer to <u>exclusion lists</u> that contain part numbers (PNs), suppliers, "where used" cells, or any other list used to eliminate items based on an attribute or condition. Generally the kanban calculator fills a "Kanban Exclusion" column with a "1" when a match is found between an item in the calculator list and the exclusion list. Set excluded items equal to "1" so that it is easy to sum the column to determine how many items were excluded. Note that "1" in this case means an item is <u>excluded</u> from kanban.

Exclusion List Formula

IF [ISNUMBER (MATCH (Supplier, 'Supplier Exclusions'!A2:A999, 0)), 1, 0]

If more than one exclusion test is required, use the OR function so that a match of any condition excludes the item from kanban.

IF [OR (ISNUMBER (MATCH (Supplier, 'Supplier Exclusions'!A2:A999, 0), MATCH (PN, 'PN Exclusions'!A2:A999, 0), MATCH (Producing Cell, 'Cell Exclusions'!A2:A999, 0)), 1, 0]

This excludes an item if supplier, part number, or producing cell matches the exclusion list.

---

2. Check <u>attributes</u> that are included as part of kanban data and exclude items based on specific criteria. The calculator might exclude items that are vendor managed, any manufactured item with a lead time of less than two days, or A items that are also finished goods (FG).

Import one or more item master fields into the kanban calculator to use as exclusion comparisons. Add corresponding columns to test kanban validity, using IF statements to check various conditions and assigning "1" to items that are excluded. Note that this is how items are excluded for low daily demand (DD) or for a minimum order quantity (MOQ) that covers too many days of demand.

Kanban Exclusion Tests

Exclude for low daily demand:
IF (DD < DD On Kanban Limit, 1, 0)

Exclude for high MOQ days demand:
IF (MOQ Days Demand > On Kanban MOQ Days Limit, 1, 0)

Exclude A items that are finished goods: IF (AND (ABC = "A", Inventory Category = "FG"), 1, 0)

Final "Consider for Kanban?" Column

IF (OR (Exclusion 1 = "1", Exclusion 2 = "1", Exclusion 3 = "1", Exclusion 4 = "1"), 0, 1)

This excludes an item (exclusion = 0) if any of the four exclusion tests have "1" as the result.

Can also sum the exclusions and exclude the item if the sum is greater than one.

IF (Exclusion 1 + Exclusion 2 + Exclusion 3 + Exclusion 4) > 0, 0,1)

3. Assess smart PNs for conditions that exclude an item from kanban consideration, such as items produced by a cell that does not require kanban because the cell pushes material to the next process.

Exclude from Kanban Using Smart PNs

IF (Left (PN, 2) = "HT", 1, 0)

This excludes heat treat items from kanban

Add a Column to Summarize Kanban Exclusions

Once all tests for kanban exclusion are complete, add a column to summarize the kanban consideration status. For example, if items were excluded for low DD in one column, for a high MOQ in another column, all FG in another column, and all parts on VMI in a fourth column, create one column that aggregates all of those conclusions using an OR or SUM function.

Note that the "1" and "0" definitions might switch for *this column* versus the exclusion columns. A "1" in the final column means consider for kanban and "0" means the item was excluded. The reason for switching the 1/0 definitions at this point is that it makes it possible to sum this column to see how many items are eligible for kanban. The "1" can also be used as a multiplier. If we wanted to sum total annual spend that was eligible for kanban, we would multiply the eligibility column times annual spend then sum those for all items.

HINTS for Associates

For every method or test used to exclude items from kanban, add a column to the calculator and label the column appropriately, e.g., "Kanban exclusion for VMI status" or "Exclude from kanban based on PN list." Insert a formula in the column that checks that specific test then add a summary column at the end of the exclusion columns.

When constructing kanban exclusion or consideration formulas, be clear what "1" and "0" indicate. If a column is labeled "DD Consider for Kanban" a "1" result means the item is on kanban but in the column labeled "DD Kanban Exclusion" a "1" means the item is not on kanban.

Step 2: Determine Kanban Type for Every Item

Determining kanban type is the second step in calculating kanban solutions. A complete kanban solution requires three things.

1. Trigger timing, either empty a bin (EaB) or break a bin (BaB), for parts with two or more signals, or a calculated reorder point for parts with one card. If this is a universally defined characteristic, it might not be a necessary data column.

2. Number of cards or signals

3. Kanban order quantity (KOQ) per signal

When determining kanban type, identify items that need a nonstandard 1-card or multi-card solution, then assign two cards to everything else.

Add a column to the calculator to indicate which type of solution is required for each item. This can be done by a very long formula in one column, or by adding a column for each test (e.g., first the 1-card test then 3 multi-card tests), then summarizing that in a final column.

Identify 1-Card Kanban Types

To identify PNs that need a 1-card kanban solution, calculate the number of days of demand covered by one minimum order quantity. Then complete the IF/THEN comparison to determine if a 1-card solution is required.

1-Card MOQ Days Demand Allowance

MOQ Days Demand = MOQ / Daily Demand

IF (MOQ Days Demand > (LT + Target SS Days) * 1-card MOQ Days Demand Allowance, 1-card solution, "")

Identify Multi-Card Kanban Types

Multi-card solutions are used in three specific situations.

1. High demand variation requires frequent resizing.

2. A long lead time is broken into manageable order quantities to reduce on-hand inventory.

3. A limitation on the maximum number of parts per kanban signal necessitates more than two cards.

Evaluate multi-card requirements in the order listed above to ensure demand variation items are treated appropriately.

Demand Variation Multi-Card

Demand variation (DV) multi-cards facilitate frequent resizing, generally to accommodate seasonal demand variation.

In a site where some items need a DV solution and others don't, there should be a flag that designates which items have high DV or seasonality. If all items in a site are subject to demand variation, use the DV multi-card solution as the default kanban type, with 1-card solutions as the only exception.

Multi-Card Demand Variation Test

IF (Seasonal demand variation flag = "1", DV Multi-card solution, "")

Lead-Time Multi-Card

A part with an actual lead time of two or more times the target lead time requires a lead-time multi-card solution.

Calculate the ratio of actual to target lead time, then check to see if a lead-time multi-card solution is required. In addition to the lead-time check, some sites limit lead-time multi-card solutions to only A and B classifications, or those items that have a substantial financial benefit from a lower on-hand balance.

Lead-Time Multi-Card Test

LT Ratio = Actual LT / Target LT

IF (AND (Actual LT / Target LT > Allowed LT Ratio, OR (ABC = A, ABC = B)), LT Multi-card, "")

This checks for two conditions, an actual lead-time ratio that is greater than what is allowed plus either an A or B classification. Both conditions have to be true to qualify for a long lead-time multi-card solution.

MaxQ Multi-Card

To determine if a maximum order quantity (MaxQ) forces a multi-card solution, calculate the 2-card kanban order quantity (KOQ) based on actual lead time, current DD and target safety stock and compare that to MaxQ. If the 2-card order quantity is greater than the allowed MaxQ, assign a MaxQ multi-card solution.

2-Card KOQ

EaB 2-card KOQ = (Daily demand * Actual LT + Target SS)

BaB 2-card KOQ = (Daily demand * Actual LT + SS)/2

Remember to round each number for MOQ and SPQ limits.

IF (Rounded 2-card KOQ > MaxQ, "MaxQ multi-card", "")

Start with a data set that includes all items or just a subset of items that make sense for "early" kanban. This list might be finished goods (FG) that have to be kept in stock to meet customer lead-time commitments. The list might be work in progress (WIP) that is produced by a shared resource that should be managed more carefully to reduce inventory and stock outs, or maybe it's as simple as purchased parts.

Instead of looking for a few items or groups to eliminate from kanban, we're looking for items that would fit very well on 2-card solutions. We want easy stuff, not weird stuff!

2-Card Kanban Type

For any item that did not require a special kanban solution, assign a 2-card solution.

Kanban Type Columns

Add a column to capture kanban-type tests and the final decision. All of the type tests could be done in one formula in a single column. But, that is very complicated and the formula is difficult to write and use. (See the Tutorial for an example of using one formula to assign kanban type.) For simplicity, add a column for each test as described above, then add one final column to summarize the conclusion. Decide which kanban type is the final answer based on the order in which the tests occurred. For example, if an item qualifies for 1-card and also for a lead-time multi-card solution, the 1-card solution is the right choice.

If You Just Want Basic 2-Card Kanban, Follow These Steps

For sites that are deploying kanban for the first time, or for those that have an existing kanban system that has not been successful, it is possible to design and execute a basic kanban system to gain some success and expertise before diving into strange stuff like 1-card or multi-card solutions.

Follow these steps:

1. Set target lead times and safety stock for ABC versus purchased and manufactured status.

It would be reasonable to start with default target lead times.

Rule of Thumb

Default target lead times in workdays

	Purchased	Manufactured
A	5	3
B	10	8
C	20	18

For target safety stock, start with a percent of lead time or a basic number of days based on ABC versus P/M status. If the business is relatively stable, use 10% of lead time, so an item with a 5-day lead time would get 0.5 days of target safety stock. If demand is a little more volatile, bump it up to 20% of lead time.

Items with really volatile demand don't fit the intent of finding easy kanban items for this first kanban phase. If all of our items have high demand variation, we can't do basic kanban and we need to design a plan to tackle the hard stuff, which might mean getting external help.

If just a portion of the business is highly volatile, we can divert our effort to simpler items and save the weird stuff for later.

2. For every item, calculate the number of days of demand covered by one minimum order quantity, using [MOQ / daily demand].

3. Calculate the lead-time ratio [actual lead time / target lead time] to identify items with reasonable lead times.

4. We touched on volatility above. If demand variation is present for some but not all of the business, insert a column to identify items that exhibit seasonal or day-to-day demand variation with a "Y" or "1" entry so that those items can be skipped for now. If variation is not a concern, we can skip this step.

5. If some items have maximum order quantities, calculate the days of coverage provided by the MaxQ, using [MaxQ / daily demand].

6. We're looking for items with reasonable lead times and order quantities, and without demand variation that would require extensive analysis. Insert a column to identify items that pass all three criteria, using an IF formula.

Example: IF (OR (LT ratio > 2, MOQ Days > Actual LT *110%, Demand Variation = "Y", MaxQ days < actual LT + target SS),0,1) This formula checks all three things that we want to weed out.

First, if the ratio of actual lead time versus target lead time is greater than 2, we eliminate the item.

Second in the OR section is a check for a high MOQ. If minimum order covers more than 110% of the actual lead time, we eliminate the item so that we avoid a 1-card solution.

Third, if the item was identified as having demand variation, the OR function eliminates it.

Finally, the formula checks to see if MaxQ days of coverage is less than actual lead time plus the target safety stock.

Anything that has one or more of these characteristics is assigned "0" to mean it does not qualify for kanban right now.

7. Everything that remains should qualify for 2 cards.

8. Calculate the kanban order quantity for each item based on 2 cards. I recommend using empty-a-bin (EaB) logic so that order quantities are higher (to avoid potential MOQ conflicts). This also makes the system easier to audit. The formula is [KOQ = (Actual LT + Target SS days) * daily demand].

9. Round the calculated order quantity for minimum order quantity, maximum order quantity, and standard package quantity.

[Rounded KOQ = {MIN [MaxQ, MAX (MOQ, Calculated KOQ) }].

10. Calculate actual safety stock for each item, using the EaB formula.

[Actual SS = (2 cards - 1) * rounded KOQ - (actual LT * daily demand].

If any items have negative safety stock, either bump up the order quantity by 1 pack size, or set the item aside for future deployment.

11. If we are left with a reasonable number of items to deploy, even a couple hundred, we should start deploying cards and work through the entire list. If there are too many items to choose from, prioritize them based on one of the following:

• Calculate inventory reduction potential in currency by comparing current on-hand currency (OHC) to estimated OHC for the new solution. Then subtract to find the net reduction from each item. Start with the biggest potential. This is the only way to achieve inventory reduction with limited kanban deployment.

• Start with items or processes that need help. If purchased plastic parts frequently experience stock outs, those would be a good starting point. If an internal process always seems to make the wrong stuff, start there. Find the pain points.

• If the items on the list center around a certain supplier or process, especially a supplier that consistently has reasonable lead times and order quantities, and therefore results in lots of 2-card items, that's a safe place to start.

12. Once we get some experience with kanban, we'll tackle more items. If a certain work cell or supplier would be 100% converted to kanban by deploying a few 1-card or multi-card items, start there and add the more challenging kanban solutions later.

13. I've never seen a new or widespread kanban deployment go perfectly well from the start, so don't be dismayed or discouraged by setbacks or errors. Keep going. If something doesn't work, change it and watch the results. You'll figure it out.

Kanban Exclusion & Type Summary

Exclude items from kanban based on groups (e.g., all finished goods) or for individual characteristics (e.g., daily demand < 1).

Deciding which kanban type fits each item comes down to a couple of factors.

1. Use one card when the MOQ is high.
2. Use a multi-card solution when variation is high, lead time is long, or MaxQ is low.
3. If none of these conditions exist, use two cards.
4. If you're doing just basic kanban, follow the steps to deploy just 2-card solutions.

Figure 21-1 is the decision tree to determine kanban type based on conditions.

Figure 21-1. Kanban Type Decision Tree

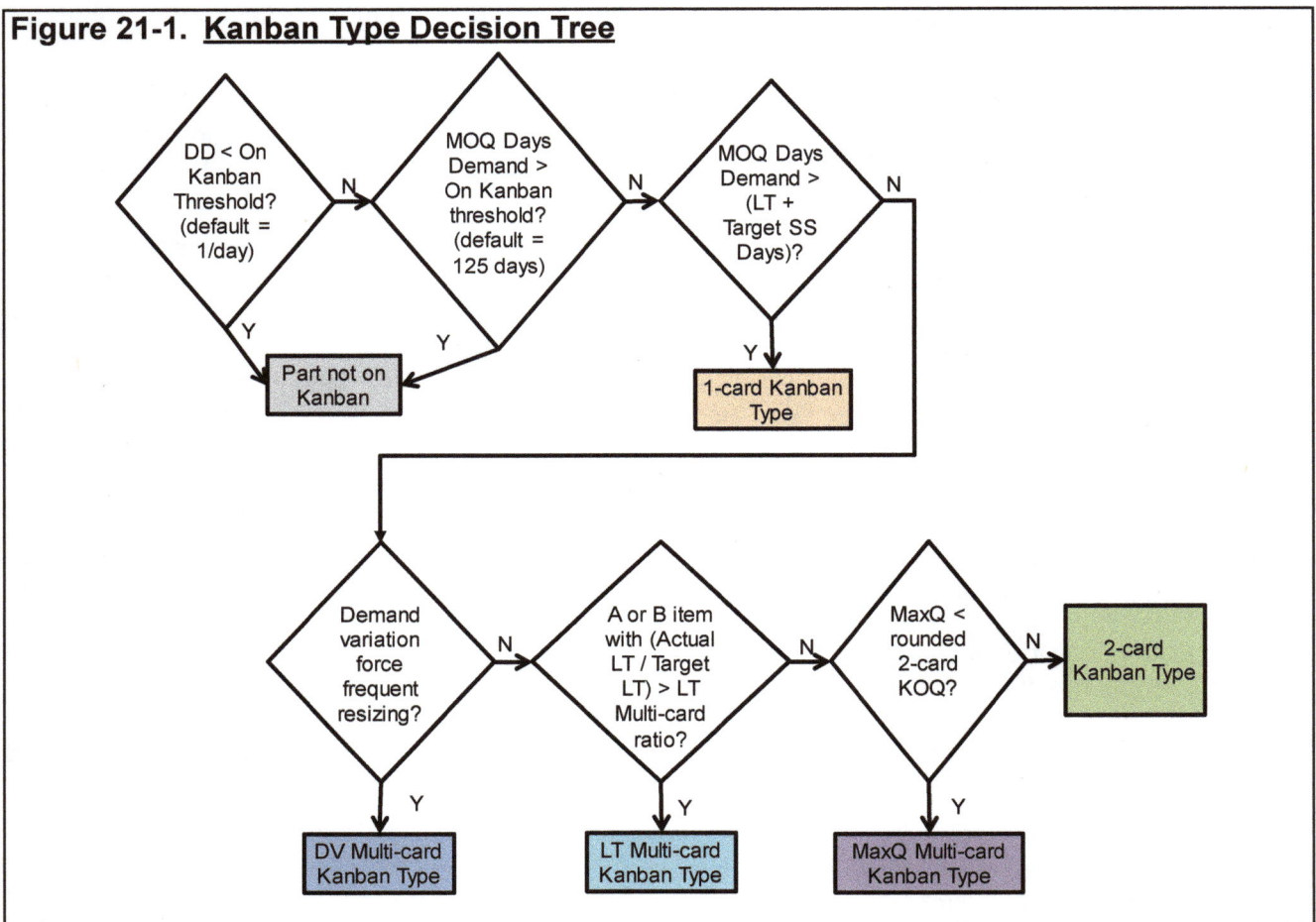

TUTORIAL: GOCO KANBAN TYPES

Mary had all the primary and secondary data, and the demand variation analysis was done. So, she was ready to assign kanban types. The formula to determine kanban type also excluded items from kanban if the "consider" flag was set to No. Because GOCO had no parts with a MaxQ limit, that kanban type was not evaluated.

She wrote one long formula, then broke it into sections to show her team what each section accomplished.

1. IF (Consider_for_Kanban= "0", "Not Kanban",

This looked at the kanban flag, and if it was "0" the part was excluded from kanban. Mary had all Automotive finished goods set to "0."

2. IF (VMI = "Y", "1 card VMI",

This set all VMI items to 1-card. There was no reason to have two cards for parts that didn't actually submit replenishment orders because a card would never hang on a kanban board. So, assigning just one card made kanban audits easier because every item had a kanban card that could stay with the VMI bin.

3. IF (OR (Annual_DD < On_KB_DD_Min, MOQ_Days_Demand > On_KB_MOQ_Days_Demand_Max), "Not Kanban",

This compared daily demand to the On Kanban DD limit to see if annualized DD qualified for kanban. It also compared MOQ Days Demand to the max allowed to determine if the MOQ qualified for kanban. The OR function at the front of the formula meant that if either case was true, the part was eliminated from kanban.

4. IF (MOQ_Days_Demand > (New_LT + Target_SS) * _1_card_MOQ_Days_Demand_Allowance, "1 card",

If MOQ was too high, or greater than lead time plus target safety stock times the 1-card MOQ factor from the Targets and Limits tab, the part got a 1-card solution.

5. IF (Seasonality = "Y", "DV Multi-card",

If the Seasonality flag was set to "Y," the item got a DV multi-card solution.

6. IF (AND (OR (ABC = "A", ABC = "B"), New_LT / Target_LT > LT_Multi_card_Multiple), "LT Multi-card",

This determined which parts belonged on an LT multi-card solution. The AND function first looked at ABC classification and selected only A or B items. Then it compared the ratio of New LT (the confirmed lead time they got from the supplier) to target lead time to see if it exceeded the allowed limit on the Targets and Limits tab. If all conditions were true, the part was on an LT multi-card solution.

7. "2 card"))))))

This was the "else" portion of the IF series, so if all the prior IF tests were false, the item was assigned two cards.

The entire formula looked like this:

=IF (Consider_for_Kanban = "N", "Not Kanban", IF (VMI = "Y", "1 card VMI", IF (OR (Annual_DD < On_KB_DD_Min, MOQ_Days_Demand > On_KB_MOQ_Days_Demand_Max), "Not Kanban", IF (MOQ_Days_Demand > (New_LT + Target_SS) * _1_card_MOQ_Days_Demand_Allowance, "1 card", IF (Seasonality = "Y", "DV Multi-card", IF (AND (OR (ABC = "A", ABC = "B"), New_LT / Target_ LT > LT_Multi_card_Multiple), "LT Multi-card", "2 card"))))))

Wasn't that fun?!

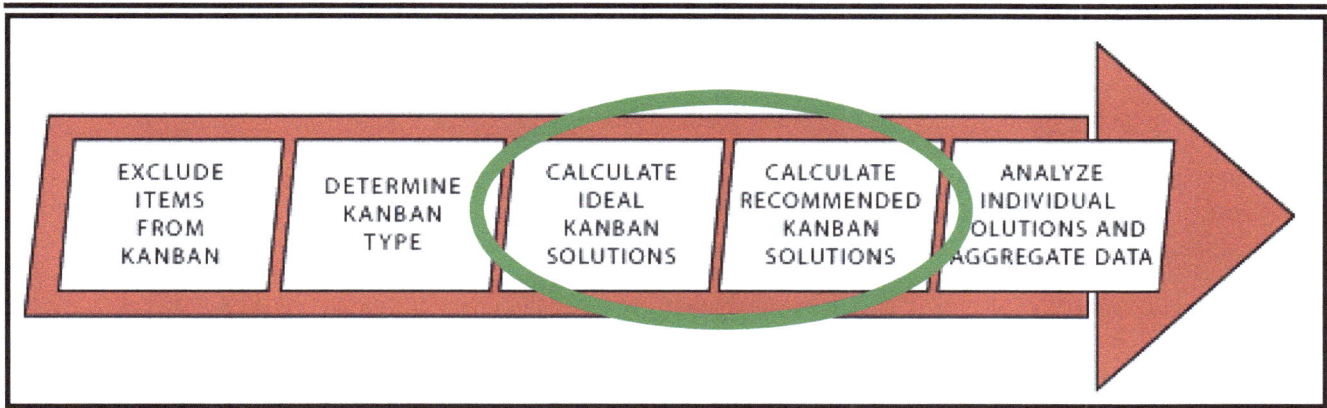

CHAPTER 22: STEPS 3 & 4 CALCULATE IDEAL & RECOMMENDED KANBAN SOLUTIONS

With the kanban type defined in the previous chapter, we're ready to calculate kanban order quantity (KOQ) and the number of cards or signals for every kanban item. The order in which these parameters are calculated (either cards first or order quantity first) depends on the situation.

Step 3: Calculate Ideal Kanban Solutions

Every perfect kanban solution is two cards with an order quantity that is based on target lead time. The order quantity is not rounded for minimum order, maximum order, or standard package limitations.

Ideal Kanban Order Quantity

Empty a bin (EaB) Ideal KOQ =

$$\frac{(\text{Target LT} * \text{Daily demand}) + \text{Target SS}}{(2 \text{ cards} - 1)}$$

Break a bin (BaB) Ideal KOQ =

$$\frac{(\text{Target LT} * \text{Daily demand}) + \text{Target SS}}{(2 \text{ cards})}$$

Do **not** round the calculated quantity.

Step 4: Calculate Recommended Kanban Solutions

Calculate 1-Card Solutions

Because there is just one card, the kanban order quantity equals MOQ, so we just need to calculate reorder point (ROP). These formulas do not change based on EaB or BaB.

To calculate the reorder point for a 1-card solution, or the quantity at which parts are ordered for replenishment, use the standard EaB kanban order quantity for two cards.

1-Card ROP

$$\text{ROP} = (\text{Actual lead time} * \text{Current daily demand}) + \text{Target safety stock}$$

The reorder point isn't *required* to be rounded for minimum order quantity (MOQ) or standard package quantity (SPQ) because it is an internally managed quantity, and therefore never becomes an actual order quantity to the supplier. However, if the item is held in containers of a specific size or quantity, e.g., boxes of 25 or buckets of 10 liters, it makes sense to round the reorder point <u>up</u> to the next package quantity for ease of identifying and separating the ROP quantity. This works in most situations, unless the package size is very large and would therefore increase the ROP significantly. If the calculated ROP is 40 and the package is 25 per box, round ROP up to 50 so that it equals two boxes. If reorder is calculated at 40 and the standard pack is 200, keep the ROP at

40 even though that means counting out 40 parts to set aside as the ROP.

HINT for Associates

If rounding reorder point (ROP) for package quantities, always round <u>up</u> not down, so the order timing is slightly early instead of a little late.

Calculate Demand Variation Multi-Card Solutions

Because the purpose of a demand variation (DV) multi-card solution is to accommodate ebbs and flows in demand, plan for 2 cards at the lowest demand level and size up from there. This requirement gives DV multi-card solutions a little more complexity than other multi-card solutions. It is also why this kanban type is the first test after the 1-card check, to ensure that any item that needs to accommodate high variation is poised to do so, whether or not it has a long lead time or a maximum order quantity (MaxQ).

Recall the Rule of Thumb for verifying that demand variation is significant enough to warrant a multi-card solution.

Rule of Thumb

Benchmarks vary from site to site, but if an entire population of items exhibits [Standard deviation units / Lead-time demand] ratios of less than about 0.2 to 0.3, the volatility is manageable without special handling. Don't force multi-card solutions unless variation is greater than 0.3 times total lead-time demand.

To identify highly volatile items, consider a cut-off of [standard deviation / lead-time demand] greater than 2 times the average standard deviation ratio for the population of items.

Demand variation multi-card calculations solve for both the number of cards and the order quantity, starting with order quantity.

1. Determine low DD based on either the low seasonal demand period or the lowest expected DD for a part with nonseasonal demand variation.

Low Daily Demand

Low DD = Average DD in low season

or

Low DD = Lowest expected DD for a nonseasonal item

---

2. Convert the lowest target safety stock into a percent of actual lead time.

Lowest Target Safety Stock Days and Percent of LT

Lowest Target SS = Target Safety Stock days for low season

or

Lowest Target SS = Standard deviation days of demand for non-seasonal parts, from lead-time buckets in demand variation analysis

Low Target Safety Stock %
= Lowest Target SS Days / Actual LT

---

3. Calculate order quantity using low DD and low safety stock as a percent. Remember that for multi-card solutions, order quantity is always based on target lead time instead of actual lead time. This controls the sawtooth curve height and also accommodates demand variation items that have a long lead time.

DV Multi-Card KOQ

DV multi-card KOQ = (Low Daily demand * Target LT) * (1 + Low Target SS %)

Rounded DV Multi-card KOQ
= MAX [MOQ, MROUND (DV KOQ, SPQ)]

Note: If a maximum order quantity also exists, select the minimum of the above result or MaxQ.

Final DV KOQ = MIN (MaxQ, Rounded KOQ)

---

4. To complete a DV multi-card solution, calculate the required number of cards based on current DD and the DV multi-card KOQ from above.

Number of Cards for DV Multi-Card

$$\text{EaB \# cards} = \frac{[(\text{Actual LT} * \text{Current DD}) * (1 + \text{Target SS \%})]}{\text{DV Multi-card KOQ}} + 1$$

$$\text{BaB \# cards} = \frac{[(\text{Actual LT} * \text{Current DD}) * (1 + \text{Target SS \%})]}{\text{DV Multi-card KOQ}}$$

Round calculated card count based on the rounding threshold

Rounded # cards = IF (MOD (# cards, 1) > Rounding threshold, ROUNDUP (# cards, 0), ROUNDDOWN (# cards, 0))

Card count varies based on current DD, but at the lowest demand we expect one of several options.

• Card count will be 2 at low DD if the part is EaB and if order quantity wasn't rounded up too much for MOQ or SPQ.

• Card count could be 1 at low DD if the item is BaB because target lead time is not adjusted for BaB versus EaB. If it ends up as 1 card, calculate the 1-card reorder point to see if it approximates the full order quantity. If so, turn in the card as soon as the first piece is used and skip the reorder point segregation exercise.

• Card count could be 1 card if the DV order quantity had to be rounded up for MOQ or SPQ.

• Card count could be more than 2 cards at low demand if actual lead time is long, because order quantity was based on target lead time.

Rule of Thumb

The goal for DV multi-cards is 2 cards at low demand and more cards as demand climbs. It is possible to have 1 card or more than 2 cards at low demand, but 2 cards is the goal.

DV Multi-Card Example

Item HML975 has seasonal variation: High DD = 955, Medium = 710, Low = 525

LT = 10 days, Target LT = 5 days, Target SS = 2 days in low season (20% of actual LT), 4 days in medium and high seasons (40% of LT)

MOQ = 1,000, SPQ = 250, Trigger = EaB

Calculated DV Multi-card KOQ = (Low DD * Target LT) * (1 + Low SS) = (525 * 5 days) * (1 + 20% SS) = 3,150, Round for SPQ = MAX (MROUND (3150, 250), 1000) = 3,250 (rounded for SPQ of 250)

Low DD cards = [(525 * 10 days) * 120%] / 3,250 + 1 = 6,300 / 3,250 + 1 = 2.94, round to 3

Medium DD cards = [(710 * 10 days) * 140%] / 3,250 + 1 = 9940 / 3,250 + 1 = 4.05, round to 4

High DD cards = [(955 * 10 days) * 140%] / 3,250 + 1 = 13,370 / 3,250 + 1 = 5.11, round to 5

Peak Demand Multi-Card Example

In a site with seasonal variation, some products are very stable and DD varies by no more than 10% throughout a year. For these stable items, we hope to avoid seasonal resizing by setting safety stock high enough to cover the demand swing over the course of the year. Target safety stock is 20% of an item's lead time, calculated based on lowest DD [Target SS = Low DD * (20% * LT)]

For item PD-222, low DD = 10 and high DD = 11. LT = 20 days.

Low season safety stock = 20% of lead time at lowest demand = 20% * 20 days lead time * Low DD = (20% * 20) * 10 = 40 units, or 4 days of safety stock

Low season KOQ = (Actual LT * Daily demand) * (1 + 4 days SS / 20 days LT) = (20 days * 10/day) * 1.2 = 240

Calculate actual safety stock at high DD for EaB.

Safety stock at high seasons = (# cards - 1) * KOQ - (Lead time * daily demand) = (2 - 1) * 240 - (20 * 11) = 240 - 220 = 20 units, or 1.8 days at peak season, (20 parts / 11 per day)

This indicates we can cover demand variation without resizing the kanban solution because DD jumps by just 10% from low to high, from 10 to 11. At high demand we have lower safety stock, 1.8 days versus 4.0 days during low demand.

If we changed our mind and wanted 4 days of safety stock during high demand, like low demand, we must resize by adding cards during high season.

Calculate Lead-Time Multi-Card Solutions

The long lead-time multi-card solution deserves attention because most sites have parts with long lead times. Recall that actual lead time must be at least two times target lead time in order to justify a multi-card solution. And, generally just A and B items are put on lead-time multi-card solutions.

Rule of Thumb

IF [Actual LT / TLT] > 2 for an A or B item, THEN consider a lead-time multi-card solution

Like DV multi-cards, calculate both the number of cards and the order quantity. First is order quantity based on target lead time.

LT Multi-Card KOQ with Target SS Percent

Long LT Multi-Card KOQ = (Target LT * Average daily demand) * (1 + Target SS %)

Rounded Long LT Multi-card KOQ = MAX [MROUND (Long LT Multi-card Target KOQ, SPQ), MOQ]

Like DV multi-card order quantities, accommodate a MaxQ if it exists.

Final LT Multi-card KOQ = MIN (MaxQ, Rounded KOQ)

Next is card count based on actual lead time.

LT Multi-Card Number of Cards

$$\text{EaB LT Multi-card \# of cards} = \frac{[(\text{Actual LT} * \text{Current DD}) + (1 + \text{ Target SS \%})]}{\text{LT Multi-card KOQ}} + 1$$

$$\text{BaB LT Multi-card \# of cards} = \frac{[(\text{Actual LT} * \text{Current DD}) + (1 + \text{Target SS \%})]}{\text{LT Multi-card KOQ}}$$

Rounded # cards = IF (MOD (# cards, 1) > Rounding threshold, ROUNDUP (# cards, 0), ROUNDDOWN (# cards, 0))

Calculate MaxQ Multi-Card Solutions

If a PN has a MaxQ that forces a multi-card solution, order quantity automatically equals MaxQ. We just need to calculate the number of cards when a MaxQ multi-card kanban solution is required.

Number of Cards for MaxQ Multi-Card

$$\text{EaB \# cards} = \frac{[(\text{Actual LT} * \text{Current DD}) * (1 + \text{Target SS \%})]}{\text{MaxQ}} + 1$$

$$\text{BaB \# cards} = \frac{[(\text{Actual LT} * \text{Current DD}) * (1 + \text{Target SS \%})]}{\text{MaxQ}}$$

Rounded # cards = IF (MOD (# cards, 1) > Rounding threshold, ROUNDUP (# cards, 0), ROUNDDOWN (# cards, 0))

Calculate 2-Card Solutions

Calculate kanban order quantity for two cards.

2-Card Kanban Order Quantities

$$\text{Empty a bin (EaB) KOQ} = \frac{(\text{Actual LT} * \text{Daily demand} + \text{Target SS units})}{(2 \text{ cards} - 1)}$$

$$\text{Break a bin (BaB) KOQ} = \frac{(\text{Actual LT} * \text{Daily demand} + \text{Target SS units})}{(2 \text{ cards})}$$

Round for minimum order quantity (MOQ) and standard package quantity (SPQ)

Rounded order quantity = MAX (MOQ, MROUND (KOQ, SPQ))

The inside portion of the formula rounds the calculated order quantity for the SPQ and the front part of the formula selects the larger of the minimum order or the rounded KOQ.

Tangential Topic: Economic Order Quantity (EOQ)

Some inventory management systems and managers utilize an economic order quantity (EOQ) formula to set the standard replenishment quantity for an item, thinking it is better than calculating kanban order quantities (KOQs). Economic order quantity is a valid concept, but it tends to underemphasize the cost of holding inventory and often results in order quantities that are too high in a kanban world.

The variables in the standard EOQ formula are annual demand (D), total cost per order (S, for set-up cost), which includes both handling and set-up costs per order, and the annual holding or carrying cost per unit (H), in dollars per unit.

Economic Order Quantity (EOQ)

$$EOQ = \sqrt{\frac{2 * S * D}{H}}$$

Annual demand is 10,000, purchase price is $8.00, cost per order is $2.00, and carrying cost is 2% of the purchase price ($0.16), the EOQ formula results in an order quantity of 500. Assuming such a low carrying cost is what makes most EOQ formulas drive such high order quantities.

$$EOQ = \sqrt{\frac{2 * \$2.00 * 10{,}000}{\$0.16}} = 500$$

If carrying cost was 6% of purchase price instead of 2%:

$$EOQ = \sqrt{\frac{2 * \$2.00 * 10{,}000}{\$0.48}} = 288.7$$

An *underestimated* carrying cost drives *up* the recommended order quantity, and this is the usual cause for kanban order quantities (KOQs) being lower than (EOQs). For EOQ to be accurate, holding cost should include the cost of money, which is either the cost of borrowing money to buy inventory or alternatively the lost interest that would be earned on an equivalent amount of invested cash. For the cost of money, a general rule of thumb is to use the annual percentage rate that would be paid on a short-term loan to pay for inventory. Though holding cost (H) does not show up as a specific element of kanban formulas, it is accommodated in the concept of target lead time, which drives shorter sawtooth curves and therefore lower holding costs.

Carrying cost (H) should also include the cost of space. If a site leases warehouse space or is hampered for revenue growth due to a lack of space, those costs (or the lack of profit from dampened revenue) should be included in holding cost.

Kanban Calculation Summary

Figure 22-1 illustrates the calculation process. The formulas for calculating order quantity and number of cards are summarized in Figure 22-2 on page 254.

Figure 22-1. Summary of Kanban Calculations in Flow Chart

Ideal kanban solutions are two cards and order quantity is not rounded.

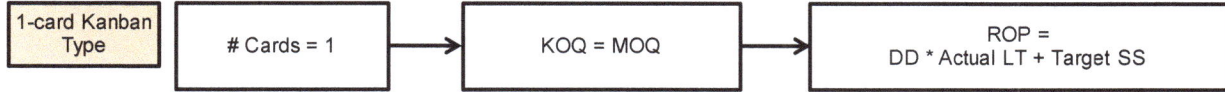

1-card Kanban Type

Cards = 1 → KOQ = MOQ → ROP = DD * Actual LT + Target SS

DD = DD for resizing, which should equal expected daily demand for the upcoming period
Actual LT = observed LT, or the time from order entry to receipt of replenishment parts
Target SS = SS in units (convert from days of demand if necessary, using Actual DD * Target SS Days)
For 1-card solutions, KOQ equals MOQ

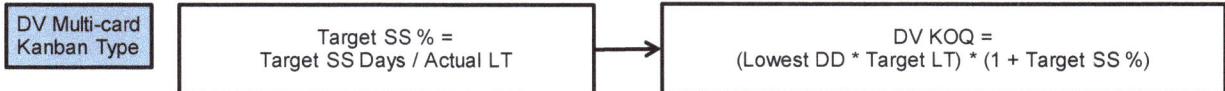

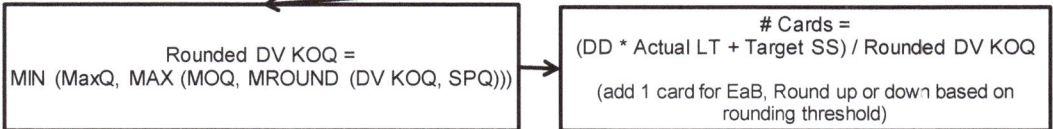

DV Multi-card Kanban Type

Target SS % = Target SS Days / Actual LT → DV KOQ = (Lowest DD * Target LT) * (1 + Target SS %)

Rounded DV KOQ = MIN (MaxQ, MAX (MOQ, MROUND (DV KOQ, SPQ))) → # Cards = (DD * Actual LT + Target SS) / Rounded DV KOQ

(add 1 card for EaB, Round up or down based on rounding threshold)

Lowest DD = DD during lowest seasonal demand period
Target SS % = Target SS as a percent of (LT * DD), = (Target SS Days/Actual LT)
Rounded KOQ is the fixed or permanent KOQ so it does not change when resizing occurs, but # of cards does.
Actual DD = DD for resizing, equals expected daily demand for the upcoming period
Round for MOQ and MaxQ, in case item has both

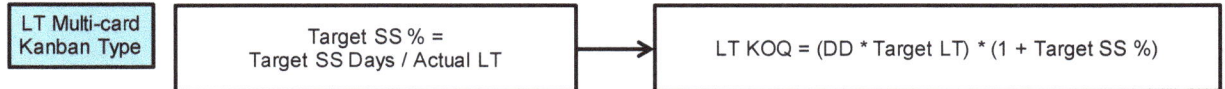

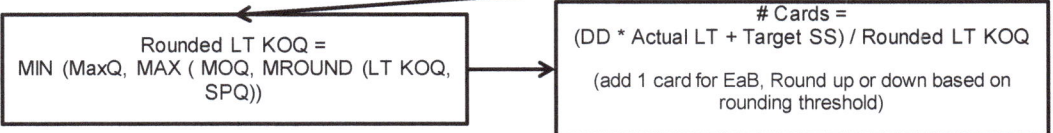

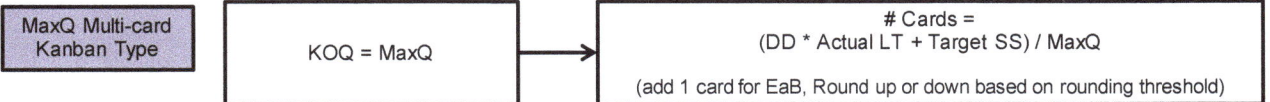

LT Multi-card Kanban Type

Target SS % = Target SS Days / Actual LT → LT KOQ = (DD * Target LT) * (1 + Target SS %)

Rounded LT KOQ = MIN (MaxQ, MAX (MOQ, MROUND (LT KOQ, SPQ)) → # Cards = (DD * Actual LT + Target SS) / Rounded LT KOQ

(add 1 card for EaB, Round up or down based on rounding threshold)

MaxQ Multi-card Kanban Type

KOQ = MaxQ → # Cards = (DD * Actual LT + Target SS) / MaxQ

(add 1 card for EaB, Round up or down based on rounding threshold)

MaxQ = maximum allowed order quantity, per the supplier

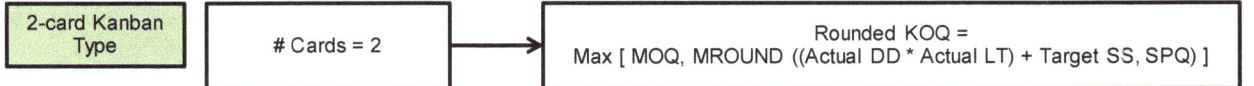

2-card Kanban Type

Cards = 2 → Rounded KOQ = Max [MOQ, MROUND ((Actual DD * Actual LT) + Target SS, SPQ)]

Figure 22-2. <u>Summary of Kanban Formulas in Table</u>

	# Cards (round to integer per the card-rounding threshold)	KOQ (always round for SPQ and MOQ)
1 card	1	KOQ = MOQ ROP = Actual LT * DD + Target SS
2-card EaB	2	Actual LT * Daily demand + Target SS
2-card BaB	2	[Actual LT * Daily demand + Target SS] / 2
DV Multi-card	Step 2. [(Actual LT * Daily demand + Target SS) / DV KOQ] Add 1 card for Empty a Bin	Step 1. BaB: [(Target LT * Low DD * (1 + Low Target SS %)] / 2 EaB: (Target LT * Low DD * (1 + Low Target SS %)
LT Multi-card	Step 2. BaB: (Actual LT * Daily demand + Target SS) / LT KOQ Add 1 card for Empty a Bin	Step 1. [(Target LT * Daily demand * (1 + Target SS %)]
MaxQ Multi-card	BaB [(Actual LT * Daily demand + Target SS) / MaxQ] + 1 (Add 1 card for Empty a Bin)	KOQ = MaxQ

1-card solutions are resized by adjusting the ROP. Multi-card solutions are resized by adjusting card count. 2-card solutions can be resized by adjusting the order quantity and maintaining two cards, or card count can be adjusted.

TUTORIAL: GOCO KANBAN CALCULATIONS

NOTES:

1. When Excel formulas are copied into this document, line breaks are inserted between sequential IF statements to make them easier to read. The final "Else" portion at the end of every IF formula is the last line or lines of the formula box.

2. Sincere apologies for the length of the formulas, but they are a bit complicated. Formulas are taken directly from Excel, and you will notice that they often use "Defined Name" references instead of cell references. A formula will say "New_ABC" instead of "V5" to reference the new ABC classification in column V and row 5. This makes formulas much easier to read and write, but it takes extra work to set up an Excel document in this manner.

3. Excel's Name Manager inserts an underline in place of every blank or special character ($, #, ?) in a defined name, so "ABC Class" becomes ABC_Class and "OH$" becomes "OH_".

4. Remember that some functions, like MAX or MROUND, require a mathematical operation in front of formula elements when using defined names. This means [MAX (MOQ, SPQ)] fails but [MAX (1 * MOQ, 1 * SPQ)] works. Go figure.

Daily Demand Values

Because GOCO had two seasons, there was more than one DD value in the data set.

1. To get average DD, Mary pulled annual demand and divided by annual workdays.

Average DD

Average DD = Annual_Demand / 250

2. Current DD was used for the current sizing exercise, pulled from the data tab.

Current DD

Current DD = VLOOKUP (PN, 'Completed Prim & Sec'!$A$1:$DZ$110, MATCH (P$2, 'Completed Prim & Sec'!$A$1:$DZ$1, 0), FALSE)

The VLOOKUP function was used numerous times in the Calculator tab to pull data from another tab. In this case, the "Completed Prim & Sec" tab contained the needed data. The MATCH function was inserted in the formula to find the column header in the data tab and to tell the VLOOKUP formula which column had the correct data. In this way, Mary could use the same formula every time she looked up data from the same source tab. For this to work, the columns had to be labeled exactly the same in both tabs.

3. Average DD for the low season was calculated in the DV tab so the data could be pulled from there.

Low Season DD

Low Season DD =VLOOKUP (PN, 'Dem Var Analysis'!$A$3:$FZ$110, MATCH (Q$2, 'Dem Var Analysis'!$A$2:$FZ$2, 0), FALSE)

4. The same approach is used for high season daily demand.

High Season DD

High Season DD = VLOOKUP (PN,'Dem Var Analysis'!$A$3:$FZ$110, MATCH (R$2, 'Dem Var Analysis'!$A$2:$FZ$2, 0), FALSE)

5. Because the data had seasonality in it, Mary used Lowest DD to calculate MOQ Days Demand, so the ratio reflects the worst case days of demand.

MOQ Days Demand

MOQ Days Demand = New_MOQ / Low_Season_DD

6. New ABC was pulled from the Primary and Secondary data tab.

New ABC

New ABC = VLOOKUP (PN, 'Completed Prim & Sec'!$A$1:$DZ$110, MATCH (T$2, 'Completed Prim & Sec'!$A$1:$DZ$1, 0), FALSE)

7. Mary used ABC as a Target SS designation, so she converted ABC into row designations for the target safety stock table.

ABC Row

ABC Row = IF (New_ABC= "A", 1, IF (New_ABC = "B", 2, 3))

Safety Stock

8. Mary pulled the correct target safety stock days for every part based on ABC and Customer Group. The first part of the formula assigned specific safety stock for VMI parts. The last part assigned target safety stock based on an index table on the Final Targets and Limits tab, where the index row was based on ABC, and column was based on the Customer Group.

Any item that was VMI had the same target safety stock of 1 day, located in cell B17 of the Final Targets & Limits tab.

For all non-VMI parts, Mary had to select the correct target safety stock reference table, either Low or High season, which was based on the time of year that resizing occurred and indicated in cell $B$1 as either Low or High. This exercise was resizing for the month of February, a High season month.

ABC_Row determined the row for the index, and Cust_Group_Column set the column number.

In the formula, if season = "Low" the calculator pulled safety stock data from cells $B$14 to $E$16 on the Final Targets & Limits tab. If not, it pulled safety stock from cells $H$14 to $K$16 on the Final Targets & Limits tab.

Target SS days

Target SS = IF (VMI="Y", 'Final Targets & Limits'!$B$17,

IF ($B$1 = "Low", INDEX ('Final Targets & Limits'!$B$14:$E$16, ABC_Row, Cust_Group_Column),

INDEX ('Final Targets & Limits'!$H$14:$K$16, ABC_Row, Cust_Group_Column)))

---

9. In addition to target safety stock for the current resizing, Mary also needed lowest target safety stock to calculate target MOQ for a seasonal item.

Lowest Target SS days

Lowest Target SS = IF (VMI="Y",

'Final Targets & Limits'!$B$17, MIN (INDEX ('Final Targets & Limits'!$B$14:$E$16, ABC_Row, Cust_Group_Column), INDEX ('Final Targets & Limits'!$H$14:$K$16, ABC_Row, Cust_Group_Column)))

For this safety stock, the formula selected the VMI value if the part had "Y" for the VMI indicator. Then it selected the minimum value from the two safety stock tables on the Final Targets & Limits tab, using ABC versus Customer Group.

10. Low Target SS % was used to multiply multi-card solutions to apply safety stock.

Low Target SS Percent

Low Target SS % = Lowest_Target_SS / New_LT

---

11. Seasonality was a Y/N (yes or no) value based on whether an item's customer group was Ag or Industrial (seasonality = "Y") or Auto and All (seasonality = "N").

Seasonality

Seasonality = IF (OR (Cust_Group = "Ag", Cust_Group = "Ind"), "Y", "N")

---

12. Mary had to assess the new lead time from updated supplier data to know if a long LT multi-card solution was required. She could have done this within the kanban type formula but that would have made that formula even longer. It was also beneficial to have a long lead-time flag as a sorting tool. If New LT was more than the allowed multiple times target lead time, the part was assigned "Y" as having a long lead time. The long LT multiple was on the Final Targets & Limits tab.

Long LT

Long LT = IF (New_LT > LT_Multi_card_Multiple * Target_LT, "Y", "N")

Calculate Kanban Solutions

13. For ideal solutions of two cards, it was easy to calculate the order quantity.

Ideal KOQ

Ideal KOQ = Current_DD * (Target_LT + Target_SS)

---

14. For recommended kanban solutions, Mary first determined kanban type: Not KB, 1-card, DV Multi-card, LT Multi-card, or 2-card. There were no MaxQ limitations.

• If DD was less than the On Kanban DD limit, the part did not qualify for kanban. Likewise, if MOQ Days Demand was greater than the On Kanban MOQ Days Demand limit, she eliminated the part from kanban consideration.

• If MOQ Days Demand was greater than (LT + Target SS Days), she assigned a 1-card solution.

• The calculator assigned 1 card to all parts on VMI since those items were refilled by suppliers and there was no need to deploy 2 cards.

• If seasonality was above the limit, it assigned DV Multi-card.

• For A and B items, if Actual to Target LT Ratio was greater than the threshold, it assigned LT Multi-card.

• All other parts were 2-card solutions.

> **Kanban Type**
>
> =IF (Consider_for_Kanban="0", "Not Kanban",
>
> IF (VMI="Y", "1 card VMI",
>
> IF (OR (Average_DD < On_KB_DD_Min, MOQ_Days_Demand > On_KB_MOQ_Days_Demand_Max), "Not Kanban",
>
> IF (MOQ_Days_Demand > (New_LT + Target_SS) * _1_card_MOQ_Days_Demand_Allowance, "1 card",
>
> IF (Seasonality = "Y", "DV Multi-card",
>
> IF (AND (OR (ABC = "A", ABC = "B"), New_LT / Target_LT > LT_Multi_card_Multiple), "LT Multi-card",
>
> "2 card"))))))

15. Once type was determined, Mary calculated the target KOQ, without rounding. Multi-card solutions used "Low Target SS % of LT" as the safety stock multiplier.

> **Target KOQ**
>
> =IF (Kanban_type = "Not Kanban", 0,
>
> IF (OR (Kanban_type = "1 card", Kanban_type = "1 card VMI"), (New_LT + Target_SS) * Current_DD,
>
> IF (AND (Kanban_type = "DV Multi-card", Long_LT = "Y"), Low_Season_DD * Target_LT * (1 + Low_Target_SS___of_LT),
>
> IF (Kanban_type = "DV Multi-card", Low_Season_DD * Target_LT * (1 + Low_Target_SS___of_LT),
>
> IF (Kanban_type = "LT Multi-card", Average_DD*Target_LT * (1 + Target_SS / New_LT),
>
> Current_DD * (New_LT + Target_SS))))))

16. They rounded target order quantity for SPQ and MOQ.

> **Rounded KOQ**
>
> =IF (Kanban_type = "Not Kanban", 0,
>
> IF (AND (MROUND (1 * Target_KOQ, 1 * New_SPQ) < Target_KOQ, MOD (Target_KOQ - MROUND (1 * Target_KOQ, New_SPQ * 1), New_SPQ) < Rounding_Threshold * New_SPQ), MAX (1 * New_MOQ, MROUND (1 * Target_KOQ, 1 * New_SPQ)),
>
> IF (MROUND (1 * Target_KOQ, 1 * New_SPQ) > Target_KOQ, MAX (1 * New_MOQ, MROUND (1 * Target_KOQ, 1 * New_SPQ)),
>
> MAX (1 * New_MOQ, New_SPQ + MROUND (1 * Target_KOQ, 1 * New_SPQ)))))

This wasn't as straightforward as one might hope. Mary wanted to round the calculated order quantity up or down for SPQ based on the rounding threshold. But, the MROUND formula doesn't work that way. Because MROUND uses standard mathematical rounding, she had to insert logic that used the rounding threshold to round Target KOQ up or down correctly.

Here is the formula logic, in plain English.

First section in the formula: Assign a KOQ of zero if the part is not on kanban.

Second Section in Formula:

Check to see if Target KOQ was rounded down, and accept or reject the rounding based on the rounding threshold:

• Target KOQ was rounded down for SPQ

  » This meant Rounded KOQ, which was rounded mathematically for the package quantity using the MROUND function, was less than Target KOQ. So, Target KOQ was rounded down to the next multiple of SPQ.

• The remainder of [Target KOQ - Rounded KOQ] divided by the New SPQ was less than [rounding threshold * New SPQ]

  » When we divide [Target KOQ minus its rounded value] by SPQ, we get a remainder that falls below the rounding threshold. If Target KOQ was rounded down, which is the only way this clause matters, then the quantity that was rounded or subtracted from Target KOQ to get to the Rounded KOQ must be compared to SPQ. If the remainder was less than the rounding threshold, we let it round down.

» Example: If Target KOQ was 1025 and SPQ was 250, the MROUND function rounds down to 1,000 because that's the right mathematical solution for rounding. We look at how much was taken off Target KOQ, or 1025 - 1000, and we have 25 units versus SPQ of 250, or 10%. This is smaller than the rounding threshold of 20%, so it should be rounded down, as was done by MROUND.

IF both are true, THEN select the MAX of either the New MOQ or the Target KOQ rounded for SPQ. This accepts a Target KOQ that was correctly rounded down as long as it exceeds MOQ.

Third Section in the Formula:

IF the rounded Target KOQ is greater than Target KOQ, which means it was rounded up,

THEN select the MAX of the New MOQ or the rounded Target KOQ.

This makes sure that a Target KOQ that was rounded up for SPQ is greater than the New MOQ.

Last Section in the Formula:

The only parts that remain are those that got rounded down and should have been rounded up. For those parts, select the maximum of the New MOQ or Target KOQ rounded for SPQ (which will round down), and then add one SPQ to increase it as if it was rounded up.

Yes, that was a bit challenging.

17. With a rounded KOQ, Mary could calculate the required number of kanban cards. "Not Kanban," 1-card, and 2-card solutions were easy, so she put them at the beginning of the formula and then assigned multi-card types.

Number of Cards

=IF (Kanban_type= "Not Kanban", 0,

IF (OR (Kanban_type = "1 card", Kanban_type = "1 card VMI"), 1,

IF (Kanban_type="2 card", 2,

(New_LT + Target_SS) * Current_DD / Rounded_KOQ + 1)))

Remember, GOCO was on EaB, so they added one card for all multi-card types.

---

18. They rounded the number of cards to the correct integer. Mary had to accommodate the rounding threshold, so she couldn't use a simple ROUND formula that relies on mathematical rounding. Like rounding KOQ, she calculated the remainder for the calculated number of cards and compared that to the rounding threshold. This formula divided the calculated number of cards by one to get the remainder, or the "decimal value" after dividing by 1 with the MOD function. If that remainder was less than the rounding threshold, it rounded card count down, and if not it rounded up.

Rounded Number of Cards

=IF (MOD (Calc_KB_Cards, 1) < Rounding_Threshold, ROUNDDOWN (Calc_KB_Cards, 0),

ROUNDUP (Calc_KB_Cards, 0))

---

19. She finally defined the ROP for 1-card solutions. This formula assigned ROP to only 1-card solutions, and left others blank.

ROP

= IF (Round___cards = 1, Current_DD * (New_LT + Target_SS), "")

Yes, these formulas really work.

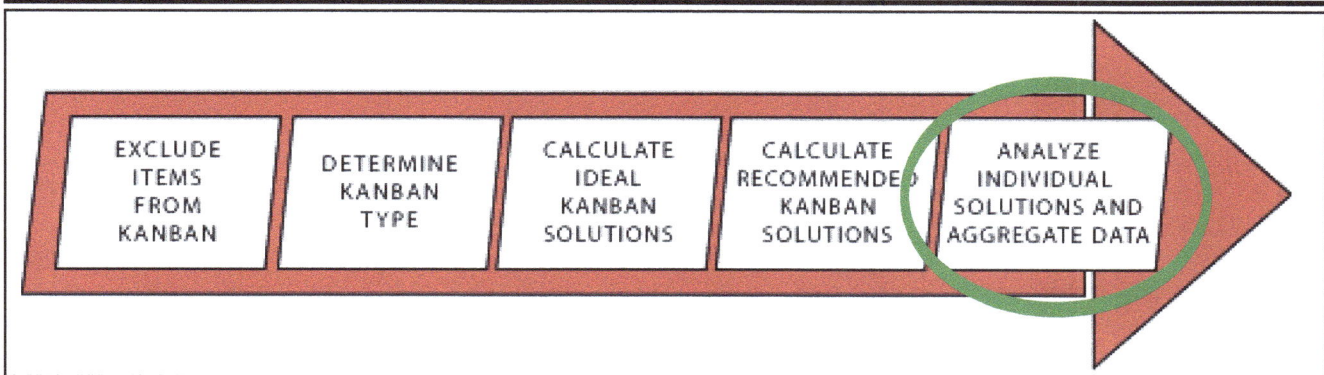

CHAPTER 23: STEP 5A ANALYZE KANBAN FOR ERRORS & ESTIMATE INVENTORY LEVELS

Once kanban solutions have been calculated, it is necessary to review the results and plan follow-up actions. But before we do anything, we have to correct any errors that occurred.

Once the results are correct, we can predict inventory levels and design action plans for delivery improvement and inventory reduction.

Fill in Missing Kanban Results & Fix Errors

The most common calculator errors are missing kanban solutions, generally due to a quirk in a formula or previously-undetected data errors.

Fill in Missing Kanban Solutions

Before deploying kanban solutions, ensure that each item that qualified for kanban received a valid solution. A quick review of the calculator tab reveals rows where a solution is missing. If the spreadsheet is long, sort or filter by number of cards or kanban order quantity and review rows where no kanban solution was assigned, yet the items qualify for kanban.

For items that should have a kanban solution but do not, create a kanban solution manually or determine why the formulas failed, and then make

corrections accordingly. If formulas are changed, remember to copy the new formula to all cells in the effected column, then recheck for errors.

Fix Errors

Sad but true: errors occur in kanban calculators. If the list of items in the calculator is short, it's feasible to do a visual check of the spreadsheet. But, with thousands of items, it's necessary to find errors in an automated way.

Mathematical functions such as SUM, MIN, or AVERAGE will fail if any of the values in the selected data set are nonnumeric, which gives errors such as "#NAME?" or "#N/A". Several columns will be summed in upcoming steps, so errors will be revealed as the analysis is performed. If a function performed on a column results in an error, usually #N/A, there is at least one cell in the column that is not a number. Find rows that contain errors and correct them until all summary functions work correctly.

Another way to find errors in each column is the filter function. If a row should have a numeric result but instead has an error, filter the column to narrow the list to just those with nonnumeric results.

> **HINT for Associates**
>
> When writing formulas, the best approach for excluded items, those items that don't need a data entry from the formula, is to assign a blank result to those cells. This makes it easy to see that blanks are for items that are not on kanban.
>
> Example: IF (KOQ > 0, MROUND (KOQ, SPQ), "")

Modify Kanban Solutions to Fix Actual Safety Stock Gaps

Calculate actual safety stock for every kanban item to ensure they were given adequate safety stock after rounding kanban order quantities and card counts. This step is essentially checking the final form of the sawtooth curve, specifically the safety stock that should be present at the bottom of the curve.

The formulas for safety stock vary for EaB and BaB triggering methods and also for 1-card solutions.

Actual Safety Stock

2 or more cards, EaB Actual SS = (# cards - 1) * KOQ - (Actual LT * Current DD)

2 or more cards, BaB Actual SS =

(# cards * KOQ) - (Actual LT * Current DD)

1-card Actual SS = Reorder Point - (Actual LT * Current Daily Demand)

Divide units of safety stock by daily demand (DD) to convert to days of safety stock.

Solutions with just 1 card should never have negative safety stock, because that could only happen if the calculator rounded ROP down for standard package quantity, and frankly the formula should not have allowed that to occur. ROP should never be rounded down, it can only be rounded up.

If a modified solution is needed to fix negative safety stock for a 2-card solution, there are two options. To keep the item on 2 cards, insert a column in the calculator for a modified order quantity and increase order quantity by one standard package quantity (SPQ), or by some reasonable quantity if SPQ is really low. We must adhere to MOQ, MaxQ, and SPQ limitations, so check the new order quantity against those values. Insert another column and calculate safety stock for 2 cards at the modified order quantity and see if that fixes the negative safety stock.

If increasing card count is an option for 2-card items, insert 2 more columns and increase card count by 1 in the first new column. Leave order quantity alone. In the second new column, calculate safety stock for the higher card count and the original KOQ, then review both possible modified solutions and decide which is best, either modified card count or order quantity. Use the best modified solution as the final kanban recommendation.

Rule of Thumb

NEVER deploy a kanban solution with negative safety stock.

To protect delivery, every resizing exercise should calculate actual safety stock for current kanban solutions, or the kanban solutions already deployed and active today. Identify any items that have negative safety stock and resize those items immediately!

Fix Negative Safety Stock

Negative safety stock means the calculated kanban solution orders fewer parts during the lead-time period than will be consumed, so it is essentially a stock-out certainty. This was likely caused by rounding the order quantity or card count down.

For multi-card solutions, there is no need to evaluate a modified order quantity because those solutions were carefully calculated around a frozen order quantity. The option for a multi-card solution with negative safety stock or really high safety stock is to add or subtract one card.

Review Low Safety Stock & Modify If Necessary

Low safety stock isn't as dangerous as negative safety stock, but it should still be reviewed. Add a column to the spreadsheet and divide actual safety stock by target safety stock for every item. Sort or filter on this new column to find items that missed their target safety stock by a wide margin, e.g., items with less than 50% of the target safety stock as measured in units or days of coverage.

Actual Safety Stock as Percent of Target Safety Stock	=

Actual SS % of Target SS
= Actual SS Days/Target SS Days

Rule of Thumb 👍

Any item with [actual safety stock < 50% of target safety stock] should be reviewed.

Review High Safety Stock

High safety stock is not a delivery risk, but it will harm inventory performance and cash flow. If the calculator rounded up for card count or order quantity, high safety stock is the result.

Unlike negative safety stock, high safety stock solutions can be deployed without impacting delivery, but they increase average inventory. To reduce unplanned safety stock, perform the process described above for card count and order quantity, but subtract from order quantity and card count. If the adjusted solutions result in negative safety stock or safety stock less than 50% of the target, use the originally calculated solution with higher safety stock.

HINT for Associates 📌

Remember that low or high actual safety stock often comes from rounding order quantity to accommodate minimum order or standard package requirements, so focus on reducing those limits!

HINT for Associates 📌

Ideal kanban solutions should always achieve target safety values because they are not rounded for minimum order or standard package quantities.

SPQ Rounding Example (continued in next box) e.g.

The calculated multi-card solution is 54 parts on 6 EaB cards. The supplier allows order quantities that are multiples of 10, so 50 or 60 but not 54. Lead time is 25 days, DD is 10, and target SS is 20 pieces.

Estimated average inventory = KOQ/2 + Actual safety stock = 54/2 + 20 = 47

Since the calculated solution is not possible, we might guess a few possible solutions:

6 cards at 60: SS = (6 - 1) * 60 – (10 * 25) = 300 - 250 = 50, Average = 60/2 + 50 = 80

5 Cards at 60: SS = (5 - 1) * 60 – (10 * 25) = 240 - 250 = -10, NOT VALID

7 cards at 50: SS = (7 - 1) * 50 – (10 * 25) = 300 – 250 = 50, Average = 50/2 + 50 = 75

Target safety stock is 20, so 50 pieces of safety stock in the first and third options is really high. But, the other solution has negative safety stock, so it isn't a valid option.

Target average on-hand inventory is 54/2 + 20 = 47, and both options are far above that.

Ideally we want to buy 270 pieces in the lead-time period [25 * 10 + 20], which is evenly divisible by 3, so let's try 4 cards at 90. (Remember to add 1 card for EaB, so 270/90 + 1 = 4 cards.)

Actual safety stock = (4 - 1) * 90 – (10 * 25) = 270 - 250 = 20

Average Inventory = 90/2 + 20 = 65, which is better than the first three options.

This gives us the exact safety stock target but a higher KOQ. The drawback is that if we have to resize in the future to accommodate higher demand, we add cards at a rate of 90 pieces per kanban card.

SPQ Rounding Example (continued from prior box) **e.g.**

270 is close to 280, which is evenly divisible by 70, so try 5 cards at 70 or [270/70 + 1 = 4.9]

Actual safety stock = (5 cards - 1) * 70 – (10 * 25) = 280 - 250 = 30, which is slightly above our target of 20.

Average Inventory = 70/2 + 30 = 65, which is the same as 4 cards at 90, so it's a matter of choosing which solution we prefer. The advantage to 5 cards at 70 is that each card is just 70 pieces, so resizing up or down by 1 card is a smaller jump for the kanban solution.

MOQ and SPQ Rounding Example **e.g.**

Part number MSP-505 has daily demand of 8, lead time of 10 days, target lead time of 10 days, and 2 days of target safety stock. Minimum order quantity is 120 and standard package is 12.

EaB Ideal order quantity = (Daily demand * Target lead time + Target SS units) = (8 * 10) + (2 * 8) = 96

If the kanban solution is 2 cards at 120 each, there are 24 pieces of unintended safety stock due to rounding up the order quantity from the ideal 96 to the minimum order quantity of 120.

EaB SS @ ideal KOQ of 96 = (# cards - 1) * KOQ - (DD * LT) = (2 cards -1) * 96 - (8 *10) = 96 - 80 = 16

Actual EaB SS @ MOQ of 120 = (2 cards - 1) * 120 - (8 * 10) = 120 - 80 = 40

Average on-hand balance for 2 cards @ 96 = KOQ/2 + SS units = 96/2 + 16 = 64

Average OHB for 2 cards @ 120 = 120/2 + 40 units of SS = 100

The sawtooth curve exhibits a dramatic upward shift: average inventory jumps by 36 units, due to 24 additional SS units and 12 additional units for the higher order quantity divided by 2.

Estimate On-Hand Inventory

Inventory minimum, average, and maximum levels can be estimated mathematically. Add columns to complete the analysis, and remember that inventory levels must be in currency when aggregating inventory data across multiple items.

Estimate On-Hand Balances for Kanban Items

Calculate estimated minimum, average, and maximum inventory levels.

Estimated On-Hand Inventory

Estimated Minimum Inventory
= Actual Safety Stock units

Estimated Average Inventory
= KOQ/2 + Actual SS

Estimated Maximum Inventory
= KOQ + Actual SS

To get estimated inventory dollars, multiply inventory units by standard cost.

Estimate On-Hand Balance for Items Not on Kanban & with Zero Demand

Items that were excluded from kanban due to zero demand will stay at the current inventory level until an inventory write-off occurs. So, current on-hand balance equals the future minimum, average, and maximum expected balances.

Estimate Minimum On-Hand Balance for Items Not on Kanban But with Some Demand

For any item, minimum inventory equals estimated safety stock. If non-kanban items are managed very tightly, with parts arriving just in time, safety stock is essentially zero. Therefore, the estimated minimum on-hand balance is also zero.

If orders are scheduled to arrive before inventory drops to zero, which is the definition of safety stock, that safety stock should be planned and managed. For non-kanban items with active demand, estimate safety stock in days or units and use that estimate as the expected minimum on-hand balance. It isn't as easy to estimate this for non-kanban items as it is for kanban, since the items might not be as predictable in their replenishment, but find a way to estimate planned safety stock.

Estimate Average On-Hand Balance for Items Not on Kanban

Non-kanban items that have active demand are logically expected to be in stock in the future, yet they were excluded from kanban due to a low DD, high minimum order quantity (MOQ), or some other attribute.

Items that were excluded due to a high MOQ or low DD will probably be purchased in a quantity equal to the MOQ, whether on kanban or not. If no safety stock is planned and inventory drops to zero just as replenishment parts arrive, a reasonable estimate of average on-hand balance is [MOQ / 2]. If non-kanban parts are planned to arrive before inventory drops to zero, add corresponding safety stock to estimate average inventory.

Estimated Average On-Hand Balance,
Non-kanban with Demand

Est Avg OHB
= Order Quantity/2 + Actual SS

Items that were excluded from kanban due to a reason other than MOQ or DD might be in stock at any time, so assume average inventory based on how flow occurs. For example, half of one day's production might be expected in stock from a certain cell. Or, two days of finished goods might be planned for a certain customer. Use your best judgment.

Estimate Maximum On-Hand Balance for Items Not on Kanban

For non-kanban items with demand, estimated maximum inventory equals the order quantity plus any safety stock units. The thought process about safety stock and expected average inventory from above applies to maximum inventory.

Estimated Max On-Hand Balance

Non-kanban with demand, Estimated
Max OHB = Order Quantity + Actual SS

Add Summary Data to the Calculator

With estimated inventory levels by item, we can now evaluate aggregate results.

Total Estimated OH Currency

When predicting total or aggregate inventory, on-hand balances (OHB) must be in currency instead of units of measure. Note: For ease of discussion, we will assume on-hand currency is in dollars and OH$ stands for on-hand dollars.

To predict total or aggregate OH$ for all items, sum the estimates for all individual items. The sum across all items assumes that every kanban recommendation is executed successfully and immediately. Any kanban deployment delays or deviations are not reflected in these numbers, but if kanban deployment is successful the inventory sums should be reasonable benchmarks for reality.

Total Estimated On-Hand Dollars (OH$)

Total Estimated OH$
= SUM (Estimated OH$ for all items)

for minimum, average, or maximum inventory

Total Average Estimated (OH$)

When planning inventory reduction activity, compare total on-hand currency, or what is actually on site, to the sum of all estimated average balances. Based on the Central Limit Theorem, the sum of actual inventory across a large population of items should approximate the average expected

inventory for those same items. More on this in the next chapter.

Total Maximum Estimated OH$

For an initial kanban deployment, it is possible for actual OH$ to exceed the sum of all *maximum* inventory, meaning current inventory is higher than it would be if *every* item was at the top of its sawtooth curve. Yikes! This is most likely to occur when kanban is being deployed for the first time because kanban often reduces inventory dramatically. But, this can also occur when resizing a large number of items, particularly if demand, minimum order quantities, or lead times have changed.

If On-Hand Currency Is Always Too High

In cases where kanban is already deployed and has been sized regularly, if on-hand inventory is consistently higher than the <u>maximum</u> expected values, there is a <u>systemic</u> and <u>widespread</u> breakdown of the materials management system.

There are a few failures that can occur:

1. Kanban is not being utilized to generate replenishment orders, even though kanban cards are deployed. Something - maybe human intervention or MRP signals - is overriding kanban, so orders are not linked to consumption, actual lead times, and so on. Kanban is not functional.

2. The kanban calculation process provided incorrect solutions, and, therefore, deployed solutions are not based on reality. This can come from data errors or calculation mistakes.

3. Replenishment orders arrive too early or too often, which adds unintended safety stock. This might be from processing kanban cards early (e.g., the bin isn't empty but the card is scanned anyway), or from data errors. Possible errors include using a lead time that was longer than actual lead time, or suppliers who ship too fast (shorter lead time than what is planned). Don't allow suppliers to ship early!

4. Actual replenishment quantities are higher than calculated KOQs, which might be due to MOQs or SPQs being higher than what was used to plan kanban quantities. Or it might be due to suppliers not adhering to order quantities, e.g., actual quantity in excess or order quantity, which should be caught when reconciling purchase orders. Don't let suppliers ship excess quantities!

5. Demand was overstated in kanban calculations, or it has subsequently declined and resizing did not occur in response to the decline.

HINT for Associates

For any <u>individual</u> item, current on-hand inventory might exceed expected maximum by a small margin, perhaps up to 10%, simply due to ebbs and flows in supply and demand. But, actual on-hand balance should never be dramatically greater than estimated maximum inventory.

If site-wide on-hand currency is consistently higher than the estimated total OH$ for a population of kanban parts, find the root cause for the gap and fix it. This is a <u>major</u> failure!

Percent of Annual Purchased Spend on Kanban

Sites that utilize kanban should measure the depth or breadth of kanban deployment. The best method is percent of annual purchased spend on kanban, *not* percent of total part numbers on kanban. This distinction is particularly important at sites with a high number of active but low usage parts. For example, if a site has 10,000 active purchased items but 5,000 are used once a year or less, it isn't reasonable to expect 90% of all purchased <u>part numbers</u> to be on kanban. However, 90% of annual purchased <u>spend</u> is probably fair.

Kanban deployment as a percent of annual spend for manufactured parts is less insightful than for purchased parts. A site might achieve widespread "flow" and therefore eliminate the need for planned inventory for WIP. Finished goods might also be excluded from kanban if customer lead times are longer than the internal processing times. Eliminating finished goods from kanban takes the highest value manufactured items out of kanban consideration. For these reasons, at some sites, the percent of annual manufactured spend on kanban <u>should</u> be low.

To get the denominator for spend on kanban, sum total annual spend for all purchased or external parts using a "SUMIF" function.

Total Purchased Annual Spend

IF Purch/Mfd = "P", Sum Annual Spend $

Sum total annual spend for all purchased parts *on kanban* and compare that sum to the total annual purchased spend calculated above.

Because the formula checks two parameters—purchased vs. manufactured and whether an item is on kanban or not—the SUMIF function won't work at the bottom of the annual spend column. Instead, insert a new column in the calculator and use an IF formula with AND to check for both a kanban solution and "P" status. If both conditions are true, grab the annual spend.

Purchased Spend on Kanban by Part Number

Purchased Spend $ on kanban
= IF (AND (# Kanban cards > 0, Mfg/Purch = "P"), Annual Spend $, "")

Sum that column to get total spend for purchased parts on kanban.

Sum of Purchased Spend on Kanban

Total Purchased Spend on Kanban =
SUM (Purchased Spend on Kanban) for all items

Divide the sum of kanban purchased spend by total purchased spend to get percent of purchased spend on kanban.

Percent Purchased Spend on Kanban

% Purchased Spend on Kanban
= SUM (Purchased Kanban Spend)/ SUM (All Purchased Spend)

Rule of Thumb

Target at least 80% of annual purchased spend on kanban for an initial kanban deployment. Eventually get above 90% as high MOQs and other kanban hurdles are addressed.

Don't bother with percent of annual spend for manufactured items.

ABC Percent Spend on Kanban

Kanban deployment effectiveness can also be assessed based on percent of annual spend on kanban by ABC classification. The procedure is the same as for percent of purchased spend on kanban, but add a check for ABC in addition to purchased versus manufactured.

If the goal is to manage the biggest piles of money by kanban, A items should be 100% on kanban, while C items might be less than 50%. If A items cover 80% of annual spend, then putting 100% of A items on kanban puts 80% of annual spend on kanban. If all B items are on kanban, the percent of kanban coverage jumps to 95%. This demonstrates that A and B items should be high priorities for kanban deployment.

> ### HINT for Associates
>
> Summary data can be added to the Calculator tab at the bottom of the relevant columns. But, if the item list is long with thousands of rows in the spreadsheet, it will be tedious to use summary data at the bottom of columns. Instead, add a Summary tab to the Excel spreadsheet and put summary data there.

Summary of Analyzing Kanban Errors & Estimating Inventory Levels

It is extremely important to verify that kanban solutions are assigned to every eligible item and that safety stock is never negative.

Inventory planning should occur as an output of the kanban process, so take time to calculate estimated inventory levels for individual items, then sum those for aggregate predictions.

TUTORIAL: GOCO KANBAN ANALYSIS FOR ERRORS & ESTIMATED INVENTORY

Mary added columns to the Excel tab to add part number details, starting with estimated on-hand balances (OHB) and dollars.

1. Actual safety stock was needed to get to estimated inventory levels. For items not on kanban, Mary assumed zero safety stock.

> Actual Safety Stock (SS) Units
>
> =IF (Round___cards = 0, 0,
>
> IF (Round___cards = 1, ROP - (Current_DD * New_LT),
>
> (Round___cards - 1) * Rounded_KOQ - (Current_DD * New_LT)))

Remember that the defined name for rounded number of cards drops the "#" symbol in the name for "Round # cards".

Note: If we had both BaB and EaB triggers, we would add a column for trigger type and define EaB = 1 and BaB = 0 for trigger method, which would force us to modify the formula above to [(Round___cards - *Trigger*) * Round_KOQ - (Average_DD * Std_LT)], where EaB would subtract a card but BaB would not.

2. Convert actual safety stock units into SS days, using current daily demand as the divisor.

> SS Days
>
> SS Days = Calc_SS_units / Current_DD

3. If current SS was negative, Mary had to adjust the kanban solution. Three items were negative.

Part Number	Target SS	Kanban type	Rounded KOQ	Calc KB Cards	Round # cards	Calc SS units	Calc SS Days
100.50 Trim	0.7	DV Multi-card	13,000	2.17	2	(1,317.2)	-1.1
DBrace1	2.2	DV Multi-card	50,000	2.17	2	(976.0)	-0.3
FlowSens	0.4	2 card	4,000	2.00	2	(11.0)	-0.1

For the 2 multi-card items, Mary added a card even if it spiked safety stock above the target. For the first two items, Mary entered the corrected number of cards in the "Rounded # Cards" column and highlighted them in yellow as a reminder that they were manually adjusted.

The third item was a 2-card solution, so Mary bumped up the order quantity by one package quantity, taking it from 4,000 to 4,500, which solved the negative safety stock problem and maintained the 2-card solution. She entered the adjusted KOQ in the "Rounded KOQ" column and also filled that cell with yellow highlight.

Part Number	Target SS	Kanban type	Rounded KOQ	Calc KB Cards	Round # cards	Calc SS units	Calc SS Days
100.50 Trim	0.7	DV Multi-card	13,000	2.17	3	11,682.8	9.8
DBrace1	2.2	DV Multi-card	50,000	2.17	3	49,024.0	14.4
FlowSens	0.4	2 card	4,500	2.00	2	489.0	2.4

4. Estimated on-hand balance or expected average inventory was based on whether the part was on kanban or not, which was checked by looking at the rounded number of cards. She assumed zero safety stock for items not on kanban, so average on-hand balance equaled [MOQ/2].

> Estimated Average Inventory or On-Hand Balance (OHB)
>
> Est_Avg_Inv = IF (Round___cards = 0, New_MOQ / 2, Rounded_KOQ / 2 + Calc_SS_units)

5. Using OHB, she calculated the estimated OH$.

> Estimated On-Hand Dollars (OH$)
>
> Estimated OH$ = Est_Avg_Inv * Std_Cost

6. Mary then calculated maximum expected inventory using the logic that zero cards or items not on kanban would have maximum inventory equal to the MOQ with zero safety stock.

Estimated Max On-Hand Balance

$Est\_Max\_OHB = IF (Round\_\_\_cards = 0, New\_MOQ, Rounded\_KOQ + Calc\_SS\_units)$

7. She added estimated maximum on-hand dollars.

Estimated Max On-Hand Dollars

$Estimated\ Max\ OH\$ = Est\_Max\_OHB * Std\_Cost$

8. She pulled current on-hand dollars from the data tab to compare to estimated <u>maximum</u> on-hand dollars, using MATCH in the VLOOKUP formula to get the OH$ data for every item.

On-Hand Dollars

$OH\$ = VLOOKUP (PN,\ 'Completed\ Prim\ \&\ Sec'!\$A\$1:\$DZ\$110,\ MATCH (OH\_,\ 'Completed\ Prim\ \&\ Sec'!\$A\$1:\$DZ\$1,\ 0),\ FALSE)$

Actual OH$ was $23,212,755. Wow! Inventory was still really high. The estimated maximum OH$ for the new kanban system was $10,181,931. Even at maximum on-hand dollars, inventory should come down by more than half!

Current OH$	$23,212,755
Estimated Max OH$	$10,181,931
Estimated Average OH$	$ 6,129,420
Reduction Current to Max	$13,030,824 (56% reduction)
Reduction Current to Average	$17,083,335 (74% reduction)

Yippee!!

9. Mary wanted to see what percent of annual spend for purchased items would be covered by kanban so she inserted a column that captured annual spend for items with a rounded card count greater than zero and a "P" under purchased or manufactured status. She summed that column and divided it by total annual spend to get the percent on kanban.

Annual Purchased Spend on Kanban

$Annual\ Spend\ on\ Kanban = IF (AND (Round\_\_\_cards > 0, P\_M = "P"), Annual\_Demand * Std\_Cost, 0)$

$Percent\ Annual\ Spend\ on\ Kanban = Annual\ Spend\ on\ Kanban\ /\ Total\ Annual\ Spend$

Total spend on kanban was $69,116,750, which was the entire annual spend. They would manage 100% of purchased parts with kanban!

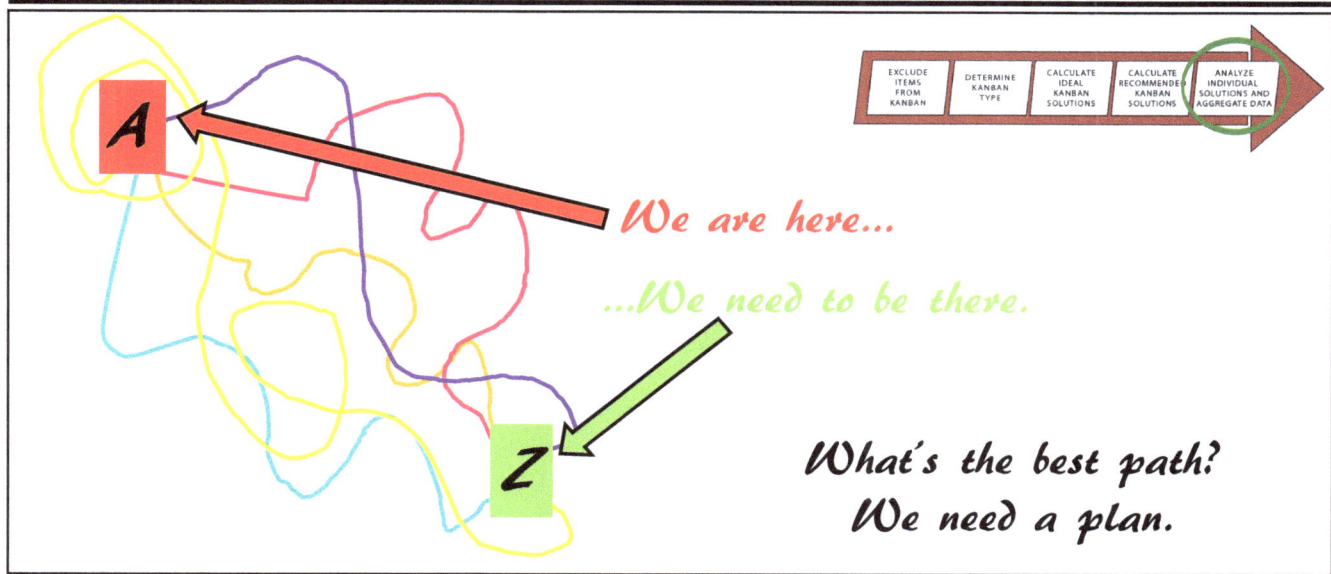

We are here...

...We need to be there.

What's the best path?
We need a plan.

CHAPTER 24: STEP 5B PREDICT & PLAN INVENTORY REDUCTIONS

Close your eyes and throw the dart. Wherever it lands will set the goal for inventory reduction!

Are you kidding me? Did you even try to aim at 250,000 or 300,000 ?!?

You told me to close my eyes!

I thought you'd know enough to keep **one eye open**!!!

I'll send the new goal to the boss, then I'll start updating my resume.

One of the most compelling kanban advantages is the potential for inventory reduction. Most sites set annual goals for revenue, profit, cost reduction, inventory performance, and on-time delivery. But, it is amazing how haphazard that goal setting process can be. Too many sites set performance goals before a single action plan is defined, resulting in a goal that is essentially a random number. The cartoon to the left seems like a gross exaggeration of the goal-setting process, but in many sites it isn't too far off. Too many managers have random goals that are not at all based on a scientific or mathematical foundation.

The best approach is to first set specific goals at lower levels, e.g., by value stream, work cell, or supplier. Second, aggregate those to predict site-wide performance. This is more tedious, but it provides a goal based in *fact* rather than *fantasy*. It is ludicrous to estimate inventory reduction with no details to back it up. So, start at the bottom by part number (PN) and aggregate up from there by ABC class, inventory class, product family, site, etc.

We can do this with kanban results.

Estimated Average Inventory Is the Benchmark

To evaluate inventory reduction, use estimated <u>average</u> inventory summed across all items, not maximum estimated inventory.

Across a large population of parts, total <u>actual</u> on-hand dollars (OH$) should hover near the <u>expected</u> average inventory for the sum of those items.

In Figure 24-1, individual sawtooth curves (blue lines) are stacked. Black vertical lines indicate points in time when a snapshot of inventory was taken. Green dots mark where each sawtooth curve was at the time of the various snapshots. Pink lines mark average inventory for each item.

Figure 24-1. Stacked Sawtooth Curves

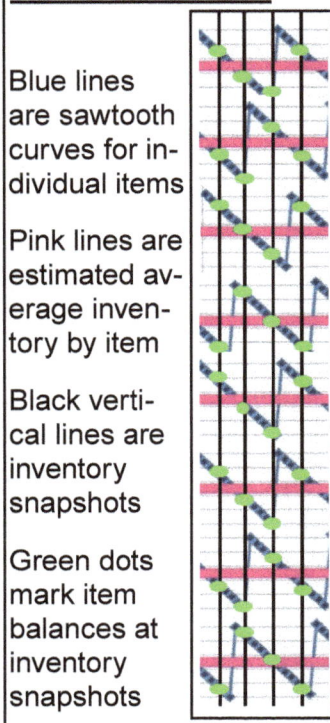

Blue lines are sawtooth curves for individual items

Pink lines are estimated average inventory by item

Black vertical lines are inventory snapshots

Green dots mark item balances at inventory snapshots

Individual items are rarely at the midpoint of their sawtooth curve. In the diagram, for each item at or near the top of its sawtooth curve (high inventory), another item is at the bottom (low inventory), so total inventory should settle near the sum of estimated averages by PN. It's the Central Limit Theorem.

Rule of Thumb 👍

<u>Actual</u> on-hand inventory dollars for a large population of parts, usually 1,000 or more, should approximate <u>estimated</u> average dollars for the sum of those parts. If total estimated OH$ for a population of parts is $5 million, at any given time we expect <u>actual</u> dollars to be about $5M. If the two sums differ by more than 5-10%, find the root cause for the gap, e.g., kanban process not being used correctly, demand has shifted, suppliers not following the rules, etc.

Estimate Potential Inventory Reduction

Predict Reduction By Item

Calculate the potential inventory change for each item by comparing current OH$ versus estimated average on-hand dollars.

> Estimated Inventory Reduction
>
> Estimated Inventory Reduction
> = Estimated Average OH$ - Current OH$ =

Note that an item that is currently at the low point of the sawtooth curve will show that inventory needs to <u>increase</u>. But, at the macro level that item should be offset by another item at the top of the sawtooth curve, which indicates inventory should come down. In general, the only inventory that is truly "too low" is at zero—a stock out situation. An item that is "too high" is anything above the estimated maximum on-hand balance (OHB) for that item. Because current or actual inventory for every item is compared to estimated average inventory, both positive and negative gaps are *expected* for individual items.

HINT for Associates 📌

Be clear and consistent as to whether a negative number is an estimated inventory decrease or increase. If financial and operational reporting follows a convention that a positive number *always* represents a desired result, subtract expected OH$ from current OH$ so that an inventory reduction is a positive number.

Predict Total Inventory Reduction

Calculate the potential reduction of the entire population, assuming every kanban solution is deployed immediately.

Total Potential Inventory Reduction

$$\text{Total Potential Inventory Reduction} = \text{Sum (Estimated OH\$ - Actual OH\$) for all items}$$

Every kanban update or deployment should make a point to fix stock out situations immediately, which will trigger urgent replenishment orders. Additionally, any items that expect an inventory increase due to being near the bottom of the sawtooth curve will also receive a replenishment order in the near future.

This means that the early impact from kanban updates is often for overall inventory to go up!

Total Reduction Might Not Be 100% Achieved

The sum of all individual reductions might not be achieved because the calculated number is the mathematically possible reduction, so it shouldn't be the immediate goal for a site. It is directionally correct and fundamentally achievable, but don't get hung up on getting down to the exact calculated inventory number.

1. Any delays in launching kanban solutions will delay inventory reductions for impacted items. If there are hundreds of kanban solutions to deploy, it will certainly take time to get all the solutions on the floor.

2. We might purposefully choose to limit kanban deployment in early days to items that will have the most impact on inventory reduction, instead of immediately deploying 100% of the new kanban solutions. If so, assume that prioritized items will achieve good results but delayed items will not see any reduction.

3. Non-kanban items probably won't achieve an inventory reduction if their current replenishment methods remain unchanged.

4. If internal or external suppliers don't perform to kanban order quantity and lead-time requirements, inventory performance will be impacted either up or down. If they over-ship or ship early, inventory goes up. Watch supplier performance after kanban solutions are deployed to ensure they are in compliance and that solutions are working as planned.

Define Negotiation Plans for Ideal Kanban Solutions

It's easy to ignore ideal kanban solutions and focus on deploying recommended solutions, simply because ideal solutions require a lot of work. However, ideal solutions are key to achieving the highest inventory reduction because they are built on target lead time with no kanban quantity limitations.

There are three types of negotiations to identify and prioritize for ideal kanban deployment.

1. Achieve lower package limits, either minimum order quantity (MOQ) or standard package quantity (SPQ), which should reduce inventory.

2. Shorter lead times should reduce inventory.

3. Longer lead times will reduce inventory *transactions*, though inventory levels will go up.

Determining which items should be high priorities for internal or external negotiations can be a daunting task because it requires analysis at the PN level. To prioritize negotiation priorities, estimate how much inventory would be reduced if all negotiation targets were achieved.

1. Calculate estimated on-hand currency for every item's ideal solution.

2. Calculate the potential inventory reduction for the sum of ideal versus recommended solutions.

Potential Ideal Kanban Inventory Reduction

$$\text{Potential ideal kanban inventory reduction} = \text{Ideal kanban OH\$ - Recommended kanban OH\$}$$

With this formula, an inventory reduction is a negative number.

Sort items to put the highest reductions at the top of the list, or insert a column that flags parts that exceed a certain inventory reduction threshold, using "1" for Yes and "0" for No.

Flag Items with High Reduction Potential

High reduction flag = IF (Ideal reduction < -10,000, "1", "0")

Sum this column to see how many items qualify as high reduction, which scopes the level of effort required to address those items. If 23 items each achieve a reduction of at least $10,000, those items would be a great place to start.

3. After flagging items that exceed a certain reduction threshold, use "SUMIF" to total the inventory column for flagged items.

Sum Reduction from High Potential Items

Total high reduction potential = SUMIF (Y2:Y1000, "1", W2:W1000)

This formula checks the reduction flag in column Y for the value "1" then sums the potential reduction in column W for all items that equal "1."

4. For every item that is a high priority, review the data to determine if the item requires a shorter lead time, a lower MOQ, a lower package quantity, or a combination of the three.

Rule of Thumb

Items that require a longer lead time are <u>usually</u> lower negotiation priorities because the advantage to be gained from longer lead times is in lower transaction costs.

However, if Receiving is always behind due to the high number of transactions per day, prioritize longer lead-time items in order to help the dock.

5. Create negotiation lists for high priority items.

• It is logical to tackle each supplier all at once, both high and low priority items, so that the supplier understands the breadth of what is requested of them. Start with suppliers that have the biggest potential impact, then sort each supplier's list to put high impacts at the top so the biggest movers get first attention.

• For internal parts, it is wise to divide workloads judiciously across planners and work cells. If one planner has 1,000 parts to tackle and another has 150, try to even the workload.

HINT for Associates

Remember that it is better to achieve a low MOQ versus a short lead time because a multi-card solution can address a long lead time, but that requires a reasonable MOQ.

It is likely for some ideal kanban solutions to predict higher average and maximum inventory than the recommended solution.

For example, if an item's current lead time is shorter than the target lead time, perhaps two days versus a target of 10 days, the ideal solution with the longer lead time will have a higher order quantity and therefore higher estimated inventory.

HINT for Associates

In the kanban calculator, create new tabs to manage action plans. Each tab can be sorted or filtered to fit the specific action plan category. So, a site might have a tab for every planner, a tab for every supplier, a tab for each cell that uses or stores kanban items, etc.

Effectively executing action plans is one of the most challenging assignments when managing a kanban system. Take time to sort and prioritize action plans. Assign those plans to specific people with specific due dates, then track progress versus the plan. As mentioned before, use action planning tabs to prioritize and track progress and ensure no one has more activity to tackle than they can handle.

If it isn't possible to deploy some of the *ideal* kanban solutions due to the need for external negotiations and internal improvement, deploy the *recommended* solutions to immediately match kanban solutions to current demand and supply conditions.

Follow this general order of deployment:

1. Resize items with negative safety stock for the *current* kanban solution. This has to happen rapidly! Right now! Today!

2. Resize items with potential for significant inventory reduction. These items often require time to bleed off inventory, as covered in the next section, so get the new kanban solutions on the floor as soon as possible.

3. Deploy kanban solutions for items being added to kanban, to expand kanban scope.

4. Update items that no longer qualify for kanban, which might entail taking kanban cards off the floor.

Inventory Reduction Timing

For every inventory reduction project, there is a bleed-off period during which excess on-hand inventory is consumed and replenishment parts are not ordered. This period varies for every item that has excess inventory, depending on how many excess parts are on hand at the start. It is common for some items to require months or even more than a year to bleed off excess inventory.

Therefore, it is wise to analyze inventory reduction plans very soon after kanban solutions are available in order to prevent an unreasonable inventory improvement assumption, such as a full reduction in 30 days or less. Many sites erroneously assume they can achieve "immediate reductions" from kanban deployment because they overlook or underestimate the bleed-off period. Even when kanban solutions are deployed immediately, it takes a while to bleed off excess inventory and achieve the predicted reduction.

Follow these steps to predict the timing for inventory reduction.

1. OH$ Reduction: Calculate the inventory reduction for each item by comparing current on-hand dollars to expected average inventory for the new kanban solution, from above.

Excess OH$

Expected Inventory Reduction $
= Current OH$ - Expected Average OH$

For this formula, a reduction is a <u>positive</u> number.

2. Each part can consume or "bleed off" a certain number of parts per week, so predict weekly bleed-off potential in both units and currency.

Weekly Bleed Off

Weekly bleed-off units
= Daily demand * # workdays per week

Weekly bleed-off dollars
= Weekly bleed-off units * standard cost

3. For every item, calculate the number of weeks required to bleed off excess inventory.

Number of Weeks to Bleed Off

Weeks to bleed off = Inventory Reduction $ / Weekly bleed off $

This divides the reduction in currency from Step 1 by weekly bleed off in Step 2. This assumes kanban solutions are fully deployed, and processes are in place to consume excess inventory *before* new material is ordered.

4. If a specific time period is under review for inventory reduction, such as "within the next 12 weeks" or "by the end of the fourth quarter," calculate how much reduction will occur in that time period.

For any item, bleed off over a certain period might be the entire estimated bleed off or it might be just a portion of the total reduction. Insert a column to capture the correct amount of reduction for the defined time period.

Excel Logic for Potential Reduction in a Certain Time Period

IF (# Weeks to Bleed Off Inventory < # of Weeks in Time Period, Estimated Inventory Reduction, Weekly Burn * # Weeks in Time Period)

This limits the predicted reduction to just what will occur within the evaluated time period.

Part Number Inventory Reduction

Item 08R32-V6 has an OHB of 1,975. The calculated EaB kanban solution is 2 cards at 500 pieces each. DD is 22, lead time is 20 days, and standard cost is $1.

Actual Safety Stock = KOQ * (# cards -1) - (LT * DD), = 500 - (22 * 20) = 500 - 440 = 60 parts

Expected OHB = KOQ / 2 + Actual SS, = 500/2 + 60 = 310 parts

Excess inventory is technically the amount above the expected maximum inventory, but let's see when we'll get to the right average inventory.

Excess inventory = Current OHB - Expected average OHB = 1975 - 310 = 1,665

Weekly burn = Workdays per week * Daily Demand = 5 * 22 = 110

Weeks to burn off excess = Excess Inventory / Weekly burn = 1,665 / 110 = 15.1 weeks

Standard cost is $2, so the expected inventory reduction is $3,950 - $620 = $3,330.

HINT for Associates

Getting down to the "estimated average inventory" is a deeper reduction than what is necessary to get within steady state for the kanban solution. As soon as OHB gets to estimated *maximum* balance, the item is operating within its sawtooth curve. Because we estimate <u>total</u> OH$ across an entire <u>population</u> of parts, bleed-off analysis measures the drop necessary to get to *average* inventory.

5. To obtain a site's total target reduction for a time period, sum the reductions for all items from Step 4.

6. For some parts, current inventory might be too low, meaning the resizing analysis revealed a kanban solution that increases on-hand inventory. If current inventory is lower than it should be, assume the increase to the new level occurs <u>immediately</u> and replenishment parts will arrive tomorrow.

7. Sum the total reduction for items with inventory to bleed off (Steps 1-5), and add back inventory for items that will increase (Step 6). The result is the expected aggregate change.

Inventory Reduction Example
(continued on next page)

We calculated ideal on-hand balances (OHB) and dollars (OH$) for every item and summed a total reduction of $1.2 million from the kanban data. We sorted the data in descending order of impact, or biggest inventory reductions at the top.

1. Purchased parts account for 72% of potential savings. (See table on next page.)

a. One supplier is responsible for 23% ($199,000 out of $864K) of the potential purchased part reduction, or 17% of the total reduction. But, that supplier is based on the other side of the world so long lead times can't be changed. That limitation takes those reductions off the table unless we re-source those parts closer to home. The team agrees to get quotes from regional suppliers to see if the off-shore supplier can be replaced for all or even a portion of the items. They estimate that just 20% of the parts can be re-sourced regionally at a reasonable cost.

b. Another supplier accounts for 15% ($130,000) of the potential purchased reduction and that supplier is less than 1 day's drive away. The Materials Manager believes they can get half of the desired lead time reduction, which equals 7% (50% * 15%) of the purchased parts target or 5% (7% * 72%) of the total reduction.

c. Twenty other random parts from various suppliers add up to 12% ($103,000) of the total. Each of those parts will be negotiated individually, with a goal of capturing 75% of the target.

d. Remaining items have reduction potential of less than $10K each, but they account for $432K of the possible reduction. Materials will try to get 10% of this potential, or $43K.

Inventory Reduction Example (continued from previous page and to next page)

e.g.

2. Internal parts account for the remaining 28% of possible savings.

a. One group of parts accounts for half of the identified reduction, but they go through an external process that adds 2 weeks to the lead time. Operations agrees to contact the outside source to see if it can be reduced to 1 week, which would capture 25% of this category or 3.5% (25% * 14%) of the total possible reduction.

b. The remaining reductions are random internal parts with long lead times. The Operations Manager agrees to cut at least 1 week from the longest parts, or 25% of the average lead time for those parts. This gives another 3.5% (25% * 14%) of the total reduction.

	Total Ideal Reduction	Predicted Success	Predicted $ Reduction
External	$864,000 (72% of $1.2M)		$225,250 (19% of $1.2M)
Overseas Supplier	$199,000	1a) 20%	$39,800
Long LT Supplier	$130,000	1b) 50%	$65,000
Random Parts	$103,000	1c) 75%	$77,250
Remaining Parts	$432,000	1d) 10%	$43,200
Internal	$336K (28% of $1.2M)		$84,000 (7% of $1.2M)
	$168,000	2a) 25%	$42,000
	$168,000	2b) 25%	$42,000
Total	$1,200,000 (100%)		$309,000 (26%)
$1.2M is the best case inventory reduction goal.		$309K is just 26% of the total potential reduction, but it is based on specific, achievable action plans.	

The intent of this exercise was to define what is <u>possible</u>, which is a different answer than what would be done in a <u>perfect</u> world if every ideal kanban solution was deployed. To define what reduction was likely, the team needed to create action plans for each group of parts.

Look at the numbers for a sanity check.

1. Purchased parts account for 72% of our total reduction potential. Do they also account for about 72% of the OH$? If not, we might have some erroneous data or assumptions.

The action plan cuts $3 in purchased parts for every $1 of internal parts, or $225K versus $84K, which is close to the 72%/28% split of the potential reduction. This indicates we're asking both internal and external items to contribute to the reduction. A plan should <u>never</u> beat up external suppliers while ignoring internal opportunities.

2. If current on-hand inventory is a lower number, say $2 million, a reduction of $300K is a huge success. But, if current OH$ is high, perhaps $10 million, it's a much smaller impact. Therefore, review the potential reduction versus current OH$ to determine the percent of inventory reduction that will occur, as well as the number of days on hand (DOH) that will be taken out of inventory.

a. If we have $2M on hand and expect to drop to about $1.7M, that's a 15% reduction in inventory dollars, and we can confirm this by calculating DOH before and after the reduction. If daily cost of goods sold (COGS) is $37,700, current inventory performance is 53 DOH, or $2M divided by $37,700. With the reduced OH$, DOH will drop to 45 [$1,700K / $37.7K = 45 DOH], which verifies the 15% improvement.

Aggregate Inventory Reduction Example (continued from previous page)

a. If we have $10 million in inventory, we'll drop to about $9.7M after kanban solutions are deployed, a drop of just 3%. If daily COGS is $190K, we'll go from 52.6 DOH [$10,000K / $190K] to 51.0 DOH [$9,700K / $190K], an improvement of 1.6 days, or just 3%.

Don't lose sight of overall DOH performance. To achieve 20 turns, which is a reasonable inventory performance target, we need to get to about 12.5 DOH, assuming 250 workdays per year. If we're currently in excess of 50 DOH, we need very aggressive plans to reduce overall inventory dollars, and 3% is not a big enough impact. Revisit the action plans.

HINTS for Associates

To prevent delays in bleeding off unneeded inventory, ensure that replenishment parts can't be ordered during the bleed-off period. Place "Do Not Order" stickers on kanban cards or insert some type of manual or electronic stops in the purchasing system.

Do not underestimate how long it will take to bleed down inventory! We can't launch a kanban project in November with 65 DOH and parts already on order and expect to hit a year-end reduction target of 20 days on hand!

The only way to accurately estimate bleed-off timing is to calculate estimated timing for individual parts, and then sum those items for aggregate inventory. This analysis is tedious but necessary.

If a kanban project or deployment is delayed, it will certainly delay the initiation of the bleed-off period. So, be aware of bleed-off challenges and delays. If the current ordering system is what resulted in high DOH, and that ordering system will be in place until kanban replaces it, there is no reason to believe the old system will magically start reducing on-hand inventory. Get busy!

Summary of Predicting Inventory Reduction

A robust kanban system aids in planning inventory reductions.

- Set reduction goals based on available data and specific action plans.
- Analyze the potential reduction from ideal kanban solutions and create a reasonable negotiation plan.
- Understand the timing it will take to bleed off inventory.

Predicting and managing activities to reduce inventory are critical aspects of *any* inventory management system. Please give this high attention and effort.

Tutorial: GOCO Kanban Analysis for Inventory Reduction

1. Mary added a column for Inventory Reduction.

> **Inventory Reduction**
>
> Inventory Reduction = Est_OH_ - OH_

This subtracted current OH$ from the Estimate, so a negative number meant inventory was projected to come down. Note that the defined names cut off the $ symbol at the end of each name in the formula. The actual column headers were Est OH$ and OH$.

2. She calculated how much would bleed off in 1 week for every PN.

> **Weekly Bleed Off**
>
> Weekly bleed off = -1 * Annual_Demand / 50 * Std_Cost

GOCO worked 250 workdays or 50 weeks per year, so Mary divided annual demand by 50 weeks to estimate weekly bleed off. This number was lower than the burn rate during peak season and higher than low season consumption, but it was "directionally correct" at any time of the year. Mary converted bleed off to a negative number by multiplying annual demand by (-1).

3. Mary wanted to know how many weeks it would take to bleed off every item and reach estimated average inventory. For any item that would increase inventory, she assumed additional inventory would be in place immediately, in Week 1. This wasn't entirely accurate because it would take time to order and receive parts. But, it was a safe assumption. It also communicated that early days of kanban deployment would show an increase in inventory.

> **Weeks to Bleed Off**
>
> Weeks to bleed off = IF (Inv_Reduction > 0, 1, Inv_Reduction / Weekly_Bleed_off)

4. Mary chose to calculate a 4-month bleed-off target, or 16 weeks of bleed, to provide a reason-

able target for the end of June's inventory balance. Any item with an inventory increase would see the entire effect immediately, so positive numbers were brought over as calculated. Any item that would achieve its entire bleed off in 4 months or less would pull the entire reduction, and those that exceeded 16 weeks would pull just 16 weeks of impact.

> **4-Month Bleed Off**
>
> 4-month bleed off = IF (Inv_Reduction > 0, Inv_Reduction, MAX (1 * Inv_Reduction, 16 * Weekly_Bleed_off))

When looking at 16 weeks of bleed off versus the entire possible reduction, Mary selected the MAX of the 2 numbers because they were both negative and she wanted the smaller impact. Yes, working with negative numbers can mess with your brain.

Remember that defined names don't work with functions like MAX, so [1 * Inv_Reduction] is how to force the MAX formula to work with defined names.

5. To identify items that had an MOQ high enough to drive a 1-card solution, she added a column to flag these parts for negotiation.

> **Negotiate MOQ**
>
> Negotiate MOQ = IF (MOQ_Days_Demand > (Target_LT + Target_SS) * _1_card_MOQ_Days_Demand_Allowance, 1, 0)

6. Next Mary found items that needed a shorter lead time using her defined cutoff parameter (LT_Multi_card_Multiple) that was equal to 2.0, or any lead time greater than twice the target lead time was on the negotiation list.

> **Negotiate Shorter LT**
>
> Negotiate Shorter LT = IF (New_LT > LT_Multi_card_Multiple * Target_LT, 1, 0)

7. Mary identified items that required a longer LT, though she knew those would be her lowest priority because they wouldn't reduce inventory dollars. The "Negotiate_Longer_LT" cutoff of 0.5 put any item with current lead time less than 50% of the target on the negotiation list.

Negotiate Longer LT	
Negotiate Longer LT = IF (New_LT < (Negotiate_Longer_LT * Target_LT), 1, 0)	⊜

Prioritize Action Plans

The team was ready to prioritize kanban action plans and summarize expected results. At the bottom of certain columns she inserted a SUM function to capture inventory totals, negotiation counts, etc. She created a new tab for summary data and added three summary tables, as shown in Figure 24-2.

Figure 24-2. **Summary Tables**

Inventory Data	Estimate		Kanban Solution Data	Count
Current OH$	$	23,212,755	Not Kanban	9
Estimated Avg OH$	$	6,129,420	1-card	7
Est Inventory Reduction	$	(17,083,335)	1-card VMI	9
4-Month Inv Reduction	$	(16,987,618)	2-card	39
Reduction %		-74%	DV Multi-card	41
			LT Multi-card	3
Negotiation Priorities	**Count**			108
MOQ	33			
Shorter LT	10			
Longer LT	0			

These tables put insightful statistics at Mary's fingertips.

1. The inventory reduction potential was enormous. Mary hoped to cut inventory in half by mid-year and the data indicated that goal should be possible.

2. Just 9 parts were not put on kanban.

3. Almost a third of the items needed a lower MOQ, but only 10 parts needed a shorter lead time.

With such high potential, Mary had to initiate action plans in the right order. She created a pivot table of inventory reduction sums by inventory category—raw material (RM), work in progress (WIP), and finished goods (FG)—versus ABC, in Figure 24-3.

Figure 24-3. **Inventory Reduction by Raw Material, Work in Progress, or Finished Goods versus ABC Classification**

Sum of Inv Reduction	Column Labels ▾			
Row Labels ▾	A	B	C	Grand Total
FG	$ (2,642,908)	$ (411,381)	$ (52,668)	$ (3,106,956)
RM	$ (1,431,346)	$ (1,796,267)	$ (1,036,215)	$ (4,263,827)
WIP	$ (4,067,902)	$ (2,752,782)	$ (2,891,868)	$ (9,712,552)
Grand Total	$ **(8,142,156)**	$ **(4,960,429)**	$ **(3,980,751)**	$ **(17,083,335)**

The highest potential was in WIP, which was not a surprise because the current-state value stream map (VSM) showed very high inventory, particularly out of Metal Forming. To confirm if Metal Forming itself showed up as a high priority in the data, Mary created a pivot table of supplier (Metal Forming is a supplier in the kanban system) versus ABC, in Figure 24-4. Metal Forming had an inventory reduction potential of more than $4M, while the highest potential for an external supplier was for GTP, with reduction potential of $1.4 million.

Figure 24-4. Inventory Reduction by Supplier & ABC

Sum of Inv Reduction Row Labels	A	B	C	Grand Total
Metal Form	$ (799,825)	$ (1,960,595)	$ (1,783,372)	$ (4,543,791)
Pack Assembly	$ (2,642,908)	$ (411,381)	$ (52,668)	$ (3,106,956)
GTP	$ (116,577)	$ (991,108)	$ (301,504)	$ (1,409,189)
Instrument Subassy	$ (1,181,491)	$ (80,330)	$ (13,067)	$ (1,274,888)
Meter Housing	$ (586,443)	$ (143,353)	$ (354,671)	$ (1,084,467)
Instrument Housing	$ (612,708)		$ (345,586)	$ (958,294)
Meter Subassy	$ (751,148)	$ (177,964)		$ (929,112)
Metal Works	$ (682,402)	$ (137,815)	$ (69,110)	$ (889,327)
Sensor Supply	$ (368,434)		$ (205,670)	$ (574,104)
Doodle Housing		$ (227,019)	$ (301,584)	$ (528,604)
Universal Display	$ (188,216)	$ (245,657)		$ (433,873)
Doodle Subassy	$ (136,286)	$ (163,521)	$ (93,588)	$ (393,395)
Hardware Runners		$ (194,999)	$ (189,966)	$ (384,965)
RPS	$ (75,717)	$ (121,294)	$ (112,134)	$ (309,145)
B&B General Supply		$ (105,393)	$ (155,697)	$ (261,090)
MPS			$ (2,134)	$ (2,134)
Grand Total	**$ (8,142,156)**	**$ (4,960,429)**	**$ (3,980,751)**	**$ (17,083,335)**

Metal Form had several inventory storage locations throughout the plant, so Mary realized that deploying Metal Form would impact numerous areas but none of them would be entirely converted to kanban until all internal and external parts were done. She elected to start with all Metal Form items despite this challenge, hitting items that fed the Instrument cells first. See Figure 24-5 on page 280 for where the biggest reductions would occur.

For the negotiation activity, Mary decided to wait a few months before contacting internal or external suppliers to request any changes because they had just responded to the GOCO data request with what should have been their best effort. Negotiating lower MOQs would be a good project once all of the kanban solutions had been deployed. Yes, it would drive resizing activity, but that could be timed to coincide with seasonal resizing and therefore would not add extra deployment effort.

Figure 24-5. <u>Inventory Reduction by Supplier vs. Where Used</u>

Sum of Inv Reduction — Column Labels

Row Labels	Assy	Doodle Assy	Doodle Housing	Doodle Subassy	Instrument Assy	Instrument Housing	Instrument Subassy	Metal Form	Meter Assy	Meter Housing	Meter Subassy	Pack	Sensor Assy	Grand Total
Metal Form			-$497,594	-$406,722	-$243,714	-$1,006,123	-$708,385		-$246,889	-$777,089	-$657,275			-$4,543,791
Pack Assembly												-$3,106,956		-$3,106,956
GTP													-$1,409,189	-$1,409,189
Instrument Subassy					-$1,274,888									-$1,274,888
Meter Housing									-$1,084,467					-$1,084,467
Instrument Housing					-$958,294									-$958,294
Meter Subassy									-$929,112					-$929,112
Metal Works								-$889,327						-$889,327
Sensor Supply													-$574,104	-$574,104
Doodle Housing		-$528,604												-$528,604
Universal Display													-$433,873	-$433,873
Doodle Subassy		-$393,395												-$393,395
Hardware Runners	-$179,938							-$71,235					-$133,792	-$384,965
RPS								-$309,145						-$309,145
B&B General Supply													-$261,090	-$261,090
MPS												-$2,134		-$2,134
Grand Total	-$179,938	-$921,999	-$497,594	-$406,722	-$2,476,896	-$1,006,123	-$708,385	-$1,269,707	-$2,260,468	-$777,089	-$657,275	-$3,109,090	-$2,812,048	-$17,083,335

SECTION VI. DEPLOY & MAINTAIN KANBAN SOLUTIONS

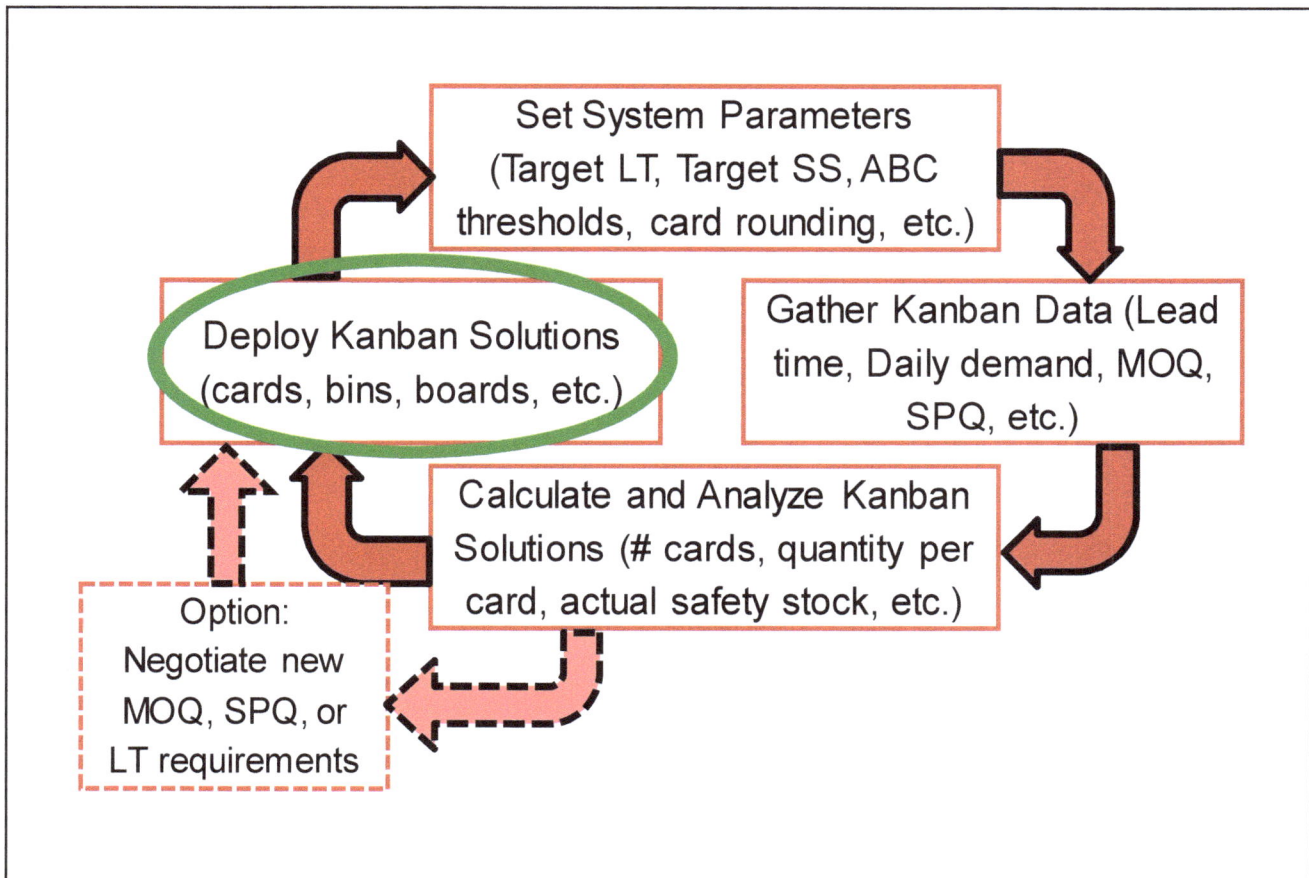

Set System Parameters (Target LT, Target SS, ABC thresholds, card rounding, etc.)

Gather Kanban Data (Lead time, Daily demand, MOQ, SPQ, etc.)

Calculate and Analyze Kanban Solutions (# cards, quantity per card, actual safety stock, etc.)

Deploy Kanban Solutions (cards, bins, boards, etc.)

Option: Negotiate new MOQ, SPQ, or LT requirements

Once kanban solutions are ready, it's time to design and deploy kanban boards, cards, and any other visual signals.

▌▌▌▌▌▌▌▌	KOQ: 1,000
P/N: 1234567	SPQ: 200
½" Round Steel Rod	ROP: N/A
Supplier: Acme Tools	Boxes/Card: 5
Planner: Metal Commodities	Total Cards: 2
Location: Welding B-3-4	LT: 10 days

CHAPTER 25: DESIGN & DEPLOY KANBAN CARDS

Once kanban solutions are finalized, it's time to print and deploy cards. In many sites this is a very frustrating part of launching or resizing kanban because it's tedious, time consuming, and prone to annoying errors. Errors might include a font that is too big to fit all the data on the card, type that's too small to read, a barcode that won't scan, incorrect information in one of the data fields, or the wrong color paper or ink used to print cards. Designing and deploying cards takes careful thought and planning.

What to Include on Kanban Cards

Must Have

See the top of this page for an example of a kanban card.

1. Part Number (PN) is an item's identifier in the financial or operational systems.

2. Description is an aid for associates because it avoids the need to memorize what every PN is. It helps ensure that cards are stored with the right items at point of use.

3. Supplier name can be either an internal cell or an external supplier.

4. Kanban contact is the person who manages the replenishment of the item, and this applies to both internal and external items. This is the item's go-to person for stock outs, order management questions, supplier questions, etc.

The risk with putting this on a kanban card is that if PN assignments change and actual *names* are on the cards, new cards have to be printed and deployed. Instead of using names, create planner codes for groups of parts and print those codes on cards. For example, if all wire harnesses are assigned to one buyer, create a buyer code called "Wire Harn."

5. Location, or where parts are stored. This makes it easy to put parts away.

6. Kanban order quantity (KOQ) is the quantity ordered each time a kanban signal is processed.

7. Standard package quantity (SPQ) is the quantity per box or container.

8. Reorder point (ROP) is the inventory level at which a replenishment order is triggered for a 1-card solution. This is not required for solutions with more than 1 card.

9. Containers per card indicates how many packages make up one kanban order. This is necessary whenever more than one container makes up one kanban order, or when 1 card covers more than one container. This might be labeled boxes per card, totes per card, buckets per card, etc., depending on the type of container.

10. Total cards or maximum cards is the highest number of cards that can be deployed for an item. This information is required for card audits. If a multi-card solution has 5 cards, we must find a total of 5 cards: cards with inventory, plus cards on the kanban board, plus cards pulled off the floor in "inactive" status.

11. Lead time (LT) is the number of workdays from order entry to receipt of a replenishment order. Lead time is in workdays.

Other Fields to Consider

1. Barcode, or any type of scannable image, is necessary if triggers or receipts are accomplished by a scanning system.

2. ABC classification is beneficial if ABC is used to manage parts on the floor. For example, if the cycle count process tracks ABC classification for every item that is counted, having it on the card makes it easy to verify.

3. <u>Card revision,</u> or print date, is when the kanban solution was established. When deploying new cards to replace existing cards, having the revision number or print date on the cards makes it easier to tell which cards are the old ones and which are new. It seems simple, but sorting old cards from new can be challenging without this aid.

4. <u>Supplier PN</u> is helpful if the item has one part number internally but a different number from the supplier.

Vary Content By Kanban Type

Utilizing more than one card layout adds complexity, but it can streamline card content for items that don't need all data fields. For example, re-order point (ROP) is needed for 1-card solutions but not for any other card. Supplier part number is never required for an internal part. So, sometimes it makes sense to have unique card layouts or content for certain kinds of cards.

Card Layout

Ensure that card layout is organized and easy to read. Do not use small fonts on kanban cards. Cards should be easy to read, even for people over 40. A kanban card is not an eye test!

Despite the need for a readable font that isn't too small, don't use over-sized cards. Cards that approach a quarter of a sheet of paper (about 4 x 5 inches or 10 x 12 cm) are too big because the large size has negative implications for kanban board design. A kanban board requires 31 date positions plus places for cards to be scanned, stock outs, past due orders, and orders due in more than 31 days. Large kanban cards result in very large kanban boards, which are more difficult to physically position and visually audit. When designing kanban cards, try to utilize a layout that is about the size of a credit card or business card.

Real-World Observation

I worked with a site that used 8½" x 11" orange paper for finished goods cards. They thought large cards would be easy to read when items were stored in tall racks, which was somewhat true, and that cards wouldn't get lost because they were bright orange and very large. Even after a couple of months on kanban, they still had to reprint cards periodically to replace those that were shipped with finished goods. (No, they weren't very good at adhering to standard work.)

This proves that large cards are no more safe from being lost than small cards. Losing cards is based on discipline and process management, not card size and color.

Card Material

Paper Cards

For many years the only reasonable option for kanban cards was printing on white or colored paper followed by either laminating the cards or placing them in plastic sleeves to make them durable enough to survive on the floor. This is still a viable way to produce cards, but there are advantages and disadvantages.

Advantages

+   It's easy to utilize different colors of paper, but remember to check the printer for the right color paper before you submit a print job.

+   Printing black text on colored paper can be relatively cheap and quick.

+   Anyone can generate new kanban cards if they are connected to a good printer, so cards don't have to be managed by one central person.

Disadvantages

- Even in the most benign environments, like hospitals, paper cards must be protected to provide any kind of durability, so lamination or plastic sleeves are necessary. Don't ignore the cost of preparing paper cards for deployment, both the material and time required.

- It takes a lot of time to print cards and sleeve or laminate them, which causes a delay from when kanban solutions are ready until cards can be deployed. Preparing new cards is what makes some sites delay kanban resizing due to the number of labor hours required to create new cards.

- Full sheets of paper make very large kanban cards, so paper cards have to be cut to size or separated at predefined perforations, which adds extra work.

- A printed kanban card in a trash can looks like any other piece of wastepaper, even if laminated or in a sleeve, so it is possible for them to be disposed of accidentally.

Disposable Paper Cards

Disposable cards are paper cards that are printed every time an order is either generated or received, and they are generally not put in sleeves or laminated. These cards are temporary so as soon as the order is consumed or received, depending on the specific process, the card is thrown away. Unlike traditional cards, disposable cards may or may not stay with inventory at point of use.

The risk with these cards is that it is difficult to accurately time the "keep" and "destroy" steps, making kanban audits more challenging. Generating a card for every order also adds a lot of work.

Plastic Cards

Printed plastic cards (imagine a credit card or plastic hotel key card) have gained in popularity as one of the best kanban card options. A good "card" printer with either white or colored cards allows them to be printed and deployed with no secondary processes, i.e., no lamination.

In addition to the durability and ease of printing, these cards can be written on with a dry erase marker or a grease pencil so it's easy to write due dates or other information on the card, as in Figure 25-1.

Figure 25-1. Plastic Cards with Due Dates Written on the Back

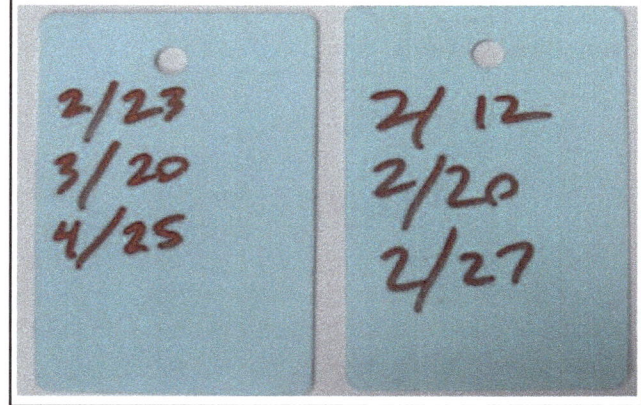

Plastic cards are cost effective and durable and many sites discover additional uses for the card printer, such as employee identification cards or visitor badges.

The disadvantage is that plastic cards require a special printer and specific cards, but these are readily available.

Some people question the small size of plastic cards, thinking they would be easy to lose, but losing cards generally has less to do with the size of the card and more to do with a lack of robust processes for card travel and placement, as described in the Real-World Observation on the prior page.

Card Color

Consider using various colors to assist kanban processes on the floor.

• Purchased parts vs. manufactured items

• Spike cards

• Material from certain suppliers

• Material for specific cells or value streams

• Material that goes to an outside partner for processing then returns to our site for final steps

• 1-card solutions that require special handling to manage reorder point (ROP) counts

---

HINT for Leaders

At a minimum, consider color coding the following kanban card features:

Color 1 = Purchased parts
Color 2 = Internal parts
Color 3 = Spike cards

Virtual Cards

Some sites operate without physical cards, using "virtual" or electronic signals instead. A virtual card means there are no physical cards. Instead, "cards" are records in a computer system.

Some virtual systems break the link between replenishment triggers and consumption, allowing the electronic system to issue orders based on inventory balances in the system. This has the same risks as MRP, specifically on-hand balance and order management errors.

Other virtual systems trigger orders based on consumption, like traditional kanban. One common approach is to put each item's barcode at point of use, e.g., on the bin itself, to scan when a bin is opened or emptied. This can work but there is a risk that triggers can get out of sync with orders and inventory, since the permanent "card" is always on the front of the bin.

It is impossible to visually audit virtual kanban cards to determine how many cards are assigned to parts or waiting for orders versus the total allowed cards for an item.

To audit virtual cards, follow these steps:

1. Look at records in the electronic system to see how many open replenishment orders exist.

2. Compare the number of open orders to the total number of cards. Any card that isn't linked to an order should represent current inventory.

3. Check physical on-hand inventory—not inventory in the system—to see if current inventory matches what the system expects to find, based on card count from step 2.

A virtual kanban audit is essentially a computer check versus what is on the floor, which is a tedious version of a cycle count.

Some sites that utilize virtual cards choose to forego any type of card audit. In that case, consider increasing target safety stock to cover system and process errors that won't be caught by regular kanban audits.

Place Kanban Boards

• Kanban boards should be near where inventory is stored so that associates don't have to travel too far to retrieve cards when material arrives or to put "to be scanned" cards on the board.

• Boards should be easy to reach, with nothing in front of them to get in the way of interacting with the board.

• Boards should not be too high or too low from the floor, for ease of managing the pegs or slots.

• Provide good lighting so associates can read cards at the board.

• If cards are scanned to generate a replenishment order, put a scanner at the board so cards don't leave the area. This reduces the risk of lost cards.

Decide How Many Boards Are Needed

Boards should manage a reasonable number of kanban cards to ensure that any date peg won't have to hold too many cards. In many sites this doesn't come into play, but it can be a factor for areas where a high number of items is managed by one kanban board.

One disadvantage to having too many cards on 1 board is that when replenishment orders arrive, someone has to find the right kanban cards to put with incoming material. They might have to shuffle through 15-25 cards on any given peg to find the right one. But, if cards are well designed and easy to read this should be quick.

Follow these steps to decide if a board can handle a group of kanban items.

1. At any given time, 31 date pegs on a kanban board equal approximately 22 workdays and 9 weekend days, the ratio of 5 workdays for every 2 weekend days for a plant with a 5-day work week.

2. Estimate how many cards 1 slot or peg can hold. If 1 peg can hold 10 kanban cards, 22 workday pegs can hold 220 cards. Orders are always due on a workday, so weekend and holiday pegs don't count.

3. EaB and BaB have different card paths.

» For every EaB card on a board, there is usually another associated card at point of use with on-hand inventory. So, in general there is an equal number of cards at point of use as are on the board. This varies based on the number of 1-card or multi-card solutions, but an EaB kanban board should plan to store half of the cards for a designated inventory store.

» BaB cards are often both on the board, so plan for the board to be capable of holding all kanban cards as a maximum load.

Number of Kanban Boards Versus Number of Cards

A production cell has 500 EaB cards to cover 190 PNs, made up of a combination of 1-card, 2-card, and multi-card solutions. With 500 cards, the kanban board for this cell must be able to store about 250 cards. A nearby production cell has 400 cards for 210 PNs. If we combine the 2 cells onto 1 kanban board, the board must be able to store about 450 cards.

We use plastic cards, and a stack of 20 cards is 0.75" high. The date pegs easily hold 1.5" of cards, so 40 cards per peg is reasonable. If 22 pegs are workdays and 9 are weekend days, and each workday peg holds 40 cards, the board can hold [40 cards per peg * 22 pegs = 880 cards]. This board should easily accommodate both sets of cards.

Rule of Thumb

An EaB kanban board should be sized to hold 50% of the maximum number of cards that could be simultaneously deployed for the items that are managed by the board. BaB boards should handle up to 100% of assigned cards.

Prioritize Kanban Deployment

Once kanban boards are up and cards are ready, determine the card roll-out sequence, both for first-time kanban deployment or resizing.

Kanban Deployment Priority: Prevent Stock Outs

If existing kanban solutions are deployed and some have negative safety stock, begin by resizing those items to prevent delivery issues.

Kanban Deployment Option: Purchased Parts

Many sites begin first-time kanban deployment activity with external suppliers, and there are a couple of good reasons to do this.

+ Because purchased parts are delivered in batches and flow can't be sustained, they are perfect for kanban.

+ Many sites have high on-hand dollars in raw material, so it's a logical place to seek inventory reductions.

As usual, there are also some risks to starting with purchased parts and external suppliers.

- If kanban deployment fails, for example due to replenishment quantities that are sized incorrectly, inaccurate lead-time data, trouble deploying cards, or failing to process orders correctly, our internal errors impact the suppliers. This can cause strain on suppliers' processes and our working relationship with them.

- Deploying *just* purchased parts means any cell that consumes both purchased and manufactured items will be partly on kanban (purchased parts) and partly on MRP (manufactured parts), which can be confusing for floor associates who execute replenishment orders or audit kanban cards.

- Sites often have many external suppliers so deploying purchased parts is a big commitment. Some suppliers are naturally a higher priority for kanban due to high annual spend, better kanban readiness, or a need for delivery improvement, so they are a great place to start.

Kanban Deployment Option: Specific Cells

Select one to three cells with a reasonable number of items for initial kanban deployment.

+ This is usually a good approach because it tackles internal and external items so the work cell is 100% converted to kanban.

- Some sites get hung up on making the first kanban cell "perfect" and they delay kanban deployment for additional cells. To avoid this trap there should be a clear list of deployment priorities to follow the first cell. Those next projects should be initiated within four to six weeks after the first cell is completed.

- Internal and external suppliers will see some items convert to kanban while others stay on MRP. To most suppliers this is invisible because the primary change for them is that kanban orders are always for the same quantity and at the standard lead time, so this should be easily managed. It's generally easier to have suppliers on both kanban and MRP than to have a production cell on both kanban and MRP.

HINT for Leaders

Some sites set out to build a "model" Lean cell and get it to perfection before expanding Lean to the next cell. What they actually build is an isolated island of Lean activity surrounded by a wide moat of Lean ignorance and apathy. This approach insulates most workers from Lean, and the model cell becomes nothing more than a delay tactic while leaders chase perfection instead of continuous improvement.

Don't get hung up on perfection!

Kanban Deployment Option: Value Stream

Select a value stream or product family that crosses numerous cells, which usually stretches from Receiving through finished goods.

+ This can significantly aid a product family that is struggling with delivery or inventory issues. If a certain value stream is a high priority for operational improvement, kanban is a good tool to assist in that endeavor.

- The risk with this approach is that it touches several cells and suppliers so it can be a daunting task, particularly if kanban is new for a site.

- Like other approaches, this can be risky if kanban deployment impacts a shared resource, where some items in a cell are put on kanban while others stay on MRP. This is the same type of risk as deploying purchased parts before manufactured parts.

HINT for Associates

If you select a value stream or product family that contains numerous cells and thousands of parts, prioritize the deployment plan. An entire value stream is usually too big to do all at once, so select one or two cells within the overall stream as the first deployment areas. This blends "focus on specific cells" with "focus on a value stream."

Deploy Kanban Cards

This process is rather straightforward, but it is time consuming and requires sound logic. The goal is to match every card with either on-hand inventory or incoming orders.

Card Deployment Logic

Every kanban card represents a certain number of pieces, e.g., 100 pounds per card, so the goal of deployment is to divide open orders and OHB into right-sized buckets as defined by the kanban quantity. This links all cards to either inventory or orders.

Many items will have too little or too much inventory. So, when the deployment process is complete, we have three groups of items based on actions that need to be taken.

1. Bleed Off: Parts with excess inventory must bleed off inventory before another replenishment order is processed. If there are space limitations where the part will be stored under the new kanban plan, establish a temporary excess location and clearly mark it as such. As associates consume parts at point of use (POU), they will go to the excess location to replenish instead of processing an order. Do not allow a card to be processed or scanned until all excess parts have been used.

Find a way to visually flag these parts as bleed off, such as covering the barcode with red tape or including a "DO NOT ORDER" label on the kanban card.

2. Expedite: Items that don't have enough inventory on hand or on order must be expedited. These parts have high stock-out risk, so orders should be processed immediately.

Issuing orders for a multi-card item is the most challenging scenario. Ideally it makes sense to stagger multi-card replenishment orders with reasonable gaps between sequential orders that approximate standard lead time. For example, a 5-day lead time would have 1 order due in 1 week and the next due in 2 weeks. But, this can be difficult to coordinate because figuring out due dates and spacing orders over time can be tedious to calculate and to enter in the system. If exact spacing can't be achieved, place all needed orders at once—but as individual orders—and explain to the supplier that they are multiple orders and therefore should not arrive all at once. Ask the supplier to spread them out at lead time pacing, or at least with reasonable gaps. When parts arrive, match them to cards and get the system working as designed.

3. Steady State: For items that are in some kind of normal pattern, for example, no excess parts and no shortages, assign every card either to inventory or to an incoming order. These parts might be out of balance, such as when all the cards are with inventory at POU and nothing is on order or when too few are on the shelf but there are plenty on order. Those abnormal conditions will work out as parts are consumed and new orders are processed.

> **Rule of Thumb**
>
> If employees are new to kanban, deploy no more than 500 cards—not part numbers—as a first step. Don't overwhelm them!

Point-of-Use Storage & Multi-Card Solutions

Even for a multi-card solution, don't *expect* or *plan* for all cards to be on-hand at the same time but instead expect to have about one or two kanban quantities on hand at any given time, or maybe up to a day of inventory.

Never plan room for extra parts at POU! Extra or unnecessary storage space shouldn't be provided because it adds to the required space allocation and can cause associates to walk more to cover their work area.

For an Extremely High Card Count at Point of Use

Use common sense and logic when designing storage space for very high card counts. Suppose an item has a maximum order quantity (MaxQ) that forces a very high card count on a multi-card solution. If an item has 50 cards to cover 20 days of lead time, the receiving cell will use about [50 cards / 20 days] = 2.5 cards of material per day. So, the consuming cell will process 2 or 3 cards per day and the supplying cell will receive 2 or 3 orders per day. Plan accordingly and allow for about 1 day of inventory at POU, or 3 to 4 kanban bins.

Real-World Observation

An internal item had daily demand (DD) of 1200, but a MaxQ of 800. Lead time for the item was 15 days, plus target safety stock of 4 days.

For a 2-card BaB, KOQ = [(1200 * 15 day LT) + (4 day SS * 1200)] / 2 = 11,400

Yikes! The MaxQ of 800 is just 7% of what is required by two cards. This item needs a multi-card solution. But, we can't calculate card count based on BaB order quantity, so we must use the lead-time demand formula.

cards = [(1200 * 15 day LT) + (4 day SS * 1200)] / 800 = 28.5, round up to 29 cards

The cell that used this item processed 1.5 cards per day (consume 1200 per day versus 800 per order) so the supplying cell had to produce 1 or 2 orders per day. Therefore, there were never more than 2-3 kanban "bins" on the shelf at the consuming cell even though there were 29 cards.

Match Cards to Orders & Parts

When deploying physical cards, each card ends up in one of three places:

1. On a kanban board waiting for parts to arrive, on the due date for the associated purchase or manufacturing order.

2. With inventory at the storage location.

3. Designated as "to be ordered." These will end up on the kanban board as soon as orders are issued.

When deploying cards, match orders and inventory to cards until all cards are assigned.

1. Match cards to open orders, either purchase orders for external parts or manufacturing orders for internal parts. These cards go on the appropriate date peg on the kanban board to wait for parts to arrive. To complete this step we need an accurate list of incoming parts, both due date and quantity per order, sorted by PN. Existing replen-ishment orders will likely be for quantities that do not match new KOQs, so it might be necessary to match more than 1 card to upcoming orders, unless open order quantities can be adjusted by suppliers.

Always start with matching cards to orders, not to on-hand inventory! This prevents cards from being processed on the floor if excess orders already exist.

2. Match remaining cards to on-hand parts by allocating the correct quantity to each available card. Every inventory piece has a card for EaB, but only full order quantities have a card for BaB.

3. Process new orders for any remaining cards, and put cards on the board on the correct date for the new order.

Deploy Empty-a-Bin Cards

When deploying kanban cards for the first time in an EaB kanban system, it can be confusing to match cards to on-hand pieces due to the flexible number of on-hand parts associated with one card. A quantity equal to the KOQ gets 1 card, but 1 piece in stock also gets a card. If the total OHB is [KOQ + 1] we need 2 cards, 1 for the full KOQ and 1 for the single additional piece.

Divide on-hand parts into quantities equal to the KOQ. Every quantity equal to 1 kanban order quantity gets 1 card and any partial quantity also gets a card. If there aren't enough on-hand parts to cover the number of cards, scan the leftover cards to place new orders and hang those cards on the kanban board to wait for parts to arrive.

It is possible, and even likely, that some items will have more parts on hand than there are cards to cover them, which is called "excess inventory." This requires special procedures to avoid ordering replenishment pieces before they are needed.

EaB Excess Inventory

If excess inventory exists, follow this general process:

1. When deploying cards for excess inventory, put inventory at POU in standard kanban quantities with kanban cards. When a kanban bin is

emptied, refill the kanban quantity using internal excess inventory. Do not allow cards on the floor to generate purchase or manufacturing orders until all excess inventory is consumed and the item is within "steady state" conditions. This might mean putting tape over the barcode, or attaching a "Do Not Order - Pull From Excess Inventory" label to the cards.

2. Do not "oversize" allowed storage space to accommodate excess inventory. If we do this, when the excess is gone we have to shrink the storage areas down to the right size. Instead, store the correct amount of inventory at POU, and put excess inventory in a well-marked and easily accessible area.

3. Audit excess items very carefully until excess inventory is consumed to ensure that cards do not get delayed after excess inventory is gone.

> **Empty-a-Bin Trigger Example**
>
> An EaB item has a KOQ of 200 and the item arrives in boxes of 100, so 1 order equals 2 boxes. To assign cards to parts on the floor, every quantity of 200 parts gets a card, and any remaining quantity from 1 up to 199 parts equals a card. So, an on-hand quantity from 1–200 equals 1 card, from 201–400 is 2 cards, 401–600 is 3 cards, and so on. If an item has just 2 cards but more than 400 pieces on hand, we have excess inventory.

Deploy Break-a-Bin Cards

Because one BaB card always equals a full KOQ, it's easier to deploy cards for BaB than for EaB. If a card equals 2 boxes of 100 pieces, a BaB card always has 2 full boxes with the card.

Like EaB, start by sorting on-hand parts into quantities equal to the KOQ. Put a card with every full order quantity and leave any remaining parts that sum to less than a full KOQ without a card. Like EaB, unassigned cards are scanned and hung on the kanban board, and excess inventory is handled with care.

BaB Excess Inventory

If excess inventory exists, follow the process described above for EaB.

> **Break-a-Bin Trigger Example**
>
> A BaB item has a KOQ of 200 parts. It arrives in boxes of 100, so 1 order equals 2 boxes. To link cards to parts, any quantity of exactly 200 parts equals a card. So, an on-hand quantity from 1–199 equals 0 cards, 200–399 is 1 card, 400–599 is 3 cards, and so on.

> *Do not rush the card deployment process. Kanban won't work in an atmosphere of "make something up and deploy some cards." If that's the case, cancel all deployment activity and get the kanban process right first.*
>
> *Deploying cards takes a lot of time and effort. It is often the first time the broader organization is exposed to kanban, so get it right. Do not complete this process with bad cards or haphazard kanban standard work.*

Card Deployment Examples

Review the following examples to see how to handle various deployment situations.

> **Card Deployment, Excess on Order**
>
> For item ABC123, each card equals 100 parts, and there are 2 cards. We have 255 parts on order, due in 2 weeks as a single order. This quantity does not match the new KOQ, so we need to decide how to assign parts to 2 cards.
>
> It's easiest to place 2 cards on the board on the due date for the open order. When parts arrive, parts are placed in 2 bins of 100 each with a kanban card with each bin. The extra 55 pieces are placed in the front bin because they are considered excess inventory since we assigned them to a card that needed 100 parts but received 155 parts.

Card Deployment, Low Replenishment Quantities on Order

e.g.

PN 56789 has 1200 parts per card, and we have an open order for 200 due tomorrow. There are 2 ways to handle an order for such a low quantity.

Option 1: Put 1 card on the board for tomorrow, the due date. When parts arrive place them at point of use with the card, behind any other inventory so we adhere to first-in-first-out (FIFO). The card will cycle faster than a typical card due to the low quantity of parts. The risk is that if there are several small open orders due on different dates, we use up a lot of cards by putting 1 card with each small order. Don't commit too many cards to small orders.

Option 2: Don't assign a card to that order, and when the parts arrive put them in an existing bin with the card that is already linked to on-hand inventory, adding new parts to what is already on hand.

For EaB, this works if there are parts on the floor with at least 1 card. Put the incoming 200 new pieces in the current active bin so that they get consumed before a card is processed. We essentially treat these as excess inventory. If we must strictly obey FIFO, put them with the last bin so that they are used last but are still included with an existing card on the floor.

For BaB, if there are parts on the floor the new parts can go with those. But, if no parts are on the floor then these new parts should have a card when they go to the floor so that it can be triggered when the first piece is consumed.

These situations are really risky so watch them carefully. No matter how they are handled, these orders do not follow standard kanban processes for how an incoming order is matched to a card. Do not use non-standard processes for more than 1 or 2 orders per PN or for more than a couple of weeks after initial kanban deployment. Sometimes it helps to create a temporary card for these orders (e.g., "place with current inventory with an existing card") to remind associates of the special handling.

Card Deployment, Cards Assigned to Incoming Orders

e.g.

Part NU45678 has 100 parts per card and 2 cards. We placed 2 cards on the kanban board for incoming orders. So, there are no cards for on-hand inventory, which is in an over-stock situation. This means all on-hand inventory should be consumed without placing a new order because we have material on the way that covers the 2 available cards.

When new orders arrive, material goes to the floor with the card from the kanban board. Put material behind existing inventory to honor FIFO. If inventory can't be placed at POU but is stored in excess storage, new parts are added to the back of that excess storage area so that all excess inventory is used before a card is processed.

There is a potential risk with this scenario if incoming orders are for low quantities and we put cards on the board for quantities that are less than the standard KOQ. Suppose we have 60 parts coming in 1 week and 50 parts coming in 2 weeks, and we assigned 2 cards to those orders. We will eventually run out of inventory or be in an expedite situation because cards are undersized (50 or 60 parts per card instead of 100) due to the low quantity assigned to these 2 cards. For this reason, be careful when assigning cards to incoming orders.

Card Deployment, Insufficient on Order

e.g.

Part BE35791 has 100 parts per card and 5 cards on EaB. We assigned 1 card to an incoming order, so there are 4 cards to match to parts on the floor, but only 62 parts on hand.

Place 1 card with inventory and the other 3 in the "To Be Ordered" stack. Ideally, we would stagger these orders so that they arrive periodically, with gaps that approximate the lead time. But, the simplest approach is to process all 3 cards at once. Inform the supplier that replenishment orders got behind but we are catching up and these are separate orders and parts should not arrive all at once.

Put parts with cards as they arrive to get into a steady state sawtooth curve pattern.

Card Deployment, Overstock

e.g.

Part HI46810 has 100 parts per card and 4 total cards. We assigned 2 cards to incoming orders and there are 652 parts on the shelf. We are in a severe overstock situation because 2 cards on the floor must cover 652 parts versus the 200 that should be covered. For steady state kanban to be achieved, we need to put 552 parts with 1 card at the front of POU and 100 parts with the second card. It isn't reasonable to expect that 552 parts will fit at POU, so utilize an excess storage area and mark the bin at POU with "DO NOT ORDER. PULL FROM EXCESS" so that associates know to pull parts from excess versus placing an order.

When new parts come in for open orders, place them in the back of excess storage, behind the card of 100 parts we already established so that they are last in the FIFO line.

Be very diligent when bleeding off excess parts to ensure that some level of FIFO is maintained and excess parts are consumed before new orders are placed.

HINT for Associates

Don't lose track of the excess inventory situation. If it takes months to get to steady state, someone must keep an eye on the bleed off occurring in excess inventory. Make excess inventory storage this part of kanban audits.

HINT for Leaders

The reason we deploy cards to open orders before assigning them to on-hand inventory is to avoid excess inventory. If existing open orders cover all available cards for an item, we don't want any cards at POU that could be scanned to create more orders.

Break-a-Bin Versus Empty-a-Bin Card Processing

The mechanics for consuming parts and managing cards is different for BaB versus EaB.

Break a Bin

1. The "front" or active bin is where parts are being pulled, and the card is turned in as soon as the first piece is used.

2. When the front bin is emptied, the second bin is pulled forward.

3. The "second" card, the one just pulled to the front or "active" position is triggered as soon as the first piece is used.

4. When the next replenishment order arrives, the one that was ordered days ago when the first piece came out of the first bin, the card is taken from the board and placed with the bin to the rear of the active bin.

5. The active bin has no card (it was turned in at Step 3) and the second bin has a card (it was put with parts on the shelf in Step 4). When the active bin is emptied and the second bin is opened, the second bin's card is turned in and for a time period both cards are on the kanban board waiting for orders to arrive.

Empty a Bin

1. A card stays with the parts until the bin is empty. The front or active bin has a card, and the second card is either hanging on the board waiting for a replenishment order or with a second bin of parts on the shelf.

2. When the active bin is emptied, the card is scanned and hung on the board, and the back bin is pulled forward with its card.

3. EaB doesn't have both cards on the board simultaneously <u>unless</u> we run out of parts.

Point-of-Use Space Limit

e.g.

A cell uses large parts that can't be stored in full kanban quantities at point of use due to space limitations. To accommodate this, parts are stored on a rack outside the cell and transferred to point of use as needed. An entire kanban order quantity can't be moved at once so manageable quantities are moved at the request of the cell.

The best way to manage this is to trigger replenishment orders at the storage location instead of at point of use. Replenishment orders will arrive there, so the kanban board should also be there. Processing cards at the storage point instead of the consuming cell separates physical consumption from generating a new order but it maintains the visual integrity of matching parts to cards, or knowing when a card should be triggered or when a replenishment order has arrived.

Note that orders will be triggered before parts have truly been consumed because triggers are linked to <u>moving</u> parts not to when the cell <u>uses</u> parts. This introduces unintended safety stock but if parts are moved in low quantities it should be minimal.

Triggering orders at point of use instead of at the storage location will work if cell associates get cards with parts. This requires storage associates to track empty a bin or break a bin status to send the card to the cell at the right time. When the storage team either opens a new order quantity (BaB) or empties a bin (EaB), they send the card with the parts to the cell. At the cell, if a part is on EaB and the card comes with parts, they know to trigger an order when they use the last piece in that group of parts. For BaB, when the cell gets the card they trigger an order as soon as they use the first piece from that group of parts. One major downside to this approach is that cards are held at two locations, both storage and point of use, which makes audits more difficult and also increases the risk of lost cards.

Special Kanban Cards

There are special kanban card designs or processes that apply to some situations.

Spike Cards

Spike cards insert extra inventory into a kanban solution to address a temporary increase in demand. Spike cards should <u>not</u> be used as an alternative to resizing kanban solutions.

There are several reasons spike cards can be required.

Spike for Past Due Demand

One of the most common reasons to deploy spike cards is to catch up with past-due customer demand.

Suppose a piece of equipment broke down and stopped production in a cell for 2 weeks. Daily demand is 100 pieces, and the cell missed 10 workdays, so when the equipment is repaired they are past due by 1,000 parts.

While the cell was down, they couldn't cycle kanban cards based on consumption. So, when the cell starts back up, they have enough inventory to run 100 per day as planned. At that level of material, they can't increase output to catch up on 1,000 late pieces. They need a higher level of inventory.

The cell has to decide how quickly they will produce the 1,000 late pieces or how much their daily output will increase in their state of accelerated production. They normally work 37.5 hours per week, or 8 hours per day minus 30 minutes per day for breaks and clean-up.

They need to be caught up with all past due orders in 4 weeks, so they must cover 2 weeks of past due orders, or 75 hours of work [37.5 work hours per week * 2], in 4 weeks, which is 18.75 hours of overtime per week.

If they add 2 hours of overtime per day plus 8 hours on Saturday, they work 10 daily hours per week plus 7.5 Saturday hours, or 17.5 *extra* hours per week. They decide to add an extra hour to every Saturday (9-hour days) to give them 18.5 hours of overtime per week. This misses the goal of 18.75 by a small margin. They hope they can increase output slightly by reducing changeover as a percent of total time due to the longer runs they will have while producing at a higher level.

During this 4 week period, they need 250 more pieces than what they would normally use, or [1,000 / 4 = 250 per week].

For every item impacted by the shutdown, they want to order spike quantities equal to the kanban order quantity (KOQ) of 100 to ensure that suppliers can utilize existing set-up plans and packaging.

• Week 1: Plan orders for 3 spike cards for 100 each. At the end of Week 1, they have 50 spike parts left from the 300 they received from 3 orders.

• Week 2: 2 spike orders plus the 50 parts left from Week 1, and end the week with zero extra spike parts.

• Week 3: 3 spike orders, and end the week with 50 extra parts.

• Week 4: 2 spike orders, and end the week with no extra spike parts.

Some sites handle past due situations by artificially scanning kanban cards while the cell is down, so suppliers continue to see replenishment signals. This works, but it takes just as much effort as the post-breakdown spike card approach, and inventory piles up while the cell is down. Inventory storage can also be an issue for many cells, so the "artificial scanning" approach is often not physically feasible due to limited storage space.

Remember to adjust the spike card plan for any items used at more than "one per" for a past due item. If a screw is used at the rate of 4 per motor assembly, order 4 times as many screws as motors.

Spike for Short-Term Demand Increase

Spike cards are also issued to address a short-term increase in demand when there is no need to resize the permanent kanban solution. Suppose a customer informs us that they are opening a new warehouse and need to increase their order quantities by 30% for 4 weeks to fill the new site. Address this temporary increase with spike cards for the affected parts, using logic similar to the above example.

Spike for Prebuild & Capacity Management

Sometimes spike cards are issued in advance of a high demand season as a way to manage capacity. Suppose a cell can produce 100 parts per day at maximum output. During low season they only need 80 per day, but during high season they need 120. So, they elect to prebuild inventory during the low season to cover the future spike. These orders can be covered by spike or "reserve inventory" cards, and during peak season the prebuilt inventory is held in reserve until regular kanban inventory is consumed and a stock out occurs. Reserve inventory is essentially an emergency supply to cover demand that exceeds capacity.

For sites that manage a capacity shortage by utilizing prebuild as a regular course of action, design specific prebuild or reserve cards for capacity management. These cards should be distinct from spike cards that are used for temporary demand spikes.

Using Spike Cards

There are a few general rules that define how spike cards work.

1. Notify the supplier that demand will be higher than normal, and give them an estimate of the scope of the increase, such as number of pieces and time duration.

2. Order the standard KOQ for every item.

• Ordering the standard quantity ensures that MOQ and SPQ requirements are met and that POU space allowances and containers will work.

• Ordering KOQs might mean that more than 1 spike order is required to address the increased demand. But, this is advantageous because it allows orders to arrive periodically instead of all at once in a large quantity. If order quantity is 1,000 and we need 3,000 spike pieces, it's better to order 3 cards of 1,000 each instead of 1 card for 3,000.

» Kanban order quantity is easier for the receiving cell because inventory arrives periodically in normal batch sizes that can be stored more easily than 1 huge quantity.

» In a spike scenario, getting pieces as they are completed by the supplier can be a huge advantage versus getting a large quantity all at once at a later time. Receiving 1,000 pieces received 3 times is better than waiting a longer time to receive 3,000 all at once.

» Supplier lead time is not artificially extended by a large order quantity, such as 3,000 versus the normal 1,000.

3. Handle spike cards in the same manner as regular kanban cards, except for scanning.

• When a spike order is placed, hang the spike card on the correct due date peg on the kanban board.

• When parts arrive, send spike parts to the floor with the spike card and put spike inventory at the rear of POU storage or in an area where they will be used only when regular kanban parts run out.

• Do not insert spike parts in front of regular kanban parts, or normal kanban parts will not get consumed and "regular" kanban cards won't be triggered as they should be. Spike cards are driven by a temporary surge, but don't let that surge disrupt regular kanban signals.

4. Spike cards address a temporary situation, so a manual review of every spike card that gets turned in should be part of standard work for spike cards. Therefore, automatic scanning is not preferred. If these cards have a barcode, it's too easy to scan a spike card and issue an order that exceeds what is required for upcoming demand, so don't put barcodes on the cards.

5. Find a way to make spike cards visually different from regular cards, like using a different card color.

Transfer Cards

Transfer cards are used when one point-of-use location signals another internal location to send parts. This signal does not generate a replenishment signal to the internal or external supplier.

Suppose 3 assembly cells in 1 plant use the same part, PN 1234567. Assembly A uses the highest number per day, followed by Assembly B, then Assembly C. So, parts are stored at Assembly A's point of use. When Assembly B and Assembly C need PN1234567, they send a transfer signal to Assembly A to request parts to refill their POU stock.

For the transfer cards in Figure 25-2, Assembly B gets 50 parts per request, and Assembly C gets 25 parts per request. They each allow 2 days for Assembly A

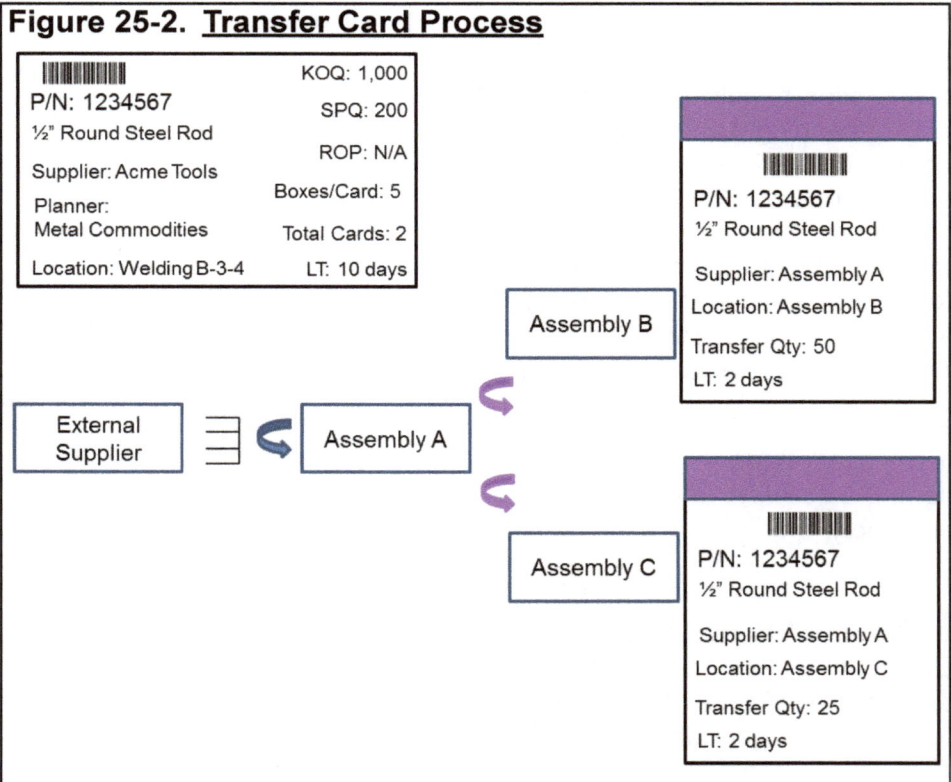

Figure 25-2. Transfer Card Process

	KOQ: 1,000
P/N: 1234567	SPQ: 200
½" Round Steel Rod	ROP: N/A
Supplier: Acme Tools	Boxes/Card: 5
Planner: Metal Commodities	Total Cards: 2
Location: Welding B-3-4	LT: 10 days

P/N: 1234567
½" Round Steel Rod
Supplier: Assembly A
Location: Assembly B
Transfer Qty: 50
LT: 2 days

P/N: 1234567
½" Round Steel Rod
Supplier: Assembly A
Location: Assembly C
Transfer Qty: 25
LT: 2 days

to fill the requests. So, they must request parts while they still have enough on-hand inventory to cover 2 days of demand, using either a reorder point approach or a 2-card system.

Assembly A is the only place that generates replenishment orders to the external supplier, using the standard kanban card in the upper left of Figure 25-2.

The transfer cards at cells B and C are a vertical layout instead of horizontal. They have a purple stripe across the top to differentiate them from regular kanban cards, as shown in the lower right of Figure 25-2.

Transfer cards might not need a barcode if the card is physically sent to the holding cell to signal the need. However, a barcode is necessary if the request for parts is handled by an electronic signal.

There are other circumstances that require transfer cards, such as centralized storage warehouses that store parts instead of keeping them at point of use. But, transfer cards should be used only when parts are stored outside a cell's POU <u>and</u> when replenishment orders are not generated at that POU.

Serialized Kanban Cards

Serialized cards have sequential numbers for all the cards in a kanban solution. An item with 5 cards would have card 1 of 5, card 2 of 5, etc. The most commonly claimed logic for serialized cards is that sequential numbers make audits more valuable because it is clear if a card has gotten out of sequence, which means it might be lost or hung up for some reason.

Yes, that's the academic theory of how it's *supposed* to work. The real world isn't quite so neat and orderly.

1. Serialized cards are deployed in order.

• The first card goes to the oldest open order, or the replenishment order with the earliest due date.

• Subsequent sequential cards are assigned to other open orders in order of due date.

• Remaining cards are put with on-hand parts with the lowest numbered card in the front bin, the bin that contains parts that are currently being consumed.

• Any remaining cards are scanned to generate more orders.

This deployment process puts kanban cards in order. The theory is that if kanban works as planned, the cards should remain in this order for their entire lives.

2. When an audit occurs, cards should be in order. Cards #3 and #4 might be on the floor while cards #1 and #2 are on the board. Or cards #2 and #3 are on the floor while #1 and #4 are on the board with #1 due after #4. But, the sequence must be in numeric order: 1, 2, 3, 4, 1, 2, 3, 4, etc.

Auditors no longer verify just the card count to confirm the right number of cards are active, but they also confirm that cards are in sequence. Any card that is out of sequence is considered an error that triggers root cause analysis. The challenge with a serialized audit is deciding which card failed. If card #3 is ahead of card #2, did #2 fall behind or did #3 skip ahead?

In the real world, cards get out of sequence. (Yes, it happens. No, it isn't the end of the world.) The situation of having cards out of sequence is particularly likely for multi-card solutions when cards are activated or deactivated in response to demand changes. If serialized cards get out of sequence, it could be that 2 bins were emptied on the same day and those 2 cards were processed at the same time, and card #3 got ahead of card #4 when they were scanned. Maybe the supplier had a quality issue and delayed the shipment for card #2 and it ended up arriving after card #3.

Does having serialized cards help us manage kanban? No. They are a waste of time and effort. This is a great example of the waste category "over-processing," to use the Lean vernacular.

Serialized cards add enormous complexity to the audit process and can also drive root cause analysis or rework (reordering the cards) that adds no value.

Suppose a kanban card audit reveals that PN45678 is missing a card, that card #4 out of 5 can't be located on the kanban board or with on-hand inventory, and we have to find that 1 card. Does it help us to know that the missing card is labeled "#4 out of 5" when we're looking for it? No. Does knowing that card #4 comes between card #3 and card #5 help us find the card? Not really. Serial numbers don't assist with the audit process.

The most common justification for serialized cards is the need for absolute adherence to first-in-first-out (FIFO) or lot traceability, perhaps in environments governed by the Food & Drug Administration or other strict regulations. By themselves, serialized kanban cards will not force FIFO, so if strict FIFO or lot traceability is required, design the entire order management process to adhere to the FIFO requirement. This might mean "order" paperwork is included with each kanban card so users can refer to the receipt or the production date for each batch of parts in order to use oldest material first. Maybe POU storage never has more than 1 order on the shelf at any given time and the next order is only delivered based on a transfer request.

The bottom line is that there are many FIFO options that are easier to manage than serialized cards.

> I've never seen serialized cards work well, nor have I seen a situation that justifies the associated complexity. Don't implement serialized cards in an attempt to solve other process or business issues! They introduce immense amounts of extra work with no added value.

Kanban Training & Deployment Practices

Training should occur before the first card is deployed.

1. At least two weeks in advance of the first deployment, communicate upcoming kanban deployment plans and dates to everyone who will be involved.

2. The week before deployment, train associates in all areas that will be impacted. They need to understand what kanban is, how cards work, what the kanban board tells them, how to process an order, and how to identify a situation that is abnormal or divergent from kanban standard work. There must be written standard work when training occurs, e.g., kanban card processes, kanban board procedures, audit steps, etc.

3. Matching cards to incoming orders should be done a day in advance so that the correct number of cards goes to the floor for each item. This can't be done too far in advance or the open order list will be invalid due to orders that arrived, were entered as new, or were changed in the system between the time of reviewing the list and the time deployment occurs. A day in advance is usually acceptable for matching open orders to cards.

4. For card deployment, have associates from the affected area match cards to parts. They have the best knowledge and should also have a vested interest in doing it correctly so that their work cell is not destroyed. This process also contributes greatly to their kanban training and understanding.

5. Deploying cards includes getting point-of-use inventory established or corrected. We might have 2 feet of shelf space for a part that needs only 6 inches, or vice versa. Don't assume that the current storage location (where an item sits) or plan (how an item is stored, such as in a box, tub, or skid) is correct. Be willing and able to fix these scenarios as they arise.

6. When matching cards to parts, identify the standard storage type (box, plastic bin, cardboard tube, shelf spot, etc.) and space (front-to-rear storage, side-by-side storage, top-to-bottom storage, etc.) for every part. Use visual cues at POU such as signs, arrows, movable barriers, etc.

7. Do not leave extra spots or open space at POU unless there are valid reasons, such as new items that will launch soon and be stored in this area. Manage space as tightly as possible so that it is easier to navigate and audit with less walking, fewer shelves, etc.

> *Train associates before deploying cards so that they don't draw the wrong conclusion about their role in kanban, such as, "I heard they're doing kanban, but it must not pertain to me" or "I don't have to understand it," or "This isn't important," or "Kanban must be temporary."*

HINTS for Associates

1.   If a site is new to kanban, do not plan a series of deployments in sequential weeks because that will overwhelm the site, the suppliers, and the Materials team. Do one event (a cell, a supplier, etc.) and let it run for 2 to 6 weeks before proceeding to the next deployment.

2.   Point-of-use storage won't always be easy to establish or finalize. Let associates live with the first guess for a while and give them permission to make adjustments. This is particularly true if the point-of-use layout or design underwent a major overhaul as part of kanban deployment.

3.   Be prepared to make adjustments rapidly and cheerfully. Support associates on the floor! When associates say, "The supplier just changed its packaging to 20 per box instead of 24," correct the kanban calculation and the cards within 1 day.

4.   The first 2 or 3 weeks after deployment are critical for sustaining kanban, particularly if this is the first deployment in an area, so tweak anything that doesn't work as planned. The leader of the area and the Materials Manager or kanban owner should tour the new deployment area <u>at least</u> daily for the first 2 weeks to specifically check on kanban. Just walking by and looking at the board is not enough.

   a. Talk to the people. Ask them how kanban is working and if they have any questions or suggestions. Ask if they have made any improvements, and, if so, have them describe the changes. Report on any corrections or findings from questions they asked yesterday.

   b. Do a visual scan of POU inventory (cards with parts? parts with cards?) and the kanban board (cards waiting to be scanned? cards on the right peg? past due orders moved to the past due peg?). Then coach associates if errors exist.

   c. Ensure that kanban standard work and 5S rules (Sort, Set in Order, Shine, Stabilize, Sustain) are being followed.

   d. If cells have daily management or metric boards, check relevant metrics to see if action or support is required. If "daily stock-out count" is a key metric due to an ongoing issue, ask them what is causing them to run out of parts. If they don't know or if they give an answer like "We told them they weren't ordering enough," flag the issue for root cause analysis.

5.   Deployments that go poorly generally suffer from one of several root causes.

   a. Kanban solutions were not sized correctly.

   b. No standard work was established, so everyone is confused and no one is properly trained. This can show up as one cell operating one way and another doing it totally different.

   c. Associates are not thoroughly trained, so no one understands what kanban is, why it's needed, what it's supposed to do, or how it works. People can't embrace what they don't understand.

   d. High error rates on printed cards (wrong MOQ, SPQ, LT, supplier name) indicates pre-work was not done satisfactorily, usually the data gathering. Confidence in the kanban system plummets to zero when errors are high.

6.   Don't do "communist kanban," where common sense is thrown out the window in favor of rigid mandates. Standard work <u>should</u> accommodate valid differences in cells instead of one universal, inflexible, one-size-fits-all solution. For example, a cell that has containers of parts headed to a heat treat oven might not have a kanban card in every basket. But, a cell using nuts and bolts might have a card with every bin of parts. These differences are valid and acceptable. Employees should believe common sense has a major role in kanban design, so please let it be true.

7.   Always remember that kanban is not as simple as it seems. Keep all the brains engaged!

Tutorial: GOCO Kanban Deployment

Mary and the team decided to use plastic kanban cards in three different colors. Purchased parts would be pink, manufactured parts white, and spike cards would be yellow. They inserted a new tab in the kanban spreadsheet to create the card print file with the following fields on the cards.

1. Barcode part number

2. "Readable" part number

3. Description: This wasn't in the Calculator tab, so when they created the Card Print tab, they pulled it from the Data tab.

4. Supplier

5. Planner (Buyer code): This wasn't in the calculator file, so they added it as a new column.

6. Location (Where used)

7. Kanban order quantity (KOQ)

8. Standard package quantity (SPQ)

9. Containers per card: This wasn't part of the calculator, though it could have been included to ensure that order quantity was a multiple of package quantity.

10. Reorder point (ROP)

11. Max # Cards

12. Lead time

They created 3 sample cards to check the layouts, in Figure 25-3. To print cards, they needed a card design for every item, but each item had to receive the right number of cards. Mary used the Microsoft Word® Mail Merge function with the new Excel tab as the source data. Once the merged file was created, she printed all purchased part cards once, all the 2-card solutions a second time, all 3-card solutions a third time, etc. until all purchased cards were printed in pink. Then Mary repeated the process for manufactured parts, for a total of 236 cards.

Mary decided not to print spike cards until she knew they were needed to support high demand season. The first kanban priority was Metal Forming due to the department's high on-hand balances. Purchased parts were also a priority, so they planned to deploy Metal Forming while they worked out deployment schedules with individual suppliers.

Mary created kanban education material for Buyer/Planners, Material Handlers, and other key associates. She helped operations managers lead a series of training sessions to introduce associates to kanban. These sessions were completed in the two weeks leading up to the first deployment.

Figure 25-3. Kanban Cards

Purchased Part, Standard Card

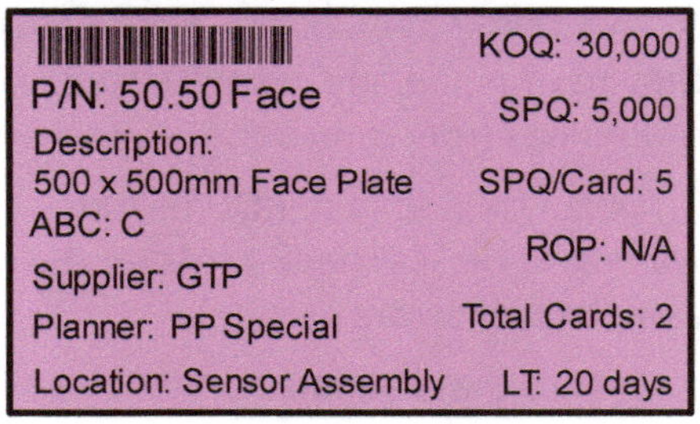

P/N: 50.50 Face	KOQ: 30,000
	SPQ: 5,000
Description: 500 x 500mm Face Plate	SPQ/Card: 5
ABC: C	ROP: N/A
Supplier: GTP	
Planner: PP Special	Total Cards: 2
Location: Sensor Assembly	LT: 20 days

Purchased Part, Spike Card

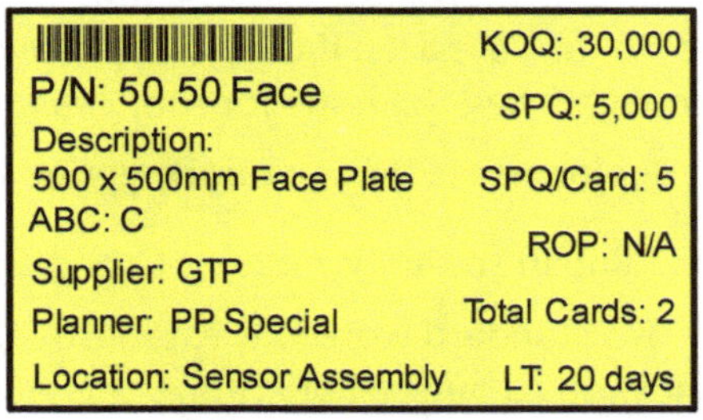

P/N: 50.50 Face	KOQ: 30,000
	SPQ: 5,000
Description: 500 x 500mm Face Plate	SPQ/Card: 5
ABC: C	ROP: N/A
Supplier: GTP	
Planner: PP Special	Total Cards: 2
Location: Sensor Assembly	LT: 20 days

Manufactured Part, Standard Card

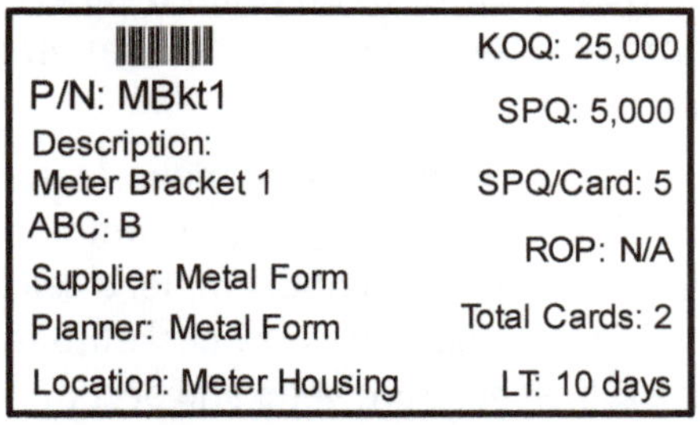

P/N: MBkt1	KOQ: 25,000
	SPQ: 5,000
Description: Meter Bracket 1	SPQ/Card: 5
ABC: B	ROP: N/A
Supplier: Metal Form	
Planner: Metal Form	Total Cards: 2
Location: Meter Housing	LT: 10 days

CHAPTER 26: KANBAN VISUAL MANAGEMENT

Kanban is a visual system.

• The design of the kanban board, the layout and color of each kanban card, and how cards are placed at point of use (POU) are all examples of the visual elements of a kanban system.

• Managing kanban bins and cards on the floor is both art and science. So, consider visual management when designing cards, POU containers, reorder-point (ROP) indicators, kanban boards, etc.

• Store cards directly with associated parts whenever possible. Remember that EaB always has a card with parts, while BaB parts only have a card when the bin is full.

Figure 26-1. <u>**Kanban Card Storage with Parts: Empty-a-Bin vs. Break-a-Bin Cards**</u>

Empty a Bin: 2 bins, 2 cards

Both bins have at least one part, so they each have a card. We always expect to find a card with EaB parts.

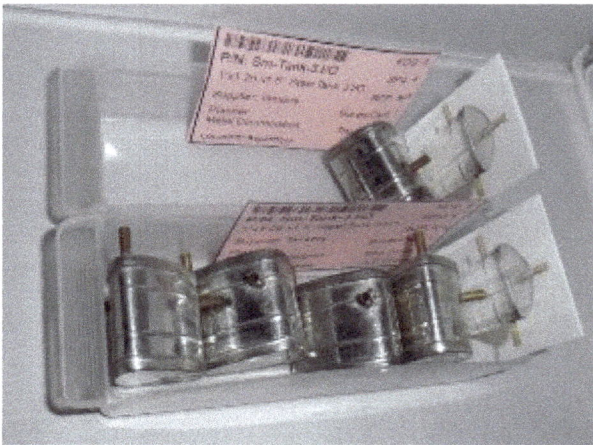

Break a Bin: 2 bins, 1 card

The top bin is not full, so it has no card. But the full bin below has a card. For BaB, we only expect to find a card with a full bin.

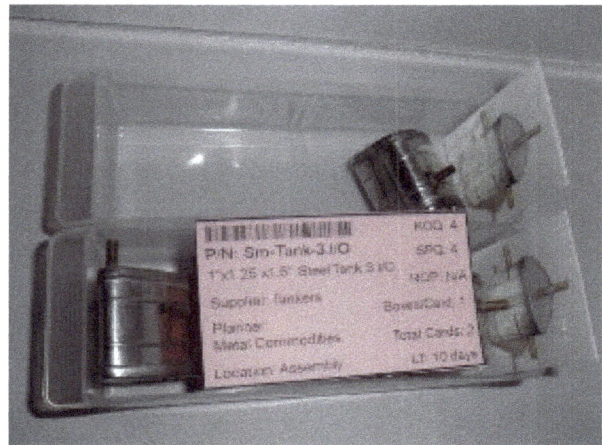

When auditing kanban bins, it's easier to see a kanban card error in an EaB kanban system because every bin should have a card. So, any bin without a card indicates a missing card, which is an error.

Figure 26-2. <u>**Kanban Card Storage with Parts: Front of the Rack or Shelf**</u>

During a kanban audit it's important to be able to spot cards quickly.

Sometimes the best way to store cards is on the front of the shelf or rack that holds the parts instead of inside the bin. This is beneficial if the card would get dirty in the bin, if the card is difficult to see or find inside the bin, or if the card would be a risk to the parts, such as electrostatic discharge or part damage risk.

Figure 26-3. <u>Kanban Card Storage: Cards Stored Away from Parts</u>

When kanban parts are stored in warehouse racks, it might be necessary to store corresponding cards on a nearby board and not physically with parts. This is not ideal for two reasons. First, large racks and centralized warehouses should be avoided, and second, cards should be stored at POU with parts whenever possible.

When cards must be separated from parts, use a well-organized and visual method for the cards. An example of a storage board is below. Parts are stored in large racks, and it isn't feasible to put cards on the containers. This board hangs on the end of a row of 9 racks. Rack designations are across the top of the board, letters A through I, and shelf numbers are listed down the side. The stack of cards for items stored on shelf 4 of rack G is circled.

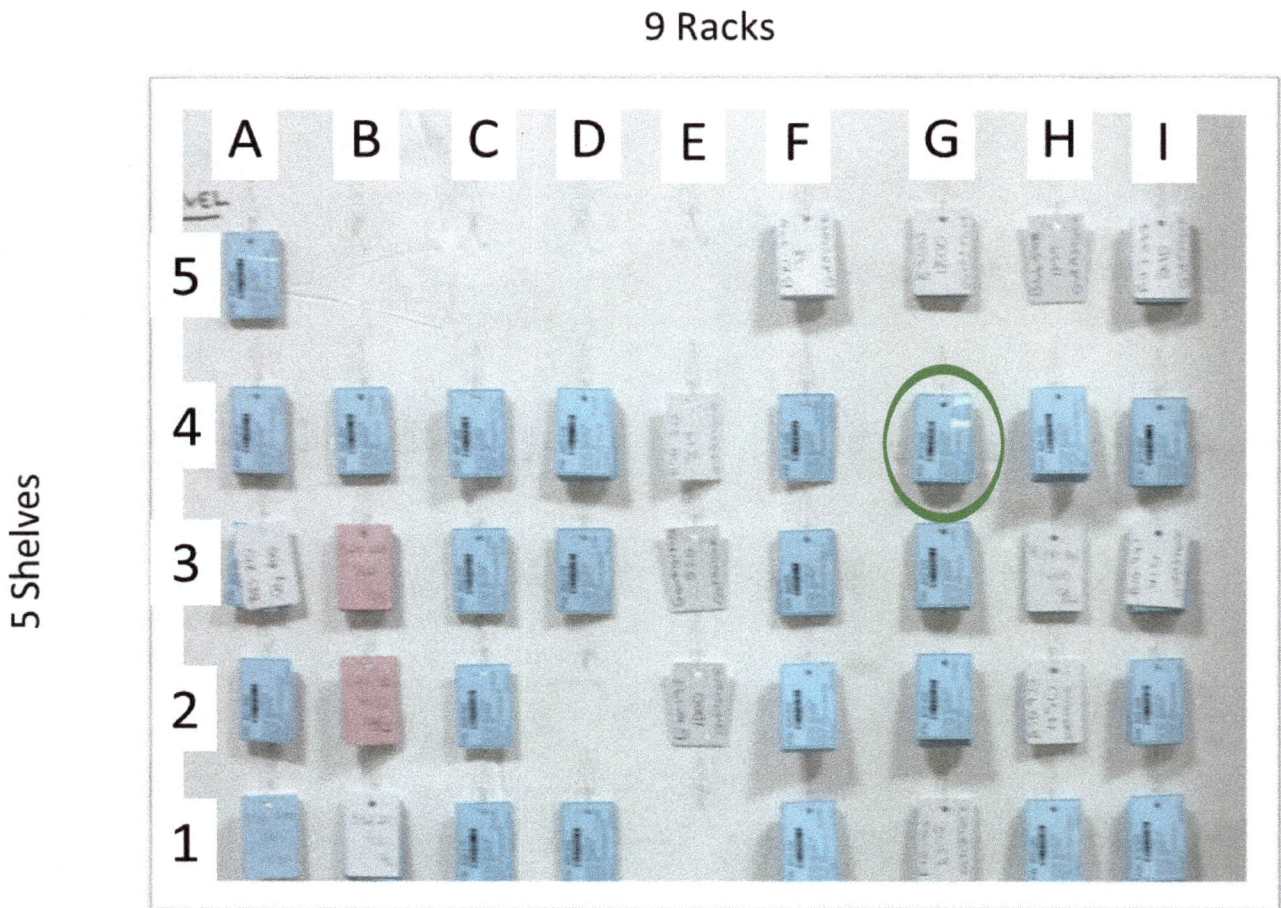

9 Racks

This kanban system uses colored kanban cards to add to the visual information provided by the kanban cards, with specific colors for purchased parts, internal items, and spike cards.

Figure 26-4. Clear Containers Make It Easy to See the ROP Line

Yellow reorder-point line is not reached, so don't order yet.

Yellow reorder-point tape is visible on the inside; time to reorder.

With a clear bin, the reorder-point line is visible from inside or outside the container. This is helpful if associates view the bin from the side (bottom right photo), but also look down into the bin (top right photo).

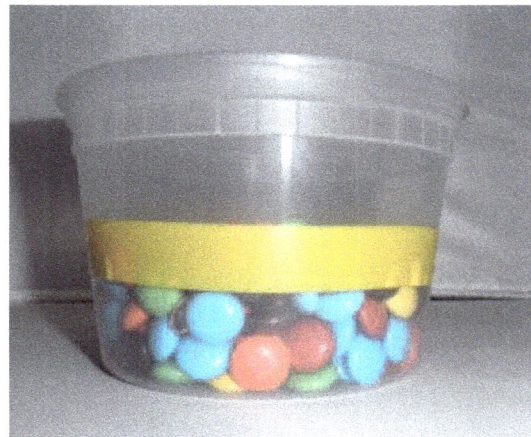

Figure 26-5. ROP Color Selection

Choose a reorder-point line color that is visible against both the color of the container and the color of the parts. Note how much more visible the white tape is in the container on the right versus the black tape on the left.

Black ROP line   **White ROP line**

CHAPTER 27: RESIZE KANBAN SOLUTIONS

When calculating solutions for the first kanban deployment or for a major overhaul, use the approach described in the section about calculating kanban solutions. But, if current kanban solutions are deployed, modify the calculator's logic to ensure that currently-deployed "fixed" or "frozen" kanban order quantities aren't altered by the resizing process. Other than that change, resizing is the same process as calculating kanban solutions from scratch.

Steps to Obtain Current Kanban Data

1. Open the kanban file and copy the Calculator tab to a new Resizing tab.

2. In the new tab, perform "Copy / Paste Special" on columns that contain the current kanban solution, the solutions that are currently deployed and will be analyzed for resizing. Paste these values into new columns to preserve what is currently deployed. Label the new columns appropriately so it's clear that these are current conditions.

3. Insert a column to indicate which items have a fixed KOQ, that is, "Y" or "1" means the order quantity is frozen, so a new card count is calculated when resizing. Remember that order quantity is fixed for all multi-card solutions, but it might not be fixed for 2-card solutions.

Use kanban type instead of number of cards to determine if order quantity should be fixed. A multi-card solution might have 2 cards as the card count, yet it still has a frozen order quantity as a multi-card solution. In other words, don't assume that any solution with 2 cards is a 2-card solution with a flexible order quantity.

4. Calculate actual safety stock for all current kanban solutions using the latest lead time and daily demand. Any item with negative safety stock for the current kanban solution should be resized <u>immediately</u> to address the stock-out risk.

Resize Kanban Solutions

Multi-card solutions assume order quantity is fixed. So, calculate the number of cards required for current demand and target safety stock.

1-card kanban solutions also retain the order quantity unless demand has risen enough that a 2-card solution is required. Assume 1 card with the same order quantity and calculate a new reorder point (ROP). If the new ROP approximates or exceeds MOQ, calculate a 2-card solution and see if safety stock is reasonable, then select 1 card or 2 cards as appropriate.

To resize 2-card solutions that will stay at 2 cards, adjust order quantity up or down as necessary. If card count can fluctuate from 2 cards, follow multi-card logic.

Multi-Card Resize

KOQ = Current KOQ

Number of cards = [(Current daily demand * Actual lead time) + Target safety stock] / Current KOQ

Add 1 card for EaB

1-Card Resize

KOQ = Current KOQ (should equal MOQ)

ROP = [(DD * Actual LT) + Target SS]

If ROP >/= MOQ, evaluate 2-card or multi-card solutions.

2-Card Resize

EaB KOQ = (Daily demand * Actual LT) + Target SS

BaB KOQ = [(Daily demand * Actual LT) + Target SS] / 2

Round for MOQ and SPQ

Verify the process by calculating new actual safety stock in units and days. If the result is negative, follow the process described in the kanban analysis chapter to address negative safety stock. Analyze new solutions as described before.

TUTORIAL: GOCO KANBAN RESIZING

In October, GOCO had to resize existing kanban solutions for the low demand season. Mary loaded kanban data in the original calculator, but knew she had to update the logic to protect current order quantities for multi-card solutions.

Mary copied the original kanban Calculator tab and renamed it "Resize."

1. She didn't want ABC to update, even if annual demand or standard cost had changed. So, she froze current ABC values by eliminating the ABC formula and replacing it with the assigned classifications. Mary also froze kanban type so that it wouldn't adjust. She knew there was a risk to this because some items might have to go from 2-card to 1-card solutions. But, she would see an indicator for that change in actual safety stock.

2. She pulled kanban data from the original kanban calculator sheet, using "Paste Special" to protect the values in those columns.

- Kanban type
- Current number of kanban cards
- Current KOQ
- Current ROP

3. She pulled October's daily demand into the "Current DD" column.

4. Mary added a column to calculate actual safety stock units and days based on current deployed kanban solutions and October's DD.

5. She inserted a column to mark solutions that required a fixed KOQ. She set all 2-card kanban types to zero, for "not fixed," and all others to one.

Fixed KOQ Designation
= IF (Kanban_type = "2 card", 0, 1)

6. The new target KOQ was based on the Fixed KOQ designation. If the KOQ was fixed, order quantity stayed the same. If it was not fixed, Mary calculated a new quantity based on DD, lead time, and target safety stock days.

Target KOQ
= IF (Kanban_type = "Not Kanban", 0,
IF (Fixed_KOQ=1, Current_KOQ,
Current_DD * (New_LT + Target_SS)))

7. Mary rounded order quantity for MOQ and SPQ.

Rounded KOQ

= IF (Kanban_type = "Not Kanban", 0,

IF (Fixed_KOQ = 1, Current_KOQ,

IF (AND (MROUND (1 * Target_KOQ, 1 * New_SPQ) < Target_KOQ, MOD (Target_KOQ - MROUND (1 * Target_KOQ, New_SPQ * 1), New_SPQ) < Rounding_Threshold * New_SPQ), MAX (1 * New_MOQ, MROUND (1 * Target_KOQ,1 * New_SPQ)),

IF (MROUND (1 * Target_KOQ, 1 * New_SPQ) > Target_KOQ, MAX (1 * New_MOQ, MROUND (1 * Target_KOQ, 1 * New_SPQ)),

MAX (1 * New_MOQ, New_SPQ + MROUND (1 * Target_KOQ, 1 * New_SPQ))))))

This formula was similar to the original kanban calculation, with one small change. The second line of the formula was inserted to check the Fixed KOQ setting and it returned "Current KOQ" if "Fixed KOQ" was equal to 1. If not, it proceeded with the regular rounding logic.

8. As before, "non-kanban" and "1-card" solutions were finished first, then the calculator looked at the fixed KOQ setting, and if KOQ was fixed (meaning it was a multi-card solution), it used the standard formula to calculate the number of cards. Otherwise it assumed 2 cards.

Number of Cards

= IF (Kanban_type = "Not Kanban", 0,

IF (OR (Kanban_type = "1 card", Kanban_type= "1 card VMI"), 1,

IF (Fixed_KOQ = 1, (Current_DD * (New_LT + Target_SS)) / Current_KOQ + 1,

2)))

9. Number of cards was rounded as usual. The formula divided the calculated number of cards by 1 to get the remainder, or the value of the decimal. If that remainder was less than the rounding threshold, it rounded down, and if not it rounded up.

Rounded Number of Cards

=IF (MOD (Calc_KB_Cards, 1) < Rounding_Threshold, ROUNDDOWN (Calc_KB_Cards, 0),

ROUNDUP (Calc_KB_Cards, 0))

10. Mary then defined the reorder point for 1-card solutions.

ROP

=IF (Round___cards=1, Current_DD * (New_LT + Target_SS), "")

11. Next she calculated actual safety stock units and days using the typical formulas, as in the original calculator.

Actual SS Units

=IF (Round___cards=0, 0,

IF (Round___cards = 1, ROP - (Current_DD * New_LT),

(Round___cards-1) * Rounded_KOQ - (Current_DD * New_LT)))

SS Days = Calc_SS_units / Current_DD

12. Mary adjusted every kanban solution that had negative safety stock, as in the original calculations.

13. All subsequent calculations for finishing and analyzing kanban solutions proceeded as before. Mary removed the 4-month bleed-off analysis (from the initial calculation exercise) because inventory was already down to reasonable levels.

14. Mary noticed that a few parts had actual inventory above the estimated maximum inventory. She subtracted estimated maximum OH$ from actual OH$ and filtered it to find high positive dollars, or parts that were at least $5,000 above the maximum inventory, and found 7 parts that totaled about $92,000 of excess inventory. Each part required root cause analysis. See Figure 27-1 for an excerpt of Mary's Excel sheet.

Figure 27-1. Inventory Reduction by Supplier vs. Where Used

PN	Supplier	Est OH$	Est Max OH$	OH$	OH$ - Max OH$	Inv Reduction	Weekly Bleed-off
DD 75.50	Universal Display	$ 49,698	$ 73,405	$ 84,487	$ 11,082	$ (34,789)	$ (45,271)
Rand2	RPS	$ 28,858	$ 42,583	$ 48,482	$ 5,899	$ (19,624)	$ (7,060)
MHous1	Meter Housing	$ 86,960	$ 165,962	$ 176,960	$ 10,999	$ (90,001)	$ (72,118)
MHous2	Meter Housing	$ 74,026	$ 111,326	$ 133,246	$ 21,920	$ (59,220)	$ (115,973)
MSub3	Meter Assy	$ 204,092	$ 276,472	$ 295,933	$ 19,461	$ (91,841)	$ (267,793)
ISub3	Instrument Assy	$ 343,363	$ 495,563	$ 501,310	$ 5,747	$ (157,947)	$ (386,993)
OSub2	Instrument Assy	$ 84,927	$ 159,967	$ 177,496	$ 17,530	$ (92,570)	$ (68,733)

Two parts came from Meter Housing, and Mary remembered hearing that their lead times were going to come down. So, she made a note to verify Meter Housing lead times before kanban solutions were deployed. If they were shorter, she would have to update those kanban solutions.

She also noted that 2 parts were from Instrument Assembly, which was rumored to be "working ahead" of kanban signals. She decided to tour the area and confirm if standard work was being followed.

She assigned root cause analysis tasks to buyers and planners to determine why inventory was high on the other parts.

Overall, Mary was very pleased with kanban. Inventory was down by more than $16 million dollars in 6 short months, and the GOCO owners were very pleased with the results. She hoped her annual bonus would reflect their delight.

CHAPTER 28: ELECTRONIC KANBAN

The topic of electronic kanban, or eKanban, often generates strongly negative or wildly positive responses, or complete and utter confusion. Let's define what electronic kanban is and what it is not.

eKanban is <u>not</u> an MRP-driven system of fixed reorder points that replaces a physical kanban system. That's simply an extension of MRP.

Instead, eKanban supplements a manual kanban system with automated processes to reduce errors, increase human productivity, capture kanban data in real time, or calculate kanban solutions.

There are a few basic functions and benefits to consider from eKanban.

eKanban Functions

Think about all the processes and tasks that are performed on a regular and repeated basis to support

Figure 28-1. Kanban Process

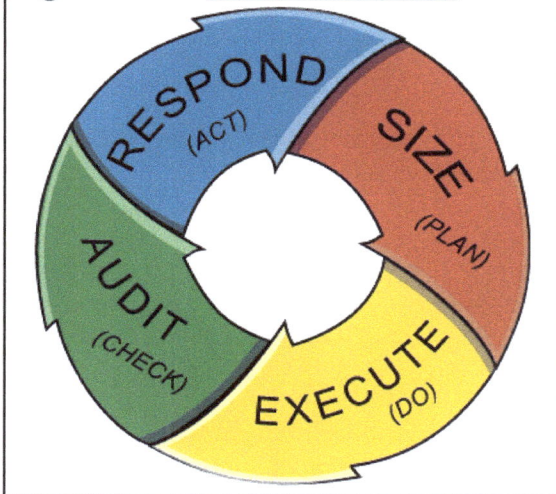

kanban, everything from sizing to responding to process and audit findings, as illustrated in Figure 28-1. Kanban is loaded with tasks that depend on accurate data and human effort, as in the process loops and checklists for the four components of the process.

Electronic kanban can perform or support many of the functions in kanban. At its very foundation, eKanban is a great data repository, and any electronic kanban system should have searchable and sortable reports and data records to facilitate data reporting and upkeep. This data should feed resizing logic, order management, card management, kanban audits, and so on.

Resizing (Size = Plan)

The sizing process is the most data-intensive and mathematically challenging part of a kanban system. Data gathering is a huge undertaking, and, if it is manually performed, it is difficult to do well. Likewise, the sizing process requires numerous decision trees and formulas. Users must define preferences and thresholds in order for decision trees to work as designed, which necessitates a centralized place to store preferences and settings.

A <u>good eKanban calculator is probably the most sophisticated and beneficial aspect of electronic kanban</u> due to the intelligence that must be present to handle various situations and functions, as shown in Figure 28-2 on page 310.

• eKanban can provide enormous benefits for accurate kanban solutions if data is pulled from real-time data repositories.

• eKanban calculators can be utilized in real time to add incredible flexibility. Instead of scheduling a quarterly resizing event to review the entire population of kanban parts for potential resizing, a site can resize any time they choose and everything can be quickly evaluated. If a site has easy resizing, every buyer and planner can be assigned a "resizing week" during the month to get their sizing activity accomplished. The possibilities are endless, and very exciting.

Figure 28-2. Sizing Loop: The Kanban Calculator

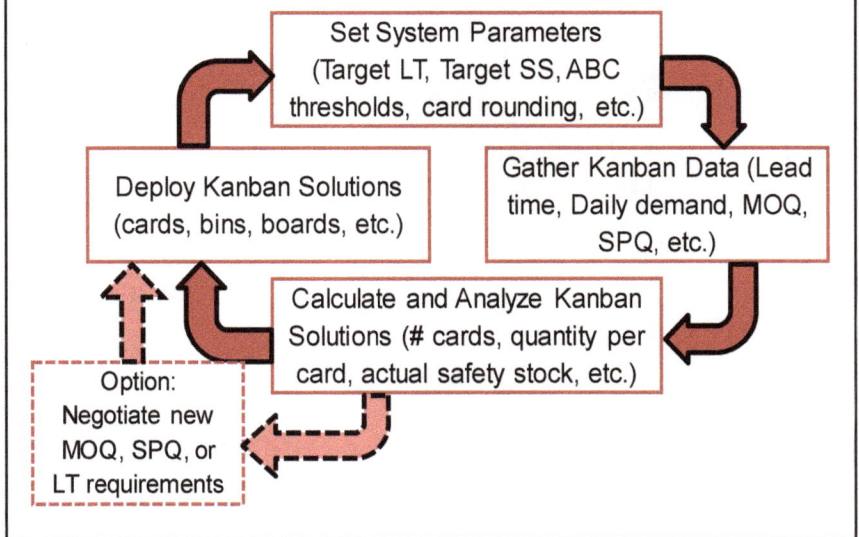

Set System Parameters (Target LT, Target SS, ABC thresholds, card rounding, etc.)

Gather Kanban Data (Lead time, Daily demand, MOQ, SPQ, etc.)

Deploy Kanban Solutions (cards, bins, boards, etc.)

Calculate and Analyze Kanban Solutions (# cards, quantity per card, actual safety stock, etc.)

Option: Negotiate new MOQ, SPQ, or LT requirements

• eKanban should provide kanban solutions that are rounded for minimum order and standard package limits and are also in compliance with lead time and daily demand assumptions. This sounds simple and mandatory, but not all eKanban tools round for minimum order or package limitations.

• eKanban solutions should evaluate current kanban solutions and flag parts that have a stock-out risk, so those items are at the top of the deployment plan to prevent delivery risk.

• Every item should have actual on-hand currency as a comparison. This allows eKanban users to determine where resizing or negotiation efforts will provide the biggest return. In a perfect world, the eKanban system would prioritize items or action plans based on inventory reduction measured in currency.

• Aggregate data should be provided by eKanban in order to scope overall opportunities (e.g., inventory reduction) or workload (how many MOQs or lead times need to be negotiated).

• An eKanban system can assist with deploying new kanban solutions, including designing and printing cards, activating or deactivating cards in multi-card solutions, assigning the right card layout based on PN or kanban solution settings, etc.

» Sites that resize frequently due to demand variation can gain great benefits from electronically activating and deactivating cards during the deployment process. Adding cards manually is easy (scan the extra card and hang it on the board), but reducing card count is much more difficult without an electronic aid. An electronic system knows how many cards are active. If a scan is attempted for a card that has been electronically deactivated, the system reports an error that tells the user to pull that card off the floor. This is a tremendous benefit versus manually finding cards and pulling them off the floor to reduce card counts after resizing for lower demand.

Order & Card Management (Execute or Do)

The order and card management loops in Figure 28-3 are repetitive processes that are performed every day by associates across the organization. Any error or delay in a step ripples through the kanban system, so automation is an advantage for error-proofing and speed.

Figure 28-3. Order & Card Loops

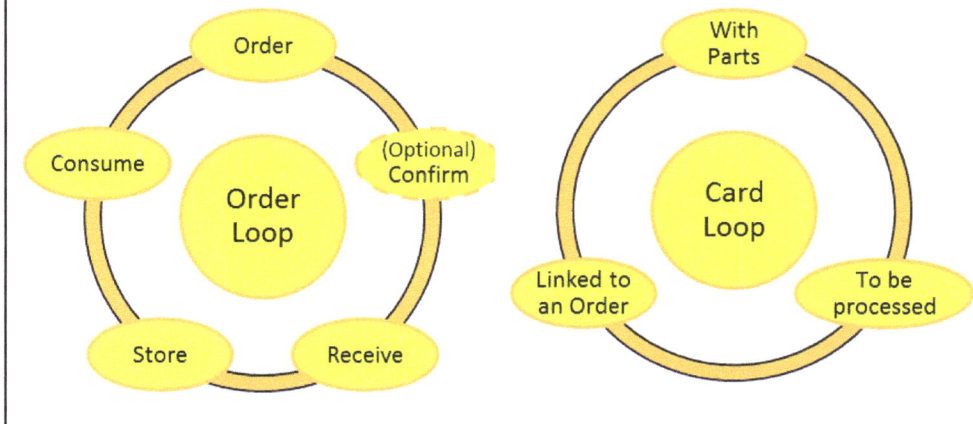

1. Barcode scanning is a basic feature of eKanban and is faster and less error-prone than manual order entry.

• Some scanning functions send an order based on a card scan, but order details are updated based on real-time data. So, any changes in lead time, order quantity, or supplier name are automatically captured due to the link to the data repository. This is essentially real-time resizing, and it minimizes errors in purchase and manufacturing orders.

• For sites that use fixed 2-card solutions and resize order quantities to adjust for demand changes, real-time updates allow them to deploy generic cards with no printed kanban order quantity (or perhaps an order quantity range on the card, such as 400-500). But, every order is issued for the latest assigned order quantity from the most recent resizing.

2. Order confirmation or acknowledgement for either internal or external suppliers is a great eKanban function because it can all be done electronically.

• This allows a supplier to confirm an order as received or to modify the due date or order quantity when accepting an order, which eliminates the back-and-forth phone calls or emails that can take hours per order. In sites with poor supplier performance or mandatory supplier acknowledgements, automating this process can save thousands of work hours per year.

3. Automated order receipt, where a barcode is scanned to receive incoming parts at the dock, allows the system to automatically capture receipt date and quantity. This is another productivity enhancement for closing open orders, updating card status, and adding material to inventory.

Kanban Audits (Check) & Responses (Act)

Robust kanban systems have built-in methods to find and repair errors or implement process updates in the audit and response processes, as in Figure 28-4 on page 312. These processes are greatly aided if electronic processes guarantee error-free, real-time, and data-driven transactions.

1. Order tracking is a key function for electronic systems, with easy access or reporting for past due, new orders, open orders, etc.

2. Audits can be streamlined by providing basic reports that list the number of active cards; total number of card; open orders by part number, date, or supplier; orders due today; orders received today, and so on. These basic reports can reveal gaps (late orders) or errors (duplicate orders) to assist with audits or responses.

Figure 28-4. Audit & Response Processes

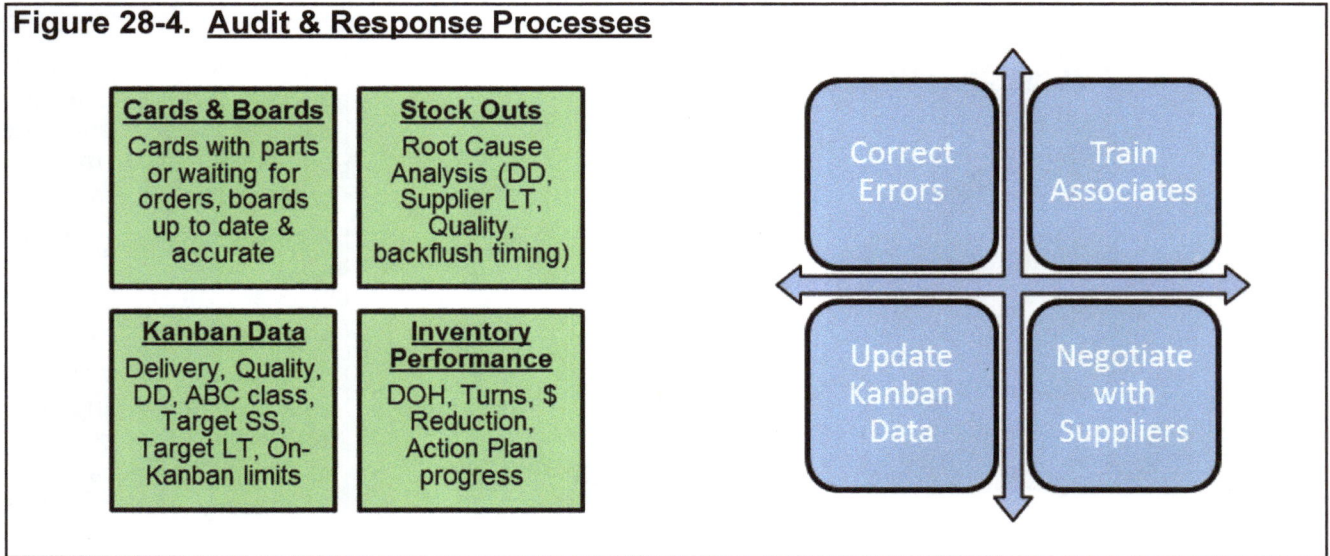

Cards & Boards	Stock Outs
Cards with parts or waiting for orders, boards up to date & accurate	Root Cause Analysis (DD, Supplier LT, Quality, backflush timing)

Kanban Data	Inventory Performance
Delivery, Quality, DD, ABC class, Target SS, Target LT, On-Kanban limits	DOH, Turns, $ Reduction, Action Plan progress

Correct Errors	Train Associates
Update Kanban Data	Negotiate with Suppliers

HINT for Associates

Don't abandon the physical aspects of kanban (cards, boards, audits), even with a great eKanban system. Doing so might seem streamlined and efficient but it violates one of the key success attributes of kanban: visual management. If eliminating cards means orders are triggered automatically based on system-reported consumption or inventory balances, as in virtual cards, we're back to relying on MRP and its inherent data gaps (on-hand balance, incoming orders, and upcoming demand). Eliminating cards or boards reduces the visual aspect of kanban, making it less tangible to associates and also more difficult to audit.

eKanban Benefits

eKanban Advantage: Error Reduction

In kanban systems, human errors occur when a process is poorly defined, if standard work is not robust, when processes are executed with errors, or when data entry is incorrect.

Data entry is probably the most common error in kanban systems. If an order is entered for part number 1234**5** instead of 1234**6**, or an MOQ is entered as 1,000 in the kanban calculator instead of 100, the kanban system suffers due to human error. Electronic processes such as scanning cards or importing kanban calculator data from direct sources versus manual data entry can prevent these issues.

The lack of standard work and the failure to follow standard work are human errors that can be aided by electronic systems such as scanning a barcode at point of use (POU) instead of keying data or sending the card to a central office and hoping it doesn't get delayed or lost on the way from POU to the MRP desk.

eKanban Advantage: Productivity Increase

Productivity gains come from automating tasks that can be more efficient and just as effective.

Scanning barcodes to generate new orders is a great example. Scanning sounds trivial, but if we process 100 orders per day and save 10 seconds for each order, we save 1,000 seconds per day, or 17 minutes of work.

Order confirmation is another repetitive activity that isn't complex or difficult but is repeated so frequently that it can be a major productivity drain. Some sites spend several work hours per day confirming orders that were sent to outside suppliers. Phone calls, emails, and other follow-up methods are used to inquire about order receipt (Did you get it?) and acceptance (Can you meet the date? Is the quantity OK?). In sites with large numbers of purchased parts, this activity can account for one or more full-time people.

eKanban Advantage: Data Accuracy

Maintaining accurate data is one of the most common weaknesses in inventory management systems.

1. Even though inventory orders are issued and received over and over, many ERP or MRP systems don't capture—or don't make available—the time period between order entry and receipt. Therefore, actual lead time by part number is unknown.

2. Many sites have inadequate processes to capture and update MOQs, SPQs, and other supplier requirements.

3. Daily demand (DD) data is available from most MRP systems. But, it often requires system manipulation that takes time and special access or expertise, which means it isn't readily available to all associates. It is also common for system-generated demand data to be calculated in ways that don't work for kanban, such as using calendar days instead of work days to calculate DD.

4. Variation analysis is a data-intensive exercise that relies on piles of demand data in lead-time buckets. I've never seen properly calculated demand variation (DV) data come directly out of an MRP or ERP system. The lead-time bucket requirement trips them up every time!

eKanban systems generally provide some level of data management that increases accuracy and effectiveness.

eKanban Advantage: Resizing

Calculating kanban solutions is a time-consuming process that requires scientific methodology. Automating calculations or card printing can save lots of employee hours. Even with a great Excel tool to calculate kanban solutions, the process is often so cumbersome and time-consuming that it is executed only when tackling identified challenges such as stock outs or adding new items to kanban, versus performing resizing as a standard and regular process.

An automated resizing process that assists with data crunching and calculations, and maybe enables or disables active cards, can be a huge benefit for resizing. <u>This might be the biggest potential benefit from eKanban if the calculation tool is designed correctly</u>. Please let me know if you need help.

Dynamic Kanban Calculation Software

At the risk of being self serving, if you need assistance with kanban calculations, or if you'd like to have an assessment of your current inventory performance and the potential reduction that could be achieved, please visit www.kanbancalculator.com and see what we have to offer.

Dynamic Kanban software was designed to serve several purposes.

1. Calculate kanban solutions for even the most complicated scenarios.

2. Provide flexibility for the user by allowing them to customize the targets and limits utilized by the calculator, so solutions are appropriate for each situation.

3. Predict inventory performance for both recommended and ideal kanban solutions, to allow users to set reasonable inventory reduction goals, both dollars and timing.

4. Generate action plan lists to manage inventory activity such as resizing, adding items to kanban, correcting ABC classifications, and negotiating minimum order quantity and lead time limitations.

With the standard outputs and reports from Dynamic Kanban, a site can assess their current and potential inventory performance. This can be done as a one-time service to give you a snapshot of what is possible, or it can be done repeatedly over time as part of a subscription.

Contact me at Josette@dynamickanban.com or visit www.kanbancalculator.com for more information.

SECTION VII.
SUMMARY & INDEX

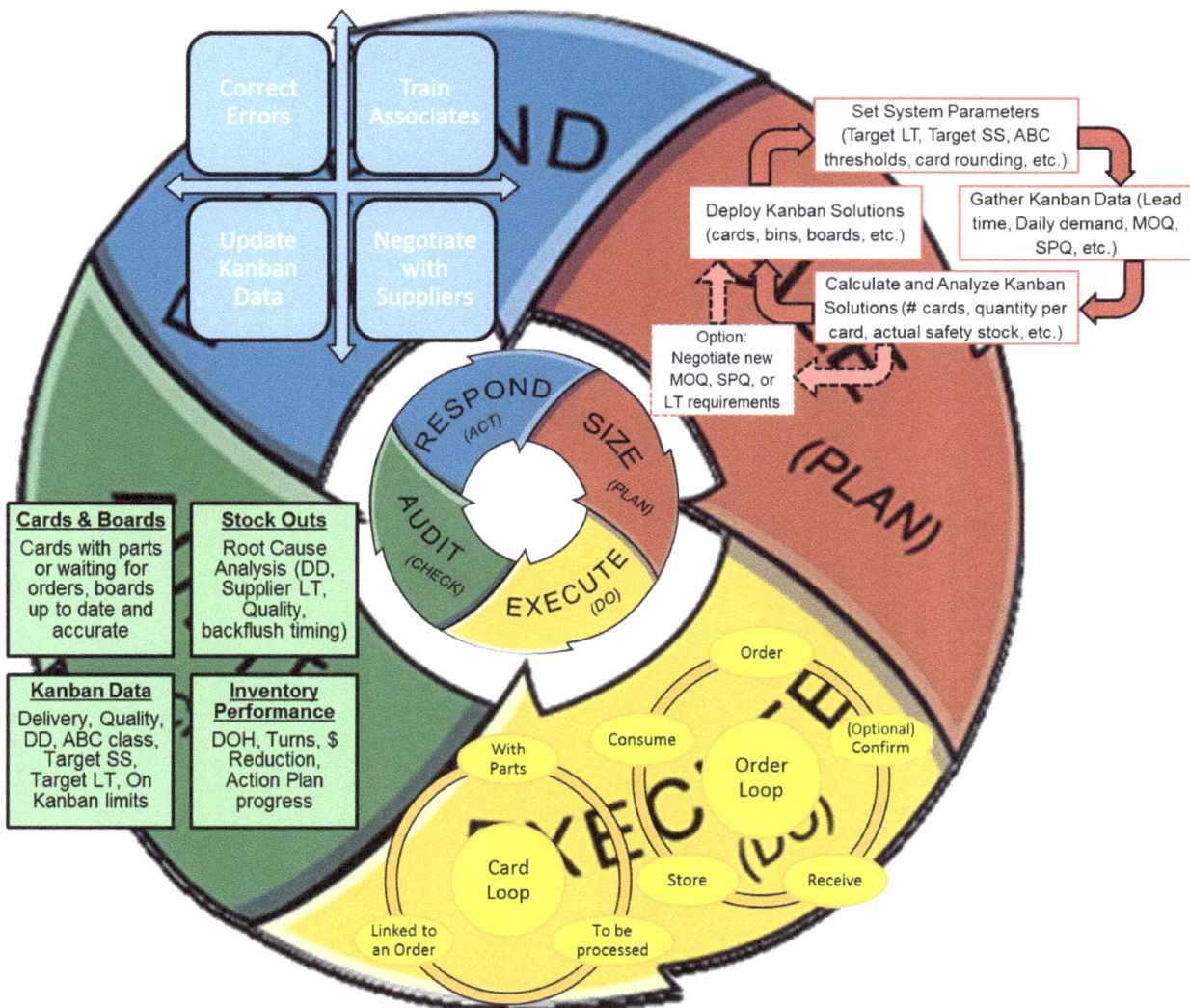

Correct Errors

Train Associates

Update Kanban Data

Negotiate with Suppliers

RESPOND (ACT)

SIZE (PLAN)

AUDIT (CHECK)

EXECUTE (DO)

Cards & Boards
Cards with parts or waiting for orders, boards up to date and accurate

Stock Outs
Root Cause Analysis (DD, Supplier LT, Quality, backflush timing)

Kanban Data
Delivery, Quality, DD, ABC class, Target SS, Target LT, On Kanban limits

Inventory Performance
DOH, Turns, $ Reduction, Action Plan progress

Set System Parameters (Target LT, Target SS, ABC thresholds, card rounding, etc.)

Deploy Kanban Solutions (cards, bins, boards, etc.)

Gather Kanban Data (Lead time, Daily demand, MOQ, SPQ, etc.)

Calculate and Analyze Kanban Solutions (# cards, quantity per card, actual safety stock, etc.)

Option: Negotiate new MOQ, SPQ, or LT requirements

(PLAN)

Order

Consume

(Optional) Confirm

With Parts

Order Loop

Card Loop

Store

Receive

Linked to an Order

To be processed

SUMMARY OF *BANKING ON KANBAN*

Remember where we started. If we want to boost cash flow, minimize inventory, and maximize delivery performance, we need a scientific way to plan and manage inventory. The best answer is often kanban.

Kanban is much more than a simple inventory management device. It is a proven tool that defines prudent replenishment plans based on scientific analysis. Yes, it requires effort and intelligence. It is tedious and time-consuming when done correctly and thoroughly. It is data-intensive and it can be mathematically complex. It's not for the faint of heart or mind, but you can do it. I have faith in you.

To succeed with kanban, master the fundamental concepts.

Understand the Sawtooth Curve

The sawtooth curve is the essential nature of an item held in inventory, with ups and downs caused by receipts and consumption as in Figure Summ-1. The sawtooth curve is a great way to explain the concepts of minimum, average, and maximum inventory values and the role that safety stock plays.

Figure Summ-1. <u>Steady State Inventory Sawtooth Curve</u>

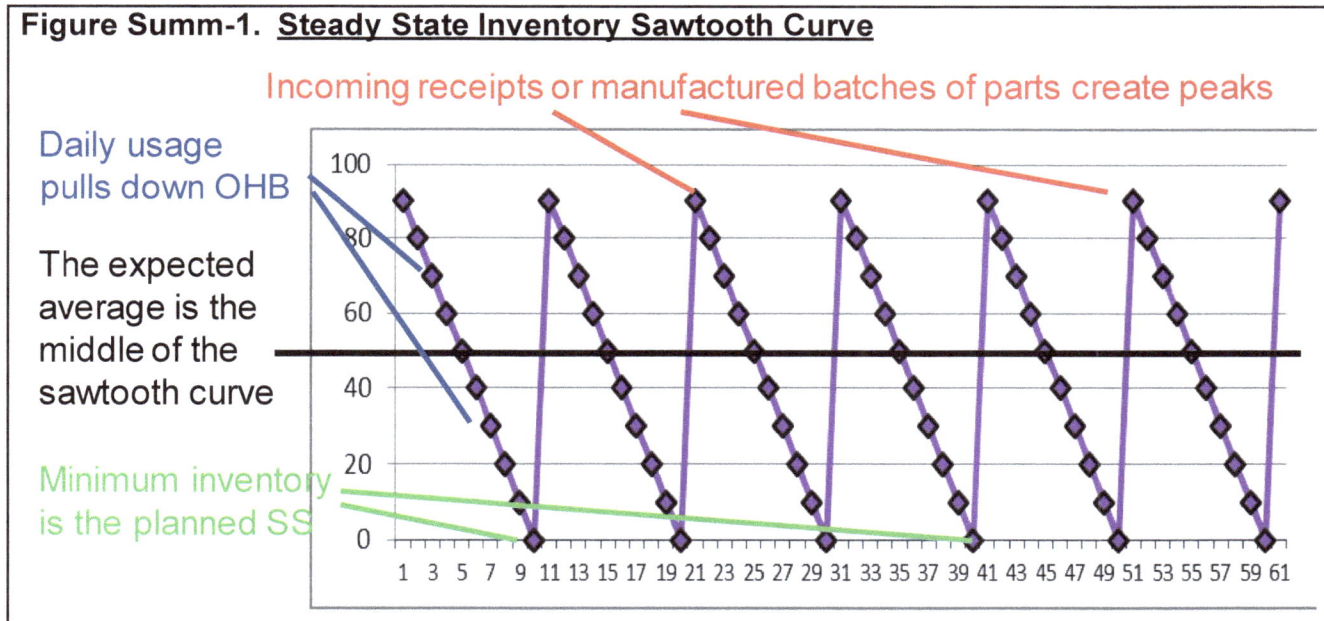

Incoming receipts or manufactured batches of parts create peaks

Daily usage pulls down OHB

The expected average is the middle of the sawtooth curve

Minimum inventory is the planned SS

Measure Inventory Management

Many operations or materials specialists underestimate the direct correlation between delivery performance and inventory performance. Both of them require underlying processes that are robust and based on accurate data.

To successfully plan and manage inventory we must keep an eye on both types of metrics. On-time delivery *must* be measured to assess kanban performance with regards to serving customers, and OTD should be measured versus the market's definition of an appropriate lead time instead of to an artificial internal lead time. In addition to delivery, add either inventory turns or days on hand to assess cash management.

Manage All Aspects of the Kanban Plan-Do-Check-Act Loop

Kanban processes are performed over and over in a type of plan-do-check-act loop as shown in Figure Summ-2. Calculating and deploying kanban solutions is the Plan phase. Executing kanban processes to replenish material is the Do phase. Auditing kanban processes and results is the Check phase. Finally, responding to kanban findings and results is the Act phase.

Each of the phases of the kanban loop has its own diagram of activities to represent the work to be accomplished.

Figure Summ-3 is the sizing loop. This is the foundation for all kanban activity so if it's incorrect or incomplete the system will falter or utterly fail.

Remember that resizing is just as important as the initial sizing activity. Don't let kanban solutions get bogged down by old data or out-of-date system assumptions. Resize often enough to keep the system synchronized with business conditions.

Figure Summ-4 and Figure Summ-5 are the execution loops for orders and cards. Managing the usage and replenishment processes are perhaps the most visible parts of a kanban system and these systems and processes should be well defined and never left to chance.

Figure Summ-2. Kanban Process

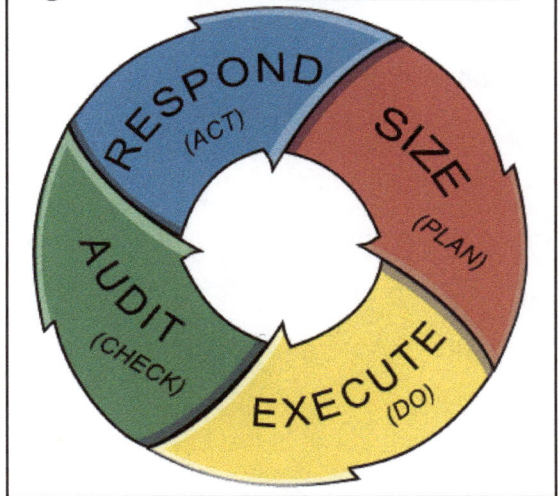

Figure Summ-3. Sizing Loop: The Kanban Calculator

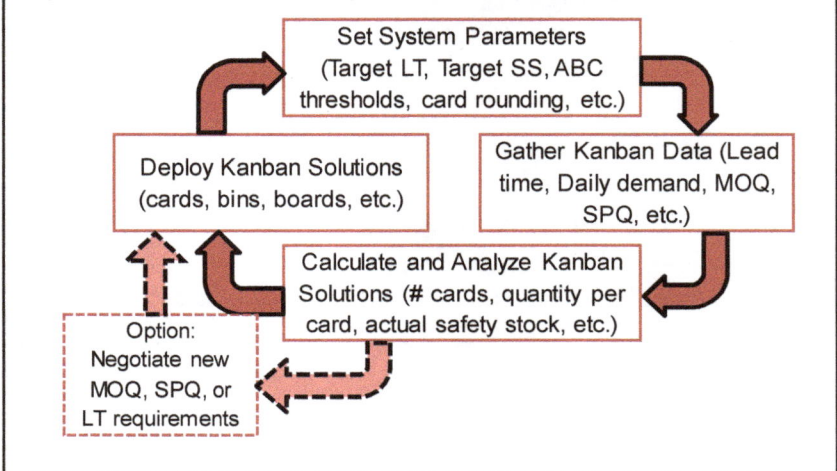

Set System Parameters (Target LT, Target SS, ABC thresholds, card rounding, etc.)

Gather Kanban Data (Lead time, Daily demand, MOQ, SPQ, etc.)

Deploy Kanban Solutions (cards, bins, boards, etc.)

Calculate and Analyze Kanban Solutions (# cards, quantity per card, actual safety stock, etc.)

Option: Negotiate new MOQ, SPQ, or LT requirements

Figure Summ-4. Order Loop

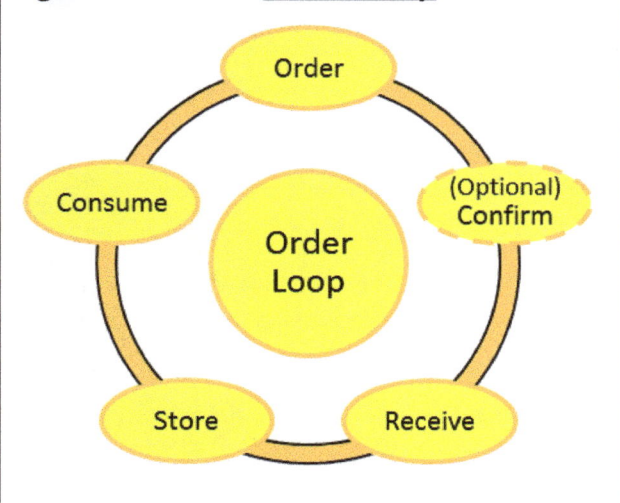

Order Loop

Order

Consume

(Optional) Confirm

Store

Receive

Figure Summ-5. Card Loop

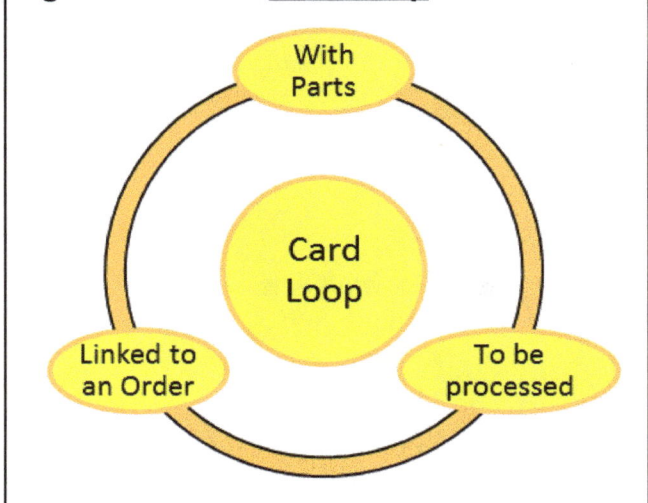

Card Loop

With Parts

Linked to an Order

To be processed

Figure Summ-6 is the audit process and Figure Summ-7 is the response list. To keep a kanban system healthy, the associated data, processes, and people must be kept up to date and in tune with reality.

Figure Summ-6. Audit Categories

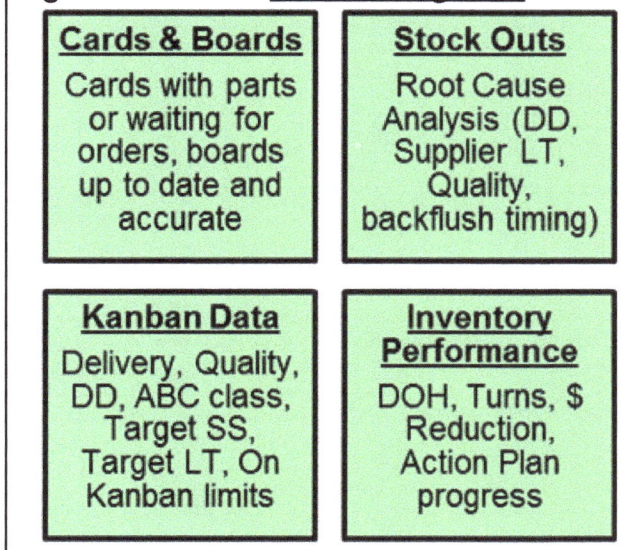

Cards & Boards

Cards with parts or waiting for orders, boards up to date and accurate

Stock Outs

Root Cause Analysis (DD, Supplier LT, Quality, backflush timing)

Kanban Data

Delivery, Quality, DD, ABC class, Target SS, Target LT, On Kanban limits

Inventory Performance

DOH, Turns, $ Reduction, Action Plan progress

Figure Summ-7. Respond

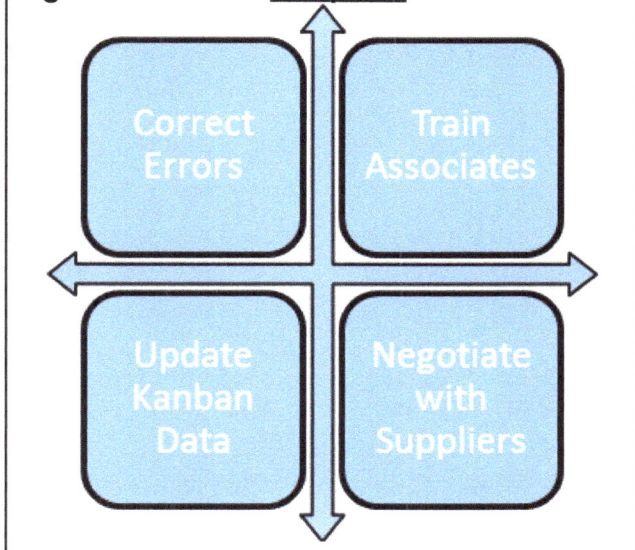

Correct Errors

Train Associates

Update Kanban Data

Negotiate with Suppliers

Maintain Accurate & Thorough Kanban Data

Kanban is data-intensive even before kanban solutions are calculated, due to the sheer amount of information that is required to populate the kanban Calculator tab and the Targets & Limits tab. But, it is even more data-intensive during and after calculating solutions. In addition to mathematical kanban solutions, analysis should be performed on individual kanban solutions, the overall kanban system, and the projected results.

Because kanban requires so much analysis, it benefits greatly from automated kanban calculators. At the very least, an Excel model must be created, but whenever possible an automated or electronic kanban calculator should be utilized.

Utilize Wise Kanban Types & Triggers

Some items don't belong on kanban and must be sorted out of the kanban list for low daily demand, high MOQ coverage, or other attributes that exclude the need for kanban, such as the presence of flow or short processing lead times versus customer promise lead times. Don't skip the step of eliminating items from kanban!

For items that are on kanban, different scenarios require different kanban types, for example, one card, two cards, or multiple cards. It is imperative to understand the conditions that drive each kanban type so that calculated kanban solutions work effectively to manage delivery and inventory performance.

• A 1-card solution is assigned when the MOQ covers more days of demand than the quantity [lead time days + target safety stock days].

• A multi-card solution is utilized for high demand variation, long actual lead time versus target lead time, or a MaxQ that is lower than the required order quantity for 2 cards.

• Two cards are assigned to all other scenarios.

Kanban orders can be triggered at the beginning (BaB), middle (ROP), or end (EaB) of a kanban bin. Empty a bin is easier to audit so it is generally preferred, but break a bin can reduce inventory levels.

Summary of Kanban Formulas

Calculating kanban solutions is a mathematical exercise, so there are many formulas.

Kanban Formulas

<u>1-card</u> reorder point (ROP) = [Actual LT * Current Daily Demand + Target safety stock]

<u>2-card</u> Kanban order quantity (KOQ)

Empty-a-Bin (EaB) KOQ = [Actual LT * Current DD + Target SS]
Break-a-Bin (BaB) KOQ = [Actual LT * Current DD + Target SS] / 2 cards
Round for MOQ, MaxQ, and SPQ.

<u>Demand Variation (DV) Multi-Card KOQ</u>

DV multi-card KOQ = (Low Daily demand * Target LT) * (1 + Low Target SS %)
Rounded DV multi-card KOQ = MIN {MaxQ, MAX [MROUND (DV KOQ, Std Pack Qty), Min Order Qty]}

Number of cards for DV multi-card

EaB # cards = [(Actual DD * LT + Target SS) / DV KOQ] + 1
BaB # cards = (Actual DD * LT + Target SS) / DV KOQ
Round based on card rounding threshold.

<u>Long Lead-Time Multi-Card KOQ</u>

KOQ = (Target LT * DD) * (1 + Target SS %)

Round for MOQ, MaxQ, and SPQ.

Number of cards for Long LT multi-card

EaB LT multi-card # of cards = [(Target LT * DD + Target SS) / KOQ] + 1
BaB LT multi-card # of cards = (Target LT * DD + Target SS) / KOQ
Round based on card rounding threshold.

<u>Number of cards for MaxQ Multi-card</u>

(Note: KOQ = MaxQ)

EaB # cards = [(Actual DD * LT + Target SS) / MaxQ] + 1
BaB # cards = (Actual DD * LT + Target SS) / MaxQ
Round based on card rounding threshold.

Analyze & Deploy Kanban Solutions

To predict inventory levels for individual items or an entire site, estimate average, minimum, and maximum inventory for every item. Sum average inventories in currency to estimate performance across numerous items or for an entire site.

Kanban analysis should also create prioritized action plans. Items should be filtered or sorted to address stock-out risks first, followed by resizing to reduce inventory, along with negotiating better lead times and order quantity limits. Remember to put items on kanban and take items off kanban, as appropriate.

Be aware of the time it will take to bleed off excess inventory and get down to steady state sawtooth curves for items that have too much on-hand inventory. An inventory reduction goal should include the potential reduction, but also the time required to get there.

Free up cash by executing the action plans that come out of kanban analysis! Kanban solutions provide a wealth of actionable information - don't ignore that intelligence.

Actual Safety Stock and Estimated Inventory

<u>Actual Safety Stock</u>

$$\text{1-card Actual SS} = \text{ROP} - (\text{Actual lead time} * \text{Current DD})$$
$$\text{EaB Actual SS} = (\text{\# cards -1}) * \text{Kanban order quantity} - (\text{Actual lead time} * \text{Current DD})$$
$$\text{BaB Actual SS} = (\text{\# cards} * \text{KOQ}) - (\text{Actual lead time} * \text{Current DD})$$

<u>Inventory Levels</u>

$$\text{Estimated Minimum Inventory} = \text{Actual SS units}$$
$$\text{Estimated Average Inventory} = \text{KOQ} / 2 + \text{Actual SS}$$
$$\text{Estimated Maximum Inventory} = \text{KOQ} + \text{Actual SS}$$

A solution is valid only if it is deployed, which requires wise card layouts and robust processes for deploying kanban cards. Kanban is a visual system, so cards, bins, boards, and other elements should be carefully planned.

Kanban requires all players to be informed and engaged in the process, so ensure that training is widespread, timely, and thorough.

Bank on Kanban!

As we wrap up this book, I hope you're a fan of kanban, even if you didn't start out that way. I also hope you gained the necessary insight and confidence to tackle and succeed at your kanban project.

Yes, I know the processes and formulas scattered throughout the book can be daunting and moderately frightening. As I said in the Introduction, get help if you need it. Kanban will go much faster and more smoothly if you have the right expertise at your fingertips in order to avoid some of the pitfalls and common mistakes.

If you want to start kanban slowly, consider starting with the easier stuff, as described in the chapter about excluding items and assigning kanban type, on page 242.

I'd love to hear about your kanban projects. Please don't hesitate to contact me to share success stories, or if you need assistance. www.kanbancalculator.com

Good luck! Be a kanban master. It's <u>really</u> fun.

Josette Russell

Index

hold inventory as far upstream as possible, *203*

ideal solution is 2 cards, target LT, no rounding of order quantity, *103*

IF [Actual LT / TLT] > 2 for A or B item THEN consider LT multi-card solution, *250*

IF [actual MOQ / target MOQ] > 2.0, THEN qualifies for MOQ negotiation, *113, 224*

IF [High DD/Low DD or High DD/Med DD] > 130% then seasonality is significant, *136, 223*

if new to kanban, deploy up to 500 cards in first deployment, *289*

IF [Std dev units / LT demand] < 0.2 to 0.3 THEN no DV multi-card solution, *163, 223, 248*

items that need longer LT usually lower negotiation priorities, *272*

kanban calculator targets and limits, *219–226*

for LT buckets, limit long LT to 6-8 weeks of demand, *145*

LT categories (short, medium, long), *111*

LT negotiation, *109, 224*

measure Safety, Quality, Delivery, & Cost, *37*

never deploy kanban solution with negative SS, *260*

no supply quality SS if supplier reject rate < 1%, *131*

OHC goal must be > sum of expected ideal inventory, *106*

optional to set minimum hurdle for negotiation efforts, *224*

push + pull = kanban signal goes back to first upstream inventory store, *201*

rare to find zero inventory between VSM process boxes, *184*

resizing generally occurs quarterly, but DV can increase frequency, *80*

review any item with [actual safety stock < 50% of target SS], *261*

scan kanban cards in real time at POU, *84*

target for changeover time is < one takt time, *186*

target SPQ = 20% of target MOQ, *113, 224*

use future demand in COGS to calculate DOH or turns, *43*

S

safety stock (SS). *See also* target safety stock (TSS)

definition, *13*

fix SS gaps in recommended kanban solutions, *260*

Formula: actual SS, *122, 233, 260*

Formula: current SS days, *233*

HINT: can add reasonable extra SS to 1-card solutions to avoid frequent resizing for DV, *95*

HINT: don't add supplier SS without first contacting supplier to clarify expectations, *132*

HINT: never add SS to cover for erroneous kanban calculator data, *130*

"on kanban" actual safety stock data, *233*

replenishment plan with SS orders more than LT demand, *29*

Rule of Thumb: never deploy kanban solution with negative SS, *260*

Rule of Thumb: review any item with [actual safety stock < 50% of target SS], *261*

SS in a sawtooth curve, *41*

sales, general & administrative

definition, *14*

sawtooth curve

1, 2, or 5 Orders Per Lead-Time Period, **_35_**

consumption is a sawtooth design factor, *24*

definition, *14*

elements of a sawtooth curve, *28–29*

Examples, *29–33*

predict min, average, and max inventory levels for sawtooth, *29–30*

replenishment LT and quantity are sawtooth design factors, *29–31*

Sawtooth: Delayed Receipt, 30

Sawtooth: Demand Variation, Delayed Receipt, **_30_**

Sawtooth: Higher Order Quantity, Correct Trigger, Demand Variation, Delayed Receipt, **_32_**

Sawtooth: Higher Order Quantity, Demand Variation, Delayed Receipt, **_31_**

SS in a sawtooth curve, *41*

Steady State Sawtooth Curve, *24, 29, 28*

tangent about charting sawtooth charts, end-of-day or beginning-of-day balances, *26–27*

things that impact a sawtooth curve, *34–36*

seasonal demand variation

current DD used to resize seasonal items, *136*

demand variation for seasonal demand, *151*

how to handle seasonality and other demand shifts, *162*

description, *133*

Formula: seasonal daily demand, *135*

Formula: seasonal DD by percent change, *135*

Formula: seasonality assessment, *135*

HINT: DV can differ from season to season, *136*

HINT: for seasonality, review graph or data table and look for steep inclines or declines in daily revenue, *135*

how to check for, *133*

Rule of Thumb: IF [High DD/Low DD or High DD/Med DD] > 130% then seasonality is significant, *136, 223*

Seasonal Variation diagrams, **_133_**

standard cost

definition, *14*

as internal primary data, *229*

used to calculate on-hand currency, *263*

standard deviation

definition, *120*